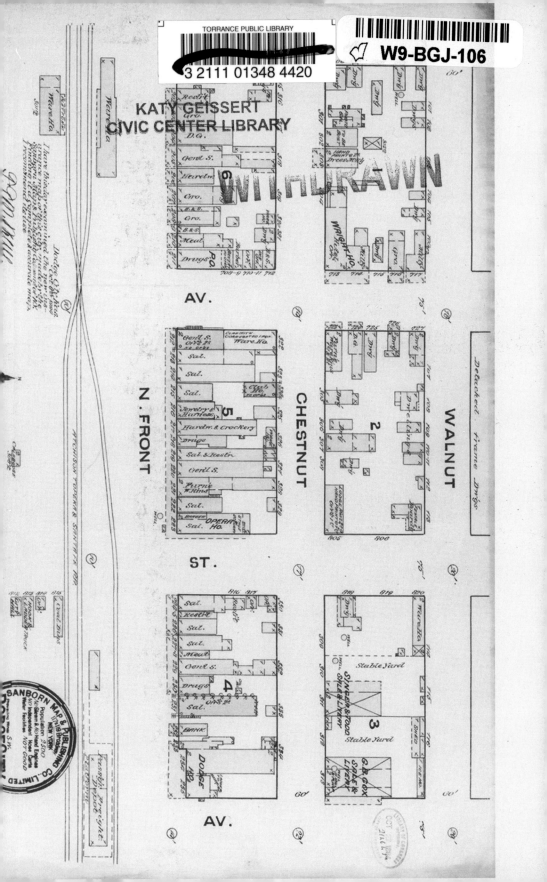

Western Lands and Waters Series
XXIII

FRONT STREET LOOKING EAST FROM THE CORNER OF SECOND AVENUE, CIRCA 1880. Wright, Beverley & Company and the Long Branch, two doors to the right, are clearly visible, as is Zimmerman's hardware, marked by the stylized rifle atop the building. The Dodge House can be seen at the far end of the street. The city well in the foreground bears the proclamation "The Carrying of Fire Arms strictly prohibited," a worthy sentiment seldom enforced.

DODGE CITY

The Early Years, 1872–1886

by

Wm. B. Shillingberg

THE ARTHUR H. CLARK COMPANY

An imprint of the University of Oklahoma Press

Norman, Oklahoma

2009

ALSO BY WM. B. SHILLINGBERG
Tombstone, A.T.: A History of Early Mining, Milling, and Mayhem (Spokane, Wash., 1999)

Library of Congress Cataloging-in-Publication Data
Shillingberg, Wm. B. (William B.)
  Dodge City : the early years, 1872–1886 / by Wm. B. Shillingberg.
  p. cm. — (Western lands and waters ; v. 23)
  Includes bibliographical references and index.
  ISBN 978-0-87062-378-3 (hardcover : alk. paper) 1. Dodge City (Kan.)—History—
19th century. 2. Frontier and pioneer life—Kansas—Dodge City. I. Title.
  F689.D64S55 2009
  978.1'76—dc22

2009007680

Dodge City: The Early Years, 1872–1886 is
Volume 23 in the Western Lands and Waters series.

The paper in this book meets the guidelines for permanence and durability
of the Committee on Production Guidelines for Book Longevity
of the Council on Library Resources, Inc. ∞

1 2 3 4 5 6 7 8 9 10

In Memory of

W. H. Hutchinson

1911–1990

and

John D. Gilchriese

1923–2004

Contents

Illustrations

Illustrations courtesy of the Kansas State Historical Society.

ENDPAPERS
Map of Dodge City, October 1884
S. T. Coit, insurance surveyor,
Sanborn Map & Publishing Co., Ltd.
Courtesy Geography and Map Division,
Library of Congress.

Chapter 1

SETTING THE STAGE

Dodge City sits atop a plot of ground on the High Plains of western Kansas, at the point where the hundredth degree of longitude crosses the Arkansas River. One of America's longest rivers, beginning high in the Colorado Rockies and flowing south and then east nearly fifteen hundred miles, the Arkansas has been largely ignored due to the absence of sustained river traffic much beyond Wichita.[1] Crossing into Kansas a hundred miles before reaching Dodge City, the river widens. In summer, with no major tributaries in the vicinity of the old town, it can even lose volume in the sandy soil. Shallow-draft vessels from canoes to keelboats exerted little influence over much of its course, unlike the majestic steamboats and wild adventures associated with the Missouri or the mighty Mississippi. There are no Mike Fink legends here, nor did there exist a Mark Twain to chronicle its virtues.[2]

The High Plains are more arid than the prairies farther east, a condition conducive to gama, wire, and buffalo grasses, which provided a natural ingredient to fuel Dodge City's economic success. Fluctuations in weather make this a land of powerful extremes. Savage winter storms sweep across the tabled landscape from the arctic north, dropping temper-

---

[1] Editors of the Rivers of America series tried giving the Arkansas its due, but overall efforts have been sparse. Clyde Brion Davis, *The Arkansas* (New York: Farrar & Rinehart, Inc., 1940). Another oddity concerning this river is that its name has two distinct pronunciations. Across the High Plains, until reaching the Oklahoma line, it is pronounced "R-Kansas." Citizens of Arkansas took exception, and in 1881, after spending years debating the point with many an impetuous Yankee, passed legislation to have the river's name conform to their state's pronunciation. Predictably, the people of Kansas ignored this faraway dictum, just as they would a futile 1932 attempt at uniformity suggested by the United States Board on Geographic Names. The standoff continues to this day.

[2] James H. Thomas and Carl N. Tyson, "Navigation on the Arkansas River, 1719–1886," *Kansas History: A Journal of the Central Plains* 2, no. 2 (Summer 1979): 135–41. One early emigrant guide reported somewhat optimistically: "A steamboat has ascended the Arkansas, during high water, for nearly a hundred miles above the south line of Kanzas." Edward E. Hale, *Kanzas and Nebraska . . . An Account of the Emigrant Aid Companies, and Directions to Emigrants* (Boston: Phillips, Sampson and Company, 1854), 161. More realistically, French traders had poled small boats upstream at least as far as Great Bend. Taking advantage of the spring runoff, others came down the river by canoe. Most often, however, there simply was not enough water to sustain traffic, as Ceran St. Vrain discovered to his chagrin in 1843, after unsuccessfully trying to ship beaver pelts east from Bent's Fort. The arrival of the Atchison, Topeka & Santa Fe Railroad in the early 1870s opened fresh possibilities.

atures and paralyzing everything before them. The spring snowmelt from the Rockies can turn the placid Arkansas into a raging torrent, although yearly rainfall seldom tops twenty inches at Dodge City. Wind from the southwest carries with it summer heat, wilting thousands of square miles as it passes over Kansas from Texas and Oklahoma.

This can be an unforgiving land. Yet it once teemed with millions of buffalo, elk, antelope, wolves, and countless other creatures. Humans came late, those of European origin some of the last to arrive. Hoping to repeat the successes of Cortez and Pizarro and seduced by visions of nonexistent cities of gold, Spanish adventurers were the first Europeans to penetrate central North America.

When the young conquistador Francisco Vásquez de Coronado reached the area in 1541, western Kansas appeared devoid of human habitation. Traveling less than a dozen miles a day and cooking food over dried buffalo dung, it is thought these intruders crossed the Arkansas River somewhere between the later sites of Fort Dodge and the town of Ford. If so, they stood a mere ten miles or so east of later Dodge City. The date was July 29, 1541, the Feast of San Pedro y San Pablo.[3]

Following custom, a priest celebrated Mass on a nearby rise. The Spaniards named the river in honor of the two saints but also called it the River of Quivira.[4] One of the expedition's officers, Lt. Juan Jaramillo, described the setting, noting the richness of the soil as being "well watered by arroyos, springs and rivers. . . . It is not a hilly country, but has tablelands, plains, and charming rivers with fine waters. . . . I am of the belief that it will be very productive of all sorts of commodities."[5]

Those few Indians encountered by the Spanish proved far different from the ones occupying these same lands when the Americans arrived three hundred years later. Gone then were the descendants of two small bands of Querecho Apache hunters seen along the Texas–New Mexico border.

---

[3] Herbert Eugene Bolton, *Coronado: Knight of Pueblos and Plains* (New York: Whittlesey House and The University of New Mexico Press, 1949), 288. Interestingly, on pages 285–86, Bolton outlines the route using calculations on the declination of the compass from Coronado's day to his own.

[4] John Rydjord, *Indian Place Names: Their Origin, Evolution, and Meanings, Collected in Kansas from the Siouan, Algonquian, Shoshonean, Caddoan, Iroquoian, and Other Tongues* (Norman: University of Oklahoma Press, 1968), 75–76. Rydjord notes: "The Arkansas River has had native Indian names, Spanish names, religious names, French names, Americanized names, an Arabic name, and nicknames."

[5] As quoted in Louise Barry, *The Beginning of the West: Annals of the Kansas Gateway to the American West, 1540–1854* (Topeka: Kansas State Historical Society, 1972), 2.

The next two centuries witnessed the arrival of the Comanches. Cousins of the Utes, these stocky invaders moved on to the plains from the mountains of Colorado and parts of northern New Mexico by the turn of the eighteenth century. Rebounding from the 1780 smallpox epidemic and driving out most of the Apaches by 1840, the Comanches established themselves from the Arkansas River south into Texas, becoming "the only great division of the Shoshonean family who lived entirely on the plains."[6] From this new homeland gained by conquest, they raided at will. Not even Mexico escaped Comanche forays.

Other tribes moving along the Arkansas included the Kiowa and Kiowa-Apaches. The Comanches and Kiowas made peace around 1790, thereafter jointly occupying lands south of the Arkansas while developing trading ties with various bands farther north. Also represented along the river were the Southern Cheyenne, Pawnee, and small bands of Arapahoes. All would play a role in the early history of Dodge City.

THE RECOGNIZED BOUNDARY between lands claimed by the United States and Spain shifted west with the Louisiana Purchase in 1803. Not without controversy, specifically the right of Napoleon to make a deal in the first place, the new line in southwestern Kansas was eventually seen as running along what became the eastern side of the Texas Panhandle, following the 100th meridian to the Arkansas River. Formalized under provisions of the 1809 Adams-Onís Treaty (ratified by the United States and Spain in 1821 and by Mexico in 1822), the boundary followed the river upstream into central Colorado, then shifted directly north to the 42nd parallel and westward to the Pacific Ocean. The point where the 100th meridian meets the river would later mark the eastern edge of the original Dodge City townsite line.

The United States was interested in exploring its new domain. Just as President Thomas Jefferson had sent out Captains Meriwether Lewis and

---

[6] Rupert Norval Richardson, *The Comanche Barrier to South Plains Settlement: A century and a half of savage resistance to the advancing white frontier* (Glendale, Calif.: The Arthur H. Clark Company, 1933), 16. Richardson assumed that "The word Comanche or Cumanche is probably of Spanish origin, but its meaning is unknown." More recent scholarship, however, assigns it to the Ute word *Komántcia*, meaning, roughly, "Anyone who wants to fight me all the time" or "Those Who Are Always Against Us." Ernest Wallace and E. Adamson Hobel, *The Comanches: Lords of the South Plains* (Norman: University of Oklahoma Press, 1952), 4; and T. R. Fehrenbach, *Comanches: The Destruction of a People* (New York: Alfred A. Knopf, 1974), 90. Sign language used on the plains signified Comanches as Snakes, identified by moving the right hand and forearm, palm down, across the body in a wiggling motion.

William Clark to explore the northern regions, an army expedition commanded by Zebulon Montgomery Pike headed farther south.

After visiting a Pawnee village in Nebraska, Pike and his men pushed on,
striking the Arkansas River near Great Bend, Kansas. Resting ten days, Pike's
small band of explorers, now numbering less than two-dozen men, continued
upstream, crossing over the future Dodge City townsite in the fall of 1806.
Credited with helping characterize the plains as the Great American Desert,[7]
Pike wrote on November 3, "passed numerous herds of buffalo, elk, some
horses &c. all traveling south. The river bottoms, full of salt ponds; grass similar to our salt meadows," adding to his journal the following day: "In the afternoon discovered the north side of the river to be covered with animals; which,
when we came to them proved to be buffalo cows and calves. I do not think it
an exaggeration to say there were 3,000 in one view. It is worthy of remark, that
in all the extent of country yet crossed, we never saw one cow, and that now
the face of the earth appeared to be covered with them. Killed one buffalo."[8]

Continuing their exploration, the Americans discovered Pikes Peak, the
upper South Platte River, South Park, and several mountain passes, as well
as the Royal Gorge of the Arkansas. In early 1807 Pike and his men were
arrested by Spanish soldiers and taken to Santa Fe, then jailed in Mexico for
criminal trespass. They were released four months later near Natchitoches,
Louisiana.

Although military exploration introduced Americans to the later site of
Dodge City, it would be commerce with New Mexico that drew them in
numbers. Trade with Santa Fe guaranteed a Yankee presence along the
Arkansas River, and this fact alone influenced events leading to the founding
of the famous town. Without the Santa Fe Trail it might never have existed.

The French in Louisiana had often circumvented Spain's prohibition
against trade with its citizens. American traders at Santa Fe, proving less
agile than the French, often found themselves arrested or had their goods
confiscated. Robert McKnight and a small party suffered that fate in 1812,

---

[7] Donald Jackson, ed., *The Journals of Zebulon Montgomery Pike: With Letters and Related Documents* (Norman: University of Oklahoma Press, 1966), 2:27, 27–28n5. Pike's view, shared by Thomas Jefferson and others at the time, was
that the Great Plains would restrict American migration, thereby stabilizing the Republic by protecting its western borders from foreign incursions. Others helped popularize the Great American Desert appellation, namely
Stephen Harriman Long. Richard G. Wood, *Stephen Harriman Long, 1784–1864: Army Engineer, Explorer, Inventor*
(Glendale, Calif.: The Arthur H. Clark Company, 1966), 116–17.

[8] Jackson, *Journals of Zebulon Montgomery Pike*, 1:342–43. As for linking specific geographic locations with dates,
Jackson admits, "Pike gives us little to go on except his usually inexact distances."

not being released from house arrest in Chihuahua until after the Mexican Revolution of 1821. Regardless of the reluctance to encourage commercial ties between the two North American powers, goods from the United States, especially manufactured items and other luxuries, were much in demand at Santa Fe. Not only could Americans supply a wider range of products, often of higher quality than those shipped from Mexico, they did so below the prevailing market price, the result of lower costs at point of origin and shorter distances traveled.

On the first of September 1821, William Becknell and thirty others left Arrow Rock, Missouri, ostensibly seeking trade with Indians. By chance they happened upon a patrol of Spanish-speaking soldiers on the Upper Canadian. Hearing details of Mexico's independence, they rode together into New Mexico's capital city. Becknell sold his goods at a handsome profit and returned home in January, carrying news that American traders were now welcome. Two other groups preceded Becknell's announcement and had reached Santa Fe under similar circumstances.

Becknell started back almost at once, but this time abandoning pack mules in favor of three wagons.[9] In the process he opened a new era in Southwest commerce. To avoid the hazards of Raton Pass—the traditional route into New Mexico—Becknell and his men tried a more direct route. Turning south about twenty-three miles beyond the future site of Dodge City, this small caravan crossed the wastelands of the Cimarron, blazing a trail favored by traders for the next five decades. Called the Cimarron Cut-off, it reduced travel time from seventy-three to sixty-two days.

Others followed, one group creating a Dodge City landmark. James Baird, one of those jailed with Robert McKnight in 1812, had formed his own Santa Fe trading company. With at least twenty men he left St. Louis late in the season with sixty pack animals.[10] They reached the Arkansas River only to be trapped by a powerful storm. The desperate men huddled together for three months on an island some half-dozen miles west of later Dodge City, a site chosen as offering protection against Indians. Most of

---

[9] Only one of these three wagons belonged to Becknell, a vehicle he acquired for $150 but later sold at Santa Fe for $700, a fact that helped encourage other more reluctant traders. Apparently the other two were also sold, as the men returned to Missouri without wagons. Mark L. Gardner, *Wagons for the Santa Fe Trade: Wheeled Vehicles and Their Makers, 1822–1880* (Albuquerque: University of New Mexico Press, 2000), 3–4.

[10] Other contemporary estimates claim fifty men were involved, while still later the number forty was given. Apparently no one knew for sure, but whatever the total, they were in for a hard journey. Barry, *The Beginning of the West*, 109.

their animals perished from cold or starvation well before spring. Feeling lucky just to be alive, they buried their goods at a spot called Gravel Rocks, just opposite their winter island refuge, before stumbling on toward New Mexico. Purchasing pack animals at Taos, they managed to return and retrieve their hidden merchandise. The company's luck failed after Mexican authorities stepped in and halted their trading arrangements with Indians.

The place where they buried their trade goods on the north bank of the Arkansas River became famous as "the Caches" and served for many years as a local point of reference. Veteran trader Josiah Gregg later recalled, "Few travelers pass this way without visiting these mossy pits, many of which remain partly unfilled to the present day."[11] Eighteen-year-old Susan Magoffin passed the site in 1846, describing it as "a celebrated place . . . situated about a quarter mile from the river, on rather an elevated piece of ground, and within a hundred yards of the road, which runs at present between them and the river."[12] Since then all evidence of the site has vanished.[13]

As trade increased—from twenty-six wagons in 1824 to one hundred only four years later—so did contact with Indians, chiefly Comanches, Kiowas, and Cheyennes, as well as some Arapahoes and Pawnees. Nomadic peoples all, they welcomed the activity as providing fresh opportunities to steal horses, as well as trade for tobacco and other scarce commodities. But suspicion soon strained tribal councils. Bands of disaffected warriors began attacking wagon trains moving along the trail in both directions. Worried traders demanded protection.

The War Department ignored their pleas until 1829, when it authorized a six-company infantry escort (the army having surveyed the route in 1826). This half-hearted effort failed to impress the traders or the Indians. At that time the United States had no mounted troops—the entire army numbered only six thousand—and congressional political alliances delayed their reintroduction by claiming the cost unjustified by current levels of Santa Fe trade. Objections behind the scenes centered on the fact that a single state, Missouri, benefited most from the enterprise. A second infantry escort in 1833 included a company of the short-lived Mounted

---

[11] Josiah Gregg, *Commerce of the Prairies: or the Journal of a Santa Fé Trader* (New York: Henry G. Langley, 1844), 1:68.

[12] Stella M. Drumm, ed., *Down the Santa Fé Trail and into Mexico: The Diary of Susan Shelby Magoffin, 1846–1847* (New Haven: Yale University Press, 1926), 53–54.

[13] David Dary, *The Santa Fe Trail: Its History, Legends, and Lore* (New York: Alfred A. Knopf, 2000), 82.

Rangers, soon reorganized as United States Dragoons.[14] Still, aside from these two feeble efforts, only four other military escorts took place before the Mexican War.[15]

Traders feared Indian attacks, but by 1843 Texas mercenaries added to their concerns. Freed from Mexican rule just seven years before, the new republic claimed as its sovereign domain all of New Mexico east of the Rio Grande.[16] Ignoring their lack of physical control over the region, Texas patriots demanded the right to collect custom duties from hapless Santa Fe traders all the same.

Texans had already launched one ill-fated expedition against Santa Fe in 1841, in which the entire command was apprehended. Despite this embarassment, Jacob Snively, a one-time store clerk and surveyor from Nacogdoches—now serving as acting secretary of war and inspector general for the Republic of Texas—supported Sam Houston's strategy of harassing New Mexicans by intercepting caravans along the Santa Fe Trail. Houston remained convinced that the route trespassed Texas public lands.

Earlier raids heightened fears. Demands for escorts poured into Washington from Missourians and Mexicans alike. To help break the impasse, Col. Stephen Watts Kearny ordered two patrols into the field. The first of these, commanded by Philip St. George Cooke, consisted of four companies of the First Dragoons. Daniel Boone's youngest son, Nathan, led the second party, three companies of dragoons from Fort Gibson. Both commanders were under orders to provide escorts while patrolling the Arkansas River crossings.

While traveling to Missouri, Charles Bent and his partner, Ceran St. Vrain, stumbled upon Snively and his band of self-styled "Texas Invincibles." From the Texans they learned of an earlier encounter with Mexican forces—mostly Pueblo Indians pressed into service at Taos—sent to meet an incoming caravan. Suffering causalities, the Mexicans withdrew under a Texas promise of safe conduct.

---

[14] Richard Wormser, *The Yellowlegs: The Story of the United States Cavalry* (Garden City, N.Y.: Doubleday & Company, Inc., 1966), 390–43; and James M. Merrill, *Spurs to Glory: The Story of the United States Cavalry* (Chicago: Rand McNally & Company, 1966), 17.

[15] Leo E. Oliva, *Soldiers on the Santa Fe Trail* (Norman: University of Oklahoma Press, 1967), 25–54.

[16] Texas president Sam Houston based his arguments on provisions of the Treaty of Velasco, a document of questionable legality that he nevertheless claimed as ending the Texas Revolution. This agreement with Santa Ana, conceded by Houston's latest biographer as being "somewhat coerced" following the Battle of San Jacinto, included lands extending "as far north as later Wyoming" and as far south as the Rio Grande. James L. Haley, *Sam Houston* (Norman: University of Oklahoma Press, 2002), 266, 297.

Bent and St. Vrain continued their journey under similar assurances. Spotting a westbound caravan guarded by Captain Cooke, the two traders shared their knowledge of Snively's plans. On June 26, 1843, a detachment of Cooke's dragoons came across some of the Texans at Jackson's Grove, a place north of the river and fifteen miles east of the Caches. Some still questioned the exact spot where the 100th meridian crossed the river, clouding Texas land claims, but everything north of the Arkansas was United States territory. Another patrol verified the main body across the river.

Cooke ordered an officer into the Texans' main camp to learn their intentions. Most felt the intruders should at least be disarmed, despite Snively's assertion that he camped on Texas soil. Threatening an attack by ordering his Dragoons across the river in battle formation, while preparing two cannon for action, Cooke demanded the Texans surrender their firearms.

Facing overwhelming force, Snively complied. Cooke's men gathered up all the weapons they could find—though perhaps not all, as trader Josiah Gregg later recalled: "Having concealed their own rifles, which were mostly Colt's repeaters, they delivered to Capt. Cook [sic] the worthless fusils they had taken from the Mexicans; so that when they were afterwards released, they still had their own valuable arms."[17] In a conciliatory gesture, Cooke allowed ten of the Texans to rearm themselves for protection in that hostile country.

However embarrassing for Snively and his Invincibles, Texans did stop raiding Santa Fe commerce, any residual desire to do so ended with the admission of their republic into the federal union in late 1845. Even as that threat faded, Washington could not come up with a workable plan to protect this important commercial highway. Unforeseen events provided the solution.

Old Santa Fe veterans were startled to find themselves competing for road and forage with swarms of new faces during the summer of 1846. Strangers crowded the trail in numbers never before imagined. War had broken out between the United States and Mexico. Commanding what was called the Army of the West, American general Stephen Watts Kearny launched his country's invasion of New Mexico and California with a

---

[17] Gregg, *Commerce of the Prairies*, 2:174. The weapons mentioned were Colt revolving carbines of the Paterson design. Although few were manufactured, these early products of Samuel Colt found an enthusiastic market in Texas, where the government had purchased one hundred Ring Lever Rifles and nearly twice that number Model 1839 Revolving Carbines just prior to the Snively affair. R. L. Wilson, *The Colt Heritage: The Official History of Colt Firearms from 1836 to the Present* (New York: Simon and Schuster, 1979), 18.

force of 1,658 men, together with various hangers-on, including hunters, traders and teamsters.[18]

Kearny's acting assistant adjutant general, Capt. Henry Smith Turner of the First Dragoons, recorded their progress in his private journal. Passing Walnut Creek at the Great Bend of the Arkansas, he reported poor grazing along creek beds. But then, near the later site of Fort Dodge, where a large portion of the army camped on July 19, Turner wrote: "Grazing better than seen yet—the hunting party saw blacktail hare and wild horses. Buffalo are abundant and fat. Made a visit to the Sand Hills on the south side of the river—found among trees the Chickasaw plum in great abundance—a delicious fruit. The grass improves as we ascend the river, more and of a better quality. Passed Jackson's Grove about noon, the spot at which Capt. Cooke disarmed a party of Texans in 1842 [sic]."[19]

By the time Kearny and his small army reached Santa Fe on August 18, the forces of American commerce stood ready to make money. New Mexico's capital swarmed with troopers and entrepreneurs. Missouri volunteers under Alexander Doniphan and Sterling Price joined with members of the Mormon Battalion (soon under the command of Philip St. George Cooke)[20] in swelling the population of this adobe frontier outpost. Through all the confusion rumbled an endless parade of wagon trains, each piled high with merchandise of one sort or another and led by hardened men dreaming of inflated prices and cold cash.

To the Indians, watching the unfolding spectacle of this military and commercial invasion, the Mexican War left them more apprehensive than hopeful. If they worried about the soldiers, they watched with more appreciative eyes the many supply wagons lagging behind. Comanches,

---

[18] Dwight L. Clarke, *Stephen Watts Kearny, Soldier of the West* (Norman: University of Oklahoma Press, 1961), 113–14.

[19] Dwight L. Clarke, ed., *The Original Journals of Henry Smith Turner: With Stephen Watts Kearny to New Mexico and California, 1846* (Norman: University of Oklahoma Press, 1966), 63. For additional comments concerning this site, following the outbreak of the Mexican War, see Ralph P. Bieber, ed., *Marching With the Army of the West, 1846–1848* (Glendale, Calif.: The Arthur H. Clark Company, 1936), 132–34, 306–308.

[20] The original commander of the Mormon Battalion, Lt. Col. James Allen, had died of "congestive fever" on August 22, 1846. As Cooke's biographer then explained, "Stephen Watts Kearny was of no mind to have Allen replaced by an elected colonel; the battalion faced a hard march to California where it was to act as a strategic reserve, and required a disciplinarian of the first order merely to ensure that it arrived. Kearny sent for Captain Cooke." Otis E. Young, *The West of Philip St. George Cooke, 1809–1895* (Glendale, Calif.: The Arthur H. Clark Company, 1955), 183; also see David L. Bigler and Will Bagley, ed., *Army of Israel: Mormon Battalion Narratives* (Spokane, Wash.: The Arthur H. Clark Company, 2000), 91–92, 120–21.

Pawnees, and other tribes began raiding both military and civilian caravans. Reflecting the demands of war, troops could not be spared for escort duty. Civilians fell back on their time-honored system of traveling in caravans, loaded weapons within easy reach. The resulting struggles, costly in both money and blood, would stretch out over three decades, building resentment and distrust among all the parties that lasted far longer.

It seemed obvious that only a threat of force could guarantee an uninterrupted flow of military and commercial merchandise into the Southwest. If no soldiers were available, traders at least hoped that small garrisons might be established to help protect their interests. When the army did authorize a site between Fort Leavenworth, Kansas, and Fort Marcy, New Mexico, they confused some and amazed others by not stationing a single company of regular soldiers there. Capt. William M. D. McKissack, the assistant quartermaster at Santa Fe, concluded that a simple repair facility placed somewhere near the midpoint, and not a full-blown military encampment, would stifle complaints. In early 1847 he ordered wagonmaster Daniel P. Mann and forty teamsters to build a depot near the Arkansas River crossings. Mann selected a spot he was familiar with, having been attacked there by a large band of Pawnees some months before, between the Caches and the future Dodge City townsite.

Adding to the general collapse of confidence, the army disappointed everyone by announcing it had never intended the location, soon called Mann's Fort or Fort Mann, to be anything more than a convenient place to repair wagons. McKissack explained: "Owing to the great number of wagons abandoned on the plains I made arrangements to erect Wheelwright, Smith & Store houses near the crossing of the Arkansas: the work was performed by Teamsters, and occupied by them."[21]

Fort Mann's physical appearance offered little comfort. Lewis H. Garrard, who arrived with an eastbound caravan on May 15 and helped build the place, later recalled, "The fort was simply four log houses, connected by angles of timber framework, in which were cut loopholes for the can-

---

[21] As quoted in Barry, *The Beginning of the West*, 669. McKissack made a number of annoying decisions. Indian Agent Thomas Fitzpatrick complained in a report to the commissioner of Indian Affairs that the assistant Santa Fe quartermaster had appropriated all the gifts from Bent's Fort intended for peaceful Cheyennes, and instead "the goods had all been taken to Santa Fe, and mostly distributed no doubt to those Indians who are now devastating the county." Appendix to Fitzpatrick's original report, September 18, 1847, in David A. White, comp., *News of the Plains and Rockies, 1803–1865* (Spokane, Wash.: The Arthur H. Clark Company, 1997) 3:391.

non and small arms. In diameter the fort was about sixty feet. The walls were twenty in hight [*sic*]."[22] He went on to say that the men assigned there wanted nothing more than to flee.

Six days before Garrard's arrival a small band of Comanches shot and lanced a man they caught fishing. His armed but surprised comrades watched from a distance as the Indians lifted the unfortunate angler's scalp and rode away unopposed. Two days later others drove off fifteen yoke of oxen and forty mules. This time there was an exchange of gunfire, wounding one Indian. Garrard reported, "In consequence of the above forays, timidity became a second nature to the teamsters, and they ventured not to show their uncomfortable countenances outside the gate."[23]

The young English traveler George Frederick Ruxton saw Fort Mann about the same time as Garrard's thirty-day sojourn: "We found the fort beleaguered by the Pawnees, who killed everyone who showed his nose outside the gate. They had carried off all the stock of mules and oxen, and in the vicinity had, two or three days before, attacked a company under an officer of the United States Engineers, running off with all the mules belonging to it."[24] By June 1846, after hoping to discourage desertion by raising everyone's pay ten dollars a month, authorities relented and ordered the seven survivors to destroy what they could. Doing so in haste, the disillusioned mechanics loaded up two wagons, one displaying a small cannon, and joined some government caravans bound for Santa Fe, leaving "the fort to the mercies of the Indians."[25]

The War Department finally recognized the need to protect the nation's valuable southwest commerce. A request had already been sent to the governor of Missouri in late July calling for five companies of volunteers. What evolved was the creation of the so-called Indian Battalion.[26] It was

---

[22] Lewis H. Garrard, *Wah-To-Yah and the Taos Trail* (Glendale, Calif.: The Arthur H. Clark Company, 1938), 331. Some disagreed with Garrard's claim of walls twenty feet high. Thomas Fitzpatrick, who had seen the results in early July, later described the place as "nothing more than rough, uneven, and very crooked cotton wood logs, raised eight or ten feet high, without form or design." Report of Thomas Fitzpatrick, December 18, 1847, as quoted in Barry, *The Beginning of the West*, 670.

[23] Garrard, *Wah-To-Yah and the Taos Trail*, 669.

[24] LeRoy R. Hafen, ed., *Ruxton of the Rockies* (Norman: University of Oklahoma Press, 1950), 279. George Frederick Ruxton died of dysentery at St. Louis on August 29, 1848, at the age of twenty-seven.

[25] For this quote, as well as most of the material used for this brief summary of activities around Fort Mann, see Barry, *The Beginning of the West*, 670–71.

[26] Available records are somewhat vague concerning the official name for his unit. At least five wide-ranging variations exist, including, for some unspecified reason, the "Oregon Battalion." For the sake of consistency, Indian Battalion will be used here.

assigned the most troublesome area, between the Indians' favorite Arkansas River crossing points: Mulberry Creek, seventeen miles east of later Dodge City, and Cimarron Crossing, some twenty-three miles to the west.

William Gilpin, a former executive officer for Col. Alexander Doniphan, served as the unit's commander.[27] Unable to convince enough veterans to sign on, Gilpin's roster included three companies of non-English-speaking German immigrants plucked off the streets of St. Louis, along with some ill-trained Americans. All they shared in common was a desire for the free land promised volunteers in time of war.

Gilpin characterized their departure as being "Ordered into the wilderness naked."[28] The motley band of 850 men rendezvoused at Fort Mann in the fall of 1847. The place had been reoccupied briefly that July, but Gilpin found it once again abandoned by government employees.[29] Before reclaiming the site, the Indian Battalion drove off a number of Pawnees using the place as a private refuge. The colonel estimated losses for the summer of 1847 to include 330 wagons destroyed and 6,500 animals stolen, as well as an unknown number of human casualties. Concerned with rumors of the major tribes on the southern plains joining an alliance, Gilpin and his cavalry set out for Bent's Fort, hoping that the Bent brothers' intimate contacts could help prevent a major outbreak.

Gilpin made the mistake of leaving behind his infantry and artillery units under the command of Capt. William Pelzer, who proved incapable of leading troops or dealing with Indians. After just two days in charge Pelzer ordered his men to open fire on a group of Pawnees looking for handouts, killing two and wounding a couple dozen more. Only one company commander refused to allow his soldiers to participate in this shameful episode.

---

[27] Thomas L. Karnes, *William Gilpin, Western Nationalist* (Austin: University of Texas Press, 1970), 191. At least Gilpin had some experience with Indians, first in Florida during the Seminole War and more recently against the Navajo. Coming from an influential Philadelphia family, he had also developed valuable political friendships during the course of his career, from Andrew Jackson, who awarded him an appointment to West Point in 1834, to Missouri senator Thomas Hart Benton. Gilpin also knew something of the West, having traveled to Oregon in 1843 with Benton's son-in-law, John C. Frémont. Along the way he met Lucian B. Maxwell, Thomas Fitzpatrick, cartographer Charles Pruess, and celebrated scout Kit Carson.

[28] Thomas L. Karnes, "Gilpin's Volunteers on the Santa Fe Trail," *Kansas Historical Quarterly* 30, no. 1 (Spring 1964): 4.

[29] The scant evidence of reoccupation comes from a single letter written by an unidentified Missouri volunteer dated July 23, 1847: "The report that this fort had been consumed by the Indians proves to be erroneous. . . . Mann, who built it, and has charge of it, says he will abandon it, unless he can get some 30 men from our battalion to remain with him—of which I think there is no probability." As quoted in Barry, *The Beginning of the West*, 706.

For his part Pelzer settled in at Fort Mann for a winter of alcoholic debauch. He denounced his absent commander, misdirected supplies, and allowed discipline to collapse. He further undermined morale by swindling his soldiers out of most of their pay. Pelzer even fought a saber duel with one of his German company commanders.

American and German troops threatened one another with open violence. The battalion's peacekeeping role seemed pointless. The ultimate breech involved Lt. Amandus Schnabel and his pliable concubine, Caroline Newsome, a rough-hewed specimen of womanhood, later described by teamster George Rutledge Gibson as "a strange character. . . . There is nothing in her appearance suspicious and she mixes with the Teamsters as one of them, and smokes, chews and acts the man." Disguised as a recruit in Company D, she performed those duties assigned by the amorous lieutenant until pregnancy forced her premature retirement from further military service, at which point George Gibson concluded, "Her sex being discovered she was sent back to the States by this train and furnishes rough jokes daily for these men of hardy habits. She has not yet laid aside mans clothes."[30] When informed of the tryst, Colonel Gilpin fumed but could do nothing from Bent's Fort.

Overcoming his own difficulties, Gilpin attempted a belated winter campaign against the Comanches and others camped along the Canadian River. He saw no Indians, having been warned of his approach by a party of Mexicans. And yet this small show of force did for a time discourage raids against government supply trains. Returning to Fort Mann in late May 1848, Gilpin, much to his relief, saw that many of his problems had begun correcting themselves. The sluggish War Department wanted the scandalous air cleared. Even those irascible Germans, now fearful of losing their 160-acre allotments for volunteer service, petitioned to have Captain Pelzer removed. He and four other officers, including Lieutenant Schnabel, resigned. Paying the price for gross insubordination, two enlisted men were hauled before a special court. Another was charged with murder and sent to St. Louis. Others, suspected of stealing government property, escaped punishment only for lack of evidence. Gilpin discovered that one of the hapless Pawnees wounded on Pelzer's reckless order was still a prisoner. He ordered the man's immediate release and issued an offi-

[30] Robert W. Frazer, ed., *Over the Chihuahua and Santa Fe Trails, 1847–1848: George Rutledge Gibson's Journal* (Albuquerque: University of New Mexico Press, 1981), 83.

cial apology coupled with assurances that his tormentor had suffered disgrace and discharge.

With a complete reorganization, the once-discredited Indian Battalion proved its worth that summer of 1848. Troubles along the trail continued, of course, but Colonel Gilpin and his volunteers demonstrated that most challenges could be overcome with perseverance. Victory in the Mexican War ended authorizations for volunteers. It now remained for the small regular army to police the nearly 800-mile route to Santa Fe. The army abandoned Fort Mann in September, with the old site serving as a civilian sanctuary for the next two years as worried traders again found no permanent military presence between eastern Kansas and the New Mexico highlands.

Passersby took a toll on the unoccupied property. Diarist Anna Maria Morris, the wife of an aristocratic army officer traveling to Santa Fe in a military ambulance, attended by a personal maid to meet her singular needs, scribbled on June 16, 1850: "we encamped on the Arkansas for the last time I hope – We passed Fort Mann this morning or rather its remains, a few old logs & mud chimney – the logs we had chopped up for fire wood & packed in our wagons enough to last 300 miles – We expect to cross the Arkansas tomorrow – The heat to day is intolerable."[31]

As the United States Army abandoned the trail, the Comanches and their allies returned in force. Exasperated traders again pleaded with Washington. Adj. Gen. Roger Jones recommended that the secretary of war authorize a series of forts. Officials dithered, not having learned a thing from earlier attempts at stabilization. In June 1850 they responded by again ordering the establishment of a single post.

The War Department left the selection to Lt. Col. Edwin V. Sumner of the First Dragoons. He picked out a temporary spot at Cimarron Crossing. Named Camp Mackay, in honor of an influential officer in the quartermaster department, Sumner and his soldiers occupied the place at the end of August. Not satisfied, Sumner scouted other sites before picking one just east of old Fort Mann. Grass was plentiful but there was no wood for construction. The colonel ordered the fort made of stone and then abandoned the idea owing to the lateness of the season. Instead, disheartened soldiers built crude shelters from sod blocks chopped from the

---

[31] Anna Maria Morris, "A Military Wife on the Santa Fe Trail," in Kenneth L. Holmes, ed., *Covered Wagon Women: Diaries and Letters from the Western Trails, 1840–1890* (Glendale, Calif.: The Arthur H. Clark Company, 1983), 2:29.

prairie. In jest they christened their new home Fort Sodom. Early post returns used the unceremonious "New Post Arkansas River."[32]

Before year's end Gen. Winfield Scott ordered that the new post be made permanent, endorsing Sumner's plan to use stone. By June 1851 the army high command named the place Fort Atkinson. Its commander, Capt. William Hoffman, complained of insufficient building materials, wood or stone, pointing out that sod would not do: "In a recent snow storm, the snow was three to five inches deep inside some of the quarters."[33] Hoffman preferred to move his entire command to Pawnee Fork, arguing that supplies of all sorts, for construction or other uses, would be available at lower cost to the government with troops stationed that much closer to Fort Leavenworth. Orders were in fact issued, but for whatever reason the move never took place. Capt. Robert Hall Chilton replaced Hoffman as post commander.

Despite indecision, Fort Atkinson did occupy an ideal spot for protecting travel and trade along the Santa Fe Trail. Traditionally the Indians concentrated their attacks between Walnut Creek and the Cimarron Crossings. The real trouble came from those who believed that a single company of infantry could suppress what was essentially a guerrilla war on the Great Plains.

With spring, camps of Comanches and Kiowas—all interested in promised allotments—ringed Fort Atkinson. Huddled inside, terrified soldiers pondered the possibility of massacre. A company of dragoons arrived early that summer and relieved the tension, as did large numbers of military personal moving down the trail to New Mexico. After their departure the fort survived with its single company of infantry. Almost as an insult, field mice soon overran the place. Cats requisitioned from Fort Leavenworth helped diminish the annoyance, but within two years they themselves were driven mad by an infestation of fleas.

Simon Bolivar Buckner, a former West Point philosophy instructor and future Confederate lieutenant general, took command in late 1851. Watching Santa Fe traffic taper off during the winter months, he advised a withdrawal to Fort Leavenworth. Buckner wished both to economize and improve the morale of his men. He also questioned the use of infantry,

---

[32] Many travelers called the place Fort Sumner or Fort Mackay, as if moving the site automatically transferred the name. Neither of these designations was ever used officially.

[33] As quoted in Oliva, *Soldiers on the Santa Fe Trail*, 96–97.

convinced that only mounted troops could face the tribes on anything approaching equal terms—an interesting concession coming from a professional infantry officer.

Late spring 1852 again saw large numbers of Comanches, Kiowas, and others—some estimates claimed an astounding ten thousand individuals—congregating around Fort Atkinson, waiting for Indian Agent Thomas Fitzpatrick. Growing restless, some even roughed up a sentry and forced their way into the fort, but they left without causing series damage.

In the midst of this drama, William Bent arrived with a small wagon train, followed by a party of Georgia excursionists searching for adventure and another group of Englishmen touring the Great Plains. Giving up on Fitzpatrick, the Indians demanded the contents of Bent's wagons. The trader's emphatic refusal alarmed everyone, soldiers and vacationers alike, to the possibility of violence. Four enlisted men deserted, spreading rumors that Fort Atkinson had been destroyed and its garrison massacred.

Of course nothing of that sort happened, but in frustration Buckner criticized his superiors, bringing about temporary improvements. Maj. Winslow F. Sanderson arrived with a fresh battalion on July 20, assuming command for twelve days. Mounted troops were also ordered into the field. Captain Chilton returned with a company of the First Dragoons before Sanderson left for Fort Laramie, accompanied by the still apprehensive but much relieved civilian pleasure seekers. Chilton and his dragoons stayed on for most of the trading season.

Meanwhile, Gen. James Carleton came up from Fort Union, New Mexico. His soldiers had been patrolling the western half of the trail with some success. This belated display of force allowed the infantrymen a respite to prepare for winter. The dragoons withdrew in September, but by then the Indians—at least those with the patience to wait—had been appeased. Fitzpatrick arrived in late August, dispensing goods and arranging for treaty negotiations the following year. Lt. Henry Heath commanded Fort Atkinson during the winter months. With the Indians bundled away in their own camps the situation quieted down, but with spring 1853 everyone expected the familiar cycle of defiance.

As if announcing the opening of the season, Chilton and his dragoons returned with orders to protect traders and mail contractors. With mounted troops serving as escorts, the number of successful raids diminished, a situation helped by Thomas Fitzpatrick arranging an accommodation with the tribes. One observer of the proceedings later acknowledged, "A volume might be written of this so-called treaty, a renewal of faith, which the Indians did not have in the Government, nor the Government in them."[34]

Military bureaucrats missed the point of maintaining a presence. Still mumbling about the cost of winter garrisons, they ordered Fort Atkinson abandoned that September, transferring soldiers from the center of activity to faraway Fort Riley, a year-old site at the confluence of the Smoky Hill and Republican rivers. Concerned now with protecting mail services, worried traders and merchants persuaded the New Mexico legislature to petition Congress to reopen the post. Washington responded with a brief occupation by two companies of the Sixth Infantry the following summer and early fall. The ruins of Fort Atkinson were left undisturbed and the troops camped in tents nearby. Years later Jacob W. Reed, a physician and mapmaker interested in the Pikes Peak gold fields, dismissed the site as "now unoccupied, and a mass of ruins."[35]

The closing of Fort Atkinson ended any permanent military presence in the area around Dodge City until nearly the last day of the Civil War. The war itself shifted the emphasis from the Santa Fe Trail to new battlefields in the East. Troops left on the frontier faced renewed threats with diminished resources. By 1864 some commanders exhibited a day-to-day ambivalence of purpose. Ordered to keep the trail open, they did their best. But they saw themselves acting more as policemen outnumbered by rowdy lawbreakers than soldiers preparing for battle. Everyone knew real battles were being fought not on the Kansas frontier, but at places like Antietam and Gettysburg. They would have preferred marching to glory with Generals Grant and Sherman to chasing scattered bands of Comanches or Kiowas.

Personal and professional frustration moved the debate into a dangerous area. Although never official policy, some officers began toying with the idea of extermination, a frightening frame of mind that would resurface from time to time in the early history of Dodge City. Even Samuel R. Curtis, commanding general of the Department of Kansas, declared that peace was not possible until the Indians suffered more, and he stated

---

[34] Hon. Percival G. Lowe, "Kansas, As Seen in the Indian Territory," *Transactions of the Kansas State Historical Society*, vol. 4, *1886–1888* (Topeka: Kansas Publishing House, 1890), 365.

[35] White, comp., *News of the Plains and Rockies*, 7:420.

emphatically that no negotiations could take place without his personal approval.[36]

Within a year Gen. Patrick Edward Connor, a frustrated Irishman serving under Grenville M. Dodge as commander of the new District of the Plains at Fort Laramie, wrote one of his subordinate commanders, on— of all dates—the Fourth of July: "You will not receive overtures of peace or submission from Indians, but will attack and kill every male Indian over twelve years of age."[37] After reviewing a copy, an outraged district commander, Gen. John Pope, sent a blistering directive to Grenville Dodge: "These instructions are atrocious, and are in direct violation of my repeated orders. You will please take immediate steps to countermand such orders. If any such orders as General Connor's are carried out it will be disgraceful to the Government, and will cost him his commission, if not worse. Have it rectified without delay."[38]

By early September 1864 the Cheyennes and Arapahoes, fearing reprisals, approached Indian Agent Samuel E. Colley at Fort Lyon, Colorado. As a point of negotiation they agreed to surrender all their captives. Edward Wynkoop, a skeptical major with the Colorado Volunteers (but later an Indian agent himself), marched on the camp, demanding their release. Surprised by Wynkoop's boldness, four captives were given up on the major's assurance of a peace conference with Colorado governor John Evans. A meeting did take place in Denver but, acknowledging the position taken by General Curtis, Evans declined to discuss specifics: "I do not

---

[36] Even Gen. William T. Sherman, in private correspondence with his brother, a senator from Ohio, later offered widely contradictory views on Indians. At one point he would write: "The Sioux and Cheyennes are now so circumscribed that I suppose they must be exterminated, for they cannot and will not settle down, and our people will force us to it." And yet, less than eight months later his tone had softened: "I agree with you that Indian wars will not cease until all the Indian tribes are absorbed in our population, and can be controlled by constables instead of soldiers." W. T. Sherman to John Sherman, December 30, 1866, and August 8, 1867. Rachel Sherman Thorndike, ed., *The Sherman Letters: Correspondence Between General and Senator Sherman from 1837 to 1891* (New York: Charles Scribner's Sons, 1894), 287, 293.

[37] Brig. General P. Edw. Connor, Commanding District of the Plains, to Col. N. Cole, Second Missouri Light Artillery, July 4, 1865. *The War of the Rebellion: A Compilation of the Official Records of the Union and Confederate Armies* (Washington: Government Printing Office, 1896), Ser. 1, 48, Pt. 2, 1049.

[38] Maj. Gen. John Pope, Headquarters Department of the Missouri, to Maj. Gen. G. M. Dodge, August 11, 1865. Ibid., Pt. 1, 356. Despite the odious nature of his order, Connor had earlier that year been awarded the rank of brevet major-general for gallant and meritorious service. He had seen hard service all the way west to California, and from Texas to the northern plains. Connor was honorably mustered out April 30, 1866, and died December 17, 1891. Francis B. Heitman, *Historical Register and Dictionary of the United States Army* (Washington: Government Printing Office, 1903), 1:321–22.

deem it advisable to take any steps in the matter until I hear the result of his expedition."[39]

While Evans vacillated in the governor's mansion, troops from Fort Larned routed large numbers of Cheyennes, Arapahoes, and Kiowas, easing tensions in western Kansas. Kit Carson, then serving as a colonel of New Mexico volunteers, rode into the Texas Panhandle with over three hundred men, plus seventy-five Jicarilla Apaches and their Ute allies serving as scouts. In late November they withstood several attacks from large numbers of Kiowas, Comanches, and some Plains Apaches and Arapahoes near the Bent brothers' abandoned trading post known as Adobe Walls. Cool-headed leadership, together with army artillery, saved the day. Carson lost only two soldiers and one of his Indian scouts killed outright, with many others wounded, some seriously. The Indians lost a great many more in the drawn-out affair. It all ended with deserted villages going up in flames, their former inhabitants left to face the coming winter without adequate shelter. As Capt. George H. Pettis explained, "The lodges were found to be full of plunder, including many hundreds of finely finished buffalo robes. Every man in the command took possession of one or more of these, while the balance were consumed in the lodges. There were found some white women's clothing, as well as articles of children's clothing, and several photographs; also a cavalry sergeant's hat, with letter and cross-sabers, cavalry saber and belts, etc."[40]

By the spring of 1865, worried army officers began scheduling caravans from Fort Larned, Kansas, and Fort Union, New Mexico, on the first and fifteenth of each month. All were to travel under heavy guard. The military acknowledged the need for more permanent facilities. One of these would be situated a dozen miles east of old Fort Atkinson, but nearer the confluence of the Dry and Wet Routes of the Santa Fe Trail south from Fort Larned. This new post was Fort Dodge.

---

[39] Gov. John Evans to Agent Samuel Colley, September 19, 1864, as quoted in Harry E. Kelsey, Jr., *Frontier Capitalist: The Life of John Evans* (Denver: State Historical Society of Colorado, 1969), 296n57.

[40] As quoted in Edwin L. Sabin, *Kit Carson Days, 1809–1868* New York: The Press of the Pioneers, Inc., 1935), 2:744–45.

Chapter 2

FORT DODGE

Maj. Gen. Grenville Mellen Dodge, spymaster and railroad builder for Generals Ulysses S. Grant and William T. Sherman, took command of the Department of the Missouri in December 1864. His area of responsibility included the old Department of Kansas, placing much of the central plains under his jurisdiction. Samuel R. Curtis had been relieved at his own request and transferred to the less stressful Department of the Northwest.

Grenville Dodge was at heart a railroad man, with much of his adult life associated with that industry.[1] As part of the Union Pacific's transcontinental ambitions before the Civil War, Dodge conducted surveys west of Council Bluffs. Even now his immediate supervisor, Maj. Gen. John Pope (sent west after defeat at Second Manassas and eventually given command of the Military Division of the Missouri) also had experience as a railroad surveyor in Indian country. Even President Lincoln's secretary of the interior, John P. Usher, enjoyed railroad connections early in his career.

Many of those now making decisions concerning tribes along the Arkansas owed a special allegiance to the railroad. Assuming conspiracy may be too harsh, but just how much these associations influenced decisions on the frontier is difficult to assess. Still, it seems naïve to turn a blind eye to the obvious benefits of ending Indian troubles along proposed rights of way. Railroad companies needed customers. Vacant land offered little chance of commercial development so long as potential settlers and ranchers believed it to be dominated by bands of lawless savages.

For bureaucrats, there seemed only two ways to handle Indians, aside from leaving them alone: treaties or open warfare. Military men were not

---

[1] T. Addison Busby, ed., *Biographical Directory of the Railroad Officials of America* (Chicago: The Railway Age, 1901), 142; Stanley P. Hirshson, *Grenville M. Dodge: Soldier, Politician, Railroad Pioneer* (Bloomington: Indiana University Press, 1967); Maury Klein, *Union Pacific: Birth of a Railroad, 1862–1893* (Garden City, N.Y.: Doubleday & Company, Inc., 1987); and David Haward Bain, *Empire Express: Building the First Transcontinental Railroad* (New York: Viking, 1999).

of one mind on this issue. Few placed much faith in treaties. Others held ambivalent views concerning tribes on the central plains, an attitude that brought with it occasional acquiescence to the peace process. These conflicting positions within the army helped set the pattern of intermittent negotiations interrupted by periods of distrust and hostility.

At Fort Leavenworth General Dodge discovered only two volunteer cavalry regiments in the whole of Kansas. Undaunted, he ordered these reluctant warriors into the field for a winter campaign to reopen communications along the South Platte River. They succeeded all too well, driving many Indians southward to threaten the old Santa Fe trade route. Dodge then ordered Brig. Gen. James Hobart Ford of the Second Colorado Cavalry,[2] and commander of the District of the Upper Arkansas at Fort Riley, to keep the trail open with a convincing show of force.[3] The Indians declined battle and Ford withdrew to winter at Fort Larned while making preparations for a spring offensive.

Meanwhile, Dodge argued departmental policy with Upper Arkansas Indian agent Jesse H. Leavenworth. An 1826 graduate of West Point, as well as a former civil engineer, Chicago lumber merchant, and recent colonel of the Second Colorado Infantry, Leavenworth was no stranger to the frontier. His deep sympathy for the tribes dated from the 1830s, when he accompanied his father, Col. Henry Leavenworth, on various western expeditions.[4]

---

[2] James H. Ford, an Ohio-born officer who entered the military as a Colorado volunteer, is referred to rather loosely in various sources as either "colonel" or "general." He was appointed a colonel of the Second Colorado Volunteers on December 5, 1863, but received a brevet brigadier general's rank on December 10, 1864. Officially discharged from service on July 19, 1865, he died a civilian at Akron, Ohio, on January 12, 1867, before learning that Ford County, Kansas, had been named in his honor. For a brief look at his military record, see Heitman, *Historical Register and Dictionary of the United States Army*, 1:429. For more detail, see Military File and Widow's Pension Records, James H. and Arabella Ford, National Archives and Records Service.

[3] As General Dodge explained his use of Colorado volunteers: "The three-months' Regiments enlisted in Colorado for the Indian service had been discharged, their time having expired, and there had been no troops sent to take their places. My only resource was to utilize the Colorado Militia until I could send troops 600 miles to take their places." Major-General Grenville M. Dodge, *The Battle of Atlanta and Other Campaigns, Addresses, Etc.* (Council Bluffs, Iowa: The Monarch Printing Company, 1910), 66.

[4] The colonel established a cantonment in 1827 that became Fort Leavenworth, the oldest army post still in operation west of the Mississippi. Robert W. Frazer, *Forts of the West: Military Forts and Presidios and Posts Commonly called Forts West of the Mississippi River to 1898* (Norman: University of Oklahoma Press, 1965), 56. In 1834, assigned a command on the southwestern frontier, Colonel Leavenworth led an expedition against the Pawnees and Comanches, his attitude toward whom profoundly influenced his son. Henry Leavenworth died on July 21, 1834, without knowing of his promotion to brigadier general. As a sign of respect, Indians escorted the body from Cross Timbers, near the falls of the Washita River. *Transactions of the Kansas State Historical Society*, vol. 7, 1901–1902 (Topeka: W. Y. Morgan, State Printer, 1902), 577–78; and Elvid Hunt, *History of Fort Leavenworth, 1827–1927* (Fort Leavenworth, Kans.: The General Service Schools Press, 1926), 286–90.

Jesse was convinced that military action only encouraged further atrocities, and recognized how easily the military could be politically manipulated.[5]

Leavenworth pleaded with Ford to keep his soldiers north of the Arkansas while he hurried plans for a peace conference. The worried agent had already interviewed representatives of the tribes, who again promised not to molest Santa Fe commerce or attack Kansas settlers. Ford sent Leavenworth's request on to Grenville Dodge. The general repeated his order to at least prepare for a spring campaign.

Adding to the confusion, a congressional mission headed by Wisconsin senator James R. Doolittle arrived at Fort Larned and immediately took up the cause of Agent Leavenworth. None of this should have surprised anyone. Responding to revulsion over the brutal Sand Creek massacre in 1864—the deliberate killing of children shifting the focus of public opinion—Congress created the committee to investigate the condition of Indians on the frontier, with emphasis on their treatment by the authorities.[6]

At Fort Larned Senator Doolittle got a little carried away, reporting, "After a long consultation, it was agreed that the [Ford] expedition should be abandoned, and Gen. [Alexander McD] McCook accordingly issued the order." The senator went on to explain, trying to justify personal involvement in military affairs: "It is not my province to criticize the official acts of major generals, but . . . I have since heard that the order was approved by Gen. Pope."[7] Dodge complained to Pope, who informed him from his headquarters at St. Louis of Senator Doolittle's mistaken impression: "You must do as you think best about Ford. General McCook had no authority from me to interfere in any manner with your troops."[8] Wanting to be kept informed, General Pope had insisted McCook accompany Doolittle.[9]

Grenville Dodge had no more patience for meddling legislators than he did for periodic promises from Indians to live in peace, and formed his

---

[5] William E. Unrau, "Indian Agent vs. the Army: Some Background Notes on the Kiowa-Comanche Treaty of 1865," *Kansas Historical Quarterly* 30, no. 2 (Summer 1964): 133.

[6] Robert M. Utley, *Frontiersmen in Blue: The United States Army and the Indian, 1848–1865* (New York: The Macmillan Company, 1967), 309.

[7] Lonnie J. White, ed., *Chronicle of a Congressional Journey: The Doolittle Committee in the Southwest, 1865* (Boulder, Colo.: Pruett Publishing Company, 1975), 21.

[8] Major-General John Pope to Major-General Dodge, June 3, 1865. *War of the Rebellion*, Ser. 1, 48, Pt. 2, 754.

[9] Major-General John Pope to Hon. E. M. Stanton, Secretary of War, April 22, 1865. Ibid., 157. Stanton responded that same day: "Send General McCook if he desires to go." For more on John Pope's position in all this, see Peter Cozzens, *General John Pope: A Life for the Nation* (Urbana: University of Illinois Press, 2000), 253–56; and Richard N. Ellis, *General Pope and U.S. Indian Policy* (Albuquerque: University of New Mexico Press, 1970), 82–85.

own ideas on what to do in dealing with both. Dodge shared the common failing of many contemporaries of being unable to distinguish between warring and peaceful bands within the same tribe. Not every Comanche or Kiowa raided the Santa Fe Trail. Even Jesse Leavenworth considered the Kiowas more troublesome than the Comanches.

Dodge saw the problem from a military point of view: "In my opinion there is but one way to effectually terminate these Indian troubles . . . to push our cavalry into the heart of their country from all directions, to punish them whenever and wherever we find them, and force them to respect our power and to sue for peace. Then let the military authorities make informal treaties with them for a cessation of hostilities." The general trusted officers more than he did outsiders: "If we can keep citizen agents and traders from among them we can, I am confident, settle the matter this season, and when settled I am clearly of the opinion that these Indians should be dealt with entirely by competent commissioned officers of the Army. . . . The cavalry now moving into the Indian country will, I doubt not, if allowed to proceed and carry out the instructions given them, accomplish the object designed by bringing about an effectual peace and permanent settlement of our Indian difficulties."[10]

General Ford began moving south in mid-March after scouts reported large numbers of Comanche, Kiowa, and Plains Apaches gathering on the Cimarron River. More Arapahoes camped on Crooked Creek. He wrote his departmental superiors, reiterating the position taken by Grenville Dodge about keeping agents and traders "out of the way until the fighting was over."[11] From St. Louis, Ford's letter traveled up the chain of command until it reached Henry W. Halleck, the army's chief of staff. Dodge, preparing his own campaign, was ordered to stand down by General Pope, who had scribbled on Ford's original document: "An expedition against these Indians was halted at the suggestion of Major Genl. Halleck, to allow Col. Leavenworth to make peace with these Indians. Leavenworth assured Genl. Halleck as I understand that he could do so. I do not believe that any sat-

---

[10] Maj. Gen. G. M. Dodge, Headquarters Department of the Missouri, to Maj. Gen. John Pope, Commanding Military Division of the Missouri, June 17, 1865. *War of the Rebellion*, Ser. 1, 48, Pt. 2, 911–12. Dodge thought so much of the points raised that he reproduced the entire text of this letter in his later reminiscences: Dodge, *The Battle of Atlanta and Other Campaigns*, 84–85. Regarding the policy position as outlined by General Dodge concerning Indian troubles on the Great Plains, General Pope's latest biographer concluded, "Pope could not have stated his purpose better himself." Cozzens, *General John Pope*, 254.

[11] Bvt. Brig. Gen. James H. Ford to Maj. J. W. Barnes, Asst. Adj. Gen., Department of the Missouri, April 12, 1865. *War of the Rebellion*, Ser. 1, 48, Pt. 2, 84.

isfactory peace can be made until the Indians have been punished and the property they have plundered from the trains of traders returned."[12]

Despite personal beliefs later expressed to General Pope that Leavenworth would fail,[13] Dodge issued orders to Ford on March 18, 1865: "Make arrangements to put a post at or near old Fort Atkinson as soon as practicable."[14] Growing impatient, he wrote again five days later, "I shall send you two additional companies of infantry as soon as I can replace them here [Fort Leavenworth], which will enable you to place a strong garrison at Fort Atkinson. I also desire you to . . . give freighters notice when the escorts start."[15] A frustrated Grenville Dodge wanted everything in place to launch his sidetracked Indian campaign the moment Jesse Leavenworth's peace efforts failed.

Complaining of inadequate protection, disgruntled traders characterized that portion of the trail west of Fort Larned as the Long Route. Aware of the grumbling, General Ford ordered Capt. Henry Pearce,[16] together with a company each of the Second U.S. Volunteer Infantry and the Eleventh Kansas Cavalry,[17] to march from Fort Larned to the confluence of the Dry and Wet Routes of the Santa Fe Trail and pick out a suitable military camp site.

Dismissing Atkinson and a place called Five-Mile Point, Pearce settled on a site known as Adkins' Ranch,[18] about nine miles east of the Fort Atkinson ruins. A stage stop had occupied that spot in 1863, but within a year Indians

[12] John Y. Simon, ed., *The Papers of Ulysses S. Grant, Volume 14: February 21, April 30, 1865* (Carbondale: Southern Illinois University Press, 1985), Calendar, April 24, 1865, 494. General Pope's endorsement, scribbled on Ford's original letter to Maj. J. W. Barnes, does not appear on the document as reproduced in the Official Records as cited in note 11 above.

[13] Major-General G. M. Dodge to Maj. Gen. John Pope, June 6 and 8, 1865. *War of the Rebellion*, Ser. 1, 48, Pt. 2, 796–97, 820–21.

[14] Major-General G. M. Dodge to Colonel Ford, March 18, 1865. Ibid., Ser. 1, 48, Pt. 1, 1211.

[15] Major-General G. M. Dodge to Bvt. Brig. Gen. James H. Ford, March 23, 1865. Ibid., 1246.

[16] Henry Pearce, an early resident of Emporia, Kansas, had served as a corporal in the Union Army. On December 10, 1862, he became a first lieutenant with Company C, Eleventh Regiment, Kansas Volunteer Cavalry. One year and nine days later he received his commission as captain. With the rest of his company he mustered out of service on August 7, 1865. *Report of the Adjutant General of the State of Kansas, 1861–1865* (Topeka: J. K. Hudson, State Printer, 1896), 199, 388.

[17] After seeing combat against Confederate forces, the Eleventh Kansas Cavalry was ordered to Fort Riley in December 1864. Companies C and E left for Fort Larned in February 1865. The remainder of the regiment moved to Fort Kearny, Nebraska, and then to Fort Laramie, Wyoming, to guard telegraph poles and confront Indians. Frederick H. Dyer, *A Compendium of the War of the Rebellion* (Des Moines, Iowa: The Dyer Publishing Company, 1908), 1184; and *Official Military History of Kansas Regiments During the War For the Suppression of the Great Rebellion* (Leavenworth, Kansas: W. S. Burke, 1870), 338.

[18] Scout H. D. Janes, In the Field, Fort Larned, to Lieut. J. E. Tappan, Fort Riley, April 11, 1865. *War of the Rebellion*, Ser. 1, 48, Pt. 2, 74–75.

burned it to the ground. Evidence suggests that the proprietor did more than simply aid stage travel. John Adkins, who later served as an interpreter and guide at Fort Dodge, had joined up with Fred Jones, Frank Walker, and John Cleveland to operate, it was said, a guerrilla band on that section of the trail, smuggling their illicit booty south into Texas.[19] After Indians destroyed the place a period of calm settled in, followed by an unimportant skirmish in August 1864, involving elements of the First Colorado Cavalry.[20]

On April 10, 1865, the day after Robert E. Lee surrendered to Ulysses S. Grant at Appomattox, Captain Pearce reported: "I hereby Establish and assume Command of Fort Dodge, Kansas."[21] Despite claims that the place was named in honor of Col. Henry Dodge,[22] one-time commander of the First Dragoons and later governor of Wisconsin, it was actually named for Grenville Mellen Dodge,[23] who later joked: "The Colonel of the regiment was very much incensed at my sending them out there without proper preparations and he said the place was so unpleasant and uninviting that they named it Camp Dodge. The Government afterwards established it as Ft. Dodge."[24] The general was confused; the place was called Fort Dodge from day one. His account does suggest the bleakness of the location. The army admitted drawbacks: "The place is weak in a military point of view, being commanded by the bluffs, and liable to surprise on account of the numerous ravines in the rear. In a sanitary point of view the location is bad, the low land being difficult to drain and flanked by a creek and low marshy ground. Malarial diseases are frequent during the autumn months."[25]

At first soldiers lived in tents, before high winds shredded the canvas,

---

[19] Louise Barry, "The Ranch at Cimarron Crossing," *The Kansas Historical Quarterly* 39, no. 3 (Autumn 1973): 349n14; and Oliva, *Soldiers on the Santa Fe Trail*, 163.

[20] Dyer, *A Compendium of the War of the Rebellion*, 1004. The author mistakenly identifies the site as "Atkins' Ranch."

[21] Headquarters Records, Fort Dodge, Kansas, General Order No. 1, April 10, 1865. Records of United States Army Continental Commands, 1821–1920.

[22] Henry Gannet, *The Origin of Certain Place Names in the United States* (Washington: Government Printing Office, 1902), 95; and *History of the State of Kansas* (Chicago: A. T. Andreas, 1883), 1560. This source, normally quite reliable, claims Henry Dodge "located a fort on the north side of the Arkansas which was named Dodge . . . some four miles below where Dodge City is now located," while returning from his 1835 expedition to the Rocky Mountains. This is not true, although Fort Dodge, Iowa, was named for him.

[23] Even the Kansas State Historical Society had difficulty deciding which Dodge the fort was named for. Yet they, too, settled on Grenville Mellen Dodge, "the authority being 'Circular No. 4, U.S. Surgeon General's Office, 1870.'" *Transactions of the Kansas State Historical Society*, vol. 7, 1901–1902 (Topeka: State Printer, 1902), 579.

[24] Grenville M. Dodge to Joseph B. Thoburn, October 24, 1910. Manuscripts Department, Kansas State Historical Society.

[25] *Report on Barracks and Hospitals, with Descriptions of Military Posts, Circular No. 4* (Washington: Government Printing Office, 1870), 301.

forcing dugouts to be built along the riverbank, each just large enough to house four cramped men. Some seventy of these, intended for the enlisted ranks, were completed that first year. Officers occupied mostly sod buildings. The hospital, too, was built from blocks of earth. The nearness to the river did guarantee an uninterrupted supply of water in case of siege. Lumber shipped from army depots farther east allowed some improvement. Roofs were raised, with walls reinforced with scraps of canvas.

A small stand of trees a dozen miles distant helped with roof beams, corrals, and firewood, but heavy rains stressed the already saturated sod walls. Poor food and limited diversions added scurvy and boredom to the list of complaints. During that first winter, with travel suspended and Indians in camp for the season, troops at Fort Dodge could do little more than struggle to stay warm. Seven men died that first year. Afterward spring weather helped slow the desertion rate by suppressing feelings of self pity. Soldiers, falling victim to spring fever, built a small sod rectangle for a sutler's store, imagining shelves stocked with goods, chiefly whiskey, to help break the cycle of monotony.

By early summer 1865, following a formal recommendation by the Post Council of Administration, sutler J. William Ladd opened for business. He received supplies from his partner, Theodore Weichselbaum, who held trading rights at other Kansas outposts. The joy over Ladd's arrival was short-lived, as he followed the old practice of offering second-rate merchandise at inflated prices. It seemed pointless to complain, but traders could at least supply, at the behest of the commanding officer, liquor, beer, and wine.

The secretary of war, caught up in a sea of moral righteousness following the Civil War, inadvertently helped civilian entrepreneurs by refusing to allow whiskey to be issued through the army's commissary or subsistence departments. Commanders might wish to discourage drunkenness, but keeping whiskey and other spirits separated from the thirsty garrison proved impossible. Civilian caravans provided a steady supply, welcoming the chance for making a profit. Men smuggled gallons at a time past sympathetic sentries. After all, enlisted men often found sutler's supplies restricted, or at least rationed by superiors. Restrictions of that sort seldom applied to officers, many of whom suffered the same problems with alcohol as did lesser ranks. In time local "whiskey ranches" dominated the trade, before being superseded by the saloons and other distractions of Dodge City.

No sooner had Fort Dodge been garrisoned than General Ford's replacement, John B. Sanborn, received word that representatives from the Comanches, Kiowas, Cheyennes, Arapahoes, and Plains Apaches were camped on Cow Creek awaiting another council. General Sanborn suspended operations until the peace commissioners, including himself, along with Jesse Leavenworth, Kit Carson, and William Bent, came together. The result was the so-called Treaty of the Little Arkansas, one of many ineffectual instruments negotiated during the Indian wars.[26] The success of the treaty process was prematurely compromised when some Indians carried out raids on their way to the peace talks, with one band of Kiowas killing five traders from a Mexican caravan near Fort Dodge.

No surge of confidence resulted from these negotiations. Not only were the Arapahoes and Cheyennes assigned lands already given to the Cherokees, the biggest blunder came from promising Comanches and Kiowas a reservation in the Texas Panhandle.[27] But the commissioners failed to realize they had no jurisdiction in Texas. It took the federal government four years to untangle this mess. When Texas became a state it retained all its public lands, allowing no exception for reservations or other federal incursions, an important point for Dodge City in 1874.

With questions of peace undecided, but hoping to improve conditions, officers at Fort Dodge commandeered government wagons and side-tracked them to haul in quarried limestone. Using civilian labor, construction began on two barracks, each designed to house fifty men, a formal headquarters and commanding officer's residence, a hospital, a quartermaster's depot, and supply buildings. And none too soon, as one commander, Maj. Henry Douglass, bitterly complained: "the house I lived in was no palace but a hovel. I never moved from it until I was a wasted cholera convalescent, my wife died in it and a want of proper comfort was in my opinion, the main cause of her death."[28]

Black troops reporting for duty were segregated into quarters doubling as a general supply area. Hospital accommodations, too, allowed no mixing of the races. Nor did it help that two companies of black infantry, traveling

---

[26] Charles J. Kappler, comp., *Indian Affairs, Laws and Treaties* (Washington: Government Printing Office, 1904), 2:887–95.

[27] David Kay Strate, *Sentinel to the Cimarron: The Frontier Experience of Fort Dodge, Kansas* (Dodge City: Cultural Heritage and Arts Center, 1970), 26.

[28] Major Henry Douglass to Asst. Adj. Gen, District of the Upper Arkansas, December 21, 1866. Headquarters Records, Fort Dodge, Kansas. Letters Sent.

through from Fort Harker during the summer of 1867, may have introduced the cholera that killed twenty-two solders and civilians at Fort Dodge, out of thirty-four reported cases.[29] The last of the cases was Robert M. Wright, who would survive to become one of the founders of Dodge City.[30]

In 1868 President Andrew Johnson authorized the creation of the Fort Dodge Military Reservation to try and keep the area free of civilians. The land chosen extended from the river northward, covering more than forty-three thousand acres, large enough to encompass adequate supplies of water, grass, and wood. Yet with the post located on the reservation's southern boundary, civilian activity directly across the Arkansas could not be controlled. This oversight caused trouble from the beginning.

Even before the president's intervention, others hoped to limit the army's jurisdiction to just four square miles. Major Douglass suspected his post chaplain, Alvin G. White, of supplying sensitive information to outside parties. One of these, a man named E. P. Wheeler, squatted for a time near the fort's flagpole, building himself a ramshackle trading post. Douglass assumed greed as the motivation behind White and his associates—including a fellow appropriately named Crook. Their pleas of innocence fell on deaf ears after Douglass discovered most of Wheeler's goods hidden in the chaplain's quarters. Without offering specifics, White claimed these items were repayment of a personal debt. Douglass thought otherwise. The disgruntled holy man and his cohorts would be heard from again, launching endless salvos of wild accusations and lawsuits, and for a time causing the army more trouble than the Indians.

Civilians had been a source of trouble from the start, a pattern of behavior that would lead directly to the founding of Dodge City. Two years before, a Mr. Boggs convinced one naïve Cheyenne to accept in trade eleven $1 bills for eleven $10 notes. Boggs chuckled over his cleverness, but his tri-

[29] Records of the Adjutant General's Office, Field Records of Hospitals, Fort Dodge, Kansas (RG 94), "Special Report of Cholera Patients at Fort Dodge, Kansas, July–August 1867," 229–35; and Ramon Powers and Gene Younger, "Cholera on the Plains: The Epidemic of 1867 in Kansas," *Kansas Historical Quarterly* 37, no. 4 (Winter 1971): 378–79.

[30] Field Records of Hospitals, Fort Dodge, Kansas (RG 94), "Register of the Sick and Wounded, 1867," Patient No. 131, "Robert M. Wright, Citizen"; and Robert M. Wright, *Dodge City, the Cowboy Capital and the Great Southwest* (Wichita: Wichita Eagle Press, 1913), 62–63. It may be useful to some readers to explain that two early printings of this book exist. Although the content is the same, the pagination differs. True 1913 first editions have 344 pages, while the subsequent reprint has only 342. As a result, citations quoted as coming from the first but actually pulled from the second, may not precisely correspond with one another by page number. All references here are from an original first edition.

umph was short-lived. Discovering the swindle, the enraged Indian and three friends waylaid Boggs's son six miles from Fort Dodge. There they murdered the helpless boy, leaving his scalped and mangled corpse on the riverbank as if presenting public testimony. Soldiers buried the boy's remains at the post cemetery. Not knowing his full name, a clerk scribbled the words "Boggs child" to record the interment in a military burial ledger.[31]

Officers at Fort Dodge worried about the large quantities of arms and ammunition reaching Indian camps. Suppliers included agents authorized by the Interior Department as well as independent traders, putting them at cross purposes with the military. Major Douglass complained in particular about one future Dodge City luminary: "Charley Rath, a trader, who lives at Zarah has armed several bands of Kiowas with Revolvers and has completely overstocked them with Powder."[32] Later, Douglass passed on information from a man named Baker, who claimed the Cheyennes had "an almost inexhaustible supply of ammunition . . . [and] used it more lavishly than he had ever seen Indians use it before." When the trapper asked why they wasted so much firepower, "they said they had *plenty more* of it *at home*."[33]

Fort Dodge veterans viewed Baker's comments with disgust, reflecting their own troubles obtaining supplies. Allotments always favored the short side. In the spring of 1866, one desperate commander watched his stocks of ammunition dwindle to 3 rounds per man. A special inspector of cavalry arrived on an unscheduled tour and loaned the garrison 336 rounds. Quartermasters at Fort Leavenworth seemed in no hurry to fill requests from commanders guarding the all-important Arkansas crossings. Civilians remained more responsive to their clients' needs.

Indians wanted white men off the High Plains. In February 1867 Kiowa chief Satanta so informed Henry Douglass, claiming that all the area's land, timber, and water belonged to him. This rather formidable individual also demanded an end to all construction, withdrawal of all troops, and specified that no roads or railroads be pushed beyond Council Grove. The major explained he could do nothing, having been ordered by the president to pro-

[31] "List of Interments made in the Post Cemetery, Fort Dodge, Kansas," No. 22, Boggs Child, February 1866. Records of the Adjutant General's Office, Medical History of Post, Vol. 81, Records Relating to Fort Dodge, Kansas (RG 94), National Archives and Records Service.

[32] Maj. Henry Douglass to Asst. Adj. Gen., Department of the Missouri, January 13, 1867. Fort Dodge, Letters Sent.

[33] Maj. Henry Douglass to Major Henry E. Noyes, Headquarters, District of the Upper Arkansas, March 19, 1867. Ibid.

tect the trail and punish anyone, Indian or white, who plundered the road. Troops from Fort Dodge pursued Indians, to be sure, but they also hunted down horse thieves, whiskey peddlers, murderers, and other riff raff.

As if exercising his right of ownership, Satanta, already familiar with procedures at Fort Dodge, led a raiding party against its corrals in June 1867. Killing one man, they succeeded in driving the stolen horses across the river. Satanta's own horse was shot, but soldiers recovered only two of their own animals. A week later Douglass admitted, "I certainly expected no attack from this source so soon after his solemn protestations, & promises to be peaceable," adding with some frustration, "There is no doubt, but that all the Indians of the Country are at war with us. Their peace promises were only mere pretexts to gain time. . . . They are all at war, and I do not believe it would be proper to make any distinction."[34]

Stranded without mounts, embarrassed soldiers at Fort Dodge stood powerless to counter Indian unrest. Civilians blamed everything on departmental inefficiency, without taking into account the limitations of an overburdened garrison. About the same time two civilian teamsters opened fire on each other. One man died, and the other nursed his wounds in the guardhouse. In less than a month two wood contractors reenacted the drama with identical results: one dead, one wounded. Within weeks both survivors were shuffled off to Fort Harker to stand trial in Ellsworth County. Later in the year members of the Thirty-Seventh Infantry quarreled with employees of the Southern Overland Mail and Express Company at Cimarron Crossing. More gunfire ensued and a soldier and two civilians lay dead. Two other soldiers faced charges.

Major Douglass learned that a member of Bishop Jean Baptiste Lamy's caravan to New Mexico was a suspected cattle thief. The owner identified both his property and the guilty party. Douglass ordered full restitution. Tongue-in-cheek, he reported to his superiors: "The Bishop agreed to this & commended my sense of justice and left with many expressions of his regard. From a conversation Lieut. [Stanley A.] Browne had with him after he left the post, I should judge that the Bishop has changed his opinion on the subject."[35]

Frustrated by civilian lawbreakers, the military hoped to at least reach some sort of agreement with the tribes. After a series of false starts every-

---

[34] Maj. Henry Douglass to Bvt. Brig. Gen. Chauncey McKeever, Headquarters, Department of the Missouri, June 18, 1867. Ibid.

one seemed ready to try. By late October 1867 the government engaged representatives from the Comanches, Kiowas, Arapahoes, Cheyennes, and Plains Apaches in peace talks at Medicine Lodge Creek. The result called for an end to hostilities and the establishment of reservations, albeit linked with promises from tribal leaders to surrender all claims north of the Arkansas.[36] Everyone expected the military to enforce the treaty.

Those familiar with conditions along the frontier greeted the Medicine Lodge Treaty with skepticism. Spring saw the Indians again crossing the river on their annual pilgrimage. Army scout and interpreter John Simpson Smith reported possible trouble with the Kiowas, claiming Satanta "has just returned from a trip into Fort Dodge, and appears very much dissatisfied with his treatment while there."[37]

Recalling Satanta's earlier attack against his stockade, Major Douglass rejected Smith's remarks outright, insisting instead, "No Indian has been so well treated at Fort Dodge as this same Indian,—he was fed while here and ten days rations apiece was given to him and his party." He then made the point, "I refused him liquor which made him angry. He walked into my room when I was absent and drank a Bottle full of El Paso wine,—he contrived in some way to obtain liquor and became intoxicated. . . . [W]henever he saw a bottle he assumed the privilege of drinking from it no matter what was the nature of the Contents." Douglass concluded— not without a smile, one can assume—"And the last thing he did, was to go the Stage Station, and seeing a Bottle he seized it, and pouring out a tumbler full of the contents drank it down,—it happened to be some medicine that . . . the Road Agent had prepared for physicking [sic] a horse."[38] The resulting intestinal distress convinced Satanta that officers at Fort Dodge had conspired to poison him.

---

[35] Maj. Henry Douglass to Asst. Adj. Gen., Department of the Missouri, July 23, 1867. Ibid.

[36] Kappler, comp., *Indian Affairs, Laws and Treaties*, 2:977–89; and Douglas C. Jones, *The Treaty of Medicine Lodge: The Story of the Great Treaty Council as Told by Eyewitnesses* (Norman: University of Oklahoma Press, 1966), passim.

[37] John S. Smith to Thomas Murphy, Supt. of Indian Affairs, February 23, 1868. Copy in Fort Dodge Headquarters Records. John Simpson Smith had been at Fort Mann, arriving there along with Lewis Garrard on May 15, 1847. Authorities prevailed upon Smith to replace Daniel Mann as the person in charge. Smith did not last long, pulling out a week later after deciding the proffered sixty dollars a month inadequate compensation for the dangers involved. Ann W. Hafen, "John Simpson Smith." LeRoy R, Hafen, ed., *The Mountain Men and the Fur Trade of the Far West* (Glendale, Calif.: The Arthur H. Clark Company, 1968), 5:333–35; and Stan Hoig, *The Western Odyssey of John Simpson Smith* (Glendale, California: The Arthur H. Clark Company, 1974), 62–65.

[38] Maj. Henry Douglass to Bvt. Brig. Gen. Chauncey McKeever, Headquarters, Department of the Missouri, March 1, 1868. Fort Dodge, Letters Sent.

With whiskey ranches dotting the countryside, Satanta's escapade was no isolated incident. Douglass had earlier ordered a detachment to inspect troops stationed between Dodge and old Fort Aubrey (opened in September 1865 near the later site of Syracuse, Kansas, then abandoned seven months later). The soldiers carried special authorization: "As there is sufficient evidence to prove that liquor has been sold to escorts in violation [of standing orders] by the Ranche men belonging to Bluff Ranche; you will cause all liquors, wines, beer, or any other intoxicating drink found at that ranche to be destroyed, and the proprietor to be warned, that should he again resume the sale of liquor in the manner prohibited, his establishment will be closed & his person seized."[39]

Soon afterward seven Indians attacked a Mexican wagon train near Nine-Mile Ridge, long known as a dangerous point, and ran off most of the stock. The Mexicans demanded protection from Major Douglass, who responded that he lacked sufficient numbers to escort every wagon train and stagecoach, adding that fifty armed men with fifteen hundred rounds of ammunition should be able to protect themselves, "provided they will only fight."[40] What troubled Douglass were reports that the Mexicans carried a large inventory of whiskey that they sold in lots of a gallon or more to anyone, including soldiers, willing to pay the asking price. Eastbound passengers and stage company employees complained of drunken escorts, as did Robert M. Wright, co-proprietor of the ranch at Cimarron Crossing, some twenty-eight miles west of Fort Dodge.[41]

Because whiskey from the Mexican train "was not dealt out in small quantities but sold . . . by the gallon, sometimes ten gallons at a time," Douglass ordered it destroyed. His decision did not come in time to help everyone, most of whom "were almost continually drunk, disorderly & riotous: in fact one affray was of a very serious character: it commenced at Bluff Ranche & ended at the Ranche at Cimarron Crossing, costing the lives of two citizens & one soldier & greatly jeopardizing the lives of stage

---

[39] Maj. Henry Douglass to Lt. H. M. Karples, 37th Inf., September 15, 1867. Ibid. Lieutenant Karples may not have been the best man to deliver such a stern disciplinary warning, as he would be cashiered from the army himself less than a year later.

[40] Maj. Henry Douglas to Sénor Gonzalez, 10 Miles above Cimarron Crossing, September 14, 1867. Ibid.

[41] For more on these locations, see: 1st Lt. D. W. Wallingford to Lt. L. Schonborn, August 23, 1868. Headquarters Records, Fort Dodge, Kansas. Reports of Detachments: "I proceeded to Cimarron Crossing some Twenty-Eight (28) miles West of this post . . . at this Crossing there was a Ranche and a stack of hay, containing about Seventy five (75) tons." The second site referred to was then operated by Bob Wright and A. J. Anthony.

passengers one of whom was a lady. This affray is traceable to liquor pro-
cured from this train."[42]

Reaching New Mexico, the owners fired off complaints to their influential congressional representative, José Francisco Chaves, demanding he
intercede with General Grant. Chaves insisted the military had refused to
protect peaceful traders under attack by swarms of hostile warriors. Free-
ing themselves after a frantic daylong battle, they moved on, only to be
overtaken by soldiers intent on destroying their cargo of whiskey. Chaves
characterized the whole affair as a "great outrage." Of course he made no
mention of the big whiskey sale at Bluff Ranch, the next station beyond
Cimarron Crossing.[43]

Douglass made light of Chaves's version of events: "The . . . attack was
but a small affair at best: the *desperate character* of the fighting may be
inferred from the casualties, the loss on both sides consisting of one
Indian pony Killed by a soldier." Then, after detailing the troubles surrounding whiskey sales, the major concluded: "The right to transport
liquor . . . I have not in this act disputed—but when those in charge of
trains 'lay to' no matter for what cause, & give away, traffic, or sell liquor
in an Indian Country & without license—it is clear to me that the [June
30, 1834, statute] in relation to the introduction & sale of spirituous
liquors in the Indian County, is thereby violated."[44] Mr. Chaves kept quiet,
although disputes involving civilian commerce continued.

The major then faced problems closer to home. Chaplain Alvin
White—who had earlier plotted with E. P. Wheeler to take over valuable
portions of the Fort Dodge Military Reservation—decided to reinvent
himself as a trader using Wheeler's goods. The post adjutant informed
him, "You have no right to negotiate for the sale of goods on this reservation or to receive payment in your house for the delivery of goods thus
negotiated. Any goods purchased from Wheeler's Ranch must be negotiated for at that place or at some place outside of the Reservation. No
Agent of that establishment will be permitted on this Military Reserve."[45]

---

[42] Maj. Henry Douglass to Bvt. Brig. Gen. Chauncey McKeever, Headquarters, Department of the Missouri,
January 24, 1868. Fort Dodge, Letters Sent.

[43] Louise Barry, "The Ranch at Cimarron Crossing," *Kansas Historical Quarterly* 39, no. 3 (Autumn 1973): 365.

[44] Maj. Henry Douglass to Bvt. Brig. Gen. Chauncey McKeever, Headquarters, Department of the Missouri,
January 24, 1868. Fort Dodge, Letters Sent.

[45] 2nd Lieut. Thomas Wallace to Rev'd. A. G. White, March 11, 1868. Ibid. Wheeler's so-called "ranch" was not
a ranch in the traditional sense, but simply a small plot of ground south of the river and opposite the fort on
which he squatted to carry out his own ideas of a business enterprise.

The errant chaplain did not accept this reprimand with grace, choosing instead to confront Major Douglass. White soon learned that his partner E. P. Wheeler, along with scout William "Apache Bill" Seamans, faced charges of introducing liquor into Indian country. Douglass also ordered the interpreter Fred Jones and a civilian named Ben Howell arrested, but later relented, despite their threats of vengeance. The United States marshal at Topeka requested White's appearance in the Wheeler case.

Ignoring official channels, White sent a letter to the army's adjutant general at Washington, attacking Douglass for running a saloon and billiard parlor, while also allowing lewd theatrical performances. The major responded by pointing out that billiards "is now considered a respectable game." He went on to describe how White used his quarters to store goods, including whiskey, and that he "devoted almost his whole time to the acquisition of money."[46] White and his friends conspired to have Douglass and two other officers indicted by a federal grand jury at Topeka for selling liquor to Indians. An embarrassed 2nd Lt. Philip Reade of the Third Infantry, a newly appointed deputy U.S. marshal, carried out the arrests.

Wheeler sent a letter to Kansas governor Samuel J. Crawford, leveling additional charges against Henry Douglass and much of the officer corps at Fort Dodge. Wheeler claimed, among other things, that an officer had forged a quartermaster's check and then blamed him; that he was jailed without sufficient food; and that officers had joined forces to stop service of a federal warrant on one of their friends, all guilty of misappropriating government property.

Douglass answered with documentation showing that the incident surrounding the quartermaster's check involved Wheeler and a man named Moore: "There being good reason to believe that Wheeler and Moore were the forgers or implicated in the forgeries. Lieut. Reade arrested the parties and requested the Comdg. Officer to hold them until he heard from the Civil Authorities."

The major explained how White drafted Wheeler's letter to Governor Crawford: "It would be a moral absurdity to attribute the authorship to Wheeler or Moore. The former has neither the brains or [sic] stamina and the latter is a simple half witted individual, and as such a ready tool to fulfill the mandates of the Master mind of this trio. I have seen similar let-

---

[46] Maj. Henry Douglass to Bvt. Maj. Gen. E. D. Townsend, Asst. Adj. Gen., Washington, April 1, 1868. Ibid.

ters before, which have been proved to have been taken from the Chaplain's rough drafts."[47]

Belittling the charges against him, Douglass outlined his troubles with Wheeler and his friends. Regarding the accusation of selling a quart of whiskey to an Indian, the major wrote: "the charge of selling a quart is simply ridiculous, an officer might as an act of hospitality have given an Indian visiting his quarters a drink, as Gen. Sheridan has done, as some of the Peace Commissioners did, but the charge of giving a quantity even a pint is absurd."[48] References to Philip Sheridan and the peace commissioners did not go unnoticed. In mentioning both Douglass placed himself and his officers in good company.

The whole affair became a bizarre mixture of charges and countercharges. Wheeler and the others, including the disgruntled interpreter Fred Jones, a one-time associate of reputed smuggler John Adkins, claimed Douglass got drunk with Satanta, and cavorted with an Indian girl underneath a billiard table. Capping the performance, they shocked everyone with a display of suggestive dancing. His accusers outdid themselves—not even Douglass's detractors within the army could picture that scene.

The case against Douglass and his officers collapsed, although proceedings continued from the June through October terms of the district court at Topeka. Alvin White, in declining to resume his clerical duties at Fort Dodge, claimed he suffered from bronchitis and typhoid symptoms. For his reward, the less-than-devout chaplain suffered a court-martial and was booted out of the army.[49] Fred Jones recovered and got himself hired on as an interpreter at Fort Hays, though Douglass warned the post's commander against retaining Jones in government service.[50] Douglass survived

---

[47] Maj. Henry Douglass to Bvt. Brig. Gen. Chauncey McKeever, Department of the Missouri, July 29, 1868. Ibid.

[48] Maj. Henry Douglass to Bvt. Maj. Gen. E. D. Townsend, Asst. Adj. Gen., Washington, July 30, 1868. Ibid.

[49] Post Returns, Fort Dodge, Kansas, December 1868, and Special Order No. 2, January 3, 1868: "The present Post Treasurer will allow the council free access to the retained papers of A. G. White U.S.A. (since Dismissed [from] the service)." Headquarters Records, Fort Dodge, Kansas. Also see Heitman, *Historical Register and Dictionary of the United States Army*, 1:1027; and Strate, *Sentinel to the Cimarron*, 66. Some people, including Sam Radges, the deputy postmaster at Fort Dodge in 1867, insisted White was innocent, presenting him as the one falsely accused. *Topeka Daily Capital*, October 8, 1905, as quoted in John W. Ripley, ed., *The Legacy of Sam Radges, Publisher and Historian* (Topeka: Shawnee County Historical Society, 1973), 4–5.

[50] Nor was General Sheridan impressed with the various specimens hired for government service: "In those days the railroad town of Hays City was filled with so-called 'Indian scouts,' whose common boast was of having slain scores of redskins, but the real scout—that is, a guide and trailer knowing the habits of the Indians—was very scarce, and it was hard to find anybody familiar with the country south of the Arkansas." P. H. Sheridan, *Personal Memoirs of P. H. Sheridan, General United States Army* (New York: Charles L. Webster & Company, 1888), 2:299.

the upheavals at Fort Dodge and later served as superintendent of Indian Affairs in Nevada.[51]

THROUGHOUT THE INDIAN WARS of the late 1860s, Fort Dodge served chiefly as a supply depot and clearinghouse for military communications. The volume of supplies shipped was remarkable. Unfortunately, not all cargoes were military, as the area still supported a lucrative trade in illegal spirits, a large volume of which flowed southward into Indian Territory. John Simpson Smith, the army scout and interpreter, warned that whiskey peddlers were single-handedly heightening tension. He seemed to be in a position to know, and not just through his official duties, for he once "distinguished his visit [to Fort Dodge] by remaining for the greater part of it in a state of intoxication." Smith claimed to know the names of guilty traders, but was dismissed as "utterly unreliable when truth is to be ascertained.—And is besides addicted to hard drinking."[52] Officers acknowledged, however, their own inability to stamp out the illegal traffic. Problems with whiskey traders would plague the area for years.

At the end of the 1860s a quiet period settled over Fort Dodge, with its commanders concerned more with civilian lawbreakers than marauding Indians. The situation became so tense that one commander issued an order to his adjutant to rid the post of vagrants. By the spring of 1872 temporary post commander Tullius C. Tupper complained directly to the United States marshal about stolen government rifles, claiming that John Hunt's nearby ranch served as the main repository. Troublemakers did not restrict themselves to stealing government property and selling liquor, but also engaged in the wholesale theft of horses, mules, and cattle.

Nor could officers keep trouble of another sort from disrupting the routine at Fort Dodge. Tensions continued among those hoping to monopolize trading rights. As early as August 1868, Robert M. Wright, until then content to run a trading and hay ranch at Cimarron Crossing with his part-

[51] By early 1869 Douglass was acquitted of all charges Wheeler and the others leveled against him. Awaiting reassignment he directed all communications be sent in care of his older brother, Andrew E., vice president of the Hazard Powder Company in New York City. Andrew Douglass later became an archaeologist specializing in American Indian remains. One wonders how much his brother's frontier experience influenced him. Henry Douglass retired as a colonel from the Tenth Infantry in 1891. George W. Cullum, *Biographical Register of the Officers and Graduates of the U.S. Military Academy at West Point, N. Y.* (Boston: Houghton, Mifflin and Company, 1891), 2:501–502.

[52] Maj. Henry Douglass to Bvt. Brig. Gen. Chauncey McKeever, Department of the Missouri, March 24, 1868. Fort Dodge, Letters Sent.

ner A. J. Anthony, asked permission to open a store at Fort Dodge. Since he held no authorizing warrant, the post adjutant refused. The enterprising Mr. Wright then did took the necessary steps, and within months he and John E. Tappan, another who had finagled trading rights, began competing.[53] Wright, dreaming of unopposed profits, continued to lobby hard for a monopoly. In early June 1869 the Department of the Missouri ordered Capt. Andrew Sheridan to remove all traders not holding written authorization. Tappan, a one-time lieutenant at Fort Riley, found himself out of business, but his partner C. F. Tracy proved just as resourceful as Bob Wright and weaseled a fresh appointment for himself.

Assistant post surgeon William S. Tremaine filed a formal complaint demanding that both Wright and Tracy stop selling liquor to hospital patients. Despite closing Wright's bar on occasion, or imposing a by-the-glass limit on enlisted personnel, officers demanded special treatment, including a private bar. Wright complied, knowing the advantages of exchanging favors, while still scheming for monopoly status. But that frontier entrepreneur worried about more than trading rights. Indians attacked and killed three of the men he employed as woodchoppers near Mulberry Creek. Wright soon faced troubles closer to home.

One incident erupted in late 1871 between two officers who had been conducting a personal feud for nearly a year. Capt. Orlando H. Moore came through Dodge on his way from Fort Hays to Camp Supply. Stopping to refresh himself at Wright's store, he spotted Capt. Joseph B. Rife, who had transferred to Fort Dodge only nine days before. Rushing to his quarters, Rife returned with a rawhide whip and small pocket pistol. The two traded insults before Rife uncoiled his whip. Moore answered with his fists. Bystanders separated the enraged combatants. Undeterred, Rife pulled his pistol and fired. The ball glanced off Moore's pocket watch, saving his life. Captain Rife was arrested and sent to Fort Hays for trial. In the end authorities allowed him to resign, owing to meritorious service at the

---

[53] Capt. Andrew Sheridan to Bvt. Brig. Gen. Chauncey McKeever, Department of Missouri, May 3, 1869. Ibid. Here it was pointed out that John E. Tappan had been appointed post sutler by the Council of Administration, but that "Mr. R. M. Wright the Post Trader is here by virtue of authority granted him to open a trading establishment at Fort Dodge, Kas., Special Order No. 222. Ext. VII Headqrs. Dept. of the Mo., Fort Leavenworth, Kansas, November 12th, 1868. No order of any Kind in regards to permission to trade here is on file in this office, in relation to Mr. J. E. Tappan." Nearly two years later the War Department reaffirmed Wright's appointment, and he was so notified on October 7, 1870. Capt. Edward S. Moale, Post Commander, to Asst. Adj. Gen., Department of the Missouri, January 3, 1871. Ibid.

battle of Antietam. Moore retired a lieutenant colonel in 1884. This would not be Bob Wright's last experience involving army officers and violence.

Together with all his predecessors, Maj. Richard Irving Dodge, a by-the-book officer with the Third Infantry who assumed command on June 4, 1872, understood problems of civilians congregating near the fort.[54] These people now seemed more organized than ever. Within two weeks of taking over, Major Dodge requested that the military reservation be expanded one mile south of the Arkansas, explaining, "This is absolutely necessary for the preservation of discipline and good order at this post. Rum shops and disreputable resorts are being established on the South bank of the river, which will cause great trouble as soon as the river becomes fordable."[55] Within days word traveled down the chain of command: "the Commanding General directs me to inform you that your recommendation is *not approved*."[56] The major's disappointment was short-lived. Within weeks the beginnings of Dodge City ended the controversy. Those crowding south of the river hurried to the new site, west of the military reservation.

The major also addressed the issue of whiskey, ordering his adjutant to inform Bob Wright: "you are authorized, until further orders, to open your Store for the sale of Spirituous Liquors. . . . The commanding officer grants this permission with great reluctance, as he is convinced that the post is better off without whiskey; and he will withdraw it as soon as he finds you are unable to regulate the sale of your Liquor so as to prevent drunkenness."[57] Despite precautions, whiskey continued to cause trouble, so much so that the summer of 1872 witnessed a climax.

As a prelude, Capt. Edward Moale informed the commander at Camp Supply about a delay in forwarding the mail. On the morning of their departure, men assigned to the detail were found to be hopelessly drunk. After the mail did move south Bob Wright was asked by what authority he had sold liquor by the bottle to a Third Infantry private. Wright's reply satisfied no one, and he was ordered to close his bar and discharge his bartender. His new friend, Major Dodge, later granted a reprieve.

---

[54] General Order No. 16, June 4, 1872. Headquarters Records, Fort Dodge, Kansas, General Orders and Circulars, Volume 1, and Post Returns, Fort Dodge, Kansas, June 1872. Maj. Richard I. Dodge, acting pursuant to Special Order No. 89, Department of the Missouri, May 27, 1872, arrived on June 3 and assumed command the following day.

[55] Maj. Richard I. Dodge to Asst. Adj. Gen., Department of the Missouri, June 18, 1872. Fort Dodge, Letters Sent.

[56] Asst. Adj. Gen., Department of the Missouri, to the Commanding Officer, Fort Dodge, Kansas, June 24, 1872. Fort Dodge, Registered Letters Received.

[57] 1st Lieut. William Krause, Post Adjutant, to R. M. Wright, June 19, 1872. Fort Dodge, Letters Sent.

Then, on July 29, 1872, 2nd Lt. Edward Palmer Turner and a detachment of Tenth Cavalry troopers rode in from Camp Supply to serve as escort for Ezra B. Kirk, the assistant quartermaster. While crossing the Arkansas their wagon and team bogged down in the river's soft bottom. Rather than correct their carelessness—and thinking instead of whiskey—Turner and his men abandoned the animals and wagon and headed straight for Bob Wright's sutler store. The young lieutenant, together with two sergeants and several troopers, soon staggered from the effects. Turner fired off his revolver in the store, rode a horse into the billiard room, and then tried repeating the performance at Wright's private residence. Major Dodge leaped into the fray but was himself assaulted, as was the officer of the day. The indignant post commander responded by clubbing Lieutenant Turner into submission with a billiard cue and ordering him dragged to the guardhouse.

That September Turner faced court-martial at Fort Hays. Though he was convicted, the final result must have frustrated Major Dodge. The lieutenant's family enjoyed close ties to the powerful. His military record shows that he rose in rank from private to second lieutenant on General Sherman's personal recommendation. The general had acted on a request from Turner's father, a former rear admiral, and at the time of his son's troubles on the Kansas frontier, the retired commander of the South Pacific Squadron. Nor did it hurt the young man's chances that his uncle, Henry Smith Turner, a West Point graduate and one-time assistant treasurer of the United States at St. Louis, had been a banking associate of Sherman's in San Francisco during the gold rush. This was the same man who had served as acting assistant adjutant general of Stephen Watts Kearny's Army of the West during the conquest of New Mexico and California in 1846.

With these connections, Turner's punishment turned out to be nothing more than the lowering of his name on the army's promotion list.[58] The secretary of war made the decision after Sherman's old friend U. S. Grant reviewed the case. Turner would have other difficulties with the army, or they with him. Five years later he threatened to kill a major at Fort Concho, Texas, and resigned under pressure in 1878. When he heard about it, as he would have in such a small army, Richard Dodge must have relished the justice of it all. And yet, in a roundabout way, Lt. Edward Palmer Turner deserves some credit for forcing the decision to organize Dodge City.

---

[58] Military Record of Edward Palmer Turner, National Archives and Records Service; and Heitman, *Historical Register and Dictionary*, 1:974.

Chapter 3

A Town, a Railroad,
and the Buffalo Trade

Maj. Richard Dodge had grown weary of those abusing his dignity as post commander. The antics of Lieutenant Turner and his comrades only accelerated plans already under way at Fort Dodge to induce civilians to abandon their lawless enclave south of the river. At the same time, and perhaps more important for those involved, was the chance to make some money. And money was a possibility owing to the advance of the Atchison, Topeka & Santa Fe Railroad through the Arkansas River Valley. Its construction crews had already reached Pawnee Rock.

Expecting swarms of railroad workers to augment the buffalo hunters already starting to congregate on the site, Robert Wright and Dodge finalized plans to organize a town off the military reservation—five miles to the west, as the major wanted more distance between his soldiers and all those saloonkeepers and brothel owners who were dug in opposite the fort. The site chosen lay less than a mile within the western fringes of what was then known as the Osage Lands, a huge rectangle of territory spawning intrigue amongst railroad moguls, state politicians, and potential settlers. In what was good news for Dodge City planners, an obscure rider attached to the 1871 Indian appropriations bill by lame-duck Kansas congressman Sidney Clarke, allowed "that the laws . . . relating to town sites be extended over all the lands obtained of the Osage Indians in the State of Kansas."[1]

Henry L. Sitler, a thirty-five-year-old freighter and hay contractor who

---

[1] U.S. Statutes, 16, March 3, 1871, "An Act making Appropriations for the current and contingent Expenses of the Indian Department . . . ," 41st Cong., Sess. 3, Chap. 120, 557. For an idea concerning the extent of the Osage lands, see Homer E. Socolofsky and Huber Self, *Historical Atlas of Kansas* (Norman: University of Oklahoma Press, 1972), 13. Concerning the actual Osage land swindle, see H. Craig Miner and William E. Unrau, *The End of Indian Kansas: A Study of Cultural Revolution, 1854–1871* (Lawrence: The Regents Press of Kansas, 1978), 121–32; and Anna Heloise Abel, "Indian Reservations in Kansas and the Extinguishment of Their Title," *Transactions of the Kansas State Historical Society*, vol. 8, 1903–1904 (Topeka: State Printer, 1904), 107–109. The original Osage Reserve was established by treaty in 1825 and extended no farther west than present-day Wichita. Surveyors then (continued, next page)

had been in the area since 1868, was the first to occupy what became Dodge City. One of thirteen children, Henry would find his future far from his Pennsylvania birthplace. While serving in the Civil War as a cavalry sergeant, he was captured in June 1864 and spent several months in various Confederate prison camps from Virginia to Georgia. Included in a prisoner exchange at Savannah, following Sherman's historic march to the sea, a revitalized and discharged Henry Sitler drifted into Kansas. He tried farming in the Solomon Valley without much success before moving farther west with others intent on hunting buffalo. He finally established a small ranch west of Fort Dodge, contracting with the government "to supply the several Forts, along the stage line, with hay."[2] Sitler's house, nothing more than a low-slung pile of sod, wins the distinction as the first structure on the Dodge City townsite that summer of 1872.

Two important newcomers—George M. Hoover, a twenty-four-year-old Canadian, and his partner, John G. McDonald—heard rumors of the new town and hoped to get situated before the rush began. Whether they learned the particulars while coming down the trail, or as two of the crowd south of the river that caused Major Dodge so much distress, is not clear. Whatever the source of the rumor, they opened a tent saloon on June 17, 1872.[3] Planks supported by piles of sod blocks served as their makeshift bar.

While Hoover and McDonald rolled out whiskey barrels and dreamed of making a fortune, two grading contractors named Cutler and Wiley— employed by the AT&SF, but who subcontracted much of their work to Edward Masterson and his younger brother, nineteen-year-old William B., through a man named Raymond Ritter—started a general supply store south of the proposed rail line.

(*continued from previous page*) arbitrarily extended the boundary out to what they thought was the 100th meridian, the old line dividing United States and Spanish territory, but they were in error, marking the meridian about fifteen miles too far west. Surveyor Joseph Brown had made his calculations in the summer of 1825 based on incorrect information given him regarding the actual longitude of Fort Osage. Army engineers later corrected the error. Kansas cartographers, however, placed the 100th meridian all over the map for the next several decades. Barry, *The Beginning of the West*, 80; and "Field Notes by Joseph C. Brown, United States Surveying Expedition, 1825–1827," *Eighteenth Biennial Report of the Board of Directors of the Kansas State Historical Society* (Topeka: State Printing Office, 1913), 120–21. For example, a map of Ford County printed in 1879 has the meridian several miles west of Dodge City, while the map accompanying A. T. Andreas's popular *History of the State of Kansas* in 1883 still places it west of town, just not quite so far. Modern mapmakers managed to get it right, placing it at the eastern edge of the original Dodge City townsite line.

[2] Affidavit of Andrew Johnson, Ford County, Kansas, December 1917. Henry L. Sitler Pension File, National Archives and Records Service. Also see Henry Sitler's pension declarations, July 9, 1890, February 11, 1891, and May 20, 1912. Ibid.; and *History of Crawford County, Pennsylvania* (Chicago: Warner, Beers & Co., 1885), 1086.

[3] "Some Reminiscences of the Early Days of Dodge City," *Dodge City Democrat*, June 19, 1903. This article was based on an extensive interview with George M. Hoover.

At the same time, George O. Smith and J. B. Edwards, a merchant from Abilene, worked their way through a succession of rowdy railroad camps. As Edwards recalled, they "hauled by wagons from Great Bend two loads of lumber and two of merchandise . . . and built one of the first three buildings erected in Dodge City, in the month of June, 1872."[4] They put up a 16-by-24 foot shack near Hoover's and McDonald's saloon and began selling groceries and other provisions to the buffalo hunters crowding together awaiting the railroad. Wedging himself between the busy grocery store and the saloon that never closed, Daniel Wolf built a general store. As Edwards recalled, he and his partner "outdid others getting a stock of goods on the shelves but only a day or two ahead of Wolf hauling by wagons from the end of track near Pawnee Rock."[5]

Meanwhile, buffalo hunter George W. "Hoodoo" Brown—a former freighter and army scout who had served alongside the legendary "Comanche Jack" Stilwell—opened a small saloon "about fourteen feet square." As he later recalled, "The buffalo got so scarce on the north side [of the Arkansas] that we quit and hauled our hides in to where Dodge City now stands. There was no Dodge City there at that time, but the Santa Fe Railroad was just building it there. Then Dodge City was run off into town lots and the company began to sell their lots." Along with his partner, Charley Stewart, Brown traveled to Hays City and Russell, Kansas, looking for lumber. "We put up a small house, on the south side of the track, without any floor in it. It was the second house built in Dodge City. . . . Whisky was twenty-five cents a drink."[6]

Frederick C. Zimmerman arrived during those early days. A knowledgeable gunsmith, he became an instant success, a welcomed addition to a place largely supported by buffalo hunters. Born in Freiburg, Saxony, Zimmerman honed his skills working in various gun shops in Paris and London. While in the French capital, the twenty-six-year-old German served as foreman for the famous gunmaker Gastrine Renett. In America he found work in several eastern cities before heading west, surviving on commissions as a firearms salesman first in Wyoming and then in Sheridan, Kansas, a wild and dangerous railroad town. After two years wandering Colorado's

---

[4] J. B. Edwards to the editor, *Dodge City Daily Globe*, September 25, 1922.

[5] J. B. Edwards to H. B. Bell, October 25, 1936. Manuscripts Department, Kansas State Historical Society.

[6] William E. Connelley, ed., "Life and Adventures of George W. Brown, Soldier, Pioneer, Scout, Plainsman and Buffalo Hunter," in *Collections of the Kansas State Historical Society, Vol. XVII, 1926–1928* (Topeka: B. P. Walker, State Printer, 1928), 116.

mining camps, he bought lumber along the Kansas Pacific Rail Line, and together with his wife, small son, and infant daughter headed south to Great Bend. From there they followed the grading crews to Fort Dodge.

At the new settlement, at first called Buffalo City, Zimmerman joined others hammering together primitive structures along what would become Front Street. He opened for business with firearms and ammunition valued at three thousand dollars. Within months, thanks to the appetites of those swarming the buffalo range, it was reported he was selling fifty to seventy-five guns a week and ordering cartridges in lots of seventy-five thousand. Zimmerman soon added stoves and tinware to his crowded inventory.[7]

Everyone found plenty of ways to make money. As J. B. Edwards explained, "We had a good trade from the start—soon buying buffalo hides loomed up and 'ye gods' what a trade that became."[8] Contributing to the boom, hunter Billy Dixon saw Dodge City in its infancy, recalling years later, "The buildings were mostly box affairs, and built in the quickest possible way. But a palace does not make happiness, and I am sure that in the rough, frontier towns of those days there was lots of contentment and good cheer in the rudest shacks."[9]

As this ramshackle settlement began taking shape, a dozen folks headed by Robert Wright and Richard Dodge, along with other officers at the fort, a few local civilians, and some outside businessmen with good political connections, pushed their own plans under a charter dated August 15. That document established the Dodge City Town Company as a private corporation for the sole purpose "of crating [sic] a town" on 320 acres, "more or less."[10] Stymied by provisions of the March 2, 1867, townsite law

---

[7] *History of the State of Kansas*, 1562; *The United States Biographical Dictionary, Kansas Volume* (Chicago: S. Lewis & Co., Publishers, 1879), 516–17; Ford County Register of Deeds, Book A, 39–40; Kansas State Census, Ford County, 1875, Schedule 1, 7, Schedule 2, 1; and *Leavenworth Daily Commercial*, November 19, 1872.

[8] J. B. Edwards to H. B. Bell, October 25, 1936. Manuscripts Department, Kansas State Historical Society.

[9] Olive K. Dixon, *Life of "Billy" Dixon: Plainsman, Scout and Pioneer* (Dallas, Tex.: P. L. Turner Company, Publishers, 1927), 78.

[10] Ford County Register of Deeds, Book A, 493–95. This document, establishing the townsite organization as a joint stock company, begins with the words: "Be it Remembered that on this 15th day of August, A.D. 1872." As a witness, however, notary Herman J. Fringer claimed the twelve members actually signed the document on July 8. A clarification from Justice of the Peace Lyman B. Shaw confirms all this. July 8, rather than August 15 is undoubtedly correct, since Major Dodge—who signed his name to the document—was absent in mid-August: "on a scout south of the Arkansas River from the 12th to 18th inst." He was available on July 8, however, before beginning a six-day special inspection tour to Camp Supply on July 9. See Post Returns, Fort Dodge, Kansas, July and August 1872. Despite all this, August 15 is still largely regarded as the legal date for the Town Company's organization. Also see "Dodge City Town Company," *Dodge City Democrat*, January 1, 1887.

requiring at least one hundred people to claim that much of the public domain, they scaled back their proposal to a modest eighty-seven acres.[11] Railroad companies did what they could to encourage towns along their rights of way, and AT&SF construction engineer Albert A. Robinson had already drawn up a townsite plat.

Those who formed the Dodge City Town Company were an interesting lot, in terms of frontier experience. Robert Marr Wright remains the most important to the history of Dodge City. Wright left his Maryland home as a teenager in 1856. Heading west, he worked first on a farm near St. Louis, but in 1859 traveled to Denver by ox team and started hauling shingles from Cherry Creek. Deciding he could make more money along the Santa Fe Trail, Wright worked for three years with stagecoach veterans and mail contractors Barlow, Sanderson & Company. He agreed to build seven stations (little more than primitive dugouts) for the company between Fort Larned, Kansas, and Fort Lyon, Colorado, and supply them with coal and forage.

By 1864 Wright and his partner, Joe Graham, located at Spring Bottom Ranch near Fort Lyon, but a seven-hour Indian battle convinced Wright to abandon the site and move his family farther east along the Arkansas. That summer he and a new partner, James Anderson, established a ranch near the later site of Fort Aubrey.

After two years Wright closed the place and relocated farther east with A. J. Anthony, his third partner in as many years, whom he later described as having "seen lots of ups and downs with the Indians on the plains, and rather enjoyed them."[12] Born in Virginia, Anthony, a man who never drank and preferred to retire before 8 P.M., came to Lawrence, Kansas, from Ohio in 1857. He worked as a stage driver before joining the Southern Overland Mail and Express Company as a conductor and express messenger operating between Missouri and Santa Fe.[13]

Anthony's association with Robert Wright, both as a friend and partner, proved a lasting one. They set themselves up as hay contractors for the

---

[11] U.S. Statutes, 14, March 2, 1867, "An Act for the Relief of the Inhabitants of Cities and Towns upon the Public Lands," 39th Cong., Sess. 2, Chap. 177, 541.

[12] Robert M. Wright, "Personal Reminiscences of Frontier Life in Southwestern Kansas," *Transactions of the Kansas State Historical Society*, vol. 7, 1901–1902 (Topeka: State Printer, 1902), 55. For an earlier view, see "A Noted Plainsman; Reminiscences in the Life of R. M. Wright, Esq., of Dodge City, Kan.," *Kansas Daily Commonwealth*, April 19, 1874.

[13] Morris F. Taylor, *First Mail West: Stagecoach Lines on the Santa Fe Trail* (Albuquerque: University of New Mexico Press, 1971), 104. For more information on A. J. Anthony, who lived to age eighty-nine, see *History of the State of Kansas*, 1560; and Kansas State Census, Ford County, 1875, Schedule 1, 1.

stage company at Cimarron Crossing, twenty-eight miles west of Fort
Dodge. In late August 1868 Indians burned them out, destroying seventy-
five tons of hay.[14] Both men found work as civilian contractors for the
army before Wright maneuvered his position as post sutler, but even then
their relationship endured. For a year, beginning in August of 1869,
Anthony served as postmaster at the fort.[15]

Richard Irving Dodge was the leading military member of the Town
Company. A native of North Carolina and an 1848 graduate of West
Point, the major already had western experience. Between 1848 and 1856 he
served at ten separate locations in Texas and skirmished with the
Comanches on the San Saba River. During the Civil War he saw action at
the first Battle of Bull Run but spent the next half-decade desk bound.
Soon after the war Dodge reported for duty in Colorado, the Dakotas,
and finally at Fort Larned, Kansas. After a brief assignment in New York
working on army regulations, he arrived at Fort Dodge in 1872 and
assumed command.[16] Richard Dodge wrote three books about life on the
plains, two of which are still widely quoted.

Two other officers got involved in the scheme. Maryland-born Edward
Moale commanded an infantry company. During the war he had fought in
several major battles, including Gettysburg. Yet not even the isolation of
Fort Dodge diverted his attention from possible investments. Organizing
a town offered tempting possibilities for this second wealthiest officer on
the post; one able to employ a twenty-two-year-old Irish girl as a servant
to help his wife look after the household and their three small children.[17]

---

[14] 1st Lt. D. W. Wallingford to Lt. L. Schonborn, August 23, 1868. Headquarters Records, Fort Dodge, Kansas.
Reports of Detachments.

[15] Post Office Department, Records of Appointment of Postmasters, Vol. 33, 1867–74, Fort Dodge, Kansas,
868–69. National Archives and Records Service. On the 1870 United States Census for Fort Dodge, both Wright
and Anthony listed themselves as merchants. They also estimated their worth in real and personal property at
twenty-two thousand dollars each.

[16] Cullum, *Biographical Register of the Officers and Graduates of the U.S. Military Academy at West Point*, 2:356–57; Heitman,
Historical Register and Dictionary of the United States Army, 1:337; and James Grant Wilson and John Fiske, ed., *Appleton's
Cyclopaedia of American Biography* (New York: D. Appleton & Company, 1888), 2:194.

[17] 1870 United States Census, Fort Dodge, Ford County, Kansas, page 5, lines 16–21. Captain Moale claimed
real estate valued at twenty thousand dollars. By contrast, fellow officer 2nd Lt. Phillip Reade claimed thirty thousand dollars in real estate holdings. Ibid., page 4, line 35. Interestingly, the 1870 census gives Moale's place of birth
as North Carolina and that of his wife as Maryland. Military sources, however, show Edward Moale born in and
appointed from Maryland. For two examples, see Guy V. Henry, *Military Record of Civilian Appointments in the United
States Army* (New York: Carleton, Publisher, 1869), 1:396–97; and William H. Powell, *Records of Living Officers of the
United States Army* (Philadelphia: L. R. Hamersly & Co., 1890), 408.

Post surgeon William S. Tremaine, commissioned from New York in August 1863 and originally assigned as an assistant surgeon to the Twenty-fourth Massachusetts Volunteers, joined his two fellow officers in Kansas with thoughts of finally making some money. He could use some, surviving on army pay surrounded by a wife, two young sons, and an infant daughter. Born on Canada's Prince Edward Island thirty-four years before becoming involved with the Dodge City Town Company, Dr. Tremaine would play an active role, serving as its first town-lot agent as well as secretary and treasurer of the company. Eight years later he was admitted to the Ford County bar and permitted to practice law.[18]

Rounding out this group were Wright's partner A. J. Anthony; Herman J. Fringer, a quartermaster clerk and former deputy U.S. marshal from Hays City; Alfred J. Peacock, a sutler clerk who had also come down from Hays; local freighter and rancher Henry Sitler; veteran trader Samuel Weichselbaum (Theodore's brother); Maj. David Taylor, a lawyer and paymaster at Fort Leavenworth; Alexander S. Johnson, land commissioner for the railroad; and Lyman B. Shaw, who served the organization briefly as a justice of the peace. The Town Company directors were Wright, Fringer, Sitler, Shaw, Major Dodge, Dr. Tremaine, and Captain Moale.

Only a county judge could act as townsite trustee. Ford County was still unorganized five years after being designated, and therefore had no judge or other county officials qualified to act.[19] Ignoring this temporary setback, but one that would lead to frenzied activity within a year, members of the Town Company filed their charter with Kansas secretary of state William H. Smallwood on August 20, 1872. Smallwood attached the state seal to the document ten days later. Bureaucrats seemed willing to allow the new town to develop more or less on its own, without interference.

Of course, those associated with the town believed in its future. Still, Dodge City might have gone the way of other now-forgotten towns, had not a group of men, ten years earlier, dreamed of a railroad connecting the

---

[18] Henry, *Military Record of Civilian Appointments in the United States Army*, 1:120; Powell, *Records of Living Officers of the United States Army*, 602; 1870 United States Census, Ford County, Fort Dodge, Kansas, page 5, lines 22–27; and Records of the Fort County District Court, Judge's Journal, Book A, 245. Unlike fellow officers Phillip Reade and Edward Moale, Tremaine listed no real estate holdings on the 1870 census, instead acknowledging only one thousand dollars as the "Value of Personal Estate."

[19] Helen G. Gill, "The Establishment of Counties in Kansas," *Transactions of the Kansas State Historical Society*, vol. 8, *1903–1904* (Topeka: State Printer, 1904), 456. Before 1867 this area, indeed more than the entire southwest quarter of the state, had been identified first as Peketon and then as Marion County.

capital of Kansas with those profitable markets in the Southwest. Many people claimed credit for developing the idea for the Atchison, Topeka & Santa Fe Railroad Company,[20] but most agree the honor belongs to Cyrus K. Holliday. That transplanted Pennsylvanian wrote the railroad's charter for presentation to the Kansas legislature in 1859. Getting beyond the planning stage proved a monumental undertaking. The drought of 1860 discouraged investment, then came the Civil War, followed by organizational problems, in addition to difficulties lining up the necessary political support and financial backing.

A generous land grant bill written by Holliday and championed by Senator Samuel Pomeroy proved key to the railroad's success. Passed by both houses of Congress and signed by President Lincoln on March 3, 1863, this legislation allowed the company "every alternate section of land, designated by odd numbers, for ten sections in width on each side" of the proposed route.[21] Thus, nearly three million acres of Kansas public land were involved. In order to qualify the railroad needed to be operating between Atchison and the border of Colorado Territory by March 3, 1873. Even so, it took years after obtaining the president's signature before the company broke ground at Topeka. The date was October 30, 1868, and it was a long way to Colorado.

The AT&SF left Topeka not for Atchison or even Santa Fe, but straight south to Pauline and Wakarusa, crossing a river of the same name to Carbondale and its Osage County coal deposits: coal to fuel the company's two locomotives and help generate freight revenues. By crossing the southern boundary of Shawnee County, the railroad qualified for local subsidy bonds, voted by residents as a commercial bribe to guarantee rail service.

The company spent little time congratulating itself. With an important deadline to meet, the railroad began its journey west. In mid-September 1869 tracks pushed through Burlingame and on toward Emporia. By March 1871 the Santa Fe reached Cottonwood Falls. Four months later it arrived at Newton, which became the major end-of-track supply point. Prostitutes and gamblers abandoned Topeka to auction their services there

[20] The company was originally called the Atchison and Topeka Railroad Company; the addition of "Santa Fe" did not come about until the November 24, 1863, stockholders' meeting.

[21] United States Statutes at Large, 37th Cong., 3rd Sess., 1862–63, 722. As quoted in Joseph W. Snell and Don W. Wilson, "The Birth of the Atchison, Topeka and Santa Fe Railroad," Kansas Historical Quarterly 34, no. 2 (Summer 1968): Pt. 1, 117.

to all those seduced by all the excitement. On August 20, 1871, six men died and another half-dozen wounded during a wild shooting spree still known as "Newton's General Massacre." One of the victims was City Marshal Mike McCluskie, who tried keeping the peace in Hide Park, a clever euphemism for the town's red-light district.

Construction stopped at Newton, as the company concentrated on linking Topeka with Atchison. As the temporary end of track, Newton hoped to break the Kansas Pacific's monopoly of shipping Texas cattle. In early September 1870 it was reported at Topeka, "We understand that it will be the policy of the company to donate a site to the Texas interests, which are expected to develop the locality and to make the town the great depot and emporium of their colossal traffic."[22] Despite all the enthusiasm, Wichita usurped Newton's dreams of glory.

Beyond Newton, officials worried about grading crews and surveyors as they entered Indian country. Former governor Samuel Crawford contacted the Department of the Missouri on behalf of the railroad. General Pope agreed to furnish an infantry escort to protect company employees. Surprisingly, Indians caused little trouble, becoming instead more of a nuisance. They might burn a bridge or two, steal some tools, or chase small groups of workers, but nothing happened that was in anyway comparable to the difficulties with Indians faced building the Union Pacific.[23]

By January 1872, the Santa Fe planned on pushing beyond Newton toward Cow Creek and the new town of Hutchinson. Severe weather, together with a storm at sea that sank a shipload of English rails (enough for twenty-five miles of track), delayed the celebration. Despite these setbacks, workers began grading the route beyond Cow Creek over the great bend of the Arkansas and on to Fort Larned. They hoped to reach that point by early May, then push on to Fort Dodge. This was the longer of two proposed routes. Critics claimed the railroad planned it that way to increase its land-grant holdings. By following much of the traditional route to Santa Fe, however, the company found easier grades, helping to reduce costs, as well as having the river alongside to provide reliable water.

Tracks arrived at Hutchinson on June 8, then pushed on at the rate of a mile a day. Once on the High Plains construction foremen demanded

---

[22] *Kansas Daily Commonwealth,* September 16, 1870.

[23] L. L. Waters, *Steel Rails to Santa Fe* (Lawrence: University of Kansas Press, 1950), 48.

more.[24] By July 12 crews reached the settlement of Great Bend, three miles east of Fort Zarah. The AT&SF had no intention of missing its March 3, 1873, Colorado deadline. Daily the company proved its ingenuity. Anxious officials rushed prefabricated bridges out from Topeka. One overly optimistic report told of the railroad constructing an 805-foot boom designed to swing across the river with hopes of snagging ties: "Mr. Green cuts the ties in the Rocky Mountains, near Fair Pine post office, and proposes floating them six hundred miles down the Arkansas."[25] That man had a contract to supply two hundred thousand of these.

By July 20 the railroad reached Pawnee Rock, only to be slowed by a string of summer storms. One reporter described another reason for delay: "Out towards the end of the track of the A.T. & S.F. railroad horse thieves abound."[26] Horses had been stolen from a party of graders only weeks before. Major Dodge ordered his soldiers to chase the outlaws: "The citizen who reported the loss was confident that the thieves were Indians; but a careful examination of the facts satisfies me that it is but another exploit of the white thieves who infest this country." The troopers, including an experienced tracker, failed because "the country in the vicinity of the R. R. has been so marked with tracks of animals that it is impossible to follow the trail of those stolen."[27]

Dodge had previously complained to officials at the Department of the Missouri about one particular "gang of horse and cattle thieves" headquartered at Albert Boyd's ranch, four miles below Fort Larned.[28] Boyd tried blaming Indians for every outrage, despite contrary reports published at Topeka: "The many Indian depredations reported are the work of the imagination of mischief-makers, circulated for selfish or vicious ends; or the magnified operations of white horse thieves. The abduction of a half dozen horses and mules is amplified like a rolling snowball. . . . An Indian

---

[24] Even so, none of this represented any sort of record, despite an exaggerated claim in the July 16, 1872, issue of the *Kansas Daily Commonwealth*: "Three miles and four hundred feet of track were laid on the A.T. & S. Fe road last Saturday. This beats anything in the previous history of track-laying in the west." In fact, on April 28, 1869, the Central Pacific completed ten miles and fifty-six feet in a single day. Then, on August 15, 1870, the Kansas Pacific claimed ten and a quarter miles. On that day the fastest single mile was laid in fifty-five minutes. George Kraus, *High Road to Promontory: Building the Central Pacific Across the High Sierra* (Palo Alto, Calif.: American West Publishing Company, 1969), 248; and George L. Anderson, *Kansas West* (San Marino, Calif.: Golden West Books, 1963), 63.

[25] *Hutchinson News*, July 18, 1872.

[26] Ibid., August 29, 1872.

[27] Maj. Richard Dodge to Asst. Adj. Gen., Department of the Missouri, July 1, 1872. Fort Dodge, Letters Sent.

[28] Ibid., June 18, 1872.

story is introduced, and the affair becomes . . . the scalping or taking to captivity of the entire engineer corps on the road. The truth is, not an Indian has been seen north of the Arkansas river this season for eighty miles west of Fort Dodge."[29] Railroad graders became the latest victims of those lawless gangs crowding the border counties.

With Indians blamed for everything, Dodge tried explaining to his superiors the difficulties faced bringing anyone to justice: "The white thieves are difficult to manage, as they go along the grade ostensibly in search of work, or roam about the country in the guise of Buffalo hunters." Still, the major did not lose faith: "I propose to keep out scouts almost continually, and hope to make this horse stealing a dangerous pastime—either for white men or Indians."[30]

Success encouraged the rustlers. On July 29, 1872, they conducted what was called a "grand steal" against the railroad, grabbing between seventy-five and one hundred animals, halting work and frustrating grading crews. Assuming the thieves planned on selling their booty at Wichita, officers from various jurisdictions took up the chase. They recovered sixteen head lost by the outlaws as they tried fording the Arkansas, and the next day found eight other animals wandering the plains. If caught, an editor at Hutchinson speculated wistfully, "Judge Lynch will hold a court that will place them beyond such pranks hereafter. The deputy of the county, Al. Updegraff, accompanied by H. C. McCarty and others, left here early Monday to assist in the pursuit. It is thought the herder in charge was the ringleader of the raid."[31]

Soldiers at Fort Dodge responded, but not just to please the railroad. The gang had robbed two members of the Fifth Infantry, taking their weapons, clothing, and mules. Sgt. Pettis L. Beatty and thirteen others from the Sixth Cavalry rode out in pursuit, along with civilian tracker Thomas Sherman. Joined later by Deputy U.S. Marshal Charley Collins, they followed the trail for over three hundred miles before overtaking the outlaws at night near the head of the dry Cimarron, at a place called Oak Spring Canyon. "The thieves replied to the demand for their Surrender by a volley," Major Dodge

[29] "From the Southwest," written by a "Correspondent of the Commonwealth," identified only as "A.A.R.," from a camp fifty-five miles west of Fort Dodge, on the Arkansas River, July 4, 1872. *Kansas Daily Commonwealth*, July 18, 1872.

[30] Maj. Richard Dodge to Asst. Adj. Gen., Department of the Missouri, July 1, 1872. Fort Dodge, Letters Sent.

[31] *Hutchinson News*, August 1, 1872. Al Updegraff later moved to Dodge City and would play a small role in its colorful history.

advised headquarters. "After a sharp fight the gang was completely routed and broken up, one killed another captured." He made a point of noting "the Soldierly conduct of Sergeant Beatty" and the others. "All the stolen property except one Springfield Rifle Musket has been recovered."[32]

Despite the thievery, the railroad made it to Larned. By the end of August tracks came within four miles of Fort Dodge, somewhat ahead of schedule. Major Dodge welcomed the event, not just because of his interest in the Dodge City Town Company, but because he knew it would expedite delivery of military cargoes. Heretofore supplies had been shipped to Fort Hays on the Kansas Pacific, and then freighted overland. Of course, troops still marched from Hays to Fort Dodge. Concerned with costs, officials declined to spend the money to have them travel roundabout by rail.[33]

In early September the company opened its line to Dodge City, but for that first month there were no paying passengers, only company executives and selected dignitaries. Regular service was not scheduled until October 7. An exception was made for Dr. S. G. Rodgers, who planned on establishing a colony of six hundred families northeast of Dodge City. This piqued the interest of railroad directors, who took pains to praise the agricultural advantages of the Arkansas River Valley. Unfortunately, the plan fizzled and the area chosen lay vacant for two years, until the small town of Kinsley sprang up in its place.

Railroad crews struggling across Kansas helped Dodge City acquire its reputation as a wide-open town. Civil War veterans from both armies mingled with Irish immigrants, disillusioned farm boys, and small-town clerks seeking excitement. It was largely physical—raw muscle built the line. Men toiled for day-labor wages on a diet of bread, salt pork, beans, and buffalo meat. On Saturday nights they succumbed to temptation at the end of track, a hodgepodge of tent saloons, gambling dens, and brothels keeping pace with their progress. Exhausted and weary, they tried sobering up on Sundays with less strenuous chores, laundry and the like, but come Monday morning not even the most optimistic crew boss expected a full mile of track.

At Dodge City railroad workers found a spot of ground boasting a twenty-four hour schedule and a liberal atmosphere much to their liking.

---

[32] General Order, No. 24, August 29, 1872. Ford Dodge, General Orders and Circulars, Vol. 2; and Maj. Richard Dodge to Asst. Adj. Gen., Department of the Missouri, September 3, 1872. Fort Dodge Letters Sent.

[33] Minnie Dubbs Millbrook, "An Old Trail Plowed Under—Hays to Dodge," *Kansas Historical Quarterly* 43, no. 3 (Autumn 1977): 278.

The town had, of course, yet to expand to the boundaries drawn for it by Albert A. Robinson, but it had gotten started —at least two blocks' worth.

Robinson's plat called for the major thoroughfare to straddle the tracks from east to west. This became Dodge City's notorious Front Street (actually two of them, North Front and South Front). Running parallel from that point north were Chestnut, Walnut, and Spruce streets. To the south were Locust (sometimes called Santa Fe Trail Street, since it more or less followed the worn ruts of that famous highway), followed by Maple, Pine, and a strip next to the river originally called Water Street. A fifteen-foot alleyway ran between Maple and Pine, as did one between Walnut and Spruce. Crossing these streets north to south were Railroad Avenue, at the far eastside of the original townsite, followed by numbered avenues First through Fifth. The blocks themselves were laid out in 250-by-125-foot rectangles; those from Walnut Street south to Maple divided into ten lots, with blocks farther out containing only eight.[34] On either side of the tracks, Front Street enjoyed a width of 125 feet, with the other streets only 60 feet wide. All north-south avenues measured 75 feet, except for Second Avenue, which was 80 feet in width. Filling in all this space with businesses and housing would take time.

Newcomers saw Dodge City either as a buffalo hunters' rendezvous, or as a convenient place for the transshipment of military supplies, but they all scrambled to corner their share of the market. Aside from Hoover and McDonald's tent saloon, Zimmerman's hardware, the south-side emporium of contractors Cutler and Wiley, grocer J. B. Edwards, and general merchandiser Daniel Wolf, members of the Town Company joined everybody else struggling to establish themselves. Herman J. Fringer and A. J. Peacock threw together a claptrap building on the northwest corner of Front Street and Second Avenue and opened a drug store. The two

---

[34] "Original Plat of Dodge City," Ford County Register of Deeds, Book A, 550; and Fredric R. Young, *Dodge City: Up Through a Century in Story and Pictures* (Dodge City: Boot Hill Museum, Inc., 1972), 26. The original plat was filed with the Register of Deeds on January 8, 1873. It should be noted that an inconsistent numbering system was used for individual town lots. For example, east to west along the north side of Front Street, lots in the first half-dozen blocks were all even numbered: 2 through 110. Conversely, on the south side of Front Street odd numbers were used in the same fashion. Farther out, on the north side including Chestnut and Walnut streets, and to the south starting with Locust Street, lots were numbered in sequence, 1, 2, 3, 4, etc. Yet lots on the south side of Spruce again used only odd numbers. There are other minor but still exasperating exceptions to all this, making it somewhat difficult to use property records to find specific clues concerning the town's development and to determine what slivers of real estate were owned by which individuals at any given time.

remained partners until June 14, 1873, after which Peacock left the firm to begin running a series of saloons full time.

Next to the drug store Leavenworth veteran Isaac Young opened a harness shop. For a time this location marked the western edge of the town's business district. Besides mending harness, the Colonel, as Young was known affectionately, performed one other important service for the yet unorganized community. Acting as "the high Justice of the Peace," reported a visiting newspaper correspondent, "The Col. is the Court, and the rapidity and fidelity with which the Colonel decides intricate cases of law, forces the conclusion that the Court 'knows herself.' He can sell a mule to satisfy a judgment with more satisfaction and less ceremony than any other court in the land."[35]

Following the lead of Fringer and Peacock, others rode down from Hays City along the old military road. These included Alonzo B. Webster, a twenty-nine-year-old New Yorker who would later serve as mayor during a particularly important transitional period. A former corporal in a Michigan cavalry regiment, Webster was discharged from service in 1866. He came to Kansas that same year with his friend Patrick Carroll and found work as a government teamster at Fort Leavenworth. A quarter of a century later Carroll recalled, "My impression is that Webster put in some time as a courier from Fort Hays. Our business took us to Fort Hays, Hays City, Fort Harker, Ellsworth, Wichita, Fort Dodge and other posts and towns along the border. In the winter of 1866 and 1867 we put in wood at Ellsworth Kansas for the Union Pacific (afterwards the Kansas Pacific) railroad."[36] After serving as a courier between Forts Hays and Dodge, Webster settled at Hays City in 1867. He found employment with Richard W. Evans, another early Dodge City businessman, then clerked for merchant Sol H. Kohn.

In the fall of 1872 Webster moved to Dodge City with his wife of six months and put up a building on the northeast corner of Front Street and First Avenue for a grocery and dry-goods business. He claimed that while serving with the Army of the Potomac, he contracted rheumatism fording rivers in northern Virginia. Whatever the cause, he suffered such painful attacks in his hips and knees that many people thought him lame.

[35] *Leavenworth Daily Times*, November 7, 1872. This issue also noted that town lots in Dodge City, depending on how near to the central business district, could expect to sell for fifty to two hundred dollars.

[36] Affidavit of P. W. Carroll, Alameda County, California, February 5, 1891. Alonzo B. Webster Pension File, National Archives and Records Service.

Next to Webster's grocery, Moses Waters and James Hanrahan opened a saloon and billiard parlor. Its popularity made the location an early landmark for a host of tired and thirsty travelers. Hanrahan played a significant role in the early doings in and around Dodge and remained one of the town's more popular citizens.

Richard W. Evans, a former postmaster at Hays City, filled a store east of Waters and Hanrahan with all kinds of supplies for buffalo hunters. Evans's background was typical of those businesspeople now descending on Dodge City. Born in north Wales in 1839, the fifth of eight children, he came to the United States with his family in 1853 and settled in Illinois. Leaving school, Evans found employment in a confectionary shop at nearby Galena. He later worked as a messenger boy on a Mississippi steamboat but "contracted an obstinate ague." Convalescing in Wisconsin and at Dodgeville, Iowa, he renewed his efforts to get an education. Working with a general merchandising firm for two years, he carefully studied the business. Evans crossed the plains for the first time in 1859, intrigued by the excitement of the Pikes Peak gold rush. For the next three years he honed his business skills while dabbling in mining properties.

Evans enlisted in the Second Colorado Volunteer Cavalry, a regiment later commended by James Hobart Ford. After serving as a recruiter at Central City, he saw action in Missouri but spent much of the time on sick call. Evans later claimed to have been wounded at the Battle of Honey Springs in 1863. Two years later his regiment fought Indians in the Arkansas River Valley, after which Evans mustered out at Fort Riley. For six months he worked for the post sutler before opening an eatery in Kansas City, Missouri. Failing as a restaurateur, Evans ended up working for a lumberman in Ogden, Kansas. He and a partner then became general merchandisers at Ellsworth, before moving on to Hays City. Buying out his partner, Evans remained there for five years, becoming postmaster in 1869. Political misfortune forced his resignation in 1870—he had supported Congressman Sidney Clarke's unsuccessful reelection bid. Having become involved supplying buffalo hunters along the Kansas Pacific, Evans shifted those operations south in 1872.

Dodge City appealed to Evans from the start. Watching events unfold amid all the noise and bustle, he saw a future for himself in this raw frontier settlement. Helped by his older brother, Griffith, Evans worked hard building his business. Griffith returned to Colorado in 1874. Richard joined him there from time to time, but always came back to Dodge.[37]

One of the important early arrivals was Charlie Rath, an experienced Indian trader and buffalo hunter. Operating under the name Charles Rath & Co. (the "& Co." being Robert M. Wright and, for a time, A. J. Anthony), Rath bought up three lots on the northeast corner of Front Street and Second Avenue. Rath & Co. only occupied the corner lot, but the partners made money from the start, selling to locals and supplying surrounding camps of hunters while catering to the needs of railroad workers swarming through Dodge City in their mad dash for the Colorado line. Despite certain personal flaws, Rath maintained the respect of most of those he met, one admirer going so far as to describe him as the "bravest man of all the plains."[38]

Rath himself was a trader of long standing in western Kansas. Although born in Germany, he came west in 1853 from his family's home in Hamilton County, Ohio, finding work in the commissary at Bent's Fort as a teenager. He mastered the rudiments of Indian trading and the Cheyenne language, soon marrying a woman of that tribe and fathering a daughter. He moved his family into Kansas and began freighting out of Fort Riley, even making trips into New Mexico. Four years later they settled at Walnut Creek Ranch on the great bend of the Arkansas. Rath took over ownership of the property after Satank, another Kiowa war chief, killed the previous owner, an old Santa Fe trader named George H. Peacock, in retaliation for a blundered practical joke.[39] By 1860 Rath got himself elected a constable of the short-lived but sprawling Peketon County.

[37] *The United States Biographical Dictionary, Kansas Volume*, 411–12; and Richard W. Evans Pension File, National Archives and Records Service. For more on this family's background, see *Portrait and Biographical Album of Jo Daviess County, Illinois* (Chicago: Chapman Brothers, 1889), 467–68. Many foreign-born persons claimed American birth; Evans was no exception. While at Hays City in 1870, and again at Dodge in 1875, Richard gave Indiana as his birthplace. Yet by 1879 he abandoned the deception and freely admitted his Welsh origins.

[38] Judge Frank Doster, "Eleventh Indian Cavalry in Kansas in 1865," *Collections of the Kansas State Historical Society, Vol. XV, 1919–1922* (Topeka: State Printing Office, 1923), 528. For a detailed but generally uncritical view of Rath's long and interesting life, see Ida Ellen Rath, *The Rath Trail* (Wichita: McCormick-Armstrong Co., Inc., 1961).

[39] Wright, "Personal Reminiscences of Frontier Life in Southwest Kansas," 49. Satank had asked his friend Peacock to write him a favorable letter of introduction. Instead, in a moment of carelessness, Peacock penned the document that lead to his death: "This is Satank, the biggest liar, beggar and thief on the plains. What he can't beg of you he will steal. Kick him out of your camp, as he is a lazy, good-for-nothing Indian." Discovering its contents, Satank returned to the ranch and killed George Peacock and two others, leaving only one injured man unmolested, stating, "Good-bye, Mr. Peacock; I guess you won't write any more letters." For more details on all of this, see Louise Barry, "The Ranch at Walnut Creek Crossing," *The Kansas Historical Quarterly* 37, no. 2 (Summer 1971): 138–40; and James R. Mead, *Hunting and Trading on the Great Plains, 1859–1875* (Norman: University of Oklahoma Press, 1986), 171–73. Here the Indian who killed Peacock is misidentified as Satanta.

Charlie Rath traded with Indians, but not without the authorities challenging both his business practices and trading status.[40] His friendly relations with the tribes more or less continued, even though a Cheyenne war party swept down and carried off his wife and daughter during the 1864 troubles. Three years later George Bent—the half-Cheyenne son of William Bent—recalled how he and Rath traded for buffalo robes with "Kiowas and Prairie Apaches" camped on Bluff Creek: "I was staying in Kicking Bird's lodge, and Rath in Satanta's."[41] It was about this time that Major Douglass complained about Rath arming "several bands of Kiowas with Revolvers and . . . completely overstock[ing] them with Powder."[42] Despite his sympathy for Indians, hostilities along the border forced even Rath's retreat.

Visiting his family in Ohio in 1870, the old plainsman met and married a local girl nearly twenty years his junior and returned to Kansas. Settling first in Topeka and then at Osage City, he invested in real estate and seemed resigned to the quiet life. Cash-flow problems forced him back onto the plains, searching for profit and adventure. He divided his time supplying buffalo meat to the hungry railroad construction gangs and hauling wood for Theodore Weichselbaum at Fort Dodge. Seeing fresh opportunities along the Arkansas, Charlie Rath moved his wife to Dodge City during that busy month of September 1872 and began reinventing himself as a commercial entrepreneur.

Another arrival, a man who exercised a profound and some say disastrous influence on the town's political history, was twenty-seven-year-old James H. "Dog" Kelley. A short, disheveled man with dropping mustache, Kelley acquired his distinctive sobriquet attending George Armstrong Custer's ever-present pack of greyhounds—some of which he brought with him to Dodge City, along with a gold watch, another gift from the

---

[40] Charles Rath and C. H. Whittaker, Walnut Creek, Kansas, to the Commissioner of Indian Affairs, February 6, 1862. Letters Received by the Office of Indian Affairs, Upper Arkansas Agency, 1855–64, National Archives and Records Service; and Council Grove *Kansas Press*, June 29, 1863.

[41] George E. Hyde, *Life of George Bent: Written From His Letters* (Norman: University of Oklahoma Press, 1968), 267. George Bent will appear in our story again, but it is interesting to note that Robert Wright at one point seems to have characterized him as "the notorious half-breed . . . who was a leader of the Dog Indians, composed of the scalawags and outlaws of various tribes." Of course, at the same time Wright apparently thought, "Colonel Chivington gave the rascals such a merited thrashing" at Sand Creek. "Reminiscences in the Life of R. M. Wright, Esq.," *Kansas Daily Commonwealth*, April 19, 1874. This account was written by someone identified only as "T" and characterized as "A Regular Correspondent."

[42] Maj. Henry Douglass to Asst. Adj. Gen., Department of the Missouri, January 13, 1867. Fort Dodge, Letters Sent.

general. Kelley sported a checkered career before and during his years in Kansas, and seems to have enjoyed his reputation for foolishness. Henry H. Raymond, a former blacksmith turned buffalo hunter, described him as a "good hearted Irishman, but when full of booze he got on the warpath and made trouble for himself."[43]

This particular good-hearted Irishman came to Kansas from New York after serving in the Confederate army. He joined up with Custer as an erstwhile Indian scout and dog handler. Learning more about the plains trading with buffalo hunters, Kelley showed up in Dodge by way of Leavenworth and Hays City, hauling with him pieces of a frame building that he reassembled on the northwest corner of Front Street and First Avenue. There he busied himself with plans to open a saloon and restaurant with local rancher John Hunt, the same man earlier accused by Captain Tupper of hiding stolen government property.

During those hectic early weeks a man named John J. Hines toured the Arkansas River Valley. He recorded his impressions in a letter dated September 14: "Saturday evening we reached Dodge, or Buffalo City, as it is called, a small town on the A.T. & S.F. road, five miles west of Fort Dodge. The 'city' consists of about a dozen frame houses and about two dozen tents, besides a few adobe houses. The town contains several stores, a gunsmith's establishment, and barber shop. Nearly every building has out the sign, in large letters, 'Saloon.'" A fortnight later, still fascinated by the number of saloons, Hines estimated the town's population at "three or four hundred souls."[44]

Despite all the emphasis on saloons, Dodge City seemed just as interested in getting a post office as in draining whiskey barrels, even if it meant grabbing the one from Fort Dodge. Postal service was vital to the town's future, mail representing the only reliable link with the outside world. In isolated country people went out of their way to find a post office. At Dodge City the office opened on September 23, with Robert M. Wright its first postmaster. He served until February 10, 1873, when Herman J. Fringer took over. Since the office shared space in his and Peacock's drug store,

---

[43] Joseph W. Snell, ed., "Diary of a Dodge City Buffalo Hunter, 1872–1873," *Kansas Historical Quarterly* 31, no. 4 (Winter 1965): 361n46.

[44] *Leavenworth Daily Commercial*, October 5, 1872. This issue contains two letters from Mr. Hines, the first, dated September 14, was written from a "Surveyor's Camp on the Osage Indians lands," while the second was sent from Wichita on October 3.

Fringer handled most of the day-to-day work anyway, so that even contemporary sources often misidentified him as the town's pioneer postmaster.[45]

During one of his many trips to Missouri, purchasing supplies for Wright's sutler store, the temperate A. J. Anthony met a transplanted Louisiana widow named Calvina Chambliss. With nature taking its normal course, the two married at St. Louis in late September 1872.[46] Anthony returned to Dodge City with his bride and her three young children on October 10. Over the years Mrs. Anthony jotted down impressions of her new home. Of her first few days in Dodge she wrote:

> Just before our marriage the town of Dodge City was started, on what might be called the borders of Sahara. Very few families had yet shown the courage to locate in this frontier town. The morning I arrived I looked around in vain for a woman's face, and did not see one until I was taken into the Dodge House [then called the Essington House] and introduced to the landlady. We sat down to our first breakfast with a great crowd of long-haired hunters, with their buckskin suits and pistols. All was excitement and trading. A man stood by the door as they went out and collected a dollar from each one for their meal.
>
> Dodge City was then a great freighting town to all points south and west, and while yet a border hamlet in size, became a great camp for cowboys, freighters, traders, and speculators of every sort.
>
> In the nature of things a good many rough characters herded here, and the early life of the city took a decidedly eventful turn. Trade grew into splendid volume, money flowed freely in all channels. Business and social excitement carried all along. The revolver being a very strong factor in all departments of social life, differences and disputes often ending in violence, as Boot Hill could testify, if it could speak. Every few days we used to hear of some poor soul gone to his account, from sudden death.[47]

Progress was what appealed to those crowding the railroad's boardroom at Topeka. They named Dodge City the terminus for the company's Third

[45] *Leavenworth Daily Times*, November 7, 1872. Also see Post Office Department, Records of Appointment of Postmasters, Vol. 33, 1867–74, Fort Dodge–Dodge City, Kansas, 1154, Vol. 40, 1874–83, Dodge City, Kansas, 560. National Archives and Records Service; and Robert W. Baughman, *Kansas Post Offices* (Topeka: Kansas Postal History Society & Kansas State Historical Society, 1961), 36, 182.

[46] Marriage Record, Andrew Jackson Anthony and Calvina Chambliss, September 26, 1872. Recorder of Deeds, City of St. Louis, Missouri, Book 15, page 392.

[47] *Dodge City Globe-Republican*, June 30, 1898. A slightly different version of Mrs. Anthony's reminiscence appeared in the *Dodge City Daily Globe*, September 25, 1922, in which she said of Boot Hill: "called so because men shot down in disputes unknown and uncared for, were buried there hurriedly with their boots on with no one to say a prayer over their remains."

Division (the section west of Newton), with W. H. Bancroft, formerly of
the Kansas Pacific, appointed division superintendent. The railroad constructed extensive sidetracks and used two converted freight cars for its
headquarters. Toward year's end it would build a depot north of the main
line, at a point just west of where Railroad Avenue crosses the tracks. The
company's decision assured Dodge City's status as a major shipping point
for military goods moving south to Camp Supply. The government encouraged freighters by building a large warehouse within the town's limits.

One month after the company opened scheduled passenger service, a
Topeka correspondent paid Dodge City a visit and reported to his editor:

> This is virtually the frontier town of the southwest at present, its chief
> article of export being buffalo hides, and its imports, lumber, flour, ready-
> made clothing, poor whiskey and sardines. It has a creditable restaurant kept
> in a tent, a poor hotel under shingles, a number of frame stores, a good water
> tank and wind mill, a sod house and a dance house.
>
> It is a very primitive village of perhaps two hundred resident population
> domiciled in tents, sod houses, dug-outs, frame shanties and freight cars.
> The depot, express and telegraph offices, consist of two freight cars,
> anchored alongside a platform. A good hotel is being built, and as the loca-
> tion of the city is one of the finest on the road, and a fine country for graz-
> ing and agriculture surround it, the day is perhaps not far distant when this
> now crude trading post will become a thriving city.[48]

That November twenty-five-year-old Dr. Thomas L. McCarty arrived
with his wife and became the town's first civilian physician. A native of the
Midwest, McCarty had graduated from the Jefferson Medical College at
Philadelphia two years before and practiced briefly in St. Louis. He
arrived in western Kansas just in time: Dodge City was about to wallow in
a spree of senseless violence, the rougher elements of the population
adopting the practice of trading gunshots with one another, a less than
tranquil pastime often requiring a surgeon's hands.

Few were discouraged by social upheavals. J. L. Leavitt came to town
and set up a lumber yard; Cotsworth and Armitage sold liquor and cigars;
McKwort and Mitchell handled groceries, liquor, and clothing; and Crawford and Cook also sold groceries as well as produce and harness supplies,
shipping merchandise south to Camp Supply. H. P. Niess, a Civil War vet-

---

[48] *Kansas Daily Commonwealth*, November 8, 1872.

eran from Leavenworth, became the town's first boot maker. Other arrivals included Morris Collar, a thirty-year-old Austrian clothing merchant who came in from Colorado. His younger brother, Jacob, followed from Lincoln County, Nevada. In Dodge City Jacob Collar began as a wholesale and retail dry goods, clothing, and furniture dealer. Eventually he established the Blue Front Store and became the first to offer coffins and other undertaking supplies, providing a steady income more in keeping with Dodge City's growing reputation.

Harry Lovett started the town's first dance hall. Others followed. One of the most successful belonged to Thomas Sherman, a New Yorker and former government tracker whom Major Dodge had hired to help Sargeant Beatty trail horse thieves after the "grand steal" against railroad grading gangs that summer. Sherman was not yet thirty when he opened for business in Dodge City. Located south of the tracks, between First and Second avenues, Tom Sherman's place became notorious. He always saw to it that choruses of young women, nearly all in their teens or early twenties, were on hand to guarantee customer satisfaction.

Dodge City ignored criticism of its saloons, dance halls, and brothels, but felt pride in its first hotel, seen by all as a sign of progress amid the squalor common to isolated frontier towns. The Essington House offered not only beds to tired travelers, but a popular bar presided over, according to one charmed reporter, by "Doc Riley, well-known by all western men. Doc is as good a boy as ever mixed a cocktail, and always full of fun." The writer described the hotel's feverish beginnings: "The Essington House, the only hotel in the place, was built a little at a time, and as fast as lumber could be got over the road. As soon as the shell was up, and before either the roof was on or floor laid, it was ready for business. A tent served as a kitchen, the carpenters proceeded with their work between meals, and the roof was put on and floor laid while the hotel was running full blast. The work inside is still going on, and in thirty days it will be finished. The patronage of the house, in the meantime, will almost pay for the entire expense of building and furnishing. . . . This is what I call a rare specimen of Western enterprise."[49]

Progress slowed in late November after the proprietor, J. M. Essington, who doubled part-time as a carpenter and building contractor, was shot

[49] *Leavenworth Daily Commercial*, November 19, 1872.

through the head during a drunken argument with his cook.[50] After Essington's burial in Boot Hill, Sincox and Sloane ran the place. Soon afterward George B. Cox and Albert H. Boyd bought the property, located near the corner of Front Street and First Avenue, conveniently north of the makeshift depot, and renamed it the Dodge House. The new proprietors remodeled at a cost of more than $11,000. Boasting thirty-eight rooms, the partners celebrated their grand opening on January 18, 1873. Much later they negotiated an $800 purchase from Peter Taschetta and his wife for the corner lot directly east.[51] Those two had come out from Leavenworth and opened a restaurant. Cox and Boyd turned that site into a two-story frame building housing a billiard parlor and saloon. Government climatologists used the roof of the Dodge House for their weather instruments.

George B. Cox, known to all his friends as "Deacon," had drifted after the Civil War. In 1871 he married a New Jersey woman and ended up in what would become Larned, Kansas. Albert Boyd arrived at the same place somewhat earlier, but in a more roundabout fashion. Actually the two presented an interesting contrast. Both served in the army during the Civil War, but on opposite sides. Cox enlisted in the infantry from his native Georgia, while Boyd joined a regiment of Illinois cavalry, seeing action at Antietam and Gettysburg. After his enlistment ended, Boyd headed west. At Fort Leavenworth he found a job with the quartermaster's department and helped take the first wagon train to Denver after the Indian troubles of 1864. From there he guided another train to New Mexico. In 1866, after a second trip to Santa Fe, he spent six months at Fort Dodge as a wood contractor.

Two years later Boyd bought a ranch near Fort Larned and began outfitting groups of hunters and dealing in hides, before opening a freighting business between Forts Larned and Dodge north to Ellsworth and Hays City. An Indian attack destroyed the property and left Boyd in debt. Major Dodge saw some justice in it, since he had accused Boyd of organizing

---

[50] *Newton Kansan*, November 28, 1872.

[51] "Lot No. (2) in Block No. (2) being twenty five feet front in Front Street and Extending through (125) one hundred and twenty five feet to Chestnut Street in the town of Dodge City as designated by the recorded map of said town." Indenture dated August 14, signed August 17, and recorded August 20, 1874. Ford County Register of Deeds, Book A, 59–60. Peter Taschetta and his wife had already returned to Leavenworth by the time they sold their corner lot in Dodge City to Cox and Boyd. Jesse A. Hall and Leroy T. Hand, *History of Leavenworth County, Kansas* (Topeka: Historical Publishing Company, 1921), 588. Their son, also named Peter, would become the assistant chief of the Leavenworth Fire Department.

stock raids with the hope of blaming Indians.[52] Albert Boyd hauled wood and began raising cattle, while acquiring real estate. He then joined up with George Cox. Together the Yankee and Confederate built the first structure on the Larned townsite. Both were chosen commissioners in the first Pawnee County elections in November 1872.

Still involved with affairs at Larned, Boyd opened a stable at Dodge City soon after the election, while at the same time becoming more involved with the buffalo trade. The partners took advantage of Mr. Essington's sudden departure from life to expand their own earthly holdings. Boyd's younger brother, Fred, who had been at Andersonville Prison during the war, joined him, as did other members of the family, including their father and married sister. For a time Fred worked at the stable, but raised cattle later on.[53]

Most everyone congregating at Dodge City in 1872 owed his or her livelihood, in one way or the other, to the idea of killing buffalo. Indians, of course, had hunted these creatures since prehistoric times, but by the early 1870s destruction had reached alarming proportions. Earlier, animals supplied only robes and meat to a limited market, making little or no impact on the herds themselves. Suddenly European and American tanners began experimenting with buffalo as a source of leather for industry—belts to keep machines running during the post–Civil War manufacturing boom. Traditional methods used on buffalo hides produced a spongy product of little value, but newer techniques, especially those developed in Germany, succeeded in making a strong but elastic product perfect for industrial uses. The process proved cheaper than depending on hides from domestic cattle, which alone could never have met demand and would have required imports from Latin American countries as far south as Argentina. Other tanners in Europe, England, and America began realizing the buffalo's potential. Orders for hides flooded the central plains.

---

[52] Maj. Richard I. Dodge to Asst. Adj. Gen., Department of the Missouri, June 18, 1872. Fort Dodge, Letters Sent. Dodge wrote, referring to a "Mr. Hudson" while describing a particularly dubious Indian raid against local livestock: "Instead of Indians the attack was undoubtly [sic] made by white cattle thieves. . . . This man Hudson is one of a gang of horse and cattle thieves who made their Headquarters at Boyds [sic] Ranche four miles below Fort Larned."

[53] For more on Cox and Boyd, see George H. Woodruff, *Fifteen Years Ago: Or the Patriotism of Will County* (Joliet, Ill.: Joliet Republican Book & Job Steam Printing House, 1876), Pt. 4, 48, 68; *Souvenir of Settlement and Progress of Will County, Ill.* (Chicago: Historical Directory Publishing Co., 1884), 173, 213, 233; *The United States Biographical Dictionary, Kansas Volume*, 669–70; and *History of the State of Kansas*, 1561.

William T. Hornaday, writing for the National Museum two decades after the event, attributed the primary cause of the buffalo's demise to "the descent of civilization, with all its elements of destructiveness, upon the whole of the country inhabited by that animal." Hornaday listed five secondary causes: man's reckless greed, the absence of governmental protection, the preference of both white and Indian hunters to slaughter cows instead of bulls, the stupidity of the animals themselves, and the development of breech-loading firearms. To all this Hornaday added, "Had any one of these conditions been eliminated the result would have been reached far less quickly. Had the buffalo, for example, possessed one-half the fighting qualities of the grizzly bear he would have fared very differently, but his inoffensiveness and lack of courage, almost leads one to doubt the wisdom of the economy of nature so far as it relates to him."[54]

Before the 1870s, trade in buffalo hides proved a haphazard affair, with the financial return versus the product's weight making large-scale efforts unprofitable. Early trappers negotiated for hides only to oblige Indians to supply more valuable furs, primarily beaver. This pattern began to change after steamboats appeared on the upper Missouri, but until railroads penetrated the central plains, trading in hides and robes seldom exceeded a hundred thousand specimens a year, and the Indians supplied most of these.

At the close of the Civil War, hunters killed buffalo mostly for the meat, tongues, and robes, shipping only small numbers of hides to dealers such as William C. Lobenstine of Leavenworth,[55] as well as J. N. DuBois and Bath & Zingling at Kansas City. These middlemen, and others headquartered in St. Louis, sold specimens to eastern and European tanners interested in experimentation. By the early 1870s conditions changed with the unleashing of an unprecedented era of industrial expansion.

Hunter J. Wright Mooar, after filling a subcontracted order from

---

[54] William T. Hornaday, "The Extermination of the American Bison, with a Sketch of its Discovery and Life History," *Smithsonian Report, 1887* (Washington, 1889), Pt. 2, 464–65.

[55] Often misspelled "Lobenstein," even in some of his own advertisements! German-born William Christian Lobenstine had seen much of the West, including California during the gold rush, before settling in Leavenworth as a hide and leather dealer. He was, perhaps, more responsible than any other individual for initiating the slaughter of the Kansas herds. J. Wright Mooar claimed he "was the biggest hide dealer in the United States. Some people wondered why he was located [at Leavenworth]. It was because that was a centrally located point for business." J. Wright Mooar, Snyder, Texas, to J. Evetts Haley, November 25, 1927. Walter Stanley Campbell Files, Box 98A, File 6, 7. Manuscript Division, Western History Collection, University of Oklahoma Library. Also see T. Lindsay Baker and Billy R. Harrison, *Adobe Walls: The History and Archeology of the 1874 Trading Post* (College Station: Texas A&M University Press, 1986), 295n3.

Charles Rath for five hundred hides sought by William Lobenstine for an English firm, sent his remaining haul of fifty-seven specimens to his brother in New York City. A tanner from Pennsylvania offered John Wesley Mooar $3.70 each, or fifteen cents a pound. Within weeks this same man ordered another two thousand. Mooar accepted the commission and joined his brother in Kansas. Orders poured in, not in hundreds, but in the thousands. One English firm demanded ten thousand in a single order. The Great Buffalo Hunt was underway.

Railroads made it possible for hunters to kill animals without pause. The companies not only offered direct routes to the East, they also shipped out all the supplies hunters demanded. Traffic figures for the Kansas Pacific to the north and the Atchison, Topeka & Santa Fe to the south attest to the systematic nature of the assault in western Kansas. Men took up this bloody calling by the hundreds. There was money to be made, adventure to be experienced. By the winter of 1872 a large percentage of these men were drawn to the hunting grounds around Dodge City. Traditional robe hunters limited their kills to the autumn and winter months, when the animal's coat was thickest. Now, with manufacturers demanding leather belts for their machines, hunters stalked their prey year round.

Potential profits seemed enormous, especially for men accustomed to the $2.50 day wage paid to common laborers on the Kansas frontier. Hordes of these men, with their big guns and bigger dreams, descended on the unsuspecting herds. Cases of surplus Civil War weapons and even slug-loaded shotguns were shipped out. Experienced shooters preferred the Remington or the Sharps. Early on, during the 1872–73 season, these rifles in calibers .44/75 and .50/70 Government were the most prized. Within three years, with fewer animals and longer ranges required for the kill, heavier Sharps rifles came into fashion with their thirty- and thirty-two-inch octagon barrels. About a quarter of these sported telescopic sights, a feature that lost favor, as did the .50 caliber, replaced by a .45 caliber cartridge nearly three inches long.[56]

Herds of buffalo stretching from Kansas into Colorado stood little chance, even against these early parties of disorganized hunters. Carcasses rotted after more animals were killed than the men could process, forcing

---

[56] For the best overview of this historic weapon and its relationship to the near-demise of the American Bison, based on the company's own records of demand and production figures, see Frank Sellers, *Sharps Firearms* (Los Angeles: Beinfeld Publishing, Inc., 1978), 303–18.

an adjustment in technique. A more efficient system detailed a single shooter, two skinners, and a hostler for cooking and other camp chores. Experienced hunters killed only those animals their skinners could handle. Still, the level of waste remained high.

Years later Dodge City hunter Frank H. Mayer calculated, "I wouldn't do the same amount of hard work, take the same chances again for any man's $50,000. . . . On my first two years, deducting interest on investment, overhead, and so forth, I barely came out even; I think my net for the two years was around $2,800. And a little over $100 a month is mighty poor pay for the financial and physical output, not counting liability to disease and violent death!" After nine years Mayer had only $5,000 on deposit. Even then, he claimed, "I am quite confident that I was among the highest rewarded five men on the range. I have since talked to a dozen of the runners I knew and one and all remarked, 'Well, you got more out of it than any feller I know of.' "[57]

Men approached the herds downwind to avoid stampedes. They tried killing each animal with a single shot. Others ate up profits by wasting ammunition. Totals for some hunters reached staggering proportions. More than one claimed a yearly average of three thousand kills. Dodge City hunter George W. Reighard said he once killed that many in a single month. Exaggerations were common, but other accounts were all too accurate.[58]

Every hunter dreamed of a successful "stand," that single spot from which to fill his daily quota of dead animals. Often, after a few went down others nervously moved away, either by stampede or by just shifting a few hundred yards. Before they resumed grazing, the shooter gathered up his accoutrements and followed, stopping only when they stopped, to renew the process. The herds never had a chance.

The slaughter reached frightful levels. Major Dodge "counted 112 carcasses of buffalo inside of a semi-circle of 200 yards radius, all of which were killed by one man from the same spot, and in less than three-quarters of an hour."[59] William Blackmore, an English sportsman who wrote the

---

[57] Frank H. Mayer and Charles B. Roth, *The Buffalo Harvest* (Denver: Sage Books, 1958), 64.

[58] Frank Gilbert Roe, *The North American Buffalo: A Critical Study of the Species in Its Wild State* (Toronto: University of Toronto Press, 1951), 419–23. Also see George W. Reighard (as told to A. B. MacDonald), "What an Old Buffalo Hunter Saw Who Helped To Exterminate the Herds That Darkened the Plains," *Kansas City Star*, November 30, 1930.

[59] Richard Irving Dodge, *The Plains of the Great West* (New York: G. P. Putnam's Sons, 1877), 136.

introduction for the major's *The Plains of the Great West*, traveled the Arkansas River Valley in 1872 and recalled that "whilst on a scout for about a hundred miles south of Fort Dodge to the Indian territory, we were never out of sight of buffalo." On a later trip, Blackmore reported, "the whole country was whitened with bleached and bleaching bones, we did not meet with buffalo until we were well into the Indian territory, and then only in scanty bands. . . . The hunters had formed a line of camps along the banks of the river, and had shot down the buffalo, night and morning, as they came to drink."[60]

Naturalist William Hornaday declared, "Could the southern buffalo range have been roofed over at that time it would have made one vast charnel-house. Putrifying [*sic*] carcasses, many of them with the hide still on, lay thickly scattered over thousands of square miles of the level prairie, poisoning the air and water and offending the sight. The remaining herds had become mere scattered bands harried and driven hither and thither by the hunters, who now swarmed almost as thickly as the buffaloes."[61]

Just counting hides failed to show the magnitude of what was happening. As Major Dodge recalled, "Though hundreds of thousands of skins were sent to market, they scarcely indicated the slaughter that, from want of skill in shooting, and want of knowledge in preserving the hides of those slain, on the part of these green hunters, one hide sent to market represented three, four, or even five dead buffalo."[62] Yet, as more skinners perfected their technique, 100 hides ready for sale represented only 125 dead animals. Such proficiency came late. Dodge estimated that for the 497,163 hides delivered from the Kansas frontier in 1872, nearly 1.5 million buffalo had to die.

Not everyone approved. As early as that first full season of 1872, some raised their voices in protest. At Leavenworth it was said, "we cannot but hope that our legislature and that of Colorado will do something this winter to put a stop to this wanton destruction of the poor buffalo."[63] A similar response came from the *Denver Tribune*, reprinted in several Kansas newspapers: "We second the protest for the hundredth time. It is an outrage that the law should stop. . . . Let Kansas and Colorado enact strict laws

---

60 Ibid., Introduction by William Blackmore, xv.
61 Hornaday, "The Extermination of the American Bison," 496.
62 Dodge, *The Plains of the Great West*, 131–32.
63 *Leavenworth Daily Commercial*, November 23, 1872.

and the evil will be abated if not eradicated."[64] Of course neither legislature did a thing, the powerful railroad lobby stifling all protest to protect their profits.

The position taken by military men is more difficult to assess. Opinion appears divided—excluding those ambivalent to the question—depending on where the officers making their thoughts known stood in the official scheme of things: whether at the War Department in Washington, Headquarters of the Department of the Missouri, or commanding one of the many posts scattered along the frontier. General Sherman, in a letter to his brother, explained his feeling about the Indians and the buffalo: "The great bulk of the Sioux have agreed to move to the Missouri where they will be too far away from the railroad to be provoked to do it damage. . . . [T]he same as to the Cheyennes, etc., below the Arkansas. The commission for present peace had to concede a right to hunt buffaloes as long as they last, and this may lead to collisions, but it will not be long before all the buffaloes are extinct near and between the railroads, after which the Indians will have no reason to approach either road."[65]

Years later John Sherman tried justifying the process described by his famous brother: "It is sad to reflect that all these animals have been exterminated, mainly in wanton sport by hunters who did not need their flesh for food or their hides for leather or robes. This destruction of buffaloes opened the way for herds of domestic cattle, which perhaps in equal numbers now feed upon the native grass of the prairies."[66]

More recently, nineteenth-century attitudes have been explained as a callous indifference over the fate of these animals, or as an official conspiracy to subdue Indians by depriving them of their mobile commissary. Although elements of both existed, this apparent shallowness of purpose is belied by circumstances. Hunters exploited the vast herds of bison for their own benefit and for whatever profit they envisioned, and not to please Sherman, the railroad, or any other official. The general may have been pleased by the outcome, but he certainly had no hand in directing the campaign. Men hunted buffalo because of the willingness of others to pay for the result, namely leather demanded by American industry.[67]

---

[64] *Denver Tribune*, as quoted in *Newton Kansan*, November 28, 1872.

[65] W. T. Sherman to John Sherman, July 17, 1868. Thorndike, ed., *The Sherman Letters*, 320.

[66] John Sherman, *John Sherman's Recollections of Forty Years in the House, Senate and Cabinet: An Autobiography* (Chicago: The Werner Company, 1895), 1:392.

[67] Andrew C. Isenberg, *The Destruction of the Bison: An Environmental History, 1750–1920* (Cambridge, U.K.: Cambridge University Press, 2000), 129.

Not everyone saw the demise of the bison as a necessary step in subduing the tribes. Some officers supported the hunt, to be sure, but others seemed indifferent, while still others opposed the slaughter. In early June 1872, Col. De Lancey Floyd-Jones of the Third Infantry, then stationed at Fort Hays but earlier in command at Fort Dodge, wrote his friend, Philip Sheridan, commander of the Military Division of the Missouri, at Chicago:

> While visiting at your house this spring . . . you gave some statistics in regard to the Buffalo, that convinced me of your interest in this animal. I have just come into possession of some facts which may be of interest to yourself as also the Genl. Government. It has been demonstrated that the hide of this animal is available for leather, and in consequence a trade has sprung up which will if continued, destroy the whole herds south of the K.P.R R. in the course of two years. Within the last thirty days twenty-five thousand hides have been shipped over the K.P. Road . . . at this rate the destruction will be in twelve months three hundred thousand: one half the herd as estimated by yourself. One gentleman stated to me that there was a continuous line of fire on this animal from this to the Arkansas river.
>
> I write this unofficially, but you can make such use of it as you deem best.[68]

Sheridan responded a week later by sending a copy of the letter to the secretary of war, adding, "I am of the belief that the destruction of the Buffalo that he mentions has been exaggerated to him, but respectfully request authority to put a stop to it, should it: upon examination prove to be as great as Colonel Floyd Jones seems to think."[69] A reply came from the chief clerk of the War Department: "The Secretary has received your note of the 11th . . . respecting the destruction of the Buffalo upon the plains, and desires me to return Col. Jones' note, and to say that he approves your request for authority to put a stop to their wholesale destruction if that officer's suppositions are correct."[70] Sheridan alone had no jurisdiction over civilian activity in Kansas. With Congress bowing to commercial pressure, nothing was done.

Astride the front lines of this commercial and cultural upheaval, Richard Irving Dodge refused to excuse the buffalo hunters, nor did he blame Indians for every reported outrage. Soon after assuming command of Fort Dodge, he wrote to his superiors: "a citizen named Nixon reported that five

---

[68] Col. DeL. Floyd-Jones to Gen. P. H. Sheridan, June 3, 1872. Copy found in Headquarters Records, Fort Dodge, Kansas, Unregistered Letters Received.

[69] Lieut. Gen. P. H. Sheridan, Chicago, to Hon. Wm. W. Belknap, Washington, D.C., June 11, 1872. Ibid.

[70] John Polls, Chief Clerk, War Department, to Lieut. General P. H. Sheridan, June 22, 1872. Ibid.

head of animals had been stolen from him by Indians the night before. He with a party of five citizens were hunting Buffalo South of the Arkansas, some twenty miles above this post. . . . He claimed to see moccasin tracks. I refused to send out any party in pursuit, or to assist him in any way."

Shifting emphasis, Dodge added, "I respectfully invite the attention of the Department Commander to these hunting parties. They claim to be citizens of Kansas, that they have a right to go where they please and be protected. They are killing countless numbers of Buffalo, simply for their hides, exasperating the Indians by the wanton and wholesale destruction. To let them go on as at present is to invite depredation and outrage by the Indians." The major, however, was only too aware of the forces lined up against that policy: "To bring them in by force will cause an outcry from all the newspapers and politicians of Kansas. I think, under the provocation of these hunting parties, the Indians have been singularly forebearing [*sic*]."[71]

J. Wright Mooar, then working with his brother, alongside John Joshua Webb and two or three hired hands, decided to test the possibilities of hunting below the Kansas line all the way into Texas. Sometime during July 1873 he and Webb rode south and found a country "that was just loaded with buffaloes." They described conditions to other hunters, but were told, "they couldn't go down there."[72]

Returning to Dodge City they spoke with Charles Rath and Charlie Myers about what they had seen. Neither merchant offered encouragement about hunting all the way into Texas. Undeterred, Mooar claimed that he and Webb decided to visit the fort and learn the views of the military firsthand. Ushered into the presence of Major Dodge, Mooar recalled, they "told him what we had seen, and I asked him if we crossed the Neutral Strip into Texas to hunt buffalo, or perhaps kill a few in the Neutral Strip, what would be his policy toward us, what would he do about it."[73]

---

[71] Maj. Richard I. Dodge to Asst. Adj. Gen., Department of the Missouri, June 10, 1872. Fort Dodge, Letters Sent. Dodge found some support in official circles. The adjutant general, E. D. Townsend, responded to Dodge's letter by writing directly to Lt. Gen. Philip Sheridan in Chicago: "Referring to the communication of the commanding Officer, Fort Dodge, Kansas, forwarded by endorsement of the 25th ultimo from your Headquarters, relative to the Killing of buffalo by hunting parties who claim to be citizens of Kansas and have the right to protection; I have the honor to invite attention to communications addressed to you from [the] War Department, June 22, 1872, which contains the requisite authority to correct the evil herein referred to." Adjutant General E. D. Townsend, War Department, Washington, to Commanding General, Military Division of the Missouri, Chicago, July 3, 1872. Copy found in Headquarters Records, Fort Dodge, Kansas. Unregistered Letters Received.

[72] J. Evetts Haley interview with J. Wright Mooar, Snyder, Texas, March 3, 1939. Walter Stanley Campbell Files, Box 98B, Folder 14A, 45. Manuscript Division, Western History Collection, University of Oklahoma Library.

[73] Ibid.

According to Mooar, the major ignored the question. Instead, for the next couple of hours, Dodge, scribbling notes in shorthand with a pencil on large sheets of fools cap, talked with them in detail about the buffalo, questioning how the animals behaved, their migration patterns, how they acted in a stampede, the procedures used in hunting them, and the monetary rewards for all the trouble. Mooar said they all had a grand time, but when preparing to leave he stated, "you have never answered our question yet." Dodge asked what it was, and as Mooar claimed, "I repeated it. If we crossed the Neutral Strip to go into Texas to hunt buffalo and maybe kill a few in the Strip, what was his policy going to be towards us. What was going to be the penalty. What were we laying ourselves liable to, if anything, and he says, 'Boys,'—I'll never forget how that expression struck me, calling us boys—we hadn't been called boys for a good while. He says, 'If I was a buffalo hunter, I'd hunt buffalo where buffalo are.' "[74] Later Mooar explained, "he wished us success and shook hands with us and bade us goodbye. And we come back well satisfied that we could cross the strip. And I did cross it. I didn't cross it right then, crossed it in September or the first of October. I began preparing to go south, yes, and we did go south."[75]

All this seems contrary to earlier statements from Major Dodge, but a similar episode supposedly took place years before in Nebraska. During the fall of 1867 Sir William Butler, a British military man enjoying a tour of the central plains, arrived at North Platte. There he "found a distinguished officer of the army in command, Colonel Dodge." Confessing that he and his party had killed more than thirty buffalo bulls, and afterward felt "some qualms of conscience at the thought of the destruction of so much animal life," Butler received official absolution from the colonel: "Kill every buffalo you can," he said; "every buffalo dead is an Indian gone."[76] It has

---

[74] J. Wright Mooar, Snyder, Texas, to J. Evetts Haley, July 28, 1937, ibid., Box 98A, File 13A, 3. Recalling all the questions Major Dodge asked regarding the habits of buffalo, while "he set there pecking with that pencil," Mooar later explained: "Here about ten years ago I heard an article read that purported to be his report to the government at Washington about the vast buffalo herds that was out here, and the way they migrated and so on, and I recognized that conversation that I had with him in that report that he made to the government." Ibid., 2.

[75] J. Evetts Haley interview with J. Wright Mooar, Snyder, Texas, March 3, 1939, ibid., Box 98A, Folder 14A, 47.

[76] Lieut.-General The Rt. Hon. Sir W. F. Butler, G.C.B., *Sir William Butler: An Autobiography* (New York: Charles Scribner's Sons, 1913), 97. Sir William gives no specific point of identification besides referring to his Colonel Dodge as "one of the foremost frontier men of his time, and the descendant of officers who had prepared the road for the army of settlement in the West." This description hardly points to Richard Irving Dodge. Besides, during that period and later he always gave his rank as major. Despite being brevetted a lieutenant colonel in 1865, he never used that distinction until promoted to that position in the regular army on October 29, 1873.

since been suggested that the officer of whom Sir William spoke was Richard Irving Dodge, although that has never been confirmed.[77]

In any event, although currently accused of failing to prevent buffalo hunters from invading Indian lands below the Arkansas,[78] the record supports the commander at Fort Dodge. It must be remembered that Major Dodge was one of those by-the-book officers whom others find so tedious. Indeed, before assuming command at Fort Dodge, he spent the months from July 1871 until May 17, 1872, in New York City helping "perfect a system of Army Regulations."[79]

Now, stationed on the frontier in the middle of the buffalo slaughter, Richard Dodge found himself trying to carry out orders from the Department of the Missouri. In early September he ordered Capt. Joseph Kerin of the Sixth Cavalry to scout along portions the Cimarron River and the road to Camp Supply. If he encountered Arapahoes or Cheyennes "on the Cimarron making their fall hunt they will *not* be *molested*."[80] Others, especially Kiowas and anyone else traveling without their families, would be ordered back to their reservations. As it turned out, Captain Kerin saw more than just bands of Indians below the Kansas line.

In his report, submitted twenty days after being ordered out, the captain detailed conditions. In speaking with a Cheyenne leader, he reported, "White Head . . . came to camp and informed me he was out hunting or looking after buffalo . . . that he had no permission to be off the reservation, but as whites were hunting buffalo on the reservation he came across the Cimarron River. . . . That parties of white men were then hunting on Beaver Creek and far into the Indian Territory. . . . They are hunting on the Wichita River, South of the Wichita mountains."[81] White Head talked of attempts by young Kiowas to enlist Cheyennes to join them on raids into Texas. The growing pervasiveness of illegal hunting parties provided most of the basis for unrest.

Responding to the captain's observations, the department's assistant adjutant general informed Major Dodge, who had endorsed and forwarded Kerin's report: "The Department Commander directs me to call

[77] Isenberg, *The Destruction of the Bison*, 155.

[78] Ibid.

[79] Cullum, *Biographical Register*, 2:357.

[80] Special Order, No. 133, September 7, 1873. Fort Dodge, Special Orders, Vol. 4.

[81] Capt. Joseph Kerin to Post Adj., September 27, 1873. Fort Dodge, Reports, Journals, and Memorandums of Scouts and Marches.

your attention to the fact, that inside of the limits of the State of Kansas, these hunters, like other citizens, are subject to the laws of Kansas, but that below the southern line of Kansas, in the Indian Territory, and particularly on the Indian reservations the military authorities have control of the matter and have full power to remove, therefrom, all or any of these parties of hunters, who may be discovered in the Indian Country."[82]

By mid-autumn 1873 an exasperated Richard Dodge again described conditions for his superiors: "[T]he whole country is covered with Buffalo hunters. They are in parties of from three to twelve, thoroughly armed, and relying partly upon the protection of the Government, and partly upon the forbearance and peaceful disposition of the Indians, they roam at will through the southern portion of the State of Kansas, and through the Territory and Reservations of the Indians, slaughtering the Buffalo by hundreds and thousands, immediately in the presence, and almost in the very camps of the Indians."

The major spelled out the consequences of inaction: "The Indians kill Buffalo slowly, as they can cure the meat and skins. The hunters kill all they can at a time, and skin afterwards. The Indians cannot compete with these hunters, and if some steps are not at once taken to stop the hunters, one of two things must occur. Either the Indians, becoming exasperated, will drive out the hunters, probably with bloodshed, which will inaugurate a war, or they will fail to obtain their winter's supply of meat and skins, which means to them starvation, or extreme suffering."

Despite the impression made by J. Wright Mooar that he sympathized with the hunters, Dodge reported: "I warned all the hunters out of the Indian Territory and off the Reservations. They move their camps back north, to the state line of Kansas, or south to the state line of Texas, and from thence hunt in the Indian Territory and reservations as before. I may arrest trespassers in the Territory or Reservations, but must release them as soon as I reach the State line, there being no law to prevent their hunting either in Kansas or Texas." Clearly concerned, Dodge ended the report with a prophecy: "In my opinion very serious consequences will result unless immediate steps are taken to arrest the work of these hunters in the Indian Territory and Reservations."[83]

---

[82] R. Williams, Asst. Adj. Gen., Department of the Missouri, to Maj. Richard Dodge, October 3, 1873. Fort Dodge, Registered Letters Received.

[83] Major Richard I. Dodge to Asst. Adj. Gen., Department of the Missouri, October 27, 1873. Fort Dodge, Letters Sent.

Too few civilians shared these concerns. Merchants in small frontier rail towns like Dodge City, often strapped for cash, owed their existence to the buffalo trade. Hunters not only sold cured hides to these men or their agents, they purchased supplies from them. Many in Dodge City were involved in this trade, but the most important practitioners remained Charles Rath and his partner Robert Wright, as well as A. C. "Charlie" Myers, whose Pioneer Store south of the tracks gave Rath & Co. its heaviest competition in those early days. Buffalo had become big business. At Pawnee Fork Myers built a smokehouse, where his men divided the animals' hindquarters into thirds, after which they sugar-cured and smoked the meat. Sewn into canvas sacks, this product commanded premium prices not only among frontier retailers but at several eastern markets as well.

Business was good, but Dodge City would experience desperate and troubling times. The hunters and others attracted to the place for rest and amusement soon created an atmosphere that made the very name Dodge City a catchphrase for bloodshed and anarchy on the Kansas frontier.

Chapter 4

MURDERS AND MAYHEM

From the start Dodge City's streets swarmed with restless young men of various persuasions and temperament. One inventory of the gathering, composed for county organizational purposes in January 1873, enumerated a population that averaged just twenty-seven years of age and was 86 percent male.[1] Jamming this floating consortium into a world dominated by firearms and alcohol, and without any of the restraints common to civilized society, helped create an atmosphere openly indifferent to violence and suffering. The terrible scenes that unfolded at tiny Dodge City were, in their brutal frequency, without precedent on the central plains during those wild days of building railroads and slaughtering bison.

As a wide-open railroad town, Dodge City attracted a host of shady characters, professional gamblers, prostitutes, and bummers, all dreaming of easy pickings. As one contemporary described the menagerie: "There is a peculiar people located on the south-western frontier of Kansas—real genuine roughs—men from all portions of the world. . . . Men of cool daring enterprise; men of lawless, reckless lives and murderous disposition. . . . The class of people who follow immediately in the wake of the track builders, are a cosmopolitan class—a medley made up of roughs, rowdys, gamblers, speculators, saloon keepers, Jews and founders of towns, all sharp gritty 'git up and git' sort of people, who care for nothing except the almighty dollar."[2]

Veteran plainsman Billy Dixon seemed charmed by the colorful citizenry: "Like moths drawn by the flame of a lamp, a picturesque lot of men gath-

---

[1] Ford County Census, January 1873. Typescript, Manuscripts Department, Kansas State Historical Society. "Dodge City will be the county seat of Ford County. The census supervisor recently appointed by Governor Harvey informed us that the county had the requisite number of inhabitants for organization, and there was no doubt of its immediate admission as soon as the census was completed. Col. [Isaac] Young, formerly of this city, is engaged in taking the census, and will have his census roll completed before the Legislature convenes." *Leavenworth Times*, November 7, 1872.

[2] *Kansas City Times*, February 15, 1873.

ered at Dodge. Practically all of them were looking for adventure and excitement, rather than for opportunities to become preachers, lawyers or merchants. They came from the border towns that dotted like beads that western
fringe of civilization. Dodge City belonged mostly to the under-world in
those days, and its ways were the ways of men and women who stayed up all
night and slept all day. Buffalo-hunters, railroad graders, gamblers, dance
hall actors and dancers and that nondescript class that lived without doing
any kind of work predominated." Dixon was kind enough to add: "But there
were good men and women in Dodge, and as in most genuine American
communities, they finally won out, despite its revelries and dissipations."[3]

Buffalo-hunter-turned-saloonman George W. "Hoodoo" Brown remembered what he thought was "the first shooting scrape in Dodge City" taking place even before the railroad arrived. The principals were Johnnie
Langford and a gambler named Charley Morehouse. According to Brown,
"They pulled Morehouse out of bed one night, where he was enjoyin' himself with a dance-hall girl, and made him drink with them." Half an hour
later everyone but Morehouse showed up at Brown and Charley Stewart's
place, "My saloon at that time was plumb full of men," Hoodoo recalled.
"I was tendin' bar myself." Langford and two friends left to find drinks in a
less crowded place. They hadn't gone far before Morehouse and some
friends showed up. Unaware of any trouble, Brown explained that Langford
and the others had just left.

The gambler and his party stepped out onto the street and spotted the
three men walking off into the shadows. Saloonman Brown described the
resulting melee:

> The Morehouse party opened fire on them. Langford returned the fire and
> the bullets were flyin' around pretty thick, and I laid down behind the
> counter and tried to crawl into the ground. One man was shot in the heel as
> he was goin' out the back door. A man was on a cot near the door on the out-
> side. Next morning they found five bullet holes through his coat, and the
> man wasn't touched. In all this shootin' there wasn't a man killed straight out.
> John Langford was shot five times, but he crawled off and hid himself in
> some brush down near the river. He was rescued next morning and was taken
> to the hospital at Fort Dodge, where he was for quite a while and finally
> recovered. Morehouse had one shot through the fleshy part of his arm.[4]

---

[3] Dixon, *Life of "Billy" Dixon*, 78–79.
[4] Connelley, "Life and Adventures of George W. Brown," 116.

The first actual homicide, Robert Wright admitted, involved a black man, known either as Tex or Black Jack, and a gambler called Denver. As Wright remembered the details, Tex was standing on the street in front of the elevated platform at Kelley and Hunt's saloon and dance hall when a crowd gathered. Someone pulled out a pistol and fired. Tex dropped to the street dead. Years later Denver claimed he "shot him in the top of the head just to see him kick."[5] George Hoover recalled, "Black Jack was shot through the head and instantly killed. He was planted, as they called it, with his boots on on Boot Hill. . . . During the winter of 1872 and spring of 73 no less than 15 men were killed in Dodge City and were planted on Boot Hill."[6]

Early September witnessed another battle: "Shooting Affair at Dodge.—We learn from persons who came down the road yesterday, that there was a lively shooting affray at Dodge on Tuesday, in which four or five persons were wounded, one or two perhaps fatally. We did not learn the names of any of the parties concerned."[7]

Two days later more of the same, this time involving a well-known tough named Jack Reynolds, who a few days before had shot a man at Raymond, a railroad camp near the Colorado line. Described as "a notoriously mean and contemptible desperado," Reynolds had been pushing his way around "by murderous threats, backed by a six shooter." Sometimes he failed to intimidate. He tried it on a railroad conductor, who instead of retreating, tackled Reynolds, disarmed him and tossed him off the train. At Dodge City, the bad man resumed his old habits and started a quarrel with a tracklayer, "who, without any 'ifs or ands' put six balls, in rapid succession, into Jack's body. The desperado fell and expired instantly; and thus the law-abiding people of the southwest were rid of a terror."[8] Kansas newspapers treated Reynolds's death with predictable irreverence.

By mid-November another tale of Dodge City violence made the rounds. At Kelley and Hunt's dance hall a Texan grabbed some cash from a game run by Matt Sullivan. The gambler pulled his revolver and smashed

---

[5] Wright, *Dodge City, the Cowboy Capital*, 169.

[6] "Early History. Some Reminiscences of the Early Days of Dodge City," *Dodge City Democrat*, June 19, 1903. Based on an interview with George M. Hoover.

[7] *Hutchinson News*, September 5, 1872.

[8] *Kansas Daily Commonwealth*, September 8, 1872. Five days later the Wichita *City Eagle* remarked that Reynolds, "in attempting to dead-beat his way on the division west of Newton, was forever quieted at Dodge City . . . by a track layer, who put six balls through him before he could say scat."

the offender on the left temple, the hammer spur penetrating the skull. Two friends rushed to the man's defense. One drew a revolver behind Sullivan, whose partner, identified only as Billy, shot him dead. Sullivan also fired, striking the last attacker through the neck, causing an ugly wound.

A visiting reporter from Leavenworth, who described Sullivan as "one of the quietest men" in Dodge, claimed the three were only wounded. Earlier his paper had given a more conventional account: "Dodge City is winning the laurels from Newton. Three men were shot at a dance house there the other night and thrown into the streets, while the dance went merrily on."[9] It was an image no newspaperman could resist. In far-off Missouri a Kansas City editor wrote: "three men were shot and thrown out into the frost. One of these men was brought to this city last night to be forwarded to his friends in New Orleans. They make no trouble about killing a few men at Fort Dodge. It is mere pastime at a dance house fandango."[10]

Most of the trouble centered on a single class of desperate men, but one row in early December involved locals and a squad of off-duty soldiers from Fort Dodge. A twenty-four-year-old private named James W. Hennessy saw himself as the best fighting man in his outfit. Carousing with his comrades, the Irish-born New Yorker decided to prove the point with his fists. Instead, a general melee erupted in Scott and Peacock's saloon near the depot, with some forty or fifty shots fired. Private Hennessey was already dead, but his friends rushed him to the Fort Dodge hospital all the same. Army records listed the cause of death as murder, stating without a hint of remorse that Hennessey "was shot dead while participating in a drunken Brawl at Dodge City Kansas Dec 4th 1872."[11]

During that particular episode the gambler Charley Morehouse, the same man wounded some weeks before during the wild street fight with Johnnie Langford near Brown and Stewart's saloon, was fatally shot through the left lung. He ended up on Boot Hill, prompting the remark: "Dodge City is making herself notorious as a fast frontier town. Four men were shot in that place last week, all of whom were killed or have since

[9] *Leavenworth Daily Commercial,* November 21, 1872.

[10] *Kansas City Times,* November 17, 1872.

[11] Records of the Adjutant General's Office (RG 94), Fort Dodge, Kansas, "Register of the Sick and Wounded," December 4, 1872, No. 1797; "Monthly Reports of Sick & Wounded," December 1872; and "List of Interments in Post Cemetery," No. 103.

died."[12] Watching the Morehouse burial, Hoodoo Brown claimed, "many more of my old-time friends lay near him."[13]

Disgusted by all the violence, a Fort Dodge wood contractor named John Fletcher suggested a vigilance committee. Weeks passed before anything was done. Meanwhile, a fortnight after the Hennessey killing, a former city marshal from Newton, William L. "Billy" Brooks, exchanged shots with W. P. Brown, the ex-railroad yardmaster there. Citizens probably wished both men had stayed in Newton. Instead they opened fire on Front Street, each wounding the other. The press reported Brown's demise, but instead he was sent to Topeka to have a bullet removed from his head. Bob Wright explained that the trouble grew out of both men's infatuation for a woman called "Captain Drew"—probably Jessie Drew, a nineteen-year-old prostitute then known to be living in Dodge City.

While describing Dodge as "smaller than its reputation would warrant," a Hutchinson editor noted in late December the town's seamier social customs: "A 'break down' is had every night. Occasionally, yes, often, these mazy entertainments wind up in a shooting affray, which if only one or two men are killed, are regarded as stupid episodes. Some ten men have received their quietus at Dodge in the last few weeks, and a dozen more are liable to the same fate at any time, for desperadoes are abundant and there is but little law."[14]

A week later residents took a brief respite from shooting one another and turned their hostility toward the hapless Cheyenne chief Spotted Wolf. It all began when he and William McDole Lee, a trader and freighting contractor from Camp Supply, broke camp after visiting various trading sites. Their carriage, piled high with merchandise, rolled over, injuring the Indian. Since orders from the Department of the Missouri did not allow assistance at Fort Dodge, Lee headed for Dr. Thomas McCarty's office in Dodge City. A bad idea, since buffalo hunters looked upon all Indians as potential assassins—a rather strange complaint, considering the many killings in Dodge since the gambler Denver shot Tex through the head "just to see him kick."

Riding along Front Street, William Lee and Spotted Wolf caught everyone's attention, especially a buffalo hunter of local renown called

[12] *Newton Kansan*, December 4, 1872.

[13] Connelley, "Life and Adventures of George W. Brown," 116.

[14] *Hutchinson News*, December 19, 1872.

Kirt Jordan, described by Bob Wright as "a very desperate man." Jordan nursed a special hatred of Indians. Only weeks before he had lost two brothers and a sister-in-law when hostiles attacked their isolated hunting camp. Everyone knew the story, if not all the details. Bob Wright exaggerated the circumstances by claiming Jordan's "sister, brother-in-law, and whole family had been wiped out by the savages, and their home and its contents burned and every vestige of stock stolen."[15] Now, the vengeful hunter convinced himself Spotted Wolf was wearing his sister-in-law's ring. Aroused to fever pitch, Jordan led a group of hunters and other drunken followers into McCarty's private office. Taking advantage of the confusion, Charlie Rath managed to hide Spotted Wolf in his own living quarters, a single-room apartment just to the north.

Rath, Lee, and Bob Wright slipped Spotted Wolf out of town, sending a message for help to Fort Dodge. Wright and Lee piled the carriage with buffalo robes to conceal their passenger before making a frantic dash for the fort. About a mile from town Capt. Tullius C. Tupper and several Sixth Cavalry troopers intercepted them. Wright was relieved, later noting, "There were no more Indians seen in Dodge except under big escort."[16] Sensing her fear, Spotted Wolf sent Mrs. Rath a pair of beaded moccasins in appreciation of her kindness.[17] She proudly kept them as a personal memento.

With Spotted Wolf gone, Dodge City resumed its normal state of anarchy. On the last day of 1872 the *Daily Commonwealth* at Topeka printed a column lead alerting its readers to a now familiar story: "SHOT DEAD—

---

[15] Wright, *Dodge City, the Cowboy Capital*, 163. Four months before the incident on Front Street involving Spotted Wolf, Cheyenne raiders attacked the family's isolated camp, killing Kirt Jordan's brothers, Richard and George, along with Fred Nelson, a Swedish hired hand. The brothers' Newfoundland dog, Queen, escaped the raid. It arrived home days later, its presence providing evidence to others that something terrible had happened. The Indians carried off Mary Jordan, Richard's young wife; later thought to have been murdered and her body discarded "fifty miles south of Fort Dodge." Asst. Adj. Gen., Department of the Missouri, to the Commanding Officer, Fort Dodge, Kansas, January 24, 1873. Fort Dodge, Registered Letters Received. Although Bob Wright mistakenly placed this incident in the northwest portion of the state, it actually took place, according to a reward proclamation issued by Gov. James M. Harvey, "in or near the county of Ness." *Kansas Daily Commonwealth*, October 15, 1872. For more details concerning this tragic episode, see: Minnie Dubbs Millbrook, "The Jordan Massacre," *Kansas History: A Journal of the Central Plains* 2, no. 4 (Winter 1979): 218–30.

[16] Wright, *Dodge City, the Cowboy Capital*, 164. Captain Moale, temporarily in command while Major Dodge was on leave, reported this incident to his superiors. That report generally substantiates Wright's version. Capt. Edward Moale to Asst. Adj. Gen., Department of the Missouri, December 28, 1872. Fort Dodge, Letters Sent.

[17] *Dodge City Daily Globe*, September 25, 1922. This story was included in a letter written to the editor by Carrie Rath Bainbridge, the former Mrs. Charles Rath.

Another Tragedy at Dodge City." Three days earlier someone fired a shotgun through a window at Matt Sullivan, killing him instantly. Editors at Topeka suggested a suspect: "It is supposed that the unknown assassin was a character in those parts called Bully Brooks, but nothing definite is known concerning the affair, or what led to it." Interviewing the news agent for the AT&SF, a Kansas City reporter uncovered other particulars concerning Sullivan, the same man characterized only six weeks before as "one of the quietest men in the place." He was now described as being a "cowardly rough" who "has shot quite a number of men during his sojourn on the frontier, and most of his deeds have been done similar to the one that brought him to his untimely end." Sullivan had pistol-whipped a railroad express messenger, fracturing his skull, all in retaliation for his mistress talking to the man. "It is thought that this affair had something to do with his assassination."[18]

A break in the violence came as the hunters left to resume their work, prompting speculation of a 150 percent increase in the buffalo harvest for the 1873 season. Depending on their quality, hides at Dodge City still brought between $1.50 and $2.50 apiece, while meat sold for around two cents a pound. Figures published at Topeka in mid-January listed a total of 43,029 hides shipped from Dodge City between September 23 and the end of the year.[19] Seventy-one railroad cars, carrying 1,436,290 pounds of meat, also traveled east—most consigned to Kansas City, with other shipments destined for St. Louis, Chicago, and Indianapolis. All this came from kills made after mid-November, when the cold weather helped reduce spoilage during shipment.

Another statistic bode ill for the buffalo's chances for survival. Tallies of buffalo bones gave a clearer picture of the magnitude of what was happening than simply counting hides shipped. Mountains of bones at railroad sidings would convince any reasonably observant person that the buffalo's days were numbered. The railroad sent east seventy-five cars loaded with bones picked from the plains of western Kansas: "A large part of them have gone to Wilmington, Del., where the best are selected for combs, knife-handles, &c.; the next best are ground into dust, and used in refining sugar; and the refuse is ground into meal for fertilizing purposes."[20]

---

[18] *Kansas City Times*, January 1, 1873.

[19] *Kansas Daily Commonwealth*, January 14, 1873.

[20] *Newton Kansan*, January 2, 1873.

THE YEAR 1873 BROUGHT WITH IT celebration. The Atchison, Topeka &
Santa Fe Railroad finally reached the Colorado border, but not without
difficulty. Crews located a site they christened State Line City. The railroad reached that spot on December 19, working through snow and freez-
ing rain. Exhausted crews had laid 271 miles of track in 222 days. Everyone
crowded the saloons of State Line City to celebrate. Merriment continued
until government surveyors dampened the revelry with news they had
missed their mark by four miles. Lacking rails and ties to close the gap, a
locomotive pushed flatcars back along the route as a skeleton crew tore up
siding. Despite the cold, they pushed the tracks across the Colorado line.
Not wanting to advertise their miscalculation, officials changed the name
of State Line City to Sargent—in honor of the railroad's general freight
agent. Years later they renamed it again, this time for Santa Fe president
Thomas Jefferson Coolidge.

For a time this new town rivaled Dodge City as the center of mayhem:
"It is said that the bullies and beauties of Dodge City are already flocking
to Sargent."[21] Another report claimed: "All the roughs, black legs and six-
shooters of Dodge and other places are now there."[22] Sargent's wildness
encouraged one inaccurate estimate: "Parties recently from Dodge City
inform us that that famous rendezvous of buffalo hunters is sick and rapidly 'played out'. The buffalo have left the neighborhood and with them
the army of hunters. The gamblers and roughs, with their frail, fair associates have gone to Sargent, whither the merchants are also going. Sargent
for the next few months, will be the 'red hot' town of the A.T. & S.F. railroad to give way in turn to Lyon, or some other place."[23] Some merchants
did move to Sargent, while others, such as Charlie Rath and Bob Wright,
as well as liquor wholesalers Hoover and McDonald, satisfied themselves
opening branches there. Wright, anticipating the railroad's eventual
advance, did the same at Granada, Colorado.

The railroad planned an excursion to the end of track with an appro-
priate celebration on New Year's Day. Along with Cyrus K. Holliday and
other company officials, Gov. James Harvey signed on to make the trip.
Several army ambulances waited at the government siding near Fort Dodge
to transport these dignitaries to the post for an evening of light-hearted

---

[21] *Hutchinson News,* January 30, 1873.
[22] *Kansas City Times,* January 15, 1873.
[23] *Hutchinson News,* January 30, 1873.

entertainment, including a welcoming thirteen-gun salute. Captain Moale and Dr. Tremaine traveled with the others for the state-line festivities. Once there, Governor Harvey picked up a hammer and did his duty: "This morning the last spikes were driven by the governor. By the governor's certificate of the completion of the road to this point, this company comes in possession of three million acres of land in the Arkansas valley, among them the best in the World. Buffaloes and thousands of heads of cattle are seen grazing on the hills and prairies hereabout."[24]

Returning from the festivities, the train stopped near Hollidaysburg—a small farming colony made up of families from Syracuse, New York, and soon renamed for that place, some seventeen miles east of Sargent—and picked up a young couple that planned on getting married at Dodge City. Instead, everyone aboard, including the railroad moguls, the state's chief executive, and a visiting judge from Great Bend, orchestrated the ceremony. Everyone participated, as the "wine flowed freely in their honor." Farther along on their journey, one of the reporters wrote, "The Larned folks got up a shooting scrape—for our benefit, I suppose. A young man named Johnny Morris was killed in a dance house, and a Mrs. Buck was accidentally shot in the thigh by the keeper, a man named Murray. It is supposed that the woman will die from her wound this morning."[25] The dignitaries pushed on, content to leave southwest Kansas to its own devices.

Those shootings may have excited the excursionists, but Dodge City did not surrender its reputation that easily. Other passengers arriving at Kansas City on January 5 described yet another killing at Dodge the previous Thursday. Billy Brooks, by now invariably referred to as "Bully" Brooks, had, it was said, "walked into a saloon where his victim was in the act of taking a drink, placed a carbine to his ear and shot a bullet clear through his head from ear or ear, killing him instantly. The man had said he intended to kill Brooks, so Brooks took this summary way of preventing it. No arrests have been made as yet."[26]

Another melee erupted on January 17 in one of the local Woodhulleries—a journalistic euphemism for whorehouse—involving five or six men in various stages of intoxication. Sexual rivalry over a twenty-year-old prostitute from Hays City named Nell St. Clair (also known as Nell Sin-

---

[24] *Kansas Daily Commonwealth*, January 3, 1873.

[25] Ibid.

[26] *Kansas City Times*, January 7, 1873. The newspaper chose to caption its story "More Border Pastimes."

clair and Nellie Rivers) supposedly caused all the trouble. Whatever the reason, when the smoke cleared Edward Hurley and a railroad employee named Barney Cullen lay dead. A third victim, a man named Southers, was so seriously wounded that most felt he had little chance to survive his encounter with Dodge City violence.[27]

J. Wright Mooar claimed a man named Jack McDermitt was chiefly responsible. If so, he did not last long as the town's latest man-killer. Within ten days he was shot to death by saloonman John Scott, the partner of A. J. Peacock, some said in revenge for the killing of Ed Hurley. "At the far end of the saloon there was a wheel of fortune running, and there was thirty or forty people around it," Mooar recalled. "Scotty caught his attention to something down there, and he turned his head and McDermitt turned his head and looked, and Scotty pulled his pistol out and put it up to his ear and killed him." As his body hit the floor, Nell St. Clair, described by Mooar as a beautiful specimen in face and form, well educated but "the hardest woman I ever saw," leaped from her perch on one of the room's six billiard tables and began making noises like a rooster. Dipping her hands in the spreading blood she slapped them together, splattering her white dress and smiling face as she pranced around the room. "Oh, that was a wicked bitch," Mooar remembered.[28]

With all the violence, Dodge City became the talk of the frontier, with one editor noting that the town "is scarcely four months old, and has in that time attained considerable notoriety for liveliness, especially in the lively extinguishments of disputes and disputers at point of arms."[29]

Indiscriminate gunfire was not the only danger. In early February reports told of five hunters carried into town frozen to death. During harsh winter months, such stories repeated themselves throughout southwest Kansas. Not only did men die, others lost fingers, toes, and whole limbs. One particularly grisly case involved six hunters—one a curious railroad employee—trapped by a vicious storm while stalking buffalo sixty

---

[27] *Kansas Daily Commonwealth*, January 23, 1873; and *Leavenworth Daily Commercial*, January 23, 1873. It should be noted that not everyone was convinced of Cullen's demise. Over the next several weeks many papers reported sightings, including the Leavenworth paper on February 26: "For men that have been killed several times, Cullen and Elan are the healthiest looking men we ever saw. Like Banqua's ghost, they will not go down, and now that the roughs have taken their departure, we hope we may not have to again record their deaths for some time to come."

[28] J. Wright Mooar to J. Evetts Haley, April 12, 1936. Walter Stanley Campbell Files, Box 98A, Folder 10, 14. Also see: Ibid, November 25, 1927, Box 98A Folder 6, 11; and July 28, 1937, Box 98A, Folder 13A, 73–74. Manuscript Division, Western History Collections, University of Oklahoma Library.

[29] *Kansas Daily Commonwealth*, January 14, 1873.

miles to the southwest on the north branch of Crooked Creek. Blinded by
the blizzard, the men lost their way. In panic they abandoned their provisions and staggered northward. For a week, with frozen feet and empty bellies, these half-dozen unfortunates dragged themselves toward Dodge City.

They arrived in a frightful state: "Their hands, feet and legs are terribly
swollen—in fact, are a perfect mass of corruption—creating a stench
which drove us from the room. . . . [O]ne of the number lost his ear, which
fell from his head a putrid mass."[30] Dr. McCarty examined each man in
turn. Unable to handle so many desperate cases at once, he hustled the
men off to Leavenworth, where five surgeons worked late into the night.
One patient died, but the others "bore their afflictions manfully and displayed a nerve that characterizes Western men."[31]

In Dodge City peace proved more difficult to find than a skilled surgeon.
As Bob Wright remembered, "Now, to protect ourselves and property, we
were compelled to organize a Vigilance Committee. Our very best citizens
promptly enrolled themselves, and, for a while, it fulfilled its mission to the
letter and acted like a charm, and we were congratulating ourselves on our
success. The committee only had to resort to extreme measures a few
times."[32] Members convinced most troublemakers to simply "get outta
Dodge." They did not fancy becoming victims of summary justice. Others
foolishly hung around and ignored the warnings.

Then, after another killing on Sunday evening, February 9, twenty committee members moved against the toughs by raiding the dance halls. They
killed a man named Ed Williams and wounded Charles Hill, who ran into
Tom Sherman's place seeking shelter. The vigilantes followed and shot him
dead. It was said of both ruffians: "These two men were the ringleaders of
a gang that have kept the town in an uproar ever since it has been started, but
we think they have got them pretty well cleaned up now."[33] Using bodies to
prove their point, the committee suggested to five others that they should
leave before sunrise. Those subdued desperadoes accepted the invitation.

---

[30] *Leavenworth Daily Commercial*, February 18, 1873.

[31] Ibid., February 20, 1873.

[32] Wright, *Dodge City, the Cowboy Capital*, 171.

[33] *Kansas Daily Commonwealth*, February 11, 1873. Of this event the *Newton Kansan* reported on February 13: "Three more men last Sunday night died with their boots on at Dodge City and two at Sargent. The vigilance committee is said to have put two of the Dodge City crowd out of the way, and hung one at Sargent to a tele-graph pole in the daytime." Also see the February 13, 1873, issue of the *Hutchinson News*: "Dodge bids fair to be more quiet for a spell," and the Wichita *City Eagle*, February 20, 1873: "Dodge City has organized a vigilance committee which have commenced work."

Years later one man claimed the vigilantes had killed fourteen men that night, burying them Monday morning two bodies per grave—a colorful tale but hopelessly exaggerated.[34]

On the day following the double murder by the forces of law and order, a fellow called Pony Spencer, an ex-railroad worker turned gambler who was one of the leaders of the 1868 Bear River Riot in Wyoming, rode into Dodge City with some friends. They did not stay long, being told to get out within ten minutes or be shot dead. One of them "declared that he had enough of that part of the country, and that the vigilantes extended from Dodge City to Pueblo."[35] Indeed they did, one report explaining the prelude to the killing of Williams and Hill with details of a violent outburst at Sargent.

That incident involved several transplanted Dodge City toughs who tried killing saloonman Chris Gilson. Instead, he killed three of his attackers outright while severing the arm of another with a shotgun blast. The remaining desperadoes fled in panic. As the smoke cleared everyone rushed out and cheered. Citizens awarded their righteous killer an expensive shotgun, and the railroad provided a travel pass. Gilson took his new weapon and used the railroad's generosity to go to Dodge City, where he helped kill Charles Hill and Ed Williams. The press reported: "Verily they have a 'sweet time of it' at the 'front.' "[36]

With stories of homegrown law enforcement making the rounds, the *Leavenworth Daily Commercial* informed its readers on February 22 that "The Vigilantes of Southwest Kansas are determined to hang enough horse thieves to fence a quarter section this spring." Outsiders sympathized: "Dodge City has obtained an unenviable notoriety for murders and scenes of lawlessness. Not less than sixteen persons have met with violent deaths at Dodge City alone since last August. So intolerable did life become in this place that a number of men, who could not be called first-class citizens, have taken grounds against the roughs. Among all those killed there were none who could not be well spared."[37]

Not content with actual homicides, someone started a rumor that Wild

---

[34] Harry (Sam) Young, *Hard Knocks: A Life Story of the Vanishing West* (Chicago: Laird & Lee, Inc., Publishers, 1915), 64–65. Young, a night watchman at the government warehouse, claimed, without any verification, "during the six months that I lived in Dodge, sixty-five men were buried there."

[35] *Newton Kansan*, February 13, 1873.

[36] *Hutchinson News*, February 20, 1873. The editor took time to crow, claiming his town "never has such bits of 'unpleasantness' because there is not a saloon or house of ill-fame in Reno county, and consequently not a desperado."

[37] *Kansas City Times*, February 15, 1873.

Bill Hickok was "Killed in Galveston, and Riddled With Bullets at Fort Dodge."[38] Others disagreed: "Wild Bill has never been at Dodge City since it has been built."[39] Hickok himself, in an apparent attempt at humor, declared, "For the benefit of the Kansas City papers, I hereby acknowledge that I am dead."[40] Not to be upstaged by a mere shootist, one editor fired back, "The Kansas City TIMES announces that 'Wild Bill' is dead . . . at the same time he was about here on a general drunk. He puts a note in the *Advertiser* this week, acknowledging that he is really dead. We suppose he means dead drunk."[41]

Fanciful killings soon gave way to the real thing. A convicted murderer from Missouri, known as Old Jester, had conveniently escaped that jurisdiction before being hanged. He then tried killing a man near Dodge City but, failing, he drew the attention of some Texans and several buffalo hunters. Together they "over took Jester, who seeing them coming, took his gun out of the wagon and endeavored to unharness one of the horses to escape. But they were too quick for him, and he received the contents of several well aimed revolvers, killing him instantly. They left him lay unburied upon the spot where he fell."[42]

By now Dodge City's reputation sparked humorous, if uncomplimentary, remarks in the public press: "A gentleman wishing to go from Wichita to Dodge, applied to a friend for a letter of introduction. He was handed a double-barreled shot-gun and a Colt's revolver."[43]

As if to prove the wisdom of that advice, reports told of yet another killing: "A man by the name of Burns was killed at Dodge City last week; he was shot from his horse by a government guide. . . . Burns fell from his horse shot through the brain; the guide went up to him and stuck the muzzle of his carbine to his bosom and slid another half pound ball through his form to kill him good. The man was left lying an entire day where he struck the ground."[44] Buffalo hunter Henry Raymond noted this incident with an offhand remark in his diary on March 13: "Tom Sherman shot Burns last night." In the previous entry he recorded another episode of

---

[38] *Kansas City News*, as quoted in *Kansas Daily Commonwealth*, March 1, 1873.

[39] *Kansas Daily Commonwealth*, March 4, 1873.

[40] Springfield (Missouri) *Advertiser*, as quoted in *Kansas City Times*, March 11, 1873.

[41] Springfield (Missouri) *Times*, as quoted in *Kansas City Times*, March 13, 1873.

[42] *Newton Kansan*, March 6, 1873.

[43] *Kansas Daily Commonwealth*, March 18, 1873.

[44] Ibid., March 21, 1873.

excess: "last night the vigilance committee shot McGill, a buffalo hunter for firing pistol in dance hall." The vigilantes had become uncontrollable. Raymond suspected a desire to eliminate competition, "so they could divide and plunder."[45]

The killing continued. After J. B. Patten murdered a Council Grove hotel-keeper visiting Pierceville—another railroad shantytown to the west—citizens delivered him to Dodge City for trial before a justice of the peace. Instead, "He was confined in a room and a guard placed over him, but during the night he made his escape, and the next day some said he had died with his boots on, some that he has ascended a telegraph pole, and others that he had twisted a limb around his throat and expired. It is morally, religiously and emphatically certain, however, that he now sleeps in the valley."[46]

Even when the town managed to relax, it did so in roughhouse fashion. One visitor in early April interrupted his counting of graves on Boot Hill to watch James H. Kelley, the saloon and dance hall proprietor, drive in a buffalo yearling with the help of a half-dozen of his ever-present hounds. Surrounded on Front Street by yelling men and barking dogs, the beast was roped and tied to a nearby post. For the raw amusement of onlookers, several men rolled empty beer kegs toward the terrified animal, just to watch him kick them back into the street.

The area's only legitimate peace officer was Deputy U.S. Marshal Jack L. Bridges, who had come to town with his wife and infant daughter in the fall of 1872. As a federal officer, however, Bridges had little or no authority over most crimes plaguing the city. His job, and that of other deputies passing through, was restricted to federal offences, mostly liquor violations and the persistent horse-thieving epidemic carried on in Indian Territory. Bridges had been a federal officer since 1869 in and around Hays City. In February 1871 he was wounded in an encounter with J. W. Ledford at Wichita.[47] Sub-

---

[45] Snell, ed., "Diary of a Dodge City Buffalo Hunter," 363n53.

[46] *Kansas Daily Commonwealth*, April 1, 1873.

[47] From contemporary accounts it seems that Bridges approached Ledford's hiding place, the privy behind the Harris House, with scout Lee Stewart and a lieutenant from Fort Harker: "Ledford seeing them advancing immediately threw open the door and came out; both parties immediately commenced firing, after emptying their revolvers at Ledford the three persons, Bridges, Lee Stewart, and the Lieutenant, turned and ran; Bridges being badly wounded fell fainting; Ledford walked across the street into Dagner's store, mortally wounded." *Walnut Valley Times*, El Dorado, Kansas, March 3, 1871. Later Bridges claimed, in a letter sent from the hospital at Fort Harker for publication in the *Daily Commonwealth* at Topeka on March 9, 1871, that neither he nor his two companions "had their pistols in their hands . . . at the time Ledford fired at them." Because of this incident many had their doubts about Jack Bridges. For both items cited, see Nyle H. Miller and Joseph W. Snell, *Why the West Was Wild: A Contemporary Look at the Antics of Some Highly Publicized Kansas Cowtown Personalities* (Topeka: Kansas State Historical Society, 1963), 43, 44.

sequent events at Dodge City suggest this episode may have dampened the deputy marshal's resolve, although in March 1873 it was reported he had come in from the Indian Territory "with fourteen persons whom he had arrested on warrants sworn out by Indian Agent John D. Miles, for violating the intercourse laws of the Cheyenne and Arapahoe agency."[48]

Rumors have long persisted that Jack Bridges served as the first quasi-marshal of Dodge City. Legally "unorganized" the town lacked authority to hire a full slate of municipal employees. The truth concerning any status for Bridges is unclear, but some citizens—most likely the vigilance committee itself—did hire people to try and establish some semblance of law and order and protect private property. For the most part the identity of these "officers" is unknown, except for one rather poor choice.

Perhaps accepting the maxim that only one of their own could control the rough element, William L. "Bully" Brooks, of all people, found himself called upon to keep the peace.[49] As with many small-minded men given a taste of power, Brooks abused his fragile authority by habitually parading his fighting image. Hunter Henry Raymond, who had arrived in Dodge City on November 16, 1872, recalled years later his first glimpse of this troublemaker turned town-tamer. Raymond joined a crowd watching an all night poker game: "The man sitting with his back to the door as I entered wore two big revolvers, whose ends showed beside the stool on which he was sitting. I learned afterwards that he was Bill Brooks, a gambler and all around crook."[50]

In the course of things, Brooks added to the growing menagerie atop Boot Hill. Details remain elusive, but it appears he *may have* killed four men in a single encounter. Unfortunately, the incident is described by Emanuel Dubbs (an old buffalo hunter not immune to exaggeration) in a memoir published nearly forty years later. As Dubbs recalled, Brooks had earlier

---

[48] *Kansas Daily Commonwealth*, March 4, 1873.

[49] The best sources on this shadowy Kansas frontier personality remain Miller and Snell, *Why the West Was Wild*, 51–57; and Gary L. Roberts, "From Tin Star to Hanging Tree: The Short Career and Violent Times of Billy Brooks," *The Prairie Scout* (Abilene, Kans.: The Kansas Corral of the Westerners, Inc., 1975), 1–85.

[50] Henry H. Raymond to Merritt L. Beeson, September 25, 1936. Raymond Collection, Manuscripts Department, Kansas State Historical Society. Before serving as city marshal at Newton, Brooks worked as a stage driver between that place and Wichita. Then, as marshal, he was reportedly wounded during an altercation with some Texas men: "One shot passed through his right breast, and the other two were in his limbs. We learn from a driver here that he will recover. Bill has sand enough to best the hour-glass that tries to run him out." Wichita *City Eagle*, June 14, 1872. It appears that less than two months later Brooks may have received payment as a policeman at Ellsworth, before traveling to Dodge City: "W. L. Brooks service as Police 17.50." Minutes of the City Council, Journal Book, 1871–80, Records of the City of Ellsworth, August 7, 1872.

killed a man named Berry over a disputed card game. Seeking revenge, the victim's four brothers came down from Hays City determined to settle things. Dubbs claimed Brooks stepped from a dance hall, "the nightly resort of . . . lewd women," firing a brace of revolvers, "and when the smoke cleared away two of the four were dead, and the other two were mortally wounded. Billy Brooks escaped as usual with only a slight wound in the shoulder. One girl in the room was seriously wounded by a stray shot."[51]

How much truth there is to this story, if any, will probably never be known, but Dubbs did claim that Brooks, within weeks of his arrival, "had established a reputation as the killer. He was wonderfully quick with a gun. He carried two, one on each hip (as did nearly every one else), and in the flash of an eye he could draw one in each hand and fire. In less than a month he had either killed or wounded fifteen men."[52] Dubbs did not claim to have personally witnessed any of this gunplay, but his figure of fifteen victims for a single shooter is preposterous, even for Dodge City.

Billy Brooks did get involved in enough violent episodes to find himself reported killed on at least three occasions. Within weeks of his supposed demise, he nearly died for real tangling with buffalo hunter Kirt Jordan. Tradition suggests that Jordan went gunning for Brooks because Dodge City's erstwhile lawman had killed one of his friends. Whatever the reason, on March 4, 1873, Jordan waited for Brooks in a doorway along Front Street. When Brooks showed his face, Jordan stepped forward and took aim. At that very moment an innocent bystander stepped between the two men. Jordan lowered his rifle. Brooks sensed the movement and dove behind two water barrels set along the street in case of fire. As Brooks tried pulling one of his revolvers Jordan fired a single shot. The bullet struck the third metal barrel loop. Slowed by the water, the heavy bullet broke through the far side, lodging in the metal ring. Water gushed out as Jordan mounted his horse and rode away, convinced he had killed his man. A soaked and chagrined Billy Brooks retrieved the spent bullet and gulped whiskey in a nearby saloon to steady his nerves.

Many in Dodge City thought this bloodless encounter was nothing more than an accidental reprieve. A committee of citizens arraigned a hurried compromise. "Jordan came riding in unarmed," hunter Henry Ray-

---

[51] Emanuel Dubbs, "Personal Reminiscences," in Charles Goodnight, Emanuel Dubbs, John A. Hart and others, *Pioneer Days in the Southwest from 1850 to 1879* (Guthrie, Okla.: The State Capital Company, 1909), 37.

[52] Ibid., 35.

mond recorded. "I heard him say 'Boys, you've got me into it!' Just then from a nearby building came Bill Brooks in white starched shirt, and with no gun on him. I never saw him thus before. He approached Jordan with a broad smile offering a friendly handshake. Jordan gave his hand, but there was no friendly smile on his face. Jordan says, 'What we've got to say we don't need to say to this crowd. Let's go inside!'"[53] Their private truce held.

This episode failed to tarnish the reputation of Brooks as a man-killer, but he hung around several more weeks and surprised everyone by behaving himself. Dodge City was beginning to change—its leading citizens wanted less violence. Tiring of repeated images of bloodshed, they dreamed of greater things for their town than being described as "A row of wooden shanties, their sameness relieved by one or two two-story frames, a dozen dugouts, a depot and water tank, a United States warehouse, a side track of empty cars, a government mule train, a thousand buffalo hides, some in piles and some staked on the ground to dry, one or two hundred men in various stages of roughness and a score of abandoned women—these complete the inventory of Dodge City."[54]

Most everyone understood that tales of violence discouraged capital investment and migration into the Arkansas River Valley. To entice both, the area longed for some semblance of law and order. From the beginning people in Dodge City had petitioned for the official organization of Ford County. To help smooth the process by proving there were enough people to warrant consideration, local harness-maker, hide dealer, and erstwhile justice of the peace Isaac Young conducted two private censuses, completing the first by October 1872 and finishing the second in January.

Finally, on April 5, 1873, the new governor, Thomas A. Osborn, issued the proclamation declaring the organization of Ford County, based on a memorial signed by forty resident householders.[55] The governor selected Dodge City the temporary county seat, appointing Charles Rath, John G. McDonald, and Daniel Wolf special county commissioners, with Herman J. Fringer selected as county clerk. Unfortunately, Wolf and his partner, Mike Murphy, had already skedaddled with his family to Sargent, preparing to sell groceries, provisions, and outfitting goods. Back in Dodge, saloonman James Hanrahan joined Rath and McDonald as a county com-

---

[53] Snell, ed., "Diary of a Dodge City Buffalo Hunter," 362n50.

[54] *Solomon Valley Pioneer*, March 8, 1873.

[55] Ford County Commissioners Journals, Book A, 1.

missioner. They met on April 30, electing Rath chairman and scheduling a special election for June 5, 1873, to fill the various positions in the new Ford County government.

Two days before the election a particularly brutal murder took place. Several rowdies killed William Taylor, a black restaurant owner from Leavenworth, who had arrived in Kansas in 1862. Following years of hard work he had become a man of property: expanding his investments to take advantage of the buffalo trade, Taylor and his brother opened a small eatery at Dodge City. They also operated a makeshift express service between the town and Fort Dodge.

On the night of June 3, A. J. Peacock's partner, saloonman John Scott, the same man who had murdered Jack McDermitt in their place some months before, joined up with several drunken friends and hired Taylor's wagon to haul them down to the fort. Leaving town the group decided to return for more whiskey. The driver protested but agreed to start back. As he turned the team, one of the passengers struck him in the face with a pistol. The drunken men took charge of the rig after kicking the driver off his exposed perch.

Hearing details from his injured employee, Taylor began searching for his property. Finding his wagon and team near the depot, he tried pacifying the men by agreeing to take them to the fort, provided they would not harm his animals. That said, someone shot and killed one of his mules. A second shot was heard and the depot watchman cried out, "The damn negro has shot me." Everyone opened fire on Taylor. Soaked in blood, the wounded man made his way to the house of another black family. Perhaps fearing retaliation if she got involved, the woman there refused aid.

Taylor staggered to Dr. McCarty's office at Herman Fringer's drug store. The brother of the wounded watchman followed with murder in mind. Fringer and McCarty pushed him out of the office and began working on Taylor. Within minutes John Scott and his friends forced their way in, Scott declaring, "Here you are, you black son of a bitch." The saloonman fired point-blank with a buffalo gun. Taylor's cries for mercy went unheard as the sound of heavy gunfire filled the room.

McCarty and Fringer fled for their lives as Scott and the others dragged their victim out into the dirt. Emptying a half-dozen revolvers into the already dying man, they finished him off by pounding the corpse with boot heels and pistols before stealing his money and watch. Taylor's mutilated body lay on the deserted thoroughfare until morning. No one dared come near. Evidence showed that the depot watchman, who had helped incite the mob by claiming he had been attacked, had actually shot himself by accident.

As if trying to justify this foul deed, someone signing himself "Scotty's Friend," wrote from Dodge City to an editor at Topeka about "a good joke that took effect here last night." He then went on for six more paragraphs, ending, "The best joke was that after killing the nig we took his hat and put it on the mule that was killed. What do you think of that for high? If any of you boys want to have a real good time, and a chance of killing somebody without danger, tell 'em to come out. Every once in a while we meet some d—d fool who don't carry arms, and it is splendid fun to go for him."[56]

The editor at Topeka was not amused, nor did ordinary citizens of Kansas share that twisted view from Dodge City. The killing of William Taylor caused an uproar. It made little difference that he was black. What mattered, beyond the nature of the offense, was his position as a man of means, "a peaceful, educated and worthy man, much respected by all."[57] For him to be murdered with impunity was unacceptable. Men of property expect protection. They now demanded retaliation, legal or otherwise, as the railroad carried Taylor's broken and unrecognizable body home to Leavenworth. There his grieving family and a large crowd of mourners awaited its return for burial in Greenwood Cemetery.

The hideous nature of the William Taylor homicide prodded several citizens to beg Major Dodge for help. The major, who in theory agreed with the occasional need for vigilante justice on the frontier but who was also aware of its dangers,[58] telegraphed Governor Osborn: "A most *foul* &

---

[56] *Kansas Daily Commonwealth,* June 7, 1873.

[57] *Leavenworth Daily Commercial,* June 10, 1873.

[58] Maj. Richard I. Dodge to Gov. T. A. Osborne [*sic*], July 5, 1873. Governors' Correspondence, Manuscripts Department, Kansas State Historical Society. Dodge understood the vigilante process: "So long as these organizations confine themselves to the legitimate object of punishing crime, they are not only laudable but absolutely necessary." But, the major also noted, "There is a difficulty. It is not often that the property owning and valuable class of Citizens are strong enough to do this work alone. They are obliged to receive into their organization some of the toughs. These in turn take in others worse then themselves until as I have often seen it a vigilance committee organized by good men in good faith may become after a while simply an organized band of robbers and cutthroats. . . . The Town of Dodge City is under the control of such a band of vigilantes."

cold blooded murder committed last night by ruffians in Dodge City—County organized but no election yet had—no body with power to act—please authorize the arrest of murderers."[59] The governor replied by telegram that same day: "Until Ford County is fully organized you are authorized to arrest and hold, subject to the orders of the civil authorities of the proper Judicial District, all persons notoriously guilty of a violation of the criminal laws of this State. I desire that you should exercise this authority with great care, and only in extreme cases."[60]

The commander of Fort Dodge did not assume these responsibilities lightly. The very next day, in a letter to the governor, he took pains to explain: "It is hardly necessary to invite your attention to the fact that I am not the proper person to exercise civil authority." Citing a regulation denying an officer's right to become involved in civil matters, Dodge sidestepped its provisions by explaining that, although the regulation "provides that any officer of the Army on the active list, who shall exercise the function of a civil office shall thereby vacate his commission," he insisted, "In making the arrests of the murders in the Taylor case, I exercised no function of Civil Office, but simply as a Citizen [who] obeyed the order of the Chief Magistrate of the State."[61]

Technically, Richard Dodge may have been operating under the auspices of Governor Osborn, but he did order Deputy U.S. Marshal Jack Bridges to take up the chase. He even supplied men for that officer's posse. Bridges arrested William Hicks and several other suspects, but not without criticism: "There is a United States deputy marshal in the place who is afraid to do anything in an organized county without warrant of a magistrate. 'The consequence is,' says our private informant 'that these disreputable murderers—at least a dozen of them—walk the streets of Dodge City regarded as little less than heroes, for killing an unarmed, inoffensive negro.' "[62]

Major Dodge moved fast, but not fast enough. A military sweep of the town netted suspects, but the chief culprit, John Scott, was not apprehended. It was later suggested he found refuge in the icebox of his and A. J. Peacock's saloon until friends arranged his escape. Rumors speculated that

---

[59] Maj. Richard I. Dodge to Gov. Thos. Osborn, Western Union Telegram, June 4, 1873. Ibid. Years later, Bob Wright claimed—incorrectly as it turned out—that Taylor was actually a servant to Major Dodge, and that fact alone ignited his outrage. Wright, *Dodge City, the Cowboy Capital*, 172.

[60] Governor Thomas A. Osborn to Major Richard I. Dodge, Western Union Telegram, June 4, 1873. Ibid.

[61] Maj. Richard I. Dodge to Gov. T. A. Osborne [*sic*], July 5, 1873. Ibid.

[62] *Kansas Daily Commonwealth*, June 7, 1873.

Deputy Marshal Bridges helped Scotty, "as he was seen on the back streets when the arrests were being made."[63] To facilitate Scott's arrest, Governor Osborn issued a proclamation on July 21 offering a $500 reward. Nothing came of the offer—a sizable sum at the time—for Scott remained at large.[64]

Two days after Taylor's murder, Major Dodge ordered a sergeant and six soldiers of the Third Infantry into Dodge City. They pitched a tent inside the town's limits and established a sentry system. The sergeant carried specific instructions "not to permit any soldier of his party to enter any Bar room, Saloon or other disreputable place in the town except under orders."[65] The major hoped his soldiers would intimidate troublemakers, but he realized the delicate legal position in using troops against civilians. Even with the governor's approval, Dodge was careful not to allow his men to interfere, but to only arrest flagrant violators of the state's criminal code. To make certain his own men did not cause trouble, Dodge restricted their access to the town through a system of passes. The men needed to sign in with the Dodge City detail before commencing their off-duty revelry.[66]

What made the William Taylor affair even more reprehensible was the discovery of involvement by members of the Committee of Vigilance. "The murder of Taylor was committed by these Vigilantes who were called together on the first alarm, then dispersed to search for Taylor," Major Dodge informed Governor Osborn. "And while Scott & Hicks (vigilantes both) dragged him from the drug store, and shot him to death, at least a dozen other vigilantes stood by ready—and obliged—to take a hand in the shooting if necessary. Among these were good men, who would be shocked at the thought of committing individual crime, and yet who aided, abetted, and became 'participi criminis' in the most cowardly and cold blooded murder I have ever known in an experience of frontier life

---

[63] *Kansas City Times*, July 15, 1873.

[64] This state reward of five hundred dollars was not an uncommon amount. Only a month later the same was offered for William Thompson, brother of the notorious Ben, for killing Ellsworth County sheriff C. B. Whitney with an errant shotgun blast; and the same was offered for the apprehension and conviction of the chief culprit in the murder at Caldwell of former Wichita police chief and Deputy U.S. Marshal Michael Meagher in late 1881. The five hundred dollars offered for the arrest of John Scott in the William Taylor case stayed on the books. Bat Masterson wrote Gov. John P. St. John on October 7, 1879, asking if that was so. The governor's secretary assured him that it was. Unfortunately, Masterson had no more luck than anyone else in apprehending Scotty. Miller and Snell, *Why the West Was Wild*, 395.

[65] Special Order No. 79, June 5, 1873. Fort Dodge, Special Orders, Vol. 4.

[66] Special Order No. 80, June 6, 1873, Ibid., and 2nd Lt. Thomas B. Nichols, Post Adjutant to Sgt. Elfner, "In charge of Detachment at Dodge City, Kansas," June 7, 1873. Fort Dodge, Letters Sent.

dating back to 1848."[67] Even Bob Wright, a supporter if not outright member of the committee, was forced to admit, "They got so notoriously bad and committed so many crimes, that the good members deserted them, and the people arose in their might and put a stop to their doings."[68]

The United States Army had already begun the process, but to forestall further threats of anarchy, the governor dispatched Judge William R. Brown from the Ninth Judicial District to Dodge City as an examining magistrate, along with Sheriff F. E. Smith of Chase County. Judge John Foster served as prosecutor, with Newton attorney C. E. Millard handling the defense. They stayed in town four days. Judge Brown conducted preliminary examinations, but found sufficient evidence against only two defendants, William Hicks and the absent John Scott. Few locals volunteered to testify, despite brave talk years after the event. A contemporary noted, "Parties from Dodge report the law abiding citizens in the majority, but they are of the milk and water order."[69]

The effect of Judge Brown's visit was short-lived. Major Dodge wrote to Governor Osborn: "Since Judge Brown held court here there have been two more attempts at murder in Dodge City—a Negro being the sufferer in each case. The man shot last night will probably die, being wounded in head and lungs."[70] The other victim was a fellow named Wallace Dade, shot through the hand and pistol-whipped about the face. Dade fled to Newton, where he told everyone who would listen: "The roughs did it from no cause whatever." A local editor replied, "we can hardly credit the story."[71]

Details of Taylor's murder brought reactions. The *New York Tribune* not only condemned the crime but also attacked Major Dodge, charging inaction. Kansas editors judged the *Tribune*'s position as scandalous. While New Yorkers criticized Major Dodge for doing nothing, others condemned him with equal passion for moving against the murderers. The objections were not so much that these ruffians did not deserve justice, but that the military

---

[67] Maj. Richard I. Dodge to Gov. T. A. Osborne [*sic*], July 5, 1873. Governors' Correspondence, Manuscripts Department, Kansas State Historical Society.

[68] Wright, *Dodge City, the Cowboy Capital*, 172. Of course, it was not that "the people rose in their might and put a stop to their doings," but action by state authorities and the power of the United States Army that broke the back of the vigilantes.

[69] *Newton Kansan*, June 12, 1873.

[70] Maj. Richard I. Dodge to Gov. T. A. Osborne [*sic*], July 5, 1873. Governors' Correspondence, Manuscripts Department, Kansas State Historical Society.

[71] *Newton Kansan*, July 10, 1873.

had no right interfering in civilian affairs. The better class of citizens voiced no objections, feeling only relief that something had been done.

Defense attorney C. E. Millard wrote his hometown editor expressing dismay over the use of military force at Dodge City.[72] He wrote in the couched language of a seasoned advocate, reducing the event to its basic elements—indeed, poor William Taylor hardly seemed to matter. Millard appeared more concerned with how all this would reflect on commerce and migration into the Arkansas River Valley than worrying about questions of law and order. To the attorney, William Taylor and Major Dodge represented more of an embarrassment than leading players in a tragic drama. Millard's position is easy to explain. He was, after all, a lawyer from a small railroad town who understood the advantages of identifying himself with important local issues of financial stability. Millard, a former district attorney in Iowa, was not so much being devious—and certainly not righteous—but he was being practical.

Richard Dodge had not heard the last of the William Taylor case. In early 1874 saloonman Henry V. Cook, one of those arrested and subsequently released by Judge Brown, filed a civil suit against the major, charging false arrest. Cook waited until Dodge was posted to Arizona before filing his complaint, a point not overlooked by jeering locals. The government assigned U.S. District Attorney George R. Peck for the defense. After fighting the case through Ford County courts for nearly a year, Peck got it transferred to the United States Circuit Court.[73] A year passed before the case reached a federal jury. Deliberating five minutes, they brought in a verdict favoring the defendant.

Amid the turmoil surrounding the Taylor murder, Ford County held its special election on June 5, 1873. After counting the ballots, officials designated Dodge City the new county seat, and declared Frederick Zimmerman, Charles Rath, and A. C. Myers county commissioners; Herman J. Fringer, county clerk and clerk of the district court; A. J. Anthony, county treasurer; Charles E. Bassett, sheriff; M. V. Cutler, county attorney; Harry Armitage, register of deeds; George B. Cox, probate judge; Morris Collar, trustee of Dodge Township; Dr. Thomas L. McCarty, county coroner; and P. T. Bowen and Thomas C. Nixon, justices of the peace.[74]

---

[72] Ibid., June 19, 1873.

[73] Henry V. Cook vs. Richard I. Dodge, Records of the Ford County District Court, Civil Appearance Docket A, 10; and Judge's Journal, Book A, 17.

[74] Ford County Commissioners Journals, Book A, 1.

If the people of Kansas felt relief that Ford County had created a government, they had misjudged Dodge City. The frontier version of musical chairs started when M. V. Cutler posted bond as county attorney just five days after the election. A month later he resigned, having been chosen a county commissioner to fill the vacancy created by the "nonqualification" of Charles Rath. Four days after that political surprise, J. H. Mulgreny was appointed register of deeds, "to fill vacancy." What became of Harry Armitage was not explained. That same day, on Cutler's motion, A. J. Anthony was appointed county treasurer, again "to fill vacancy." No one asked why, which seemed an obvious question since Anthony was the man elected to the position in the first place. On July 24, A. C. Myers resigned as chairman of the board, replaced by Cutler. By October 6, however, Myers was back serving as chairman pro tem—with no official explanation given as to how and why all this took place.

Political gymnast M. V. Cutler did scribble out his own version of events in a rather newsy letter to Governor Osborn. Ignoring the two assault cases described by Major Dodge after the murder of William Taylor, Cutler claimed that "the Town has been very, and I may say, remarkable [sic] quiet, no disturbance having taking [sic] place since of any note." Not exactly true, but Cutler went on to explain certain political developments in more convincing detail: "It is true that several Co officers elect failed to qualify, owing to several of the Merchants here being absent, who they desired as Bondsmen. Since then the Board of Commissioners have appointed parties to fill vacancies caused by non qualification." Citing certain organizational difficulties, Cutler continued: "Several of the officers elect were very dillitory [sic] about entering upon the duties of their respective offices, owing to the writ of Quo Warrento [sic] served upon the commissioners, but if the County Organization is sustained I have not the slightest doubt but what every officer will do his utmost to maintain law & order."[75]

On October 13 the commissioners ordered a regular general election for county offices for November 4. At that time, Charlie Rath was again elected one of three county commissioners, no mention being made of his previous difficulties. One week after the election, Herman J. Fringer resigned as clerk of the county and district court, effective November 15.[76] As it turned

---

[75] M. V. Cutler to Governor Thomas A. Osborn, July 14, 1873. Governors' Correspondence, Manuscripts Department, Kansas State Historical Society.

[76] Ford County Commissioners Journals, Book A, 2–4.

out this was the sort of political turmoil the citizens of Ford County would come to expect in the months and years to come. Whether all this offers an example of pure democracy, or a case of democracy run amok, is more difficult to assess. Of course, the people of Dodge City always took pride in their ability to charge headlong against prevailing winds.

All this political maneuvering lay in the future. Of singular interest to voters in the June 5, 1873, special election, considering the area's short but violent history, was Charles E. Bassett becoming Ford County's first sheriff. Officially, Bassett could not assume his duties until posting bond as required by state law—which he finally did on June 10, to the tune of three thousand dollars[77]—but Judge Brown sidestepped that formality from day one, ordering Bassett to carry out his duties in the interim. Thus, for a time, Charlie Bassett answered only to Judge Brown and not to Ford County's elected commissioners.

Bassett proved a man to be reckoned with. Standing just below six feet, the new sheriff carried a powerful build. Born in New Bedford, Massachusetts, in late 1847, the son of a sail maker, Bassett joined a Pennsylvania infantry regiment near the close of the Civil War. At war's end, he drifted west, showing up in Dodge City in late 1872. Now, as the chief peace officer in the county, Bassett set an example. Townspeople had found a man they could trust, and loyalties to the discredited vigilance committee began to fade. As the people turned to Bassett, the vigilance movement collapsed.

The law may have come to Dodge City, but problems over the organization of Ford County and the installation of its elected officials continued. Immediately a campaign to discredit the county's status began, charging fraud and claiming insufficient population for legal recognition. This was not true, but the legitimacy of county government was challenged in court. Major Dodge suspected the railroad, fearing local tax assessments, of orchestrating this controversy.[78] Elected officials offered a united front against those hoping to derail their right to organize. Still, it took time to extricate Ford County from this mess—so much so that between July 24 and October 6 the county commissioners could transact no business owing to their clouded status. As county government stalled, Dodge City's troubles continued.

---

[77] Ibid., 2.

[78] Maj. Richard I. Dodge to Gov. T. A. Osborne [sic], July 5, 1873. Governors' Correspondence, Manuscripts Department, Kansas State Historical Society.

On the evening of July 20, William Ellis, the young son of a furniture clerk in Leavenworth, staggered into the bar of the Dodge House with butcher Charles S. Hungerford and two prostitutes. Intoxicated, Ellis—who had only been in the county six months, working for Bob Wright and A. J. Anthony as a part-time sutler clerk and stock tender—demanded drinks for himself and his three companions. Bartender Daniel W. Burrell refused service. They exchanged words, after which Ellis and his friends retired to French Peter's saloon for more beer. Later they passed the Dodge House. Seeing Burrell on the porch, they reopened the argument. Staggering, young Ellis challenged that he could whip any son-of-a-bitch around the hotel. Burrell called him a goddamn liar.

As the bartender started down the steps expecting to overpower his adversary, Ellis pulled a .44 caliber Colt revolver. Seeing the gun coming into play, Burrell reached for his own weapon. Ellis fired first, striking Burrell in the left arm, the ball passing into his chest. Burrell got off a shot as he stumbled, hitting his assailant in the right leg. William Ellis bled to death within the hour. Burrell, far more seriously wounded, died two days later. At Leavenworth, the press reported that Ellis's father "had been apprehensive of the contamination of the boy's morals, and had written to him desiring him to give up his dangerous employment, and return to Leavenworth. But . . . the young man has gone suddenly into another world, his body and soul wrecked."[79]

The inquest, held before Justice of the Peace P. T. Bowen, ruled that Burrell had acted in self-defense. Some witnesses thought that John J. Murray, known locally as "Curly," had actually killed Ellis. Scattered testimony suggested three shots, not two. As the shooting began, according to this version of events, Murray had jumped from the hotel's porch and grappled with Ellis. Some believed that during the struggle Ellis was shot with his own pistol. In any case, the coroner's jury ended its work by granting absolution to Daniel Burrell's memory, blaming the whole affair on the indiscriminate carrying of firearms.

It all sounded like a fine lesson in civic responsibility, but it lacked conviction since the coroner's jury included Tom Sherman, whose saloon and dance hall had itself been the scene of so many disturbances, as well as ex-officer Billy Brooks, who had personally contributed so much to Dodge

---

[79] *Leavenworth Daily Commercial*, July 23, 1873.

City's instability. But then, this was the frontier, and when it came to discussions of violence both men were experts. All five jurors were allowed fifty cents for their time and trouble. Others, too, pocketed coin for doing their duty. Dr. McCarty collected twenty-five dollars for "professional services rendered." Yet, with all the county's troubles, no payment could be authorized for anyone until October 6.[80] It is doubtful whether Brooks ever collected his half-dollar. He left town soon afterward to open a whiskey ranch along the border and begin a fateful association with area horse thieves.

While burying its latest victims, Dodge City began solving its own problems associated with Ford County's organizational crisis. From the beginning, property owners held real estate titles on the strength of temporary agreements between themselves and the Dodge City Town Company. By early June, charges of fraudulent organization jeopardized this delicate balance. Residents needed a county judge to legalize the townsite, but Ford County still had no one allowed to act in that capacity, nor was anyone quite sure when that might happen. Townsite organizers solved the problem by maneuvering their attachment to Ellis County for judicial purposes. The courthouse lay a hundred miles to the north, with portions of three other counties intervening, but the choice was a good one. Many of Dodge City's businessmen came from Hays City and still had many friends there, including the probate judge, H. J. McGaffigan. Town Company officials convinced the Ellis County magistrate to act in an "ex-officio" capacity for Dodge City's benefit.

So it was that from Hays City Judge McGaffigan took the necessary steps on behalf of that growing community along the Arkansas and entered the filing fee of $108.75 with the Wichita Land Office on June 25, 1873. The procedure covered an initial 87-acre tract,[81] "in trust for the Several use and benefit of the occupants of the Townsite of Dodge City."[82] Following state law, McGaffigan ordered the three Ford County commissioners to resurvey the site. On August 21, for the sum of one dollar, the judge conveyed the townsite, by now expanded to 302.78 acres, to its nineteen legal occupants—that is, members of the Dodge City Town Company. At Hays City, McGaffigan filed a plat at the courthouse, levied a tax

[80] Ford County Commissioners Journals, Book A, 4.

[81] House Misc. Doc. No. 45, 47th Congress, 2nd Sess., Pt. 4, "Town-site and County-seat Acts," 301.

[82] Ford County Register of Deeds, Book A, 62.

on Ford County as reimbursement for his time and expenses, and then washed his hands of the whole affair.[83] Nine days later the nineteen "occupants" deeded their holdings—the entire townsite—to the Dodge City Town Company for a nominal one-dollar consideration.[84]

Within weeks the Town Company had grown far beyond the original dozen members to include Charles Rath, Morris Collar, Patrick Ryan, George B. Cox, Richard Evans, Alonzo B. Webster, John Haney, Jacob Collar, Frederick Zimmerman, James H. Kelley, George M. Hoover and two other army officers, Captains Tullius C. Tupper and Ezra B. Kirk. Ford County's new register of deeds, M. J. Bruin, recorded the Town Company's holdings on November 12, 1873, and issued many of the indentures to occupants of town lots six days later. By May 1, 1874, even the United States government acknowledged the Dodge City townsite by issuing Osage Indian Land Certificate No. 5145, a document filed with the United States General Land Office in Washington.[85]

One visitor in mid-August 1873 found a quite different Dodge City: "This place is quiet now, compared to what it was one year ago. . . . I was greatly surprised to find religious services being held in the dining room of the Dodge House—a real Sunday school, and a preacher conducting it. There were in attendance some thirty persons."[86] Less violence attracted new business. Hutchinson residents Charles Collins and the McMurray brothers opened a stage line between Dodge City and Camp Supply, traveling south on the old government road each Friday and returned the following Monday.

---

[83] This process may appear unnecessarily complex, but it remained serious to those involved. Eighteen months later, while in the state legislature, McGaffigan, at the behest of cattleman John E. Farnsworth, temporarily blocked the organization of Ness County—two counties north of Ford—because "The county was not properly organized and a very great fraud was perpetrated." "Some of the Lost Towns of Kansas," *Collections of the Kansas State Historical Society, Vol. XII, 1911–1912* (Topeka: State Printing Office, 1912), 469–70n36. The instigator of all this turned out to be Dr. S. G. Rodgers, who had earlier planned a community between Fort Dodge and Larned. Rodgers, who had come out from Chicago with a half-dozen families, "made up a fraudulent census showing a population of 600 and sent a petition to the governor which he had signed with a lot of names taken from a Kansas City directory." Frank W. Blackmar, *Kansas* (Chicago: Standard Publishing Company, 1912), 2:352. For McGaffigan that number of supposed citizens must have been vaguely reminiscent of Dodge City's petition. Colonel Young came up with what seems an exaggerated 604 residents during his January 1873 enumeration.

[84] Ford County Register of Deeds, Book A, 491–92. Controversy persisted even to the point of court rulings against the procedure used. For an example from late 1874, see: Mary Gowdy vs. R. W. Evans, Records of the Ford County District Court, Judge's Journal, Book A, 18–19. Since cases such as these were just individual complaints, everything proceeded much as before.

[85] Ibid., 62–63.

[86] *Junction City Union,* August 30, 1873.

But that September financial panic gripped the nation. After the Civil War, the United States experienced a period of overexpansion in business. At the same time dividends lagged, with more than 100 of the nation's 364 railroads paying none in 1872. The country also suffered a dangerous trade imbalance, together with a top-heavy credit structure that undermined the system. Banks offered high-interest loans faster than they acquired deposits—seven times faster, by some estimates. The flow of capital from productive enterprises into speculative ventures of all sorts worried thoughtful investors. Business failures nearly doubled between 1871 and 1872. On September 8, 1873, the crash began with the failure of the New York Warehouse & Security Company. Within a fortnight the Wall Street banking firms of Kenyon Cox & Company and Jay Cooke & Company followed. The Great Panic of 1873 had begun. The New York Stock Exchange closed its doors for ten days to save itself from ruin.

People in southwestern Kansas were not immune to the vicissitudes of Wall Street. Orders for buffalo hides fell. Declining revenues, even counting cash generated by cattle shipments from Wichita, halted construction on the AT&SF. Commerce slowed in Dodge City, ending those big spending days noted by Mrs. Anthony on her arrival the year before. Still, all was not doom and gloom: "Yet, aside from the stagnation of the buffalo hide business, this little city presents a lively appearance, and the merchants and business men generally are doing a good and lucrative business."[87] Luckily the town still served as the chief shipping point for military cargoes moving south into Indian Territory.

Dodge City's major hide and meat merchants branched out into other areas. A. C. Myers expanded into groceries, outfitting goods, and other essentials. Charles Rath and Robert Wright did the same, adding dry goods as well as boots and shoes. Another dealer associated with the buffalo trade, Cutler & Company, followed suit. Of course, Dodge City's saloonmen continued to do a thriving business as men gathered around the town's watering holes to drown their financial woes with a fine selection of whiskey, cognac, beer, wine, and an assortment of liqueurs. Drunkenness continued, but the level of violence heretofore associated with these places fell dramatically. Charlie Bassett had temporarily suppressed the lawless element.

---

[87] *Kansas City Times,* October 29, 1873.

In the midst of that chaotic autumn of 1873, Dodge City found time for civic improvements. With much of the town's commerce now pointed south toward Camp Supply and the Indian agencies, town planners decided to build a toll bridge across the Arkansas. With the contract awarded to a Leavenworth builder, construction began in October. In February 1874 the commissioners authorized the formation of the Dodge City Bridge Company after voters, by a margin of 111 to 14, approved the issuing of bonds in a special election.[88] The county charged tolls to outsiders, but townspeople enjoyed free access. Since the structure crossed the river at Second Avenue, that thoroughfare became known as Bridge Street.

By late October it could be said: "The town of Dodge is quiet compared to last winter. The desperadoes have all taken their departure, leaving the peace-loving citizens in possession."[89] On November 4, 1873, Ford County voters went to the polls, casting ballots in the first regularly scheduled general election. Charlie Bassett retained the office of sheriff. Rath, Peacock, and A. J. Anthony became commissioners, with Peacock chosen chairman. Others included Alonzo B. Webster, treasurer; John G. McDonald, clerk of the district court; and Dr. McCarty again elected coroner. James Hanrahan, the pioneer billiard-parlor impresario, became the county's first representative to the state legislature.[90] Organized government had come to Ford County.

Dodge City seemed willing to grow up. Yet the town failed to break completely with its past. On December 4, 1873, the *Hutchinson News* reported, "Harry Lovett, one of the early citizens of Newton, was shot through the left breast at Dodge City, Monday night, and is not expected to live." With the Lovett affair the town crossed over into a new and eventful year. Within months many residents in and around this small speck of a town on the Arkansas River would help start an Indian war.

---

[88] Ford County Commissioners Journals, Book A, 21; and Ford County Register of Deeds, Book A, 34.

[89] *Kansas Daily Commonwealth*, October 22, 1873.

[90] Ford County Commissioners Journals, Book A, 8.

Chapter 5

Dodge City and the Red River War

By late October 1873 Dodge City businessmen had formed a committee to contact newspaper publishers, with hopes of finding one willing to relocate. The town's remoteness and violent reputation tended to frighten the faint-hearted, but to its credit, the state still boasted more newspapers per capita than any other: "Kansas is perhaps the only place on the face of the earth of which it has been said that a newspaper was started before there was any news to print."[1] Since Dodge City had plenty of news—granted, much of it bad—supporters felt confident they could corral "some good live newspaper man . . . who would write up the town and county, and give Eastern men an idea of this great agricultural and stock-raising valley of the Arkansas."[2]

Accepting the challenge, Alonzo W. Moore sold his interest in the *Jackson County News*, a paper he had founded at Holton in 1867. He kept everything but its good name, hauling the press and all the type south to Topeka for loading aboard the AT&SF and the journey west.[3] Never one to dither when there was work to be done, Moore was handing out issues of the *Dodge City Messenger* by February 26, 1874. The new paper was a standard four-page, six-column weekly with subscription rates posted at three dollars a year, payable in advance, or six months for two dollars.

---

[1] Statement made in 1906 by early journalist Henry King, making reference to the *Kansas Weekly Herald*, first published in 1854. As quoted in Nyle H. Miller, Edgar Langsdorf, and Robert W. Richmond, *Kansas in Newspapers* (Topeka: Kansas State Historical Society, 1963), iii.

[2] "Journalists, Take Notice. DODGE CITY, Oct. 31, 1873." *Kansas City Times*, November 4, 1873. This short article ended on an encouraging note: "Nearly all present were in favor of advertising and subscribing liberally. A committee was appointed to correspond with any journalist that they might know on the subject," adding as the clincher, "A good opportunity now presents itself for some enterprising young man of small capital."

[3] *History of the State of Kansas*, 1342. On June 30, 1870, Alonzo W. Moore told the federal census enumerator that he owned two thousand dollars' worth of real estate and one thousand dollars in personal property—not paltry sums at that time for a small-town businessman. 1870 United States Census, Holton, Jackson County, Kansas, 320, lines 10–12.

In Dodge City the new editor, a forty-eight-year-old Pennsylvanian, began lining up advertisers. Moore, who had come to Kansas during those bloody years before the Civil War, was not shy about demanding support: "Let every man in the county show his appreciation of our efforts in publishing a paper in this sparsely settled region—by subscribing and paying for the Dodge City Messenger. Do it now! Don't wait for some other time!" Moore appreciated melodrama, but he also helped create an optimistic mood while adjusting to his new surroundings: "The city has gained an unenviable name, far and near—but now, instead of these terrible scenes that we read of, being reenacted, quietude reigns supreme."[4] It all sounded wonderful, and some of it was even true, as the economic climate began changing.

Eastern hide dealers, many of whom had panicked during that fall's financial crisis, recovered some of their courage with the new year. Orders for buffalo hides again filtered west, if in smaller numbers, but there were other problems. Billy Dixon remembered, "All the hunters assembled at Dodge were convinced that never again would there be a big run of buffalo that far north, because of the enormous slaughter on that part of their range in 1872 and 1873."[5] With fewer animals close by, the hide men shifted operations farther south. They continued congregating at Dodge City because of the railroad, the town's recreational offerings, and its proximity to Fort Dodge in case of trouble. Ignoring the provisions of the Medicine Lodge Treaty, which set aside portions of the southern herds for the exclusive benefit of Indians, these men pushed deeper into Indian Territory. Stretched thin, the army could offer little opposition. Making matters worse, some officers sympathized with the hunters, despite departmental directives ordering treaty enforcement.[6]

Indians did not know what to think. Behind the roar of guns they saw their way of life disappearing. Fear and hate intermingled as tribes gath-

---

[4] *Dodge City Messenger*, February 26, 1874. Editor Moore also promised, "We dislike a long Salutatory with more words than sense—promising great things which cannot be fulfilled—(as is too often the case with editors in Kansas)—but we merely say that we are here, in Dodge City, Ford County, State of Kansas, for the purpose of publishing a newspaper, earning and receiving our 'chuck,' and doing what we can towards promoting the interests of [the] county. The 'Messenger' is an Independent—or Neutral, paper—reserving the right, however, to criticize the actions of our public servants both in high and low places—to denounce public robbery and wholesale stealing—and speaking a good word for those who merit it."

[5] Dixon, *Life of "Billy" Dixon*, 111.

[6] R. Williams, Asst. Adj. Gen., Department of the Missouri, to Maj. Richard Dodge, October 3, 1873. Fort Dodge, Registered Letters Received.

ered to face their most visible foe: the hunters, those heavily armed, long-haired, bearded, and unwashed—yet formidable—opponents. They had blasted such a wide swath of destruction across the central plains that southern herds no longer migrated in any appreciable numbers much beyond the Cimarron. Months earlier Major Dodge had warned his superiors: "In my opinion very serious consequences will result unless steps are taken to arrest the work of these hunters in the Indian Territory and Reservation."[7] The crisis seemed to offer no solution but the old dream of waging war against these unprincipled invaders.

The tribes drew strength from societies that for generations had glorified struggle and personal combat. Indeed, many of their ancestors came to the southern plains only after suffering defeat at the hands of more powerful northern tribes. Others, chiefly the Comanches, displaced earlier inhabitants by force. From their new homes, tribes fought one another, while at the same time confronting old enemies from Mexico. After the Council House Massacre in 1840, Comanches fought the hated Texans with renewed vigor. They drew a distinction between Texans and Americans, a view reinforced by the Civil War when each side fought the other. At war's end the tribes at first failed to recognize Americans and Texans as one people. Many seemed willing to keep promises made to Americans as best they understood them while continuing, with no apparent contradiction of purpose, to raid settlements, ranches, and isolated travelers within Texas.

The cult of the warrior became the theme of the hour. Most of those harassing the tribes either came from Dodge City or found supplies and encouragement at that place. The alcohol flowing into Indian Territory passed from the town's wholesalers to the whiskey ranches dotting the Fort Dodge–Camp Supply road. Sources also included Texas entrepreneurs and traders from New Mexico called Comancheros, first described by Josiah Gregg in 1844 as commercial groups, "usually composed of the indigent and rude classes of the frontier villages."[8] Stumbling in on the heels of the whiskey sellers, gangs of horse thieves felt at home raiding unsuspecting Indian camps or tramping through the saloons, gambling dens, and brothels

---

[7] Maj. Richard Dodge to Asst. Adj. Gen., Department of the Missouri, October 27, 1873. Fort Dodge, Letters Sent.

[8] Gregg, *Commerce of the Prairies*, 2:54. For more on the Comancheros, a term invented by Gregg to identify Mexicans who traded with the Comanches, see: Charles L. Kenner, *A History of New Mexican–Plains Indian Relations* (Norman: University of Oklahoma Press, 1969), 78–97, 155–206.

defining life in Dodge City. Profits and the potential for trouble mirrored the amount of whiskey sold and the number of horses stolen.

Concerns over alcohol heightened as dealers in Ford County got better organized. One commander at Camp Supply complained in late 1873 that "whiskey ranches are established up the road from this Post to Fort Dodge, one at Bluff Creek, two on Bear Creek, and one at the Cimarron, and that whiskey is being sold to the Indians by their owners. As these ranches are all within the Kansas line, and I believe in unorganized counties, I respectfully request to be informed what action, if any, can be taken by me to have them broken up."[9]

Authorities failed to do anything. Responding to complaints from Arapaho chiefs that some of their young men traded ponies and buffalo robes for whiskey, Quaker Indian agent John D. Miles requested twenty soldiers and three wagons from Lt. Col. John Davidson at Camp Supply, to proceed "in charge of a trusted officer" along the road to Dodge City, arresting offenders, seizing their property and holding them for civil authorities.[10] No authorization to do so was ever granted.

The tribes grew apprehensive about the denizens of Dodge City. Not only did hunters congregating there slaughter their major source of food, but some of them, with no consideration for the consequences, killed Indians whenever possible. Only the year before, Spotted Wolf escaped with his life on the streets of Dodge City, being whisked out of town with the help of Charlie Rath. A less violent incident followed. President Grant and the Indian Commission had promised the tribes a gift of horses. John Miles hoped to persuade the Indians to accept the animals at Camp Supply in the spring. Excited, they refused to wait. Mindful of the incident with Spotted Wolf, Miles wanted the horses sent to Wichita. Instead, the freight agent arranged shipment to Dodge City.

Eighteen Indians and their agent arrived in town mid-morning on December 3, 1873, only to discover the animals delayed three days. Maj. Charles E. Compton, in command at Fort Dodge since November 14, informed Agent Miles that under orders he could not give permission to camp on the military reservation, but could only offer wagons and an

---

[9] Lt. Col. J. W. Davidson to Asst. Adj. Gen., Department of the Missouri, December 7, 1873. Camp Supply, I.T., Letters Sent.

[10] John D. Miles to Lt. Col. J. W. Davidson, January 23, 1873. Camp Supply, I.T., Letters Received.

escort for their return trip.[11] Fearing a change in weather, Miles rejected the idea of camping on the prairie and foolishly tried finding shelter in town. Rebuffed, he and his Indians retreated to the railroad depot, where local toughs gathered, hurling taunts and other insults. Someone tossed pungent red peppers on the hot stove, causing a general retreat. Miles found temporary shelter at Richard Evans's store, before the railroad gave grudging permission to use an empty freight car.[12]

While the Indians and their agent huddled in that unheated shelter on a Dodge City siding, a group of English sportsmen left town with plans to hunt south of the Arkansas. At Fort Dodge they hired a teenager named Jacob Dilsey to haul supplies. Along with scout Thomas Levi, everyone arrived safely at Camp Supply. Traveling down the North Fork of the Canadian they came upon a small party of Kiowas between Cottonwood Grove and Sheridan's Roost. A Mexican interpreter warned that Big Tree and Satanta camped nearby. Unconcerned, the sport hunters moved on.

The Englishmen sent their hired man back to pick up more provisions, giving him specific instructions to meet again in four days. No rendezvous took place. Concerned, they returned to Camp Supply and asked the military to conduct a search. The cavalry made a sweep of the surrounding country and found the burned-out wagon. The young teamster had been scalped, with both his arms and legs hacked away. Soldiers buried the remains before following the trail of stolen animals to a Kiowa camp. None of the perpetrators could be identified.

The murder of Jacob Dilsey caused hard talk in Dodge City: "The excitement in and around Fort Dodge is intense, and the old trappers and hunters in that vicinity vow that if the government does not inflict summary punishment upon the incarnate fiends, they will take the matter into their own hands and commence a war of extermination."[13] Not everyone blamed the Kiowas: "it is observed that this party was filled out at Dodge City," noted the chief clerk at the Central Superintendency at Lawrence, "and that they were in the Indian Country contrary to the treaty and without any legitimate

[11] Maj. C. E. Compton to John D. Miles at Dodge City, December 6, 1873. Fort Dodge, Letters Sent. Although regulations did not allow Compton to give the agent a requested three-day bread ration, he did notify Miles two days later: "The Post Treasurer of this post will however, if you desire, furnish you with the number of rations (of bread) required at the rate of five (5) cents per ration cash."

[12] Agent John D. Miles to Enoch Hoag, Superintendent, Office of Indian Affairs, Central Superintendency, Lawrence, Kansas, sent from Dodge City, December 7, 1873. Letters Received by the Office of Indian Affairs, Upper Arkansas Agency, 1855–74, hereafter cited as "Upper Arkansas Agency."

[13] *Kansas Daily Commonwealth,* December 12, 1873.

business, that the teamster who was killed was alone, and there being many white desperadoes in that country, I see fully as much to convince me that he met his death at the hands of some of those, as by Indians."[14]

Reporting the young teamster's death, Agent John Miles also complained of whiskey among the Cheyennes. Federal law-enforcement officers in Kansas had no authority regarding illegal whiskey sales or any other infractions south of the state line. By an act of Congress that jurisdiction belonged exclusively to the United States District Court for the Western District of Arkansas—soon the private bailiwick of the famous hanging judge, Isaac Charles Parker.[15] From Fort Smith deputy marshals confronted serious problems, including an epidemic of murders committed by whites against Indians. Even so, whiskey cases filled most dockets: "the disposal or attempted disposal of liquor to the Indians of the Indian Territory, has been the cause of more than one-half of the criminal cases tried by the Federal Court at Fort Smith."[16] Complicating matters, Fort Smith was three hundred miles east of Camp Supply.

Despite concerns over buffalo hunters and whiskey peddlers, others feared the presence of government surveyors, hordes of whom now came through Dodge City to blanket the Indian Territory. Kiowas, in particular, felt a superstitious revulsion against these men, as they did toward any form of census tally. Alarm heightened as more and more of these men marked the land with piles of stones and scribbled indecipherable gibberish into notebooks. Anger rose, and with it threats of violence. On March 18, 1873, forty or fifty Cheyennes rode in and destroyed the McDongall camp while everyone was absent except the cook. Wrecking everything in sight, they beat that unfortunate man over the head with clubs and struck him at least once with an ax. Miraculously he survived.

The following day Indians killed four surveyors near the Cimarron River. Others were closely watched as they continued working. With eleven

---

[14] Cryus Beede, Chief Clerk, Office of Indian Affairs, Central Superintendency, Lawrence, Kansas, to Edward P. Smith, Commissioner of Indian Affairs, Washington, D. C., December 21, 1873. Letters Received by the Office of Indian Affairs, Kiowa Agency, 1864–80. The Kiowas denied involvement: "It will be observed that Kiowas still deny any Knowledge of the murder of the teamster between Cheyenne Agency and Camp Supply. . . . no evidence whatever has been received at the agency fastening guilt of said murder upon the Kiowas." Enoch Hoag to Edward P. Smith, January 2, 1874. Ibid.

[15] For a convenient summary of what went on there, see Edwin C. Bearss and A. M. Gibson, *Fort Smith: Little Gibraltar on the Arkansas* (Norman: University of Oklahoma Press, 1969), 313–32; and Glenn Shirley, *Law West of Fort Smith: A History of Frontier Justice in the Indian Territory, 1834–1896* (New York: Henry Holt and Company, 1957).

[16] S. W. Harman, *Hell on the Border; He Hanged Eighty-Eight Men* (Fort Smith, Arkansas: The Phoenix Publishing Company, 1898), 34n.

isolated parties still in the field, plans were hastily drawn up to concentrate them into three or four large groups. Commanders from Fort Dodge and Camp Supply offered escorts to protect surveyors between the southern Kansas border and the north fork of the Cimarron. Despite precautions, surveying Indian land remained a dangerous business. Civilians blamed Indians for all the violence. Some military officers, including Major Dodge, reacted with skepticism. As an example, back in April 1873 a hunter named Samuel E. D. Parker came north with a wagonload of buffalo hides and a wounded leg. He told of fighting off a half-dozen warriors, killing one, thirty-five miles south of the Arkansas near the mouth of Sand Creek. The major questioned Parker's worthiness as a chronicler: "He has the reputation of being one of the most accomplished liars in this country. However Capt. [Henry B.] Bristol saw him and he is undoubtedly wounded."[17]

Meanwhile, following the direct intervention of the United States attorney general and the commissioner of Indian Affairs, Agent John Miles reported in early January 1874 the appointment of two special deputy U.S. marshals from Kansas to help patrol the border. One of these was an old friend named John H. Tally. The other was Edward C. Lefebvre, a thirty-one-year-old French-born engineer. Although outnumbered and outgunned by the outlaw bands, both men proved themselves. Six weeks later, using his authority as Indian agent, Miles appointed agency blacksmith Benjamin Williams to patrol Indian lands. He did so, however, without an official commission.

In early March a group of Cheyennes under Little Robe and Bull Bear reported forty-three head of stock, including five mules and many recognizable white and spotted ponies, stolen from their camp along the Cimarron. Authorities suspected William A. "Hurricane Bill" Martin and his gang of border ruffians. The Indians followed the outlaws into Kansas but failed to find their animals. Frustrated, they returned south. John Miles predicted serious consequences: "These lawless whites . . . must be restrained or we shall not be able to control the Cheyennes."[18]

As Little Robe traveled north searching for his animals, a party of younger warriors-to-be, including his own son, overtook him. Little Robe felt uneasy about controlling these young men among the whites in

---

[17] Maj. Richard Dodge to Asst. Adj. Gen., Department of the Missouri, April 28, 1873. Fort Dodge, Letters Sent.

[18] Agent John D. Miles to Superintendent Enoch Hoag, March 28, 1874. Upper Arkansas Agency.

Kansas. He withdrew, leaving the others to continue on toward Medicine Lodge. In the course of their travels, these young men ran off stock and skirmished with locals. In this instance James French, a well-known troublemaker along the border, rode with the Indians.

Complicating matters, units from Fort Dodge intercepted the raiders. On April 11, 1874, Capt. T. C. Tupper struck the Cheyennes after they stole eighteen horses, two mules, and fifty-five head of cattle from settlers near Sun City, southeast of Dodge in Barber County. After a short exchange of gunfire, a couple dozen miles below the salt flats of the Cimarron at the mouth of Bull Bear Creek, the soldiers recovered most of the animals. The Indians returned to the agency with some of the stolen stock, together with tales of their novel adventure. Little Robe's son bragged of his wounds, inflating his standing amongst the more militant Cheyennes. The animals originally stolen from Little Robe's band were sold at Dodge City within weeks.[19] The frustrated Indian agent continued to blame whiskey traders and stock thieves for his troubles.

Deputy marshals Tally and Lefebvre located Hurricane Bill Martin, along with a half-dozen confederates, at J. W. Baker's ranch on Turkey Creek. Outnumbered by the outlaws in their fortified camp, the officers withdrew. George Bent, working as an interpreter at the Cheyenne-Arapaho Agency, wrote of Bill Martin's activities, noting his practice of stealing from both Indians and whites, while selling "whiskey, arms, ammunition &c. to Indians." Bent lost several head of stock to that marauder in late April and began pursuing the missing animals himself. Indians offered to help, but Bent declined, fearing possible confrontations with innocent settlers in Kansas.

George Bent knew from experience that the buffalo hunters and whiskey peddlers were not the only sources of trouble along the border in 1874: "Another of the primary causes for the disturbance of the peace in the south was the presence of a number of white horse thieves who made their headquarters at Dodge City, Kansas, and raided the Indian camps at every opportunity. These bands of thieves were made up of the roughest and most lawless men of the border."[20]

Hurricane Bill Martin's gang consisted of fifteen to twenty of these

---

[19] Agent John D. Miles to Edward P. Smith, Commissioner of Indian Affairs, Washington, D.C., Third Annual Report, Upper Arkansas Agency, September 30, 1874.

[20] Hyde, *Life of George Bent*, 354.

tough frontier types. After running off George Bent's stock, other outlaws raided White Antelope's band of Cheyennes and took eleven more horses, before stealing another five animals from some Plains Apaches camped nearby. Deputy U.S. Marshal Lefebvre begged for assistance from authorities at Camp Supply. Lt. Col. John R. Brooke, the new commander, answered by citing a Department of the Missouri directive that troops could not be used to enforce civil laws without a direct order from the president.[21] The colonel seemed to ignore questions of his own jurisdiction over the Indian Territory.

Bill Martin, along with Texas Bob Hollis, Jackson "Slippery Jack" Gallagher, Charles McBride, and one-time Dodge City peace officer Billy Brooks, had established himself at Baker's Ranch, northeast of Indian agency headquarters on the Fort Sill–Caldwell road. They even arranged mail delivery. Others congregated nearby at a place called Black Jack Woods, bordering Turkey Creek, a tributary of the Cimarron. Baker's Ranch served as a rest stop for the Southwest Stage Company, leading to suspicions that company employees aided the outlaws. Not that it did them any good, if true. On May 3, 1874, outlaws stole four horses from the company's station in King Fisher County and grabbed another from Baker's Ranch.

After Deputy U.S. Marshal Michael Meagher, on special assignment from Wichita, finally made some arrests, Agent Miles ordered Baker to close his place and leave the Cheyenne Agency. The order did not accomplish much. Nor did boldness always favor the outlaws. In late May, Ben Williams confronted Samuel "Apache Sam" Walker at Smith and Ford's trading post on the North Canadian. Walker reached for a revolver and was shot dead. It was just as well, as arresting offenders made little impact; the commander at Fort Sill released them, claiming no authority to hold federal prisoners.

Despite Williams's proving himself during the encounter with Apache Sam, William S. Tough, the United States Marshal for Kansas (a man whose name belied his resolve), refused a request from Agent Miles for a permanent appointment: "If I could believe that in appointing Mr. Williams it would in any way aid or assist the two already appointed, I would certainly [do so], but I can see nothing to be accomplished by such

---

[21] Headquarters Records, Department of the Missouri, General Order, No. 3, February 4, 1874.

appointment. I think two deputies are as good as three, and less expensive to the government. . . . Why not call upon the Marshal of the United States for the Western District of Arkansas for assistance."[22]

Amid jurisdictional bickering, Indians not only watched their herds plundered, but did so on empty bellies. In mid-June Miles noted with alarm that supplies allowed only half-rations of beef. The agent reminded his superiors that in contrast to the agency, the Panhandle of Texas offered both whiskey and buffalo in abundance. Fearing these temptations, Miles refused to allow anyone still on the reservation to leave, even on hunting expeditions. A general uprising seemed likely when measured against false promises and starvation rations.

Authorities did manage to arrest the notorious James French, busy trading liquor with agency Indians on the Fort Dodge–Camp Supply road. Sent to Dodge City under military escort, French bribed his three guards with forty dollars. Frustrated, John Miles wrote: "Since his escape this man French has continued his whiskey traffic with the Cheyennes, living with them and dressing in Indian costume."[23] Concerned with troubles along the border, a situation exacerbated by his own behavior, French abandoned the Cheyennes, traveling toward Sedgwick County with more stolen horses. Deputy U.S. Marshal Mike Meagher arrested him on June 14, while the outlaw tried auctioning off the animals on the streets of Wichita.

Indian leaders blamed Miles for not keeping horse thieves at bay. With only three overworked deputies at his disposal, the agent seemed trapped by circumstances. The army was forbidden to interfere in civilian jurisdictions outside the Indian Territory. The United States government failed its treaty obligations. It could not stop the buffalo hunters and fielded a less than adequate force to oppose horse thieves and whiskey peddlers. Agency Indians had shown a willingness to try reservation life, but staying at the agency meant hunger and humiliation for these once-proud warriors.

The Arapahoes had lived more or less at peace with settlers since signing the Medicine Lodge Treaty. Even as tensions rose along the border, Major Compton reported from Fort Dodge that one hunting party had carried on friendly relations with whites while bivouacked in Kansas. The Cheyennes, too, followed much the same course. Leaders tried to exclude troublemakers, including members of the Dog Soldier Society, and accepted direction

---

[22] United States Marshal W. S. Tough to John D. Miles, June 17, 1874. Upper Arkansas Agency.

[23] John D. Miles to Edward P. Smith, June 18, 1874. Ibid.

from American representatives. Even some Comanches and Kiowas seemed ready for peace, at least if it did not involve compromise with the hated Texans. Examining attitudes throughout the Indian Territory, it seems likely that without the buffalo hunters, whiskey traders, and outlaws, there would have been no major Indian war on the southern plains in 1874.

Corruption and mismanagement within the government's supply system crippled efforts to find peace. With the demise of the bison, Indians were more dependent than ever on insecure agency rations. One of the army's most successful commanders, Nelson A. Miles, understood: "They were sometimes for weeks without their bread rations. Their annual allowance of food was usually exhausted in six or seven months. Thus they were either overfed or half-starved. . . . [T]hey would usually remain peaceable during the winter, but an outbreak in the spring and summer was the usual result."[24]

Watching events deteriorate, a frustrated John Miles sent a prophetic warning to his Washington superiors while reporting the killing of three men near Medicine Lodge: "These people know no other way of avenging their wrongs only by retaliation. . . . They of course claim that their raids shall be confined to 'the exterminating of the Buffalo Hunters.' "[25] Unbeknownst to Miles, he wrote those words three days after Indians had attacked an encampment of those men in the Texas Panhandle.

Facing unanswered complaints, tensions mounted at tribal councils. Talk, lubricated with illegal spirits, turned to war. Many dreamed of one huge outburst to sweep the whites off the plains forever. Those who had seen the power of their enemy—from visits to the great cities of the East—warned of the futility of battle. Overwhelmed by indignities, most participants ignored these words of caution.

Still, the drive toward war remained a slow process. Ordinary Indians awaited word from their leaders, men who themselves failed to achieve consensus. Many of the Comanches, a secretive people in the best of times, stayed on the move across such a wide area that other tribes could only guess their intentions. The Kiowas appeared obsessed with intertribal bickering. Arapahoes could not make up their minds, and the Cheyennes lacked strong leadership. Indecision vanished in the spring of 1874, after the tribes fell under the spell of a young Quahadi Comanche medicine man called Isa-tai

[24] Nelson A. Miles, *Personal Recollections and Observations of General Nelson A. Miles* (Chicago: The Werner Company, 1896), 157.

[25] John D. Miles to Edward P. Smith, June 30, 1874. Upper Arkansas Agency.

(a name roughly translated as Wolf Shit or Coyote Droppings) who rose as a symbol of defiance, standing resolute in defense of traditional ways.

This man's sudden rise worried Kiowa and Comanche agent James Haworth, who informed his boss, Enoch Hoag, at Lawrence: "They have a new Medicine man, who can accomplish wonders. Horse Back says he can furnish them an inexhaustible supply of cartridges, suited for any gun, from his stomach. Certainly a very valuable man to have around in time of war. He can also raise the dead, having recently done so. He is himself, and can render all others bullet-proof. I am yet at a loss to know what kind of an opinion to give."[26] In that superstitious world surrounding Indian daily life, Isa-tai's medicine seemed strong stuff indeed. The young man now called for all Comanches to assemble on Red River, near the mouth of Sweetwater Creek, for a Sun Dance. Unlike other tribes on the southern plains, the Comanches did not practice this ritual, though they had watched performances by their Kiowa allies. The significance of all this was not lost on knowledgeable whites.

The Sun Dance ceremony produced a decision for war. At first the Comanches favored an attack on the Tonkawas in Texas—Indians who had allied themselves with the whites against other tribes. Then they joined the Kiowas proposing a huge raid into Texas to avenge the death of Lone Wolf's son, Tau-ankia, and his favorite nephew Gui-tain, who were killed along with eight others in early December 1873 by a detachment of troopers from the Fourth Cavalry.[27] Weighing the merits of each argument, the Indians narrowed their choice to a more practical target.

It was obvious to everyone that buffalo hunters represented the primary enemy. Kicking Bird had already explained the Indians' deep resentment toward these men in terms any American could understand. To Agent Haworth the Kiowa chief compared the buffalo to money, saying, "they loved them just as the white man loved his money, and just as it made a white man's heart feel to have his money carried away, so it made them feel, to see others killing, and stealing their Buffalo."[28] As the whiskey flowed and the debate grew more intense, leaders decided to strike at the very heart of their insoluble dilemma. They would rise up and attack an

---

[26] James M. Haworth to Enoch Hoag, May 6, 1874. Kiowa Agency.

[27] 1st Lieut. Charles L. Hudson, 4th Cavalry, to Post Adjutant, Fort Clark, Texas, December 15, 1873. Ernest Wallace, ed., *Ranald S. Mackenzie's Official Correspondence Relating to Texas, 1873–1879* (Lubbock: West Texas Museum Association, 1968), 67–69.

[28] James M. Haworth to Enoch Hoag, June 6, 1874. Kiowa Agency.

encampment of buffalo hunters and Dodge City traders in the Texas Panhandle, at the place called Adobe Walls.

To get nearer the southern herds, hide dealers selected a grassy meadow two miles north of the Canadian River, in present-day Hutchinson County, as a convenient point of rendezvous. Spaniards from New Mexico had used the place as a trading site long before William Bent and Ceran St. Vrain arrived in the early 1840s to build what became known as Fort Adobe.[29] Bent's employees, including John Simpson Smith, skirmished with the Comanches and other tribes almost from the start. Continual unrest convinced the owners to destroy the site. Kit Carson fought a desperate battle there in 1864 against a combined force of Comanches, Kiowas, and Kiowa-Apaches. Ten years later history seemed ready to repeat itself.

Dodge City merchants planned a trading post near the old ruins. Dependent on buffalo for their livelihood, they worried over herds disappearing from the plains of western Kansas. They gambled on Texas for salvation. Experienced hunters, such as J. Wright Mooar and Billy Dixon, had long praised the Panhandle as a prime killing ground. A. C. "Charlie" Myers and his new partner, Fred J. Leonard, warmed to the idea, ignoring the obvious risks of moving so far into hostile territory. They arranged for the hunters to haul their supplies south in return for a small fee and assurances that prices would stay at Dodge City levels—a promise not always kept. Hoping for a monopoly on shipping below the Cimarron, the two partners bought eight Murphy wagons and eighty oxen from Henry Sitler for $4,066.67, payable in three notes of trust.[30] They hired Charles E. "Dirty Faced Ed" Jones and Joseph Plummer to mark the route back to Dodge City, giving birth to the famous Jones and Plummer Trail.[31]

The main expedition, made up of "100 teams all loaded and about 110 men," according to Emanuel Dubbs, left Dodge City in March 1874 and camped that first night on Crooked Creek, one of many streams marking routes into the Panhandle.[32] Two days later they reached the Cimarron River, known to all as the "dead line," marking entry into Indian country.

---

[29] The exact date for construction of Fort Adobe is unknown. For a good discussion of this point, see Hyde, *Life of George Bent*, 356n3; and David Lavender, *Bent's Fort* (Garden City, N.Y.: Doubleday & Company, Inc., 1954), 405n10.

[30] Ford County Register of Deeds, May 21, 1874, Book A, 49. Payment dates were August 9, November 9, 1874, and February 9, 1875.

[31] For more on this important trading route and cattle trail and its importance to the history of Dodge City, see C. Robert Haywood, *Trails South: The Wagon-Road Economy in the Dodge City–Panhandle Region* (Norman: University of Oklahoma Press, 1986), 64–99.

[32] Dubbs, "Personal Reminiscences," Goodnight et al., *Pioneer Days in the Southwest*, 46.

Crossing the Neutral Strip, the party arrived on Beaver Creek, a main tributary of the North Canadian, by the fourth day. Moving west they struck
the mouth of Palo Duro Creek, taking time to refill water barrels before
pushing south to the source of Moore's Creek, which they followed down
to the Canadian. Traveling another dozen miles or so, on that seventh day
out from Dodge City, they reached West Adobe Creek, about a mile from
the old ruins. Camping for the night, they waited until dawn to survey the
abandoned site. "When we first saw Adobe Walls," Billy Dixon remembered, "there were parts of walls still standing, some being four or five feet
high. The adobe bricks were in an excellent state of preservation."[33] The
new arrivals set themselves up 1.2 miles north of the old site, on a broad
meadow nestled between Adobe and Bent creeks.

The Dodge City merchants, more or less under the leadership of Charlie Myers and James Hanrahan, dominated everything at Adobe Walls.
Myers and Fred Leonard starting laying out a 130-by-210-foot picket corral and hide yard, using upright cottonwood logs hauled in from Reynolds
Creek, six miles across the Canadian. At the northeast corner of this
north-south rectangle they constructed a two-room picket building for
their trading business. At the opposite corner of the enclosure was a small
kitchen and mess hall. North of that, along the west side of the hide yard,
the partners erected a roofed but otherwise open-air stable large enough to
accommodate forty horses. On all but the southwest corner, ten-foot circular bastions were added. As it turned out they offered only the illusion
of security, as did the corral's picket construction, prompting carpenter
Andrew Johnson to remark years later, "If you ever build a place to with-
stand an Indian attack, don't build your stockade like we did."[34]

South of Myers and Leonard, Thomas O'Keefe built a small picket blacksmith shop. Just below O'Keefe's James Hanrahan opened a saloon, a rectan-
gular sod structure lying roughly along an east-to-west line and measuring
42 by 23 feet. Not to be outdone by their rivals Myers and Leonard, Charlie
Rath and Bob Wright opened a branch of their Dodge City store. James
Langton, Wright's partner at Fort Dodge, managed the Panhandle property.

---

[33] Dixon, *Life of "Billy" Dixon*, 132. Emanuel Dubbs had a similar reaction: "We found 'Adobe Walls' consisted
of the remnant of broken down and decaying Adobes, possibly constructed by the Mexicans, the true history of
which is not known." Dubbs, "Personal Reminiscences," Goodnight et al., *Pioneer Days in the Southwest*, 46.

[34] Statements of Andrew Johnson, as quoted in Baker and Harrison, *Adobe Walls*, 56. The picket corral, Johnson explained, was "of more protection to the Indians than it was to the white men."

Rath oversaw construction of a three-room building, measuring some 22½ by 59 feet, with a 13-by-12-foot bastion added later to the southeast corner. The sod walls at Rath & Co. were three feet thick at the base, tapering to eighteen inches at the top. The store itself was located on the east side of a corral and hide yard that was never finished. Sod blocks were cut from the prairie in chunks three to five inches thick, using a special plow fashioned by pioneer Dodge City blacksmith and Town Company member Patrick Ryan. Set about two hundred feet south of Hanrahan's saloon, Rath & Co. was somewhat isolated from the rest of the compound. Yet the entire complex covered only about six hundred feet of ground on a slightly northeast-to-southwest axis.[35]

Elsewhere, those Indians preferring peace warned agents of the coming danger, blaming tensions on the government's failure to face its responsibilities. By early June others, who had given up on peaceful relations, attacked Joseph Plummer's party some fifteen miles southeast of Adobe Walls, killing Dave Dudley and Tom Wallace. The attackers, thought to be Kiowas under Lone Wolf but possibly Cheyennes, mutilated the bodies—leaving them scalped and castrated, with noses, ears, and toes severed, brains removed, and skulls stuffed with grass. A wooden stake was driven through the body of each man, pinning them to the ground.

Other attacks followed. On a small tributary to the Salt Fork of Red River, two more hunters lost their lives. Their skinners escaped before the camp was destroyed and the horses stolen. An Englishman, John T. Jones, and a German, W. "Blue Billy" Muhler, were murdered and mutilated in their camp near the Canadian. Their partner, Anderson Moore, found the remains and recited the sad details to a subdued audience at Adobe Walls. Returning from Dodge City with a wagonload of whiskey, James Hanrahan and his teamsters came under attack while resting their stock along Sharp's Creek. Surprised, they returned fire, surviving with their lives and valuable cargo but losing all but one horse to the Indians. Stranded until the following afternoon, they were helped by another group, including Charlie Myers, heading back to Adobe Walls.

Deputy U.S. Marshals Edward Lefebvre and John Tally rode into the Texas Panhandle in early June, searching for two mules stolen from George

---

[35] For the best description of the Adobe Walls complex, see Baker and Harrison, *Adobe Walls*, 14–23. Business was good from the start. On June 25, 1874, the *Dodge City Messenger* reported, "Ten wagons loaded with buffalo hides, from the Canadian, came in Tuesday morning last. The hides belong to Myers & Leonard, of this city."

Bent. They learned what was happening: "The movement against Buffalo hunters seemed to have been well-planned," Lefebvre wrote. "The Indians divided themselves into small parties and made simultaneous attacks on the different camps."[36] Within a few miles of those sites, the officers met a party of railroad surveyors under Frank Maddox returning to Camp Supply. They described helping Joseph Plummer bury the remains of his friends Dudley and Wallace (Plummer missed the massacre by hauling buffalo hides to Adobe Walls). Maddox suggested the deputies join his party. Both accepted, but on the night of June 11 they lost their horses to Indians, about a day and a half from their destination.

A palatable sense of danger hung over the Panhandle buffalo range. Fearing raids, isolated hunters began drifting toward Adobe Walls. J. Wright Mooar and his brother John, along with Lemuel Wilson and Phillip Sisk, fought off two attacks. On June 19 four warriors fired on a military mail escort between Fort Dodge and Camp Supply, wounding one man. Others struck Sun City, a small hamlet on the north side of Medicine Lodge Creek, near the mouth of Turkey Creek. The place itself, consisting of no more than a dozen buildings and a small stockade, "was burned and five men killed and scalped, and the settlers driven off."[37]

It all made good sense from an Indian's viewpoint. Two weeks before, in a report filed at Fort Dodge, it was said that "Sun City, and the three inhabited ranches on Mule Creek of which Smallwood is the centre, have the reputation of being the Head Quarters of a band or bands of Horse thieves. From what could be gathered it is the impression that the people on Mule Creek are hardly worthy of Government protection."[38]

More rumors about murdered whites circulated, including the story of four mutilated corpses near the Canadian River. At Dodge City a general uproar surrounded the death of freighter L. L. Warren, who was killed and scalped just eight miles south of town. Most everyone blamed Indians. Major Compton expressed doubts, pointing out that horse thieves hoping to implicate Indians often scalped their victims and reminding his superiors, "The citizens, especially of Dodge City, are using their best efforts to keep up an undue excitement and seem only to be anxious to crowd rumor upon rumor regardless of truth of facts. I merely enclose the slip within,

[36] Edward C. Lefebvre, writing from Camp Supply, to John D. Miles, June 14, 1874. Upper Arkansas Agency.

[37] *Dodge City Messenger*, June 25, 1874.

[38] 2nd Lt. Austin Henely, Sixth Cavalry, to Post Adjutant, Fort Dodge, June 10, 1874. Headquarters Records, Fort Dodge, Kansas, Reports, Journals, etc., Scouts & Marches.

cut from the Dodge City Messenger, to show you the source from which the news eminates [sic] as probably the article will be copied in other journals, losing nothing in its travels."[39]

Amos Chapman, a twenty-seven-year-old army scout and interpreter (and a civilian recipient of the Congressional Medal of Honor for action at the Buffalo Wallow fight three months later), carried a warning to Adobe Walls with James McAllister, then running a bull train for Camp Supply traders Lee and Reynolds. McAllister said they were trailing two thieves who had stolen horses from his employers. Thinking they may have crossed the Panhandle on their way to New Mexico, the two men rode to the encampment on the Canadian. The threat of an Indian attack was an open secret, as McAllister recalled years later: "The Indians around Fort Supply would be in to the fort every day, and they told us that they were going down to Adobe Walls and kill the buffalo hunters. When we passed there we told the hunters what the Indians had said, and that they were coming, but they wouldn't believe us. They weren't even looking for them when they came."[40] Some hunters doubted Chapman's veracity because of his relationships. Indeed, his Cheyenne father-in-law would take part in the fight at Adobe Walls.

Another version has Lt. Col. John Davidson, then commanding the Tenth Cavalry at Fort Sill, learning about the attack from some disaffected Comanches. He passed on the intelligence to traders Lee and Reynolds, who in turn tried warning their friend Charlie Rath. Escorted by a sergeant and six or seven troopers, at least according to J. Wright Mooar, Chapman and McAllister secretly reported to A. C. Myers, James Hanrahan, and Charlie Rath.[41] Or so the story goes. Since it is not clear when the two men arrived, it must be noted that Rath had already returned to Dodge City three weeks before the attack. Charlie Myers also left before the fight. So, they may not have been there to hear any warnings from Chapman and McAllister. Back

[39] Maj. C. E. Compton to the Asst. Adj. Gen., Department of the Missouri, June 19, 1874. Fort Dodge, Letters Sent.

[40] James E. McAllister to J. Evetts Haley, July 1, 1926. As quoted in Baker and Harrison, Adobe Walls, 58–59. Another student of these events stated flatly that Amos Chapman specifically warned Rath, Myers, and Hanrahan to "expect a massive Indian attack on the morning after the next full moon: Saturday, June 27," and that "The three merchants decided at once to keep the secret to themselves; if word got around, the hunters might clear out, leaving the valuable stock of supplies defenseless." James L. Haley, The Buffalo War: The History of the Red River Indian Uprising of 1874 (Garden City, N.Y.: Doubleday & Company, Inc., 1976), 61. If true, it does not say much for Myers and Rath, both of whom departed Adobe Walls well before the battle.

[41] J. Wright Mooar to J. Evetts Haley, April 12, 1936. Walter Stanley Campbell Files, Box 98A, Folder 11, Manuscript Division, Western History Collection, University of Oklahoma Library, 1.

in Kansas, Myers described conditions in the Panhandle to a reporter from the *Dodge City Messenger*: "There are quite a large number of hunters in that locality and they are 'red hot' to pitch into the Indians. That he (Myers) never saw a set of men so eager for a fight—so anxious to exterminate the whole race of Indians, as the hunters now on the Canadian are."[42]

They would soon have their chance. At Adobe Walls some of the men were up and about on that morning of June 27, 1874, not wrapped in their blankets as Isa-tai had promised. There is still controversy surrounding all this. The accepted explanation has the cottonwood ridgepole at Hanrahan's saloon cracking around two in the morning from all the fresh sod piled atop the building the day before. Afraid of being buried alive, the men repaired the damage by setting several support beams in place.[43]

J. Wright Mooar—who had left the encampment by this time—offered a more conspiratorial theory, one that has been repeated many times. Mooar claimed that James Hanrahan, aware of the impending attack, hoped to trigger an alarm. He had not done so earlier for fear the hunters would abandon the compound, jeopardizing his valuable inventory, as well as those of Myers and Leonard and Rath & Co. Trying to disguise his motives, or so Mooar reasoned, Hanrahan fired off a revolver and fooled the waking men about the ridgepole. In the confusion he convinced them to carry out repairs. At first light he offered free drinks in appreciation, but the men were now up and alert.[44]

On that Saturday morning hunter Billy Dixon planned an early start

---

[42] *Dodge City Messenger*, June 25, 1874.

[43] As Billy Dixon explained: "Had it not been for the cracking of the cottonwood ridge pole in Hanrahan's saloon, the Indians would have come upon us unawares and all of us would have been killed, yet we never could find a single thing wrong with the log. Every hunter that came in after the fight, as well as every man at the Walls, examined that cottonwood ridge log over and over to find the break, but it could not be found. The two men who were asleep in the building declared that the noise sounded like the report of a rifle." Dixon, *Life of "Billy" Dixon*, 187. According to an account written by John Coulter of the *Leavenworth Times* and republished in the *Dodge City Times* on November 24, 1877, the men located at Hanrahan's "were startled by the falling of a portion of the roof, which had given way." Also see, *Dallas Morning News*, March 13, 1888.

[44] J. Wright Mooar claimed years later: "In all former accounts of the battle, much has been made of the providential cracking of the ridgepole in Hanrahan's saloon. The real cause for the night alarm was kept a secret by a group of men, including myself, who knew the truth. Under a solemn oath, we agreed to keep this secret until there should be but one survivor. He was then to be released from his oath. I am that last survivor, and will give the facts." Robert F. Pace, ed., *Buffalo Days: Stories from J. Wright Mooar As Told to James Winford Hunt* (Abilene, Texas: State House Press, McMurry University, 2005), 50. For yet another version of this story, see J. Wright Mooar to J. Evetts Haley, July 28, 1937. Walter Stanley Campbell Files, Box 98A, Folder 13A, Manuscript Division, Western History Collection, University of Oklahoma Library, 18–19. It is also interesting to consider that if Hanrahan had indeed fired a gun in his saloon hoping to approximate the sound of a cracking ridgepole, why did the waking hunters, all keenly knowledgeable about firearms, not notice the distinctive sulfur smell from the black powder then used in cartridges, or the smoky atmosphere thus created? On this point J. Wright Mooar, along with other more recent critics, is strangely silent.

and sent William Ogg, a skinner who also worked part-time for Hanra-han, to round up the horses grazing near the creek. Tying his bedroll and tossing it into the wagon, Dixon picked up his rifle and glanced toward the horses. "They were in sight," he later recalled, but

> Something else caught my eye. Just beyond the horses, at the edge of some timber, was a large body of objects advancing vaguely in the dusky dawn toward our stock and in the direction of Adobe Walls. Though keen of vision, I could not make out what the objects were, even by straining my eyes.
>
> Then I was thunderstruck. The black body of moving objects suddenly spread out like a fan, and from it went up one single, solid yell—a warwhoop that seemed to shake the very air of the early morning. Then came the thudding roar of running horses, and the hideous cries of each of the individual warriors who engaged in the onslaught. I could see that hundreds of Indians were coming.[45]

Hoping to save his favorite horse, Dixon grabbed the terrified animal and tied him to his wagon—not that it mattered, all the animals at Adobe Walls were either killed or stolen, only the dogs, including Billy Dixon's "highly intelligent setter bitch, named Fannie," managed to escape.[46] Dixon fired a random shot toward the attackers and ran for Hanrahan's saloon. Young William B. Masterson, awakened at Myers and Leonard's corral and at first mistaking the sound of distant hoofs for buffalo, also sprinted for Hanrahan's place, a structure taking on all the trappings of a fortress. Billy Ogg, another survivor of that desperate race, reached the building just in time. Witnesses claimed that had Ogg's spirited gallop been timed, punctuated as it was with flying lead, he would have forever set a world's record.

Inside the saloon the men barricaded themselves. There was little time to ponder strategy as waves of Indians circled the compound, the rooms filling with acrid smoke from dozens of black powder cartridges, mixing with the smells of fear, sweat, and vomit of more than one terrified defender. Warriors rode closer with each turn, firing against the thick sod walls of Hanrahan's and Rath & Co. Others dismounted and started shooting into Myers and Leonard's place from fixed positions.

When the battle opened an estimated twenty-nine persons occupied Adobe Walls, including Hannah Olds, the cook at Charlie Rath's and the only woman present. Two of the men, brothers Isaac "Ike" and Jacob "Shorty" Scheidler, camped in their already packed freight wagon north of

---

[45] Dixon, *Life of "Billy" Dixon,* 157.
[46] Ibid., 197.

Myers and Leonard's corral. Unaware of the earlier commotion at Hanrahan's, they now found themselves surrounded by screaming Indians. Lying motionless the brothers and their large black Newfoundland retriever escaped notice until one curious Comanche peered under the canvas, only to be blown to bits by a buffalo gun fired at pointblank range. Enraged, others mobbed the wagon, overpowering the men and their dog. Impressed by the animal's ferocious defense, warriors lifted a patch of the dog's hair, as if acknowledging a worthy foe.

Defenders were scattered across the compound. Eleven fought from Myers and Leonard's picket building. Nine others, including Billy Dixon, Bat Masterson, and Jim Hanrahan, held the saloon. At the far southern end of the complex, seven more, including the hapless Mrs. Olds, took refuge at Rath & Co. Isolated by the flow of battle, the three groups shouted encouragement to one another. Later they all remembered hearing bugle calls coming from the Indian ranks. In reminiscence, the Comanche Quanah Parker described the bugler as a black army deserter—a curious development, since a bugler had also made an appearance on this same battlefield during the fight with Kit Carson ten years earlier.[47]

From behind barricades defenders recovered their wits. They began fighting back, first with sidearms fired at close range—a frantic fusillade that helped save the day—before reaching for those deadly buffalo guns.[48] As the battle opened Indians found refuge behind the picket fence of Myers and

---

[47] Thelma S. Guild and Harvey L. Carter, *Kit Carson: A Pattern for Heroes* (Lincoln: University of Nebraska Press, 1984), 253; and Edwin L. Sabin, *Kit Carson Days*, 2:742, 958n53. More recent speculation suggests: "Carson thought this was a white man, but it was more likely Satanta, a leading chief and warrior, who was noted for playing a bugle." Tom Dunlay, *Kit Carson and the Indians* (Lincoln: University of Nebraska Press, 2000), 332. Ten years later Satanta was at Fort Sill suffering from some undisclosed illness and was not on hand for the second fight at Adobe Walls. Baker and Harrison, *Adobe Walls*, 68. Regarding the bugler at the 1874 fight, Bat Masterson wrote years later, "The negro was killed late in the afternoon of the first day's fighting as he was running away from a wagon owned by the Schadler [*sic*] brothers, both of whom were killed in this same wagon. The negro had his bugle with him at the time he was shot by Harry Armitage. Also he was carrying a tin can filled with sugar and another filled with ground coffee under each arm. Armitage shot him through the back with a 50 calibre Sharps rifle as he was making his escape. That ended the negro bugler." W. B. Masterson to Frederick S. Barde, October 13, 1913. As quoted in Miller and Snell, *Why the West Was Wild*, 320.

[48] A detailed archeological investigation of the site during the 1970s revealed evidence concerning the types of firearms, including both muzzle loading and cartridge types, used to defend Adobe Walls. Recovered bullets, cartridge cases, percussion caps, paper wadding, and other debris, shows a range of weapons from the small .32 rim fire to the massive .56 Spencer. In between are examples of the .44 Henry rim fire, .44 Long, .44 Smith & Wesson American, .45 Colt, and other center fire pistol cartridges, alongside a variety of rifle ammunition, the most widely represented being the .45-70 and .50-70 Government, along with many .50-90 Sharps center fires. Musket balls span the range from .38 to .56. There is even evidence suggesting shotguns were used during this desperate battle; various sized pellets being recovered, from No. 2 to No. 3 buckshot. For a complete listing of what was found, see Baker and Harrison, *Adobe Walls*, 193–95.

Leonard's hide yard. From there they gunned down Billy Tyler, a hunter turned teamster who was trying to reach one of the bastions with Fred Leonard. Bullets whizzed through the dried grouting of the trading post, shattering canned goods and turning the hardened dirt floor into a makeshift skating rink for those less than sure-footed defenders huddling inside.

Other attackers, including Quanah Parker, swooped down and tried smashing doors open using the weight of their horses, but having been reinforced by Dodge City carpenter Andrew "Andy the Swede" Johnson, they held firm. Undeterred, the Indians continued their strategy of first charging then circling the buildings, all the while firing at the stubborn walls. They withdrew only to regroup and continued shooting from a safer distance. Repeated exposure to buffalo guns in the hands of experienced hunters took its toll. Indians went down trying to retrieve bodies of dead and wounded comrades, a feat held in high regard among tribes on the southern plains but a tactical flaw under conditions of this desperate battle.

Around noon the men barricaded in the saloon discovered that the morning's fight had consumed most of their ammunition. Jim Hanrahan and Billy Dixon dashed for Rath's store, where eighteen thousand cartridges crowded the inventory. Hanrahan loaded a sack with this precious commodity and returned to his place amid ineffective long-range fire. Dixon stayed behind at Rath's, the weakest point in terms of numbers and experience in the whole complex, occupied as it was by a store manager, his clerk, bookkeeper, a cook, a carpenter, a blacksmith, and the like—but not one professional hunter. With Dixon's help the eight defenders continued the fight with renewed spirit.

By early afternoon the attacks subsided. Many of the warriors now doubted Isa-tai's magic; he had, after all, promised they would kill all the hunters as they slept. Instead they were awake and responded with force. From the number of dead and wounded, it was clear that the promised immunity from bullets was somewhat off the mark. Adding to their list of grievances, observers concluded from Quanah Parker's wound, received between his shoulder and neck, that their enemy possessed some mysterious weapon capable of turning bullets in flight. The physical laws of trajectory and the fickle nature of ricochet played no role in the Indians' reliance on superstition to explain otherwise natural phenomenon.

Worried chiefs berated Isa-tai, who tried diverting criticism with another dose of smoke and mirrors, this time explaining that while en route to Adobe Walls a Cheyenne had killed a skunk, thereby unraveling all his magical formulas. No sooner had he finished that story than a stray bullet struck his horse squarely in the head. Witnesses feared the whites capable of hitting targets they could not see. Younger warriors tried to attack their discredited miracle worker. Rescued by the chiefs, who felt the man's shame sufficient punishment, Isa-tai conceded the day was lost.[49]

Late that afternoon it appeared as if the Indians had withdrawn, at least beyond rifle range. Some defenders stepped outside for the first time since the dawn attack. Dead animals and dead Indians littered the ground. These buffalo hunters, so accustomed to blood and killing, hurried to collect souvenirs from their defeated enemy, even before bothering to bury fallen comrades Billy Tyler and the two Scheidler brothers in a common grave along the north wall of Myers and Leonard's hide yard. Fearing renewed attacks the men abandoned Hanrahan's and, after strengthening the makeshift barricades, divided themselves between the two stores. No attack came but the men had a rough night. Many, including Billy Dixon, admitted having nightmares. One nervous lookout, convincing himself that a moving shadow was an Indian, shot and killed one of the dogs wandering back to the compound.

None of the larger animals had done well during the attack. Billy Dixon made a point of describing their suffering: "Before long there were a large number of wounded horses standing near the buildings. A horse gives up quickly when in pain, and these made no effort to get away. Even those that were at a considerable distance from the buildings when they received their wounds came to us, as if seeking our help and sympathy. It was a pitiable sight, and touched our hearts, for the boys loved their horses. I noticed that horses that had been wounded while grazing in the valley also came to the buildings, where they stood helpless and bleeding or dropped down and died."[50]

Even on that first morning it was obvious large numbers of Indians were still around. They did not renew frontal attacks on the trading post,

---

[49] Haley, *The Buffalo War*, 75; and Baker and Harrison, *Adobe Walls*, 72. Finally forgiven, Isa-tai surrendered with other Comanches in 1875 and settled down near Fort Sill, where he raised a family. He died on November 10, 1914, at his home near Lawton, Oklahoma. He was seventy-two years old. In 1963 his grandson, James Eschiti of Waters, Oklahoma, donated Isa-tai's buffalo-horn headdress and ceremonial shield and lance, together with other of his grandfather's personal belongings, to the ethnology collection of the Panhandle-Plains Historical Museum. Baker and Harrison, *Adobe Walls*, 73, 319n108.

[50] Dixon, *Life of "Billy" Dixon*, 167.

but occasionally fired their guns in the general direction of the compound. It became a nuisance more than a danger. But the defenders were trapped, after all, without horses or any reasonable hope of rescue. Tensions eased with the smells of breakfast drifting from Myers and Leonard's kitchen. There the company cook, known to everyone simply as "Old Man" Keeler, was frying buffalo meat to accompany yeast powder biscuits and gallons of strong coffee, the first taste of food anyone enjoyed since the fight began more than twenty-four hours before.

Many hunters out on the Panhandle heard the muffled sounds of battle on June 27. Some packed up and skedaddled back to Dodge City. Others, concerned for the welfare of friends at the trading post, drifted towards Adobe Walls. Approaching the site, Frank J. Brown and his outfit spotted Indians everywhere they looked: "The Indians were thick on every side but I noticed that they kept out of range of the guns from the stockade." Brown could not forget his reaction: "We whipped up our horses and went in on the run. The men had the gate open. If they hadn't come to meet us and shot so well from inside, I don't believe we'd ever made it."[51]

Falling victim to the relentless heat of late June, it did not take long for the bodies of the Indians and the carcasses of those animals not driven off by the attackers to begin decomposing, adding to the rot of smashed canned goods at both stores. It all created a putrid assault on the senses. Hoping for relief, both from the smells of death and billions of flies, the newcomers used their horses to haul away dead animals and dead Indians, eleven of the latter, according to Fred Leonard.[52]

Overcome by the passions of the battlefield, all somewhat reminiscent of the mutilation of Dave Dudley and Tom Wallace, hunters scalped and decapitated the Indian corpses. "Twelve Indian heads, minus hair, feathers and other *thum mim*, now adorn the gate-posts of the corral," read an account published at Topeka. "The collection is diversified by the *caput* of a negro, who was killed among the Indians with a can of yeast powders in his hand. He didn't 'raise' worth a cent after that."[53] Hunter Orlando A. "Brick" Bond, a later Dodge City dance hall proprietor whose outfit J. Wright Mooar considered "outlaws and rustlers . . . a hard bunch," saw the results

[51] Statements of Frank J. Brown, as quoted in Baker and Harrison, *Adobe Walls*, 97.

[52] *Leavenworth Times,* July 10, 1874.

[53] *Kansas Daily Commonwealth,* August 8, 1874.

and remembered years later, "they were a hideous looking sight, for they looked like they had been laughing when their heads were cut off."[54]

Amid the uncertainty, someone hoisted a flag fashioned by Andy Johnson from discarded Indian blankets, a gaudy affair sporting a large five-pointed star. Dixon remembered: "A black flag was flying from one of the buildings," and within hours a German-born Civil War veteran named George Bellfield came in by wagon up the valley from the Canadian, "and when Bellfield and his companion saw it they thought we were playing some kind of joke on them," Dixon added. "But when he drew nearer and began seeing the dead horses, he put the whip to his team and came in at a dead run."[55]

English hunters James and Robert Cator, having endured long-range skirmishing, rode into Adobe Walls from their camp twenty-five miles to the south. Later arrivals, seeing the flag from a distance and unaware of the events of June 27, assumed, as had Bellfield, that the hunters were having fun. It was, of course, no laughing matter, and now, not knowing if the Indians planned renewing their assault, defenders questioned the odds of rescue. Tempted by a cash offer, Henry Lease volunteered to ride for Dodge City under cover of darkness on George Bellfield's saddle horse. Days later a man named Reed made a second attempt. Both got through safely.

On the third day fifteen Indians rode to the crest of a high bluff east of Adobe Walls Creek. Tradition claims Billy Dixon spotted them, and at the urging of his friends shouldered his Sharps rifle. As his wife remembered her husband's account: "I took careful aim and pulled the trigger. We saw an Indian fall from his horse. The others dashed out of sight behind a clump of timber. A few moments later two Indians ran quickly on foot to where the dead Indian lay, seized his body and scurried to cover. They had risked their lives, as we had frequently observed, to rescue a comrade who might be not only wounded but dead. I was admittedly a good marksman, yet this was what might be called a 'scratch' shot."[56] If the story is true, and

---

[54] Statement of Orlando A. "Brick" Bond, as quoted in Baker and Harrison, *Adobe Walls*, 98. For J. Wright Mooar's 1939 characterization of Bond and his outfit, see Ibid., 6.

[55] Dixon, *Life of "Billy" Dixon*, 179–80.

[56] Ibid., 180–81. Although not present as a witness himself, J. Wright Mooar disputed Dixon's claim: "It was Charlie Armitage that killed that Indian. It wasn't Billy Dixon by any means," J. Wright Mooar to J. Evetts Haley, July 28, 1937. Walter Stanley Campbell Files, Box 98A, Folder 13A, 12, Manuscript Division, Western History Collection, University of Oklahoma. It should also be noted that Mooar had mixed feelings about Dixon: "Red Lummis, Brick Bond, and Fred Singer had outfits and belonged to the other class from us. Billy Dixon was with this other class, but he was a rather better man than the outfit he ran with, though he was of that stripe." Ibid., November 25, 1927, Box 98A, Folder 6, 12. Similar controversies surround other aspects of the fight at Adobe Walls, and it is doubtful they will ever be explained to everyone's satisfaction. For a fair and reasoned discussion of this particular episode, see Baker and Harrison, *Adobe Walls*, 66–68.

there are many who doubt the specific details, especially the reported distance of 1,538 yards, it remains, at least in legend, the final defensive act in the Battle of Adobe Walls.

FIVE DAYS LATER WILLIAM OLDS STARTED down the ladder from his perch atop Rath & Co. Negotiating his decent with difficulty, while entertaining friends with a story of seeing a party of Indians riding by at a distance, the store clerk turned Indian fighter tripped the trigger of his rifle by accident, sending a bullet though his skull and splattering blood and brains across the room. Mrs. Olds, who during the battle had overcome her initial terror to reload rifles for the defenders, rushed into the room just in time to see her dead husband tumble to the floor. "Her grief was intense and pitiable," recalled Billy Dixon. "A rough lot of men, such as we were, did not know how to comfort a woman in such distress. We did the best we could, and if we did it awkwardly, it should not be set down against us."[57]

That gun's killing power, better than his own, impressed young Bat Masterson. He was encouraged to ask the grieving widow if he might borrow it in case the Indians returned. Hannah Olds agreed and Masterson retired to Hanrahan's. Learning that Bat was planning on pulling out for Dodge City, Mrs. Olds sent Frank J. Brown to retrieve her husband's rifle. There are two versions of what happened next. In neither one does Mr. Masterson fair particularly well, as both suggest he failed to return the gun to Mrs. Olds when asked.

As Billy Dixon recalled the details, Bat promised he would return it in the morning, Masterson's word guaranteed by James Hanrahan. At that point Frank Brown questioned everyone's honesty and was ejected from the saloon at gunpoint. As Brown told the story, he and Fred Leonard went to Hanrahan's with a note from Mrs. Olds asking for her husband's gun. Both were roughed up, Brown thrown out a window. He tried climbing back in, revolvers in hand, but was discouraged by a buffalo gun to the temple. A siege followed with actual shots fired. Sanity reasserted itself, a white flag displayed, and the rifle of Williams Olds returned.[58]

Where the truth lies in all this no one can say. Perhaps what it repre-

---

[57] Dixon, *Life of "Billy" Dixon*, 182–83.

[58] Baker and Harrison, *Adobe Walls*, 102–103. For more on this less than complimentary incident in the life of Mr. Masterson, see Robert K. DeArment, *Bat Masterson: The Man and the Legend* (Norman: University of Oklahoma Press, 1979), 46–48.

sents is clear evidence of the tremendous pressure everyone felt after being attacked by so many determined warriors, as well as not knowing if their adversaries planned to return.

The exact number of Indians involved in the fight at Adobe Walls, almost all Comanches and Cheyennes, is unknown, but evidence suggests between 200 and 300. The Indians attacked in small waves rather than commit their full strength to a single assault. Three days after the battle Fred Leonard wrote his partner Charlie Myers, saying, "There were 200 of them."[59] Two professionals from Fort Sill, interpreter Horace B. Jones and veteran scout "Comanche Jack" Stilwell, a survivor of the desperate fight at Beecher's Island in 1868, reported back to Colonel Davidson that 200 or 250 Indians had assaulted the compound.[60] These two reported the death of seven Comanches and four Cheyennes, adding, "The Indians themselves admit that a large number of their people were wounded and they fear a great many mortally. They claim to have killed 3 white men."[61] Later arrivals on the battlefield told of counting thirty graves on the surrounding hills. Despite an accurate count, the Indians had clearly suffered a major defeat.

As the days passed, others drifted into Adobe Walls for protection. With no help from Dodge City and evidence mounting that most of the Indians had withdrawn, the men decided to send out an expedition under James Hanrahan. Avoiding the main road, he and the others, thirty-five in all, including Billy Dixon, Bat Masterson, and Frank Brown, headed north.

---

[59] Fred Leonard to A. C. Myers, July 1, 1874. As reprinted in *Leavenworth Times*, July 10, 1874. Leonard also commented on the Indians' timing of the attack: "We were completely taken by surprise. Our men behaved like heroes. If the Indians had come one hour later, we would have been killed, and Dixon and Jim Hanrahan and their men would have been started on a hunt, leaving the place with only 17 men, and only half armed." At Topeka the *Kansas Daily Commonwealth* reported from their Dodge City correspondent on July 19, 1874, "From parties of buffalo-hunters who have just come in from Adobe Walls, I learn that a force of Indians, estimated at about 300, have laid siege to the trading ranches on the Canadian."

[60] Comanche Jack was also the older brother of Frank Stilwell, killed by Wyatt Earp in 1882 over his involvement in the murder of Earp's brother, Morgan. "Comanche Jack," whose actual name was Simpson E., traveled to southern Arizona shortly afterward to learn the circumstances surrounding his own brother's death. Wm. B. Shillingberg, *Tombstone, A.T.: A History of Early Mining, Milling and Mayhem* (Spokane, Wash.: The Arthur H. Clark Company, 1999), 320–21; and Capt. Robert G. Carter, *The Old Sergeant's Story* (New York: Frederick H. Hitchcock, Publishers, 1926), 116, 129. One contemporary offered the opinion, conceding Stilwell's reputation as "a downright law and order man," that he "would hate to be in Wyatt Earp's place if they met face to face in the open prairie." *Arizona Daily Star* (Tucson), April 30, 1882.

[61] Lt. Col. J. W. Davidson, Commanding Fort Sill, I.T., to Asst. Adj. Gen., Department of Texas, July 7, 1874, "I have the honor to submit the following reports of Messrs. Jones and Stilwell." Copy filed with Letters Received by the Office of Indian Affairs, Central Superintendency, after first being sent from the War Department to the Secretary of the Interior, August 1, 1874. In addition to statements from Jones and Stilwell, Fred Leonard estimated, "About 25 or 30 Indians were killed—we found 11." *Leavenworth Times*, July 10, 1874.

These refugees arrived at Dodge City on July 17, "getting through without being molested."[62] They carried with them Indian trophies from the battlefield (many of them destined for museums as far away as Chicago) and, for those who actually took part in the fight, incredible tales of danger and survival.

Still, no help arrived on the Canadian. Charlie Rath and A. C. Myers had telegraphed Governor Osborn on July 8, demanding that the military protect their supplies and employees. Concerned for the fate of those still in the Panhandle and fearing a general uprising along the Kansas frontier, Osborn communicated with General Pope. After reassuring the governor of his intention to protect settlers in Kansas, the general dismissed aid for Adobe Walls: "In relation to the trading firms at Dodge City who have, in violation of law and to the incalculable injury of the peaceful and honest farmers and frontier settlers of Kansas, established trading posts, or rather grog-shops in the Pan Handle of Texas, seventy-five miles south of the Arkansas, to trade with the buffalo hunters and ruffians who have invaded the Indian country and committed violent and inexcusable outrages upon the Indians, I have no word of sympathy or concern. They have justly earned all that may befall them, and if I were to send troops to the locality of these unlawful trading establishments, it would be to break them up and not to protect them."[63]

Pope reported to General Sheridan his contacts with the Kansas governor and his refusal "to send any troops down to the Pan Handle of Texas . . . to protect the illegal trading establishment and the buffalo hunters whose operations have, no doubt, largely contributed to this general outbreak."[64] At odds with his stubborn subordinate, Sheridan replied with

---

[62] *Leavenworth Daily Commercial*, July 26, 1874, as reprinted from the *Dodge City Messenger.* This article lists the names of all thirty-five men who left the Panhandle as part of the Hanrahan expedition. They made it through safely, but on their second day out, along San Francisco Creek, the men discovered the mutilated body of Henry Lease's partner, Charlie Sharp. They buried the badly decomposed remains before pushing on to Dodge City.

[63] W. M. Dunn, Jr., Acting Asst. Adj. Gen., Department of the Missouri (letter dispatched at the behest of Gen. John Pope) to Gov. Thomas A. Osborn, July 8, 1874. Headquarters, Department of the Missouri, Letters Sent. There was much false information circulating along the frontier concerning the true nature of the activities at Adobe Walls: "According to the best information I can obtain," wrote Thomas Battey, a Quaker schoolteacher among the Kiowas, "the object in establishing this outpost appears to have been to build up an illicit trading-post, where whiskey, arms, and ammunition may be exchanged with Indians for their stolen stock." Thomas C. Battey, *The Life and Adventures of a Quaker Among the Indians* (Boston: Lee & Shepard, Publishers, 1875), 311.

[64] Gen. John Pope to Gen Philip Sheridan, July 10, 1874. Headquarters, Department of the Missouri, Letters Sent. Also see Cozzens, *General John Pope*, 313–15. Some suggest that Pope, as commander of the Department of the Missouri, had no real authority at Adobe Walls. By this time, however, department boundaries had been redrawn to include all land in Texas and present-day Oklahoma north of the Canadian River, thus giving the general complete jurisdiction over the battlefield.

some heat that while in Texas the Dodge City men had every right to hunt or trade. Sheridan wrote General Sherman, complaining about Pope. As the army began gearing for war, Sherman insisted his two frontier commanders compose themselves.

Rath, Bob Wright, and Charlie Myers had been trying to arrange transportation into the Panhandle ever since couriers Lease and Reed reached Dodge City. The traders took it upon themselves to organize an expedition. Wright's old partner and independent freighter A. J. Anthony arranged the lease of twenty wagons and recruited an army of teamsters. Led by Thomas Nixon, nearly sixty armed men served as escorts. They left Dodge City on July 16 and reached Adobe Walls within a week.

The main purpose of this expedition was to retrieve buffalo hides abandoned after the fight. That such emphasis placed human lives on the second tier of concern mattered little to those still trapped in the Panhandle. To them the sight of the Dodge City caravan seemed a vision of salvation. Everyone helped with the work, which was made more difficult because hides had been scattered after June 27, to help eliminate places of concealment should the Indians return. For a fee even wagons belonging to other hunters were pressed into service for this important work. Thousands of hides were salvaged. Everyone and everything arrived back in Dodge City on August 5, except for a handful of men paid to stay behind and guard the buildings. Among the hide dealers hope survived that tensions would ease, allowing a renewal of the hunt, with the trading post at Adobe Walls again the main point of rendezvous.

EVENTS OFTEN ASSUME ACCELERATED momentum in times of crisis. War had come to the southern plains. In hindsight it seemed so unnecessary. If only a small portion of the energy and resources now unleashed against the tribes had been used to discourage buffalo hunting below the Kansas line, and to stop horse thieves and whiskey peddlers from invading Indian Territory, the uprising could have been avoided. U.S. Marshal William Tough's claim that "two deputies are as good as three, and less expensive to the government" appears all the more tragic and shortsighted, although Pope's indictment of Dodge City's trading firms was accurate.

Residents of that community not only helped start this war, they now reaped its rewards. Both Fort Dodge and the town became major supply points for the ensuing campaign. Great numbers of troops and civilian contract workers overran the town's limited resources, including saloons and other centers of amusement.

In overall command, Col. Nelson A. Miles launched his campaign from Fort Dodge. On August 11 he ordered Major Compton, along with four companies of cavalry and one of infantry, to scout the country between Camp Supply and Beaver Creek. Lt. Frank D. Baldwin of the Fifth Infantry, chosen chief of scouts, was detached from Compton's command and sent to Adobe Walls with eighteen soldiers and twenty Delaware Indians. Billy Dixon and Bat Masterson signed on as civilian scouts and they reached the battlefield on August 18. The lieutenant, nursing a decidedly sore rump, blamed on too much time as an infantry officer, questioned the caretakers before selecting a campsite for his men on Beaver Creek, just north of the original ruins.

The morning after Baldwin's arrival he and four others witnessed a dramatic encounter. Fifteen Indians were chasing five hunters back toward Adobe Walls. Two rode horses while the others urged their wagon and team forward. Bringing up the rear, hunter George Huffman was unhorsed, killed, and scalped within rifle range of the five soldiers. Baldwin and his men, caught unawares by the suddenness of the attack, ignored protocol and followed the others scrambling to safety. The lieutenant organized an expedition against the raiders, but only captured some Indian ponies.[65]

That night everyone—soldiers, hunters, and civilian scouts, along with their Delaware Indian allies—camped behind the picket walls of Myers and Leonard's hide yard. By morning all the hangers-on had decided to follow the soldiers out of the Panhandle. And so it was that on August 20 the Adobe Walls trading post, conceived at Dodge City amid so much enthusiasm that spring of 1874, was finally abandoned. Henceforth, only military units and occasional passers-by even bothered to stop and look around. With the place deserted at last, Indians returned and destroyed most everything left behind. They burned what they could; only the sod walls of Hanrahan's saloon survived this first attempt at destruction. The Indians also left behind the severed heads still decorating Myers and

[65] Baker and Harrison, *Adobe Walls*, 105–107; and Robert H. Steinbach, *A Long March: The Lives of Frank and Alice Baldwin* (Austin: University of Texas Press, 1989), 65–68. For another version of this episode, see Lemuel T. Wilson, "Scouting with Baldwin on the Texas Panhandle," Pampa (Texas) *Daily News*, September 29, 1933, as quoted in Peter Cozzens, ed., *Eyewitnesses to the Indian Wars, 1865–1890: Conquering the Southern Plains* (Mechanicsburg, Penn.: Stackpole Books, 2003), 507.

Leonard's corral gate. Indeed, for years afterward visitors walking the battlefield uncovered bones scattered over the ground, remains of the twelve
decapitated and unburied corpses, for as hunter W. C. Cox recalled, "we
pitched out their headless bodies like you would a dead dog's."[66]

Surviving the famous Buffalo Wallow fight on September 12, 1874 (for
which he and Amos Chapman became civilian recipients of the Congressional Medal of Honor), Billy Dixon joined an expedition from Fort
Dodge that stopped at Adobe Walls in late October. While there the hunter
welcomed an unexpected visitor. His dog, which had fled the battlefield in
panic with the other canines, reappeared. Dixon "was sure that she had
been killed by the Indians or wandered away and starved," but now,

> After we had petted her and fed her, Fannie disappeared. But her absence was
> brief. She came back with something in her mouth and stood wagging her tail,
> to attract attention. When we saw what she had brought to us every man
> grinned and was as tickled as if he were a boy. Fannie had brought a fat,
> bright-eyed little puppy in her mouth. Dropping the little fellow gently on the
> pile of bedding, she frisked about with delight as each of us tried to get hold
> of the pup and fondle it. Fannie bounded away while we were "fussing"
> among ourselves to see who should play with the pup. She came with another
> pup in her mouth, leaving it beside the other one. She made two more trips,
> until finally her family of four little ones were playing with each other on our
> bedding. The father of these pups was the big Newfoundland that belonged
> to the Shadler [sic] brothers, which the Indians killed while he was trying to
> defend his masters at the very beginning of the Adobe Walls fight. When we
> pulled out, Fannie and her babies were given a snug place in the mess wagon.[67]

With Adobe Walls abandoned, the influence of Dodge City's hide merchants along the Canadian faded, much to the relief of Camp Supply
traders Lee and Reynolds. Some suggested that those two approved the
attack, hoping to drive out competitors. One accuser, Judge O. H. Nelson,
an early resident of the area, went so far as to say they "hired Quanah
Parker to run the hunters out of Adobe Walls."[68] But by 1874 Indians
needed no encouragement to strike out against buffalo hunters. Besides,
the Camp Supply traders were the ones who sent Chapman and McAllister into the Panhandle with warnings for Charlie Rath and the others. Lee

---

[66] W. C. Cox to Ethel McConnell, interview, Childress, Texas (no date), as quoted in Baker and Harrison, *Adobe Walls*, 98. Cox, who arrived at the compound shortly after the battle, claims to have seen the bodies of thirteen Indians littering the field—one higher than Fred Leonard's count.

[67] Dixon, *Life of "Billy" Dixon*, 197–98.

[68] For this quotation from Judge O. H. Nelson, as well as for a fully documented discussion of this whole controversy, see Donald F. Schofield, "W. M. D. Lee, Indian Trader," *Panhandle-Plains Historical Review* 54 (1981): 58–60.

and Reynolds were in Dodge City many times afterward—each enumerated there on the 1875 Kansas State Census. They even formed a partnership with Charlie Rath in 1876 to hunt whatever buffalo still roamed the southern range—a strange association if any of their contemporaries suspected them of helping instigating the attack of June 27, 1874.

Dodge City businessmen profited from all the trouble, but they also feared its consequences, as did others along the Kansas frontier. From Ford County, frantic requests to Governor Osborn demanded arms to stiffen resolve. Following their repulse in the Panhandle, the Indians raided Kansas, Texas, New Mexico, and Colorado in the opening moves of the last great outbreak on the southern plains. Cheyennes placed the road between Fort Dodge and Camp Supply under siege. Larger settlements were safe, but isolated travelers and hunting parties, as well as ranchers and small bodies of soldiers, faced serious risk.

In early July, Agent John Miles reported the murder and mutilation of freighter Pat Hennessey and three others just north of Baker's abandoned ranch: "they had three wagons loaded with sugar & coffee for Agent Haworth all of which was destroyed or taken away. All the men were scalped. Hennessey had been tied to his wagon and burned."[69] Miles and his party buried the bodies and moved on. Deputy U.S. Marshal William Malaley rode with them but was troubled by the number of boot tracks found at the ambush site. At Buffalo Springs he began making inquiries. He discovered that former Dodge City troublemaker Billy Brooks and a couple of his horse-thieving friends claimed to have witnessed the attack. Pressed for details, Brooks grew evasive. The discovery of a wagon filled with Hennessey's supplies at a campsite used by the outlaws, along with two of his horses and six mules taken from Vail & Company, shifted blame from the Indians.[70] No one could prove if Brooks was guilty of murder or whether he or someone else had simply helped themselves to the abandoned cargo after the killings. Even though Malaley always suspected whites as being the ones responsible, other evidence suggested the possibility of a Cheyenne war party.[71]

---

[69] Telegram from John D. Miles to Edward P. Smith, July 7, 1874; and Miles to Smith, July 10, 1874. Upper Arkansas Agency.

[70] Roberts, "From Tin Star to Hanging Tree," 75. Also see *Sumner County Press*, July 10, 1874, and Wichita *City Eagle*, August 6, 1874.

[71] Roberts, "From Tin Star to Handing Tree," 65–68. For some of Malaley's activities surrounding this incident, see G. D. Freeman, *Midnight and Noonday; or, The Incidental History of Southern Kansas and the Indian Territory* (Caldwell, Kans.: G. D. Freeman, 1892), 234–36.

By early June, reports from the frontier filled Kansas newspapers with enough authentic news to convince anyone that there was serious trouble at hand. Whites tended to blame all the tribes, though most Kiowas and Arapahoes stood out of harm's way at their agencies.

One correspondent, J. T. Marshall, stopped at Dodge City and gave Alonzo Moore and his fledgling *Messenger* a friendly plug: "Like most managers of country papers, his duties are varied and complex, officiating as editor, compositor, pressman, bookkeeper and 'devil.' When he makes a 'strike' it is for a higher standard of excellence in the composition of his paper."[72] Other observers were not so generous: "It also struck us that [the] Dodge City Messenger must have tried to scare every body off the A. T. & S. F. Road from the manner in which it published wild rumors as 'reliable information.' In view of the real facts it must now feel rather cheap."[73]

Ignoring the vicissitudes of journalism, Indians raided all along the Santa Fe line. Soldiers from Fort Dodge guarded stations all the way to Granada, Colorado, but could not patrol everything in between. Even the outlaw element took notice: "Bully Brooks, formerly of Dodge City, and a number of ruffians of that kidney, have been driven in from the territory by fear of Indians, and are hanging around the cavalry and militia, casting wistful eyes at their horses."[74]

But the days of Billy Brooks eyeing horseflesh were numbered. After some animals stolen at Caldwell turned up for sale in Dodge City, authorities in Sumner County issued warrants for the arrest of several suspected stock thieves, including Brooks. Sheriff John G. Davis moved against the gang near Caldwell, arresting five. Brooks surrendered after some resistance. Fifteen other citizens rode into Indian Territory and arrested a sixth outlaw, the one-armed Charlie Smith.

At a preliminary hearing, Judge James A. Dillar discharged one prisoner outright before releasing another on bond. Billy Brooks and L. B. Hasbrouck, a local attorney suspected of aiding the outlaws, were tossed into the county jail along with Smith. The fourth prisoner was held elsewhere. Although men guarded the jail, a mob overpowered this meager force around midnight on July 29. They escorted the unrepentant trio of Brooks, Smith, and Hasbrouck toward the bridge over Slate Creek. There,

[72] *Kansas Daily Commonwealth*, July 11, 1874.

[73] *Hutchinson News*, July 2, 1874.

[74] *Kansas Daily Commonwealth*, July 11, 1874.

self-satisfied locals left the bodies of all three dangling from the same tree, facing Indian Territory, the scene of their most recent escapades.

Trying to calm those more concerned with Indians than outlaws, correspondent J. T. Marshall wrote: "The air is full of rumors of massacres, but they are so vague and contradictory as to create a doubt of their correctness."[75] Others explained the opening moves of what would be called the Red River War as simple exaggerations. Veteran Indian traders, such as James R. Mead and William Griffenstein, downplayed reports of three thousand Cheyennes, Arapahoes, and Kiowas going on the warpath. So did Dodge City merchant Richard Evans, then in Leavenworth buying supplies, who assured his listeners that back home the Indian scare was over.[76]

The press noted that all the trouble, including the brutal murder of Pat Hennessey, took place below the Kansas line—scant comfort to those living along that open border. Others blamed Hurricane Bill Martin with spreading rumors in order to frighten settlers into abandoning their homes, leaving behind property ripe for plunder. Concern mounted for ten herds of Texas cattle moving north between Red River and the stockyards at Wichita. Civilians all along the line formed militia companies and began stockpiling arms and ammunition. Yet, even amid all the seriousness, a note of levity crept in: "The Indians have invented a new method of scalping victims, so that now a bald-headed man stands no more show than any one else. This is as it should be."[77]

In early July, too late to make a difference, Wichita lawmen arrested Bill Martin and charged him with threatening an unarmed man. Perhaps fearing his reputation, no witnesses came forward to testify against the enterprising Hurricane Bill. Authorities released him from custody following fifty-six days behind bars. The next day the press jokingly remarked: "He proposes to take a hand in the Indian War as a scout and guide if a regiment is raised."[78]

As Nelson A. Miles prepared his own expedition at Fort Dodge, journalist Marshall wrote of the controversy between John Pope and the trading firms and hunters from Dodge City blamed by the general for the

---

[75] Ibid., July 12, 1874. For a sampling of Marshall's reports, expertly edited by Lonnie J. White, see J. T. Marshall, *The Miles Expedition of 1874–1875: An Eyewitness Account of The Red River War* (Austin: The Encino Press, 1971).

[76] *Leavenworth Daily Commercial,* July 18, 1874.

[77] *Kansas Daily Commonwealth,* July 14, 1874.

[78] Wichita *City Eagle,* September 3, 1874.

outbreak, and for whom he had "no word of sympathy or concern."[79] Not surprisingly, Marshall sided with the locals, claiming Dodge City merchants were in no way responsible for the outbreak: "They are shrewd, go-ahead business men, and the imputations of the general are unwarranted, to say the least."[80] Later Marshall claimed, prematurely as it turned out, "a more quiet, orderly town is not found on the frontier."[81]

Changes had taken place. Thanks to Sheriff Charlie Bassett, Dodge City had grown comparatively quiet. Since the murder of William Taylor the year before, Ford County's chief lawman had enlisted the aid of two deputies, first hiring Jerome Sackett in early 1874, followed that summer by the addition of Edward O. Hougue from Ellsworth.

Authorities of that booming cattle town had named Hougue their chief of police two years before. Later he served as an ordinary policeman, while at the same time working as a deputy sheriff. Using entries in the Ellsworth police docket, it appears that Hougue performed well as an officer. The high point of his career came in August 1873, when he arrested the notorious Ben Thompson, after Thompson's drunken brother, William, shotgunned the county sheriff by accident. Ben held the town at bay until Billy escaped. Enraged, Mayor James Miller fired the entire police force. Deputy Sheriff Ed Hougue and two citizens stepped forward to confront Thompson, who surrendered without incident.[82] That same day Hougue was again appointed Ellsworth's police chief.

Relieved after only twelve days, he ran unsuccessfully for county sheriff a month later. Soon afterward he hired out as a night watchman to some

---

[79] W. M. Dunn, Jr., Acting Asst. Adj. Gen., Department of the Missouri (dispatched at the behest of Gen. John Pope) to Gov. Thomas A. Osborn, July 8, 1874. Department of the Missouri, Letters Sent.

[80] *Kansas Daily Commonwealth*, August 8, 1874.

[81] Ibid., August 15, 1874.

[82] *Ellsworth Reporter*, August 21, 1873. For more on this incident, see State of Kansas vs. William Thompson, Records of the Ellsworth County District Court, Interrogatories and Depositions. Returned to Kansas for trial nearly four years later, Billy was finally acquitted on September 14, 1877. It has often been suggested that future Dodge City peace officer Wyatt Earp arrested Ben Thompson on that sultry August day in 1873, but no credible evidence has ever surfaced to support the claim, first postulated in the fanciful Stuart N. Lake, *Wyatt Earp, Frontier Marshal* (Boston: Houghton Mifflin Company, 1931), 84–94. There the matter stands, or so it seems, despite Ben's alleged remark to his attorney, "Here came Ed Hogue [*sic*] and *two others* [emphasis added], supported by some citizens at a distance, all armed with muskets, pistols and guns ready for action." No name, Wyatt Earp's or otherwise, has ever been attached to those "two others." Perhaps Earp devotees find it difficult to counter Thompson's other characterization: "Hogue and his *two cubs*. . . ." [emphasis added] W. M. Walton, *Life and Adventures of Ben Thompson, the Famous Texan* (Austin, Texas: Published by the Author, 1884), 117, 119. For additional information on this disquieting episode, see Miller and Snell, *Why the West Was Wild*, 635–40; and Floyd Benjamin Streeter, *Ben Thompson: Man with a Gun* (New York: Frederick Fell, Inc., 1957), 91–115.

local businessmen. With his fortunes in decline, Hougue remained in and around Ellsworth until 1874. On the evening of May 30, with $150 paid "for services done as a detective," he left a card game looking for trouble. At the door, Hougue called to a group of unarmed Texas drovers to step forward or be shot. City marshal J. Charles Brown, joined by one policeman and a deputy sheriff, arrested the former police chief: "After a day's confinement Hogue [sic] wisely came to terms and on the promise to leave the city and to keep the peace he was allowed to depart."[83] Hougue traveled to Dodge City where Charlie Bassett, recognizing his talents when sober, hired the twenty-eight-year-old Frenchman as a Ford County deputy sheriff. Hougue satisfied his new boss and hung around Dodge City for the next three years.

Charlie Bassett and his two assistants may have quieted the streets of Dodge City, but the Indians made the country for miles around hazardous. A party from Lawrence, organized in Dodge by Capt. Oliver F. Short in late July, had contracted to survey many miles of section lines. A month later Capt. Luther Thrasher, the expedition's second in command, discovered a wagon and six bodies, including those of Short's fifteen-year-old son. Suspicion pointed to a party of Cheyennes who had chased some hunters a day or two before.

Robert Armstrong, another government surveyor who left Dodge City in early August with fourteen others, found four dead men—identified as John Doyle, John McDonald, William Graham, and an elderly fellow named Snyder—killed near old Fort Aubrey. All four were returning from the Colorado mines when overtaken; everyone but the old man traveling on foot. Snyder tried to escape toward the railroad station at Aubrey but was cut down. The Santa Fe shipped the bodies to Granada for burial.

Other Indians rode north and struck Pierceville, a small hamlet west of Dodge City. They burned one house and killed a horse. A squad of cavalry joined the pursuit, accompanied by James Hanrahan and his partner, Moses Waters. Around the same time, twenty-five Indians assaulted Henry Sitler about eight miles from town. Wounded, he survived. Others found the countryside less hazardous. Bob Wright returned to Dodge from Camp Supply without incident. He did, however, relate details of a des-

---

[83] *Ellsworth Reporter*, June 4, 1874.

[84] *Kansas Daily Commonwealth*, September 27, 1874.

perate encounter between soldiers and Indians. As events to the south grew more ominous it was said: "Fort Dodge is almost without a garrison, and the state will have, in case of an Indian incursion, to be defended by the militia."[84] Meanwhile the Fort Leavenworth quartermaster ordered two million pounds of corn and one hundred thousand pounds of oats sent to Dodge City for shipment south in support of the army.

Mindful of General Pope's statements concerning Dodge City, editor Alonzo W. Moore missed no opportunity to show his contempt for that officer. Describing another Indian raid near Pierceville, this time against some eighty head of cattle owned by S. D. Bancroft, the *Dodge City Messenger* added: "What about that 'protection' to the settlers on the frontier, that Gen. Pope talked about? Where are all these soldiers that he said he had strung along the border? Pope's protection to the settlers is a myth. The fact is, the Department of the Missouri needs a Custer."[85]

Others thought buffalo hunters could take care of themselves. In reporting James Hanrahan's party losing twenty-four head of horses and mules during a single raid, one Leavenworth editor informed his readers that Tom Nixon and other hunters had skirmished with Indians south of the Cimarron, killing one warrior and capturing sixteen horses. Nixon and his men shot six of the animals and took the others back to Dodge City: "The hunters are nearly all out after buffalo, and well armed and provisioned, and prepared to meet almost any body of the marauding Indians. The troops are doing nothing, but the hardy buffalo hunters claim that they need no protection."[86]

Despite reports of Indians waylaying surveyors, hunters, and ordinary citizens, as well as military contact with hostiles, the wheels of democracy kept turning. On November 3, 1874, the state held its general election. Thomas A. Osborn held on as governor, while in Ford County minor changes took place in local government. Robert Wright replaced James Hanrahan as the area's representative in the legislature, polling all 140 votes cast. Other offices, including sheriff and seats on the county commission, remained the same, as none were scheduled for the ballot until 1875. Dodge City showed its appreciation to Judge W. R. Brown for his efforts follow-

[85] *Leavenworth Daily Commercial*, September 26, 1874. As quoted from the *Dodge City Messenger.*
[86] *Leavenworth Daily Commercial*, November 8, 1874.

ing the murder of William Taylor, supporting his successful campaign for congress with 132 votes.[87]

As winners celebrated victory and losers drowned their sorrows, the state prepared to confront a second invasion, this time an infestation of Rocky Mountain locusts.[88] Officials at Topeka devised an aid package that of course included Ford County. The very thought of assistance caused a small revolt. Locals preferred to think of themselves as hardy individualists and turned the money down. A month later it was said, "several destitute recipients of army blankets and relief goods" had turned their backs on three dollars a day offered by the railroad to clear snow from its tracks between Dodge City and Kinsley. Instead, they demanded four dollars. Such ingratitude sparked the comment: "It strikes us that a man who can't afford to work for his bread when work is offered him, at good prices, is too well off to depend on charity."[89] Other standards stayed the same: "During the cold snap whiskey did not freeze in Dodge City."[90]

With military forces confronting Cheyennes, Comanches, and some Kiowas, the number of civilian freighters traveling between Dodge City and Camp Supply rose to record numbers. For months dusty streets echoed with the sounds of military traffic. Freighting was hard work and those so engaged played hard, all to the delight of Dodge City merchants and saloonkeepers, who watched cash boxes fill with coin and script. Many locals, including Bob Wright, got involved in this temporary but welcomed windfall. So did some not generally associated with the mule team and bullwhip: one mother and daughter worked together hauling freight between the town and Fort Dodge.

With winter close at hand, many assumed the army would suspend its campaign until spring. But the military surprised its critics with a plan that involved troops converging on the warring tribes from all directions. In the main effort Nelson Miles struck south from Fort Dodge. Col. Ranald S. Mackenzie attacked north from Fort Concho, Texas, while Maj. William

---

[87] For complete elections returns, see Ford County Commissioners Journals, Book A, 51.

[88] These terrible insects represented a maddening scourge, and yet, primarily due to inadvertent human activity, they are now gone. Grasshoppers still cause trouble, but the last swarm of Rocky Mountain locusts seen in North America, and a small one at that, took place in Manitoba in 1902. Jeffrey A. Lockwood, *Locust: The Devastating Rise and Mysterious Disappearance of the Insect That Shaped the American Frontier* (New York: Basic Books, 2004), xvii.

[89] *Kansas Daily Commonwealth*, January 19, 1875.

[90] *Hutchinson News*, January 28, 1875. As quoted from the *Dodge City Messenger.*

Price marched east from New Mexico. Supporting these thrusts, Lt. Col. George Buell drove westward from Fort Richardson, Texas, and Lt. Col. John Davidson moved in the same direction from Fort Sill. The Indians mounted a spirited defense but stood little chance against this coordinated offensive. Resistance lingered into the spring of 1875, but by the end of April it was all over, with Indian leaders awaiting their fate at the hands of a less than understanding enemy.

Forgetting they helped instigate this last great uprising on the southern plains, citizens of Dodge City rejoiced over the defeat of the Comanches and Cheyennes. As the Red River War reached its climax, the town looked forward to the future, a promising vision offering economic prosperity no longer so dependent on buffalo.

Chapter 6

Securing the
Texas Cattle Trade

By May 1875 a disgruntled Alonzo W. Moore gave up on the *Dodge City Messenger*. During its short but colorful run the paper endured its share of criticism, yet also earned grudging praise. One influential daily described it as "one of the spiciest, best edited and newsy of our exchanges."[1] Finding no buyers, Dodge City's pioneer editor simply packed up and left town, firing his final salvo on June 5: "The Messenger collapsed for the want of an appreciation on the part of the business men to sustain a good newspaper. Such is life."[2]

For a time Dodge City's former editor ran the *Harvey County News* at Newton, then moved on, prompting speculation: "A. W. Moore last week sold his interest in the *News* to his partner . . . and will possibly hunt up another worn out outfit soon like the one just disposed of, for another similar speculation." That remark may have been harsh, but it was prophetic. By 1883, after time spent at Topeka, Alonzo W. Moore was reported back in the newspaper business at Gunnison, Colorado.[3]

The headstrong publisher may have decamped too soon. Despite declining revenues from buffalo, a small item published at Topeka in early May 1875 signaled a shift in fortune: "The Atchison, Topeka & Santa Fe Railroad Company will erect stock yards near Dodge City this spring, suf-

---

[1] *Leavenworth Daily Commercial*, November 28, 1874.

[2] *Dodge City Times*, February 2, 1878. Quoted from an old copy of the *Messenger* discovered by local attorney Michael Sutton.

[3] *Newton Kansan*, December 7, 1876. Also see *History of the State of Kansas*, 773, 1560. Alonzo W. Moore spent much of his adult life in Topeka. During the years 1856 and 1857 he was elected first as door keeper and then as sergeant at arms of the Kansas State House of Representatives. He returned to Topeka after his Colorado sojourn, but eventually fell on hard times. By the turn of the century he worked as a schoolhouse janitor. He would, however, put his life back in order, and well into his seventies reestablish himself as a job printer. With frontier resilience A. W. Moore survived into his mid-eighties. Along the way he married and fathered two children, only one of whom lived to see the twentieth century.

ficient to accommodate the cattle which may be shipped from that point."[4] The AT&SF and the Kansas Pacific competed for this business: the former from its vast facilities at Wichita, and the latter at Ellsworth. Often seen as a handicap, Dodge City's geographic isolation appealed to the railroad's board of directors, men now charmed by its wide-open possibilities. Within an hour of arriving early on the evening of May 18, Capt. D. G. Stockwell, the railroad's livestock agent, ordered the construction of a small 50-by-60-foot holding pen.[5]

That summer two hundred newspapermen, some coming from as far as New York, traveled as guests of the Santa Fe on one of the company's many propaganda excursions. Crowding nine coaches hauled across the wilderness by two steam locomotives, they arrived at Dodge City tired and unkempt but ready for the grand tour. Primed by a festive reception at Fort Dodge, they were taken out and shown the grazing and agricultural possibilities of Ford County, where vegetables and grains already showed promise. Local townspeople wanted none of it: "The people of Dodge City differ from those of most places. They don't want settlers on the plains around them. They want to make their place the great cattle mart of the West."[6]

Ford County remained uninterested in the plow, some said uninterested in civilization. Fort Dodge quartermaster Ezra Kirk reported, "The Arkansas valley is infested by a bold gang of horse thieves. A vigilance committee has been organized at Dodge City, and it would not be surprising if some of the telegraph poles were found ornamented some of these days."[7] Threats had little effect on the outlaws, but Dodge witnessed other examples of discord. Following an argument of hazy origin, saloonman Thomas Sherman shot Ford County clerk William F. Sweeney. As the injured man convalesced, deputy clerk J. H. Boyle assumed those duties until his boss reappeared, somewhat subdued by the experience.

The town shrugged off criticism, but those in saloon-free Hutchinson found other reasons to complain: "The dinner at Dodge City would have been better received, if the champagne had been omitted. Wine and other liquor are a played out institution."[8] That may have been true in righteous

---

[4] *Kansas Daily Commonwealth*, May 2, 1875.

[5] *Annual Report of the Board of Directors of the Atchison, Topeka, and Santa Fe Railroad Co. . . . for the year ending December 31, 1875* (Boston: Franklin Press: Rand, Avery, and Company, 1876), 40.

[6] *Kansas Daily Commonwealth*, September 7, 1875.

[7] Ibid., July 14, 1875.

[8] *Hutchinson News*, July 1, 1875.

Reno County, but not in Dodge City, where saloons remained major institutions of free enterprise. None of this dampened enthusiasm from Texas cattlemen.

Watching the AT&SF's crowded cattle cars roll by from grazing lands in Colorado, local businessmen imagined their own profits piling high. At Topeka plans to dominate that trade—not just from Colorado, but from capturing most of the trail herds coming north from the rich grasslands of south Texas—crowded boardroom debate. The Santa Fe's scheme depended on Dodge City becoming the greatest shipping point for cattle the West had ever seen. The year 1875 proved the turning point.

The economic shift from buffalo came just in time. Scattered remnants of those once-vast herds still showed up along the railroad line, but only in numbers mocking the glory years of 1872–73. Local interest turned from bison to beef with ease, ignoring the tannery built by Charlie Rath and Bob Wright the year before, which still processed some two thousand hides annually. Reflecting the town's beginnings, buffalo steaks and venison remained popular staples in most Dodge City restaurants.

The town's economy might be changing, but its reputation worried outsiders. On Sunday, October 3, 1875, Lydia English and her family passed through on their way from Concordia, Kansas, to Prescott, Arizona. Noting the toll bridge, Mrs. English scribbled other entries into her sparse diary: "No Sabbath at Dodge. Saloons all open, and men and women hauling hay. Dodge is a very rough, dirty looking place. Saw the first large herd of Texas cattle here seen in the valley."[9] She saw no reason for decent people to settle there.

Mrs. English may have been put off by what she saw, but others found the place just to their liking. The coming of Texas cattle convinced Bavarian boot maker John Mueller to abandon Ellsworth and his seat on its city council. Friends assumed he had "gone to the new town, near the Military Post, in the Pan Handle of Texas."[10] Instead, the thirty-four-year-old arrived in Dodge City with his wife and two small children, renting space on Front Street, two lots west of the Dodge House. This veteran of Ellsworth seemed perfect for Dodge City. Two years before he got involved in a feud with a cattle dealer named Charles Stransenback. Finding them-

[9] Joseph W. Snell, ed., "By Wagon From Kansas to Arizona in 1875—The Travel Diary of Lydia E. English," *The Kansas Historical Quarterly* 36, no. 4 (Winter 1970): 374.

[10] *Ellsworth Reporter*, September 23, 1875; and Records of the City of Ellsworth, Minutes of the City Council, August 17, 1875, 181.

selves standing face to face in a Kansas City saloon, they traded harsh words and gunfire. Both survived.

On November 2, 1875, as if celebrating its changing status, Judge Samuel R. Peters of the Ninth Judicial District ordered Dodge incorporated in what the State of Kansas classified as a City of the Third Class, thus allowing formal organization of municipal government. It did not require voter registration, however, an oversight leading to repeated charges of ballot stuffing and, on occasion, the importation of fraudulent voters. Peters accepted a citizens' petition, establishing the town's boundaries and claiming some three hundred inhabitants. With no newspaper, locals satisfied the publication requirement by posting incorporation notices throughout the townsite. Judge Peters ordered the first municipal election to take place on December 1, appointing Charles Rath, Morris Collar, and Charles Bassett election judges, while naming W. F. Sweeney and Daniel Frost election clerks, with A. B. Webster, R. W. Evans, and A. J. Peacock serving as a board of canvas to count votes.[11]

On the same day that Judge Peters ordered incorporation, voters cast ballots in the regular county election. One dissenter wrote Governor Osborn, complaining: "Parties this morning with closed doors organized a board of election before the hour of eight, and the sheriff then unlocked the door from the inside and declared the polls open. Myself and colleague stepped in, and claimed our right to sit as judges of election, and were ejected with violence. What is our remedy?" The governor suggested, "I know of no remedy except to contest the validity of the election in the courts."[12] Despite this harassment charge against Sheriff Bassett, the results stood. Attorney Daniel Frost replaced Robert Wright as the area's representative in the legislature and Jim Kelley's new saloon partner, Pettis L. Beatty, continued on as township trustee.[13] And now, on the first of December 1875, Mr. Beatty won the right to serve as Dodge City's mayor.

Beatty had been a sergeant with the Sixth Cavalry at Fort Dodge before leaving the army on August 24, 1873, to cast his fortune with the year-old town. He replaced James H. "Dog" Kelley's original partner, John Hunt, in a saloon and restaurant business that became known as Beatty & Kelley. On

---

[11] Records of the Ford County District Court, Judge's Journal, Book A, 33–34. Although the formalities took place far to the east in another county, Judge Peters directed: "that this order of incorporation be entered at length in the Journal of proceedings of the District Court of Ford County Kansas and that . . . Copies of this Order be posted in conspicuous places in Said Dodge City at least one week before the election."

[12] *Kansas Daily Commonwealth*, November 3, 1875.

[13] Ford County Commissioners Journals, Book A, 105.

November 18, 1873, the Town Company granted the new partners title to the two lots on the northwest corner of Front Street and First Avenue, where Kelley's frame building already stood.[14] This gave them a fifty-foot front on the town's main thoroughfare, from the start a popular site with Texas men.

P. L. Beatty had enjoyed an interesting military career. In September 1861 he joined the Seventh Illinois Infantry as a three-month enlistee. Two years later he reenlisted, this time with the Second Cavalry from his native New York. In between, he spent nearly a year with the navy, serving on two gunboats as part of the Mississippi Squadron. Three years after the war he reenlisted in the cavalry and ended up in Kansas by way of Texas. It was Sergeant Beatty, along with scout and later Dodge City saloonman Tom Sherman, who chased the horse thieves following the "grand steal" against railroad grading crews in the summer of 1872, winning praise from Major Dodge. The following February Beatty ran afoul of the army, charged with being absent from his company "without permission from proper authority . . . until arrested in the Post Traders Store."[15] For this he forfeited ten dollars' pay. But now, in late 1875, the thirty-two-year-old ex-trooper-turned-mayor chaired meetings of the new city council and helped write Dodge City's first ordinances.

Trying to codify standards for local government, the council set meetings for itself on the first Tuesday of each month. They set the salary for city marshal (the mayor and councilmen served without compensation), established provisions for liquor licenses at one hundred dollars a year, paid quarterly, and set monthly rates for other businesses, most ranging from five to ten dollars. None of this applied to "any person selling produce of any kind raised in this County or to the Hunters selling game venison or Buffalo meat."[16]

The council tried to influence personal conduct, especially drunkenness and profanity. The law now forbade the discharging of firearms, firecrackers, and fireballs and lighting bonfires. Exceptions were made for George Washington's birthday, the Fourth of July, Christmas, and New Year's Day. Reflecting cattle town experiences elsewhere, as well as their

[14] Ford County Register of Deeds, Book A, 5–6. The saloon was called the Alhambra and the restaurant boasted "meals at all hours." Between those businesses Beatty and Kelley allowed two outsiders to open the Centennial Barber Shop: "shaving, shampooing and haircutting done in the latest fashion."

[15] Headquarters Records, Fort Dodge, Kansas; General Order, No. 3, February 6, 1873; and Maj. Richard Dodge to Judge Advocate, Department of the Missouri, February 7, 1873. Fort Dodge, Letters Sent. Also see Pettis L. Beatty, Military and Pension Records, National Archives and Records Service.

[16] Ordinance No. 5, Sec. 1, December 24, 1875. Dodge City Ordinances, Book A, 5.

own days as a hunters' rendezvous, city fathers passed an ordinance on Christmas Eve outlawing the carrying of deadly weapons—violators risked fines ranging from three to twenty-five dollars.[17]

To enforce their mandates the council hired thirty-year-old Lawrence E. Deger as the town's first city marshal. An Ohio-born son of Swiss immigrants, Larry Deger came to Kansas from Wisconsin, settling first at Hays City. Commenting on his appointment at Dodge, the newspaper there noted the novice lawman's impressive bulk: "L. E. Deger is the big man of the town, weighing 307 lbs. He wears on the lapel of his coat a badge with the word 'Marshal.' Larry takes the same interest in church affairs here as he did in Hays City."[18]

Deger proved himself a reliable officer, and by the spring of 1876 Charles E. Miller, the newly appointed United States marshal for Kansas, named him his deputy at Dodge City. The new marshal also performed less glamorous tasks. Worrying about fires, the city council ordered Deger to examine all flues, chimneys, and stovepipes, demanding owners make repairs by January 15. Violators faced a fifty-dollar fine.[19] The marshal also needed to guarantee that fire barrels along major thoroughfares remained full. For all this, including keeping the peace, Larry Deger was paid the grand sum of fifty dollars a month, a figure that later fluctuated between seventy-five and one hundred dollars, depending on the busyness of the cattle season.

Looking back, Dodge City's involvement with the Texas cattle trade seems inevitable, even with fewer than five hundred animals shipped that first year. And yet the process that brought Texas herds into Kansas, and eventually to Ford County, involved a complicated series of physical conditions tied to an appetite for political maneuvering and legal manipulation.

BEFORE THE CIVIL WAR, small allotments of Texas cattle had reached Kansas City, Westport, and other Missouri river towns, with some going as far east as St. Louis and various Illinois border settlements. Other destinations included New Orleans, then the largest market for cattle in the South, as well as Mobile, Alabama. Those animals were either driven overland into

---

[17] Ordinance No. 4, Sec. 8, December 24, 1875. Ibid., 4. The new city government merely followed guidelines established earlier by the county, see Ford County Commissioners Journals, Book A, 32.

[18] *Ellis County Star,* April 6, 1876.

[19] Ordinance No. 6, Sec. I, December 24, 1875. Dodge City Ordinances, Book A, 7.

Louisiana or shipped from Galveston, Corpus Christi, and other gulf ports. Thousands more were driven to California gold camps during the early 1850s, "the first long-distance drives in the history of the range-cattle business."[20] West Coast markets paid higher prices than New Orleans.

The war changed everything. At first large numbers of Texas cattle were sent across the Mississippi to help feed hungry Confederates. Then New Orleans fell to Adm. David Farragut and was occupied by Gen. Benjamin Butler. With U. S. Grant closing the river to Southern commerce after the surrender of Vicksburg in 1863, the wild herds roaming south Texas became virtually useless for sustenance or profit.

At war's end financially strapped Texans began eyeing northern markets for beef. Cattle were cheap in Texas and former enemies offered tempting prices for the soon-to-be-famous longhorn, an animal that was "of no undistinguished ancestry in spite of his appearance," one historian observed. "They were of light carcass with long legs, sloping ribs, thin loins and rumps, and a disproportionately large belly. In color they were nondescript, yellow, red, dun, and black, with often an iron-grey stripe along the back. Their meat was coarse and stringy, 'teasingly tough.' They were almost as wild as the buffalo that they supplanted on the plains, for behind them were generations of untamed ancestors. To drive a herd of such beasts, to work them over, to brand and ship them to market meant a business that would not be without adventure and danger."[21]

Responding to demand, novice stock raisers in central and southeastern Texas started rounding up these long-neglected animals. The year 1866 witnessed the birth of the great Texas trail drives. At first it did not go well. The plan itself, as old as cattle raising in America, envisioned the product walking itself to market, or at least to the nearest railroad. Texans and northern dealers searched for a site far enough from settlements to avoid confrontations with angry farmers and others crowding in around

---

[20] *Prose and Poetry of the Live Stock Industry of the United States* (New York: Antiquarian Press, Ltd., 1959), ed. by James W. Freeman and originally published in 1905 by the National Live Stock Historical Association, 392. The trail started from either San Antonio or Clarksville and headed west to El Paso (then called Franklin City), across New Mexico and on through Guadalupe Pass to Tucson, Arizona. From there trail bosses followed the traditional route west, passing the Pima villages, following the Gila River to Yuma, then on to San Diego or Los Angeles. From those points the animals were scattered across the state toward San Francisco, Sacramento, and into the gold regions of the Sierra foothills. This commerce continued intermittently until 1860, although the years 1853–54 saw the heaviest volume, after which rejuvenated local herds began satisfying demand.

[21] Ernest Staples Osgood, *The Day of the Cattleman* (Minneapolis: The University of Minnesota Press, 1929), 26–27.

places like Sedalia.[22] The central plains, already benefiting from the post-war railroad boom, seemed to offer a reasonable alternative to those older trails into Missouri. Even as the Union Pacific's Eastern Division, soon renamed the Kansas Pacific, continued pushing westward, questions of where to locate a shipping point remained unanswered. This confusion mirrored a legislative response to a natural phenomenon.

A disease commonly called Texas fever—but also known as Spanish, splenic, or simply Southern cattle fever—proved deadly to domesticated stock. Although half-wild longhorns enjoyed a partial immunity, they did act as carriers of the microscopic tick responsible for the disease. The earliest documented cases in the United States date from an 1814 Philadelphia report on cattle brought up from South Carolina. The source was unknown. Yet, in referring to cattle from southern Texas, one government authority noted in 1885: "So long as cattle born and raised in this Gulf section remain there, Texas fever is unknown among them. But when they are driven or transported to the northern part of Texas, or to the States and Territories of the northwest, they communicate the disease to the cattle of these more northern latitudes."[23] Cattlemen remarked that cold weather seemed to offer protection—it actually killed the parasites responsible.

Northern breeders understood the danger from south Texas stock. Cattlemen trying to overcome these fears during the summer and fall of 1866 saw their hopes blocked by legal barriers, as well as by armed bands in eastern Kansas and southwestern Missouri determined to halt the invasion. Trail bosses held their herds at Baxter Springs, Kansas, while trying to find a point of compromise. A few head made it to Chicago, while others sold at high prices to farmers as far away as Iowa. Texans made money, but nothing compared with what was to come. Some rather adroit political maneuvering needed to take place before this era that launched a legend could begin.

With their herds stalled at Baxter Springs, desperate Texans had no idea that powerful forces in Kansas, all willing to ignore the statewide quaran-

---

[22] Louis Pelzer, *The Cattlemen's Frontier: A record of the trans-Mississippi cattle industry from oxen trains to pooling companies, 1850–1890* (Glendale, Calif.: The Arthur H. Clark Company, 1936), 37. Dr. Pelzer noted, "In 1866 about a quarter of a million long-horned Texas cattle were started for Sedalia, Missouri, but the drovers meeting various obstacles and objections, diverted the herds to other points."

[23] Joseph Nimmo, Jr., "Range and Range Cattle Traffic in the Western States and Territories," House Ex. Doc. No. 267, 48th Cong., 2nd Sess. (Washington, 1885), 29. For more on this early scourge, including the views of cattleman John S. Chisum, see C. C. Hutchinson, *Resources and Development of Kansas* (Topeka: Published by the Author, 1871), 117–19; and James Cox, *Historical and Biographical Records of the Cattle Industry and the Cattlemen of Texas and Adjacent Territory* (St. Louis: Woodward & Tiernan Printing Company, 1895), 71–84.

tine on Texas cattle, had already begun working their magic along the corridors of the state capital at Topeka. The resulting legislation opened Kansas west of Dickinson County and allowed cattle to be sent east by rail. Now, cattlemen needed only a specific shipping point.

Town boosters and other commercial pirates offered choices reflecting self-interest. For a time, Ellsworth, Junction City, and Salina all looked promising. In an odd twist, the place chosen was Abilene. As the seat of Dickinson County, it lay well within the dreaded "dead line"—the popular term for the quarantine boundary. Ignoring that legal impediment, the three McCoy brothers from Sangamon County, Illinois, orchestrated the necessary behind-the-scenes political support for this clearly illegal site.

That family, of southern origin but also among the earliest settlers around Springfield, operated as William K. McCoy & Bros. They had turned from farming to livestock trading before the Civil War, at a time when Illinois produced more beef cattle than anywhere except Texas and shipped more livestock to eastern markets than any other state. After Appomattox they expanded with shipments as far away as New Orleans and New York, before shifting attention on those vast herds wandering the southern plains. Representing the family, Joseph G. McCoy traveled to Kansas. That talented young businessman—who falsely took full credit for the plan of shipping cattle off the plains by rail—found others working hard on the same idea. Because of the new quarantine law, Ellsworth County seemed favored to win the prize.

Undaunted, McCoy worked out agreements with the railroads allowing shipments as far as Chicago. With contracts in hand, he began looking for a place to begin operations. He dismissed a number of sites before joining up with Charlie Thompson, the founder of Abilene. "Abilene was selected because the country was entirely unsettled, well watered, excellent grass, and nearly the entire area of country was adapted to hold cattle," wrote McCoy, by way of justification. "And it was the farthest point east at which a good depot for cattle business could have been made."[24]

Joseph McCoy, a man with the rare ability of combining tact and brashness, traveled to Topeka and confronted Gov. Samuel Crawford, the

---

[24] Joseph G. McCoy, *Historic Sketches of the Cattle Trade of the West and Southwest* (Kansas City, Mo.: Ramsey, Millett & Hudson, 1874), 50. For more information on this important family, see John Carroll Power, *History of the Early Settlers of Sangamon County, Illinois* (Springfield, Ill.: Edwin A. Wilson & Co., 1876), 487–88; *History of Sangamon County, Illinois* (Chicago: Inter-State Publishing Company, 1881), 817; and *Portrait and Biographical Album of Sedgwick County, Kan.* (Chicago: Chapman Brothers, 1888), 676–77.

same man who had signed the modified quarantine bill less than six months before. Crawford was made to see the benefits to his state and its citizens by helping circumvent the very law he was sworn to uphold. The governor more or less supported McCoy's choice of Abilene. With the tacit approval of the state's chief executive, McCoy finalized his plans.

Ignoring the legalities, cattlemen pointed their herds north. Farmers and other settlers of Dickinson County—whose presence McCoy conveniently failed to mention in his popular memoir—rose up in protest. Supporters calmed fears by cleverly contracting county produce at prices well above market value. Resistance crumbled as everyone awaited their chance to make money. While Dickinson County ignored enforcement of the quarantine law, Abilene proclaimed itself the major shipping point for Texas cattle in the state of Kansas. Other towns tried advertising their advantages, but it was Abilene that showed the way, setting a standard of conduct that continued at other locations well into the 1880s.

Ellsworth's organizers had Texas cattle in mind from the beginning. The Kansas Pacific gave its approval. Directors understood that settlement would eventually choke off Abilene. As early as the 1872 season Ellsworth positioned itself as a major shipping point. But Ellsworth would suffer the same fate as its rivals. In time settlement and agriculture overtook the Texans. More isolated sites needed to be found farther west.

Even so, Ellsworth fought off competition from Salina, Brookville, Solomon, and other towns. With the advance of the AT&SF into the Southwest, new shipping points opened up. Newton cornered the market for one brief but eventful season, before Wichita became Ellsworth's chief rival during the early 1870s. Even so, cattle provided only a temporary windfall. Eventually all eyes turned toward Dodge City.

Those long drives from Texas represented a great gamble, an American adventure as indicative of the nation's character as any of its other endeavors. Popular romance aside, nothing can detract from this simple reality and the honest acknowledgment of what actually took place on those long dusty trails pointing north from the Rio Grande.

As buffalo hunters cleared the grasslands of western Kansas, Texas cattlemen relished the possibilities for their own industry. A few head moved over the AT&SF from Sargent and Great Bend as early as 1873. Smaller shipments were even made from Dodge City the following year. By 1875, with the Indians defeated and the local economy suffering the lostbuffalo revenues and cancelled military freighting contracts, residents welcomed the Texans. Within two years the town controlled much of the trade, helped by Wichita falling victim to an expanded dead line and pressure from wheat farmers.

Traditionally, cattle traveled into Kansas over the Chisholm Trail, moving more or less on a line running from the range lands of south Texas past Austin, Waco, and Fort Worth before crossing into Indian Territory at Red River Station. South of the eventual site of Caldwell (founded on the southern Kansas border in 1871), the trail divided at the Pond Creek Cutoff, with some herds moving on to Abilene or later Wichita and others swinging northwest to Ellsworth. With Dodge City joining the list of Kansas cattle towns a new route opened, appropriately called the Western or Dodge City Trail. From south Texas it went past San Antonio to Fort Griffin, one hundred miles west of Fort Worth, and forded Red River at Doan's Crossing in present-day Wilbarger County. The Western Trail then continued north, passing Camp Supply and on to Dodge City and Ogallala, Nebraska. Other herds bound for Ford County used part of the old Chisholm Trail, but branched off to the west after crossing the Cimarron south of the Kansas line.

Drovers riding into Dodge City risked all the pleasures and indignities offered by Kansas cattle towns: "The saloons guzzle him with whiskey, the gambler plies him with faro[,] keno and monte. The dance house surfeits him with the charms of the raw boned and blear eyed beauties of the frontier, borrowed from the slums of the cities and the keen eyed clothier tickles his uncultivated fancy with an apparel as gaudy as that of a monkey in a side show."[25]

But these Texas men were young, and driving longhorns into Kansas remained their life's great adventure. The wickedness of places like Dodge City only enhanced the memory. After weeks on the trail, not even cheap goods at inflated prices, gamblers of questionable virtue, hangovers, or occasional bouts of venereal distress could strip the luster from those wild days of youth. As one visitor noted with humor, "I have been to Dodge. I dodged down there last Thursday, and dodged out of there Friday morning. Any man who can accomplish this feat successfully, is a hero." In fairness, he conceded, "you are in no danger whatever, as long as you behave yourself. But if you are spoiling for a fight you can be accommodated in

---

[25] *Leavenworth Daily Commercial*, June 20, 1875.

short order. Three newspaper correspondents have been here during the last week and they all escaped unhurt."[26]

Preparing for the Texans, one local worried about more than stocks of liquor and cigars. On January 6, 1876, A. J. Peacock, saloon proprietor and chairman of the county commissioners, stepped from the train at Topeka and registered at the Tefft House. He soon found himself mired in controversy over $8,500 in suspected fraudulent bonds, including a small sampling from what would become Seward County (located southwest of Dodge City but attached to Ford County for judicial purposes as Seward Township), whose citizens wanted a bridge across the Cimarron. Peacock came to Topeka to register $8,000 in Ford County bonds with the state auditor in order to finance a new jail and courthouse.[27] The county was then renting courtroom space from Bob Wright. Peacock brought along the $500 bridge bonds as a courtesy to R. A. Wilson, the newly elected trustee of Seward Township.

The problem now was poor timing. Rocked by a series of bond scandals, most recently from Barber County, authorities and speculators alike viewed all new offerings with caution. Manipulating the skepticism, railroad mouthpiece Joseph G. Waters persuaded the attorney general to file a criminal complaint with the district court. The lawyer charged Peacock with conspiring with Mr. Wilson, Ford County clerk William F. Sweeney, and Sam Gallagher, the clerk of Seward Township, to issue bonds and then steal the money on the strength of a township election they knew had never taken place. One editor defended the railroad: "They are large tax payers in Ford County, and, very properly, don't intend to be swindled if they can help it."[28]

The railroad's case rested on a false premise. The commissioners of Ford County had scheduled an election in Seward Township for December 6. During a special meeting called twelve days after the balloting to certify the results, commissioners also demanded payment of railroad taxes. Then, just two days before Peacock's arrival at Topeka, the city council passed an ordinance calling for fines up to twenty dollars if the railroad continued to allow

---

[26] *Kansas Daily Commonwealth*, September 7, 1875.

[27] Ford County Commissioners Journals, Book A, 87, 107, 129; and *Kansas Daily Commonwealth*, January 8, 1876. Each of the bonds in question, those from Ford County and Seward Township, were issued in denominations of five hundred dollars. For Mr. Peacock's spirited rebuttal, see *Kansas Daily Commonwealth*, January 9, 1876.

[28] *Kansas Daily Commonwealth*, January 8, 1876. The veteran Dodge City saloonman and novice politician did receive some encouraging words from Leavenworth: "Whatever may be said of Mr. Peacock, he has the reputation of being an honest man, and we will consider him as such until it is proven otherwise." *Leavenworth Daily Commercial*, January 18, 1876.

its engines or cars to block public thoroughfares for more than fifteen minutes at a time.[29] All this helped orchestrate the case against Peacock. Back in 1873, the AT&SF had challenged the formal organization of Ford County—if the county was not legally organized, then it could not levy taxes on the railroad. Major Dodge saw through the charade, suspecting company officials even then of plotting tax avoidance.[30] Peacock survived and returned home to chair the county commissioners' special meeting on February 2.

As Peacock confronted the powerful railroad lobby at Topeka, news from Dodge City described battles of a more familiar sort: "Dodge City negroes will shoot. Two of them entered into a quarrel last week, resulting in the serious wounding of one of them. The perpetrator was sent to Great Bend for safe keeping. He is now at liberty, with the impression that shooting is no crime. Who next?"[31] That question was answered within three weeks: "Another shooting affray took place at Dodge City last week, the victim being a white man, who was sent to a premature grave on account of the reckless use of firearms in the hands of 'darkies.' If man is to be a target for the wreckles [?], then, Mr. Justice, step in—but you are so slow."[32]

THE CATTLE TRADE MAY HAVE changed Dodge City's economic climate, but older problems persisted. At the end of March eight horses stolen in Sumner County were spotted in Dodge. Unlike receptions given horse thieves in 1874, residents, their patience strained by recent forays against local stock, preferred a more practical solution. Another vigilance committee formed. Staring reality in the face the outlaws withdrew.

Perhaps encouraged by memories of Billy Brooks, people from Sumner County demanded action. A group of these, loosely commanded by a Captain Allen, rode into Dodge City. Their arrival coincided with excitement over the theft of a valuable span of horses from a local farmer. Following a suspicious trail, the Sumner County mob found two men with the stolen animals about fifteen miles from town along Saw Log Creek. Assuming guilt without trial, they blindfolded both captives, passed around a bottle of whiskey as if in celebration, and hanged the two face to

---

[29] Ordinance No. 8, Sec. 3, January 4, 1876. Dodge City Ordinances, Book A, 9. Also see Ford County Commissioners Journals, Book A, 108–109.

[30] Maj. Richard Dodge to Gov. T. A. Osborne [sic], July 5, 1873. Governors' Correspondence, Manuscripts Department, Kansas State Historical Society.

[31] Leavenworth Daily Commercial, January 5, 1876.

[32] Ibid., January 28, 1876.

face from a nearby cottonwood. Burying the bodies, identified as a man named Cole and one John Callaham, the drunken crowd returned to Dodge City and resumed their revelry.

Some were troubled by the brutality. Concern heightened after Sheriff Bassett proved Callaham could not possibly have been involved in the Sumner County raid. That man had been working for a Mr. Owens gathering buffalo bones. Callaham enjoyed a good reputation in Dodge City and no one there believed him guilty. Nothing was known about Cole. Callaham's father, a Topeka sewing-machine salesman, appealed to Governor Osborn, who wrote Charlie Bassett and Ford County attorney L. P. Henderson, demanding an investigation: "I trust you will extend to Mr. Callaham all the assistance, counsel and encouragement which it may be in your power to extend. There must be an end to mob violence in this state."[33]

Bassett's inquiries cleared young Callaham. The sheriff then asked the state for money to organize an effort to apprehend the vigilantes. Since those named included prominent citizens of Sumner County, the governor declined, as did officials of Ford County. Facing political reality, Bassett's office closed the file. This episode, followed a month later by the hanging of a man off a railroad bridge near Lakin—some seventy miles to the west—did little to encourage confidence.

In March 1876, undeterred by stories of scattered violence, another of those periodic railroad excursions traveled down the line. On this occasion two trains passed through Ford County, stuffed with politicians and journalists, one of whom was not at all impressed with Spearville: "one of the most dreary, uninviting spots on the American continent, and, unless I miss my guess, will never again contain the same number of inhabitants that it did last Tuesday." Dan Frost, Ford County's legislative representative, went along to try and stifle criticism while praising the Arkansas River Valley. At least Dodge made a better impression than Spearville: "At Dodge City both trains stopped for supper, and the way the pleasure seekers went for hot coffee and beer at twenty-five cents a drink, has not been witnessed in Kansas since the palmy days of 'Rowdy Joe' at Wichita. About two hundred of the party partook of an elegant supper at the Dodge House, kept by Cox & Boyd, which all hands united in pronouncing the *ne plus ultra* of excursion suppers." Returning from Colorado, "just twelve hours out from

---

[33] Gov. Thomas A. Osborn to the County Attorney and Sheriff of Ford County, April 24, 1876. Governors' Correspondence, Manuscripts Department, Kansas State Historical Society.

Pueblo," the excursionists stopped again at Dodge City: "Here we took breakfast, and, leaving the Hon. D. M. Frost among his native icicles and Texas cattle, we again sped onward, downward and homeward."[34]

Such trips may seem frivolous today, but they did provide small frontier towns with badly needed publicity beyond their own section. These groups always included newspapermen who could, if properly entertained, be induced to write some encouraging articles. Dodge City, scheming hard to dominate most of the cattle business on the central plains, welcomed all the kind words.

On April 3, 1876, following the annual city elections, liquor wholesaler George M. Hoover replaced Pettis L. Beatty as Dodge City's mayor. Hoover's election emphasized an old complaint: "it is a fact that all the city officials of Dodge City and Ford County . . . are bar-keepers or own-ers of liquor saloons. One of the County Commissioners owns a saloon and the Sheriff is his chief clerk. No one was elected to any position who was not a strictly anti-temperance man."[35] All true, but there was another oddity surrounding George Hoover's election. When he became mayor, Hoover was not yet a citizen of the United States, but still a Canadian subject. True, he had filed his Declaration of Intent on January 30, 1874, but the mayor did not complete the citizenship process until June 27, 1878.[36] By then he was out of office.

Soon after the election, Captain Stockwell, the AT&SF's livestock agent, returned to Dodge City to expand its stockyards to 300 by 350 feet.[37] Stockwell traveled with assistant superintendent A. A. Egbert. They arranged to have the feed yard at Hutchinson moved east to Newton, thereby making Dodge City, Newton, and Atchison the main forage points for Texas cattle moving east. On May 12, four thousand head came in from San Antonio, delighting everyone in Dodge City.

Despite all the cattle, freighting still played an important role. Demand for consumer goods and other supplies, along with small government con-tracts, kept the teamsters busy. In late April, Rufus Saxton, deputy quar-termaster for the Department of the Missouri, called for sealed bids to cover its two routes from Dodge City for the twelve months beginning on

---

[34] "Legislative Excursion," letters to the editor, signed "Pioneer," and dated March 8 and 11, 1876. *Kansas Daily Commonwealth*, March 12, 1876.

[35] *Lawrence Journal*, as quoted in *Newton Kansan*, February 18, 1875.

[36] Records of the Ford County District Court, Declaration of Intent, 1:1; and Final Naturalization Records, 1:8.

[37] *Annual Report of the Board of Directors of the Atchison, Topeka, and Santa Fe Railroad Co. . . . for the year ending December 31, 1876* (Boston: Franklin Press: Rand, Avery, & Co., 1877), 44.

the first of July. This traffic involved shipments to Camp Supply and another run farther south to Fort Elliott, Texas, established in the Panhandle the year before. Even as it welcomed the cattlemen, Dodge City remained the center of a wide-reaching commerce. Of course, it owed everything to the railroad. As freighters, cattlemen, and townspeople prospered, so did the AT&SF, which by early June 1876 employed nine to fifteen men at its machine shops at Dodge City.

As if the town needed the diversion, local dance hall proprietor and occasional township constable "Prairie Dog" Dave Morrow filed suit in the Ford County District Court against Capt. Emil Adam of the Fifth Cavalry, whom Morrow charged with burglary and destruction of property. As it turned out, the captain and his soldiers had camped at old Fort Aubrey and used wood torn from its abandoned buildings for their fire. Prairie Dog Dave, known even then as a notorious character, claimed the site as his own and instigated charges in mid-May. Morrow subpoenaed several local characters, including Edward and William B. Masterson, along with J. J. Webb, another hard case then working ostensibly as a teamster for A. J. Anthony. To counter these charges, the government dispatched U.S. Attorney George Peck from Topeka. Before that seasoned advocate even stepped off the train, Judge Samuel Peters tossed out the case.[38]

Samuel N. Wood, a longtime Kansan of mixed reputation, had joined William N. Morphy as counsel for Captain Adam. Sam entertained the court with some personal references that Dave Morrow found insulting and was knocked flat by the outraged plaintiff. But then Wood, known to everyone as Slippery Sam, never did get along that well in Dodge. Only the year before it was said, "The guests of the Dodge City hotel were much exercised . . . by the appearance of a negro woman at the first table. Col. Wood and Judge Bowen, a rampant democrat . . . to carry out the spirit of the civil rights bill agreed between themselves to set one on each side of her. This sociable action on the part of the two men caused the colored woman to inquire their names and being informed, she said she guessed she would prefer eating at the second table."[39]

Mrs. Wood enjoyed better luck than did her famous husband. During one stopover on a trip to Pueblo, Colorado, in 1876, Mrs. Wood wrote of a pleas-

---

[38] State of Kansas vs. Emil Adam, Records of the Ford County District Court, Criminal Appearance Docket A, 30; and Judge's Journal, Book A, 43.

[39] *Chase County Leader*, as quoted in *Hutchinson News*, July 15, 1875. On that same day the *Newton Kansan* commented more succinctly, "A colored woman at Dodge City refused to eat at the table with Sam Wood."

ant evening with Lt. George Spencer and his family, and of being visited at her hotel by Charlie Rath: "He is an old plainsman, well known in southwestern Kansas, among the old settlers and along the old Santa Fe trail. He is keeping a grocery, provision and general supply store at Dodge City, and is doing as well as all who know the honest, generous man would wish."[40] Mrs. Wood's only regret was learning of the death of Rath's young son.

WITH ITS SHIFT FROM buffalo to cattle, Dodge City seemed ready for another newspaper. Earlier the town had become part of the Southwest News Bureau, an organization established at Topeka by Henry King that hired "news-gatherers" along the Kansas border, Indian Territory, and eastern Colorado to supply items for its eastern clients, including some widely circulating dailies in St. Louis, Chicago, Cincinnati, Philadelphia, and New York City. Despite criticism from departing editor A. W. Moore, Dodge City understood the value of journalism in pressing its case with Texas cattlemen. Newspapers remained a valuable propaganda tool for local commerce.

Two Iowa-born newspapermen from Rice County, Kansas, stepped forward on May 20, 1876, and began publishing the *Dodge City Times*. The two men, twenty-two-year-old Walter C. L. Shinn and his younger brother, Otis Lloyd Shinn (known simply as Lloyd in Dodge City), learned the printing trade in Leon, Iowa, not far from their father's Decatur County farm. Moving to Kansas in 1873, they bought the *Rice County Herald* but sold out before year's end. Lloyd ran a grocery store at Pearce, but preferred newsprint to fresh produce. He and his brother dreamed of another frontier weekly. After toying with Great Bend, they moved to Dodge City.

Lloyd Shinn was a self-educated man, having left school at age twelve. Without a formal education, he studied law on the side and was eventually admitted to the bar. At Dodge City he owned one of the finest libraries in town, and would serve Ford County in a variety of positions. Walter speculated in real estate and became an attorney after attending lectures for six months at the University of Michigan.[41]

---

[40] *Kansas Daily Commonwealth*, May 26, 1876.

[41] Records of the Ford County District Court, Judge's Journal, Book A, 342; and *Ford County Globe*, October 14, 1879, March 30, 1880. For additional biographical material on the two Shinn brothers, see *History of the State of Kansas*, 755, 1560; and *Biographical and Historical Record of Ringgold and Decatur Counties, Iowa* (Chicago: The Lewis Publishing Company, 1887), 626–27.

The *Dodge City Times* made its debut as a tabloid-size, eight-page, four-column effort, with Walter acting as proprietor. The brothers worked together as editors. Other Kansas newspapermen gave the results high marks for style and presentation. Even the conservative editor at Hutchinson confessed, "The Dodge City *Times* manages to get up the livest and fullest little county paper on the least apparent material, of any paper we ever saw. It is red hot, so to speak, every week."[42] This new voice from Ford County courted Texas interests. The brothers enjoyed a good joke, even at their own expense, several months later writing: "The Chinaman who is trying to learn to be an editor in the Times office says he is content to follow that profession until he can strike a better job. He is looking out for an engagement at shoveling dirt."[43]

Learning from earlier experiences at Abilene, Ellsworth, and Wichita, authorities at Dodge City took precautions. On May 24, 1876, the *Wichita Weekly Beacon* published a report: "Wyatt Earp has been put on the police force at Dodge City." Over the years Earp has become something of a frontier icon; a virtual prisoner of popular culture, a heroic image showcased in books and movies that ignored the darker sides of his secretive personality and disruptive public career, including a federal indictment for horse theft in the Indian Territory, followed by two arrests in Peoria, Illinois, along with his brother Morgan, for keeping a house of ill fame.[44]

Wyatt Earp worked in a limited capacity as an officer around Wichita as early as October 1874, although he did not become a city policeman until

---

[42] *Hutchinson News,* February 22, 1877.

[43] *Dodge City Times,* as quoted in *Kansas Daily Commonwealth,* October 24, 1876.

[44] United States vs. Wyatt S. Earp, Edward Kennedy, and John Shown, for Larceny in the Indian Country. Records of the United States District Court for the Western District of Arkansas, May Term 1871, Control No. NRFF-21-3W51, Federal Archives and Records Center, Fort Worth, Texas. Earp was indicted along with the other defendants for stealing two horses from William Keys on March 28, 1871. In a deposition, the wife of John Shown swore that Earp and Kennedy got her husband "drunk near Ft. Gibson," then grabbed the animals, "& told him to ride 50 miles toward Kansas." They traveled only at night but were still overtaken by the victim's brother. "Earp and Kennedy told Keys that my husband stole the horses. They also said that if Shown (my husband) turned states evidence they would kill him." Wyatt Earp and his co-defendants did make an appearance before the court, waiving examination after hearing a reading of the charges. The record is somewhat sketchy, but it appears they were briefly held until each posted a $500 bond. The case never seems to have gotten beyond the preliminary stages, suggesting that Earp avoided prosecution and possible incarceration by jumping bail. In later life he avoided all references to this incident. It has since been suggested that Kennedy was found not guilty, and as a result authorities decided to drop the case against Earp. There is nothing in the file to support that assumption, no specific information at all regarding the final disposition of the charges against any of the defendants. Regarding Earp's Illinois troubles, see *Peoria Daily Transcript,* February 27 and May 11, 1872. Wyatt's older brother, Virgil, tended bar during this same period. O. C. Root, *Root's Peoria City Directory For 1870–'71* (Peoria, Ill.: N. C. Nason, Printer, 1870), 72.

April 21, 1875. Somewhat embarrassing to modern aficionados, aside from learning that Wyatt had once dropped his revolver and nearly shot himself,[45] was the fact that his sister-in-law Bessie, the wife of brother James, had been arrested and fined as a common prostitute in May 1874. This remained a monthly ritual through March 1875. One must assume that Wyatt's appointment to the police force, rather than his serving as a symbol of moral rectitude, was what ended Bessie's repeated enumeration on the city's prostitution list. Earlier she and one Sallie Earp were arrested and briefly jailed, before scrounging money for bail after their case was remanded to the district court following guilty pleas before a justice of the peace. The charges involved keeping "a bawdy house or brothel" on Douglas Avenue near the Arkansas River bridge. The district judge, however, would later dismiss the case on a point of law agreed to by the county attorney.[46]

Other members of the family faced legal troubles. The Wichita Police Judge's Report for August 1874 lists one J. Earp (presumably James) being fined five dollars and costs for some undisclosed offense. Then, under similar circumstances in September 1875, Morgan Earp was assessed one dollar with two more covering costs.[47]

Contemporary sources explain Wyatt Earp's departure from Wichita. On April 2, 1876, he engaged in a public brawl with William B. Smith, a former federal officer and one-time city marshal who had again announced his candidacy for that post. Smith reportedly made some rather disparaging remarks regarding Marshal Mike Meagher's plan to hire Earp's brothers as policemen. It seems likely that the unstable political atmosphere did as much to spark the trouble as did Smith's mumblings, which the press duly noted, "furnished no just grounds for an attack, and

---

[45] *Wichita Weekly Beacon,* January 12, 1876. As the press reconstructed the event: "while policeman Erp [*sic*] was sitting with two or three others in the back room of the Custom House saloon, his revolver slipped from its holster and in falling to the floor the hammer which was resting on the cap, is supposed to have struck the chair, causing a discharge of one of the barrels. The ball passed through his coat, struck the north wall then glanced off and passed out through the ceiling. It was a narrow escape and the occurrence got up a lively stampede from the room. One of the demoralized was under the impression that some one had fired through the window from the outside."

[46] The State of Kansas vs. Bessie Erp [*sic*] and Sallie Erp, Case No. 814, Proceedings of the Sedgwick County District Court, September Term, 1874, Vol. 2, 210. For the earlier case, presented before Justice of the Peace D. A. Mitchell, see The State of Kansas vs. Sallie Erp [*sic*] and Betsey [*sic*] Erp, Case Records of the Sedgwick County District Court, June 3, 1874. At Wichita, on the 1875 Kansas State Census, Bessie Earp gave her occupation as "Sporting"—a common frontier euphemism for prostitute.

[47] Police Judge Reports, Judge E. B. Hewett, Case No. 102, J. Earp, August 1874; and Judge J. M. Atwood, Case No. 170, Morgan Earp, September 1875. Miscellaneous Papers, Records of the City of Wichita.

upon ordinary occasions [they doubted if Wyatt] would have given them a second thought." Earp was arrested by Meagher and fined thirty dollars and costs for violating "the peace and order of the city."[48] Within weeks all this led to the city council dismissing their headstrong officer. Wyatt traveled to Dodge City in late May, a looming vagrancy charge serving as the primary motivation.[49] Ignoring negative speculation from Wichita, Larry Deger appointed Earp his assistant marshal.

Ford County sheriff Charles E. Bassett also recognized Wyatt's potential and named him a deputy to work alongside Under Sheriff Ed Hougue. Earp now held authority in both city and county. These duel arrangements usually worked well, causing little conflict between one's respective superiors. Yet on July 1, 1876, Wyatt Earp, acting as assistant marshal, arrested and filed a complaint against the under sheriff for "fighting and disturbing the peace and quiet of the City."[50] Of course, as a deputy sheriff the assistant marshal worked directly under Hougue. Police judge Daniel Frost fined the embarrassed county lawman ten dollars and costs. The case did not prejudice Charlie Bassett. The popular Ford County sheriff went ahead and hired Wyatt's younger brother Morgan, along with William B. Masterson, as additional deputies that same summer.[51]

Facing its second cattle season, the town needed officers, but many questioned their rectitude and professional competence. In June the notorious Dutch Henry Born stole one mule and a gelding from George S.

---

[48] *Wichita Weekly Beacon*, April 5, 1876; and Police Judge Reports, Judge J. M. Atwood, Case No. 347, Wyatt S. Earp, May 1, 1876. Miscellaneous Papers, Records of the City of Wichita.

[49] Proceedings of the Governing Body, Journal B, 107, Records of the City of Wichita; and Police Committee Report, May 10, 1876, Miscellaneous Papers, Records of the City of Wichita. There were other irregularities aside from assaulting candidates for public office, which assured Wyatt's removal. Although the newly elected city council agreed on May 8 to pay him forty dollars for twenty days' service in April, they had already blocked his reinstatement by a six-to-two vote. The police committee then stepped in two days later, recommending "That the scrip of W. Erp [*sic*] & John Behrns [*sic*] be with-held from payment until all moneys collected by them for the city be turned over to the city treasurer." That was the end of Wyatt Earp in Wichita.

[50] The City of Dodge City vs. Edward O. Hougue, Police Court Record, Daniel M. Frost, Police Judge, July 10, 1876. Transcript filed with the Clerk of the Ford County District Court, December 21, 1876. Also see Records of the Ford County District Court, Criminal Appearance Docket A, 46. There has always been some confusion concerning the spelling of this name, which appears either as "Hougue" or "Hogue." In the transcript there is a document with his signature, clearly showing "Ed. O. Hougue."

[51] It has often been said that Bat Masterson's whereabouts between March 1875 and the spring of 1877 are unknown, but documents filed with the Ford County District Court prove his as well as Wyatt and Morgan Earp's status as county peace officers during the summer of 1876. Even their father, Nicholas Porter Earp, received a nominal payment from Ford County during this period for some undisclosed service. Ford County Commissioners Journals, Book A, 146.

Emerson, a Clark County stock raiser and buffalo-bone freighter. Since the crime took place in Foote County, then attached to Ford for judicial purposes, Sheriff Bassett alerted other Kansas lawmen by telegraph. This led to Dutch Henry's capture after the sheriff of Russell County stabbed him outside a clothing store. Authorities there confiscated the stolen animals before sending the wanted man to Dodge City.

Dutch Henry enjoyed his reputation as a troublemaker. Estimates of his activities before reinventing himself as a Colorado mining man suggest no less than fifty horses stolen between the Arkansas and Saline rivers. Officers nabbed him at least twice before. Sheriff Chauncey B. Whitney of Ellsworth County did so first, "but there being some informality in the arrest he was released."[52] Born was apprehended again some five miles outside Ellsworth on June 15, 1874, this time for stealing government mules in Ellis County, despite rumors placing him at the Battle of Adobe Walls twelve days later.[53] Dutch Henry languished at Leavenworth for eighteen months before being discharged by a sympathetic magistrate. It did not take him long to resume his old habits—that is until Charlie Bassett tossed him into the small Ford County jail.

Born's luck held. Emerson swore out a complaint before Justice of the Peace Harry T. McCarty. The new county attorney, D. M. Sells, a recent arrival from Great Bend, filed charges in the district court. Deputy Sheriff Masterson began serving subpoenas.[54] But Dutch Henry simply walked away, causing consternation in Dodge City. As one visitor reported: "the door [to his cell] had been unlocked, the prisoner allowed to escape, and then relocked. . . . Strong suspicions are entertained that some one of the officers connived at his escape and for a valuable consideration let the notorious horse thief slide."[55] Speculation concerning those responsible persisted for years.

This same correspondent, complaining of Dutch Henry's sudden disappearance, described Dodge City's population as "almost altogether transient." So many travelers drifted in that hostlers Cox and Boyd expanded.

[52] *Ellsworth Reporter*, June 18, 1874.

[53] Ibid.; Baker and Harrison, *Adobe Walls*, 68–69, 76, 79; and Seth Hathaway, "The Adventures of a Buffalo Hunter," *Frontier Times* 9, no. 3 (December 1931): 133.

[54] State of Kansas vs. Henry Born, alias Dutch Henry. Records of the Ford County District Court, Criminal Appearance Docket A, 33, 40; Criminal Case No. 28, File Record; and Judge's Journal, Book A, 73.

[55] Letter from J. F. B. to the editor, sent from Kinsley and dated June 28, 1876, *Kansas Daily Commonwealth*, July 1, 1876.

Newcomers crowded the refurbished Dodge House the moment carpenters finished their work. The new Western House, opened by Silas Maley near the southwest corner of Locust Street and First Avenue, did not have trouble filling his rooms, either. Businessmen talked of starting a legitimate bank to handle growing financial commitments, contrasting an earlier report: "A bank has been started at Dodge City. It is a faro bank."[56]

People saw signs of progress springing up everywhere. By late June 1876 officials laid the cornerstone of the long-awaited Ford County Courthouse. Townspeople began bragging of their one church ("The ladies, God bless them, built it, by getting up festivals and begging."[57]), together with a small schoolhouse, which doubled for worship during the visit of Episcopal bishop Thomas Vail.

Services relied on itinerant preachers. Methodists tried starting a congregation the year before but abandoned Dodge City in disgust. In late June a few citizens signed a petition pledging a yearly salary of one hundred dollars to R. M. Overstreet, matching funds from the Presbyterian Synod at Emporia, for the good reverend to deliver one sermon a month. Some felt that was more than enough religion, with one critic observing, "Dodge City has but one church which will seat about one hundred and is never crowded."[58] Within six months it was said, "The church at Dodge City is threatened with sale for debt."[59]

The town had mellowed. Even the Topeka correspondent, after criticizing authorities over Dutch Henry's mysterious disappearance, conceded, "Dodge, of course, is lively, in a certain direction, notably its saloons and dance houses." Then, in an offhanded compliment, he added, "Of course she is not altogether bad—in fact, she is not as wicked as represented. I feel just as safe upon the streets of Dodge as in any other town in the State, though the City Marshal had a street fight or two, while I was there—but then I suppose that that was only to show the Commonwealth man, that he was on the fight, and that he must keep straight. I took the hint and got away safe."[60]

Citizens continued to focus on national and statewide affairs, especially politics. In those days before twenty-four-hour mass media, with its unfor-

[56] *Hutchinson News,* December 16, 1875.

[57] *Kansas Daily Commonwealth,* June 8, 1876.

[58] *Newton Kansan,* September 7, 1876.

[59] Ibid., February 22, 1877.

[60] *Kansas Daily Commonwealth,* July 1, 1876.

tunate ritualizing of imagery over substance, voters saw politics quite differently from their modern counterparts, ordinary people often showing a far deeper understanding of specific issues.

Citizens took the process very seriously. During the summer of 1876 both parties held statewide conventions. For the Republican hoedown, Ford County sent Frederick C. Zimmerman and Morris Collar as delegates, with Charles Rath and non-citizen George M. Hoover serving as alternates. A month later Mayor Hoover proved his versatility by also becoming a delegate to the state Democratic convention. James Langton and Larry Deger attended the congressional convention at Wichita, along with Richard Evans and Herman Fringer. Daniel Frost and city councilman D. D. Colley traveled to Great Bend for the state senatorial convention.

Interest peaked as November neared, with candidates hustling for office from township races to the presidency. Kansas office seekers did not ignore Ford County, still a part of the third congressional district, an odd cluster of counties that even included Topeka. Representatives of the two Republicans and one Democrat running for Congress made repeated pilgrimages to Dodge, regaling its inhabitants with endless promises.

As if flaunting their independence, Ford County voters cast ballots contrary to the Kansas majority. The November 4 tally favored Democratic presidential hopeful Samuel J. Tilden over Rutherford B. Hayes. Tilden did not carry Kansas, and although winning the popular vote, he was denied the White House by a special electoral commission named by the Republican Congress. Ford County may have voted Democratic in the presidential race, but for Congress everyone supported the two Republicans, with not a single ballot marked in favor of the Democrat. In the race for governor, Ford County backed Democrat John A. Martin by a lopsided margin in a losing effort against Republican George T. Anthony. Locally, Robert Wright crushed fellow Republican Daniel Frost 203 to 15 to reclaim his seat in the legislature. Michael Sutton became county attorney, beating Democrat William Morphy, a lawyer who had moved from Ellis just five months before.[61] Sutton, a twenty-eight-year-old Civil War veteran (he had volunteered one month before his sixteenth birthday), was himself a newcomer to Dodge City. Over the years he would play an important role, often operating behind the scenes, during the town's troublesome political wars.

---

[61] Ford County Commissioners Journals, Book A, 172–75.

BUSINESS HAD ROUNDED A CORNER from those financial panic days of 1873. Dealers still shipped out a few buffalo hides, Charlie Rath and Bob Wright contributing twenty-five hundred in early October. The town's position with Texas cattle seemed secure. Even sheep crowded the Dodge City stockyards. Often overlooked as a factor in the town's booming economy, these often-maligned creatures played their role.

By early autumn, the town boasted two religious congregations, Baptist and Catholic, a school, a government warehouse and signal office, and impressive stockyards. The courthouse was nearing completion. New construction gave the town a look of permanence, contrasting the shabbiness of earlier years. Rath & Co. replaced its two-story wood frame with a more impressive brick version, symbolizing its importance.

One outsider described developments: "New and substantial buildings are crowding out the rude castles of the demi-monde and gambler."[62] Many of them left in late summer to ply their trades at mining camps in the Black Hills. Dodge grew so quiet that winter it needed only one police officer, despite a report that they "hanged a man twice in Dodge City, a few nights ago, to ascertain whether he was guilty of stealing some pistols. They then threatened to shoot him, and finally concluded that he was innocent and released him."[63] Even so, it had been a good year, with more than five thousand head of beef and large numbers of sheep sent to eastern markets.

In late December the town formed a fire company. Within a week it proved its worth as flames engulfed the railroad's tank house, barn, and stockyards. A crowd milled about wondering what to do. The fire brigade saved the day. Instant heroes, members enjoyed free liquor, compliments of the Dodge House. The town also arranged a dollar-per-couple masquerade ball, with oysters supplied by Beatty & Kelley and Fred Leonard. Proceeds went to fire company. Citizens felt safe as 1876 came to an end.

Facing a new cattle season, railroads and towns across Kansas scrambled for a slice of the pie. From their editorial offices at the *Dodge City Times* the Shinn brothers accused the Kansas Pacific of hiring agents to fan out across Texas and try convincing cattlemen to patronize their road. Of course, the AT&SF did the same. After all, business was business, and Dodge City advertised along with everyone else, calling attention to lower prices on cigars, liquor, and other commodities favored by Texas men.

---

[62] *Kansas Daily Commonwealth*, September 20, 1876.
[63] Ibid., November 4, 1876.

There was still much to be done. Another fire destroyed a stable, seventy-five buffalo robes, and large stocks of finished lumber. As the railroad rebuilt its facilities, businessmen made their own preparations. Buildings got fresh coats of paint and signs refurbished to help guide customers to waiting cash drawers. Cox and Boyd repapered their billiard parlor and saloon adjoining the Dodge House, leaving manager Nat L. Haywood to stroll between its empty tables awaiting customers fresh off the trail. Saloon owners rushed to open on time, spreading the word that beginning in April drinks and cigars could be had for fifteen cents each, or two for a quarter. The railroad hauled in mountains of supplies, picked over by merchants busy stocking shelves. Boot makers sharpened their tools while blacksmiths and liverymen prepared to deal with tired and footsore mounts off the trail from Texas.

There were two new livery stables. Bob Wright's old partner, James Anderson, came over from Wichita to start one, and Hamilton Bell opened the other. This tiny town, with its few hundred inhabitants, boasted four blacksmith shops. Each employed two to four workmen, all of whom dreamed of organizing a union while glancing at the horizon, along with everyone else, for the first signs of Texas beef.

The town's transients—gamblers and prostitutes among them—reappeared from their off-season excursions. Others, too, decided to tempt fate in wide-open Dodge City. Former governor Thomas Carney, ostensibly there to buy hides and buffalo bones for a St. Louis firm but who actually came "to entice our unsophisticated denizens into the national game of draw poker, and fleece them of their loose cash," discovered instead a harsh reality. Fooling only himself, Carney believed he had corralled three unsuspecting greenhorns. This trio of poker buddies turned out to be Col. Charles Norton, Robert Gilmore—a genuine character known locally as Bobby Gill—and saloonman Charles Ronan: all three professional sporting men. It was not a good day for ex-governors. Instead of leaving with pockets stuffed with cash and coin, "The next eastbound freight train carried an old man, without shirt studs or other ornament, apparently bowed down by overwhelming grief, and the conductor hadn't the heart to throw him overboard. Gov. Carney is not buying bones and hides in this city any more."[64]

---

[64] *Dodge City Times*, March 24, 1877.

Along with gambling, drinking, and whoring, Dodge City's other diversions followed a rough-and-tumble playbook. A common form of merriment involved phony Indian attacks. Designed as a way to introduce
strangers to the uncertainties of frontier life, residents lured unsuspecting
newcomers out of town while casually mentioning the possibility of hostiles on the prowl. Once alone on the plains, the Indians—townspeople
all, dressed in authentic garb retrieved as trophies from the Adobe Walls
battlefield—charged forward in mock attack. Terrified victims galloped
back screaming out warnings of massacre. Forewarned citizens lined the
streets to greet riders with laughter and ridicule.

Other distractions proved only slightly milder in tone, ranging from
setting a man's coat ablaze while he still occupied the garment to inter-
rupting a romantic interlude between Bobby Gill and "Miss Susy Haden,
a beautiful Creole maiden of this city." The newspaper reported the climax
on its front page: "when the boys entered the Castle de Coon, Bobby was
there in person 'with both hands,' and himself and Susy were occupying
positions relative to each other of such a delicate nature as to entirely pro-
hibit us from describing in these chaste and virtuous columns."[65]

A more harmless prank was the invention of "Luke McGlue," a fabri-
cation blamed for all sorts of mischief. Everyone, including the press and
police, played along with this lighthearted farce. When St. Louis cigar
salesman J. B. McManahan discovered the theft of several sample cases, his
"suspicions were excited against Luke McGlue, and, taking Constable
[James H.] McGoodwin, he went through every saloon and business house
in the city. Everybody was smoking and praising the cigars Luke McGlue
had given them, but Luke could not be found."[66] On July 21 the *Dodge City
Times* even published "A Story in One Part" attributed to the elusive Mr.
McGlue. It took years for this game to play out.

Popular amusements included illegal prizefights among local toughs.
Early in the 1877 cattle season Nelson Whitman and Red Hanley, championed as "the red bird from the South," met in front of the Saratoga,
owned by saloon impresarios Chalkley M. Beeson and William H. Harris,
"at the silent hour of 4:30 A.M., when the city police were retiring after the
dance hall revelry had subdued, and the belles who reign there were off

[65] Ibid.
[66] Ibid.

duty." Whitman was favored among professional sporting men, and so it turned out to be: "About the sixty-first round Red squealed unmistakably, and Whitman was declared winner. The only injuries sustained by the loser in this fight were two ears chewed off, one eye bursted and the other disabled, right cheek bone caved in, bridge of the nose broken, seven teeth knocked out, one jaw bone mashed, one side of the tongue chewed off, and several other unimportant fractures and bruises. Red retires from the ring in disgust."[67]

Against this backdrop of hard-edged entertainment, Ernst von Hesse-Wartegg, a popular and prolific travel writer and a wealthy descendant of Austrian nobility, showed up hoping to witness the untamed American frontier firsthand. It is, therefore, interesting to see just what features of Dodge City tickled his cultured sensibilities. Hesse-Wartegg and his party of nameless companions stepped from the train and headed straight for the Dodge House: "The hotel was of ill-fitting boards that admitted wind in gusts. In the dining room, an expansive chamber, wooden posts supported the low ceiling. A swarm of the unbelievable billows of flies that infest the prairie greeted us and went for our noses and hands as if they were spread with sugar." Conditions did not improve as they stared at their greasy plates: "The meal was terrible; not even the roasted flies we must have swallowed with it could flavor it. Yet how to justify complaints in the middle of nowhere?"

This educated European at once recognized that "Dodge City, emporium to endless, wild prairie, is important as a commercial center. Cattle, buffalo hides, bones, and other produce are collected here for shipment by rail. Wagon routes and cattle trails lead south to Indian Territory and Texas, and shops sell goods for such expeditions: saddles, bridles, whips, and clothing. Shops are open late—part of Dodge City's night life, which greatly interests the foreigner."

The nightlife certainly fascinated the twenty-three-year-old Ernest von Hesse-Wartegg. Leaving behind their half-eaten dinner and accepting the unavoidable pangs of hunger, he and his friends strolled the streets and examined the buildings: "And such buildings! Each a house of pleasure, furnished with uncertain shapes: billiard parlors, gambling halls, and bordellos, their doors and windows open to the street, inviting passersby inside. From

---

[67] Ibid., June 16, 1877.

every door and window poured vulgar racket: clatter of bottles and clink of glasses, shouts of merrymaking and laughter of debauch. On the streets, teamsters, buffalo hunters, and frontier riffraff milled about. Women of the lowest sort, in flashy clothes, waved invitations to them."

Avoiding such temptation themselves, this party of outsiders was attracted to one particular joint near the depot, from which "through open doors, [a] revolting din blasted at us. Outside huddled groups of doubtful characters: sun-blackened fellows with disheveled hair, messy beards, and bare chests; in leather clothes and heavy boots or Mexican gaiters knee-high; with holstered revolvers belted to their waists. They eyed us suspiciously as we pushed among them into the hall."

Once accustomed to the darkened interior, a delighted Hesse-Wartegg absorbed his surroundings:

> Along the opposite wall the bar groaned under empty and half-empty whiskey bottles. To the right, three musicians crowded a table, playing bass, violin, and drums. Their cacophony offered dancers rhythms that fluctuated between cha-cha and waltz. . . . Meanwhile, in each corner, about a dozen men sat at tables and played cards. Piled on the tables were banknotes and silver coins, as well as large chips of several colors and worth from twenty cents to twenty-five dollars. The cards were Spanish and their unusual designs could be discerned only with difficulty through dirt. Spanish monte and faro were the games; the stakes, incredible. Many onlookers crowded around each table and, with the players, laid bets on the turn of a card. Feverish intensity, interesting to watch, gripped onlookers and players alike. All were silent—except for the scarcely audible, half-suppressed curse that escaped lips now and then, having burst straight from the heart.

Other colorful distractions caught the Austrian's trained eye: "In the middle of the floor, among many holes in its boards, a few couples whirled to the queer time of the music. Giant fellows, teamsters in Latin dress—sombreros, Spanish jackets, and tall hunting boots—as graceful as hippopotamuses, embraced with muscular arms their short-skirted partners. And those priestesses of Terpsichore—delicate, graceful, and mostly in bright colors—could have been nymphs dancing in joyous innocence. Yet what fallen women!"[68]

---

[68] Frederic Trautmann, trans. and ed., "Across Kansas by Train in 1877: The Travels of Ernst von Hesse-Wartegg," *Kansas History: Journal of the Central Plains* 6, no. 3 (Autumn 1983): 159–60. Mr. Trautmann, who translated this wonderful account, described Hesse-Wartegg's companions with a note of humor: "He traveled in a group whose members he neither numbered, named, nor described; but, in passing, he mentioned a professor, a military officer, and an artist."

Hesse-Wartegg may have found the display extraordinarily colorful, but locals accepted it as routine. Besides, at that moment they were too preoccupied with politics to concern themselves with descriptions of what seemed to them nightly fandangos. Voters waited the counting of ballots from the all-important April 2, 1877, city elections. James H. "Dog" Kelley replaced George M. Hoover as mayor. Two members of the five-man city council retained their seats—George B. Cox and D. D. Colley. John Newton, Fred Leonard, and Chalkley M. Beeson took the slots vacated by Charlie Rath, John Mueller, and Hamilton Bell. Kelley nominated his friend, Michael Sutton, for city attorney and city clerk. Larry Deger kept his job as city marshal, but without the full blessing of the new administration. Kelley and Deger disliked one another, and the marshal's reappointment did not lessen the animosity.

Saloonman James Kelley's political success brought with it consequences not to everyone's liking. Simply put, Major Kelley seemed possessed of an adolescent personality. He enjoyed a good time and assumed everyone felt the same, regardless of any attendant social disruption. His views concerning cattle town hospitality were certainly not original. They mirrored precedents established by a succession of political hacks, including James G. Hope, an early mayor of Wichita. While Kelley did not condone violence north of the dead line—an informal boundary insulating the better class of citizens above Front Street—he turned a blind eye to overzealous drovers on the town's south side, at least within loosely defined limits.

Ignoring the danger of allowing someone like James Kelley to hold public office, merchants could hardly contain themselves when contemplating potential profits. The newest members of that fraternity were Gordon E. Hadder and Matthew R. Draper, both in their late twenties, who had started a small store the year before with help from their former Montgomery County employers. Now hoping for more, they opened a much larger Front Street dry-goods emporium in late April 1877, two doors west of Mueller's boot shop. In time this aggressive duo would control one of the major mercantile firms in Dodge City, with branches in other towns and a stock ranch in the Texas Panhandle.

Both proprietors hailed from Ohio. Gordon Hadder arrived in Kansas in 1869, settling in Montgomery County and working for the banking house Parker, York & Company. In 1874 he went to St. Louis for a year, learning more about business as a teller at the Bank of North America.

Matthew Draper had come to Kansas in 1865, settling first near Leaven-worth. After five years as a farm laborer he, too, went to Montgomery County and found more promising employment with Parker, York. In 1873 Draper traveled to St. Louis, finding work as a messenger with the U.S. Express Company. While in the river city, the two men came together over dreams of making a fortune from the cattle trade. They singled out Dodge City as offering the best chance.[69]

To prepare for Texas drovers, petitions and recommendations for saloon licenses flooded the city council. Mayor Kelley, City Marshal Deger, and councilmen C. M. Beeson and D. D. Colley were all assured a favorable response as they joined other hopefuls currying favor at the May 1, 1877, meeting. McGinty & Deger, Garis & Tilghman, Dunhan & Dawson, Beeson & Harris, Springer & Masterson, A. J. Peacock, Beatty & Kelley, G. M. Hoover, Rule & Smith, Cox & Boyd, Langton & Newton, H. J. Fringer, H. B. Bell, Colley & Manion, Chambers & Foster, and Henry Sturm all crowded the small room demanding action. Obviously no one thought the approaching Texans need suffer from thirst.

By mid-April several flocks of sheep arrived from the southwest, keeping stockyards workers and railroad crews busy with heavy loading sched-ules. Most everyone else stared south for signs of beef. Three weeks later trail boss Mike Dalton brought in a herd of 1,200 from the Red River crossings belonging to Powers, Buckley & Company. Dalton had encoun-tered trouble from farmers in Comanche County, then within the dreaded quarantine line. "Grangers went for them like a swarm of mad hornets," reported the *Dodge City Times* on May 12, "and heavy fines and damage money had to be yielded up before the stock could proceed." Powers and Buckley held another 6,000 head in readiness, but there were questions raised whether their firm planned to ship from Dodge City or Ellis. Astride the Kansas Pacific, Ellis seemed the likely choice since Mr. Powers took money from the KP to favor that road. But Ellis could no longer be reached without crossing the dead line.

Dodge City boosters stopped worrying about the troubles plaguing Powers, Buckley & Company after learning from Henry M. Beverley and

[69] *The United States Biographical Dictionary, Kansas Volume*, 309–10; *History of the State of Kansas*, 1561; and *Gould's St. Louis Directory for 1875* (St. Louis, Mo.: David B. Gould, Publisher, 1875), 269.

others in and around Fort Griffin that 100,000 head of cattle were already moving. Nearly 59,000 of these passed Fort Worth by May 12. George W. Littlefield and J. C. "Doc" Dilworth represented the largest contingent, with herds totaling more than 15,000 head. Others—sixteen groups in all—included Dillard R. Fant with two herds numbering 6,200 head; Ellison & Dewees moving 7,100 in all; Hood & Halmsley with 5,500; and others with smaller numbers, including Mifflin Kenedy with 2,000. Reporting these figures, the *Times* ignored subtlety and openly contrasted Dodge City's quarantine-free advantage over other possible shipping points.

The year 1877 proved successful beyond simple comparisons with past years. The stockyards earned even more from the railroad's decision to hold cattle shipped from Colorado. At Dodge City the animals were unloaded, fed, and watered before being returned to trains for the journey east.

The police force seemed to increase in direct proportion to the number of saloons. In early May the mayor and council named Joseph W. Mason an officer. A month later Edward J. Masterson became the assistant marshal, replacing an absent Wyatt Earp. These appointments came none too soon, with two hundred drovers walking the streets. Marshal Larry Deger faced troubles of his own with Robert Gilmore—the ubiquitous Bobby Gill, a member of Mayor Kelley's gang and a man described by Bob Wright as "one of the most notorious characters and . . . the best all-around 'sure thing' man that ever struck Dodge City."[70] Deger confronted Gill for making a public spectacle of himself. Bat Masterson, another favorite of Mayor Kelley, intervened by grabbing the marshal around the neck, allowing Gilmore's escape. Deger, while struggling with Masterson, called on bystanders to grab Bat's gun. Officer Mason did so. With boisterous Texans offering Masterson another revolver, Deger pistol-whipped him to the ground. Gambler Charles Norton stepped forward in Bat's defense but was arrested. Later that afternoon, Edward Masterson, in his first act as assistant marshal, collared Gilmore. The next day Police Judge Daniel Frost fined Bat Masterson twenty-five dollars and costs. Colonel Norton paid ten dollars, and Bobby Gill, standing at the center of the whole mess, was only assessed five dollars.

As small as it was, the police force handled most of its duties with dispatch. It even managed to do so that season of 1877 without the services

---

[70] Wright, *Dodge City, the Cowboy Capital*, 227–28.

of Wyatt Earp, much to the annoyance of later devotees. Even some locals were disappointed: J. Wright Mooar claimed, "He was one of the best officers there."[71] Instead, Wyatt drifted in and out on gambling jaunts. Nor were Earp's experiences in Dodge City all pleasant ones: "Miss Frankie Bell," reported the *Times*, "who wears the belt for superiority in point of muscular ability, heaped epithets upon the unoffending head of Mr. Earp to such an extent as to provoke a slap from the ex-officer, besides creating a disturbance of the quiet and dignity of the city, for which she received a night's lodging in the dog house and a reception at the police court next morning, the expense of which was about $20.00. Wyatt Earp was assessed the lowest limit of the law, one dollar."[72] He was not the only former officer not on duty. Charlie Bassett's one-time deputy, Edward O. Hougue, had died of fever in Wyoming. Later Hougue's Dodge City residence was sold at a sheriff's auction for $325 to satisfy a civil judgment.[73]

Giving his own impressions of the town that June, in an article published under the banner AMONG THE LONG HORNS, one visitor remarked, "Dodge City! yells the brakeman, and with about thirty other sinners we hurry to the Dodge House to ornament the register with our autographs, deposit our grip sacks with Deacon Cox, and breakfast—but what crowd is this we elbow our reportorial nose into? And bless our soul what a sight!" Indeed it was: "We learn that everybody not at the Dodge House is at the 'Alamo.' The Alamo is presided over by a reformed Quaker from New York, and it is hinted that the manner in which he concocts a toddy (every genuine cattle man drinks toddy) increases the value of a Texas steer about $2.75." If true, the man singled out for praise, Henry V. Cook, certainly provided a service. At that very moment the Santa Fe stock agent estimated sixty thousand head grazing outside town and a like number closing in from the south: "The grass is remarkably fine, the water plenty, drinks two for a quarter and no grangers. These facts make Dodge City THE cattle point."[74]

---

[71] J. Wright Mooar to J. Evetts Haley, July 28, 1937. Walter Stanley Campbell Files, Box 98A, Folder 13A, 71. Manuscript Division, Western History Collection, University of Oklahoma.

[72] *Dodge City Times*, July 21, 1877.

[73] Michael Hoffman and J. C. Brockeck (?) vs. E. O. Hogue [*sic*]. Records of the Ford County District Court, Civil Appearance Docket A, 79; and M. Hoffman and J. C. Bronecke (?) vs. Ed Hogue [*sic*] and Louise J. Hogue, A. J. Peacock and Emma L. Peacock, Judge's Journal, Book A, 61–62. Also see notice, "Sheriff's Sale," *Dodge City Times*, July 21, August 18, 1877.

[74] *Dodge City Times*, June 16, 1877. George M. Hoover and Henry V. Cook were the proprietors of the Alamo saloon during this period. The reference to "a reformed Quaker from New York" alludes to Mr. Cook, who was born in New York in 1847. This is the same man who sued Major Dodge in 1874 as a result of being arrested during the turmoil surrounding William Taylor's murder the year before.

As if accepting the town's economic legitimacy, outsiders described Dodge City far less critically than in years past. G. C. Nobel of the *Atchison Champion*, seemed surprised by what he saw: "This being our first visit to the metropolis of the West, we were very pleasantly surprised, after the cock and bull stories that lunatic correspondents had given the public. Not a man was seen swinging from a telegraph pole; not a pistol was fired; no disturbance of any kind was noted. . . . The Texas cattle men and cowboys, instead of being armed to the teeth, with blood in their eye, conduct themselves with propriety, many of them being thorough gentlemen."[75]

Texas drovers often behaved better than the locals, including the mayor. James Kelley tended to take the power of his office too seriously. In one embarrassing incident he interfered with the arrest of Charles Ronan, a gambler and barman loosely associated with the mayor's gang. Marshal Deger and Mayor Kelley acknowleged their differences, and Kelley made it clear he wanted Larry Deger out of office since he refused to support the mayor's liberal policy on questions of law enforcement. James Kelley's animosity bubbled to the surface with his friend's arrest.

Marshal Deger had no sooner locked up Ronan than Mayor Kelley stormed in, demanding his release. Deger refused. Kelley ordered the marshal to surrender his badge and consider himself suspended. Deger ignored him. Incensed, Kelley ordered Assistant Marshal Edward Masterson and policeman Joe Mason to arrest their boss. Clearly uncomfortable, both hesitated to act. For his part, Deger pulled a revolver and refused arrest. As Mayor Kelley stuttered with rage, cooler heads prevailed. Masterson suggested Marshal Deger submit to arrest until everything could be resolved. Deger agreed and spent ten minutes behind bars before being released on his own recognizance.

Later that morning a complaint was filed against Kelley, charging him with interfering with an officer. The mayor now found himself under arrest. The two cases came before Police Judge Daniel Frost, who ruled that Deger had violated no ordinance and tossed out the case. Before Kelley could face the judge, the city council held a special session to investigate "the conduct and actions of certain city officers."[76] They meant Deger, not Kelley, who had charged the marshal with misconduct despite the court's ruling. Kelley's plan misfired. The council dismissed charges

---

[75] Ibid., July 7, 1877.
[76] Ibid., "City Council," July 21, 1877.

against Deger, and ordered him to resume his duties. Seething with resentment, the mayor could do little more than approve the council's findings. A majority of councilmen then petitioned Judge Frost, favoring a *nolle prosequi*—a dismissal of the suit—be entered in the mayor's case. Frost agreed and discharged Kelley. Unfortunately, James Kelley was not one to forgive or forget. His resentment of Marshal Deger now extended to Judge Frost.

Deger then rearrested Bobby Gill, this time for vagrancy. The prisoner confessed his sins but begged forgiveness. Testimony described him as a troublemaker, noting his preference for quarrels and street fights. Others testified in Bobby's defense, disavowing the vagrancy charge by claiming he always carried more than enough money to pay his bills. The judge seemed inclined to agree, but public opinion preferred Mr. Gilmore's deportation. Bobby agreed to leave if charity could provide him train fare at least as far as Emporia. Marshal Deger took up a collection and escorted him to the depot. A subdued Robert Gilmore would eventually return, but many of his friends, including Mayor Kelley and Bat Masterson, resented Deger's involvement in the case.

Masterson did not forgive Deger for the pistol-whipping. By now both men also worked for Charlie Bassett, Deger as a regular deputy and Masterson as under sheriff. As tensions grew between the two, Bat forced Deger's resignation from the sheriff's office in early August. Less than two months later, however, Deger actually hired Masterson as a special policeman for ten days. It seems likely he did so because of pressure from his assistant marshal, Ed Masterson, for whom Deger had great respect, along with a resentful Mayor Kelley and at least two members of the city council quite friendly with the brothers.

This rivalry continued into autumn when Deger and Masterson each announced their candidacy for sheriff of Ford County. The state constitution prohibited Charlie Bassett from seeking a third consecutive two-year term. Describing the contest, the *Dodge City Times* seemed to favor Masterson, but also offered some kind words on behalf of Deger: "He has been City Marshal of this city for a long time, and his ability to keep the peace has been often tested. Give him a fair consideration. He is a substantial, honest and upright man."[77] Another candidate, George T. Hinkle, soon quit the race and threw his support to Deger.

---

[77] Ibid., October 13, 1877.

Hoping for consensus, a so-called "People's Mass Convention" was organized for Saturday evening October 27. Interest ran high, with about two hundred voters packing Garis & Tilghman's Lady Gay saloon at the appointed hour. P. L. Beatty gaveled the meeting to order. Attorney Mike Sutton nominated councilman D. D. Colley as chairman. The purpose was to sanction a single slate of candidates for the November ballot. While votes were not binding, they did give some indication of the political sympathies of major Dodge City figures—those who supported the popular mayor's so-called gang, and those who did not. The anti-gang faction had already begun coalescing around Police Judge Daniel M. Frost.

John Means won the endorsement for county clerk, and then attention focused on the sheriff's race. George M. Hoover jumped up to nominate Lawrence E. Deger. Former city attorney Harry E. Gryden, a long-time Democrat, seconded the nomination, as did lawyers William N. Morphy and Daniel Frost. P. L. Beatty nominated William B. Masterson. Attorney Sutton, and saloonmen Chalkley Beeson and James M. Manion joined others loudly seconding Beatty's choice. Sutton followed with a rousing oration. The vote favored Masterson, although no precise numbers were given.

Beatty nominated Charles H. Lane for county treasurer, with Mike Sutton uncorking another spirited performance. Harry Gryden backed Fred Leonard for the same post, with William Morphy offering Frederick Zimmerman. No one got a majority. Convention officers ordered another ballot. Leonard withdrew, throwing his support to Zimmerman, but Lane won the nomination. The convention went on to consider other candidates. The evening's results pleased Jim Kelley. His Honor would ride an unprecedented wave of popularity, but not without opposition.

Political differences were not confined to ballot box irregularities. One dispute between William Morphy and Robert Wright ended in a scuffle two days before the election. Morphy claimed that his support for Deger and Zimmerman started the trouble. It ended with Wright pistol-whipping Morphy, then kicking the bleeding lawyer about the face and head as he lay on the street. Refusing to take this abuse lying down, so to speak, Morphy filed suit seeking $3,000 in damages. Wright denied the allegations as the sheriff's office began serving subpoenas. Ninth District Court judge Samuel R. Peters heard the case during the January 1878 term, with attorneys Sutton and Colborn representing the defendant, and Harry E. Gryden

presenting evidence for Morphy. Highlighting the informal nature of proceedings in those days, J. J. Webb, one of the subpoenaed witnesses for the
defense, also served as a juror. Not that it mattered much in the long run.
Wright was found guilty, but the court awarded the battered Mr. Morphy
a mere $4.50 and costs, just enough to cover his medical expenses.[78]

Undaunted by the People's Mass Convention, Larry Deger announced
his intention to run for sheriff as an independent. Frederick Zimmerman
ran for treasurer under the same banner. County commissioners met at the
clerk's office on November 9 to announce the results. Bat Masterson
defeated Larry Deger, but only by 3 votes.[79] In the race for treasurer,
Charles Lane turned back Zimmerman's challenge, 189 to 150. P. L. Beatty
retained his post as township trustee.[80]

Following his narrow defeat, Deger filed suit contesting the results. A
month later the city council fired Deger and promoted Assistant Marshal
Edward Masterson to the vacancy. Feeling self righteous over Deger's
downfall, the council felt no qualms hiring the likes of Prairie Dog Dave
Morrow and John Joshua Webb as temporary policeman. With Councilman Colley and others named assistant judges to reexamine the vote count
for sheriff, and with the hearing scheduled before Probate Judge Herman
J. Fringer, Deger saw the futility in facing a panel packed with the mayor's
allies and withdrew his suit.

Deger's dismissal caused some bitterness. But as the *Times* noted on
December 8, "Notwithstanding the fact that considerable feeling was man-
ifest against the removal of Mr. Deger, no one accuses Mr. Masterson of
seeking the position." The former marshal later suggested that at least one
councilman admitted voting against him for his tardiness in withdrawing
his challenge. The newspaper also acknowledged political reality: "In justice
to Mr. Deger we will say that no charge of misconduct was brought against
him. . . . The powers that be saw fit to make the change, and it was made. It
was made on the principal [*sic*] that 'there are just as good men in the party
as out of it.' "

Before taking office, Edward Masterson was wounded during an altercation in the Lone Star dance hall on the afternoon of November 5. A

---

[78] W. N. Morphy vs. R. M. Wright, Records of the Ford County District Court, Judge's Journal A, 125; and
Unnumbered Civil Case files.

[79] *Dodge City Times*, November 10, 1877. Legend mistakenly has Masterson crushing Deger "by a two-to-one
majority." Lake, *Wyatt Earp, Frontier Marshal*, 191.

[80] Ford County Commissioners Journals, Book A, 213; and *Dodge City Times*, November 10, 1877.

man from Georgia named Bob Shaw accused another of stealing forty dollars. Both men had been drinking. When Masterson arrived, he spotted Shaw "by the bar with a huge pistol in his hand and a hogshead of blood in his eye, ready to relieve Texas Dick of his existence in this world and send him to those shades where troubles come not and six shooters are not known." Masterson smashed Shaw on the back of his head with a pistol, but he refused to go down. Instead, Shaw squeezed off a shot, striking the officer under the right arm. As he fell, Masterson shifted his pistol and began firing, hitting Shaw in the left arm and leg.[81]

Two others were wounded: Texas Dick took a ball in the groin and bystander Frank Buskirk was hit in the left arm. Drs. Tom McCarty and Sam Galland treated everyone's wounds. Masterson was up and about within the week. He visited his parents at Wichita before becoming Dodge City's chief of police, despite a petition signed by Dan Frost, Fred Zimmerman, and others protesting Deger's removal. To downplay those objections, Kelley made the smart move of appointing the popular Charlie Bassett as Masterson's assistant marshal.

Perhaps overcome with confidence, Kelley and his supporters tried ridding themselves of Police Judge Daniel Frost. On the same day as the pro-Deger petition reached the city council, a second petition arrived signed by W. B. Masterson, P. L. Beatty, Robert M. Wright, and others charging Frost with being a nonresident. Frost moved back within the city limits before anything could be done. Round one between Kelley and his opponents was over.

More took place that fall of 1877 than the simple maneuvering of discordant politicians. On November 24 the pioneer mercantile firm Charles Rath & Company dissolved. The firm then reorganized as Wright, Beverley & Company, the principals being Robert M. Wright, Henry M. Beverley, and the newly elected county treasurer, Charles H. Lane. The new firm employed councilman John Newton as bookkeeper, along with a number of experienced clerks, including Jim W. Skinner, a former lightning rod agent who had worked at Rath & Company's Palo Duro store in Texas, and

---

[81] *Dodge City Times*, November 10, 1877. Shaw recovered and was allowed to return home, his wounds judged sufficient punishment for his drunken indiscretion. The newspaper noted a week later: "Shaw is not a desperado as would seem from this incident. Parties who have known him say he never was known to make a six-shooter play before this. Dr. Galland, under whose medical treatment he so rapidly recovered, has a high regard for him. Mr. Shaw's family are highly respectable people, and he has concluded to quit the far west and go back to live under the parental roof."

S. E. Isaacson, who, along with Henry Beverley, had learned the business from Mayer Goldsoll at Ellsworth and Great Bend. The Spanish-speaking Sam Samuels, put in charge of firearms and jewelry, served the large numbers of Mexican drovers.

The fifty-year-old Henry Beverley, known to everyone in the cattle business as "Judge," had been associated with Rath & Company for some time, first as a salesman, then as the firm's chief Texas agent. As such, he helped point many of the early herds toward Dodge City. Although a Virginian by birth, Beverley served in a Texas regiment during the Civil War. He later worked as a drover, and thus understood their needs. Coming to Kansas in 1870 Beverley saw the railroad towns, including wild and sinful Abilene. After settlers closed that market he drifted to Ellsworth. In May 1874 Beverley opened a restaurant before associating himself with Mayer Goldsoll in the mercantile trade.

When it became obvious that Dodge City would become the new cowboy capital, Beverley joined up with Charlie Rath and Bob Wright. Now he found himself a full partner in one of the most prosperous firms on the Kansas frontier. Celebrating his good fortune, Beverley moved his large family to Dodge. He took over a comfortable stone house built by Henry L. Sitler, who, despite his large holdings in local real estate, planned to remove his family to a farm he owned far to the east in Chase County.

The change in ownership did not leave Charlie Rath stranded. As part of the new arrangement, he took over the old company's operations in Texas: a store at Rath City, others on the Palo Duro, and one at Sweetwater that even then was being relocated to nearby Fort Elliott. Rath also owned a store at Fort Griffin in partnership with Frank E. Conrad that never was part of the Dodge City company.

While working these scattered interests in Texas, Rath kept in close contact with Dodge City through frequent visits and by reporting a schedule of cattle passing Fort Griffin. The *Kansas City Commercial Indicator* printed reports from Conrad and Rath for a number of seasons. The partners provided dates, names of owners and trail bosses, starting points and destinations, and the numbers of cattle involved, along with their brands. Since most of these herds had some contact with Dodge City, everyone awaited copies of that paper sent out from Missouri.

Other changes took place after the creation of Wright, Beverley &

Company. The *Dodge City Times* changed hands. Walter Shinn sold his interest to Nicholas B. Klaine on the first of December. On that very day, hoping that what he wrote turned out to be true, Shinn reported: "The TIMES has always been free from political rings or party cliques, and the solid business which has been built up for it will enable it to stand fearlessly and independently alone in the future." Walter's brother, Lloyd, a newly elected justice of the peace, who had also been serving as city treasurer since early September, stayed on at the *Times* for another eight months. Walter became more involved in real estate and bought the old Rath tannery. He would be in and out of Dodge City for years.

Nicholas Klaine, a friend of County Attorney Michael Sutton since 1867, came to Dodge from Warrensburg, Missouri, selling his interest in the *Standard-Herald*, a paper he helped found in 1865. Born in New Jersey to French parents in 1839, Klaine moved west as a boy. He learned the printing trade at Rock Island, Illinois, then worked as a journeyman printer on the *St. Louis Republican*. During the war he saw action with a Missouri cavalry regiment assigned to General Sherman's forces. Mustered out in 1864, Klaine arrived at Warrensburg, an area still Confederate in its sympathies, carrying with him his own ideas about journalism and politics. In spite of his obvious Republican leanings, Johnson County voters sent him to the state legislature in 1868. When he pulled out for Kansas and found a place for himself on the *Dodge City Times*, this Union Army veteran was serving Warrensburg as city clerk.[82] Ignoring Walter Shinn's promise of maintaining the paper's political independence, Klaine would turn the *Times* into an aggressive Republican organ.

Hoping to thwart what they considered the political high-handedness and other excesses of Mayor Kelley's regime, Daniel Frost and William Morphy founded the *Ford County Globe* on Christmas Day 1877. They brought out their next issue on January 1, 1878, and for some reason listed both as "Vol. I, No. 1." Morphy served as editor while Frost acted as publisher. The *Globe* appeared as a four-page, six-column weekly. In their December issue, the proprietors wasted no time getting down to business, declaring, "We owe allegiance to no man, clique, or party, and shall do our

---

[82] Hill P. Wilson, comp., *A Biographical History of Eminent Men of the State of Kansas* (Topeka: The Hall Lithographing Company, 1901), 575–77; Ewing Cockrell, *History of Johnson County, Missouri* (Topeka: Historical Publishing Company, 1918), 99, 217, 339; and *History of the State of Kansas*, 1561.

duty as to us seems best, regardless of where the axe falls." Of course they hoped the axe would fall repeatedly on the head of Mayor Kelley and his allies. Readers would enjoy years of spirited exchanges as both papers took journalistic pot shots at one another.

The thirty-two-year-old Daniel Frost had already become a political figure of sorts. A Pennsylvania native, Frost had come to Kansas from Illinois in 1868, settling at Sheridan where he clerked in a general store. He returned there in 1870, after playing the role of mining speculator at Elizabethtown, New Mexico, but soon left again, this time for Kit Carson, Colorado. There he found work as a schoolteacher and served as deputy postmaster. At the same time he became associated with one of the town's leading mercantile firms. After fire nearly destroyed the town and wiped out his livelihood, Frost visited Dodge City for the first time in late 1872. He retreated to Sargent, where he was appointed postmaster and ran a small store. Frost was elected a Hamilton County justice of the peace in late April 1874, but returned to Dodge that summer, and on December 18 was admitted to the Ford County bar. Now, together with his law practice, Daniel Frost busied himself with journalism as a major voice in opposition to James Kelley.[83]

The year 1877 had been an exciting one. Although most cattle passing through the Dodge City market were destined for stock ranges farther north (hence the term "through cattle"), records of the AT&SF showed an official tally of 22,940 head shipped, representing an increase of 13,400 animals over the total for 1876.[84] Official figures were disputed somewhat by numbers kept at Dodge City. Those sources claimed a slightly higher total shipped through December 1. The *Dodge City Times* included 498 cars unloaded and handled at the city's facilities from Colorado.[85] Whatever the actual figure, the business generated pleased merchants and ordinary citizens alike, as they looked to the future with growing confidence. For many, however, 1878 would bring disquieting memories of the past.

---

[83] *The Rocky Mountain Directory and Colorado Gazetteer* (Denver: S. S. Wallihan & Company, 1871), 411; *History of the State of Kansas*, 1561; *Kansas Daily Commonwealth*, November 7, 1873, May 6, 1874; Post Office Department, Records of Appointment of Postmasters, Vol. 33, 1867–73, Sargent, Hamilton County, Kansas, 868, National Archives and Records Service; Baughman, *Kansas Post Offices*, 188; Ford County Commissioners Journals, Book A, 26, 33; and Records of the Ford County District Court, Judge's Journal, Book A, 22.

[84] *Annual Report of the Board of Directors of the Atchison, Topeka, and Santa Fe Railroad Co. . . . for the year ending December 31, 1877* (Boston: Press of George Ellis, 1878), 26. This report also noted: "A careful estimate located about 45,000 head of cattle wintering in the counties south of this line between Newton and Dodge."

[85] *Dodge City Times*, December 8, 1877.

HENRY L. SITLER'S SOD HOUSE,
THE FIRST STRUCTURE ON THE PROPOSED DODGE CITY TOWNSITE.

In 1872 it occupied space south of the tracks, slightly north and some thirty feet east of the southeast corner of Front Street and Third Avenue. Encroaching upon Front Street assured its eventual demise.

DODGE CITY IN 1872, WAGONS LOADED WITH BUFFALO HIDES.

To the left is Daniel Wolf's general store, followed by Smith and Edwards's grocery, and one of the first dance halls. Hoover and McDonald's tent saloon stood to the left, out of view. They soon shifted operations to the north side of Front Street.

SOUTH OF THE RAILROAD'S RIGHT OF WAY, LOOKING WEST IN LATE 1872. Grading contractors Cutler and Wiley owned the long building on the right. A barbershop occupied the tent at the far left. Failing to conform with boundaries of the original townsite plat, most of these early buildings were soon dismantled.

With the AT&SF opening for business in October 1872, the company rushed operations with these two freight cars serving as its temporary depot. Located amidst its tracks at the foot of Railroad Avenue, the arrangement was replaced in 1873 with a more permanent structure. Over the years this location was improved with a series of ever-larger facilities.

(*left*) Robert M. Wright, sutler at Fort Dodge, pioneer merchant, and founding member of the Dodge City Town Company, also served as a state legislator and later as mayor. Present from the beginning, Wright saw it all, getting personally involved in many controversies. Looking back two years before his death, he published his reflections in *Dodge City, the Cowboy Capital.*

(*right*) William L. "Billy" Brooks, stage driver and former Newton city marshal. A man of small stature and sour disposition, he was chosen to keep the peace in early Dodge City chiefly because of his propensities as a killer. Those activities helped establish the town's reputation for violent excesses.

RATH & COMPANY'S HIDE YARD IN 1873.
Charlie Rath sits atop thousands of specimens being readied for shipment.

LOOKING SOUTHEAST FROM BOOT HILL IN 1873.
Rath & Company can be identified by its distinctive outside staircase.
The railroad's water tank and the Arkansas River fill in the background.

DODGE CITY NORTH OF THE TRACKS IN 1873.

The first building on the left is Isaac Young's harness shop and makeshift justice court, followed by Herman Fringer's drug store, a building that included the post office. Across Second Avenue is Rath & Company. To the right are the railroad's depot and water tank.

A PORTION OF FRONT STREET IN 1873.

From left to right, Hoover & McDonald's saloon and wholesale liquors, Frederick Zimmerman's hardware, Dr. McCarty's original drug store, Morris Collar's O. K. Clothing, and A. J. Peacock's saloon and billiard parlor. The woman seated in front of Hoover & McDonald's is thought to be Mollie Whitecamp, the prostitute known as Dutch Jake.

GOVERNOR'S
PROCLAMATION.

STATE OF KANSAS,

Executive Department,

TOPEKA, JULY 21st, 1873.

WHEREAS, William Taylor was murdered at Dodge City, Ford County, Kansas, on or about the 3d day of June, 1873, and whereas, one John Scott, alias Scotty, described as being about 28 years of age, five feet eight and one-half inches in height, brown hair, gray eyes, and strongly built, with small scar on forehead, is known to have been one of the perpetrators of said crime, and is now at large, and a fugitive from justice.

NOW THEREFORE, I, Thomas A. Osborn, Governor of the State of Kansas, in pursuance of law, do hereby offer a reward of Five Hundred Dollars for the apprehension and conviction of the said John Scott.

In Testimony Whereof, I have hereunto subscribed my name, and caused to be affixed the Great Seal of the State. Done at Topeka, this 21st day of July, 1873.

L. S.

THOMAS A. OSBORN,

By the Governor:
W. H. SMALLWOOD, Secretary of State.

REWARD OFFERED BY THE STATE OF KANSAS FOR
THE CAPTURE OF JOHN SCOTT FOLLOWING THE SLAYING OF WILLIAM TAYLOR.
This event represented the most brutal murder of an unarmed innocent
during Dodge City's early months of anarchy.

(*clockwise from above*) George M. Hoover, pioneer saloonman and liquor wholesaler. He grew with the town, reinventing himself as an entrepreneur, flourmill operator, and president of the Bank of Dodge City. Along the way he twice served as mayor and helped organize the *Dodge City Democrat* in late 1883.

Coming down from Hays City, Lawrence E. Deger served as city marshal as early as 1876. Despite his 307-pound girth he performed his duties with dispatch and was soon appointed a deputy U.S. marshal for the area.

Pioneer saloonman, restaurateur, and disruptive four-term mayor James H. Kelley (standing at left with one of his ever-present hounds) along with local butcher Charles S. Hungerford.

GUNSMITH AND HARDWARE MERCHANT FREDERICK ZIMMERMAN,
STANDING JUST TO THE RIGHT OF HIS FRONT STREET ESTABLISHMENT IN 1873.
Zimmerman holds the hand of this three-year-old son, Arthur. Matilda Zimmerman
sits next to Arthur, with her infant daughter Clarissa, born in Colorado just prior to
the family's move to Dodge City, resting in the carriage.

FRONT STREET IN 1876, LOOKING WEST FROM FIRST AVENUE.
Beatty & Kelley's saloon, the Centennial Barber Shop, and their restaurant take up the
first two lots, followed by Jacob Collar's general merchandise, the Saratoga saloon, J.
Tyler's Tonsorial Parlor (later the Lone Star saloon and restaurant), McCarty's drug
store, Morris Collar's dry goods, Zimmerman's hardware, George Hoover's saloon and
wholesale liquors, the Long Branch, the Alamo, and Rath & Company.

(*clockwise from above*) Nicholas B. Klaine, after buying the interests of the two Shinn brothers, turned the *Dodge City Times* into a champion of Mayor James Kelley and his political gang. Later, in a bizarre reversal of intent, the editor embraced religion and Prohibition reform with equal fervor.

Daniel M. Frost. Differences with Mayor Kelley convinced Frost and his partner, William M. Morphy, to launch an opposition newspaper, the *Ford County Globe*.

City Marshal Edward J. Masterson, murdered April 9, 1878, while arresting an intoxicated drover at A. J. Peacock's south side saloon.

Following the Dull Knife scare in 1878, seven Northern Cheyennes were indicted for murder in Ford County. Here, on April 30, 1879, the defendants sit on the courthouse steps with their interpreter, George Reynolds. At the top is Franklin G. Adams, the first secretary of the Kansas State Historical Society. The final disposition of the case surprised many.

(*clockwide from above*) Varieties entertainer Dora Hand, killed October 4, 1878, by a bullet quite possibly meant for the mayor.

Harry E. Gryden, lawyer and political gymnast who often landed on the wrong side of controversial issues. Despite these self-generated handicaps, Gryden remained one of the more colorful members of Dodge City's professional class.

Attorney Michael W. Sutton possessed gifts worthy of Machiavelli. With fingers in every public purse and his ear to the ground, Sutton backed Mayor Kelley's gang as long as it suited him, shifting allegiances just as quickly-ending up allied with reformers as a newly minted temperance devotee. Along the way he made enemies, even claiming Mayor Robert Wright tried to kill him while firing several shots into his house.

BIRD'S EYE VIEW OF

DODGE CITY, KANS.

COUNTY SEAT OF FORD COUNTY

1882

POPULATION 1200

1. Court House.
2. School House.
3. U. S. Signal Service Office.
4. Odd Fellows Hall.
5. A. T. & S. F. R. R. Depot.
6. Post Office.
7. Dodge City Lloyd Shinn, P. M.
X—Methodist Episcopal Church.
A—Presbyterian "
B—Roman Catholic "
C—Union "

Dodge City Grist Mill, H. F. May & Co., Prop's.

D—Dodge City Times, N. B. Klaine Ed'r and Prop.
E—Ford Co. Globe, Frost & Shinn, Ed's and Prop's.
F—Dodge House, Cox & Boyd, Prop's.
G—Iowa " W. C. Beebe, Prop.
H—South Side House, South end of Bridge.
  (Wm. Suetes, Prop.
J—Great Western Hotel.
K—Wright House.

Published by J. J. Stoner, Madison, Wis.

Beck & Pauli, Lithographers, Milwaukee, Wis.

FRONT STREET, LOOKING WEST FROM RAILROAD AVENUE IN LATE SPRING 1879.
West of the Dodge House is Mueller's boot shop, a bakery, police judge Samuel Marshall's land office, York, Hadder & Draper's mercantile, Hungerford's butcher shop, and the Occident and Old House saloons. Beyond Second Avenue Beatty & Kelley's new two-story meeting hall, restaurant, and saloon is under construction.

THE LONG BRANCH, SCENE OF THE SHOOTING DEATHS OF
HARRY T. MCCARTY AND LEVI RICHARDSON.
Later disagreements with proprietor William H. Harris and his new partner Luke Short helped precipitate the Dodge City War. Beeson and Harris had earlier moved over from the Saratoga, with Chalkley Beeson and his wife purchasing the Long Branch property in 1878. Retiring from the saloon business before all the trouble, Beeson owned the land under the Long Branch for forty years.

NORTHWEST CORNER OF FRONT STREET AND SECOND AVENUE.
Wedged between Wright, Beverley & Co. (Henry Beverley is standing on the street in front of the building) and the Long Branch is the much narrower Stock Exchange, a saloon formerly known as the Alamo, owned by one-time reform mayor A. B. Webster in 1883.

THE BULLFIGHT ARENA.
This activity served as the center of the storm highlighting Dodge City's controversial Fourth of July celebrations of 1884.

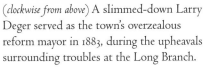
(*clockwise from above*) A slimmed-down Larry Deger served as the town's overzealous reform mayor in 1883, during the upheavals surrounding troubles at the Long Branch.

Alonzo B. Webster, early grocer and dry goods merchant who eventually recognized the profits to be made from liquor. His ownership of the Stock Exchange, along with political and personal differences with William H. Harris, linked with stiff competition from the Long Branch, helped bring about the Dodge City War.

Bat Masterson, one of Dodge City's more colorful and controversial citizens. When Dr. Galland's Great Western hotel became the scene of a bitter confrontation between Prohibition reformers and locals angry over the temporary closing of saloons in late June 1885, Bat saved the day. But not even the redoubtable Mr. Masterson could hold back the tide that would forever change Dodge City into something decidedly different from its formative years.

THE DODGE CITY PEACE COMMISSION.
Photograph taken in Charles A. Conkling's south side studio in early June 1883. (*front row, left to right*) Charles E. Bassett, Wyatt Earp, W. F. McLain, and Neil Brown. (*back row*)William H. Harris, Luke Short, Bat Masterson, and William F. Petillon.

HAMILTON BELL'S VARIETIES, A SALOON AND DANCE HALL ON THE SOUTH SIDE. George Masterson is tending bar. Note the gaming tables and the large number of well-dressed women present. In later years such establishments drew the ire of Dr. Samuel Galland and a growing retinue of Prohibition agitators.

Chapter 7

1878: Another Year of Chaos

On New Year's Day 1878 the *Ford County Globe* printed an unflattering item from the *Washington Evening Star*: "Dodge City is a wicked little town. Indeed its character is so clearly and egregiously bad that one might conclude—were the evidence in these latter times positive of its possibility—that it was marked for special Providential punishment." Of course the *Globe* took issue with this slur from the nation's capital, without knowing the town was about to give the appearance of replaying its violent past.[1]

Unsuspecting, Dodge City prepared for the coming cattle season with customary gusto. Clemence Zingsheim opened a one-man cigar factory behind Beatty & Kelley's. In exchange for some kind words, he dropped off samples at both newspaper offices. Alonzo B. Webster stopped peddling groceries and dry goods and rented his choice Front Street location to boot makers John Mueller and Walter Straeter. Those two, already employing half a dozen men, planned to service more than cattlemen's footwear. They busied themselves turning Webster's old place into the Bon Ton Saloon—soon renamed the Old House. Despite rumors of his entering the cattle business himself, Webster, anticipating a building boom, joined up with the Brinkman brothers to open a lumberyard south of the tracks.

To the casual observer Dodge City presented a façade of peaceful prosperity. Most of the residual rancor over the sheriff's race had faded by late January. Two weeks after his swearing in, William B. Masterson began proving his mettle, however slim his margin of victory. Early on a Sunday morning, five desperadoes tried unsuccessfully to rob the railroad station at Kinsley. A local posse saddled up but lost the trail in thick ground fog. Meetings at Dodge City the following afternoon with Superintendent W. H.

---

[1] Editors at the *Globe* remarked, "We think this correspondent had a sour stomach, when he portrayed the wickedness of our city." They did go on to say, however, "He . . . makes several good points, which are full of wisdom for all of those who desire to see the truth. We dislike very much to have our town spoken of abroad, in this manner, but we must expect it unless we ourselves, try to improve the present conditions of things."

Pettibone of the AT&SF ended with the railroad posting $100 rewards for the outlaws, payable dead or alive.

Frustrated, people at Kinsley pointed fingers at the Ford County sheriff's office, upsetting those in Dodge City. Even Deger supporters William Morphy and Daniel Frost joined the revolt. Testiness turned to pride after Masterson and his posse returned with two of the wanted men, Edgar West and Dave Rudabaugh. Suspicion also led to the arrest of saloonman William Tilghman, a former buffalo hunter and one-time friend of Hurricane Bill Martin and Dutch Henry Born. Retreating from its earlier stance, the Kinsley press now admitted, "We give Sheriff Masterson of Ford due credit for his activity in pursuing and capturing the brigands. He did his duty finally and no more." Reprinting this quasi-apology on February 12, the *Ford County Globe* added a sarcastic "thank you."

Learning more about the other outlaws, Masterson, Charlie Bassett, J. J. Webb, and another man—either Miles Mix or Red Clarke—armed themselves for pursuit. Forewarned, the wanted men found refuge in the rough country along the Cimarron. After enduring thirteen days in the saddle, the lawmen returned home, worn out and disappointed. Perhaps hoping to mend political fences, the sheriff visited Spearville, but without the desired result: "W. M. Sutton, Bat Masterson and Lloyd Shinn, were up here the other day. They button holed a number of our citizens, but I think did not derive much comfort. Somehow the people of the east end of the County, do not train with the 'gang.' Although Shinn labored long and earnestly, I have not heard of any new subscribers to the Times."[2]

Political frustration was short-lived. On the evening of March 15, policeman Nat Haywood spotted another of the Kinsley train suspects in a south-side saloon and hurried off to inform the sheriff. Masterson turned to his brother Edward and Charlie Bassett for assistance. At Anderson's livery stable the officers learned that two men had just ridden out, heading south. Traveling by moonlight the lawmen overtook the fugitives, arresting Tom Gott and J. D. Greene. They offered little resistance after one of them got his revolver hopelessly tangled up in his clothes. The next day, James Masterson, J. J. Webb, and Bassett took up the trail of Mike Roarke and a man known only as Lefeu, but came back empty handed.

---

[2] Correspondent "DePew" reporting from Spearville, March 1, 1878. As quoted in *Ford County Globe*, March 5, 1878.

Before trial, Dave Rudabaugh wiggled free by turning state's evidence. Officers released William Tilghman, admitting a case of mistaken identity. Edgar West, Tom Gott, and J. D. Greene pleaded guilty and were sentenced to five years in prison. The people of Ford County looked back on this messy affair with pride in their new sheriff.

Events surrounding the attempted Kinsley train robbery highlighted the volatile nature of life on the Kansas frontier. In Dodge City the availability of firearms and the chance of violence prompted a complaint from the *Globe*. Writing under the headline "The Festive Revolver," the editor noted the habit of carrying weapons in defiance of local ordinance: "An honest man attending to his own business, doesn't require the constant companionship of a six-shooter, to make him feel easy and safe. We think there is something rotten with a man's conscience when he parades the streets with an exposed six-shooter, knowing that he is violating law with impunity, simply because he is a friend of the marshal or policeman."[3]

Others were too busy with their own affairs to become embroiled in that old controversy. George M. Hoover and partner Henry V. Cook moved their saloon from the Alamo to Hoover's old site. Colley and Manion then shifted one door west from the Long Branch into the Alamo. Chalkley Beeson and William H. Harris took over the Long Branch after leaving the Saratoga. Merchants York, Hadder & Draper, having outgrown their store near Mueller's boot shop, reopened with a larger assortment of goods on the old Saratoga site.[4]

Since the attitude of city government could very well determine success or failure during the upcoming cattle season, politics dominated almost every other consideration. Capitalizing on Sheriff Masterson's performance, James Kelley ran for a second one-year term as mayor. As a recognized member of the mayor's gang, the sheriff's actions reflected favorably on the office. The profitable business climate, together with relative peace and quiet, assured Kelley's chances. Indeed, the mayor's popularity was such that no one mounted a serious challenge, despite opposition from Dan Frost and his still-small band of stalwarts.

---

[3] *Ford County Globe*, March 5, 1878.

[4] Ford County Register of Deeds, Book A, 506–507. Hadder and Draper bought this property from Ida M. Beeson for twenty-five hundred dollars. The location is identified as Lot 28, Block 4, on the north side of Front Street and four lots west of First Avenue. A. J. Anthony originally owned the site, long before Beeson and Harris opened their first saloon there.

Not that Kelley ignored all complaints. With the election in mind he encouraged the marshal to confront a persistent eyesore: "City Marshal Masterson contemplates organizing a tramp brigade for the purpose of cleaning the streets and alleys of the filth and rubbish that has been accumulating for a year or so. There are about thirty tramps now sojourning among us, all of whom have no visible means of support and are liable to arrest under the vagrant act."[5]

When voters went to the polls on April 1, 1878, they cast their ballots almost exclusively for Kelley. Independent challenger Jeems Dalton stumbled into second place with nine votes, followed by Samuel Galland with three and George Hoover with one. Editors at the *Globe* swallowed their pride and reported, "The City election passed off quietly. The gang elected their ticket without opposition which insures a perpetuation of the same condition of things as now exists."[6]

The election had taken place on April Fools' Day. Not content with political shenanigans, several of the boys ran through the streets at three o'clock that morning yelling, "Fire!" Alarm bells sounded and pistols shots punctuated the air. Sleepy members of the fire company muscled out the hook-and-ladder wagon and raced toward the Lady Gay. Turning the corner, they proceeded about a block down Bridge Street before discovering that someone had set fire to a pile of debris on a small island in the river. It proved to be a successful April Fools' prank since "everybody was out to see the fire, [but] you couldn't find a man, woman or child, over two years and a half old who would acknowledge that he had heard the alarm or was waked at all." Not everyone escaped embarrassment by a simple denial: "One of the fallen frail, ran against a wagon yesterday morning while rushing to see where the fire was, she now mourns the loss of several teeth. This is rather expensive April foolishness."[7]

Nine days later, around ten in the evening, a more serious tragedy took place. Marshal Edward Masterson and his newly appointed assistant, Nat Haywood—the one-time policeman and former manager of Cox and

---

[5] *Dodge City Times*, March 30, 1878.

[6] *Ford County Globe*, April 2, 1878. Elsewhere it was said, "The Gang got up a funny ticket at the election yesterday. They placed upon it the names of S. Galland, F. C. Zimmerman, M. Collar, Harry E. Gryden, E. S. Conwell, Garry Baldi and John Watson. This ticket was a jest of some of the boys, to us unknown, but in our opinion the above names are among the most respected in Dodge, and the betters of those who originated the ticket."

[7] Ibid.

Boyd's billiard hall—investigated a disturbance at A. J. Peacock's south-side saloon and dance hall.[8] There the two officers encountered half a dozen intoxicated drovers. Masterson noticed that at least one of them, a fellow named John "Jack" Wagner, carried a revolver.

The marshal disarmed the offender and handed the weapon to the man's boss, Alfred M. Walker (both Wagner and Walker were mistakenly described as "cattle drivers from near Hays City").[9] Assuming everything was under control, Masterson and Haywood stepped onto the sidewalk. Wagner followed. Whether he carried another weapon, or simply retrieved from Walker the gun just taken from him, was never determined. Whatever the circumstances, "a general rush was made from inside the Hall to the sidewalk; Policeman Haywood stepped forward to assist the Marshal, but just as he did so, two other 'cow men' drew their pistols upon him and held him in position. One of them snapped a pistol in his face, which fortunately missed fire."[10]

As Masterson struggled with Wagner a shot rang out, tearing an ugly hole in the marshal's abdomen. With his coat smoldering from the black powder then used in cartridges, Masterson managed to stay on his feet and fire five rounds. One struck Wagner in the bowel, while two others hit Alfred Walker, shattering his right arm and passing through the left lung. Masterson's final two shots grazed the faces of an unnamed cattleman and an innocent bystander. The wounded marshal walked unaided for nearly two hundred yards, before collapsing in George Hoover's Front Street saloon. Startled patrons carried the injured man to either his own or his brother's room and called for Dr. McCarty. Less than forty minutes later, without complaint, Edward J. Masterson died. He was not yet twenty-six years old.

After the shooting, Alfred Walker staggered through the saloon and tumbled into the dirt some distance behind the building. Friends carried him and Wagner to Charles Lane's rather luxurious bachelor apartment on

---

[8] Although the *Ford County Globe*, in its official directory, still listed Charlie Bassett as assistant marshal during this entire period, the *Dodge City Times*, in its weekly issues of April 6 and 13, correctly shows N. L. Haywood occupying that position. Also on April 6, the *Times* reported proceedings of the city council's regular meeting four days earlier. At that time they allowed Haywood seventy-five dollars as assistant marshal—the same salary paid Edward Masterson.

[9] *Dodge City Times*, April 13, 1878.

[10] *Ford County Globe*, April 16, 1878.

the second floor of Wright, Beverly & Company. Only a year older than his victim, it was said of Wagner, "Some time ago he received a fall from his horse, which it is thought rendered him partially insane."[11] Admitting his guilt, Jack Wagner died at sunrise and was planted on Boot Hill the next afternoon. Alfred Walker suffered but survived.

Responding to his brother's murder, Bat Masterson, within the hour, moved against the other four drovers at Peacock's saloon. Armed with warrants, the sheriff placed the men under arrest to answer for their part in the tragedy. They stood nervously before the bar of justice as an angry town pondered their fate. Attorneys Harry Gryden, Daniel Frost, and William Morphy handled the defense. County Attorney Michael Sutton and his law partner, Edward Colborn, prosecuted. Yet, after spending two full days listening to witnesses, Justice Rufus G. Cook released the prisoners on grounds of insufficient evidence.

The killing of Edward Masterson greatly upset townspeople, revealing a level of maturity absent from the cavalier attitude shown earlier killings. Forgetting its political differences with the city administration, the *Ford County Globe* issued a small double-column extra on April 10. It was a handbill-sized sheet printed on only one side, outlining the details then known under the headline "DODGE CITY IN MOURNING!" Later the paper eulogized: "Everybody in the City knew Ed. Masterson and liked him. They liked him as a boy, they liked him as a man, and they liked him as an officer."[12] Businessmen closed their doors from 10 to 6 on the day of Masterson's funeral and draped their buildings in black crepe out of respect for the fallen officer. Dodge City had never seen anything quite like it. Edward Masterson was buried at the Fort Dodge Cemetery.[13]

Eleven days after the marshal's death, Mike Sutton accompanied Bat Masterson to Wichita to help console his grieving parents. Others, too, found themselves suffering over this senseless tragedy. Seven weeks after being shot, Alfred Walker still lay bedridden. His father, described as "a highly respected old gentleman," came up from Texas to transfer his son to

[11] *Dodge City Times*, April 13, 1878.

[12] *Ford County Globe*, April 16, 1878.

[13] Records from the Fort Dodge Cemetery list Edward Masterson as interment No. 133. A year later his body was removed to the new Prairie Grove Cemetery at Dodge City. Many years later, when Prairie Grove gave way to residential expansion, the bodies were again moved to the newer Maple Grove Cemetery. Bat Masterson, then a sports reporter in New York City, returned to erect a suitable marker on the site but failed to locate his brother's grave.

Kansas City for better medical treatment. From there the elder Walker began his journey home, but within the week fell seriously ill and died at Fort Scott, Kansas.[14]

At Dodge City, John Brown and Joe Mason were temporarily added to the police force. The council named Charlie Bassett to fill the marshal's vacancy while increasing his salary. The distant *Peabody Gazette* reflected: "Dodge City pays its Marshal $100 per month, and from all we can learn, we should rather imagine he earns it."[15] J. Wright Mooar characterized Bassett as a "pretty good man, too, better than his associates. They were that same crowd there, all that bunch."[16] Brown replaced Nat Haywood as assistant marshal. Wyatt Earp, after visiting several places in Texas on one of his periodic gambling sprees, returned on May 8. Three days later he replaced Brown as Bassett's assistant, receiving a warm welcome from locals.[17]

None of this improved the reputation of Dodge City. The old buffalo hunter and saloonman George "Hoodoo" Brown characterized the town during these years:

> Dodge City in the seventies was wild woolly and composed mostly of saloons, gambling houses and dance halls, a few general stores, and a few respectable families. The gamblers were a rough set and mostly two-gun men, but they would pay you what you happened to be lucky enough to win against their semicrooked games. The dance-hall women and girls, some of them rather young, were mostly outcast characters from further east.... Men shot out their own difficulties; the city officials were controlled by the saloon keepers and gamblers. One day a stranger had lost his money gambling and sent to the mayor to have the gambling house raided; the mayor promptly called the marshal and had the man arrested for gambling, which he had confessed to doing, consequently he was glad to get out of town and let the matter drop.[18]

---

[14] *Dodge City Times*, June 1, 1878.

[15] As quoted in: *Ford County Globe*, May 28, 1878.

[16] J. Wright Mooar, interviewed by J. Evetts Haley, Snyder, Texas, March 3, 1939. Walter Stanley Campbell Files, Box 98B, Folder 14A, 97. Manuscript Division, Western History Collection, University of Oklahoma.

[17] "Wyatt Earp, one of the most efficient officers Dodge ever had, has just returned from Fort Worth, Texas. He was immediately appointed Asst. Marshal, by our City dads, much to their credit." *Ford County Globe*, May 14, 1878. Just the year before it was said, "Wyatt Earp, who was on our city police force last summer, is in town again. We hope he will accept a position on the force once more. He had a quiet way of taking the most desperate characters into custody which invariably gave one the impression that the city was able to enforce her mandates and preserve her dignity. It wasn't considered policy to draw a gun on Wyatt unless you got the drop and meant to burn powder without any preliminary talk." *Dodge City Times*, July 7, 1877.

[18] Connelley, ed., "Life and Adventures of George W. Brown," 127–28.

Wyatt Earp's return notwithstanding, it was thoughts of money, chiefly money from Texas beef, that swept Edward Masterson's murder from the top of the news. Reports reaching Dodge City in late April told of more than 18,000 head having already crossed the Trinity River near Fort Worth on their way to Kansas, Wyoming, and Nebraska. From San Antonio Henry Beverley announced well over 200,000 head ready for the trail. Dodge City expected most of this traffic: "It will require at least 1,300 men to bring these cattle to Dodge." In addition, "there will be 250 owners and buyers who will make their headquarters at Dodge during the season, or until their business is completed. [These men] must be fed and clothed." Hoping not to appear transparently greedy, the reporter added, "Our merchants were never before so well prepared to furnish to the trade everything needed, at a small margin of profit."[19]

With the cattle season almost at hand, the town began divesting itself of that most notorious symbol of its bloody past: Boot Hill began its final journey into history. Latecomer Nicholas Klaine chronicled the site's sordid statistics for his readers: "There are now about twenty . . . graves of persons who met death by violent means. There were a few who died from natural causes, but who possessed no money or friends to give them a more aristocratic burial place. When Gabriel blows his horn, verily it will be a motley crowd of sinners that the graves on Boot Hill send forth to attend the final judgment."[20]

The Town Company sold the Boot Hill property to Herman Fringer and Samuel Marshall, a couple of eager speculators who planned to subdivide the land for home sites. In the meantime, to satisfy a desire toward respectability, a five-acre tract situated about a half-mile north and slightly east of the courthouse and christened Prairie Grove Cemetery was chosen as a suitable replacement. All the bodies that could be found were transferred by January 1879. From the beginning the press described the plan as "an opportune project though few people in this section die with their 'boots off.' "[21]

While Dodge City tried to introduce more conventional institutions,

[19] *Ford County Globe*, May 7, 1878.

[20] *Dodge City Times*, May 4, 1878.

[21] Ibid., May 18, 1878. By late August single graves at Prairie Grove Cemetery began selling for five dollars, with 20-by-20 family plots going for twenty-five dollars. For transactions involving the sale of the sixteen town lots comprising Boot Hill, see Ford County Register of Deeds, Book A, 553–54, 559–60.

residents read with dismay negative reports of their town published elsewhere. Others saw the fun in it. After the *Kinsley Graphic* characterized
Dodge City as "the beautiful, bibulous Babylon of the frontier . . . she is no
worse than Chicago," the *Times* responded, "This we admit is a slight leverage in the social scale, to be placed in the category of Chicago's wickedness."[22] Others offered a more balanced look: "Extremes meet here, and
Dodge can show some of the best as well as some of the worst elements of
frontier life."[23]

More pleasing were reports of legendary stockman Dillard R. Fant
holding thirteen hundred head of horses on the range south of town,
while J. L. Driskill, George Littlefield, Sam Chisum, J. D. Houston, and
other Texas cattlemen crowded in to register at the Dodge House, as if
announcing the new season. As Dodge City got down to the serious business of buying and selling, the killing of Ed Masterson served only as a
sad reminder of things past. Indeed, the *Times* reported on June 22, "Look
at the light docket for the next term of the district court, and pity the
poor attorneys." Of course no one pities lawyers, but this turned out to be
a somewhat premature assessment.

During that summer of 1878, the New York firm of McKillop &
Sprague listed a number of Dodge City businesses in their national com-
mercial register. The basic criteria rated credit and financial strength. York,
Hadder & Draper received the highest score, followed closely by Wright,
Beverley & Company; Cox and Boyd's Dodge House, saloon, and livery; R.
W. Evans's general merchandise; and Frederick Zimmerman's hardware.
All carried a "good" credit listing and were estimated to be worth between
$50,000 and $75,000 in the case of York, Hadder & Draper, down to
$6,000 to $10,000 for Evans and Zimmerman. The next tier included Herman J. Fringer's drug store, Thomas L. McCarty and Samuel Galland as
physicians and druggist (Galland's Great Western Hotel fared less well),
and George M. Hoover's saloon. Hoover's credit rating was estimated a
"fair risk," but his financial standing was the same as his neighbor Zimmerman. McCarty's worth ranged between $3,000 and $4,000, while Galland fell $1,000 below his colleague. Those at the bottom garnered only a
"limited" credit risk and correspondingly had lower financial ratings. The

[22] *Dodge City Times*, July 6, 1878.
[23] *Pueblo Chieftain*, as quoted in *Dodge City Times*, June 8, 1878.

Long Branch saloon, for example, was listed between $1,000 and $2,000 in the financial category. Still, Beeson and Harris came out better than Colley and Manion, who slipped below $1,000.[24] Considering that these estimates reflected business in a small and somewhat isolated frontier community, the town made a good showing.

Had anyone taken ratings on the business of drinking whiskey, tiny Dodge City would have scored even higher. The *Times* calculated at one point, from the number of empty barrels lying around town, that residents and visitors drained three hundred a year, adding: "We don't know whether there is any credit in making this statement, and whether it reflects any credit or not, it reflects that the Bibulous Babylon keeps up its credit on a commercial commodity. The curious can estimate the number of drinks in 300 barrels of whiskey. We haven't time to make the enumeration."[25]

AROUND FOUR O'CLOCK in the morning of July 13, Deputy U.S. Marshal Harry T. McCarty strolled into the Long Branch for a drink. McCarty, a former justice of the peace, deputy county clerk, and county surveyor, as well as a draftsman and artist of some talent, had received his commission from U.S. Marshal Benjamin F. Simpson less than three months before. Now, in the warm early hours, he leaned against the bar talking with Adam Jackson.

In the far corner a group of men pestered Thomas O'Herron (alias Thomas Roach), a man described as "a half-witted, rattled-brained and quarrelsome wretch."[26] For some reason, the victim of all this abuse ran to McCarty and without saying a word lifted the deputy's Colt revolver. As McCarty turned to see who had relieved him of his sidearm, O'Herron pulled back the hammer and fired, filling the long narrow room with acrid smoke and a deafening roar. The heavy .45 caliber bullet torn through McCarty's right groin, laying open the femoral artery, passing through his thigh, and burying itself in the wooden floor. McCarty stumbled toward the door, but collapsed from shock and loss of blood. A bystander pulled his own pistol and fired at O'Herron, striking him in the right side. The

---

[24] *The Commercial Agency Register for July, 1878* (New York: McKillop & Sprague Co., 1878), unnumbered pages, Kansas Section.

[25] *Dodge City Times*, September 7, 1878.

[26] Ibid., July 13, 1878.

wounded man cried out, "I am shot," and fell to the floor, pretending to be dead.

The crowd carried McCarty to bartender Charles Ronan's nearby rooms and sent for Dr. Thomas McCarty (no relation to the wounded man). It seems that friends familiar with his quarrelsome nature when drinking had escorted O'Herron, a camp cook for the Shiner brothers also known as Limping Tom, out of town earlier than evening. He reappeared and now found himself in serious trouble, as the deputy U.S. marshal bled to death within the hour. Residents appeared genuinely shocked by this pointless murder, although McCarty had more than his share of detractors. While awaiting trial, O'Herron announced to Deputy Sheriff William Duffey his intention of starving himself to death. He may have been more serious about escaping as a search of his cell uncovered a case knife, a wire hook, and a file. Convicted of first-degree manslaughter on a plea of guilty, O'Herron was sentenced to twelve years and three months in prison.[27]

McCarty's burial did not signal an end of Dodge City's troubles. Around three o'clock on the morning of July 26, a small group of Texas drovers retrieved their sidearms and started back to camp. Moving slowly toward the Arkansas River bridge, these men, later estimated between two and four riders, decided to cap their evening with some harmless mischief. As they passed Ben Springer's newly opened Comique Theater, they fired several shots into the rear of the building, all the bullets passing over the empty stage and into the ceiling. Springer's patrons that night included comedian Eddie Foy, who years later recalled with predictable exaggeration: "Bat Masterson was just in the act of dealing in a game of Spanish monte with Doc Holliday, and I was impressed by the instantaneous manner which they flattened out like pancakes on the floor. I had thought I was pretty agile myself, but those fellows had me beaten by seconds at that trick. The firing kept up until it seemed to me that the assailants had put hundreds of shots through the building. They shot through walls as well as windows, for the big .45 bullet would penetrate those plank walls as if they had been little more than paper."[28]

[27] State of Kansas vs. Thomas O'Herron, Records of the Ford County District Court, Criminal Appearance Docket A, 60; and Judge's Journal, Book A, 194, 197.

[28] Eddie Foy and Alvin F. Harlow, *Clowning Through Life* (New York: E. P. Dutton & Company, 1928), 113. Of the commotion caused inside the Comique, the *Ford County Globe* noted on July 30, 1878, "A general scamper was made by the crowd, some getting under the stage, others running out the front door, and behind the bar."

Hearing those first few shots, Assistant Marshal Wyatt Earp and policeman James Masterson rushed toward the Comique. Once on the scene, they joined several citizens blasting away at the fleeing cowboys. The Texans managed to gallop across the bridge with Earp, Masterson, and the others in hot pursuit. On the far side one of the horseman tumbled to the ground with a badly wounded arm.

The injured man turned out to be a young drover named George Hoy. The officers carried him to Dr. McCarty's office. As McCarty dressed the man's wound and decided amputation was not necessary, reporters from both newspapers pushed their way in for interviews. Most readers felt sorry for the prisoner, despite reports of his having legal troubles in Texas. The *Times* described him as "rather an intelligent looking young man."[29] The *Globe* wrote: "He claims not to have done any shooting; be that as it may he was in bad company and has learned a lesson 'he wont forget soon.'"[30] Unfortunately, young Hoy did not respond to treatment, and "the hot weather and the nature of the wound caused mortification to set in."[31] McCarty sent for Dr. Tremaine. The army surgeon took one look and amputated the young cowboy's gangrenous appendage on August 21, only to watch his patient die that same day. Hoy was temporarily buried on Boot Hill, with a large number of Texans paying their respects at graveside.

ON AUGUST 6, 1878, the city council passed two ordinances that appeared, at first glance, to be in sharp contrast with the town's wide-open reputation—still described in some circles as the wickedest city in America. Ordinance No. 41 outlawed gambling and gambling houses, while Ordinance No. 42 did the same for houses of ill fame.[32] In actual practice these laws eliminated neither gambling nor prostitution, but did grant city officials a way to regulate both activities, thus awarding even more power to James Kelley's political machine. Dodge City, following frontier custom, selectively invoked these ordinances to rid itself of unwanted practitioners. Both laws became quasi-licensing devises for those gamblers and madams lucky enough to enjoy favor with the mayor and council. Besides,

[29] *Dodge City Times,* July 27, 1878.
[30] *Ford County Globe,* July 30, 1878.
[31] *Dodge City Times,* August 24, 1878.
[32] Ordinances No. 41 and 42, August 6, 1878. Dodge City Ordinances, Book A, 70–71, 72–73.

hitting each group with fines on a monthly basis helped satisfy righteous-minded citizens. While increasing city revenues, Mayor Kelley remained loyal to Texas interests.

Such adroit political maneuvering on the part of Kelley and his followers was in keeping with the times. Richard Evans, as chairman of the Republican Committee of Ford County, called a meeting to name delegates to the congressional convention at Wichita and the state convention at Topeka. Mike Sutton, Morris Collar, D. D. Colley, Charlie Bassett, A. J. Peacock, Michael Sughrue, and Wyatt Earp were among those representing Dodge City at the county meeting. Disappointed by the statewide party's decision to allow Ford County, then with an estimated population of more than thirty-five hundred, only one seat at Topeka, the committee passed a resolution of protest, instructing their delegates to hold out for at least two.

Ford County's Democrats held a similar meeting, naming delegates to their party's convention at Leavenworth. George M. Hoover and Harry E. Gryden were chosen, with William Morphy and Dr. Thomas McCarty on hand as alternates. The Ford County representatives hoped to nominate Henry M. Beverley for lieutenant governor. After all, Ford was the only county in Kansas to cast a majority for Tilden in 1876. Overlooking this sign of loyalty, state Democrats ignored Ford County's wishes and named Leavenworth druggist and mayor George Ummethun their candidate for the second spot on the ticket.

Amidst all the political wrangling, Lloyd Shinn, the last remaining founding owner of the *Dodge City Times*, sold out to Nicholas Klaine. Despite wishing the *Times* "every success in the future,"[33] Shinn joined the rival *Ford County Globe* within six weeks, in a move thought to be temporary, but which ended with his owning a half-interest by the first of the year.[34] Dan Frost needed the help—William Morphy, burdened by tuberculosis, the demands of frontier journalism, and a busy law practice, had retired in late September. With Morphy's departure and Shinn's arrival, the political posturing of the *Globe*, at least regarding state and national issues, became more Republican in tone. Thus, editors of both newspapers now openly supported that party's positions on most issues, beyond those mired in local rivalries.

As autumn approached, Dodge City became embroiled over escalating tensions in Indian Territory. The year before, the government had begun

[33] *Dodge City Times*, August 31, 1878.
[34] *Ford County Globe*, October 15, 1878, January 1, 1879.

trying to consolidate the Cheyennes at the old Darlington Agency near Camp Supply. Agents withheld rations from those still occupying traditional sites in Nebraska and points north, hoping to force their departure. They began arriving at the agency by August 1877, but soon two-thirds fell ill. With only one physician available to attend all these people, by the spring of 1878, a quarter of the Northern Cheyennes were dead. As they suffered, the remaining Indians dreamed of their old homelands. Soon, individually and in small groups, they began deserting the Indian Territory. When Dull Knife, Wild Hog, Little Wolf, and other respected leaders decided to leave, it caused panic along the Kansas and Nebraska frontier.

Agent John Miles had called the northern bands to agency headquarters to conduct a census. They refused. Miles then issued a September 7 deadline, only to be ignored. Two days later, leaving tepees standing and campfires burning to deceive prying eyes, Dull Knife, Little Wolf, and the others slipped away. In all 353 Indians were missing: 92 men, 120 women, 69 boys, and 72 girls. Following a clear trail, the army marched out in pursuit. Four days after the breakout, the two sides fought a skirmish near the Cimarron, north of Camp Supply. Three troopers and an Arapaho scout were killed and three soldiers wounded. Refusing to surrender, the warriors held their ground while their women and children crossed the river. With darkness everyone abandoned the fight.

At Dodge City people learned of Dull Knife's breakout from reading a special September 14 noon edition of the *Times*: "Our extra was gotten out for information, and not to excite the fears of any one. The wild Cheyenne chafe under their poor treatment in the Territory. Their home is on the wild desert of the North. They wish to return to their happy hunting grounds and savage life. The only probable scalps they would take on these marches would be the scalp of a Texas steer."

Three days later the *Globe* printed more ominous rumors telling of attacks against Texas herds grazing south of the city. A drover for Henry Kollar was killed, along with two others guarding Driskill stock. Horses were stolen and cattle shot. A man named Bates, who carried these stories into Dodge City, also warned that former Great Western Hotel proprietor Silas Maley and his wife were among the victims. To protect their herds, Bud and Tobe Driskill, together with more than a dozen other cattlemen, armed themselves and rode to Driskill's camp near the mouth of Bluff Creek.

Soldiers at Fort Dodge responded by marching out to intercept the hostiles. There was no panic in Dodge City. Concern heightened only after Indians came uncomfortably close to town. By September 18, more people rode in from the south with tales of theft and murder. Early that afternoon, as a general warning, city officials ordered the fire bell rung. Men rushed to the engine house prepared to defend their town. An anxious Mayor Kelley telegraphed Governor Anthony: "Three hundred Indians are driving off stock and killing herders. They are now within six miles of our city. We are without arms, having equipped members who have gone south. Can you send us arms and ammunition? Situation alarming. We are powerless without arms and ammunition."[35]

Trying to imagine Dodge City bereft of firearms must have been quite an exercise for people in Topeka. Nevertheless, while the governor and his advisors pondered the situation, another telegram arrived from an alarmed James Kelley: "No U.S. troops here, and no arms at post. The country is filled with Indians. Send arms immediately. Breech-loaders."[36] With no reply forthcoming, five other citizens sent a third message: "Indians are murdering, and burning houses within three miles of town. All the arms we have have been sent. Can you send us arms and ammunition immediately?"[37]

The truth to all this is much harder to sort out. As reports spread beyond Dodge City, several families, including those of H. P. Niess, George Horder, and Harrison Berry, abandoned their homes, seeking shelter in town. That afternoon smoke was seen rising from Berry's house on an island in the river three miles away. A trainload of volunteers rushed to save the property: "P. L. Beatty, Chalk Beeson, Wyatt Earp and S. E. Isaacson were principals in extinguishing the flames," reported the *Times*.[38] This was the incident referred to in the third telegram to Governor Anthony. Some thought the Indians responsible while others blamed the family for leaving a fire unattended.

Giving in to what must have seemed exaggerated pleas, the governor

---

[35] Telegram from Mayor James Kelley to Gov. Geo. T. Anthony, September 18, 1878. "Marking an Epoch—The Last Indian Raid and Massacre," *Eighteenth Biennial Report of the Board of Directors of the Kansas State Historical Society* (Topeka: State Printing Office, 1913), 23. C. W. Willett, H. E. Gryden, and D. Sheedy also signed Kelley's telegram.

[36] Telegram from Mayor James H. Kelley to Gov. Anthony, September 18, 1878. Kelley alone signed this telegram. Ibid.

[37] Telegraph to Gov. Anthony signed by H. (?) Shinn, R. W. Evans, C. W. Willett, T. L. McCarty, and James C. Connor, September 18, 1878. Ibid.

[38] *Dodge City Times*, September 21, 1878.

ordered his adjutant general to Dodge City with two hundred stands of arms and ammunition, but with specific instructions to issue nothing, except "upon receipt of officers of county or city, joined by five responsible citizens."[39] Anthony sent a telegram to Mayor Kelley advising him of the shipment, but adding, perhaps in an attempt to defuse the situation, that General Pope estimated only seventy-five warriors involved in the breakout. The next day Adj. Gen. Peter Noble turned over a hundred rifles and six thousand rounds of ammunition to a relieved James Kelley. Noble distributed the rest at other points, such as Cimarron, while reporting the situation quiet. Representatives from one group known as the Pennsylvania Colony came into Dodge City for their allotment of arms, only to be ignored. Disgusted, they returned to their families empty-handed.

Despite Major Kelley's concerns, the Indians had no intention of attacking Dodge City. But the town hardly enjoyed peace and quiet. On the evening of September 18, after all the telegrams demanding arms and ammunition, former policeman John Brown argued with barman Al Manning. Brown punctuated his argument by spitting in Manning's face. "Al very properly responded to this insult by emptying a six-shooter at Brown, who being an expert runner and dodger, evaded the bullets," reported one editor under the familiar heading "The Festive Revolver."[40] While running and dodging, Brown pulled his own pistol and starting shooting. Perhaps exhausted by all the gymnastics, Brown's aim was off. Instead of killing Manning, he wounded an innocent bystander named William Morton in the left instep. As the smoke cleared, Manning was arrested and hauled before Judge Cook, who set bond at $560.

The very next evening a drunken muleskinner and part-time cattle herder named H. Gould—known as Skunk Curley—fired a shot that struck a visitor from Great Bend in the right shoulder. The bullet passed "across the backbone to the left shoulder, making four holes and inflicting an ugly wound. The wounded man is doing well. His friends say he was an entire stranger to Curley, who was drunk, and that it was probable the shot was intended for some one else."[41] Four days later an unknown assailant shot Frank Trask, the brother of former policeman Charles Trask, after he crossed the tracks on his way to Beatty & Kelley's restaurant, "the ball strik-

---

[39] Gov. Geo. T. Anthony to P. S. Noble, Adj. Gen., September 19, 1878. "Marking an Epoch," 23.

[40] *Ford County Globe*, September 24, 1878.

[41] *Dodge City Times*, September 21, 1878.

ing him in the right side, passing half way around the body and making a very painful wound."[42] Officers arrested Daniel Woodward as a suspect.

All this led the *Globe* to note on September 24: "No less than half a dozen shooting scrapes occurred in our city during the past week. We are glad to state, however, that no one was seriously hurt. The last one occurred night before last. There seems to be more danger of being shot in the city than there is danger of being scalped by the Red Men out on the plains." By October 5 the *Times* reported, "The city is remarkably quiet this week. There has been no blood, and the wounded of last week are walking about. There is a calm after the storm."

For those living outside the city, Dull Knife's breakout seemed like serious stuff indeed. Leaving the reservation with few horses and limited supplies, the Cheyennes intended to secure both from whites in Kansas. Besides raiding the camps of Henry Kollar and the Driskills, the Indians struck other outfits at Bluff Creek and Cimarron Station. Others attacked a man and his wife traveling to the Texas Panhandle. Both managed to reach a nearby ranch and thus survived the encounter, but the Indians ransacked their belongings, taking what they needed and leaving the rest scattered across the plains.

Indians attacked Pat Ryan's ranch at the mouth of Mulberry Creek, eighteen miles southeast of Dodge City. Routed, they turned against the camp of Chapman and Tuttle, two miles farther out, killing the cook. Warriors then raided John Frazer's camp, stealing twenty horses, before attacking Dennis Sheedy and running off ten more. On September 19 they hit S. B. Williamson's sheep flock on Crooked Creek, killing 250 of the harmless animals. The next day they attacked Boynton's sheep camp, thirty-two miles to the southwest, and continued the slaughter. The Indians killed six men in Comanche and Barber counties.

The following week, cattlemen, led by the Driskill brothers, joined forces with Capt. William Hemphill's company. They engaged the Indians for about an hour along one of the feeders of Crooked Creek before the captain ordered a withdrawal, much to everyone's disgust. Lt. Col. William H. Lewis, commanding at Fort Dodge, sent fresh units into the field, accompanied again by civilian volunteers. Encounters took place but without much success on either side. "The soldiers were anxious for a general fight, while

---

[42] *Ford County Globe*, September 24, 1878.

the officers seemed haunted by the ghost of Custer and were evidently afraid to take the least risk," reported the *Globe*. "On Monday the Indians, with about 400 captured horses, moved north, while the troops remained all day in camp. Not an officer or soldier was killed or wounded. The troops are not following, using precautions to prevent the track from becoming too fresh."[43]

Stung by the complaints, Colonel Lewis took to the field, leading two companies of the Fourth Cavalry and a single company of his own Nineteenth Infantry. The colonel discovered the Indians' trail where they had crossed the Arkansas near the town of Cimarron. Pushing northward, he overtook them some thirty miles south of Fort Wallace. An engagement took place at a spot called Punished Woman's Fork. Lewis, a frontier veteran with wide experience—mostly in Texas before the Civil War—was fatally wounded.[44] He died the next day.

The Indians continued north, but circumstances overtook their best efforts. On October 23 Dull Knife and a number of his followers surrendered at Fort Robinson in northwest Nebraska. Many officers there sympathized with the Indians, much to the displeasure of Generals Sheridan and Sherman. Those two, fearing a mass outbreak, wanted the Northern Cheyennes returned to Indian Territory. Dull Knife's people refused to go. Capt. Henry W. Wessells, Jr., a thirty-one-year-old officer assigned to the Third Cavalry, ordered them confined under guard in a barracks with little food or water and no heat. In desperation, and using weapons hidden by their women, they tried to make their escape on a cold night in early January 1879. In a series of engagements over the next dozen days, sixty-four Indians, including women and children, lost their lives.[45] As the news spread, a sense of shame rippled across much of the nation.

The government, perhaps responding to all the negative publicity, allowed Dull Knife and many of his followers to settle for a time in the Dakotas, sharing space with the Sioux on the Pine Ridge Agency. Little Wolf, one of Dull Knife's trusted lieutenants and chief tactician, surren-

---

[43] Ibid.

[44] Cullum, *Biographical Register*, 2:382–84. Aside from Texas, William H. Lewis also saw service in Florida against the Seminoles and took part in the Utah Expedition of 1858–59, then engaged the Navajo in New Mexico.

[45] For a sympathetic and then the official view of these proceedings, see George Bird Grinnell, *The Fighting Cheyennes* (Norman: University of Oklahoma Press, 1956), 414–27; and Lt. Gen. P. H. Sheridan, *Record of Engagements with Hostile Indians within the Military Division of the Missouri from 1868 to 1882* (Washington: Government Printing Office, 1882), 83–84.

dered near his old home in Montana. Along with his ragged band he was escorted to Fort Keogh. There, somewhat ironically, many of the survivors, including Little Wolf himself, became scouts for Nelson Miles during that officer's subsequent Indian campaigns. In fairness to the colonel, he did help Little Wolf and his people find a new home along the Tongue River in 1884. Dull Knife, embittered by life, had died on the Rosebud in 1883.

Not all the Indians involved in the 1878 breakout did as well as Little Wolf. As early as November 11, Governor Anthony wrote the War Department demanding that the principal chiefs be turned over to civil authorities for trial in Kansas. In so doing he cited as precedent the 1872 Texas case against Satanta and Big Tree, but noted, "if there is no precedent, public necessity and simple justice would, I believe, be ample justification for this demand."[46] Thirty-one people lost their lives during the Dull Knife raid, and nearly $190,000 in claims would be filed, with the state approving more than $101,000 of these within a year. The largest individual claims came from Ford County, with cattlemen Evans, Hunter & Evans topping the list. They calculated their loss at $23,075 and received $17,760 in compensation. Similar figures for J. L. Driskill & Sons came to $21,125, and $13,700. For sheepman Dennis Sheedy the figures were $11,591 and $5,596. Even Harrison Berry, whose house burned down, either through carelessness or direct action by the Indians, claimed an $805 loss and was paid $625.[47]

Seven Cheyennes—Wild Hog, Run Fast, Frizzle Head, Young Man, Tall Man, Old Man, and Crow—were eventually indicted in Ford County for the murder of Washington O'Connor at Meade City.[48] All had missed the Fort Robinson breakout and massacre "by having been confined in the guardhouse at that post."[49] Getting the Indians released from army custody in Nebraska took time. But by February 1879 all were sent to Fort Leavenworth, shackled and under heavy guard. Authorities dispatched Sheriff W. B.

---

[46] "Marking an Epoch," 30.

[47] Ibid., 31. For a complete list of claims submitted and the amounts paid, see: "REPORT—Of the Commissioners Appointed to Investigate the Indian Raid Claims," *Ford County Globe*, September 9, 1879. For whatever reason, Nicholas Klaine and the *Dodge City Times* ignored the story, leaving it to their rival to report the commission's findings in full. For more on all this, see Ramon S. Powers, "The Kansas Indian Claims Commission of 1879," *Kansas History: A Journal of the Central Plains* 7, no. 3 (Autumn 1984).

[48] State of Kansas vs. Wild Hog et al., Records of the Ford County District Court, Criminal Appearance Docket, Book A, 63; and, *Dodge City Times*, February 15, 1879. The names of the prisoners used here are those listed in the original indictment. Other variations were common, including: Wakabish, or Tangled Hair; Manitou, Left Hand, or Rain in the Face; Porcupine, Left Hand, or White Antelope; Muskekon or Blacksmith; Old Crow; and Noisy Walker. Miller and Snell, *Why the West Was Wild*, 239.

Masterson, along with Charlie Bassett and James Masterson, to retrieve the wanted men. Capt. A. J. French, together with buffalo hunter George "Kokomo" Sullivan, accompanied the Ford County lawmen to Leavenworth as witnesses, "who, it is believed, can identify the prisoners."[50]

At the June 1879 term of the district court, Judge Peters listened to arguments. He granted County Attorney Michael Sutton's request that the charges against the defendant Crow be dropped and "said information . . . against him be discharged."[51] Defense attorneys then pleaded for a change of venue in the case of *The State of Kansas vs. Wild Hog et al.* Again Judge Peters agreed and transferred the proceedings to Lawrence in faraway Douglas County.[52] The final outcome surprised many, and not just along the Kansas frontier. After hearing numerous witnesses, Judge Nelson T. Stephens discharged all six of the remaining defendants, releasing them into the custody of Agent John D. Miles. Judge Stephens also ordered Ford County to defray the costs.

As surprising as anything else associated with this case was the reaction in Dodge City while the indicted Cheyennes occupied the Ford County jail. One contemporary noted years later: "I called upon those notable characters . . . and found them the most conspicuous and best entertained men in prison. The representatives of different illustrated newspapers were there, sketching their pictures, and treating them to cigars. It was certainly a very novel sight to me, and I thought it strange that the citizens of Dodge City had not formed a necktie party. . . . I came to the conclusion that Dodge City was a very law abiding city, and was a good town to live in (especially when one is acquainted with the early history of the place)."[53]

While leaving others to debate that point, Dodge City witnessed another killing. This time the victim was Dora Hand, a thirty-four-year-old veteran of the midwest variety circuit. She first came to town that summer of 1878, after working two years at various St. Louis theaters, primarily Jacob Esher's Varieties, following a successful run in Memphis.

---

[49] C. E. Campbell, "Down Among the Red Men," *Collections of the Kansas State Historical Society, Vol. XVII, 1926–1928* (Topeka: B. P. Walker, State Printer, 1928), 682.

[50] *Dodge City Times,* February 15, 1879.

[51] Records of the Ford County District Court, Judge's Journal, Book A, 226.

[52] Ibid., 227. For additional reflections on this unusual case, see Todd D. Epp, "The State of Kansas v. Wild Hog et al.," *Kansas History: A Journal of the Central Plains* 5, no. 2 (Summer 1982): 139–46.

[53] Dennis Collins, *The Indians' Last Fight; or, The Dull Knife Raid* (Girard, Kans.: The Appeal to Reason [1915]), 261. For more on the peaceful reaction of Dodge City residents, see *Ford County Globe,* February 17, 1879; and *Dodge City Times,* February 22, 1879.

Using the stage name Fannie Keenan, Dora continued her career in Dodge City, first at Ben Springer's Comique and then at Hamilton Bell's Variety. She enjoyed a popular following. Reporting a benefit performance by her and Hattie Smith, the press noted: "They are general favorites and will draw a crowded house."[54]

Early that fall Dora Hand returned briefly to St. Louis, this time working at Leonard Offerman's Tivoli Hall. She came back to Dodge City just two weeks before her death, announcing to her friend, fellow performer Fannie Garrettson, her plans to be married. Before doing so she needed to get rid of her first husband, musician Theodore Hand, whom she had married at St. Louis in 1871 under the name Dora Crews. Domestic discord soured the relationship. By 1877 Theodore abandoned his wife and began an adulterous relationship in Cincinnati with a woman named Suzzie Sataur. Dora claimed he had threatened her physically while confiscating most of her money and personal possessions. A year later she hired Harry Gryden and filed suit for divorce at Dodge City.[55] Set for the January 1879 term, the case never came to trial, due to circumstances beyond the jurisdiction of the court.

Early on the morning of October 4, 1878, a lone horseman approached a small two-room, wood-frame shack situated behind the Great Western Hotel that temporarily housed Dora Hand and her friend Miss Garrettson. Reining to a halt, this man fired two shots into the building, before fleeing along the road toward Fort Dodge. Wyatt Earp and James Masterson responded to the scene and found a woman lying dead in a pool of blood. Contemporary accounts provided details: "The building was divided into two rooms by a plastered partition, Miss Keenan [Dora Hand] occupying the back room. The first shot, after passing through the front door, struck the floor, passed through the carpet and facing of the partition and lodged in the next room. The second shot also passed through the door, but apparently more elevated, striking the first bed, passing over Miss Garretson [sic], who occupied the bed, through two quilts, through the plastered partition, and after passing through the bed

---

[54] *Dodge City Times*, August 10, 1878. Wyatt Earp had arrested Hattie Smith on July 19 for behaving in a "Riotous & disorderly manner." Police judge Samuel Marshall fined her a total of $11.50 in fines and costs.

[55] Marriage Record, Recorder of Deeds, City of St. Louis, Missouri, Theodore Hand and Dora Crews, November 22, 1871, Book 15, page 180; and Dora Hand vs. Theodore Hand, Records of the Ford County District Court, Unnumbered Civil Case Files. Also see "Notice of Publication—Dora Hand, plaintiff, vs. Theodore Hand, defendant," *Ford County Globe*, October 1, 1878.

clothing of the second bed, struck Fannie Keenan in the right side, under the arm, killing her instantly."[56]

A coroner's inquest named James M. Kenedy, one of the sons of Texas cattle baron Mifflin Kenedy, as the person responsible. Why he or anyone else fired those shots was never explained. The traditional version involves a personal quarrel with James Kelley, who, suffering some undisclosed illness, had traveled out to Fort Dodge to consult Dr. Tremaine. In his absence Kelley allowed Fannie Garrettson to use his rooms. Possibly the assailant thought the mayor was still in residence.

There is some evidence that the headstrong Jim Kelley may have manhandled young Kenedy for causing trouble at his saloon. An entry in the police docket shows that Wyatt Earp arrested a James "Kennedy" on July 29 for carrying a pistol. For this indiscretion Police Judge Samuel Marshall fined the defendant $3.00 and costs. On August 17 Kenedy was arrested again, this time by City Marshal Charlie Bassett, for causing a disturbance. He again pleaded guilty and paid a fine and costs totaling $17.50.[57] Whether or not any of this led James M. Kenedy to try and assassinate the mayor of Dodge City is pure speculation.

Whatever the basis of the coroner's suspicions, a posse made up of Sheriff William B. Masterson, City Marshal Charles E. Bassett, Assistant Marshal Wyatt Earp, Deputy Sheriff William Duffey, and one-time Kinsley robbery suspect William M. Tilghman, a later city marshal himself, rode out to overtake the suspect. On October 12 the *Times* characterized this group "as intrepid a posse as ever pulled a trigger." They maneuvered themselves into position astride Kenedy's route near Meade City, some thirty-five miles to the southwest. Spotting their man, they shouted for him to surrender. The fugitive hesitated and the posse opened fire, striking Kenedy in the shoulder. Three other rounds dropped the suspect's horse.

Officials delayed Kenedy's hearing for two weeks to give the prisoner time to recover from his injury. An air of mystery surrounded the proceedings, held before Judge Rufus G. Cook. On October 10 the *Globe* reported

---

[56] *Ford County Globe*, October 8, 1878.

[57] Walter Stanley Campbell Files, Western History Collection, University of Oklahoma Library, Justice Docket, Dodge City, Kansas, Notes, Box 96, 24, 39. Campbell, who wrote under the name Stanley Vestal, recorded that at the time of his own research, the police docket covering the period from July 5, 1878, through October 5, 1882, was safely in the hands of City Hall. Unfortunately, it has since disappeared and only Campbell's notes attest to its contents. Yet, even Campbell's notes only cover cases brought before Police Judge Samuel Marshall. Records of other township justices have also disappeared.

to its stunned readership that Kenedy's "trial took place in the sheriff's office, which was too small to admit spectators. We do not know what the evidence was, or upon what grounds he was acquitted. But he is free to go on his way rejoicing whenever he gets ready."

It has long since been suggested that the defendant's powerful father saved his son on this occasion. Mifflin Kenedy, an influential voice within the ranks of Texas cattle barons, did exercise some leverage over Dodge City. Born in Pennsylvania, the elder Kenedy, known as "Captain" in memory of an early voyage to Calcutta and service on a corvette during the Mexican War, had entered the cattle business early in south Texas. For a time he partnered with Richard King, later patriarch of the legendary King Ranch. The two were old friends from their steamboating days on Florida's Apalachicola. As a cattleman, Kenedy directed many herds north, much to the benefit of Dodge City.[58] In that season of 1878 another of the Captain's sons, John G. Kenedy, had organized herds totaling eighteen thousand longhorns from his father's ranch in Nueces County. Even Mayor Kelley entertained selfish reasons for wanting to stay friendly with Mifflin Kennedy.

Much to the relief of the wounded man, his father arrived on December 8. Visiting the convalescing patient at the Dodge House, Captain Kenedy began making arrangements to take him back to Texas. Before traveling the young man needed an operation to remove five inches of shattered bone from his upper arm. The elder Kenedy sent for Dr. B. E. Fryer at Fort Leavenworth to handle the delicate procedure, allowing William S. Tremaine and Thomas L. McCarty to assist. After the Kenedys left Dodge City nothing more was published about the Dora Hand affair. Curiously, the *Dodge City Times* ignored the case after Kenedy's capture. Of course, Nicholas Klaine supported the mayor's strategy of pacifying important Texans, even if one of their sons did murder an innocent woman while trying to kill the town's top elected official.

Dora Hand's murder slipped from memory as the people of Ford County prepared for election day. Both newspapers may have supported Republican principles, but locally, party affiliations meant less than regional and personal considerations. In Dodge City these were divided between supporters of the mayor's gang, backed by Nicholas Klaine's

---

[58] John Henry Brown, *Indian Wars and Pioneers of Texas* (Austin: L. E. Daniell, Publishers, 1896), 229–34; and J. Marvin Hunter, *The Trail Drivers of Texas* (New York: Argosy-Antiquarian Ltd., 1963), 2:954–58.

Times, and the People's County Ticket, championed by Daniel Frost's *Globe*. Citizens saw Texas cattle as the basis of their prosperity and tended to vote along those lines. Freighting remained the town's second most important industry.

Mayor Kelley, despite his administrative shortcomings, got most of the credit for keeping Dodge City amiable to Texas interests. With this in mind, the gang supported Bob Wright for state representative, Mike Sutton for county attorney, and Nick Klaine for probate judge. For these same positions the People's County Ticket backed Richard Evans, Dan Frost, and N. C. Jones.

Both camps courted the rural vote. Newcomers in eastern Ford County had begun the slow process of shifting unchallenged political control away from Dodge City, a fact that had not gone unnoticed. The two candidates for state representative offered any concessions they thought necessary to improve their chances with farmers. If elected, both Wright and Evans promised to have the state quarantine line shifted to the Arkansas River. They also assured farmers of their willingness to see the Fort Dodge Military Reservation opened to settlement. The *Globe* warned, "For the past week the Gang have done their best to bring about discord and dissension in the ranks of the People's party, paying daily visits to the 'dear farmer,' whom they have cursed and abused ever since those honest tillers of the soil dared to settle on our lands."[59] In fact both factions behaved hypocritically in their efforts to corner rural votes. Neither side paid any attention to the farmers until they needed them.

Much to the dismay and embarrassment of Daniel Frost and the People's County Ticket, the gang registered a near total victory. Bob Wright defeated Richard Evans 407 to 199, Mike Sutton bested Dan Frost for county attorney 398 to 213, and Nicholas Klaine became the new probate judge. H. P. Myton, the People's candidate for clerk of the district court and associate editor of the *Spearville News*, did manage to win in a three-man contest, but most other offices went either to the gang or to independent candidates, such as Dr. McCarty for school superintendent. Ford County supported the Democratic Party by a wide margin in all statewide offices—especially in Dodge City. John Frances, Republican candidate for state treasurer, proved the only exception, but even then he carried the day by only nine votes.[60]

[59] *Ford County Globe*, November 5, 1878.

[60] Ford County Commissioners Journals, Book A, 241–42. Also see *Dodge City Times*, November 9, 1878; and *Ford County Globe*, November 12, 1878.

The gang staged a victory celebration the following evening, described as "a grand jollification meeting," with Bob Wright, Mike Sutton, P. L. Beatty, and others galvanizing the cheering crowd with waves of grandiloquent oratory, followed by fireworks, whiskey, and mounds of food.[61] The losers enjoyed no fiesta. Instead, they charged fraud, pointing to nonresidents crowding the polls and the seductive influence of free liquor. While it was true that both sides welcomed fraudulent ballots if that would guarantee victory, the final outcome pretty much reflected a majority opinion in Ford County. But then, campaigners on the short side of the count seldom acknowledge the outright rejection of their arguments as the major reason for their defeat.

The election over, Dodge City resumed its routine. With the cattle season ending the town entered its quiet period, causing a disappointed Dan Frost to complain, "Our city authorities ought to begin to look at the expenses of the city a little and see if they might not be curtailed somewhat. Three policeman at this time of year seems to us a little extravagant."[62] The officers continued working for cattle-season salaries: Charles Basset earned $200 a month, with Assistant Marshal Wyatt Earp and Policeman James Masterson each getting $150. At its December 3 meeting, however, the city council reduced police costs to $200—with Marshal Bassett getting $100 and Earp and Masterson splitting the difference. At their next meeting, held on January 7, 1879, the council voted to continue the lower rate until further notice.

Dodge City's officers may have faced a cut in pay, but that tumultuous year of 1878 still offered excitement. Late in the afternoon of December 6, four men escaped from the county jail, much to the chagrin of Sheriff Masterson, who had just returned from Spearville to summon jurors for the January term of the district court. The escapees were Frank Jennings and James Bailey, both accused of stealing horses from Nichols and Culbertson's corral; W. H. Brown, arrested by the sheriff for stealing a horse from John Stevenson near Spearville; and "Skunk Curley" Gould. Early that evening, James Masterson captured the Skunk hiding in a buffalo wallow about a mile from town. A few days later Officer A. D. Cronk apprehended Jennings and Bailey at Kinsley and held them for the sheriff. Of the four only Brown eluded capture.

[61] *Dodge City Times*, November 9, 1878.
[62] *Ford County Globe*, November 26, 1878.

The apprehended escapees soon cursed their failure at freedom. Michael Sutton prosecuted all three when the district court reopened for a new term in January 1879. Judge Peters sentenced the twenty-four-year-old Gould to two years and three months' hard labor at Leavenworth. Witnesses subpoenaed in the case included Hamilton Bell, James Masterson, Wyatt Earp, and William Duffey. James Bailey and Frank Jennings both got two years and six months' hard labor.[63] All three cited liquor as contributing to their downfall. Apparently the judge considered horse stealing more serious than simple assault with intent to kill, since, of the three defendants, the Skunk ended up with the lightest sentence. Meanwhile, Sheriff Masterson got himself appointed a deputy U.S. marshal.

As Ford County dealt with its runaways, Dodge City gave a tentative nod to both religion and education. Reverend Ormond W. Wright, a twenty-five-year-old New Yorker, found the experience not altogether unpleasant. He began his efforts in late 1876 at the Union Church building, a nondenominational meeting place on the northeast corner of Spruce Street and First Avenue. Rowdiness slackened somewhat after Wyatt Earp and Bat Masterson accepted the reverend's pleas to become deacons. Only in Dodge City was there a need for someone to ride shotgun over church services.

Reverend Wright first organized the Presbyterian church on May 26, 1878. Minutes of their organization's first session show the influence of women in bringing religion to the Kansas frontier. Charter members included Mrs. A. J. Anthony, Ida Beeson, Mrs. Rufus G. Cook, Mrs. S. E. Straughn, and of course Reverend Wright's own wife.[64] By early August 1878 the Methodists, too, got started with seventeen members. A man named Adam Holm served as pastor, while alternating services between Dodge City and Cimarron.

By the end of 1878 school also became an established institution. Even in this isolated place parents demanded education for their children. As early as January 1873 the Dodge City Town Company had sold directors A. J. Anthony, James Langdon, and N. P. Niess four lots for one dollar to be used as a school site.[65] Texas herd owners, many of whom brought their

---

[63] State of Kansas vs. H. Gould, alias Skunk Curly, and State of Kansas vs. Frank Jennings and James A. Bailey, Records of the Ford County District Court, Criminal Appearance Docket A, 53, 54; and Judge's Journal, Book A, 183, 186, 189–90. Also see *Dodge City Times*, January 11, 1879; and *Ford County Globe*, January 14, 1879.

[64] Ethel E. Watkins, *Our First Century, An Historical Sketch: First Presbyterian Church, Dodge City, Kansas* (Dodge City: First Presbyterian Church, 1978), 2–3.

[65] Ford County Register of Deeds, Book A, 32–33. The lots in question were numbers 9 thru 12, Block 2.

families with them to spend the season in Dodge, helped out with the city school. By late 1878, Miss Anna Fleming's primary grades boasted forty-eight students. The high school listed thirty-eight more.

As the eventful year of 1878 came to a close, and while awaiting the court's decision on Gould, Jennings, and Bailey, Sheriff Masterson traveled to Colorado and negotiated for perennial offender Dutch Henry Born, the same man who escaped from the Ford County jail under questionable circumstances two years before. Reaching Trinidad, Masterson wired County Attorney Sutton: "Sheriff wont deliver up Dutch Henry unless I pay him $500. He says he can get that fer him in Nevada."[66] Masterson returned the dapper defendant to Dodge City on the morning of January 6. Five days later the *Globe* refused to speculate on how the sheriff managed to do so without a formal extradition or paying the extortion money. The paper simply stated: "we are not curious to know just now."

Dutch Henry had not spent all his time in Colorado since his earlier brush with Ford County authorities. The army, while helping search for suspects in the attempted robbery at Kinsley, had discovered more evidence of Dutch Henry's escapades. Lt. Cornelius Gardner wrote: "I . . . learned from reliable sources that 'Dutch Henry' was seen a few days previous to the attempted robbery making his way in a North Easterly direction with five men, also learned that Dutch Henry and his gang had a dugout in the Anderson Timber nearly opposite the mouth of Buffalo Creek on the Cimarron." Curious about the site, southeast of Dodge City near the border with the Indian Territory, the lieutenant went to see for himself: "Arrived at the 'dugout' two days later which I found unoccupied. It was well fortified, had rifle pits around it, and could easily be defended by a few men."[67]

In late May a deputy sheriff near Kearney, Nebraska, arrested Born as he tried to sell some horses stolen from Norton County, Kansas. Returned to the scene of the crime, the outlaw escaped again within the month. All that is known about him supports the characterization: "Dutch Henry is the most noted horse thief on the border—has stolen more horses, been captured oftener, wounded oftener, broken jail oftener, and been through

[66] *Dodge City Times*, January 4, 1879.

[67] 2nd Lt. Cornelius Gardner to Post Adjutant, February 7, 1878. Headquarters Records, Fort Dodge, Kansas; Reports, Journals, and Memorandums of Scouts and Marches, 1873–79.

more thrilling adventures than any other man in the west. His name is a by-word in Kansas."[68]

Now, due to Sheriff Masterson's persistence, Dutch Henry stood before Judge Peters at the Ford County Courthouse. The trial lasted two days, with many witnesses called on both sides, generating far more paperwork than is generally found in Ford County criminal cases during this period. Still, it proved a waste of time, as jury foreman Jim Skinner announced the defendant not guilty.[69] Dismissed, a smiling Dutch Henry left town, but his joy was short-lived. Soon afterward Deputy U.S. Marshal Charles B. Jones arrested the celebrated outlaw in Wichita and handed him over to the sheriff of Shawnee County, to answer for yet another jailbreak. Dodge City was not sorry to see him go.

Dutch Henry Born eventually abandoned his lawless ways. Returning to Colorado in the 1880s, he became a mining man; at Creede he made enough money on the Happy Thought Mine to go into semi-retirement with his younger brother in the remote back country of Archuleta County. Dutch Henry later settled on the shores of a trout lake—which still bears his name—in the San Juan Mountains near Pagosa Springs. He became a respected resident of the area, and then, rather late in life, married a woman thirteen years his junior and fathered four children. The man who had once been the scourge of the Kansas plains died peacefully at home on January 20, 1921.[70]

---

[68] *Dodge City Times*, June 1, 1878.

[69] State of Kansas vs. Henry Born, alias Dutch Henry, Records of the Ford County District Court, Criminal Appearance Docket A, 62; Judge's Journal, Book A, 210; and Miscellaneous Criminal Case Record Files.

[70] Baker and Harrison, *Adobe Walls*, 76. Born's last surviving daughter, Mabel Bennett, wrote to author R. Lindsay Baker in 1979: "Very few times of his past life was talked of at home. It seems it was another time and world and one he wished to forget. For the first 7 years they lived at the lake, he did not even have a gun in the house. He said he had all of the killing that he wanted." It has also been said that Dutch Henry was born of German immigrants at Manitowoc, Wisconsin. While it is true that his brother was born there in late 1863, and that Dutch Henry gave Wisconsin as his place of birth to the 1920 census enumerator, he had earlier claimed to have been born in Germany in February 1849, arriving in the United States in 1853. 1900 United States Census, Precinct 5, West of Pagosa Springs, Archuleta County, Colorado, E.D. 1, Sheet 10B, line 68.

Chapter 8

STUMBLING TOWARD THE FUTURE

Surviving another dangerous year, Dodge City tried convincing people of its wish to be more progressive. Reality offered few encouraging signs. In late January 1879 the *Ford County Globe* reported a camp revival staged by Allen Lewis, an itinerant preacher from Lebanon, Indiana, praising the services and its influence on Sunday School attendance. Some credited Christian virtue for this shift of emphasis. Optimists missed a smaller article near the bottom of the same column entitled "Scarlet Sluggers," describing a public brawl between two prostitutes: "A disjointed nose, two or three internal bruises, a chawed ear and a missing eye were the only scars we could see."[1]

Clearly, Dodge City had not abandoned its riotous past, despite all the prayers offered for its redemption. But at least one symbol of upheaval was no more: despite delays in the process, "The skeletons removed from the graves on Boot Hill were found to be in a fine state of preservation, and even the rude box coffins were as sound as when placed in the ground," rhapsodized the *Globe* on February 4. "They are now all resting side by side, like one happy family, at the lower end of Prairie Grove Cemetery, northwest of the city. The enchanting click of the festive revolver they no longer hear."

Speculators Herman Fringer and Samuel Marshall failed to turn Boot Hill into residential sites. Not surprisingly, no one wanted to live there. But the city wanted a place to build a new schoolhouse. Besides Fringer and Marshall's entry, the Shinn brothers offered two acres north of the city called Shinn's Addition (known in some circles as Poverty Ridge). Two acres owned by Daniel Frost east of town were also considered, as was a piece of land with a 250-foot front to the west owned by Morris Collar.

---

[1] *Ford County Globe*, January 21, 1879.

During a meeting on May 3, the school board could not decide. Instead they appointed a committee to study the possibilities.

Made up of Frederick Zimmerman, Alonzo B. Webster, Dr. McCarty, Morris Draper, and C. W. Willett, the group recommended Shinn's Addition. Politics intervened as County Attorney Michael Sutton suggested rejecting the report and allowing everyone present to vote the issue. Harry Gryden objected but was shouted down by Sutton's supporters, "whereupon voting commenced and a scene of boisterous confusion ensued, many leaving . . . in disgust without voting."[2] The gang had not forgotten Shinn's defection from the *Times* to the *Ford County Globe*. Sutton and his allies favored Boot Hill. Once again the gang had outmaneuvered its opposition.

The decision to build a schoolhouse on Boot Hill did not go unnoticed at Hays City: "Boot Hill in Dodge has been chosen as the site of the grand new school house. The proudest evidence of enlightenment upon the one surviving relic of barbarism! It is consistent."[3]

With Boot Hill's future all but assured, citizens turned their attention to the legislature's wish to redraw the quarantine line. Supporters of the cattle trade hoped the new boundary would close off much of the area north of the Arkansas, thus reducing complaints from farmers living in the northeast section of the county, while at the same time keeping the town open to the Texans. Businessmen preferred pacifying the farmers. First, with their crops protected from the longhorns, they need not organize against the cattle interests, as had happened elsewhere. Second, merchants began to appreciate the possibility of long-term relationships with the agricultural community. Morris Collar even renamed his place the Farmers and Settlers Store.

As Ford County's legislative representative, Robert Wright worked hard to assure the best advantage with the quarantine. In early February a petition signed by nearly every farmer in the county supported Wright's efforts. The legislature adopted changes that seemed to satisfy everyone. The *Times* outlined the new boundary as running "south through the center of Hodgeman and Ford counties, to a point just east of the stock yards at Dodge City, to the Arkansas river. It follows the Arkansas river east to the Edwards county line, and thence south to the Indian Territory. . . . The

---

[2] Ibid., May 13, 1879.
[3] *Hays City Sentinel*, as quoted in *Dodge City Times*, May 31, 1879.

time for driving cattle inside of the 'dead line' [has] been changed from October 1 to November 1."[4]

This last provision, some claimed, offered distinct advantages: "the cattle will be in good condition to stand the drive; they will arrive at a time when feeders will be ready to purchase, and they will therefore meet prompt and profitable sale. Those fit for killing will be on the market at a time when the weather is particularly favorable to packers and butchers; at that time grass will be good—far better than the thin, washy grass of spring—and the stock will certainly be in much better condition for standing the drive than they could possibly be early in the spring."[5] Much of the credit went to Robert Wright, supported behind the scenes by the railroad, determined to protect its investments at Dodge City.

Frontier towns often found themselves at the mercy of railroads. Some flaunted their power, but the Santa Fe preferred a more subtle approach. Viewed through the prism of economics, railroads needed towns and settlers to assure their growth, but towns depended on the railroad for their survival. Without the substantial investment and active cooperation of the AT&SF, Dodge City's cattle town prosperity would have been unthinkable. Officials may have disliked admitting any of this publicly and often disavowed the relationship, but they fooled no one.

The AT&SF proved its power in late March 1879. Sheriff Masterson received a telegram from its Canon City office requesting a posse be organized at Dodge City to assist the company in its long-simmering feud with the narrow-gauge Denver & Rio Grande concerning rights-of-way through Royal Gorge. Masterson and Deputy William Duffey opened a recruiting office and enrolled a volunteer company of thirty-three mercenaries. The whole idea of an elected official responding so willingly to the demands of a private corporation to do its bidding in another state may seem ludicrous today, but during the late nineteenth century, it illustrated raw power.

The struggle between the two railroads had begun years before. Only the financial panic of 1873 delayed open confrontation. Yet by 1875 the AT&SF began pushing its tracks from Granada along the Arkansas toward La Junta. In so doing, it cut across the cattle trail passing through Col-

---

[4] *Dodge City Times*, March 22, 1879.
[5] *Pueblo Chieftain*, as quoted in *Dodge City Times*, April 19, 1879.

orado to the Kansas Pacific. Undaunted by threats from the KP to build its own spur to La Junta, the Santa Fe kept laying track under its subsidiary, the Pueblo and Arkansas Valley Railroad Company, reaching Pueblo on March 7, 1875. All this jockeying for position alarmed Denver & Rio Grande president Gen. William Jackson Palmer.

Despite an agreement reached between all three roads operating in eastern Colorado, Palmer extended his tracks south from Pueblo to the small company town of El Moro. The general's decision to stop there enraged citizens of nearby Trinidad. When the Santa Fe made its move to block the D&RG from gaining access to Raton Pass—and with it an open road into New Mexico—it received help from the population of the neglected community. Construction boss A. A. Robinson, the same man who drew the original Dodge City townsite plat, effectively took control of that route, but only after some rather complicated maneuvering that ended just thirty minutes before Palmer's crews arrived. Trinidad's coal deposits added to the Santa Fe's revenues and reduced the cost of that commodity to places like Dodge City.

With the AT&SF looking southward, General Palmer shifted emphasis. The mining booms at Leadville and Silverton altered the equation. The only feasible route lay through Royal Gorge. Palmer, repeating his mistake of snubbing Trinidad, now built his road to within three miles of Canon City, another source of Colorado coal. People there reacted the same way as their brethren had at Trinidad. They pleaded with the Santa Fe to run a parallel line to their town. Complacent company directors, sitting around conference tables at Topeka plotting the future over aged whiskey and Cuban cigars, still had their eyes fixed on New Mexico. They hesitated concerning Royal Gorge until the rich silver strikes at Leadville reawakened their interest.

Palmer's company was in trouble, even facing possible bankruptcy. Revenues fell as coal shipments from El Moro faltered. Meanwhile, the Santa Fe drained off traffic from Pueblo. In desperation, Palmer tried negotiating a pool agreement with the Kansas Pacific and the troublesome AT&SF. Rebuffed, Palmer—who was by then reading the Santa Fe's telegraphic codes—decided to move into Royal Gorge while its crews busied themselves in Raton Pass.

Hearing of the plan, W. R. Morley, a former manager of the Maxwell Land Grant and a one-time Denver & Rio Grande engineer now working for the Santa Fe, made a desperate midnight ride into Canon City. There he succeeded in rousing its citizens to aid him in the fight against the hated D&RG. As Palmer's crews approached Royal Gorge, they found the Santa Fe's graders already in possession. Although the Denver & Rio Grande had surveyed the canyon in 1873, they never bothered filing a plat. Neither side backed down, as crews from both roads continued working within yards of one another.

The entire controversy was headed for the courthouse. Convoluted legal maneuvering, a slow enough process in the best of times, now worked against General Palmer's interests in the short run. As the financial underpinnings of the Denver & Rio Grande weakened, Palmer agreed with reluctance to lease his company to the Santa Fe; contingent upon it agreeing to pay D&RG stockholders 43 percent of any gross receipts thus generated. The agreement took affect at midnight, December 13, 1878.

Under provisions of the lease, the Santa Fe diverted traffic onto its own line. Income for the Denver & Rio Grande fell below the level enabling the company to pay interest on its bonds. The AT&SF even used its rival's rolling stock to transport construction supplies to crews at Royal Gorge. Palmer repudiated the agreement and refiled his original lawsuit in federal court. Before a decision could to be handed down, Palmer's men began vandalizing the Santa Fe's work in the canyon. It was then that the railroad turned to its willing allies at Dodge City. If gunmen were needed, the AT&SF knew where to turn.[6]

The Denver & Rio Grande organized its own toughs, swept up from the streets and saloons of Colorado's capital. Masterson and his men left Dodge City on March 22: "They all boarded the morning train, armed to the teeth . . . and started for the scene of hostilities."[7] The sheriff and several others returned two weeks later. "The boys report having had an easy time, nothing to do, plenty of chuck and $3 a day from the railroad," reported the *Globe* on April 8. "They spent Sunday in the city and went back on Monday to resume their duties. So far there has been no trouble, and about five miles of the road is completed. About 100 men are

---

[6] For a more comprehensive look at the details behind this struggle, at least from the Santa Fe's point of view, see James Marshall, *Santa Fe: The Railroad that Built an Empire* (New York: Random House, 1945), 144–58; Waters, *Steel Rails to Santa Fe*, 97–127; and Keith L. Bryant, Jr., *History of the Atchison, Topeka and Santa Fe Railway* (Lincoln: University of Nebraska Press, 1982), 37–53.

[7] *Ford County Globe*, March 25, 1879.

employed just to see that no attempts are made by the Rio Grande men to drive the A.T. & S.F. workmen from the disputed canyon."

During another respite, Masterson helped save Wyatt Earp's life. Three men traveling from Clay County, Missouri, to Leadville decided to have their way in Dodge City. Earp easily disarmed one of the men. As he led his prisoner by the ear toward the calaboose, one of the others convinced his partner to "throw lead" at the otherwise distracted assistant city marshal. Masterson arrived in time to disarm the would-be assassin. Two of the Missourians spent the night in jail.

The next evening, having learned nothing from the experience, all three Clay County badmen set out to even accounts. Hiding behind a store, they sent a boy to summon the sheriff. Not trusting the trio, the young messenger warned Masterson to be on guard. With the help of Deputy William Duffey, the sheriff rounded up all three. Thwarted a second time in as many days: "These fellows remarked that they 'had run things in Missouri' and believed they could 'take' Dodge City, but admitted that they were no match for Dodge City officers. Dodge City is hard 'to take.' The pistol brigands find in it a 'warm berth.' "[8]

Meanwhile, back in Colorado, the Santa Fe hoped to limit its risk by recruiting gunman Ben Thompson and several other Texans to help guard its property at Pueblo. By early June the company feared a ruling from Thomas Bowen, a federal judge friendly to the D&RG. The Santa Fe concentrated its forces at Pueblo and again called upon Bat Masterson at Dodge City.

The sheriff and nearly sixty others boarded a special westbound train on June 9. Tensions rose all along the line as the AT&SF consolidated its position. Gunfire broke out at Gucharas, killing one man and wounding another.[9] At Pueblo the county sheriff began serving officials of the Santa Fe with Judge Bowen's order to desist. Events seemed pointed toward open battle between Colorado officers and the Dodge City men. Suddenly, those guarding the Pueblo facilities surrendered.

---

[8] *Dodge City Times*, May 10, 1879. The two men involved in the original altercation were probably Henry Kaufman and Tom W. Ewen, since Justice Docket entries No. 429 and 430 list both standing before the court on May 6, to answer complaints filed by Wyatt Earp, charging each with violating the ordinance against carrying concealed weapons. Justice Samuel Marshall levied fines of $10.50 plus $3 costs against each man. Walter Stanley Campbell Files, Box 96; Justice Docket, Dodge City, Kansas, Notes, 79. Manuscript Division, Western History Collection, University of Oklahoma Library.

[9] Streeter, *Ben Thompson*, 134.

It is not clear exactly what happened. Some suggested the D&RG bribed either Bat Masterson or Ben Thompson, or both, to lay down their arms. Thompson's long-time attorney, William M. Walton—described as "a man of superb social qualities,"[10] claimed his client was offered twenty-five thousand dollars to surrender, but refused.[11] Another chronicler stated that an agent for the Denver & Rio Grande "held the belief that a man who could be hired by an entire stranger to go out and slay people for a few dollars a day could be dealt with, and so went over to the roundhouse to see Masterson, with the result that the men at the roundhouse abandoned their position."[12]

Although many in Dodge City seemed proud of their men's resolve in Colorado, others complained. They wondered about their sheriff charging off into another state at the head of a band of paid mercenaries, rather than staying behind and carrying out those duties he had been elected to perform.

Questions arose concerning other actions by the sheriff. On March 10, 1879, George B. Cox, chairman of the board of county commissioners, resigned, explaining, "the existing feelings between the County Com[missioners] and some of the County officers make the position anything but pleasant, and impossible for me to do the County the justice my official oath demands."[13] In reporting the incident eight days later, the *Globe* added, "For a long time the relations of the Sheriff and the Board have not been amicable, and frequently high words have been spoken. Mr. Cox being naturally of a very retiring disposition and not, like most men in office, always ready to maintain his opinions and enforce his ideas at all hazards, just quietly resigns and will have nothing more to do in an official capacity."

Earlier that year Chairman Cox had objected to all the costs charged county taxpayers for housing prisoners.[14] At the same meeting the commissioners appointed one of their own, A. J. Peacock, along with Charlie Bassett, to verify moneys due Ford County from the state treasury on criminal cases from unorganized counties attached to Ford for judicial

---

[10] James D. Lynch, *The Bench and Bar of Texas* (St. Louis: Nixon-Jones Printing Co., 1885), 485.

[11] Walton, *Life and Adventures of Ben Thompson*, 134.

[12] Statement from railroad historian Cy Warman, as quoted in Streeter, *Ben Thompson*, 208n10.

[13] Ford County Commissioners Journals, Book A, 253.

[14] *Ford County Globe*, January 14, 1879. The amount in question was $238.80. Ford County Commissioners Journals, Book A, 245.

purposes. The board gave Peacock and Bassett full power to examine any records they chose.

Perhaps Masterson saw it all as an intrusion. Someone signing himself "O. K. Tenderfoot" sent an open letter to Commissioners Peacock, J. W. Sidlow, and J. B. Means: "Sirs—Please answer this question: Who or which one of our county officials is it that has been playing border ruffian so far as to intimidate Mr. Cox so as to cause him to resign. . . . Gentlemen, please answer. The people have a right to know who it is that has captured you."[15] This man's question referred to the board's statement in accepting Cox's resignation: "we deeply regret that the conduct of certain parties toward Mr. Cox has compelled him to take this step."[16] Whatever the cause for bitterness, repercussions would be felt at the polls.

Trouble in Dodge City always involved more than politics. Early on the evening of April 5, Levi Richardson, a well-known freighter and a scout for the army during the Dull Knife scare, tangled with a gambler known as Cock-Eyed Frank Loving. It seems as if Cocked-Eyed Frank had for some time been living with a prostitute toward whom Richardson, too, "cherished tender feelings." This mutual admiration caused them to come to blows at least once. At that time P. L. Beatty overheard Richardson's threat that he would "shoot the guts out of the cock-eyed son of a bitch any way."[17]

Bartender Adam Jackson later testified seeing Cock-Eyed Frank enter the narrow confines of the Long Branch just as Richardson stood up to leave. The two exchanged words. Richardson pulled his .44 Remington and fired point-blank. The *Globe* described the resulting melee: "both drew murderous revolvers and at it they went, in a room filled with people, the leaden missives flying in all directions. Neither exhibited any sign of a desire to escape the other, and there is no telling how long the fight might have lasted had not Richardson been pierced with bullets and Loving's pistol left without a cartridge. Richardson was shot in the breast, through the side and through the right arm. It seems strange that Loving was not hit, except a slight scratch on the hand, as the two men were so close together that their pistols almost touched each other. Eleven shots were fired, six by Loving and five by Richardson."[18]

---

[15] *Ford County Globe*, April 1, 1879.

[16] Ford County Commissioners Journals, Book A, 253.

[17] Testimony of P. L. Beatty, Coroner's Inquest upon the body of Levi Richardson, *Ford County Globe*, April 8, 1879.

[18] *Ford County Globe*, April 8, 1879.

Hearing gunfire while at Beatty & Kelley's saloon, City Marshal Bassett raced down the block to the Long Branch, entering just as Cock-Eyed Frank fired his last two rounds. Bassett watched as "Richardson was dodging and running around the billiard table. Loving was also running and dodging around the table. I got as far as the stove when the shooting had about ended. I caught Loving's pistol."[19] Deputy Sheriff Duffey disarmed Richardson after a short struggle. Badly wounded, the popular freighter died within the hour. He was thought to be about twenty-eight years old.

Based on testimony of those present, most of whom supported the claim that Richardson fired first, the six man coroner's jury decided Frank Loving had acted in self-defense. They ignored the fact that both shooters had been armed contrary to ordinance, although the *Globe* did remind its readers: "Neither of these men had a right to carry such weapons. Gamblers, as a class, are desperate men. They consider it necessary in their business that they keep up their fighting reputation, and never take a bluff. On no account should they be allowed to carry deadly weapons."[20] Levi Richardson fared no better in death than he had in life: liabilities against his estate totaled nearly $400, but the administrator's sale netted only $199.50.

Richardson was soon forgotten. With Mayor Kelley running for a third one-year term, all eyes focused on the gang and its hold on city government. Still reeling from their November defeats, anti-gang forces lacked the confidence to mount a challenge. Conceding the futility of the moment, Dan Frost looked to the future: "Is it not about time for the businessmen, mechanics and property-owners of Dodge to consider that the town is no longer at the 'end of track?' Will it not prove to their advantage if the idea is given a place in its government at once that this is a permanent city, destined to grow within a few years to be like Topeka, Emporia, Lawrence and Atchison?"[21]

None of this made any impression on James Kelley, who stuck with the idea of keeping Dodge City a haven for Texas cattlemen. During the March 4 council meeting he had named Chalkley Beeson, Walter Straeter, and James Anderson election judges, setting the stage for his own victory.

---

[19] Testimony of Chas. E. Bassett, Coroner's Inquest . . . Levi Richardson, ibid.

[20] *Ford County Globe*, April 8, 1879.

[21] Ibid., March 18, 1879.

Supporters of the People's Party could do little more than await the inevitable. On April Fool's Day the *Globe* mused, "The 'gang' is beginning to connubiate over the spring election, which takes place next Monday. Of course they have it all their own way."

Ignoring complaints from its rival, a gleeful *Times* reported the results on April 12: "It was, indeed, like a 'funeral day,' for the opposition party is so dead that they had not strength enough to bring out a ticket." No one could help but acknowledge the gang's triumph. James Kelley received 203 votes for mayor, against only 2 ballots cast for Presbyterian minister O. W. Wright. City council seats went to Walter Straeter, C. M. Beeson, D. D. Colley, Morris Collar, and John Newton, all with totals similar to Kelley's. Scattered council votes even included one for Bat Masterson.

The council then passed new ordinances raising city license fees and setting the salaries of city officials, prompting the *Times* to declare: "The revenue derived from fines on gambling and prostitution, which will be revived next month, will pay the police force. . . . Our city government is in a prosperous condition, and the recent action of the council dispels the base insinuation 'that the people will wake up and find their fair city bankrupt by the evils of "gang" rule.' City script may now be quoted at par. Let us have more of such 'gang' rule."[22]

Worried about a $3,000 debt and depleted city treasury, others debated the point. Approving increases of a "dram shop license from one hundred to three hundred dollars," opposition leaders questioned the wisdom of raising the pay for the city attorney and city clerk, since both were the same person—Mike Sutton's law partner Ed Colborn.[23] Along with his salary, Colborn collected fifty cents for each license issued, six dollars in all police court cases where the defendant pleaded not guilty but was convicted, and three dollars for an outright guilty plea—this at a time when the police court handled at least one hundred cases a year. Adding to city expenditures, policeman cushioned their salaries with an additional two dollars for each arrest.

Concerns about money rose with rumors claiming only 179,000 head of cattle expected for the entire season. The *Times*, mirroring local panic,

---

[22] *Dodge City Times*, April 12, 1879. This last statement was in response to an attack published in the April 8 issue of the *Ford County Globe*: "[Kelley and his cronies] have the ropes and not until the people wake up and find their fair city bankrupt will they realize to its full extent the evils of 'gang' rule."

[23] *Ford County Globe*, April 15, 1879.

began predicting the end of the cattle trade. AT&SF livestock agent A. H. Johnson blamed pessimism on a particularly dry winter in south Texas. Henry M. Beverley, representing himself and Robert Wright, toured the area and seemed to confirm the decline, softening the blow with assurances that most herds would still come by way of Dodge City.

Soon, more optimistic news began filtering north from Texas. Cattlemen around San Antonio may have predicted smaller drives, but those from Goliad, Bee, and Refugio counties anticipated larger numbers than ever. Because of the drought, owners began selling off one- and two-year-old stock. Buyers in south Texas reported demands for larger down payments, suggesting a loosening of trade amid reports of cattle starving to death between Victoria and the Gulf. At the same time, veterans of the trail prepared for the journey north. The Shiner brothers assembled ten thousand head, while Dillard Fant, an old Dodge City regular, rounded up three herds for the Kansas market.

Still worrying about the numbers, businessmen tried ending another impediment to free trade. By late March, they again questioned the policy of demanding tolls on the Arkansas River bridge. Despite claims published in the old *Dodge City Messenger* in 1874 of a "FREE BRIDGE ACROSS THE ARKANSAS RIVER!" it had never happened. Settlers to the south complained about the dollar charged for each crossing. Rumors of building free bridges at Cimarron and Spearville worried some Dodge City retailers. As a countermeasure, bridge company stockholders considered reducing tolls to settlers. Dismissing the gesture, settlers demanded free access. It was not to be. As soon as the numbers of Texas cattle reached satisfactory levels, all discussion of bridge reform died.

Others dismissed negative speculation concerning the Texas trade. George Hoover not only traveled to Louisville, Kentucky, to personally contract shipments of whiskey, he built himself a warehouse for beer. Hoover planned to reduce his costs by ordering stock by the carload. Reflecting Hoover's optimism, P. L. Beatty and Mayor Kelley demolished their building to make way for a two-story affair housing a saloon known as the Alhambra, together with a restaurant and meeting hall called the Opera House. The original structure had been set up first at Leavenworth. From there it was disassembled, hauled west, and rebuilt at Junction City and then again at Ellsworth. Following another move to Hays City, the veteran wood frame finally met its end on Front Street, a victim of cattle town progress.

Ignoring fears of the future, Morris Collar, A. B. Webster, Henry Beverley, and others set out to build themselves impressive homes. Attorney Harry Gryden ordered construction of a new office. Walter Shinn rebuilt his tannery on Charlie Rath's old site. Showing no concern over rumors of a slow season, J. S. Kirk built the City Hotel two blocks from the depot. Bob Wright also started a hotel, located east of the *Times* office, rumored to be run by pioneer saloonmen Colley and Manion.

The enthusiasm encouraged others. Col. James A. Coffey and his old Indian trading partner, Oliver Marsh, had arrived in late 1878 with plans of opening a dry goods, flour, and seed emporium west of the post office. Coffey, an old Kansas veteran who had helped found the towns of Humboldt and Coffeyville, did not live to see profits from Dodge City, dying of pneumonia three months later. Oliver Marsh and his son stayed on. In early June, W. H. Lockridge opened a gentleman's store in a building owned by George Hoover, featuring a complete line of ready-made clothing, hats, boots, camp equipment, groceries, and dried fruits. John Mullin, a man with two years' experience catering to Texas cattlemen at the Ellis railhead, managed the Lockridge enterprise.

Skepticism faded after Texans George Littlefield and J. D. Houston spoke of 18,000 head expected by the end of May. Revised figures pointed to 250,000 for the season. The town again saw profits coming in on the hoof, even from "through cattle" destined for the Platte River Valley. Four months after predicting the demise of the cattle trade, Nicholas Klaine viewed the question with renewed enthusiasm: "In conversation with a prominent cattleman . . . we learn that there would be a larger drive next year than for the past two years. . . . He believes Dodge City will retain the cattle trade until that business is moved westward by reason of settlement."[24]

Cattlemen announced plans to ship from Coffeyville on the Missouri, Kansas & Texas. That road offered lower rates to Chicago, then paying higher prices for beef than either Kansas City or St. Louis. The AT&SF charged $40 a carload from Dodge to Kansas City, but from there to Chicago, because of a pool agreement negotiated by Missouri interests, rates jumped to $106.50. Dodge City worked to overcome this impedi-

---

[24] *Dodge City Times,* June 7, 1879.

ment, hoping for some relief from the just completed Chicago and Alton Railroad. "The fact of the matter is that Kansas City is the great barrier that stands between the railroads on the east of her and the stock trade of the west," groused the *Ford County Globe* on May 13. "We hope that Chicago will look into this matter and see that western stock-dealers can enter her market without paying tribute to every little city they would necessarily have to pass in going there."

Commission merchants at Kansas City resisted anyone tinkering with their system. After the threat from Coffeyville failed to materialize and longhorns began arriving again in respectable numbers, concerns in Dodge City over railroad rates dried up as a topic of conversation. The whole system was then balanced somewhat with the abandonment of the four-year-old "Cattle Eveners' Pool" in late spring 1879. Thereafter, a joint executive committee of the eastern trunk lines controlled rates.[25]

In early May butcher Charles Hungerford returned with news of a large herd of Texas cattle grazing along the Cimarron. Three weeks later reports told of 43,610 head arriving at Fort Griffin, with 73,882 more passing Fort Worth. Adding to these numbers, John Gamble held 4,900 head at Bluff Creek, along with 1,300 others owned by Tinner and Polley. Numbers within easy reach of Dodge City swelled to 30,000. Meanwhile, Bennett and Littlefield crossed 3,000 head at Bear Creek, as Snider and Caruthers drove herds totaling 12,000 animals across the Texas Panhandle, with Moore and Allen pushing 10,000 "through cattle" en route to North Platte, Nebraska.

After Col. W. C. Lewis announced another 6,000 head, the *Globe* published a list compiled by Henry Beverley in early July showing that nearly fifty cattlemen had come into Dodge City within the last ten days. A week later the paper dismissed rumors of a depressed market: "A good many buyers have been induced to go to other points for their cattle on account of current rumors that Dodge had no cattle this season. This is erroneous, and does our city a great injustice, for while some cattle have passed on

---

[25] A behind-the-scenes conspiratorial creation amongst various railroad executives for determining rates for the shipping of cattle beyond Chicago that strangled competition, even for some of those involved. Shippers especially felt themselves at the mercy of this combination. Joseph Nimmo, Jr., *Report on the Internal Commerce of the United States* (Washington: Government Printing Office, 1879), 177–78. As Mr. Nimmo notes, "The operations of the Cattle Eveners' Pool were conducted secretly, and great difficulty has been met in the various efforts which have been made to ascertain fully and completely the facts in regard to it. This fact furnishes an instructive comment upon the propriety of its existence on the ground of public policy."

and gone north, the bulk of cattle are yet to arrive, and we predict that the cattle that are held in this vicinity will bring the best figures received on through cattle for 1879."[26]

Texas men were still kings, but by the end of the 1870s the economy of Ford County began showing signs of separating itself from its total reliance on freighting and cattle. It was a slow process, but as a sign of the future a group from Decatur, Illinois, representing H. F. May & Company, had already visited Dodge City with plans to build a flour mill and grain elevator. Six months earlier the press announced the company's decision, they having negotiated favorable freight rates with the AT&SF.

From Decatur, Henry F. May and his partner John M. Rainey, shipped the old St. Clair mill to Ford County. Reassembling the machinery, the two men opened the Dodge City Flouring Mills on June 13. Located at the west end of Locust Street and costing twenty thousand dollars, the three-story structure and smokestack dominated the skyline.[27] Following tradition, dignitaries delivered windy speeches, after which the Dodge City Cornet Band entertained three hundred spectators. Almost everyone understood this structure represented the future. Agriculture was the only logical successor to the cattle trade, an exciting and somewhat romantic enterprise, to be sure, but not one that could last forever.

Emphasis on change proved premature, even if, following the Colorado troubles and the killing of Levi Richardson, the town seemed calmer than during its formative years: "Dodge City is quiet and local items are scarce," mused the *Times* on July 26. Bob Wright's new hotel, the Wright House, opened at the northwest corner of Chestnut Street and Second Avenue. Adobe Walls hero and local restaurateur Fred Leonard leased the place (rather than Colley and Manion as first expected) with A. J. Peacock running the bar. Another early pioneer, Charles Hungerford, relocated his meat market next to Beatty & Kelley's restaurant, a convenience appreciated by the mayor. A. B. Webster began building the new schoolhouse on Boot Hill, while H. F. May & Company expanded its reach by shipping flour to Colorado by late September.

Changes included the dissolution of York, Hadder & Draper on July 22. George Hadder retired from the successful partnership, which by now

[26] *Ford County Globe*, June 24, 1879.

[27] *Dodge City Times*, June 14, 1879; and *Ford County Globe*, June 17, 1879. Also see *Portrait and Biographical Record of Macon County, Illinois* (Chicago: Lake City Publishing Co., 1893), 296–97, 719–20; and *History of the State of Kansas*, 1561.

enjoyed a close association with F. B. York & Company of Fort Griffin, Texas. Hadder moved on to Colorado Springs and opened a drug store. He returned briefly to Dodge City in late October. Within six months, together with former Wright, Beverley & Company partner Charles H. Lane, and Spanish-speaking employee Sam Samuels, Hadder joined forces with George Reilly at Caldwell. They opened a large store anticipating the eventual shift of the cattle business to that Kansas border town.

Reflecting journalistic preference, a Topeka correspondent had given Dodge City's police force a heady compliment that summer: "With Charley Bassett for Marshal, Wyatt Earp for deputy, and Jas. Masterson as an officer . . . an offender might as well be beneath the nether mill stone."[28] But the old town's shifting status held little interest for Earp, who resigned his $100-a-month post in early September. The council voted him $13.32 for his last four days of service. On December 1, 1879, Wyatt and his brothers Virgil and James, together with their wives, arrived at Tombstone, Arizona. Two months after Earp's departure, City Marshal Bassett also resigned. On November 4 the city council would appoint James Masterson and Neil Brown to the positions vacated by the two veteran Dodge City officers.

Meanwhile, just four days after Earp's resignation, Barney Martin, an Irish-born tailor from Hays City, and Arista H. "Jim" Webb, a porter for York & Draper, spent the afternoon drinking whiskey at Walter Straeter's Old House saloon. The two came to blows over a chance remark that Webb found offensive. It was not a fair confrontation, Martin being described as "a remarkably small man, generally inoffensive and timid."[29] Another source noted, "When sober he was quiet and industrious; but his sprees were frequent, and while he may have been annoying as drunken men do sometimes, he was not considered dangerous or vicious."[30] Rufus G. Cook, the justice of the peace working his side job as bartender, refused to give Webb a pistol and ordered both combatants off the premises. Martin apologized for his remark, claiming he was only joking, then left to sit on a small wooden bench in front of his tailor shop next to Henry Sturm's Occident saloon—the old Waters and Hanrahan site.

---

[28] Letter from "W. M. H." to the editor of the *Kansas Daily Commonwealth*, July 15, 1879, as quoted in *Ford County Globe*, July 22, 1879.

[29] *Ford County Globe*, September 9, 1879.

[30] *Dodge City Times*, September 13, 1879.

Martin's disclaimer did not appease Webb, who demanded a pistol from Zimmerman's hardware. The clerk testified he even tried pushing his way behind the counter to get one, saying "he wanted to hit some one over the head; said he would then pay his fine and pay for the damage done to the pistol."[31] Turned away, Webb rushed home, saddled his horse and rode back with a Winchester rifle. Finding Barney Martin still sitting at his shop, he smashed him over the head with the rifle barrel. Martin died within hours, never regaining consciousness. Witnesses blocked Webb's escape. Charlie Bassett disarmed the man, finding the Winchester not only cocked but fully loaded. The marshal took his prisoner to the city calaboose, but soon transferred Webb to the county jail, owing to the mood of the crowd.

A coroner's jury viewed the body and heard testimony in the storeroom of Fred Leonard's old restaurant before deliberating in the clubroom of the Long Branch. Justice of the Peace Lloyd Shinn ordered Webb held without bond for the next term of the district court. Attorneys tried making an issue of the defendant's mental state—his father wrote from Virginia, explaining apparent hereditary problems: his brother and two of his other six children being similarly afflicted, cases serious enough for authorities to place them in the asylum for the insane at Williamsburg.

Found guilty of first-degree murder, the judge imposed a death sentence in late January 1880, the first such ruling in Ford County.[32] Left destitute, Mrs. Webb ended up at the Home of the Friendless in Leavenworth. The state never did execute her husband. Five years later the governor declared him insane and issued a pardon.

At 6:30 in the morning of September 27, 1879, President Rutherford B. Hayes, together with Gen. William T. Sherman and Gov. John P. St. John, arrived at Dodge City on one of the president's western tours, dragging with them an entourage of minor dignitaries and hordes of newspapermen. One would have expected some excitement. Instead, reported the *Globe* three days later, "we have frequently witnessed a larger and more enthusiastic crowd gather around a dog fight or a 'street broil.' "

---

[31] Testimony of James Connor, Coroner's Inquest upon the body of Barney Martin, *Ford County Globe*, September 9, 1879.

[32] State of Kansas vs. A. Howell Webb, Records of the Ford County District Court, Criminal Appearance Docket A, 71; Criminal Case Record, File No. 64; Judge's Journal, Book A, 279–82; and *Dodge City Times*, January 24, 1880; and *Ford County Globe*, January 27, 1880.

The president, his wife, General Sherman, and the governor spent about two hours at Fort Dodge, while the other excursionists "remained in the city, loafing around on the street corners."[33] President Hayes and General Sherman did address a small crowd of men and boys from the train platform; the general, cracking jokes, clearly the more popular of the two. Afterward, noted the *Globe*, "Several of our peasantry approached the President and General and gave those worthies considerable 'jaw' about irregularities in their pensions and other grievances, one old lady from the Emerald Isle demanded rations for herself and children on the strength of her husband's bravery in the army. But all great men are subject to petty annoyances."[34]

Criticism of the welcome given the president of the United States was not long in coming. Editors at the *Chicago Times* were flabbergasted: "There was no demonstration and apparently no curiosity to see the distinguished visitor. . . . They were welcomed with no flapdoodle oratory, no crowds, no bands, no cannon, no anything."[35] Frost defended Dodge City: "These critics evidently forget that Dodge is not formed on a common model. . . . In the first place, we cannot shout early in the morning. We don't get up steam much before noon. . . . Should Grant, the Emperor William, the Prince of Wales or Barnum's Hippodrome make an entry into Dodge at so unfashionable an hour as did Hayes we couldn't be there in any considerable numbers. They might catch a few who had not gone to bed yet, but our steady citizens would be missing. . . . We cannot really be expected to break in upon our habits and upset ourselves by turning out at daylight for doubtful Presidents or second class shows of any kind."[36]

People spent little time reacting to criticism. There were more important issues. County elections were scheduled for early November, and for the first time the People's Ticket realistically sensed victory. Conceding the potential strength of the agricultural vote, Dan Frost picked Spearville as the site for his party's October 18 convention. Hoping to counteract the smugness of its rivals, the gang announced their own meeting for Dodge

---

[33] *Ford County Globe*, September 30, 1879.

[34] Ibid.

[35] *Chicago Times*, as quoted in *Ford County Globe*, October 7, 1879.

[36] *Ford County Globe*, October 7, 1879. Frost's reference to "doubtful Presidents" reminded readers that Samuel J. Tilden had received most of the popular vote in the election of 1876, but Hayes became president anyway. Even stout Republican Nicholas Klaine buried his account of the visit in an uncaptioned twenty-line paragraph on the last page of his September 27 issue of the *Dodge City Times*.

City. Those attending included not only the obvious disciples—Mayor Kelley, Robert Wright, Nicholas Klaine, Michael Sutton, and A. J. Peacock—but two political outsiders: Frederick Zimmerman and Henry Tassett, both soon picked to run on the People's Ticket.

After the conventions both factions shamelessly ballyhooed their selections. The gang threw its support behind William B. Masterson for sheriff, Alonzo B. Webster for county treasurer, Otto Mueller for county clerk, Philip J. Upp for register of deeds, H. M. Clark for county surveyor, and Samuel Marshall for county commissioner from the second district. For these same positions the People's Ticket championed liquor dealer George Hinkle, Frederick Zimmerman, George Potter, William F. Petillon, Henry Tassett, and George Hoover. Both sides backed John W. Straughn for coroner and Samuel R. Peters to continue as judge of the Ninth Judicial District.

Anti-gang forces concentrated on the sheriff's office, criticizing the costs associated with jailing the seven Cheyennes after the Dull Knife scare. It did not help matters to have that case dismissed just three weeks before the election. Stirring up more dissatisfaction, the *Globe* reported on October 21: "There is a suit now pending against Ford county for a large bill of costs in this case, and as will be seen by the proceedings of the Board, J. G. Waters, of Topeka, has volunteered his services to defend the county against paying these costs, amounting to several thousand dollars. The suits against the county are brought by W. B. Masterson, Sheriff." Frost, recognizing a winning issue, kept up the attack. Praising incumbent commissioner George Hoover's candidacy, he wrote a week later: "Just think of Ford county having to pay $4000 for the simple arrest of seven lousy Cheyenne Indians and that without even an effort to convict them. Hoover is against all such frauds. Don't his vote show it on Sheriff's bills?"

Commissioners accepted the services of outside counsel, but others questioned Mike Sutton's role in all this: "Mr. Masterson has already received about three hundred dollars on the Cheyenne Indian account, and he and some others have instituted suit against Ford county for twenty-one hundred dollars more. Joe Waters, attorney for the Santa Fe, has volunteered to defend the county. Where is Mr. Sutton?"[37]

Some of these costs represented unavoidable expenses. Nicholas Klaine tried putting it into perspective by reminding his readers: "Bat Masterson is

---

[37] *Spearville News*, October 25, 1879. Regarding the acceptance of the offer from railroad attorney Joseph G. Waters during the meeting held on October 7, 1879, see Ford County Commissioners Journals, Book A, 270.

Sheriff of thirteen unorganized counties. Of course it costs something to run so much territory."[38] It was a well-reasoned argument, especially since the state did little to compensate Ford County taxpayers. Masterson's lawsuit only added to the exasperation already felt by voters. As early as mid-September, one Spearville subscriber had written the *Globe*, "Will you be kind enough to let the farmers of the east end of Ford county know . . . who the candidates are that are seeking the office of Sheriff this fall, besides Masterson? We have [had] enough of the Masterson rule."[39] Disclaimers published in the *Times* did nothing to alleviate these sentiments.

Robert B. Fry, editor of the *Spearville News*, agreed: "We understand that 'Bat Masterson' is going to shoot his way into the office of sheriff. This manner of conducting a canvass may do in Mississippi, but not in Ford county."[40] Fry spread the rumor that Masterson had charged John Stevenson twenty-five dollars to recover his stolen horse and arrest the culprit. Stevenson denied it, going so far as to support Bat's candidacy. But the damage was done, despite a retraction from Fry: "We make this voluntary correction, through justice to Mr. Stevenson, and Mr. Masterson as well, notwithstanding we are opposing Mr. M's reelection, we propose to be fair in the matter, and use such weapons, only, as he has forged himself."[41] The problems hounding Masterson helped set the tone for everything that followed. No wonder Frost and his allies looked forward to November 4 with such confidence.

The campaign was characteristically bitter. Accusing each other of the same tactics, both sides engaged in all manner of abuse, slander, and illegal maneuvering for votes. Even the *Dodge City Times*, heretofore so confident, struggled to sidetrack the advancing avalanche. It was too late. Ballots cast on November 4 swept the People's Ticket to victory. George T. Hinkle defeated Bat Masterson in all six precincts to become sheriff of Ford County by a margin of 136. Frederick Zimmerman routed A. B. Webster by 220 votes in their race for treasurer. Most margins of victory proved equally impressive.[42]

---

[38] *Dodge City Times*, October 25, 1879.

[39] *Ford County Globe*, September 16, 1879.

[40] *Spearville News*, November 1, 1879.

[41] Ibid.

[42] Ford County Commissioners Journals, Book A, 272. Also see *Dodge City Times*, November 8, 1879; and *Ford County Globe*, November 11, 1879. It should be noted that some of the totals, as reported in both newspapers, vary slightly from the official tally recorded by the county commissioners during their meeting on November 7.

Neither side handled the results with grace. Nicholas Klaine, while reporting the tally on November 8, added his own feeble excuse for defeat: "There is a good deal of speculation as to the causes of the late defeat in Ford county, of the Independent ticket. The reasons given would fill a large volume; but we conjecture the most powerful influence was in the beer keg; and of course people fighting for honesty and reform wouldn't use money." Despite that laughable defense, the gang lost simply because a majority of voters no longer wanted them in office. Dan Frost, unfamiliar with victory, gloated through the next several issues of his newspaper. On November 25, he crowed, "The 'People's' bills are all paid. What troubles the Independents is that they can't get theirs paid out of the county treasury."

Klaine tried to salvage something from the humiliation: "Henceforth the DODGE CITY TIMES shall be known as a Republican newspaper. . . . We take this step believing that the opposition have a majority in Ford county; but we wish to be connected with a party and an organization of well defined principles, whether we are in the minority or majority—in the matter of votes. . . . This step is not made for the reason of regaining lost ground in consequence to the late local defeat."[43]

No one believed him. Three days later the *Globe* responded to Klaine's ruse of wrapping the gang's future in the banner of the Republican Party: "The 'Gang' is no longer in existence. It failed to 'get to the joint' last Tuesday, and has lost its grip forever. The sickly effort of its leaders to build a Republican party upon its ruins will not succeed. The Republican party is too grand an institution to permit of such a flagrant counterfeit." Instead, Frost prophesied: "It will be the old pirate under a new flag."

With victors baiting losers, tempers cooled slowly. The *Spearville News* claimed, "We hear that Bat. Masterson said he was going to whip every s— of a b—— that worked and voted against him in the county."[44] Then, as if following through on this threat, Masterson, in his capacity as a deputy U.S. marshal, swore out a complaint on November 30 and arrested Dan Frost, alleging that he received stolen government property from a sergeant at Fort Elliott, Texas, back on May 1, 1878, to wit: "300 pounds of white lead, two gallons of varnish, three kegs of nails, a lot of stationery, to the value of $127 54."[45]

[43] *Dodge City Times*, November 8, 1879.

[44] *Spearville News*, November 8, 1879.

[45] *Dodge City Times*, December 6, 1879; also see *Ford County Globe*, December 2, 1879.

Hauled before U.S. Commissioner R. G. Cook, Frost posted a hefty $5,000 bond. The federal grand jury at Topeka indicted him several months later. The case occupied even more months of feeble maneuvering. Residents got fed up and forwarded a petition to federal authorities supporting their beleaguered colleague, signed by Fred Zimmerman, Bob Wright, George Hoover, Larry Deger, and twenty others, asking for an immediate dismissal. The combative editor escaped this politically charged episode.

Frost survived, a little worse for the experience, but this affair did not end the new regime's embarrassment. Lame-duck county clerk John B. Means, nominated with so much fanfare by Harry Gryden, William Morphy, and Dan Frost just two years before, resigned in late December mumbling something about leaving the state. It seems that Mr. Means had forged several hundred dollars in county script. Mysteriously, no charges were filed and within a month press reports had the errant public servant roaming the streets of Santa Fe. Politics in Ford County were seldom dull. Reveling in the missteps of the self-righteous, Nicholas Klaine recovered his bravado, recasting his now tainted opposition as "The Ring: A Railroad Ring, a County Script Ring, a Government Agent Ring. A Stupendous Ring, indeed."[46]

Politics divided the town more than one might expect for such a small place. It provided harmless amusement for some and a lively diversion for others. Those not bemused took small comfort from the spectacle; even making money off the Texans failed to compensate for the constant scrounging for votes. Besides, in some respects beyond mere numbers, the 1879 cattle season had proved a disappointment after all. Earlier, the *Great Bend Tribune* went so far as to suggest that Dodge City would lose its hold on the trade to Lakin, some seventy miles to the west. Frost ridiculed that idea as "a wild dream coming from the shattered and tottering mind of the Tribune editor, who knows less about the 'cattle trade' than a Texas steer knows of Chesterfield's rules of etiquette."[47] Lakin did get some of the business, but it never threatened Dodge City's dominance.

Late rains convinced some cattlemen to drive herds farther north rather than hold them in Ford County. Many buyers followed the exodus. Although numbers of cattle shipped exceeded totals for 1878, other elements

---

[46] Ibid., November 15, 1879.
[47] *Ford County Globe*, July 8, 1879.

of the business weakened. The *Kansas City Price Current* remarked, "Dodge, as a cattle market, is fast losing its prestige, and the present season has been the dullest in its history, not more than half the number having been marketed here this year than there was last. As the town depends more or less on this class of trade for its support, all branches of business have suffered, and many believe that its palmy days are over."[48] More evidence of a sluggish economy: "About 200 whiskey barrels were disposed of within the past twelve months. . . . The whiskey traffic in Dodge is on the decline."[49]

Reconciling marketing statistics with their own reduced revenues was one thing, but in early January 1880, treasurer-elect Frederick Zimmerman, was hauled before U.S. Commissioner Rufus G. Cook and charged with possessing stolen government property. The judge set bail at one thousand dollars. To many the circumstances seemed strangely reminiscent of Dan Frost's earlier predicament. Five weeks later Cook held a preliminary hearing and discharged the defendant. It was just as well. After the scandal surrounding John Means—who had written himself twelve hundred dollars in fraudulent county notes before galloping off for New Mexico—locals did not need their confidence shaken further, especially not by the new treasurer. To make matters worse, the former clerk's official bond had been misplaced, or so it was said. This development represented only part of the problem: "County script has taken a tumble since the last allowance of Indian bills. Another such batch of Indians would burst the county."[50]

Perhaps from embarrassment or simple boredom, editors turned from scandals to praising their troubled community. Exaggerating the town while ignoring its faults was nothing new, but this time the strategy backfired. Perhaps overcome by the dawning of a new decade, Nicholas Klaine got carried away as a propagandist: "Dodge City is a remarkably healthy place. There is little or no sickness here. As a health resort Dodge City offers some excellent advantages."[51]

Unfortunately, less than three weeks earlier it was reported, "Deputy Sheriff Duffey is very low with fever, and not expected to live."[52] Duffey survived, but the same could not be said for others. The day before

---

[48] *Kansas City Price Current*, as quoted in *Dodge City Times*, September 6, 1879.

[49] *Dodge City Times*, September 27, 1879.

[50] *Ford County Globe*, January 20, 1880.

[51] *Dodge City Times*, January 24, 1880.

[52] *Ford County Globe*, January 6, 1880.

Klaine's rosy pronouncement, the infant son of A. J. Anthony died of "bilious fever." A week later A. B. Webster's young son recovered from what was thought a life-threatening illness. At the end of February the infant daughter of G. W. Shannon died. During this same period, perhaps with Klaine's optimism ringing in their ears, Dan Frost, Richard Evans, John Straughn, Thomas Jones, and Mrs. Matilda Zimmerman all lay bedridden with various ailments. Dodge City also endured a measles outbreak, infecting saloonman Henry V. Cook, and forcing one of the Driskill boys to convalesce at the Dodge House. Klaine's description of the city as a health resort may have impressed uninformed outsiders, but it drew less sympathy from the coughing and feverish locals.

Dodge City had no future as a health spa, but it still enjoyed symbols of civic pride. Not everything involving government expenditures depressed taxpayers as had the scandal surrounding Indian prisoners. The town formally dedicated its new $6,000 Boot Hill schoolhouse on February 4, 1880, amid much fanfare and self-congratulations. In his address, County Attorney Mike Sutton, who had done more than anyone to force the school's location there, retraced its sordid history: "It happened in 1872 that a man was shot within a few hundred yards of where the speaker now [stands]. His body lay nearly all day without any one to care for it, when toward evening a grave was dug upon the identical spot where we have built our new school building. The grave thus made was followed by many others until this beautiful hill became dotted with little mounds to the number of twenty-five or thirty."[53] Sutton saw the contrast between graveyard and school site as a sign of progress.

Educational improvements aside, Dodge City had not lost its taste for rough humor. Nor did the disappointing 1879 cattle season dampen its appeal. In October mischief makers had so terrified a new tailor with tales of slaughter—including graphic particulars about poor Barney Martin— that "He immediately bundled up his dry goods, took down his sign, and without saying 'by your leave' to his nearest neighbor, or paying his little outstanding bills, silently stole away on the first train that left the depot. We are again without a tailor and the places for patches on our pants are growing larger and more numerous every day."[54]

---

[53] Ibid., February 10, 1880.
[54] Ibid., October 21, 1879.

Then, in February 1880 the town unfolded its most elaborate prank. A "gentleman of distinction who bore the unassuming name and title of Meredith, M.D."—"He was what the boys would call a 'daisy'"—was invited to town to deliver a lecture at the Lady Gay dance hall. A large crowd gathered, but by prearrangement began shouting insults the moment the good doctor opened his mouth. Bat Masterson, as chairman of the welcoming committee and the speaker's self-appointed champion, pulled a revolver as others tried dragging the now terrified guest off the dais.

As planned, shots were fired as the lamps went out: "It was only after the ammunition in the house was expended that the murderous carnival ceased and a lamp was lighted. . . . But the dead and wounded had ere this time escaped and even the Doctor was nowhere to be found. Search was made, and at last he was discovered coiled up under the speaker's stand with his hands over his marble features and a ghastly bullet hole through the crown of his hat." Only then could it be reported: "The meeting adjourned sine die."[55]

The town did more than stage elaborate hijinks. News filtered in from Las Vegas, New Mexico, that former freighter, deputy sheriff, and city policeman John Joshua Webb had been convicted of murder in the shooting death of a cattle buyer. Residents began collecting money for an appeal. Lawyers Sutton and Colborn, Mayor Kelley, and Bat Masterson, together with Wright, Beverley & Company each contributed twenty dollars. Within weeks, however, James Allen and Dave Rudabaugh—the same man involved in the attempted Kinsley train robbery two years before—killed the jailer in a botched scheme to free Webb. Although J. J. eventually escaped on his own, Lincoln County sheriff Pat Garrett captured both him and Rudabaugh and turned them over to Las Vegas authorities. In late 1881, Webb escaped again, with Rudabaugh and six others, by digging through an adobe wall. Never recaptured, the former Dodge City officer reportedly died of smallpox in Arkansas the following year.[56]

Concerns for J. J. Webb did not trouble Dodge City for long. The town had problems of its own. Fears of repeating the disappointing 1879 cattle

---

[55] Ibid., February 17, 1880.

[56] Lynn Perrigo, *Gateway to Glorieta: A History of Las Vegas, New Mexico* (Boulder, Colo.: Pruett Publishing Company, 1982), 71–75; and *Las Vegas Daily Optic*, February 15, December 3, 1881. Also see *Dodge City Times*, March 13, 1880, April 20, 1882; and *Ford County Globe*, April 6, 1880.

season haunted Front Street. Struggling against charges of being high-priced, the *Ford County Globe* did its part rigging a defense: "The merchants of Dodge City are to-day selling goods at a closer margin than in any town west of Newton, and more particularly is this true as to the prices of what people buy to eat and wear. . . . Dodge is a cash town. . . . The heaviest stock man as well as the farmer, can purchase cheap for cash, anything he desires."[57]

Ordinary people expected business to guarantee their prosperity. They demanded the same from politics. With the gang's fortunes in apparent decline, opponents now looked with confidence toward the April 6 city balloting to finally unseat James H. Kelley. Earlier township elections stirred little interest, but with the mayor's chair on the block things began heating up. Whom to choose as an opposition candidate remained the question. Suggestions included saloonman and council member Walter Straeter, as well as John W. Straughn, then serving as county coroner, jailer, deputy sheriff, and deputy county surveyor. Even Frost welcomed Straughn's candidacy. Yet within weeks both Straughn and Walter Straeter declined all offers of support.

Still, it seemed as if voters were ready to abandon Mayor Kelley. There was, after all, a childlike side to Kelley's character that no longer carried with it the appeal of earlier days. At one point, the mayor ordered his police to arrest nearly a dozen men for allegedly shooting one of his hogs. Knowing the mayor's fondness for foolishness, former policeman Joe Mason sent him a black bear from Camp Supply. Kelley kept the animal in the backyard of his restaurant, much to the delight of Dodge City's children, if somewhat annoying to his patrons.

By early March, a bipartisan gathering of thirty-two citizens persuaded Dr. Thomas McCarty to run. Included among his supporters were Kelley's old foes George Hoover, Richard Evans, Fred Zimmerman, Harry Gryden, George Hinkle, and his new under sheriff, Fred Singer. One might expect to see these men line up against the gang, but others were a surprise. Even old allies seemed to feel the time had come for change. Robert M. Wright, city councilmen Chalk Beeson and Morris Collar, Justice of the Peace Rufus G. Cook, and saloonman A. J. Peacock joined the effort. Important businessmen such as F. B. York and Matthew Draper, Henry

---

[57] *Ford County Globe*, March 23, 1880.

Beverley, Henry Cook, and George Cox, all urged McCarty to declare his candidacy.

The apparent avalanche for McCarty caused confusion. Trying to salvage victory from disaster, Mike Sutton, Nick Klaine, Bat Masterson, and others offered McCarty's friends a deal. The plan allowed the doctor to be elected, without opposition, if Kelley and his allies were compensated with council seats on McCarty's ticket. Smelling victory without need for compromise, anti-gang forces dismissed the idea.

Rebuffed, gang leaders met in Kelley's saloon on the day before the election to energize their forces for a political last stand. Mike Sutton, never one to concede defeat until all the votes—legal or otherwise—were counted, personally drew up the ticket: James H. Kelley again for mayor, but with William H. Harris, Henry M. Beverley, George Randall, Thomas Draper, and Dr. Samuel Galland for councilmen, with David S. Weaver for police judge. Sutton knew that many of the faithful objected to his choices for council—especially Henry Beverley, an enthusiastic supporter of McCarty. Passing the list around the room, Sutton argued that these candidates, linked with Kelley's bid for reelection, might just neutralize the opposition.

Convinced that Sutton's strategy offered the only chance, gang loyalists went to work. They were everywhere, convincing, cajoling, promising, bartering, lying—anything for a vote. McCarty's supporters dozed the deep sleep of the innocent. They awoke on election morning to find "the Kelley men [had] formed an almost solid phalanx around the polls, and it was only by a Herculean effort that Christians could vote."[58] By noon McCarty's workers gave up the effort as a lost cause. Despite charges of voter fraud—likely true—James H. Kelley won his fourth term as Dodge City's mayor with a surprising total of 242 votes against only 68 for Dr. McCarty. Sutton's handpicked candidates for city council also won with wide margins. Even David Weaver, the gang's choice for police judge, managed to squeeze by with just 2 votes more than Harry Gryden.

Daniel Frost, bemoaning the difficulty of "Christians" reaching the polls, admitted defeat with an element of grace: "While we were opposed to Mr. Kelley—always have been, and perhaps always shall be, as we 'don't belong to his pile,' yet we give him and his advisors, Messrs. Sutton,

---

[58] Ibid., April 6, 1880.

Klaine, Masterson and others, credit for winning a victory with odds against them. . . . The Deacon will now lead us in prayer."[59] Nicholas Klaine led no one in prayer, but he gloated less than usual: "We wish to remark that the so-called 'gang' don't sit on dry goods boxes when they have political work to do. They sow early and they reap later. They are indomitable and with an energy and perseverance in the search of a straggling voter that is commended by our neighbor on the corner."[60] Three days later Frost countered: "During the late city election a close observer remarked that 'even a South Carolina bulldozer could learn a trick or two by hanging around the polls during an election in Dodge City.'"[61]

Kelley retained the mayor's chair but was now on his own in the saloon and restaurant business, and he proved to be a poor businessman. His long-time associate, Pettis L. Beatty, dissolved their partnership on March 25. Within five weeks the old army sergeant took over the Wright House, replacing Robert Wright's friend James Anderson, who, in turn, had succeeded Fred Leonard after the Adobe Walls veteran left to become a representative of the *Kansas City Journal*. Unlike earlier managers, who allowed A. J. Peacock the liquor concession, Beatty ran his own place, and now, along with everyone else, anxiously awaited the longhorns.

Remembering the recent slump, residents welcomed news filtering in from Texas and eastern livestock markets. As early as February, estimates suggested seventy-five thousand more cattle than seen in 1879. Frank E. Conrad, Charlie Rath's old partner in the Drover's Store at Fort Griffin, predicted the largest drive ever. Dodge expected three-fourths of all the stock driven north to be grazing on grasslands south of the city.

Conrad boasted of ties with the Dodge City market: "I have perfected arrangements with Wright, Beverley & Co. . . . whose large and carefully selected stock was purposely selected to meet the demands of the Texas Cattle Trade, by which goods purchased from me can be settled for at their house and vice versa. Judge Beverley of that firm, like myself, lived for many years in the cattle regions of Southern Texas, which fact, together with genial business associates render their house a pleasant headquarters for Texas Cattle Men."[62]

[59] Ibid.

[60] *Dodge City Times*, April 10, 1880.

[61] *Ford County Globe*, April 13, 1880.

[62] Frank E. Conrad, Fort Griffin, Texas, "A Letter to the Drovers," February 10, 1880, as published in: *Ford County Globe*, March 16, 1880.

A unanimous vote from the Northwestern Texas Stock-Raisers' Association pleased Dodge City. The group agreed to continue driving their animals to Kansas as long as Texas railroads refused to lower freight rates. W. J. Wilbur, holding herds on the Washita in the Texas Panhandle, visited Dodge and assured listeners that cattle from that section had survived the winter and were ready to move. Reports from San Antonio listed sixty-five cattlemen preparing to come north with nearly 300,000 head. Familiar names included Mifflin Kenedy, John McAllen, Ellison & Son, and the Snyder brothers. Leaving his ranch near Tascosa, George Littlefield arrived in town on May 8, estimating a season of 350,000 head. None of this disappointed the Front Street crowd.

On May 11 the *Globe* reported: "Cattle men and cattle dealers are beginning to come in and are selecting their hotel quarters for the summer. They come to stay, to participate in the largest cattle drive ever brought from Texas." A week later, Frost noted with relief seven full days of rain. After conceding benefits to farmers, Frost got to the point: "The main dependence of the business men of Dodge City, however, will be the cattle trade, and if the rains have been as general and heavy on the plains south and west as reports indicate, grass will be in excellent condition in a few days. Up to the time of the recent rains all the cattle on the ranges were in splendid condition, and the rains of last week insure them good pasturage for the season."

The town stood by ready with fresh coats of paint, restocked liquor cabinets, cigars by the thousands, decorative paintings for the Long Branch, and the widening of city sidewalks to accommodate the anticipated thump of Texas boot heels. As an added treat, Judge Cook opened an ice cream parlor at the City Hotel.

For the *Kansas City Commercial Indicator*, Frank Conrad recorded 102,612 head passing Fort Griffin by May 20. Almost all were headed for Dodge City, with others divided chiefly between Caldwell, Ogallala, and Cheyenne. At the same time 52,300 more passed Fort Worth. By the end of May more than 53,000 cattle and nearly 3,000 horses had already crossed the Arkansas. Within a fortnight the number of longhorns crossing into Ford County reached more than 131,000, and the herds just kept coming. Business boomed along Front Street and in south side honky-tonks. Totals reached 205,311 by the week ending June 25.

Amid all the expectations of profit and prosperity, citizens of Dodge City enjoyed an opportunity to officially examine their community's standing in the scheme of things. In early June 1880 the federal government began taking the Twelfth United States Census. Ostensibly done to determine population totals for allocating seats in the House of Representatives, this process, while not always accurate, did collect interesting local data. Officials in Washington demanded statistical information on all sorts of things, including meat production and transportation questions. Thinking along much the same lines, Joseph G. McCoy, the man who had started it all at Abilene, arrived in Dodge City as the census count began. It was a busy and important time.

The town had come a long way since its sod and clapboard beginnings eight years before. The census recorded within the town's legal boundaries a population just four short of a thousand, with the entire Dodge Township tally standing at 1,854. The work force comprised more than half of those counted. Of these, one analyst calculated, the largest percentage were common laborers. These were followed by servants, railroad workers, farmers, freighters and stage drivers, drovers, construction workers, merchants, clerks and others loosely associated with the freighting industry. Then came stockmen, craftsmen, and personal-service workers such as bartenders, gamblers, and musicians, as well as professionals, lawyers and physicians, along with food processors, and miscellaneous categories such as real estate agents and city employees.[63] Women, mostly employed as servants, accounted for 10 percent of the work force.

Some have suggested that all this proves a greater importance of the railroad and freighting industries than it does for cattle. The analysis is deceiving, however, since at the time of the enumeration—from June 1 thru June 25—most cattlemen were still on the trail.[64] In fairness, Texans should not have been included, but rather enumerated back home as part of their own families or as absentee householders. Even if counted by mistake as permanent Dodge City residents, most had not yet arrived. Just a week before, the *Times* had noted, "The postoffice is daily receiving letters

---

[63] C. Robert Haywood, "The Dodge City Census of 1880: Historians' Tool or Stumbling Block?" *Kansas History: A Journal of the Central Plains* 8, no. 2 (Summer 1985): 103.

[64] For some reason, a fact hardly ever encountered examining other 1880 Census returns, Dodge City's enumerator, Walter Shinn, managed to fill out only one sheet per day. A census sheet had space for just fifty names. What else Walter was doing during those days is anyone's guess.

addressed to cattle drovers, so our city will soon be thronged with the owners and drivers of the immense cattle herds."[65] The Texas invasion thus began in earnest after the census was taken.

Black citizens comprised 3.3 percent of the population, a figure somewhat lower than for the entire state. In contrast, figures for foreign-born residents are reversed, the numbers being 13.2 percent locally but only 11 percent statewide. In Dodge the largest number came from various German and Austrian states. Although both newspapers occasionally mentioned their presence, the census recorded no Chinese. It did, however, note two Russians and one each from Hungary and Poland, as well as five Mexicans. In short, the census confirmed Dodge City's population as predominately white and western European in ancestry. Most preferred it that way. Press references concerning blacks, for instance, invariably displayed a condescending tone. Editors voiced no enthusiasm for the exodus of southern blacks into Kansas during the years 1879–80.[66]

Coming as no surprise, the 1880 census tallied a young population; nearly 50 percent of those counted were still in their twenties and thirties. Young men predominated, males accounting for more than 60 percent of the population. Married couples, too, were mostly young. This helps explain the large number of children. Thirty percent of the population was under age fourteen. More than 10 percent below the state average, that figure still represented a sign that civilization had arrived—children being a rarity during the town's explosive early years. Dodge City had come a long way, but some citizens began demanding more.

---

[65] *Dodge City Times,* May 29, 1880.

[66] Robert G. Athearn, *In Search of Canaan: Black Migration to Kansas, 1879–80* (Lawrence: The Regents Press of Kansas, 1978), 179–80.

Chapter 9

Politics, Cattle, and Money

During a tense city council meeting in June 1880, Mayor Kelley asked Mike Sutton to serve as city attorney. Sutton agreed, but resigned within the week. Harry Gryden, a critic of the regime claiming a change of heart, took up the post. Unimpressed, councilmen Henry Beverley, Samuel Galland, and George Randall resigned in protest over the mayor's handling of city affairs. Only William H. Harris and Thomas Draper stayed on. Kelley issued a proclamation calling for a special city council election to take place in thirty days.[1]

Daniel Frost offered a personal observation: "Although we have taken no hand in the controversy up to the present time, we have always believed that Messrs. Beverley and Randal [*sic*], and when not listening to false prophets, Dr. Galland also, are men who have the welfare of the city at heart, and we regret that they felt it their duty to resign." The editor continued, hoping every word was true: "It cannot be doubted that the sentiment and support of the business part of the community is with them, as against the Mayor and his advisors."[2] Even Bat Masterson was pushed aside. Less than two weeks before, Hamilton Bell replaced him deputy United States marshal.

As Kelley announced the special election, thirty-one anti-gang businessmen, including Henry Beverley, John Mueller, Albert Boyd, and Frederick Zimmerman, held a meeting at the Railroad Land Office. Called to discuss business conditions, partisans focused instead on the sorry state of city government. A committee was formed to draft resolutions for publication. Klaine snubbed the affair, but Frost jumped at the chance to publicize grievances, using nearly a full column of the June 8 issue of the *Ford County Globe*.

---

[1] Ordinance No. 9, Dodge City Ordinances, Book A, 11; and *Dodge City Times*, June 5, 12, 1880.
[2] *Ford County Globe*, June 8, 1880.

Those at the Land Office held nothing back, charging Kelley's regime as being "notoriously extravagant and incompetent." That said, the committee plunged into more specific complaints: "neglect in the collection of licenses, collection and payment of valid claims in favor of and against the city; in the unwarrantable expenditure of the funds of the city, and the careless and reckless manner in which the accounts relating thereto have been kept; in the employment of unnecessary ministerial officers at grossly exorbitant salaries, and in the encouragement of profligacy and vice, morals are corrupted, the present and future prospects of Dodge City are oppressed and discouraged and life and prosperity rendered, in a measure, insecure."

Participants grew more irate with each resolution and began demanding reform. They called for diligence in making city elections less open to complaint, since in the past they had "been carried by all manner of fraud, bribery, bull-dozing and corruption." It mattered little that both sides employed the same tactics.

Citizens may have demanded reform, but the gang still held power. Ignoring evidence of rebellion, James Kelley sat in the mayor's chair, enjoying all its prerogatives, including control of the police.

No sooner had councilman Galland resigned than he was arrested, along with his clerk, for failing to pay fees for a city license on the Great Western Hotel. Following what was described as "a short preliminary skirmish, in which the Doctor received a patronizing welt or two from the festive revolver of Policeman [Neil] Brown," the two men appeared before Judge D. S. Weaver. Weaver fined the former councilman one dollar and dismissed charges against his clerk. People saw it all as retaliation for Galland's resignation, but, in fairness, he did have a history of delinquent payments. But then, so did Mayor Kelley. Neil Brown, accused of assault and battery, paid a ten-dollar fine and costs after a jury found him guilty of simple assault.[3]

Gambling on an old strategy, Mayor Kelley identified himself with prosperity. He made a good case, reminding voters that more than 130,000 head

---

[3] State of Kansas vs. Neal [*sic*] Brown, Records of the Ford County District Court, Judge's Journal, Book A, 331. Dr. Galland was not the only person singled out for noncompliance. On June 19, 1880, just days before the special election to fill vacant seats on the city council, the *Dodge City Times* reported, "The city officers have been making things lively this week on violation of ordinances and non-payment of licenses. There is no government like a strong government."

had already passed Fort Worth by June 2, nearly doubling the number for the same period the year before. Similar reports came in from Fort Griffin.

As Dodge City awaited the Texans, the special election took place. It turned out to be surprisingly calm. Despite all the talk, only one slate of candidates was considered. Mike Sutton, Charles Hungerford, and Walter Shinn became councilmen-elect. Even Dan Frost did not seem upset with the results, writing four days later, "Messrs. Sutton and Hungerford belong to the Kelley faction, but are capable of reason. W. C. Shinn has not taken much part in politics and was placed on the ticket rather as a compromise. He is generally considered to be adverse to the present style of government."[4]

Then, somewhat reminiscent of Rutherford B. Hayes and William T. Sherman nine months before, Ulysses S. Grant passed through Dodge City just days after the election—at three o'clock in the morning. No one seemed concerned that the former president and commander of the Union Army failed to make an appearance. Locals were more consumed with self-interest than noticing the arrival and departure of celebrities in the middle of the night. After all, Bob Wright had laid a telephone line between his home and office, raising speculation about scientific wonders to come. The largest congregation yet assembled helped dedicate the new Presbyterian church. A more temporal gathering watched railroad agent W. R. Johnson direct work on the company's stockyards, making them the largest on the Santa Fe road.

Dampening the town's enthusiasm, the *Ford County Globe* described another blemish: "We have repeatedly called attention to the confidence men that have infested our city. . . . [F]orbearance has decidedly ceased to be a virtue, and the business men and citizens are unanimous in the opinion that they have had enough of the sure thing and confidence men for one season. They must go. Some very glaring outrages have been perpetrated during the past week, and Dodge City—the wicked city, as she is called—is thoroughly disgusted and indignant."[5]

Frost may have been referring to reports from Yates Center detailing how two of its young men had been swindled in Dodge. Traveling to Colorado, Isaac Bainter and Steve Taylor set up camp outside town. A man

---

[4] *Ford County Globe,* July 6, 1880.

[5] Ibid., August 24, 1880.

and woman claiming to know Bainter's brother announced themselves. Touring Dodge City with their newfound friends, Taylor grew suspicious and returned to camp. Bainter showed up within the hour, followed by three or four others claiming to hold a bill of sale on their wagon and team. Too drunk to protest, Bainter stood by in silence. Taylor gave in only after one of the men claimed to be the county sheriff. By morning the two decided to see a lawyer, but were told nothing could be done since they had no money.

Back in Yates Center Taylor told his story, a tale championed by a sympathetic press. Editors spread the blame: "The merchants and business men of Dodge City are as guilty as the men who committed the act, and should be held equally responsible in the opinion of the public. If by their sufferance they did not permit those desperadoes, robbers and murderers to live there and carry on their nefarious practices, such a condition of affairs could not exist. Let them use hemp and rid the place of such worthless villains before they ask decent people to come to their town. Strangers, passing through Kansas, beware of Dodge City!"[6]

Dr. Galland wrote the editor at Yates Center claiming the city attorney bragged about getting fifty dollars a week not to prosecute gamblers. An indignant Harry Gryden took exception, sending a heated reply to Dan Frost for publication in the *Ford County Globe*. Perhaps with a smile the editor informed his readers: "Mr. Gryden has weakened on his letter, and surreptitiously purloined it from this office, hence it will not appear in this issue."[7] Despite attacks on the city attorney, more and more citizens began thinking the most outrageous offender might be the mayor himself.

Ignoring the unrest, James H. Kelley tried introducing an ordinance during the council meeting on September 7 authorizing himself one hundred dollars a year. To make the scheme more palatable, Kelley tried including all previous mayors, his former partner P. L. Beatty and early foe George M. Hoover. Council members balked. Understanding the shifts in popular sentiment, William H. Harris, Walter Shinn, and Mike Sutton stood against the mayor. Only Draper and Hungerford supported the plan. Kelley's critics enjoyed the irony: "The prime mover of this brilliant piece of regulation for the city, we are informed, is still indebted to the

[6] *Yates Center News*, July 29, 1880.
[7] *Ford County Globe*, September 14, 1880.

city for his liquor license for the years 1879 and 1880. The Council had better turn their attention to the Mayor, and see that he too is made to conform with the ordinances of the city."[8]

Kelley's misstep refocused everyone's attention on politics. For the upcoming general election, some Republicans, Democrats, and Greenbacks preferred breaking with tradition and contesting county offices along party lines. Those loyalties worked well in national and statewide races, but local contests centered mostly on the popularity of individual candidates. Half the members of the county Democratic Committee turned away from their own convention and supported the Republican Party's nominees, including Robert Wright for state representative, Mike Sutton for county attorney, and Lloyd Shinn as probate judge.

Remnants of the gang—with Mike Sutton conspicuously absent—abandoned claims as standard bearers of the Republican Party. Calling for their own convention, they joined forces with Greenbackers, "two sorehead Republicans, and twelve straight Democrats," to field candidates under the banner of the Peoples' County Ticket.[9] George Cox accepted their nomination, by telegram from New Jersey, to run for the legislature against Bob Wright. He should have saved his money.

The *Times* gave candidates of the county ticket a glowing sendoff, enthusiasm not shared by the voters. Of all their candidates only A. J. Anthony won a seat as county commissioner.[10] Nationally, unlike the strong Democratic showing in 1876, Republican presidential hopeful James A. Garfield pulled 370 votes against 288 for Democrat Winfield Scott Hancock. Dodge City appeared to be less a one-party town.

The November election introduced an ominous state constitutional amendment restricting the manufacture and sale of alcohol except for "medicinal, mechanical and scientific purposes." In Dodge City most everyone recognized the threat. Ford County rejected the measure 516 to 24. It passed statewide by nearly eight thousand votes. Klaine forecast: "We presume there will be medicinal, mechanical and scientific shops opened, or back-doored as the case may be, for any one who is accustomed

---

[8] Ibid., September 21, 1880.

[9] Ibid., October 26, 1880.

[10] Ford County Commissioners Journals, Book A, 304–306; *Ford County Globe*, November 2, 16, 1880; and *Dodge City Times*, November 6, 1880.

to his usual glass can not be made to shut-off his supplies at once, without great detriment to his nerves."[11]

Weeks later, as the legislature wrestled with implementation, Robert M. Wright rose in hopeless opposition to deliver a tongue-in-cheek address to his colleagues:

> I cannot refrain . . . from raising my feeble voice in protest against this monstrous measure. I do not oppose this bill on account of my own love for the distilled nectar of the corn field, nor yet for the purple ambrosia of the vineyard. I admit that I like a glass of either, now and then, but I am not a slave to the demon of the cup. . . . In fact, Mr. Chairman, so great is my virtue in this direction, that I have often gone three, aye, four days without my whisky, and I am proud to relate without any special disturbing effects upon my physiological structure, but it is a dangerous experiment and should not be tried too often. . . .
>
> Now, sir, the only way out of this labyrinth of proposed injustice is to exclude Dodge City, as well as all that region west of the 100th meridian, from the provisions of this bill. If you do this it will not only be an act of justice guaranteed by the Constitution upon stern necessity, but will receive the righteous judgment of all the citizens of Dodge; harmony will again prevail upon the border, the scouts will be called in and future generations of cow boys will arise and call you blessed.[12]

Two weeks after the November elections Dodge City admitted another killing: "The report was soon confirmed and everybody felt that Dodge had still some of the bloody instinct for which she was so famous in the lawless days of her infancy, when money was a dross and whisky four bits a drink."[13] This time two men, Henry C. Heck and John "Concho" Gill, quarreled over the affections of prostitute Callie Moore.

Henry Heck had been around town for over three years. He owned a ranch at Mulberry Creek, on the road to Camp Supply. Before that he ran a dance hall and managed Hamilton Bell's livery stable when the proprietor was out of town. Most everyone liked him. During all this time the amorous Miss Moore remained Heck's "apparently faithful companion." That is until September, when in town on a shopping spree she met the gambler John Gill: "it was a dead mash at first sight. His dark brown eyes, classic features, and complexion bronzed by a southern sun, together with

---

[11] *Dodge City Times*, November 6, 1880.

[12] Ibid., February 24, 1881.

[13] *Ford County Globe*, November 23, 1880.

the indolent life of a gambler's paramour, were too dazzling to be resisted when compared with kitchen drudgery, and the society of her more homely lover."[14] Thereafter, Callie offered her talents and devoted her energies to the "festive Concho."

At about one o'clock in the morning of November 17, Heck appeared at the door of his rival's south-side boarding house. Gill later claimed he was sick in bed as Callie attended the stove. A visitor, Charlie Milde, testified that Heck kicked at the door, demanding entrance. Indisposed or not, Gill rose to the challenge, revolver in hand. Heck forced his way in and was shot through the right lung. Officer Neil Brown arrived within minutes to disarm and arrest John Gill. Henry Heck staggered to a nearby saloon, asked for whiskey, telling the surprised bartender he had just been shot. Finishing his drink, Heck walked out, only to return, collapse on the floor, and die. Thirty minutes had not passed since the fatal shot was fired.

Nicholas Klaine summarized local feelings: "It has been some time since a murder has been committed in Dodge City. . . . There was no provocation, and it is hinted that the unfortunate Heck was the victim of a conspiracy, the facts of which may be developed upon [during] the trial of the murderer."[15] The court heard from a number of witnesses, including saloon owners A. J. Peacock and James Masterson, testifying to the events in dispute, as well as the relationships of those involved. Considering the evidence, a jury found John Gill guilty of second-degree murder. His attorney petitioned for a new trial, but the court dismissed the motion and sentenced the defendant to fifteen years in the penitentiary.[16]

Forgetting the bloodshed, 125 voters petitioned for a special election to dissolve city government. At issue was city indebtedness (five thousand dollars just for the year 1880) and the high salaries paid city employees.[17] Others argued that with Prohibition the city could no longer tax saloons, a major source of revenue. Direct taxation seemed the only answer. Few

---

[14] Ibid.

[15] *Dodge City Times*, November 20, 1880.

[16] State of Kansas vs. John Gill, alias Concho. Records of the Ford County District Court, Criminal Appearance Docket A, 79; and Judge's Journal, Book A, 329–30.

[17] That fall some progress had taken place in reducing city expenditures. On October 5 the council voted to reduce the combined salaries for the marshal and his assistant by half, to one hundred dollars a month. Two months later, at the meeting on December 7, both James Masterson and Neil Brown presented bills to the city of one hundred dollars. On the motion of Walter Shinn, seconded by Thomas Draper, the council voted instead to pay each man fifty dollars.

then realized that Dodge City would for years ignore all Prohibition laws and regulations. Not prepared for outright revolution, despite the signatures on the original petition, the vote came out 109 to 44 against giving James Kelley the boot. Daniel Frost was beside himself: "We hope a greater interest may be manifested by our people when new officers are to be elected in April."[18]

By 1881 Dodge City was beginning to lose some of its founders. City councilman Charles Hungerford moved his butcher business to Trinidad. Police Judge and general merchandiser David S. Weaver left with his wife to pursue business interests in New Mexico and Colorado. As members of the gang, perhaps both realized their days of power were nearing an end. William H. Harris left for a time but did not resign from the council. He traveled to San Francisco and then on to Tombstone, Arizona, before returning to Kansas. Former police judge and real estate agent Samuel Marshall skipped out for other reasons: "The officers of Insurance companies are making efforts to capture Samuel Marshall, who absconded from this place a short time ago. They traced Sam from Kentucky to Texas. He is wanted on a charge of embezzlement. It is said that he abandoned his wife and son."[19]

EARLY IN JANUARY 1881 thirty-five-year-old Pettis L. Beatty married Ellen Herling, a nineteen-year-old waitress at the Wright House. That same afternoon Beatty and his bride entertained friends with champagne before boarding the train for their new home at Trinidad. There, along with one of Bob Wright's sons, they planned to open a hotel. The groom's colleagues from the fire department, together with the Dodge City Silver Cornet Band, followed the couple to the station for a proper sendoff honoring the town's first mayor. Beatty did not act in haste—weeks before he sold Kelley his interest in their Front Street real estate. Meanwhile Bob Wright bought all of Beatty & Kelley's other holdings outside the main business district.[20]

Besides Hungerford, Weaver, and now Beatty, others had interests in Colorado. Richard W. Evans often traveled there, involving himself in var-

---

[18] *Ford County Globe*, January 4, 1881.

[19] *Dodge City Times*, July 10, 1880.

[20] Ford County Marriages, Book A, 71; Ford County Register of Deeds, Book C, 233–34, 235–36; *Dodge City Times*, December 11, 1880, January 15, 1881; and *Ford County Globe*, January 18, 1881.

ious things with his older brother, Griffith. Another brother, the Reverend John Evans—who had "abandoned the ministry"—showed up to help Griffith in the mercantile trade.[21] Richard purchased a share of the *Mountaineer* at St. Elmo. Within weeks the more experienced Walter Shinn bought out R. W.'s interest, satisfying his responsibilities at Dodge City by replacing his brother as justice of the peace in early January 1881, after Lloyd became probate judge.[22]

Richard Evans, along with Ford County functionary John W. Straughn, began speculating in Colorado mining property. Early that year premature rumors reached Dodge that the pair had struck it rich near Leadville, prompting an apology of sorts: "Some people may have thought Mr. Evans a sleepy old rooster and that Mr. Straughn had wild hairs in his eyes, but the sequel shows that the Col. is the chief and Dick Evans a solid Muldoon."[23] Straughn became so caught up in the excitement he resigned as deputy sheriff and jailer, but held on to the office of Ford County coroner.

With Mayor Kelley and the gang losing their grip on city affairs, residents representing both sides of the political divide awaited the April 4 elections. Realizing their days were numbered, stalwarts made a fight of the township balloting. With the tide turning against them, some, including James Masterson, opened their own polling place, then raided the polling station of their rivals: "The lights were blown out and a scramble ensued over the ballot box, which was kicked around in the darkness, passing here and there, until it was finally obtained by Under Sheriff Singer. Judges and clerks dispersed and the election was over."[24]

Sensing Kelley's defeat, Daniel Frost renewed his attacks. The mayor understood the hopelessness of his situation. Making matters worse, Kelley and his police abused a visiting agent of the Adams Express Co., after the man characterized His Honor as "a loud mouthed Irishman." The ruffled representative told everybody that Harry Gryden boasted he could carry any jury in town for one hundred dollars.[25]

---

[21] *Portrait and Biographical Album of Jo Davies County, Illinois,* 467–68. The family had always experienced bursts of righteousness. It was said that patriarch Edmund Evans, a Welsh-born civil engineer and Illinois farmer, "was all his life an ardent advocate of temperance." *The United States Biographical Dictionary, Kansas Volume,* 411.

[22] *History of the Arkansas Valley, Colorado* (Chicago: O. L. Baskin & Co., 1881), 496, 513–14. Walter Shinn became justice of the peace two weeks before being admitted to the bar. Records show he was not granted the right to practice until January 21, 1881. Records of the Ford County District Court, Judge's Journal, Book A, 342.

[23] *Ford County Globe,* January 11, 1881.

[24] Ibid., February 8, 1881.

[25] *Oskaloosa Herald* (Iowa), March 17, 1881.

This incident, along with the arrogance displayed during the township election, hastened the gang's fall. What actually happened, considering the years of frustration, surprised Dodge City's political veterans. Voters entered the polls on April 4 to pass judgment on a single slate of candidates, office-seekers now supported by both factions.

Pioneer merchant and part-time deputy sheriff Alonzo B. Webster, a former gang sympathizer who had turned his back on Kelley and the others, headed the list for mayor. Four of the five men running for council seats, Albert Boyd, Chalk Beeson, George S. Emerson, and Patrick Sughrue, were equally well known. The fifth name, railroad official H. T. Drake, appears to have been a compromise candidate. Attorney Thomas S. Jones rounded out the ticket as police judge.

Webster polled all but 5 of the 250 votes cast. James H. Kelley, out of office for the first time since 1877, watched his power evaporate while convalescing after being thrown from his horse. With Kelley bedridden, Mayor Webster took charge at the April 6 council meeting. He fired City Marshal James Masterson and Assistant Marshal Neil Brown.[26] In their place he named Under Sheriff and County Surveyor Fred Singer and dance hall proprietor Thomas C. Nixon (who had come to Dodge as a buffalo hunter in the early days). Webster also fired the boastful Harry Gryden. On the motion of Councilman Albert Boyd, he ordered Marshal Singer and City Clerk H. P. Myton to inventory all city property. Not only were there new faces on the police force, they presented a new look as well. Wanting his officers to appear more professional, the mayor ordered navy blue uniforms.

To the relief of many, Mayor Webster issued a strongly worded proclamation: "To all whom it may concern: All thieves, thugs, confidence men, and persons without a visible means of support, will take notice that the ordinances enacted for their especial benefit will be rigorously enforced on and after to-morrow, April 7, 1881."[27] Reacting to complaints, the council

---

[26] For reasons not explained, the press reported both Masterson and Brown receiving $420 from the council at the time of their departure. Of course that figure may well have been a misprint. The original city council minute book has disappeared. "Council Proceedings," *Dodge City Times*, April 14, 1881.

[27] *Ford County Globe*, April 12, 1881. Also see *Dodge City Times*, April 14, 21, 1881. The actual vagrancy ordinance, passed on April 12—despite the April 7 date given by the *Globe*, provided fines of not less than five dollars nor more than twenty-five dollars for the first offense, and not less than fifteen dollars for any further disregard of the new law. Those unable or unwilling to pay could be jailed and forced by the city marshal to work cleaning the streets at the rate of one dollar a day to compensate the city for the assessed fine. Ordinance No. 52, April 12, 1881. Dodge City Ordinances, Book A, 94–95.

passed an ordinance allowing pigs found "running at large within the cor-
porate limits of this city" to be impounded, and that any dogs running free
without a collar and license tag: "shall be killed by or under the direction
of the City Marshal," an act for which the officer would receive fifty cents.[28]

Responding to indebtedness, the council passed sweeping new business
taxes, annual fees now ranging from $2.50 to $50.00. The laissez faire days
of James Kelley seemed at an end. Most residents supported Webster. In
appreciation they presented him with an expensive breech-loading shotgun. The mayor was no stranger to firearms, having killed a man twelve
years earlier at Hays City.[29] Within forty-eight hours he seemed prepared
to do so again.

Weeks before, James Masterson and A. J. Peacock, partners in the Lady
Gay dance hall—recently painted red, white, and green to help draw the
attention of expected Texans—hired the latter's friend (some claimed
brother-in-law) Al Updegraff as bartender.[30] In early April 1881 Updegraff and Masterson became embroiled in a quarrel, thick with threats and
drawn revolvers.

The cause of the trouble remains unclear, but Updegraff, the only par-
ticipant to leave a written account, claimed:

> a friend of Masterson's robbed a woman of $80 by entering her room while
> she was absent. I advised her to have the party arrested, which she did,
> through the proper officer. Masterson thereupon came to me and insisted
> that I should make the woman withdraw the complaint, which I refused pos-
> itively to do. He, Masterson, thereupon informed me that my services as bar-
> keeper was no longer needed, and I must quit. Mr. Peacock, the other
> member of the firm, thereupon insisted that I should stay, as I was right.
> Masterson having claimed to be a killer, then undertook the job of killing
> me, and attempted it on the following evening by coming into the saloon and
> cocking his revolver in my face. I got the best of him by a large majority, and

---

[28] Ordinance No. 53, April 18, 1881. Dodge City Ordinances, Book A, 96–97.

[29] During July 1869 Webster worked as a clerk for Richard W. Evans at the Hays City post office. One afternoon local tough Samuel Strawhun entered the building with Joe Weiss. They planned on punishing Webster for
his having served a vigilance committee notice for them to leave town. In the midst of this attack, Webster pulled
a revolver and shot Weiss through the bowels. He died soon afterward. Strawhun ran off. Webster would have no
further trouble, however, as Wild Bill Hickok killed the twenty-eight-year-old ruffian in a gunbattle several weeks
later. For A. B. Webster's involvement in all this, see *Junction City Weekly Union*, July 31, 1869; and Joseph G. Rosa, *They
Called Him Wild Bill: The Life and Adventures of James Butler Hickok* (Norman: University of Oklahoma Press, 1979),
146–47.

[30] Wright, *Dodge City, the Cowboy Capital*, 176. Although Wright mentioned this relationship, the *Ford County Globe*
on April 19 stated, "it seemed he [Updegraff] was a strong friend of Peacock's."

notwithstanding his reputation as a killer, he hid out and was next morning arrested upon my complaint.[31]

Updegraff may very well have bested Masterson in this instance, since James, or some of his friends, telegraphed his brother William at Tombstone, Arizona, to return home and help deal with Jimmy's upstart employee and unappreciative partner.[32] The one-time Ford County sheriff did so, arriving near noon on Saturday, April 16. Stepping from the train Masterson walked along the north side of the tracks, getting only about a block and a half west of the depot before spotting Peacock and Updegraff coming up from the Lady Gay. As those two neared the city jail, situated below the tracks between First and Second avenues, they were startled to hear Bat call out their names. All three men pulled their weapons, Masterson diving behind the railroad embankment, with Peacock and Updegraff seeking shelter at the corner of the calaboose.

Despite Masterson's later canonization as a master of the Colt revolver, all the shots went wild. With Bat's position to the west of Peacock and Updegraff, several of that duo's bullets peppered business houses on the north side of Front Street. Included among the random targets were the Long Branch saloon, George M. Hoover's wholesale liquors, and Dr. T. J. McCarty's drug store. Pedestrians dove for cover or returned fire. One of those shots hit Updegraff in the lung. James Masterson took silent comfort from his bartender's painful wound.

This so-called Battle of the Plaza lasted only a few minutes. Marshal Singer ran forward, along with Mayor Webster, toting his new shotgun. They arrested Masterson and disarmed the other two combatants. Among the three, Singer found only one unexploded cartridge, in Updegraff's

---

[31] Al. Updegraff to the editor, April 21, 1881. *Ford County Globe*, May 10, 1881. There is, however, no indication of this arrest in the notes compiled by Walter Stanley Campbell from the surviving police court docket. Of course, as noted earlier, not all of the old dockets were then available for inspection. Concerning their deteriorating relationship, the *Globe* remarked almost in passing on April 19, "Pistols were drawn and several shots fired, but no one was hurt." Updegraff made no mention of shots being fired, nor did the *Dodge City Times.*

[32] On April 19, 1881, the *Ford County Globe* stated that James "telegraphed to his brother, Bat Masterson . . . asking him to come to Dodge and help him out of his difficulties." Updegraff, in his account, speculated: "He or his friends then telegraphed an inflammatory dispatch to his brother, Bat Masterson, who arrived in due time." Years later one popular writer claimed that Wyatt Earp told him, "Bat showed me the message he received in Tombstone and it was not from his brother. It didn't say what kind of trouble Jim Masterson was mixed up in. It only said that Peacock and Updegraft [*sic*] were threatening to kill him." Walter Noble Burns, *Tombstone: An Iliad of the Southwest* (Garden City, N.Y.: Doubleday, Page & Company, 1927), 57. Unfortunately, quotes attributed to Wyatt Earp by Mr. Burns are not particularly reliable.

revolver. Had it not been for the action of armed bystanders, all three combatants might have emptied their weapons without effect, save damage done to buildings in their line of fire. Only Updegraff's wound dampened the farce.

Marshal Singer hauled Masterson before Police Judge Thomas Jones, who fined the former sheriff eight dollars and costs for discharging his pistol on a public thoroughfare. Bat pleaded guilty and paid his fine.[33] The small sum caused grumbling. Officials swore out state warrants against the two Masterson brothers, as well as Charles Ronan and Tom O'Brien, both implicated in firing shots during the melee. People were outraged. This whole affair represented the past, something the town's more progressive elements wished to forget. The negative sentiment, together with pending legal action, forced the two Mastersons to temporarily abandon Dodge City.

Even Nicholas Klaine condemned the outburst: "The firing on the street by Bat. Masterson, and jeopardizing the lives of citizens, is severely condemned by our people, and the good opinion many citizens had of Bat. has been changed to one of contempt. The parties engaged in this reckless affray were permitted to leave town, though warrants were sworn out for their arrest. . . . If they will remain away there will be no more trouble in Dodge City. Should they return they will be prosecuted." Sound advice, and as Klaine observed in another column: "Jim Masterson and Charley Ronan have gone west to grow up with the country."[34]

Six weeks later, Harry Gryden, resentful at being dumped as city attorney, wrote Bat Masterson at Pueblo. Gryden made it sound as if the whole town feared his return and blamed Mike Sutton's shifting loyalties for the trouble, ending, "Kelley is looking over my shoulder and says 'tell him Sutton is at the bottom of it all, damn him.'"[35] Klaine reprinted a supposed purloined copy of Gryden's letter, along with a lengthy poem poking fun at the whole affair. The idea of one man terrorizing Dodge City struck its

---

[33] Walter Stanley Campbell Files, Western History Collection, University of Oklahoma Library, Box 96; Justice Docket, Dodge City, Kansas, Notes, April 1881. This small fine caused the *Walnut Creek Blade* to comment: "It costs $8 to shoot a man through the lung in Dodge City—such is Bat Masterson's fine." As quoted in George G. Thompson, *Bat Masterson: The Dodge City Years* (Topeka: Kansas State Printing Plant, 1943), 39. For another complaint concerning this paltry sum, see *Ford County Globe*, April 19, 1881.

[34] *Dodge City Times*, April 21, 1881.

[35] Ibid., June 9, 1881.

inhabitants as preposterous. They did, however, enjoy the spectacle Gryden was making of himself. The gang failed to sway public opinion against the new regime. Gryden and Jim Kelley may have looked foolish, but this episode did demonstrate the Machiavellian talents of Michael Sutton.

With the election and the Masterson fiasco behind them, townspeople prepared for the Texans. Despite annual rumors of doom, 1881 promised more prosperity. Totals for cattle driven north in 1880, not just those destined for Dodge City, calculated the third-highest since drives began in 1866, and nearly 140,000 better than 1879. The AT&SF shared everyone's optimism. Not only did the company order seventy-five new locomotives while planning a roundhouse at Dodge City, it built new stock yards a short distance east of the original site.

Firms such as Wright, Beverley & Company continued collecting intelligence from sources in Texas. Henry Beverley remained especially active, making use of his many friends in the Lone Star State, including members of his wife's family, the Skiles, living near San Antonio. Subscriptions to Texas newspapers helped the process. Stock raiser A. H. Polley spent several months at Fort Griffin and kept Bob Wright informed of herd owners and stock totals passing that point. By mid-May all these contacts estimated a spring drive in excess of 235,000. Purchase contracts accounted for more than two-thirds of that number. Good news indeed for Dodge City, as these figures did not include 90,000 head expected from northwest Texas and the Panhandle. Toward the end of June hotel registers listed forty-four cattlemen and eleven sheepmen.

Money began changing hands. Mr. Montgomery, of the Kansas City firm of Quinlan and Montgomery, made several buys before the end of June, including Smith and Elliott's 4,000 head. Cattle raiser J. F. Gragon, from Wallace, Kansas, contracted for $20,000 worth of stock on the Dodge City market. Pueblo merchant J. N. Andrews sold his entire herd, bought as an investment the previous fall, to a lumberman from Muscatine, Iowa, for $100,000. J. L. Driskill & Sons, Texans with strong Dodge City ties, picked up the Fraser herd for $120,000. Amidst all this buying and selling, people standing on the sidelines began looking at events with the glitter of gold in their eyes.

Gunfire made a comeback in July 1881. Nathan Hudson, a south-side dance hall proprietor, Kelley supporter, and part-time freighter—a man earlier characterized by Major Dodge as "one of the gang of cattle thieves that makes its headquarters at Boyd's Ranch near Fort Larned"—died of consumption on the afternoon of the twenty-first.[36] Normally not the sort of thing that rated much notice, this particular death led to further tragedy late the following evening. Knowing the end was near, the thirty-seven-year-old Hudson gave money to his paramour, nineteen-year-old Sadie Ratzell. She, in turn, deposited about seven hundred dollars with George Hoover. Later that same night, while a doctor attended Hudson, Sadie thought she heard the cocking of a revolver. In the morning she was disturbed by rumors of someone planning to rob her. After Hudson's funeral Sadie moved into his other house near Andy Johnson's blacksmith shop.

Whether or not Miss Ratzell heard revolvers being cocked, she felt anxious. By nightfall her suspicions gave way to fear. Seeing three men, first near the railroad then alongside Johnson's shop, she convinced herself the rumors were true. Sadie sent her older sister, May Ingram, who along with her husband had lived in Hudson's household, to find Deputy Sheriff Thomas Bugg. Unable to find the deputy, May told her story to Assistant Marshal Tom Nixon. At the same time thirty-three-year-old Mollie Whitecamp, a one-time washerwoman supporting herself as a prostitute known to all as Dutch Jake, passed on Ingram's alarm to Tom Bugg and Brick Bond. Leaving Bond at Johnson's shop, Bugg spoke with Lillian Woodward, who had seen suspicious-looking people prowling about. City Marshal Fred Singer also made an appearance.

A young Mexican boy had found Singer sitting in front of Peacock's Lady Gay saloon. He and the marshal walked toward the scene, but spotted Sadie and Tom Bugg sitting on Lillian Woodward's porch. Singer asked Sadie to step inside. He talked to Miss Ratzell at some length: "Asked her if she had any money there; said no, that she had deposited it in town. Mrs. Peacock had before told me that . . . Sadie had $875 in her trunk, and she was mighty foolish for keeping it there."[37]

---

[36] Maj. Richard I. Dodge to the United States Marshall [*sic*], Topeka, June 19, 1872. Fort Dodge, Letters Sent.

[37] Testimony of Fred Singer, Coroner's Inquest upon the body of Jos. McDonald, *Ford County Globe*, July 26, 1881. Three years later Sadie Ratzell engaged in more foolishness. Then using the name Sadie Hudson, she was stabbed during an altercation with fellow saloon habitué Bertha Lockhart: "They had both just returned from the dance house, and the difficulty was caused by jealousy of a mutual lover. Sadie was stabbed in three different places; one wound pretty near the spinal column under the backbone, one a little forward, and one in the breast." Sparking the trouble: "It appears that the two girls had some words, when Sadie slapped Bertha in the face, and then the cutting commenced." Sadie survived. Dodge City *Kansas Cowboy*, August 9, 1884.

Stepping outside, the marshal spotted someone walking behind the blacksmith shop. With all the talk of revolvers, prowlers, and plans for robbery, Singer hurried forward. As the officer got within thirty feet of his quarry the unidentified man moved into a thick patch of sunflowers. Turning, the man raised his arm and called out, "Stand!" Fearing a gun, Singer pulled his own and fired. Startled, Thomas Bugg and the others rushed over. They carried the wounded man, who, as it turned out, was a railroad employee named Joseph McDonald, into a room at Hudson's dance hall. He died there at 3:20 that morning.

The whole thing turned out to be a tragic mistake: "This shooting was not done to simply keep up Dodge City's former reputation in the art of killing people. It was an unfortunate mishap between two individuals who had no ill will towards each other and who probably never had met before."[38]

Joseph McDonald and George Early had left Topeka to do some work for the railroad farther up the line at Syracuse. Coming back through Dodge City, Early and another man had some trouble with Marshal Singer, who testified, "I know Geo. Early as one of the two fellows that I ordered out of town. The other fellow wore eye-glasses, and was fined in the Police Court."[39] That man was not McDonald, whose name is not listed on the docket. Early and McDonald drank together but then went their separate ways hours before the shooting. A coroner's jury exonerated Singer and officials released McDonald's body for shipment back to Topeka.

Not all summer visitors turned out to be intoxicated railroad employees or famous Texas cattlemen. Many early pioneers, men such as Henry L. Sitler and Adobe Walls veteran Billy Dixon, kept reappearing. Charles Rath, holding open connections with Wright, Beverley & Company and the Texas firm of H. Hamburg & Co. at Mobeetie, was a frequent visitor. In early August he excited the children by taking delivery of a portable steam engine: "The steaming up of Mr. Rath's road engine attracted as much attention as a calliope at a circus."[40] Charlie Bassett, looking for a way into the cattle business, showed up again after eighteen months on the road. People crowded around wishing him well, remembering all the terri-

---

[38] *Ford County Globe,* July 26, 1881.

[39] Testimony of Fred Singer, Coroner's Inquest . . . Jos. McDonald, *Ford County Globe,* July 26, 1881.

[40] *Dodge City Times,* August 4, 1881.

ble times and the stability he offered as Ford County's first sheriff. The return of so many popular pioneers, each in his own way important to the past, prompted the retelling of many an old story.

DODGE WAS CHANGING. Having never shown much interest in living presidents, it reacted with respect to news of James A. Garfield's assassination. By early afternoon of September 26, the official day of mourning, every business and public building closed its doors. Nothing like it had taken place since Ed Masterson's funeral three and a half years before. A procession fell in behind an army band on its way to memorial services at the Presbyterian church. It was a day to remember: "This is the first occasion in the history of Dodge City that all the business houses and places of amusement have been closed. One place of public amusement has been open day and night, seven days a week, for five years, and its front doors never were locked until yesterday."[41] Of course nothing stayed closed for long—Wicked Dodge was soon back in business.

The president's assassination seemed far away to most people in Ford County. Sadness of a different sort followed the shooting of twelve-year-old Charles E. "Dick" Wheadon, the stepson of buffalo hunter and part-time lawman Prairie Dog Dave Morrow. The incident, involving a friendly scuffle over what turned out to be a loaded shotgun, took place at the homestead of boot maker Henry Niess. The gun discharged, peppering the boy "from the navel to the forehead." He died two days later. A coroner's jury ruled the shooting accidental. Wheadon "was buried in Prairie Grove cemetery on Monday, quite a large procession followed his remains to their last resting place."[42]

With Alonzo Webster at City Hall, visitors noticed a change in attitude. One correspondent wrote of the contrast with Kelley's lackadaisical leadership: "we took our first trip to Dodge City, since the new administration, although the temperance amendment is not recognized in that

---

[41] *Ford County Globe,* September 27, 1881.

[42] Ibid., October 11, 1881. Also see *Dodge City Times,* October 13, 1881. In reporting this sad event, the *Globe* made a point of saying, "The evidence before the coroner's jury explains the occurrence fully, and adds another instance to the many terrible accidents that have resulted from the careless handling of loaded guns." Although both newspapers identified the boy as "Dick Whedon," the 1880 United States Census listed him in Dave Morrow's household as "Charles E. Wheadon."

luxurious city we can see a marked difference and advancement." That writer pointed out other changes: "Instead of sidewalks being surrendered to hogs, dogs and fleas, and the town officered by a set of men, a part of whom could not be equaled in degree of crime and treachery, we now find the worthy Mayor, A. B. Webster surrounded by a brave set of officers, who wage a sturdy war for the protection of not only the people of Dodge City, but for the cow-boys, farmers or other transient persons."[43]

By late September Robert Wright hired mason William Hessman to rebuild the storage area behind his main building out of stone, brick, and iron, hoping to make it fireproof. Wright built an even larger warehouse near the tracks. West of Wright, Beverley & Company, across Second Avenue, Herman Fringer sold out to George Hoover for six thousand dollars.[44] The front portion of the property housed the drug store and post office. With Fringer's retirement at age thirty-six, Dr. McCarty bought the drug business but not the real estate. He kept it open, along with his own City Drug Store, in the old Alamo saloon building wedged between Wright's store and the Long Branch. Within a month McCarty reconsidered and moved everything into the larger corner lot. Mayor Webster bought out McCarty's old place and began converting the space into the Stock Exchange saloon.

That October Fringer resigned as postmaster. He had no intention of leaving Dodge City. Not in the best of health, he simply wanted a rest and to take time visiting friends and family at Canton, Ohio. Lloyd Shinn was appointed to fill Fringer's vacancy on the twenty-sixth.[45] He kept Samuel Gallagher as his assistant.

Later that same month Fred Singer, hoping to find a more profitable line of work, resigned as city marshal. Webster named a local butcher, twenty-seven-year-old B. C. "Bob" Vanderburg to the position. Singer stayed on as Ford County under sheriff, but then took charge of the Old House saloon. Even as the town's reform mayor, Webster saw no conflict with local officials, including himself, running saloons—despite statewide

---

[43] *Jetmore Republican*, as quoted in *Ford County Globe*, August 9, 1881. The reporter ended his piece with an observation that would have been unheard of not that long before: "We could not help but notice the difference in the business men and their places of business. They seemed to realize the fact that they had a government, and that their property and patrons would be protected from violence."

[44] Ford County Register of Deeds, Book C, 405–406. The property is designated Lot 42, Block 6.

[45] Post Office Department, Records of Appointment of Postmasters, National Archives and Records Service, Vol. 40, 1874–83, 560.

Prohibition and the recurring criticism of so many Dodge City and Ford County officials involved in the liquor trade.

The pursuit of money and progress did not keep people from aiding one of their own, mired in troubles far from the Kansas plains. As they had done for J. J. Webb some years before, townspeople rallied to the defense of former assistant city marshal Wyatt Earp, then mired in controversy over a gunbattle at Tombstone, Arizona. More than sixty signatures appeared on the notarized testimonial, which Earp's attorney submitted as part of his defense. Bob Wright's name topped the list, followed by Lloyd Shinn, Michael Sutton, and George Hoover. Names reflected every facet of the town's political life: Mayor Webster and four of the five city councilmen signed, as did James Kelley, both newspaper editors, and Presbyterian minister O. W. Wright.[46] Earp's Arizona troubles turned out to be one of the few times many of these men found anything to agree on.

With sweeping changes at City Hall, the 1881 county elections promised even more. Forty-nine citizens, representing all factions, called for a Peoples' Independent Delegate Convention at the courthouse on October 18. The name of Daniel Frost, so often associated with such efforts, does not appear on the list, which did include A. B. Webster, Robert Wright, and Michael Sutton. George Hoover chaired the meeting. The first item took up fraudulent votes stuffed into the Spearville ballot box by seventy-five railroad section hands. After two hours of debate, fourteen delegates withdrew and held their own meeting at the Great Western Hotel. The courthouse crowd nominated a ticket headed by George T. Hinkle for sheriff. Disgruntled delegates at the Great Western, styling themselves the straight Independent Ticket, concocted their own slate with political newcomer Michael Sughrue picked for sheriff.

Both groups came up with acceptable candidates. Editors chose sides. Nicholas Klaine jumped on the bandwagon of the Peoples' Independent Ticket, while Frost supported those chosen at the Great Western. Considering those backing the candidates from the courthouse, Frost's position seems inconsistent. But then, Dan Frost was not always that easy to figure out. By contrast, Klaine recognized the shifting whims of the electorate straight away. Getting caught up in the backlash that crushed James Kelley had been an education.

---

[46] Defense Exhibit "A," Territory of Arizona vs. Morgan Earp et al., Defendants, Document No. 94, In Justice Court, Township No. 1, Cochise County, A.T. (Hayhurst typescript, WPA), 132–33.

Compared with today's endless campaigns, Ford County's example can only be viewed with envy. With just three weeks separating the conventions from the balloting, candidates hustled support without respite. Returns confirmed a near sweep for the Peoples' Independent Ticket, but by narrower margins. For the opposition, only B. A. Jones won—defeating W. F. Petillon in the race for register of deeds.[47] Even then, noted a mildly disappointed Dan Frost, Jones "never asked for the nomination, and made no effort to secure his election."[48]

With candidates hustling votes, Dodge City shifted emphasis, winning praise as a rest-stop for health seekers: "A great many consumptives are compelled to seek a higher altitude, and their physicians prescribe Colorado and New Mexico, where they can also have the benefit of the baths," reported the *Globe* on November 1. "But coming from a lower to a higher altitude is a dangerous experience to many of these invalids, and they find it greatly to their advantage to stop over a few weeks at an intermediate point, and thus become accustomed to the change." Restaurants and hotels welcomed the business. Thanks to the cattle trade Dodge City offered superior accommodations compared with most towns along the western route.

Not everyone had the sense to take advantage of these possibilities. Since P. L. Beatty moved to Colorado, managers of the Wright House had trouble maintaining its profitability. Walter Straeter gave up and opened a saloon and small variety theater at Thomas Draper's old stand on Front Street. By July 1881 J. H. Tepfer tried running the place, with Mrs. W. H. LyBrand in charge of the dining room. She succeeded; he failed. Finally, Arthur Woodman took on the task, but he, too, closed by mid-December with creditors at his heels, attaching his goods and chattels against unpaid bills. Not even a booming economy can save a business from ruin if poorly managed. Nothing else explains the failure of one of Dodge City's better hotels.

At the beginning of that summer of 1881, the *Kansas City Commercial Indicator* had reported George Littlefield's sale at Dodge City of his LIT Ranch near Tascosa to Judge C. C. Quinlan and Alex Fraser for $248,000, including 17,000 cattle and 210 thoroughbred bulls, as well as many horses

---

[47] Ford County Commissioners Journals, Book A, 343. Also see *Ford County Globe*, November 8, 1881; and *Dodge City Times*, November 10, 1881. Regarding the victory of Jones over Petillon, editor Klaine observed: "His [Petillon's] defeat can only be attributed to the popularity of his opponent in Dodge City. In the east end, where he is well known, Mr. Petillon ran ahead of his ticket."

[48] *Ford County Globe*, November 8, 1881.

and mules. Dan Frost was beside himself: "There never has been such a boom in the sale of Texas through cattle since the drive from Texas was first inaugurated as has been exhibited on this market this season."[49]

Not only did Texans sell cattle, so did many locals, including members of the firm York, Parker & Draper, boot maker John Mueller (until he sold out to A. J. Anthony and Chalk Beeson), and Henry Beverley and his sons, as well as Robert Wright and his Fort Dodge partner James Langton, operating through their sutler store address. Former city marshal Larry Deger served as the Dodge City agent for Lee and Reynolds, the Fort Supply traders, who bred Herefords and Shorthorn cattle on their ranch in Oldham County, Texas. Even Texans saw advantages to having peripheral operations in Kansas. Using Dodge City as a secondary headquarters, J. L. Driskill & Sons owned two ranches south of the Arkansas, one on Kiowa Creek in Comanche County and the other along the Cimarron in Clark County.

The first two weeks of August saw 82 cattle cars sent east, along with 4 filled with horses. A month later 178 cars pulled out during the same two-week period. By the first week of October, 206 cars were loaded, followed within the next ten days by 257 more. From the eighteenth through the end of the month, shippers added 219 cars to the total, straining the resources of the AT&SF. As early as October 11, the *Globe* advised: "The past week has been a lively one in and about the Dodge City stock yards. It seemed as though every stock man in the country wanted to ship cattle, but of course only a limited number could do so, as cars could not be furnished by the railroad company to meet the demand." Frost added prophetically: "we feel confident that the shipments will more than double for the next two weeks." By the third week of November the season's total reached 1,572 cars.

Then averaging twenty head per car, this amounted to 31,440 cattle shipped from Dodge City so far that season. With prices then averaging thirty dollars a head, net, it brought returns to the cattlemen of nearly a million dollars. For shipping all this beef, the railroad collected its own windfall. The town congratulated itself: "The fact of the matter is, Dodge City has become the great cattle market for the west, either for through Texas cattle or a place to ship stock from to the eastern markets."[50]

---

[49] Ibid., July 5, 1881. Regarding the sale of Littlefield's LIT ranch, his biographer quoted a price of $253,000. J. Evetts Haley, *George W. Littlefield, Texan* (Norman: University of Oklahoma Press, 1943), 125.

[50] Ibid., November 22, 1881.

Counting receipts, the town took time to relax before renewing the process. Amid dreams of striking it rich, stockholders gossiped about prospects for the Dodge City Mining Company's Colorado properties. Pondering more down-to-earth subjects, the Ford County township elections—this time without the antics of James Masterson—produced few surprises. Optimism over silver mines and ballot boxes spilled over. Even the much-beleaguered Wright House reopened under the management of W. H. LyBrand and his wife.

As the LyBrands remodeled and planned their grand opening, others decided to try their luck elsewhere. Popular dry-goods merchant Oliver Marsh sold out to Gaede, Baker & Company—a firm from Rockport, Missouri—who, except for Mr. Baker, were strangers to Dodge City. Marsh planned to move his family to Las Vegas, New Mexico, joining his brother-in-law in the lumber business. Within a month he was back, buying an interest in the Dodge City flourmill. "Sending flour west and returning lumber from New Mexico is a scheme that but few people had dreampt of. The people out there want our flour and we want their lumber," complimented the *Globe*.[51]

Still savoring cattle profits, Dodge City merchants turned their attention to the first Texas State Stockmans' Convention set to begin at Austin on February 14, 1882. Bob Wright, A. J. Anthony, Henry Beverley, Mayor Webster, Jim Kelley, Mike Sutton, and nearly forty others gathered at Straeter's opera house to consider sending one or more representatives to talk up Dodge City. After much debate, some of it acrimonious, they settled on Dan Frost. They also agreed to support the National Stock Trail—one of Frost's pet projects. The editor-turned-lobbyist made the trip with S. B. Bennett, a Fort Worth cattleman who at the time held twelve thousand head between the Big Wichita and Red rivers. Nicholas Klaine could not ignore this opportunity to chide his rival, claiming poor Dan would be out of his element and hopelessly confused.[52]

---

[51] Ibid., March 21, 1882.

[52] *Dodge City Times*, February 16, 1882. Among other jibes, the paper claimed, "Mr. Frost will forget his mission, and become oblivious to cattle trails or highways, and will do the best he can to further the interests of the newspaper he represents." The National Stock Trail was little more than a fanciful dream conjuring up a federally mandated route from the northern border of Texas all the way to Canada. It may have excited some, but nothing ever came of it, owing chiefly to obvious objections and growing settlement along all the proposed routes. Besides, bureaucrats in Washington offered no support. James Cox, *Historical and Biographical Record of the Cattle Industry and the Cattlemen of Texas and Adjacent Territory* (St. Louis: Woodward & Tiernan Printing Company, 1895), 107–108.

Wright and the others sent a telegram to Texas full of warm greetings and words of support, albeit couched in phrases so patronizing it could not possibly fool anyone at Austin. Still, one doubts the Texans missed the point. They, too, understood the realities of business and their president replied to the Dodge City men with equal fervor. Dodge City needed the Texans as much as the cattlemen needed an accommodating shipping point and grazing areas such as those offered by Ford County. When the Austin meeting appointed a committee on trails, it included such old friends of Dodge City as Charles Goodnight, D. H. Snyder, and Dillard R. Fant.

As always, estimates concerning the expected numbers of cattle began filtering north from Texas and west from the Kansas City livestock markets. Early in 1882 sources around San Antonio predicted larger drives from the southern range. It seems the West brothers planned totals of 17,000 head; followed by Schiner and Lytle with 16,600; James F. Ellison, along with Read and Byler each with 15,000; and Smith and Elliott, and George Littlefield with about 10,000 more. Twenty-five other cattlemen pushed projections in mid-February to 208,000.

On February 28 Mike Sutton resigned as county attorney. Even Dan Frost was sorry to see him go: "through the instrumentality of our efficient county attorney, our laws have been so well enforced and faithfully executed."[53] It helped that he had turned his back on the gang, a strategy, one can only assume, that was helped along by his marriage three years before to Mayor Webster's niece. Sutton now stood with the forces of reform. District Judge J. C. Strang appointed Thomas S. Jones to serve out Sutton's term. The judge also named William F. Petillon as clerk of the district court, following the sudden resignation of H. P. Myton. Myton, however, stayed on as city clerk.

Alonzo B. Webster faced no opponent for reelection as mayor in 1882. Few found fault with his handling of affairs; especially after one report, released only a fortnight before the election, showed a $2,200 reduction in city indebtedness, as well as an increase in general revenues, all done without the $500 owed by James Kelley for delinquent license fees. Everyone seemed to support Webster, who ended up with 225 votes. But ballots were more evenly divided among nine candidates for city council and two for police judge. In those closer races George S. Emerson, Albert Boyd,

[53] *Ford County Globe*, February 14, 1882.

Patrick Sughrue, Hamilton Bell, and Chalkley Beeson won council seats. R. E. Burns defeated Nicholas Klaine for police judge. Since the editor supported Webster and two of the council candidates, Boyd and Bell, he claimed a small victory nevertheless.

Mike Sutton accepted a position on the legal staff of the AT&SF. The city council appointed him a special advisor to defend its interests, offering $220 a year. Luckily for the chameleon-like advocate, Sutton's other clients provided a heftier income, enough so that he needed a partner. James T. Whitelaw accepted the challenge and brought his family up from Medicine Lodge. Sutton's new man moved in with Dan Frost at the western edge of the city. One could not imagine such an arrangement during the days of Jim Kelley's regime.

Webster soon found himself standing between his town's feuding newspaper editors. The trouble involved city and county patronage. Klaine had supported J. D. Shaffer for county commissioner on the candidate's promise to favor the *Dodge City Times* for the county printing contract. Once in office, however, Shaffer supported the *Ford County Globe*. The issue turned ugly, with claims and accusations fired from all sides. The commissioners decided to give county printing to the lowest bidder. Then, at its May 2 meeting, the city council, most of whose members were not supported by the *Times*, voted to have the *Globe* publish its proceedings. Enraged, Klaine resigned as city treasurer. Soon, both city and county officials saw the silliness of it all. At the behest of George Hoover, the county modified its stand by allowing both papers to print its official business, for half the normal rate, until January 1883. At the June 10 council meeting Klaine again accepted the appointment as city treasurer. Much to the relief of Mayor Webster, this bizarre uproar fizzled out.[54]

At the same meeting that reinstated Nicholas Klaine, Harry E. Gryden was appointed city attorney—the very post from which Webster had fired him the year before. It had not been an easy time. In early December 1881 Mike Sutton had charged Gryden with vagrancy and attached his law office for an unspecified $40 debt. Three months later Gryden fled to Colorado and was soon reported stranded in Pueblo. He discovered life as a Rocky Mountain wanderer not to his liking. Hat in hand, Gryden returned to

---

[54] Ford County Commissioners Journals, Book A, 343, 347, 350. *Dodge City Times*, January 12, April 13, June 15, 1882; and *Ford County Globe*, January 24, May 9, June 13, 1882.

Dodge City in time to receive a $45 payment from the county as assistant school examiner before reopening his law office.[55] Two months later Webster decided to bring the repentant attorney into his administration.

Gryden was not the only old-timer from Dodge City who found Colorado a less than friendly place. At Gunnison, soon after Gryden's reinstatement, Adobe Walls veteran James Hanrahan was put on trial, along with two others, charged with the murder of Eliza Hopkins.[56] Hanrahan was found not guilty and eventually made his way to Idaho. There he reentered politics, serving Custer County for a couple of years in the state legislature.

After pacifying Harry Gryden, Webster appointed blacksmith Peter W. Beamer city marshal, with township constable Clark Chipman his chief assistant and Lee Harland a policeman. The mayor then named a committee, made up of City Clerk H. P. Myton, along with councilmen Beeson, Boyd, and Emerson, to settle accounts with outgoing marshal Bob Vanderburg. Beamer seemed a solid choice. A resident since 1879, he was no stranger to the West, having worked as a miner and blacksmith in Colorado for many years. Besides, as if proving his toughness, Beamer ended his Civil War service as a first sergeant in General Sherman's army.[57]

Hoping for tighter control over his police, Webster issued fourteen new regulations, some of them addressing long-standing problems. No longer could officers engage in private business outside their official duties. Gone, at least theoretically, were the days of Bat Masterson and Wyatt Earp, when policemen supplemented their salaries as professional gamblers and saloonmen. Drinking on duty was no longer permitted, nor could liquor be introduced into the city jail. To reduce favoritism shown some offenders, individual officers were not allowed to withdraw complaints without the mayor's personal authorization.[58] A. B. Webster hoped to end the practice of the police becoming a power unto themselves in local affairs.

Most everyone supported the new regulations—that is when not thinking about making money. Pondering cattle profits proved irresistible. One

---

[55] Ford County Commissioners Journals, Book A, 351.

[56] *Gunnison News-Democrat*, May 11–14, 16, 20, 1882. Years before news from Colorado was more complimentary toward Dodge City's early pioneer: "A dispatch from Lake City, Colorado, October 6th, says that Hanrahan was elected Sheriff by over one hundred majority. He is a Democrat." *Dodge City Times*, October 13, 1877.

[57] *History of the State of Kansas*, 1560–61; and *The History of Adams County, Illinois* (Chicago: Murray, Williamson & Phelps, 1879), 355–56.

[58] "Police Regulations," *Dodge City Times*, June 22, 1882.

group formed their own company, to be financed by one hundred thousand dollars in capital stock. A committee of nine, headed by George Hoover and including Henry Sitler, Richard Evans, Bob Wright, and A. J. Anthony, explored the idea of soliciting subscriptions at twenty-five dollars a share. Growing impatient, Hoover tried getting into the cattle business himself by offering to purchase Pat Ryan's herd of eight hundred animals on Mulberry Creek for twenty-five dollars a head, delivery scheduled for June 1. Hoover, in turn, sold a half interest to Herman Fringer. Some questioned the wisdom of all this since neither man had ever owned so much as a single cow.

They did, however, have money and the best wishes of Nicholas Klaine, who gave the deal such a glowing send off that Ryan backed out, concluding: "he would rather pay the $1,000 forfeit and keep his stock, than take chances in getting established in the stock business again on equally as good a range, with such a well selected and graded up herd as he now possesses."[59]

Not willing to spend time feeling sorry for himself, Hoover moved on to a fresh scheme. Riding around town in a beer wagon bedecked with the Anheuser-Busch logo (a vehicle he loaned for picnics and Sunday school parties), Hoover worked on plans of opening a bank. Heretofore businesses such as Wright, Beverley & Company, and even Hoover himself, had informally handled banking matters. With Dodge City becoming such an important commercial center, not only because of its livestock interests, but with its vast freight and trading network as well—an actual bank made sense. Hoover interested Richard Evans, Herman Fringer, and Henry Sitler in the plan. Before filing the actual charter of incorporation with the secretary of state, saloon owner and former city councilman William H. Harris signed on as a director.

The Bank of Dodge City opened with capital stock of $50,000. George Hoover served as president, with Richard Evans, cashier; Herman Fringer, assistant cashier; and Otto Mueller, clerk and bookkeeper. City councilman, hotel proprietor and budding Pawnee County wheat king Albert Boyd invested $5,000 in the venture. Then, as if to convince fellow citizens of the new institution's sound footing, the *Times* published, in a radical departure for such things: "The aggregate wealth of the stockholders is

[59] *Ford County Globe*, April 18, 1882. For Klaine's extravagant remarks on Hoover's deal with Ryan, see *Dodge City Times*, March 30, 1882.

about $250,000. Mr. Hoover's wealth is estimated at $50,000; R. W. Evans, $40,000; H. J. Fringer, 20,000, H. L. Sitler, 50,000; W. H. Harris, 40,000; A. H. Boyd, 50,000."[60]

The new bank was ready for the Texans when the usual invasion of stockmen and buyers took place. M. S. Culver, representing Foster, Clark & Culver, San Antonio commission merchants and livestock dealers, still handled much of the outside business for Wright, Beverley & Company that spring of 1882. Within the next several weeks many well-known cattlemen arrived, including W. W. and Sam Driskill, Henry Kollar, Andrew H. Johnson, and the legendary Shanghai Pierce. The railroad not only improved its stockyards and loading facilities, but also planned thirty cottages, each with five rooms, to house its employees.

Meanwhile, in open defiance of the state's Prohibition law, the Long Branch began advertising imported brandy, gin, port, sherry, claret wines, and Bass' Ale to supplement its normal offerings of whiskey and beer. In their advertisements, observing the letter if not the spirit of the law, Beeson and Harris included a half-hearted caveat: "for medical, scientific and mechanical purposes."

Anticipating thirsty cowboys, the two proprietors began a forty-foot addition to the Long Branch. While remodeling they uncovered evidence of Dodge City's unsavory past: "In tearing down the canvas on the walls . . . about twenty-five bullet holes were disclosed—mementoes of other days. In this house H. T. McCarty and Levi Richardson both fell—one by a cruel and crazed drinker, and the other by a jealous rival in the affections of a woman. At the time Richardson was killed the saloon was crowded with people—and such scampering was never before seen. The man who went through the transom of the back door, is still living in Dodge, but the man who crawled into the ice chest died the victim of drink in Colorado. The bloody scenes of Dodge are things of the past."[61] Only two weeks before, the town heard news of Cock-Eyed Frank Loving being killed during a gambler's quarrel at Trinidad, Colorado.

In May Charles Goodnight opened the shipping season. That month saw seventy-one cattle cars en route to Kansas City, with eighteen more loaded with horses for other destinations, including Colorado and

[60] *Dodge City Times,* June 22, 1882.
[61] Ibid., May 4, 1882.

Nebraska. On the range south of town, Houston and Rutledge, J. T. Lytle, C. Bennett, and the West brothers all held two herds, each estimated at 2,500 head. Less than two weeks later A. H. Polley wrote from Albany, Texas—which had replaced Fort Griffin as a major tally point—reporting fifty herds passing by on their way to Dodge City, representing nearly 150,000 longhorns.

Despite concerns about trails being cut by fencing in Texas, primarily in the Panhandle, the season looked good. On June 22 Klaine boasted: "Cattle sales are quite brisk. 15,000 head have been sold since our last report. About 75,000 head of cattle are yet to arrive." Sheep, always welcomed on the Dodge City market, declined somewhat in the spring of 1882, owing to Texans buying up the large flocks in New Mexico normally brought into western Kansas for shipment.

As the livestock bonanza reached fever pitch, and less than two weeks after accepting the appointment, Peter Beamer resigned as city marshal. His departure presented Mayor Webster with a dilemma. He did not want to promote Clark Chipman, although that officer did assume some of those duties out of necessity. Webster decided to act as his own marshal until a suitable replacement could be found. Perhaps remembering Dodge City's early years, the mayor telegraphed former deputy U.S. marshal Jack Bridges in Colorado, asking him to return and accept the post. Bridges arrived on July 8. Webster swore him in that same day.

The appointment of Jack Bridges stirred controversy, even if some were pleased with his selection: "Jack's friends speak highly of him and of his integrity and bravery. He has done some fine service for the government, and upon every occasion acquitted himself with honor."[62] Others were not convinced. An editor at Caldwell wrote, "Jack, like Wild Bill and Bat Masterson, belongs to the killer-class and it is only a question of time when he will lay down with his boots on."[63] The *Times* counterattacked on July 27, accusing the Caldwell editor, W. B. Hutchison, of being in league with Ellis County horse thieves while serving as a justice of the peace at Hays City during the late 1860s.

To some, men like Jack Bridges represented days best forgotten. Old timers around Dodge City could not help recalling rumors of Bridges

---

[62] Ibid., July 13, 1882.
[63] *Caldwell Commercial*, as quoted in *Ford County Globe*, July 25, 1882.

helping saloonman John Scott escape justice after the murder of William Taylor in 1873. Whatever the feelings in the editorial rooms at Caldwell, or spoken on the streets outside their own offices, officials in Dodge felt the need for a man like Jack Bridges to serve as city marshal.

Dodge City may have found itself an old-style lawman, but it seemed less engrossed with old-time problems. Cattlemen still swarmed the city, filling its hotels, restaurants, and places of amusement but without causing much trouble. Railroad officials arranged tickets at half price to drovers, "well vouched for as being regularly in the business," from Dodge City to San Antonio via the Santa Fe and connecting lines.

As merchants counted up their receipts, the *Times* reported on August 3: "Some idea of the increase of business in Dodge City may be had from a couple of statements. The expense for the month of July of one of the prominent saloons, was $1,634.95. The sales in June of one of the prominent stores was 55 per cent above the sales in June last year. The sales in July was 90 per cent over the sales of July last year."

Col. J. M. Day completed his purchase of the Driskill ranches south of Dodge, the last costing sixty-five thousand dollars. Cattle trading became contagious. Mayor Webster, Henry F. May, George Anderson, and Henry Sitler traveled to the Panhandle in search of rangeland. A. J. Anthony, Chalk Beeson, and his latest partner Jacob Collar, took time out to go to their respective ranches to brand calves. Thoughts of immediate profit induced Collar to sell his interest in the C.O.D. Ranch to William H. Harris for a reported twenty thousand dollars. Beeson and Harris were now ranching partners as well as proprietors of the Long Branch.

Cattle markets in western Kansas suffered a slump in early August, but then, the business always had been fickle. By the tenth the *Times* noted, "The town has been dull for several days past. The business of Dodge is sort of phenomenal. To-day there is a busy throng—to-morrow will appear like some banquet hall deserted." Despite the gloom, stock shipments totaled 36,540 head—or 1,827 cars—from July 1 to the beginning of October.

THE FALL OF 1882 witnessed the ending of an era. After a hesitant start four years before, the government finally closed Fort Dodge. The Dull Knife scare of 1878 delayed the decision, but the opening of two-thirds of the military reservation to settlement in late 1880 guaranteed the with-drawal. As had been the case from the beginning, civilians created problems for soldiers. Troops at Fort Larned complained to the post adjutant at Fort Dodge about civilian forays. Some of their fence had vanished, only to reappear on a local farm. Stockmen grazing cattle and sheep on the restricted reservation rebuffed, often by force of arms, all efforts to remove them. In one annoying instance a teenager threatened some soldiers. A sergeant disarmed the boy and destroyed his rifle with an ax. Officers preferred fighting Indians to policing unruly civilians.

Many in Dodge City, following the lead of the outspoken Daniel Frost, protested the closing. Anticipating complaints, the military had quietly issued orders on April 5 to begin preparations. And so, despite repeated rumors, people in Dodge did not hear the official news until May 20.

The *Globe* published article after article condemning the decision, claiming troops were still needed to protect settlers from Indians hoping to succeed where Dull Knife had failed. Nicholas Klaine took a more realistic approach: "Referring to the abandonment of Fort Dodge the Globe wants to know if this country must again be 'given up' to the 'Indians and the buffalo.' We hope not. We are quite confident the buffalo wont return. There are no buffalo in the country. The Indians have been subdued and the savages are in Arizona making the air ring with their whoop. We don't like to let Fort Dodge go; but we can't help it. And the Globe can't stop it by howling 'redskins and buffalo.' "[64]

Ignoring complaints from dispirited civilians, officers at Fort Dodge carried out their orders. Glancing over the procedures for closing the post allows a look into the workings of the American military in the nineteenth century, a time when government departments were far less wasteful of public funds than future generations would tolerate. Nothing was discarded: all transportation materials, except for one four-mule wagon and team, was ordered to Fort Riley; wood-sawing machines to Fort Gibson, Indian Territory; medical provisions to Fort Supply—hospital records boxed and shipped to the surgeon-general's office in Washington—medical periodicals to Fort Leavenworth; all subsistence stores, except pork and bacon, to Fort Elliott, Texas; the pork to Fort Leavenworth and the bacon to Fort Craig, New Mexico; hay to Rawlings, Wyoming, for even-

[64] *Dodge City Times*, June 1, 1882.

tual shipment to the White River Agency; corn, oats, and bran to Fort Elliott; fifteen tons of coal each to Forts Elliott and Supply, the remainder to Fort Lyon, Colorado.

As for weapons, Colt revolvers, Springfield rifles, and related items were sent to Fort Supply, along with selected ammunition and reloading tools. The four 12-pound Mountain Howitzers and equipment went to Fort Riley, but the cartridge bags for the guns went to to Fort Elliott; and the remainder of serviceable ordnance was shipped to the Rock Island Arsenal in Illinois. The wire and iron telegraph poles between Fort Dodge and Dodge City came down, much of it going to Fort Leavenworth. The remaining poles, insulators, pins, and cross-arms were shipped west for use on the military telegraph between Colorado Springs and Pikes Peak.[65] And so it went.

By October 2 it was about over. Of the three companies stationed at Fort Dodge, one marched the 165 miles to Fort Elliott, another to Fort Reno, 111 miles south of Caldwell, and the third to Fort Supply. On that day the flag came down and Capt. William Fletcher issued his final statement as post commander: "In accordance with instructions from Hdgrs. Dept. of the Mo., this post is hereby discontinued."[66] Fort Dodge may have closed, but it was not abandoned. Aside from one lieutenant and six soldiers left behind to complete the shipment of equipment and supplies, the government still owned the buildings, together with fourteen thousand acres of the old reservation. This land was not opened for settlement until 1889. The fort itself became the Kansas State Soldiers' Home that year, paid for by donations largely collected from Dodge City.

Authorities from the Department of the Missouri appointed James Langton, who also owned a cattle ranch on Sand Creek, "to take charge of the public buildings on the Fort Dodge Reservation."[67] This provided some compensation for Langton, who lost his postmaster's job when the fort closed. To further reduce losses, Wright & Langton held a closeout

---

[65] Maj. Edward R. Platt, Asst. Adj. Gen., Department of the Missouri, to the Commanding Officer, Fort Dodge, Kansas, May 31, June 1, 12, 19, July 8, 27, 1882. Fort Dodge, Registered Letters Received.

[66] Order No. 87, October 2, 1882, Special Orders and Orders, Vol. 6. Headquarters Records, Fort Dodge, Kansas. Also see: Fort Dodge, Post Returns, October 2, 1882.

[67] Headquarters, Department of the Missouri, to the Commanding Officer, Fort Dodge, Kansas, September 4, 1882. Fort Dodge, Registered Letters Received. This official acknowledgement of Langton's appointment surprised no one in Dodge City, as the *Times* had reported his selection on June 22.

sale: "laces, Embroideries, Hats, Caps, Lamps, Glassware, Stoves, &c. &c. At Prices That Will Astonish," presided over by John Chambliss at "The Cheap Store," on the corner west of the post office in Dodge City.[68]

In late September, with no thoughts of Fort Dodge, Democratic gubernatorial candidate George W. Glick held a rally at Kelley's old Opera House. Glick's warm reception, helped by his outspoken opposition to Prohibition, seemed to bode well for his party's chances. Following Glick's visit, sixty-three voters called for a Peoples' Delegate Convention at the courthouse on October 9 to nominate candidates for county offices. Both Republicans and Democrats signed on, thus giving the false impression of unity. With the Democrats smelling victory, the campaign divided along party lines. At the convention a number of Ford County Democrats, such as George Hoover, grabbed all the major nominations, using the banner of the Peoples' Independent County Ticket.

As a counterbalance, Republicans held their own convention on October 16. They named Henry May to run against Hoover for state representative; Daniel Frost to challenge James Whitelaw for county attorney; Louis C. Hartman against Herman Fringer for probate judge; and George Emerson to fight it out with fellow Republican Fred Zimmerman for Third District county commissioner. William F. Petillon, a long-time Democrat, announced as an independent for clerk of the district court, the position he already held. The campaigns proceeded without much rancor.

The November 7 results were expressed by the *Times* two days later: "FORD COUNTY GOES DEMOCRATIC BY A BIG MAJORITY." George W. Glick, who considered the Prohibition law "premature, rash, and unwise," defeated the two-term governor and anti-liquor disciple John P. St. John by a huge margin. The same was true in Ford County with Hoover, Fringer, Whitelaw, and Zimmerman. Petillon tasted victory, but only by 79 votes, defeating P. J. Upp, a man running on both formal tickets.[69]

Frost did not take Whitelaw's challenge gracefully. Trying to use his former houseguest's position as Mike Sutton's law partner as evidence against him, rumors began circulating a fortnight before the election suggesting

---

[68] *Ford County Globe*, October 10, 1882. See also ibid., October 3, 1882; and *Dodge City Times*, October 12, 1882.

[69] Ford County Commissioners Journals, Book A, 369–71. Also see *Dodge City Times*, September 28, October 12, 19, 26, November 2, 16, 1882; *Ford County Globe*, October 31, November 8, 14, 1882; and William E. Connelley, *A Standard History of Kansas and Kansans* (Chicago: Lewis Publishing Company, 1918), 2:829–31.

that it was all "a scheme of Sutton's to get control of the office." In fact, before assuming his duties in January, James Whitelaw dissolved his arrangement with Sutton, who then asked a twenty-three-year-old fellow New Yorker named Frederick T. M. Wenie to join his firm.[70]

As always, political posturing and cattle prices elbowed against one another for attention, but now a certain sadness pervaded the atmosphere. Robert Wright's popular nineteen-year-old daughter, Clara Belle, had died that August of heart failure and other complications while visiting the hot springs at Las Vegas, New Mexico. Then, on December 8, Dodge City mourned the loss of probate judge and pioneer newspaper editor Lloyd Shinn. Long suffering from tuberculosis, Shinn had dissolved his partnership with Frost in mid-July. Within days he and the new Presbyterian minister, W. P. Taitsworth, set out for a month's vacation in Colorado with hopes of improving his health, leaving his younger brother Frank to help handle affairs at the post office. Returning to Dodge City, Lloyd Shinn died shortly before his twenty-seventh birthday, attended by his sister Eva and brother Walter. Both accompanied the casket back to their parent's home in Iowa.

Herman J. Fringer finished Shinn's term as probate judge. Nicholas Klaine was named postmaster on January 2, 1883. The editor's jockeying for the nomination caused harsh words: "The breath had hardly left the body of the late Postmaster when he [Klaine] was on the street, although it was early morning, with a petition to have the appointment vested in himself. A man of less decency (save the mark) would have at least allowed some friend, if he had one, to go around with such a petition."[71]

Despite the loss of Lloyd Shinn, the people of Dodge City could look back on 1882 with pride. From July 1 the *Globe* counted a record 63,520 head of cattle shipped; the *Times* estimated the figure at 75,000. In his final report, H. T. Drake, the man in charge of the AT&SF's stockyards and shipping at Dodge City, noted 3,230 cars sent east between May 1 and the end of the year.[72] This more than doubled the total for 1881. The railroad also handled 51 cars filled with horses and another 3 of sheep. Counting "through cattle," some 200,000 head of livestock had been sold on the

---

[70] James R. Whitelaw to the editor, *Dodge City Times*, October 26, 1882; and *Ford County Globe*, January 2, 1883.

[71] Letter to the editor signed "Fair Play," *Ford County Globe*, March 27, 1883.

[72] *Ford County Globe*, January 2, 16, 1883.

Dodge City market in 1882. What mattered most, however: the local numbers topped those reported by Caldwell, Dodge City's chief rival for the Texas trade.

All this buying and selling, together with profits from a freighting industry covering the Texas Panhandle, enriched the town. A construction boom offered chances for profit as demand grew for both commercial buildings and private homes. Saloonman Henry V. Cook sold out to Charles Milde and Bob Tardy and rushed to become a lumber dealer, buying the yard once owned by Mayor Webster. At a cost of thirty-five hundred dollars, Catholics built their own church, large enough to seat two hundred worshipers. Real estate prices reflected the gains, with vacant lots snatched up by eager investors.

On November 23, 1882, the *Times* crowed: "Business is tolerably fair in Dodge. There is no town on the Santa Fe road, excepting Topeka, that will compare with Dodge as a business point. Some towns are trying to excel Dodge (notably Caldwell), but they make no comparison. Dodge is a boomer." Later reports claimed the AT&SF planned spending two hundred thousand dollars at Dodge City on a new depot and double stockyards. Even the Dodge City Mining Company rekindled interest among shareholders with reports of valuable assays from its holdings on North Star Mountain near Alma, Colorado. People had much to be thankful for, not least being the remarkable feat of having no one killed in their town during the past year. If they took this as some sort of omen, 1883 would prove that the old town had not quite broken with its past.

Chapter 10

THE DODGE CITY WAR

The year 1883 began with a successful ice harvest. People cut blocks six to eight inches thick from the frozen Arkansas. During the first week of January alone they pulled out 2,000 tons. George Hoover claimed 200, while Frederick Zimmerman and Henry Beverley each took 150, and Bob Wright 300 tons. That pioneer, having ended his partnership with James Langton, needed ice for the Wright House. His twenty-one-year-old son, Robert Henry Wright, fresh from tutelage in the hotel business under P. L. Beatty at Trinidad, now managed the property, with his mother overseeing the household. W. H. LyBrand became chief clerk at the Dodge House, after George Cox and Albert Boyd went their separate ways in late January. Boyd retired to his wheat fields and horse ranch near Larned, becoming a livestock trader there and at Dodge City.

As if giving the town a vote of confidence, disciples pointed out a hundred new dwellings built during the past year. George Cox renovated his ever-popular Dodge House. Other improvements included two more telephone lines. Dr. McCarty ordered one connecting his drug store and home, with another running between the post office building and Oliver Marsh & Company's flourmill.

Nicholas Klaine noted another transformation: "Within two years past Dodge City has undergone radical changes in her municipal character. The wayward, incredulous countryman is not fleeced by the sharp deceiving confidence operator. The unsuspecting traveler is not knocked down and robbed. There are no highway robberies, no murdering and no thieving. It is true, gambling, prostitution and whisky selling is carried on but there is some restrain, some respect, and show of decency in the illegitimate and unlawful affairs."[1]

Robert Wright set aside forty fenced acres along the river as a city park. He ordered four carloads of mature cottonwoods, box elders, honey

---

[1] *Dodge City Times*, March 22, 1883.

locusts, and other varieties hauled down the Santa Fe line. By early April he directed the planting of each tree, much to the delight of thankful citizens. Wright felt the physical appearance of the town needed as much or more attention than did its ever-changing moral climate.

On February 2, nearly two years after surviving a gunshot wound to the lung during his melee with Bat Masterson, Al Updegraff died. First reports listed the cause as "general debility." Doctors soon confirmed rumors that he had died of smallpox. Mayor Webster ordered the contents of Updegraff's room, including the furniture, burned. Officials assumed the Lady Gay's former bartender had contracted the dreaded disease during a visit to New Mexico. Next, following a week-long spree, a black barber named William Davis fell ill with what everyone assumed to be delirium tremens. Instead, he died of smallpox at Spearville.

Nine days after Updegraff's demise, ex-deputy Thomas Bugg succumbed to the same malady. The fourth victim turned out to be a confidence man and three-card-monte devotee named John S. "Jack" McCarty. Awaiting sentencing on a robbery conviction, Jack jumped bond on February 19 but got no farther than Neil Brown's ranch, forty miles south. He died there a week later. Thomas McIntire, a member of the coroner's jury during the Dora Hand inquest, returned the body to Dodge City. Officials refused entry. McIntire reluctantly buried the gambler's remains in Five-Mile Hollow south of town, leaving a simple board to mark the spot. Sometime later cattleman Joseph Morgan, a member of the posse that rode to Brown's ranch, died of smallpox at his own place on the Canadian.

Fearing that word of an epidemic might scuttle the upcoming cattle season, Dan Frost tried to downplay the outbreak. He blamed Thomas Bugg's death on heart failure. Even after smallpox was identified as the culprit, Frost tried to fault its victims: "Each one . . . were hard drinkers, and we may say did not draw a sober breath for weeks before their deaths, men who were dissipated with no regular habits, (unless it was to drink) kept late hours and with no particular place of abode."[2] Others recognized the seriousness. The railroad sent out a special "vaccination train," staffed by various physicians along its route. Dr. McCarty served the Dodge City area.

Mayor Webster and the council responded to the danger. A new ordinance listed quarantine regulations and established a board of health,

---

[2] *Ford County Globe,* February 27, 1883.

presided over by the mayor.[3] The board decided to isolate patients at Fort Dodge, ignoring objections from the government. Reported cases increased as the death toll reached six. Those infected included a child and sister-in-law of Neil Brown, an adopted child of Deputy Sheriff Fred Singer, and three children of stonemason William Hessman, one of whom died. The *Times* tried to ease fears: "It is all a mistake. The small-pox is at Fort Dodge and not Dodge City. Keep away from Fort Dodge."[4]

Frost had earlier claimed, "The four cases that were taken to the Post hospital and under the care of the Board of Health of this city, we learned last evening with one single exception were out hunting jack rabbits when the doctor called to see them."[5] Klaine disavowed the farce, admitting: "Well, well; and what does 'Dr.' Frost think about the 'small-pox business' now. Dr. McCarty had taken the photographs of the patients at Fort Dodge, and the sorry spectacle shows small-pox in the most malignant form. The features of the sick men are scarcely recognizable."[6] The disease vanished within six weeks, allowing the skittish to return from rural sanctuaries.

With the epidemic at an end, the cattle season seemed secure. January reports from San Antonio estimated a spring drive of upwards of 230,000 animals. Within a month that number had grown by another 100,000. To assure the town's appeal among Texas men, Robert Wright attended the second annual Stockmens' Convention at Austin. By mid-February he returned to report assurances from Texas allies not only that the current drive would surpass that of 1882 but also that the bulk of this traffic would benefit Dodge City. The Kansas quarantine line still allowed an open trail to the Arkansas.

To help solidify trade, stockraisers in and around Dodge City organized their own conventions for March 20. Governor Glick, a veteran breeder of shorthorn cattle, traveled out from Topeka to address the assembled delegates.[7] Bob Wright provided a room over his store for the use of C. W. Willett, secretary of the Western Kansas Stock Growers' Association. Dodge City was determined to extend all possible courtesies.

Acknowledging the importance of cattle, everyone also understood the

[3] Ordinance No. 68, February 19, 1883. Dodge City Ordinances, Book A, 129–30.

[4] *Dodge City Times*, March 15, 1883.

[5] *Ford County Globe*, February 27, 1883.

[6] *Dodge City Times*, March 15, 1883.

[7] G. A. Laude, *Kansas Shorthorns: A History of the Breed in the State from 1857 to 1920* (Iola, Kans.: The Laude Printing Company, 1920), 29, 34–37, 49, 105.

town's advantages as a freighting hub. Figures from July 1, 1882, through February 1, 1883, for W. M. D. Lee & Company and associated firms such as D. W. VanHorn & Company of Fort Elliott, Randleton & Company, and Rath and Dickson, both from Mobeetie, Texas, showed 4,626,673 pounds of goods moving through Dodge City. Of all this the *Lakin Herald* remarked: "The above is only what freight is shipped south by this one freight house, then comes Wright, Beverley & Co., York, Parker, Draper & Co., Geo. S. Emerson, and many other well known houses that receive tons of freight and ship largely to different points making Dodge City one of the most prominent towns on the road."[8]

Spring brought with it the likelihood of changes in city government. Alonzo Webster decided not to seek a third term as mayor. Politics seemed predictable. Even Frost conceded three days after the January convention nominating township officers that "this has no political significance, whatever, as the convention had a Democratic chairman, a Republican secretary and a Greenbacker on the floor to make motions."[9] Boredom soon gave way to the forces of reform.

Sixty registered voters called for a nominating convention at the courthouse on March 17. All factions were represented, but one side dominated the proceedings. Saloonman William H. Harris won the nomination for mayor, with Patrick Sughrue, Thomas J. Tate, Nelson Cary, Henry Koch, and Charles Dickerson chosen to run for city council, with W. E. Frush as police judge. This slate, supported oddly enough by James H. Kelley and the *Ford County Globe*, did not satisfy the town's more aggressive reformers.

This so-called law-and-order element called a meeting two days later. Former city marshal Lawrence E. Deger was chosen to run for mayor. Since forced from office by Mayor Kelley and the council in 1877, Deger had worked as a common laborer before getting hired to represent the Dodge City interests of traders Lee and Reynolds. He also became chief agent for the Adams Express Company until the AT&SF allied with Wells, Fargo in May 1882—Wells, Fargo had engineered an exclusive with the AT&SF. Outmaneuvered, Adams Express withdrew, leaving Deger without a position. He had now come full circle and was running for mayor. With him, Henry Beverley, Henry Sturm, Hamilton Bell, George Emerson, and H. T. Drake ran for city council, alongside R. E. Burns as police

---

[8] *Lakin Herald*, as quoted in *Ford County Globe*, March 6, 1883.

[9] *Ford County Globe*, January 30, 1883.

judge. These candidates enjoyed the support of outgoing mayor A. B. Webster and the *Dodge City Times.*

This shift in loyalties by the town's two newspapers is an interesting one. Of course both claimed to support Republican Party principles; it was just that Frost felt more comfortable as a voice in opposition. Besides, Klaine's position as city treasurer guaranteed no kind words from the *Globe.* In some ways this helps explain Frost's sympathies toward remnants of the gang as they again eyed public office. Klaine proved more pragmatic, at least at this point in his career. He saw that the days of wide-open government were over and he was not about to be left behind. Old Nick shifted his loyalties to fit the moment, as did Mike Sutton.

During the campaign Frost limited his attacks to Klaine's record as city treasurer. Klaine responded by characterizing the candidacy of William Harris and the others as a step backward, adding: "Is it Mr. Harris' money that makes Mr. Frost think Mr. Harris is such a nice man?" Klaine was enjoying himself, pointing out, "It seems that we threw a bombshell into the enemy's camp. The effluvia arising from the aforesaid explosion would indicate that the rottenness had been struck."[10]

Election Day offered some surprises: "Before 8 o'clock, the hour of opening the polls both factions went to the poll house. The Deger party outnumbered the other faction, and chose the judges of election," reported a pleased Nicholas Klaine. "Then the fray began—all day long stood one hundred men at the polls, hotly and earnestly contesting the character of the voter. No such election was ever before held in Dodge City. No election before ever created the enthusiasm, the ardor or the interest. Three hundred and fifty seven votes were polled—the largest number ever polled in the city precinct. But the earnestness and enthusiasm of the contest had drawn out all of the available and unavailable votes. And though the legal battle raged hotly, earnestly and fiercely, yet it was carried on peaceably and in apparently good spirits."[11]

Larry Deger pulled in 214 votes, defeating Harris by a margin of 71. All five council candidates running with Deger won with totals above 200, as did R. E. Burns for police judge. It was a clear victory, with serious implications for the public peace.

---

[10] *Dodge City Times,* March 29, 1883.

[11] Ibid., April 5, 1883.

On April 23, just three weeks after the election, the new city council passed two ordinances that on the surface seemed harmless, even commendable for any enlightened community. Both measures soon shattered Dodge City's complacency. The first addressed the problem of prostitution: "An Ordinance for the Suppression of Vice and Immorality." The new law defined violators as any person or persons operating "a brothel, bawdy house, house of ill-fame, or of assignation," or anyone being an inmate or resident of any such establishment. Another section disallowed advertising or plying that trade "upon the Streets or in any public place." The second ordinance took up the question of vagrancy. Section II applied to anyone without a visible means of support caught loitering around brothels, gambling halls, or any place selling liquor, including those "engaged in any unlawful calling whatever." This provision could apply to gamblers.[12]

Then, on the evening of April 28, 1883, Deger's administration made its move. City Marshal Jack Bridges, along with several special policeman and City Clerk Louis C. Hartman, a former agent for liquor wholesaler Henry Sturm, raided the Long Branch: "Three prostitutes pretendedly employed in Harris & Short's saloon, as 'singers,' but employed evidently to evade the ordinance in relation to prostitution, were arrested and put in the lockup."[13] Questions were raised about the limited scope of the action taken, with Dan Frost observing: "It was claimed by the proprietors that partiality was shown in arresting women in their house when two were allowed to remain in A. B. Webster's saloon, one at Heinz & Kramer's, two at Nelson Cary's, and a whole herd of them at Bond & Nixon's dance hall."[14]

Why single out the Long Branch? The answer involves politics, personal prejudices, and business rivalries. As part of the general shift toward reform, resentment had been growing against certain elements of the saloon trade. Deger's defeat of William H. Harris opened the door. Accepted by most businessmen, Harris felt jealousy from ordinary citizens because of his wealth. The popularity of the Long Branch troubled competitors—especially ex-mayor Alonzo B. Webster.

Adding to the uncertainty, Harris now had a new partner, one not as well thought of as Chalkley Beeson, who had retired six weeks earlier to

---

[12] Ordinances No. 70 and 71, April 23, 1883. Dodge City Ordinances, Book A, 133–34, 135–36. Although approved on the 23rd, neither ordinance legally went into effect until notice was published in the *Dodge City Times* on April 26, 1883.

[13] *Dodge City Times*, May 3, 1883.

[14] *Ford County Globe*, May 1, 1883.

devote more time to their successful C.O.D. stock ranch. The new face at the Long Branch was a gambler of mixed reputation named Luke Short, a man whose physical appearance did justice to his name. When giving notice of this change in ownership, Beeson and Harris joked, "All persons knowing themselves to be indebted to the late firm of Beeson & Harris will call and make satisfactory settlement, as talk is cheap but it takes money to buy whisky."[15] Before long there was little to laugh about at the Long Branch.

After the arrest of his three "singers," Luke Short ran into City Clerk Louis Hartman. They argued and both men reached for their weapons. The sound of at least three gunshots caught everyone's attention. During this brief melee the terrified Hartman tripped and fell. Thinking he had killed his man, Short took refuge in Tom Land's saloon. Actually all the shots went wild, but they did serve as an opening for what became known as the Dodge City War. The shooting focused attention on Luke Short rather than William H. Harris, the intended victim of the April 28 raid against the Long Branch. Some speculated that much of the trouble started after Harris asked Mayor Deger to remove Clark Chipman from the police force.[16]

Short was arrested but released on two thousand dollars' bond. Mayor Deger convinced himself that the diminutive gambler had wanted to assassinate the city clerk. On April 30 officers rearrested Short, as well as a New Mexico desperado named W. H. Bennett, a gambler from Mobeetie known as Dr. Niel, and three other members of that murky profession: Johnson Gallagher, Lon A. Hyatt, and Thomas Lane. Dr. Galland offered to post bond for Luke Short but was refused by city authorities. Luke's attorney, Harry Gryden, was also turned away. Harris telegraphed Nelson Adams at Larned to represent his partner, but he too was denied access, being "informed that the exigency of the situation did not need a lawyer, although the patient was very sick."[17]

Mayor Deger ignored the courts and, reminiscent of his action agains Bobby Gill while city marshal in 1877, offered the arrested men "their choice of trains." Short traveled to Kansas City and began telling anyone who would listen about the terrible injustice he had suffered. Nicholas Klaine argued, "the citizens of Dodge City are determined that the lawless element shall not thrive in this city. No half-way measures will be used

[15] Ibid., February 6, 1883.

[16] *Daily Kansas State Journal*, May 17, 1883. Also see Miller and Snell, *Why the West Was Wild*, 109.

[17] *Dodge City Times*, May 3, 1883.

in the suppression of either lawlessness or riot."[18] All this seems somewhat humorous coming from James H. Kelley's former champion. The editor of the *Times* also missed the irony of Deger's questionable behavior.

Luke Short had been in Dodge City for a couple of years and had worked at the Long Branch from at least August 1882. An enigmatic wanderer, Short came to Texas from Mississippi with his parents when only a child. By 1870, at age sixteen, he rode into Kansas with the trail herds but soon began peddling whiskey and learning to gamble. Six years after leaving Texas he opened a trading post in northern Nebraska but ran afoul of authorities by selling liquor to the Sioux. Short dropped from sight to avoid arrest. Following the Dull Knife scare, Luke became a dispatch rider for the army, after which he drifted into Leadville, Colorado, as a full-time gambler. Eventually he came to Dodge City and plied his trade at the Long Branch. Then, as Wyatt Earp, Bat Masterson, and William Harris had done before him, Luke Short traveled to Tombstone. In February 1881 he killed a drunken gambler named Charlie Storms but was exonerated. Short turned his back on the faro tables of Arizona and returned to Dodge City.[19]

Despite later reports of his manhandling unruly customers at the Long Branch, Luke acted with restraint not evident during his encounter with Louis Hartman. Finding himself in a pistol duel with a man of Short's reputation must have proved sobering to the city clerk and newly elected justice of the peace. Certainly no gunman, Hartman earned his living primarily as a hotel keeper, having leased the Great Western late the previous summer.

The exiled Luke Short now sat in a Kansas City hotel room contemplating his future. His immediate plans seemed to rule out returning to Dodge City. Two of the banished, Lon Hyatt and Tom Lane, tried but met stiff resistance. Meanwhile, friends kept Luke informed about conditions in Dodge. Using stationary from the Bank of Dodge City, fellow saloonman Otto Mueller wrote:

> The situation here in town is unchanged except so far as relates to public opinion, which is gradually but steadily changing in your favor. . . . Of course every movement must be made with the greatest care and caution, and as many are too timid to express themselves, it will naturally require time,

---

[18] Ibid.

[19] For more on Luke Short's early life, and his troubles in Arizona, see William R. Cox, *Luke Short and His Era* (Garden City, N.Y.: Doubleday & Company, Inc., 1961), 9–81; and Shillingberg, *Tombstone, A.T.*, 190–91.

before the organization that style themselves 'the Vigilanters' will be convinced that they must give way to public opinion. And a beautiful lot of reformers they are, these vigilanters, under the leadership of their captain, Tom Nixon of Dance Hall fame. . . . Harris and his friends feel confident that Bob Wright on his return to town will take the lead against the suppression of further outrages, and I think also that he is the best man for it.[20]

Two days later, replying to a missive from Short, George M. Hoover wrote in a more pessimistic mood concerning a suggestion that Governor Glick might be persuaded to intercede against this abuse of due process. Hoover, at least at this stage of the crisis, thought it unlikely: "You know how a Governor acts. With the church element, the Railroad officials, and part of the so called immoral element against you, he would not interfere in the ruling of a city or mob ruling. My advice to you would be to either sell your interests in Dodge, or else employ some one to look after your interests here, and make up your mind to abandon Dodge at least during the present administration."[21]

Larned attorney Nelson Adams also wrote, cautioning against Luke's return, warning that the shotgun brigade was still searching the trains: "They swore vengeance against you as I understand it."[22] Because of the outlandish nature of the proceedings, and in no small measure due to Luke Short's proximity to its reporters, the press of eastern Kansas and the Missouri border embraced the tale with gusto. Early accounts favored the deposed Long Branch saloonman. Amid this blush of favorable publicity, Luke Short felt confident enough to travel to Topeka and lay his case before Governor Glick, encouraged that some voices of dissent were being heard in Dodge.

Amid the confusion Governor Glick sent for William F. Petillon, a thirty-seven-year-old New Yorker and rising star in Ford County's Democratic Party. As such he became a political go-between, helping Luke Short prepare his case for the governor's consideration. Petillon had come a long way since his arrival from Chicago six years before. He started out as a barber at Spearville, having run a barber shop and bathing rooms in the Windy City from the late 1860s with his brother, Henry, at places such as the Tribune Building and the Grand Pacific Hotel. A life-long Democrat,

---

[20] Otto Mueller to Luke Short, May 5, 1883. Governors' Correspondence, Dodge City War File, Archives Division, Kansas State Historical Society.

[21] George M. Hoover to Luke Short, May 7, 1883. Ibid.

[22] Nelson Adams to Luke Short, May 8, 1883. Ibid.

Petillon divided his time between trimming hair and political intrigue. Before traveling to Topeka, Short and Petillon closeted themselves in a Kansas City hotel room and pored over the wording of the petition to be presented to George Glick.

In the five-page notarized document, Short outlined the trouble as he saw it. After discussing the incident with Louis Hartman, and his subsequent arrest, the gambler added: "the cause of said act of violence was not anything that your petitioner had done against the law, but arose from political differences and Business rivalry." Short also named some of those, besides City Marshal Bridges, who came to the jail to assure his departure: Larry Deger, Fred Singer, Orlando A. "Brick" Bond, Thomas Nixon, Alonzo B. Webster, Bob Vanderburg, Clark Chipman, Louis C. Hartman, and "about twenty five others all being heavily armed."[23]

Studying the document, however self-serving in Luke's favor, Governor Glick sent an inquiry to Ford County sheriff George Hinkle. That officer's reply reached the Topeka telegraph office at 6:30 on the evening of May 11: "Mr. L. E. Deger our mayor has compelled several persons to leave the city for refusing to comply with the ordinances. No mob exists nor is there any reason to fear any violence as I am amply able to preserve the peace. I showed your message to Mr. Deger who requests me to say that the act of compelling the parties to leave the city was simply to avoid difficulty and disorders. Everything is as quiet here as in the capital of the state and should I find myself unable to preserve the present quiet will unhesitatingly ask your assistance."[24]

Five minutes later another telegram reached Topeka, signed by Robert Wright and rancher Richard J. Hardesty, claiming unusual calm throughout the city. Governor Glick, annoyed and unconvinced, sent an angry message to Sheriff Hinkle: "The accounts of the way things have been going on there are simply monstrous. . . . You tell me that the mayor has compelled several parties to leave the town for refusing to comply with the ordinances. Such a statement as that if true, simply shows that the mayor is unfit for his place, that he does not do his duty, and instead of occupying the position of peace maker, [he] starts out to head a mob to drive people away from their homes and their business."

[23] Luke L. Short to Hon. Geo. W. Glick, Prepared Statement, notarized in Jackson County, Missouri, May 10, 1883. Ibid.

[24] Telegram from Geo. T. Hinkle to Hon. G. W. Glick, received at Topeka, 6:30 P.M., May 11, 1883. Ibid.

The selective manner of enforcing ordinances troubled the governor: "ever since this pretence of the mayor that he was trying to enforce two ordinances against women visiting saloons, that he had prohibited it only as to one saloon, made arrests in one case, and permitted that ordinance to be violated every day and every night, to his own personal knowledge, and that of the marshal and police officers of the city, by other men who were running saloons where women are permitted to visit, and sing and dance."

Nor was it lost on Governor Glick that there should be no saloons in Dodge City in the first place: "It is also demanded and charged by parties who are now demanding the enforcement of the liquor law, that every saloon and dance hall in Dodge City must be suppressed, and there is coming up almost a universal demand over the state, that it shall be done, if I have to station a company of troops in the city of Dodge, and close up every saloon, and every drinking place, and every dance house in that city."[25]

The governor's threat to suppress every saloon and dance hall in Dodge chilled the gaiety along Front Street. He again reminded the sheriff of his responsibility to keep the peace even if the mayor failed to discharge his duties, and offered the resources of the state. For his part, Sheriff Hinkle seems to have missed the point about the absence of due process. He replied by telegram the following morning along the lines of his previous message: "Mr. Short's expulsion from the city is the direct result of his own action and the feeling of the people generally is very strong against him. The city is as quite now as it has ever been but I fear that if Mr. Short returns trouble will ensue."[26]

To keep up the pressure, Short and Petillon manipulated the press by granting numerous interviews. Their remarks did little to ease tension, for as one Topeka newspaper reported, "Mr. Webster, late mayor of Dodge City, is also a saloon keeper, and during his term of office removed from a more remote location to one next door to Harris & Short's 'Long Branch,' on Front street. . . . As a collateral incident it is asserted the Webster-Deger party promised Nixon, in consideration of his support in the election, not only that he should be unmolested in his dance house business, but that he should have no competitor in the city."[27]

The dance hall mentioned was the old Lady Gay, once owned by A. J.

---

[25] G. W. Glick to Geo. T. Hinkle, May 12, 1883. Ibid.

[26] Telegram from Geo. T. Hinkle to Hon. G. W. Glick, received at Topeka, 11:15 A.M., May 12, 1883. Ibid.

[27] *Topeka Daily Capital*, May 12, 1883.

Peacock and James Masterson and now run by Brick Bond and Tom Nixon. The reference to Webster's saloon, because of its importance to all the trouble, is worth describing in more detail. The location spoken of was a narrow building some 16½ feet wide, wedged between the Long Branch and Wright, Beverley & Company's two-story brick building on the corner of Front Street and Second Avenue. George M. Hoover and Henry V. Cook opened a sampling room and billiard hall there on June 1, 1877, called the Alamo. After Bob Wright sold the land under the Long Branch to Chalkley Beeson's wife, Ida, on March 2, 1878, D. D. Colley and J. M. Manion shifted their saloon operations into the space, with Beeson and Harris taking over the Long Branch. In late 1879 Dr. McCarty moved his City Drug Store from its original location east of Zimmerman's hardware into the old Alamo site. There he stayed until taking over Herman Fringer's old quarters at the post office in October of 1881.

It was only after McCarty moved out that Alonzo B. Webster took over the space, turning it back into a saloon called the Stock Exchange. By early March 1883 rumors told of Webster selling out to Beeson—who had dissolved his partnership with William H. Harris less than six weeks before—for five thousand dollars. Although the *Times* reported that Webster planned to move back to his original location at First Avenue—with Walter Straeter shifting his saloon business into the Dodge House, the deal fell through. Straeter stayed at the Old House, closing down in mid-April for a month-long remodeling.

Webster's arrangement with Beeson turned sour, for on April 12, 1883, the *Times* noted, "A. B. Webster returned from Kansas City, where he purchased a number of fine pictures to adorn the Stock Exchange." Elsewhere Klaine remarked, "The Stock Exchange has been nicely fitted up. The music stand is handsomely decorated with paper of the finest designs. The paper that adorns the walls cost several hundred dollars. The proprietor must expect handsome returns from the summer's business for the outlay in refitting the interior of his house." Then, as if to complete his occupancy, Webster bought the land under the refurbished Stock Exchange from Robert Wright on April 20, 1883, for three thousand dollars.[28] Webster's

---

[28] For changes involving this particular property, see Ford County Register of Deeds, Book A, 543–44 and Book D, 123–24. Also see *Dodge City Times*, June 2, 1877, March 15, April 12, May 3, 10, 1883; and *Ford County Globe*, March 13, April 24, 1883. Many accounts of the Dodge City War incorrectly identify Webster's place next to the Long Branch as the Alamo, not the Stock Exchange. It is also misstated that A. B. Webster, rather than Larry Deger, served as mayor during this period.

desire to recoup his investment, while trying to compete with the growing popularity of the Long Branch, helped precipitate the Dodge City War.

A number of leading citizens, including Democratic county chairman M. S. Culver, concluded the governor had been misinformed. They rushed a telegram on May 13, requesting that the adjutant general or some other reliable representative be sent out to investigate all aspects of the situation. As George Glick studied this latest message, he also pondered a more ominous development:

> Yesterday a new man arrived on the scene who is destined to play a part in a great tragedy. This man is Bat Masterson, ex-sheriff of Ford County, and one of the most dangerous men the West has ever produced. A few years ago he incurred the enmity of the same men who drove Short away, and he was exiled upon pain of death if he returned. His presence in Kansas City means just one thing, and that is he is going to visit Dodge City. Masterson precedes by twenty-four hours a few other pleasant gentlemen who are on their way to the tea party at Dodge. One of them is Wyatt Earp, the famous marshal of Dodge, another is Joe Lowe, otherwise known as "Rowdy Joe;" and still another is "Shotgun" Collins; but worse than all is another ex-citizen and officer of Dodge, the famous Doc Halliday [sic].[29]

To try and calm the situation, George Hoover, Robert Wright, and Chalkley Beeson rushed to Kansas City to confer with Luke Short and Bat Masterson. Although this trio remained closed-mouthed with the press, it was reported, "One of the committeemen said that if Short were to go back he would probably be allowed to remain unmolested long enough to settle his business affairs, but if he should insist upon staying there there

---

[29] *Kansas City Journal* (Missouri), May 15, 1883. Despite a questionable career, the Georgia-born, Pennsylvania-trained dentist-turned-gambler, John Henry "Doc" Holliday remains, at least within the confines of popular culture, one of those mythical, larger-than-life characters of the Old West. His stay in Dodge City, where he did set up a small dental office at the Dodge House during the summer of 1878, was brief—only "about seven months," according to his common law wife, Mary Katherine. Soon afterward, they traveled the gambling circuit through Trinidad and Leadville, Colorado, to Las Vegas, New Mexico, and Prescott, Arizona, before ending up in Tombstone. It was there that his later status as a quasi-historical personality found its roots. In 1881 Wyatt Earp acknowledged that Holliday, while in Dodge City, "came to my rescue and saved my life when I was surrounded by desperadoes," but details are sketchy, as are facts concerning any actual reappearance on the streets during the Dodge City War. Recollections of Mary Katherine [Holliday] Cummings, original in the John D. Gilchriese Collection; and Deposition of Wyatt S. Earp, November 16, 1881, Territory of Arizona vs. Morgan Earp et al., Defendants, Document No. 94, In Justice Court, Township No. 1, Cochise County, A.T. (Hayhurst typescript WPA), 138. Doc Holliday was still with Wyatt some months after the trouble in Dodge City; Earp's nine-year-old niece saw both men at her father's house at Garden City, Kansas. She remembered the visit as Holliday gave her a brightly colored rag-doll to mark the occasion. Wm. B. Shillingberg, "The John D. Gilchriese Collection: An Introduction," *Wyatt Earp, Tombstone, and the West from the Collections of John D. Gilchriese, Part I* (San Francisco: Johns' Western Gallery, 2004), 9.

would most likely be trouble, and his life would be in danger."[30] Wondering if any solution was possible, Sheriff Hinkle organized a forty-five-man posse to meet the westbound train, fearful that Short and Masterson might be aboard.

To counter sympathies for Luke Short, Mayor Deger, along with all five councilmen, the city marshal, the assistant marshal, city clerk, treasurer, city attorney, police judge, and city physician, presented their own version to the Topeka press corps. They attacked William Harris as "a gambler by profession and living in open adultery with a public prostitute, and the interest which he has in the town is merely of a local character.[31] He could close up and settle his affairs in one day. . . . He is a man whose character no respectable man in the community in which he lives would vouch for."[32] The group went on to vilify William F. Petillon for his involvement in the case of John S. McCarty, the escaped confidence man who had died of smallpox at Neil Brown's ranch, claiming the clerk had either lost or deliberately misplaced McCarty's bond.[33]

Many questioned these narrow characterizations of William H. Harris. His critics, in portraying him as a gambler, failed to mention his position as vice president of the Bank of Dodge City, or the fact that he was one of the wealthiest men in town. Luke Short took exception to all criticism of his partner—the foul insinuations issued by Deger and the others, all probably written by Mike Sutton.

Concerned over Sutton's involvement in the troubles brewing in Dodge City, the AT&SF's general solicitor, George R. Peck, telegraphed the attorney on May 17: "Parties will not return to Dodge. Considering your relation to the Company and our large interests at Dodge City I think you should hold yourself aloof from both parties to the existing troubles. Do everything you can to allay the excitement, and to prevent any hostility to the Company."[34] Peck must have read with alarm the charge published

---

[30] *Topeka Daily Capital*, May 16, 1883.

[31] Harris's behavior in this instance was not uncommon. Former mayor James Kelley lived with a woman of considerable bulk known as the Great Eastern, an allusion to an iron behemoth of the same name designed as a trans-Atlantic ocean liner. On the 1880 census, while still serving as city marshal, James Masterson was enumerated with his sixteen-year-old concubine, Minnie Roberts. Bat Masterson was shown living with nineteen-year-old Annie Ladue.

[32] *Topeka Daily Capital*, May 18, 1883.

[33] At the time of the controversy, it was reported: "It is said that the bond [three thousand dollars] never passed into the hands of the District Clerk, so he informs us." *Dodge City Times*, February 22, 1883.

[34] Telegram from Geo. R. Peck to M. W. Sutton sent via R. R. Line, May 17, 1883. Governors' Correspondence, Dodge City War File, Archives Division, Kansas State Historical Society.

three days later in Topeka's most influential daily: "The election resulted in favor of Deger, owing to the importation of illegal railroad votes by M. W. Sutton, the railroad attorney, who is a nephew [by marriage] of Webster, assisted by [H. T.] Drake, a self-constituted guardian of railroad votes."[35] The Santa Fe had enough worries with its roundhouse and machine shop accidentally destroyed by fire on March 9.[36]

Meeting with group after group representing the two factions, George Glick must have rolled his eyes and thrown up his hands in bewilderment. He concluded that what he needed most was a neutral observer. In despair he turned to the state's adjutant general, Thomas Moonlight. On May 18, under the headline "MOONBEAMS ON DODGE," the *Topeka Daily Capital* reported, "It was learned yesterday that Governor Glick had commissioned Col. Tom Moonlight Minister Plenipotentiary to Ford county, to negotiate a treaty by which peace might be restored to that distracted community, and that Col. Moonlight was on the ground." The good colonel carried out his inquiries for the governor on May 17.

Moonlight sent the governor three telegrams that day, the last arriving at Topeka a little past nine o'clock in the evening: "Short has a right to come to his home. There will be no open riot or assault. The sheriff will do his duty but cannot protect against private attack. This is Short's danger. The agreement secures Short publicly and privately. It will be the beginning for reconciliation & harmony will follow. I implore you to accept this beginning and time will do the rest. The sheriff is earnest but should excitement continue he cannot secure men to do his bidding. I again implore you to advise Short to return on the agreement. All his friends say so and they ought to know."[37]

Thanks to Moonlight's reports, officials felt vindicated. Without incident, Bat Masterson passed through Dodge City aboard the Santa Fe on May 21, heading for Colorado, while Short traveled to Caldwell. The exiled gambler impressed the locals: "Mr. Short is a quiet, unassuming man, with nothing about him to lead one to believe him the desperado the

[35] *Kansas Daily Commonwealth*, May 20, 1883.

[36] *Ford County Globe*, March 13, 1883; and *Dodge City Times*, March 15, 1883. In its report, the *Times* noted: "Two stationary engines were also rendered useless by the fire. . . . The material is on the ground for the building of an 18-stall round house of stone and we suppose work will be done this summer." The stone used came from the company's roundhouse at Trinidad, Colorado.

[37] Telegram from Thos. Moonlight to Gov. Geo. W. Glick, received at Topeka, 9:06 P.M., May 17, 1883. Governors' Correspondence, Dodge City War File, Archives Division, Kansas State Historical Society.

Dodge mob picture him to be."[38] This mood changed with a telegram from Sheriff Hinkle to the governor: "Can you send Col. Moonlight here tomorrow with power to organize company of militia? I have ample reasons for asking this which I will give to Col. Moonlight so that he can communicate them to you."[39]

Wyatt Earp's sudden appearance had unnerved Hinkle. Chiding Nick Klaine, Dan Frost wrote: "Wyatt Earp has returned to the city. Wonder if it has any political significance? Eh, Deacon?"[40] The pace of events quickened as fresh rumors piled atop old rumors. People waited for an open clash: "Masterson, Wyatt Earp, and all the sports in the country, held a meeting at Silverton and decided to take Dodge City by storm. Short is at Caldwell but will meet the party at Cimarron, 18 miles west of Dodge, perhaps Sunday night or soon after. Horses will be taken at Cimarron and the whole party will rendezvous at Mr. Oliver's [*sic*], two miles west of Dodge."[41]

Responding to a petition signed by forty-two concerned citizens, the governor authorized a company of the state militia mustered into service under the command of Harry E. Gryden; commissioned a major back in January as a reward for his years of service to the Democratic Party. Mayor Deger, George Hoover, Fred Singer, and Bob Wright asked the governor to reconsider. Thomas Moonlight implored the people of Dodge City to come to their senses. Appealing to their love of money, the adjutant general wrote Sheriff Hinkle on June 4: "The cattle men will soon begin to throng your streets, and all your citizens are interested in the coming— It is your harvest of business and affects every citizen, and I fear unless the spirit of fair play prevails it will work to your business injury."[42]

Luke Short stepped off the train at Dodge City on Sunday afternoon, June 2. Three days later the *Ford County Globe* speculated, "and we believe he has come to stay." Sheriff Hinkle worried that a fight was imminent. Two

---

[38] *Caldwell Journal*, May 24, 1883.

[39] Telegram from Geo. T. Hinkle to Geo. W. Glick, received at Topeka, 3:00 P.M., May 31, 1883. Governors' Correspondence, Dodge City War File, Archives Division, Kansas State Historical Society.

[40] *Ford County Globe*, June 5, 1883.

[41] *Kansas Daily Commonwealth*, June 5, 1883. The rendezvous point belonged to rancher Ison Prentice "Print" Olive. He refused support. As Olive's biographer explained, nine-year-old Albert Olive claimed he saw future Dodge City marshal Billy Tilghman "slap the face of the redoubtable Bat Masterson when Bat was said to have made a caustic remark concerning the use of the Olive barn being denied them in their 'ride on Dodge.' Print Olive never knew of the incident until much later. But it would not have affected his decision to stand by the element in Dodge wanting law and order and less of the saloon life to which it had become inured." Harry E. Chrisman, *The Ladder of Rivers: The Story of I. P. (Print) Olive* (Denver: Sage Books, 1962), 319.

[42] Thomas Moonlight to Geo. T. Hinkle, June 4, 1883. Correspondence of the Adjutant Generals, Archives Division, Kansas State Historical Society.

days after Short's arrival Mayor Deger issued a temporary proclamation against gambling. "No excitement resulted," observed the *Times* on June 7, "every one engaged in the unlawful practice submitting to the authority. This step was deemed a precautionary measure, and one intended to preserve good order in the city." On the evening of June 5 Gryden scribbled out a telegram to Colonel Moonlight that arrived in Topeka early the next morning: "Everything here settled. Parties have shook hands across the bloody chasm. A number of men with a record are here but all is lovely."[43]

Any relief was short-lived. Another telegram arrived for Governor Glick just two minutes after Gryden's rosy message to the adjutant general. Signed by Hinkle, Deger, Klaine, Zimmerman, Bob Wright, and councilman George Emerson, it read: "Our city is overrun with desperate characters from Colorado, New Mexico, Arizona and California. We cannot preserve the peace or enforce the laws. Will you send in two companies of militia at once to assist us in preserving the peace between all parties and enforcing the laws."[44]

Wishing by now that he had never heard of Dodge City, the governor sent a weary Thomas Moonlight back to that troubled community. He wired Harry Gryden to use the militia if necessary, but keep the peace at all costs. It proved unnecessary. Twenty minutes after Moonlight boarded the westbound train, Glick received the hoped-for message from Sheriff Hinkle: "The difficulty is settled. Shorts [*sic*] fighters have left town. I am satisfied we will not have any more trouble."[45]

Not everyone was gone. Bat Masterson, Wyatt Earp, W. F. McLain, Neil Brown, and Charlie Bassett—who had come down from Montana—joined with Short, Harris, and Petillon (described by Daniel Frost as the "distinguished bond extractor and champion pie eater") at the south side studio of photographer Charles A. Conkling. The resulting image of those eight somber-looking frontiersmen became famous as the Dodge City Peace Commission.[46] The invasion of these six-shooter celebrities caused the *Times* to reflect: "Within the past week the city had more dis-

---

[43] Telegram from H. E. Gryden to Thos. Moonlight, received at Topeka, 8:23 A.M., June 6, 1883. Governors' Correspondence, Dodge City War File, Archives Division, Kansas State Historical Society.

[44] Telegram to G. W. Glick, received at Topeka, 8:25 A.M., June 6, 1883. Ibid.

[45] Telegram from Geo. T. Hinkle to G. W. Glick, received at Topeka, 12:20 P.M., June 6, 1883. Ibid.

[46] This term received wide circulation. Some months later William H. Harris visited the nation's capital, prompting kind words from the local press: "W. H. Harris, Esq., vice president of the Bank of Dodge City, Kansas, and a member of the Peace Commission that summarily took the law in its own hands and quelled the lawlessness that prevailed in that city last summer, which will be well remembered by the readers of the Critic, is in the city and at the National." Washington, D.C., *Critic*, as quoted in *Ford County Globe*, January 29, 1884.

tinguished visitors and more ex-city and county officers in it than we ever
saw together at any one time. It was a regular reunion of old-timers."[47]
Masterson and Earp left town on June 10.

The day before, a Topeka newspaper had reprinted a letter from Masterson describing the atmosphere. Not surprisingly Bat claimed not to
have found "a single individual who participated with the crowd" to force
Luke Short's removal.[48] Most of them had left town soon after Wyatt
Earp and the others arrived. With the departure of those "distinguished
visitors," the reformers felt it safe to show their faces. These included
Michael Sutton, who years before enjoyed regaling listeners with stories of
his Civil War exploits. In light of all this brave talk, Dan Frost could not
help having fun at Sutton's expense: "As soon as Bat Masterson alighted
from the train into this city Mike Sutton started for his cyclone building
on Gospel Ridge, where he remained until a truce was made."[49] For a time
Frost referred to the embarrassed attorney as "Cyclone Mike."

Peace had returned to Dodge City. To assure that harmony continued,
Colonel Moonlight authorized the organization of a local militia company, called—appropriately enough—the Glick Guards. The state
enrolled forty-six men. Patrick Sughrue served as captain, with Peter
Harding first lieutenant, James H. Kelley second lieutenant, Henry Wright
ordnance sergeant, and Dr. Samuel Galland as surgeon. The forty-one
remaining members of the rank-and-file included Luke Short himself,
along with William H. Harris, Neil Brown, W. F. Petillon, William Tilghman, Clark Chipman, and I. P. Olive.[50] The Dodge City War had ended,
but its repercussions persisted. Despite Luke Short's triumphant return,
Dodge City could not force the genie of reform back into its bottle.

---

[47] *Dodge City Times*, June 12, 1883.

[48] *Daily Kansas State Journal*, June 9, 1883.

[49] *Ford County Globe*, June 12, 1883. In that same issue Frost reprinted an item from the *Larned Optic*: "Mike Sutton,
my lord is an exoduster from Dodge. On the return of Luke Short and his friends, it didn't take Mike long to arrive
at the conclusion that Kinsley was a much healthier locality, and that town is now his abiding place. Net [Attorney
Nelson Adams] sends greetings to Mike, and a notification that Larned is quarantined against him. When Dodge
becomes too hot for Mike Sutton h—l itself would be considered a cool place—a desirable summer resort."

[50] *Dodge City Times*, August 30, 1883. For a comprehensive collection of the various documents and newspaper
articles relating to the Dodge City War, see Miller and Snell, *Why the West Was Wild*, 519–65; and "Dodge City 'War'
of May, 1883," Microfilm, Kansas State Historical Society, 1959.

Chapter 11

REFORM VS. REALITY

As the Dodge City War ran out of steam, the mayor demoted Assistant Marshal Clark Chipman back to policeman, eventually removing him from the force altogether. Not everyone was pleased,[1] but it seemed a reasonable response to speculation blaming some of the recent troubles on Deger's refusal to pacify William H. Harris.[2] The city then appointed "Mysterious Dave" Mather to fill the assistant marshal vacancy, a rather poor choice from those preaching reform.

Mather always seemed to be emerging from the shadows, having associated with such notorious characters as Dave Rudabaugh and Dutch Henry Born. Over the years he stood accused of everything from horse theft to train robbery, yet he did serve as an officer from time to time. In early 1880 he and Charlie Bassett prospected for gold in Colorado. At Fort Worth, authorities charged him with stealing. He had been to Texas before, running afoul of the law at Mobeetie with another Dodge City luminary: town marshal Jim McIntire recalled Mather and Wyatt Earp swindling gullible citizens with the old gold brick scam before he kicked them out of town.[3]

Mysterious Dave was still in Texas in late March 1883. Sixty days later he became Dodge City's assistant marshal at seventy-five dollars a month. Mather had not been in office thirty days before a complaint reached the governor's desk: "I was assaulted and abused on the Public Streets because I was not a Blackleg and gambler by the Officer and one of his Subordinate's [sic] They are running this town and a Decent Family Cannot be

---

[1] One of the dissatisfied wrote the *Ford County Globe* on July 17, 1883: "Why was C. E. Chipman put off of the police force. A man that was as good an officer as ever was on the force, and the only man that had any interest in the city, the only officer that pays a cent of taxes. . . . Look at the condition of our town. Has there been any reform about which Deger puffed and blowed so much? An ignorant man is not competent to tell what to do. That is what is the matter with our mayor."

[2] *Daily Kansas State Journal*, May 17, 1883. Also see Miller and Snell, *Why the West Was Wild*, 109.

[3] Jim McIntire, *Early Days in Texas; A Trip to Hell and Heaven* (Kansas City, Mo.: McIntire Publishing Company, 1902), 131–32. For details on how this incredulous scam worked, see John Philip Quinn, *Gambling and Gambling Devices* (Canton, Ohio: J. P. Quinn Co., 1912), 248–57.

Tolerated by them or their Minions the aforesaid officer was taken from a Cold Deck Table and made Assistant Marshal inside of a few hours and no questions asked. . . . [T]he Town is being run by such a Class and the State of Kansas or anyone does not say Boo."[4] There is no record of George Glick's response, if indeed there was one. Perhaps he was sick of hearing about troubles in Dodge City.

At least Mather took the job. Turning his back on the town's troubles and his own responsibilities, Sheriff George T. Hinkle sold his house and furnishings to Charles Heinz, owner of the Lone Star saloon and restaurant, and moved on to Garden City to get into the liquor business.[5] Hinkle finished his term in office, but most of the day-to-day work fell to Under Sheriff Fred Singer.

Louis Hartman gave up any ideas of helping keep the peace. Having traded pistol shots with Luke Short, the repentant Hartman retired to his justice court. He opened a tobacco shop in the Railroad Land Office after Samuel Galland took back the Great Western Hotel in early September. Hartman then moved into Sutton and Wenie's old office next to the post office. The two lawyers had found space in Bob Wright's building. Others, too, moved up from the south side to that rarified atmosphere north of the tracks. Photographer Charles Conkling, who had recorded for posterity the Dodge City Peace Commission, abandoned his canvas studio for a more substantial location on Chestnut Street, just east of the *Times* near the corner of Third Avenue.[6]

As in the past, many questioned the police force and its cost. On July 6 the mayor and council raised salaries for the city marshal to $150 and his assistant to $125. For the month of June, even before the increase, the city paid out $538.50 for police services, including bonuses for Jack Bridges and Dave Mather. During that same period Police Judge R. E. Burns collected $636 in fines. Nicholas Klaine helped boost the total by forking over $10 and costs for engaging in a public brawl. He had attacked the visiting editor of the *Garden City Herald*.

---

[4] James De Grass to Gov. George W. Glick, June 30, 1883. Governors' Correspondence, Archives Division, Kansas State Historical Society, as quoted in Miller and Snell, *Why the West Was Wild*, 454.

[5] *Ford County Globe*, July 24, 1883. The paper's editor got it right, claiming a price of eighteen hundred dollars. Ford County Register of Deeds, Book E, 254–55. Warranty Deed, Annie C. Hinkel and Geo. T. Hinkel to Charles Heinz, July 20, 1883. The property is described as Lot 12, Block 27.

[6] Conkling bought this location—the south fifty feet of Lot 28, Block 3, previously occupied by the Robbins tailor shop—from George Hoover and his wife for $275 on September 8, 1883. Ford County Register of Deeds, Book D, 156. Conkling did not open for business, however, until the end of October.

Police were criticized after the death of a cowboy named John Ballard. In an incident reminiscent of the George Hoy affair five years before, Ballard and two companions rode south along Second Avenue toward the Arkansas River bridge in the early evening of July 9. Reaching Bond and Nixon's dance hall, two of them pulled revolvers and started shooting, mostly into the air. City and county officers responded, firing at the trio as they rode for the bridge. Ballard fell from his horse near the river. A six-man coroner's jury concluded the cowboy died from a gunshot fired by one of his companions: "The ball entered the right cheek, and came out on the left side of the neck, two or three inches below where the ball entered on the right side."[7]

Frost blamed Deger for failing to enforce the law against carrying weapons: "If such men were compelled to lay aside their arms before they got under the influence of strong drink, much trouble might be avoided."[8] The council had amended the ordinance during Webster's regime, raising the fine for carrying weapons from twenty-five dollars to one hundred.[9] As with the 1876 law, its provisions were too often ignored. Editor Klaine remarked, "The custom of the border should be modified, and the pistol given up. There is a disposition to do away with the carrying of firearms, and we hope the feeling will become general. The carrying of firearms is a barbarous custom, and it is time the practice was broken up."[10]

While increasing police salaries, the council passed an ordinance against using opium, or even maintaining premises where the drug was consumed. Less than two weeks later Judge Burns levied the maximum one hundred dollars against one Chinese proprietor and fifty dollars against his associates, after "the city officers swept down on the evil in the night when the aroma of the den was stifling, and the wooers of the horrible were inhaling the dangerous poison."[11] After this exotic interlude, officers arrested E. R. Foley for shooting fellow Dodge House dishwasher Frank McBride. Reports blamed the incident on the mishandling of a small pistol, conclud-

---

[7] *Dodge City Times*, July 12, 1883.

[8] *Ford County Globe*, July 10, 1883.

[9] Ordinance No. 67, Sec. I, August 14, 1882. Dodge City Ordinances, Book A, 128. This act specified that no one could "carry concealed or otherwise about his or her person, any pistol, bowie knife, slung shot, or other dangerous or deadly weapons, except County, City, or United States officers." For the earlier provisions, approved by Mayor Hoover and the city council on September 22, 1876, see Ordinance No. 16, Sec. II, ibid., 27.

[10] *Dodge City Times*, July 12, 1883.

[11] Ibid., July 19, 1883. Also see *Ford County Globe*, July 24, 1883; and Ordinance No. 74, "An Ordinance to Amend Ordinance No. 70," Sec. 1 and 2, July 6, 1883. Dodge City Ordinances, Book A, 139.

ing: "The boys regret the circumstances and so do the citizens."[12] In July
the police court collected over nine hundred dollars in fines.

Larry Deger had more on his mind than the police. On the evening of
July 18, the thirty-eight-year-old "slimmed down" chief executive (then tip-
ping the scales at only 284 pounds) married Etta Engleman, a woman twelve
years his junior. Baptist minister N. G. Collins performed the ceremony at
the groom's home, which was outside the eastern edge of town. Therein lay
the rub: Deger's residence lay outside the city limits. Returning from a hon-
eymoon tour of Colorado, the mayor found himself in hot water. The *Globe*,
still resentful about Dan Frost's similar troubles, declared the mayor's office
vacant while calling for an emergency election. Deger outwitted them all. He
and the council passed an ordinance incorporating the whole area, thereafter
known as Wright's Addition, into the city. This four-block rectangle, northeast of the Railroad Avenue–Front Street intersection and below the residential development along Military Avenue, included Larry Deger's house.[13]

A strange sight transfixed townspeople on a Sunday morning in early
August. Along with several dozen soldiers, a band of 357 Indians, including former warriors, together with their women and children (14 Arapahoes and the rest Northern Cheyennes), rode through town and camped
six miles west. They came from Fort Reno, Indian Territory, and were on
their way to the Pine Ridge Agency near their old home in the Dakotas.
Included were Wild Hog and Crow, two men remembered from the Dull
Knife raid in 1878. Times had changed. Gone were those outbursts of violence that so often characterized contacts with Indians at Dodge City in
the early days. The contrast was unmistakable: "The cavalcade as it passed
through our city furnished no little amusement to our people, many of
whom had never before seen a real live Indian. Everybody was out and saw
them pass, and no less than one hundred people from the city paid them
a personal visit after they got into camp, where they became more familiar
with the life and habits and general characteristics of the 'noble red man'
while in camp. It was a gala day for those who never had seen the like
before, while old plainsmen had no especial cause to change their minds ·

---

[12] *Dodge City Times*, July 26, 1883.

[13] Ford County Marriages, Book A, 125; *Ford County Globe*, July 31, 1883; *Dodge City Times*, August 2, 1883; and Ordinance No. 76, August 8, 1883. Dodge City Ordinances, Book A, 142–43. On August 7 the *Ford County Globe* reported:
"As there are but two male residents upon this tract . . . we imagine they will have but little difficulty in getting their
names to the petition required. But as this move will bring in more taxable property within the city limits, we rather
favor the move." A week later the paper added, "The country residence of Hon. L. E. Deger has been attached as
an addition to our city. The monster petition was signed by one name, 'only this and nothing more.'"

on a band of roving refugees that have cost this government millions of money and thousands of lives."[14]

More pressing realities broke the spell of this historic interlude. Fearful of the effect Deger's reforms might have on business, several citizens called for an August 13 mass meeting at Kelley's hall. Supporters passed out hand-bills urging attendance that evening at 7:30. George Hoover gaveled the meeting to order. Richard Evans served as chairman, with jeweler and watchmaker Adolphus Gluck (who had come to town in 1879) chosen secretary. It did not take long to get down to business. Five resolutions were passed, the main thrust of protest outlined in item number four:

> RESOLVED, That we believe any interference by our city authorities with the present manner of the saloon proprietors and their employees in conducting their business, will be unjust to them, detrimental to the interest of our city and its merchants and citizens generally, and a movement in bad faith with the well-known understanding as to the enjoyment of certain liberties and privileges for which the city government have heretofore, and do now demand and receive monthly a money consideration.[15]

A committee carried copies of these resolutions to Mayor Deger and the city council. Back at Kelley's joint the faithful listened to speeches from William Harris and Alonzo Webster, who had broken with Deger over the mayor's pious handling of the saloon question. Dan Frost seemed to have his head in the clouds: "We hope and believe that a better feeling and greater harmony now prevails among all parties, and that our law-makers will not lend a deaf ear to the wishes of the community."[16] Deger did exactly that. Supporting the mayor, editor Klaine called the results meaningless: "Those resolutions are about as intelligent as mud."[17]

Luke Short's victory in moving back into the Long Branch strengthened the reformers. The gambler missed the point and swore out a complaint against Judge Burns, charging, "misconduct in office and the collection of illegal fees." He caused the judge to be arrested but Short's dreams of revenge fizzled.

---

[14] *Ford County Globe*, Supplement, August 7, 1883.

[15] *Ford County Globe*, August 14, 1883. Organizers called the meeting because they felt "certain parties are again agitating our city by urging the authorities to take action detrimental to the business interest of the community." Memories of the turmoil caused by the Dodge City War would not fade.

[16] Ibid.

[17] *Dodge City Times*, August 16, 1883. Editor Klaine took other pot shots at the saloon and gambling crowd, claiming: "Gambling in Dodge is on the ragged edge," and "Gambling in Dodge needs considerable bolstering." The summer of 1883 remained a period of hard feelings.

The case came before Justice R. G. Cook, who dismissed it on motion of the county attorney, fulfilling Klaine's prophecy: "The arrest of Judge Burns will not accomplish the purpose desired. On the contrary, law-breakers will feel the full power of justice." Reminding his readers of Short's confrontation with Louis Hartman, Klaine concluded, "Threats of assassination will not deter the administration of the law."[18] A week later he reported County Attorney Whitelaw's examination of the judge's docket and the dismissal of all charges, adding, "Burns will continue to inflict evil doers with the penalty of the law. This officer may not perhaps show enough leniency, but a soft heart is not equal to trying circumstances. . . . Judge Burns plunges the official harpoon into all alike. His severity may not be according to taste, but it is in keeping with the exigency of the situation."[19]

More distant rumblings for reform could be heard, carrying with them heavier weight than any rulings from Judge Burns. The AT&SF lined up with the reformers in demanding change. Considering the predatory reputations of most western railroads, this sudden concern for righteousness strikes one as somewhat hypocritical. Directors floated rumors of shifting many prized facilities to other locations if Dodge City did not heed their advice. Worried, a seven-man delegation headed by Robert Wright rushed to Topeka to learn details of the company's plans first hand.

Most of those in attendance found the proposals reasonable, with Dan Frost noting: "They have never demanded that saloons should be closed in Dodge; that gambling should cease; that houses of prostitution should be closed. . . . they have simply requested that our saloons and other places of business be closed on the Sabbath day; that gaming be removed from the public gaze; that women of easy virtue keep in their own places of business and not ply their calling upon our streets. In short, to reverse the picture and hide the evil that now exists, and show up the bright side to the public gaze."[20]

Mayor Deger and the council took the railroad at its word, passing an ordinance on September 5 ordering all businesses to close on Sundays. Mindful of the Long Branch controversy, five days earlier they had out-

[18] Ibid., August 23, 1883.
[19] Ibid., August 30, 1883.
[20] *Ford County Globe*, September 4, 1883.

lawed "vocal or instrumental Music in any Concert Hall or other public place . . . for purposes other than Literary or Scientific."[21]

Preachers welcomed the news, even as they prayed for more resistance to sinners. Nicholas Klaine, forgetting his vocal support for Mayor Kelley's philosophy of openness, noted, "The closing of public places in Dodge City, Sunday, did not augment the church attendance, but the salutary condition was pleasing notwithstanding."[22] Responding to an apparent rekindling of Christian virtues, the *Times* began printing summaries of sermons, though not without jibes from the *Ford County Globe*. Klaine tried defending himself: "We give considerable space to the Sunday doings in Dodge. . . . If there is anything else going on besides the church on Sundays we are not informed, for we do not take the pains to find out."[23]

With reform impossible to ignore, both Republican and Democratic central committees met at the courthouse within an hour of each other on the afternoon of September 8. Following maneuver and debate, both decided against proposing separate lists of party candidates for the county elections. The races would be decided by each voter's personal opinion of the candidates and their stand on municipal reform. Daniel Frost held on as chairman of the Republican Committee, despite challenges from Nicholas Klaine and Mike Sutton. Klaine tried tying Frost to the Democrats: "a few of the members of the Ford county Republican central committee also belong to the Glick Guards, a Democratic battalion, designed to boost Gov. Glick's political interests. Frost's name does not appear on the roll of the Guards, but the names of some of the committee do appear there. . . . The Republicans of Ford county are in a bad fix when the party is left to the control of Democrats and renegade Republicans."[24]

Klaine drew distinctions where none existed. The major topics in the fall of 1883 were reform and the saloon trade. Klaine and Sutton may have embraced the state Republican Party's stand on Prohibition, but other party members voiced opposition to that legislation and what seemed to

---

[21] Ordinance No. 77, Sec. 2, August 31, 1883. Dodge City Ordinances, Book A, 144–45. For closing businesses on Sunday, see Ordinance No. 78, September 5, 1883. Ibid., 146–47. Klaine got somewhat carried away with the railroad's involvement in all this, writing in the *Dodge City Times* on August 30: "We are glad the company is taking so much interest in Dodge. The company has a perfect right to do so—the company has considerable property and pays heavy taxes. It is entitled to the voice of one hundred men, and we hope it will exercise that privilege."

[22] *Dodge City Times*, September 6, 1883.

[23] Ibid., September 20, 1883.

[24] Ibid., September 13, 1883.

them other excessive reforms. These, then, remained the issues, not the supposed function or political composition of the Glick Guards.

Dodge City then witnessed a double killing at a small Negro dance hall and boarding house near the Arkansas River bridge. The victims turned out to be the proprietor, William Smith, and a customer named William Hilton. Indeed, Hilton was free on $3,000 bond, having been charged with murder in Barber County. At Smith's dance hall late in the evening of October 7, Hilton berated one of the inmates. Smith intervened to protect his girls. Hilton pulled a revolver and fired three fatal shots. Patrons responded by killing Hilton. Both men were buried in Prairie Grove Cemetery. This particular dance hall had been the scene of trouble before—three months earlier Judge Burns fined Smith $41.50 for keeping a bawdy house on the premises, and also fined three women there $5.50 each, charged with "indecent exposure of person."[25]

Such affairs encouraged the self-righteous. Describing an exodus of prostitutes to Caldwell, Klaine remarked, "What is Dodge's loss is Caldwell's gain."[26] Frost countered, "While the thieves and prostitutes are quietly departing from Dodge City, it would be a Gods blessing for this community if old 'Nick' would go too. We do not wish to place him in the above category, owing to our respect for the thieves and prostitutes."[27] Some of this moral fervor seemed less than equitable. It must have galled whiskey dealers from Coolidge, then under jurisdiction of the Ford County District Court, to read saloon and liquor advertisements in both Dodge City newspapers while they awaited fines as high as one hundred dollars for selling spirits, "contrary to law."

Frost called for a People's Delegate Convention the day after the killing of Smith and Hilton. Klaine charged the whole process rigged by opponents of reform. The convention chose a list of candidates headed by Patrick Sughrue for sheriff. He and the others received the backing of the *Ford County Globe*. Five days later opponents held their own convention under the banner of the Peoples' County Ticket. Supporters included Larry Deger, Bob Wright, A. B. Webster, and Democratic Party county chairman M. S. Culver. They selected Fred Singer to run for sheriff and received the warm support of the *Dodge City Times*.

---

[25] *Ford County Globe*, July 10, October 9, 1883; and *Dodge City Times*, July 12, October 11, 1883.

[26] *Dodge City Times*, September 6, 1883.

[27] *Ford County Globe*, September 11, 1883.

Despite an assertion in the *Times* on November 1 that "The election contest up to this date has been a sort of quiet affair," opponents made it interesting. Rumor suggested Sughrue planned to name Bat Masterson his under sheriff, the implication being a return to gang rule. Sughrue answered with a disclaimer, "not that Mr. Masterson wouldn't be fully competent and acceptable to a great many people in this county, but he is not a resident of this state and has no intention of becoming such," adding: "I am sure, however, that he would reflect as much credit to the office as Mysterious Dave, who will be Mr. Singer's right-hand man."[28] Sughrue then found himself named in a lawsuit, along with William H. Harris, to recover the bond forfeited in the old Jack McCarty case.[29]

Frost came out swinging against the Peoples' County Ticket, charging that "The fact that old 'Nick,' old Zimmerman, old Burns, Jim O'Neill, 'Wright's Bullard,' and Sutton are supporting the Singer ticket . . . ought to be enough to defeat it."[30] He then singled out Zimmerman for personal attack. The hardware man had pulled his advertising from the *Globe* in late September, helping turn the editor against him.

In a special session on October 27, the county commissioners announced returns from a special election on whether to spend thirty-five hundred dollars on a county poor house. The measure failed, but Frost asked, "What will Zimmerman do with the lot of bad lumber he has on hand and which he tried to force on the tax payers of the county with his little poor house scheme[?]" Zimmerman had also supported the successful plan to abolish the separate election precinct south of the tracks and have it absorbed into Dodge precinct. Frost attacked Zimmerman's involvement, charging that "Wright and Klaine own and control Zimmerman's every action. He belongs to them, body and soul, and he is no longer the free and fair man the people thought him to be. Had he the power he would at once declare himself king of the county."[31]

Zimmerman painted the editor as an ingrate, bringing up some embarrassing episodes from Frost's past, including his arrest for possession of stolen government property: "and only through the united efforts of the

---

[28] Ibid., October 16, 1883.

[29] Ford County Commissioners Journals, Book A, 424. Also see *Dodge City Times*, November 1, 1883. The commissioners considered all this during a special meeting held on October 25. Since McCarty was dead, the case was dismissed, but not until after the election.

[30] *Ford County Globe*, October 30, 1883.

[31] Ibid., Supplement, November 6, 1883.

respectable citizens, for humanity sake, for his family and relations, suc-
ceeded in keeping him from the penitentiary, where he belongs, long ago.
We even helped him with money to defray his expenses and attorney fees.
I even went around with a petition to parties he could not go to, to get
their signatures for his release; and this slanderer and vilifier now abuses
me."[32] Zimmerman reminded everyone of his efforts to help finance the
Ford County Globe as an opposition newspaper, since neither Frost nor
William Morphy had the money to do so.

While attacking Zimmerman, Frost claimed Mike Sutton and Fred
Singer were conspiring to intimidate voters, having told the county commissioners "That they—meaning the Singer faction—would have fifty
deputy sheriff's [*sic*] at the polls on election day." The editor, who elsewhere increased that number to sixty, allowed his imagination to get the
better of him, as no one believed fifty deputies would show up. Still, in his
attempt to portray his rivals as irresponsible, Frost implied that Sughrue
voters could expect violence: "The opposition are already putting their
artillery in order for election day. We noticed ten or a dozen pocket pistols
on the work bench of F. C. Zimmerman, on which repairs are needed."[33]

Frost tossing out political bombshells at weekly intervals produced an
unexpected result. Early on the morning of November 4 someone burglar-
ized his composing rooms and took revenge, smashing the press and
destroying much of the type. Frost also lost copies of his November 6
issue. Of those printed in advance for mailing to out-of-town subscribers,
only one copy is known to have survived. The infuriated editor gathered
up enough type to print a small four-column, single-sheet extra on
November 5. Frost labeled the person responsible a coward, a villain, and
a dirty scoundrel! while squelching a rumor that he had destroyed his own
property to create sympathy for the Sughrue ticket. In fairness, the *Times*

---

[32] *Dodge City Times*, November 1, 1883. Zimmerman went on to claim: "Where at Kit Carson [Colorado] D. M. Frost was in partnership with the postmaster there. A fire started in the neighborhood of [the] postoffice and the postoffice was consumed by fire; after which these worthies swore out a statement that they had no time to save $1,700 worth of U. S. postage stamps, when it was proved without a doubt that they saved a barrel of whisky. Fur-ther, when D. M. Frost was postmaster at Syracuse [Kansas] he paid his little bills with U.S. postage stamps. This is the record of the man who slanders respectable citizens."

[33] *Ford County Globe*, Supplement, November 6, 1883. Elsewhere Frost advised, "The artillery left with F. C. Zimmerman for repairs, last week, have all been called for, and are now carried in the hip pockets of the sixty deputy sheriff's [*sic*]."

condemned the incident, with Nicholas Klaine challenging, "Let the Scoundrel be hunted down."[34]

On Election Day Frost brought out a two-page supplement rich with sharp attacks against the opposition. He used three columns to answer Zimmerman's earlier response in the *Times*, rehashing charges of ballot stuffing in a school election, as well as the hardware merchant's own arrest for possessing stolen government property. Refusing to back off, Frost, as an added insult, reprinted the petition dated August 18, 1880, that supported him while condemning Bat Masterson's "unwarrantable charge" regarding his own troubles along those lines. Of course Zimmerman's name headed the list of two-dozen citizens, including Robert M. Wright, then standing with the editor. Despite the harshness of the campaign, Frost had reason to celebrate. Election results, with only two exceptions—register of deeds and the coroner's office—favored the Sughrue ticket. Fred Singer lost his race for sheriff by 145 votes.[35] Confident of victory, Nicholas Klaine was shaken, claiming the outcome "a complete surprise."

Disappointed but undaunted, the editor remarked: "The TIMES will continue in the course we have marked out, and will not flinch one iota. We are for moral reform, in favor of just and equitable laws, a proper restraint of vice, the observance of Sunday, and decency and good order generally. The result of Tuesday does not influence our course. We shall pursue the even tenor of our way, unbiased, and unprejudiced without fear and without favor."[36] For all their show of taking the high road, Klaine and his allies would have to wait. Dodge City did not yet feel the need to join the ranks of the righteous, disregarding an earlier plea: "all this talk that Dodge City must be a hell hole in order to succeed, is all bosh."[37]

In a conciliatory mood, Frost reported that Bat Masterson and Wyatt Earp had "quietly and unostentatiously dropped in onto our inhabitants early last Tuesday morning, and their presence about the polls on that day had a moral effect on our would-be moral element, that was truly surpris-

---

[34] *Dodge City Times*, November 8, 1883. In another column Klaine expanded his feelings: "As a matter of justice we hope citizens will not let this matter rest until the affair had been probed to the bottom. The laws of this country allow the freedom of the press. If an editor commits blunders or willfully slanders people, there is redress. If he pursues the wrong policy the people apply the remedy and withhold support."

[35] Ford County Commissioners Journals, Book A, 430–32.

[36] *Dodge City Times*, November 8, 1883.

[37] Ibid., October 18, 1883.

ing. It is needless to say every thing passed off quietly at the city precinct on election day."[38]

Reminiscent of George Hoover's status when he ran for mayor, Patrick Sughrue got elected sheriff of Ford County without American citizenship; the thirty-nine-year-old Irishman was not naturalized until March 1887.[39] A month later Sughrue sold his share of a blacksmith shop to Bob Wright and P. W. Beamer. Taking over the sheriff's office, Sughrue moved his family into the jailor's quarters.

Wright became so wrapped up in new businesses he hardly noticed the political dust settling. He rented his hotel to rival George B. Cox, who reinstalled W. H. LyBrand as manager and had John Giggs take over LyBrand's duties at the Dodge House. Wright had already resigned as president of the Dodge City Town Company, receiving a resolution of thanks and a claim from the *Times* that "no man has done more for the prosperity of Dodge City than Hon. R. M. Wright."[40]

Changes were also taking place within the ranks of the gambling and saloon crowd. Following all the turmoil of the Dodge City War, William H. Harris and Luke Short faced reality and sold the Long Branch to Roy Drake and Frank Warren on November 18. Harris stayed in town, devoting himself to his banking and cattle interests, but Luke Short knew it was time to leave. He had canvassed the gambling circuit in Texas and returned to Fort Worth with Bat Masterson. Ten days before councilman H. T. Drake had asked if "anything had been done towards having the dance halls closed [as] it was mutually agreed between the proprietors . . . that they were to close after November 1st, 1883."[41] Drake and other reformers would have to wait months for an official response.

Not all the news from 1883 concerned smallpox, saloon wars, political battles, and social reform. Cattle still reigned supreme. By December 18, despite a slow start, railroad yardmaster and amateur politician H. T. Drake reported 75,769 head shipped from Dodge City aboard 3,443 cars from June 7 through December 5. October proved the peak month with 31,517. Stockyard workers also loaded 600 sheep and 410 horses. The AT&SF shipped

---

[38] *Ford County Globe*, November 13, 1883.

[39] Records of the Ford County District Court, Declaration of Intend, 173; and Final Naturalization Records, 95. When Sughrue's twin brother, Michael, unsuccessfully ran for sheriff in 1881, he did so as a citizen, being naturalized in June. Both men had fought for the Union during the Civil War, Patrick with an Illinois regiment, and Michael from Kansas. They came to Dodge City from Leavenworth.

[40] *Dodge City Times*, October 11, 1883.

[41] "Council Meeting," Ibid., November 15, 1883.

back 8.64 million pounds of civilian goods and 3.5 million pounds of military supplies, to the benefit of Dodge City's freighting industry.

Through cattle, numbering in the tens of thousands, helped make 1883 the most prosperous year to date in the town's long association with the Texans. Looking to the future, the *Globe* championed the advantages of building slaughterhouses near Dodge City. Instead of wasting railroad space on live animals, the newsman reasoned, "forty carcasses could be placed in a refrigerator car and transported to any market reached by live stock in the east for exactly the same money as twenty five steers would cost."[42] Some warmed to the idea, but others recognized the dangers. They knew the Texas trade could not last forever. Besides, eastern packinghouses were not about to surrender their valuable monopoly to some frontier outpost.

Some saw an easier way to make money in the cattle business—steal some cattle. In late August William Byrd shipped eighteen stolen head and was arrested. The court set bond at six thousand dollars. Harry Gryden thought that figure excessive. James Whitelaw and Michael Sutton, representing the state, argued otherwise. The court reduced the amount to four thousand dollars. Byrd disagreed with everyone and skipped out for Texas five weeks later, much to the disgust of the Western Kansas Stock Growers' Association, which offered a reward of one thousand dollars. Embarrassed, Byrd's bondsmen, including Robert Wright, sent Dave Mather in pursuit. The assistant marshal's failure to apprehend his man prompted Frost to report on November 27: "Dave Mathews [*sic*] returned home yesterday from his trip to Texas, but minus the 'Byrd,' who is still in the bush. We said HE WOULD return without him, and so he did." The wanted man eluded capture for another seven months.

As Frost and Klaine growled and bickered, Democrats organized their own newspaper. Both the *Dodge City Times* and *Ford County Globe*, their personal feuds notwithstanding, represented interests of the Republican Party. Republicans had been gaining strength, but Ford County remained largely Democratic. The new paper organized as a joint stock venture known as the Dodge City Democrat Publishing Company, with George M. Hoover president. Robert Wright's former associate Charles H. Lane (having returned from Caldwell) became secretary and editor, with Dr.

---

[42] *Ford County Globe*, September 25, 1883. Belaboring the point, Frost asked a week later, "is there a point in the entire State of Kansas that would be more accessible by rail, closer to the feeding grounds, and in every way more suitable for the establishment of slaughtering houses than Dodge City? Not one. A point that sends forth to the markets of the east from 60,000 to 75,000 head of beef cattle annually is certainly worthy of consideration."

Samuel Galland serving as treasurer. James Whitelaw and William Petillon sat as company directors, with the latter fronting as business manager.

Hoover and the others rented the former Railroad Land Office, south of the tracks, and moved in the old press and type from the *Garden City Herald.* The *Dodge City Democrat* marked its debut on December 29, 1883, proclaiming: "the endeavor shall be to make the paper all that the name implies, a paper of and for the people, controlled by no clique and sub-servient to no class. The general oversight of the course of the publication is lodged in the hands of men of whose Democracy, patriotism and incor-ruptibility there can be no question in this community." Many were skep-tical. Klaine admitted the new paper "had good prospects for success," but decried its stand against Prohibition. After Charlie Rath hired Lane away to manage his business at Mobeetie, D. J. Van Meter became editor.

Not only did the new paper disagree with the *Times* on Prohibition, it also poked fun at its rival's religious conversion: "The DEMOCRAT believes in churches. When conducted in accordance with the principles of Chris-tianity, only good follows them. But the DEMOCRAT is the organ of no denomination. One 'Christian Advocate' in Dodge will suffice."[43] Cautious citizens prayed for better times. They wanted to believe the *Globe's* assess-ment: "If Dodge City can hold down internal insurrections this year, you may look for such a boom for our city as was never seen before."[44]

Ford County's new officers assumed their duties in January. For a time Sheriff Sughrue acted as his own jailor, before hiring his twin brother Michael. Two days after becoming sheriff, Patrick toured the jail and "found sundry articles that he did not care to leave in the possession of his prisoners, to-wit: A two-bladed pocket knife, and a case knife which was transformed into a saw. The first article named was supplied by Mrs. Wig-gins, who was residing in the jailors rooms, and admitted to have been so supplied by Charles Ellsworth, who is one of the inmates of the jail. Sher-iff Sughrue, since he has taken charge of the court house, has laid down some very rigid rules for the government of the temple over which he pre-sides."[45] T. J. Tate replaced Fred Singer as under sheriff. A month later Singer joined up with Tom Lahey and took back his old place on Front Street from Casimero Romero, renaming it the St. James Saloon.

---

[43] *Dodge City Democrat*, February 16, 1884.

[44] *Ford County Globe*, January 1, 1884.

[45] Ibid., January 22, 1884. Samuel Galland, Morris Collar, and James H. Kelley stood together as sureties for Pat Sughrue's $5,000 bond. *Dodge City Democrat*, December 29, 1883.

Citizens looked back on 1883 with embarrassment. They wanted no repeat of the Long Branch troubles. The Democratic Party resolved to run its own candidates in the township elections. Organizers called a meeting at Galland's Great Western Hotel. They nominated Thomas Lahey as township trustee over Henry V. Cook; Samuel Galland—holding back the challenge of A. J. Anthony by 20 votes—as treasurer; W. H. LyBrand and R. G. Cook—running as an Independent—for justices of the peace. Nelson Cary and Dave Mather, of all people, rounded out the list as constables, edging out perennial candidate Prairie Dog Dave Morrow.

Republicans, divided over Prohibition, prompted a challenge from Dan Frost: "Now, will you allow the democrats to get away with the township offices without a protest?"[46] Klaine, embracing Prohibition with the enthusiasm of the converted, saw the contest as a simple referendum on that issue: "The opportunity is now offered of taking straight Democracy and straight whisky. It would seem that the importance in this election is free whisky and free Democracy which are one and inseparable."[47]

Failing to organize along party lines, Republicans called for a Peoples' Convention. There, Hamilton Bell got the nod as township trustee. Samuel Galland, a Democrat, was again nominated for treasurer, this time by acclamation. E. D. Swan and independent R. G. Cook became candidates for justice of the peace. Spurned by the Democrats, Dave Morrow joined O. D. Wilson to round out the ticket as constables. Other dissatisfied Republicans put up their own slate of candidates, including the reluctant Louis C. Hartman as justice of the peace.

The Democratic Party had always enjoyed a majority in Ford County, and the fragmented Republicans could offer little resistance. The township elections in February turned into a sweeping Democratic victory, surprising few observers. With the exception of O. D. Wilson defeating Dave Mather by thirty-two votes, all the Democrats won by impressive margins.[48]

Frost questioned the wisdom of an independent Republican effort, claiming without explanation that the "so-called Republican ticket [was] gotten up to allow the democrats to win."[49] Conceding Democratic strength in Dodge City, Nicholas Klaine tried playing down the results: "Some of the candidates on the Democratic ticket were Republicans, and

---

[46] *Ford County Globe*, January 29, 1884.

[47] *Dodge City Times*, January 24, 1884.

[48] Ford County Commissioners Journals, Book A, 441; and *Dodge City Democrat*, February 16, 1884.

[49] *Ford County Globe*, February 19, 1884.

some of the candidates were quite acceptable to Republican voters."[50] Flush with victory, the *Dodge City Democrat* ignored the excuses.

Political recrimination did not provide the only topic of conversation that February. A woman walked to her neighbor's house on Chestnut Street, behind the *Times* building, and stood at the door annoyed when no one answered her knock. Growing more apprehensive than irritated, she peered through a window. On the floor lay the body of her friend, a middle-aged black washerwoman named Kaziah Morris—known to all her friends as Keezock. Alarmed, the neighbor summoned authorities. Near the body was a stove plate "besmeared with brains and blood."

Suspicion pointed to Keezock's lover, a man named Henry Chambers, who worked for Bob Wright as a caretaker at Fort Dodge. Learning that Chambers and the deceased often quarreled, Pat Sughrue rode out to the fort and made the arrest. Searching the suspect's belongings, the sheriff found bloodstained clothing. Sughrue determined that Chambers had visited the Chestnut Street house the night before with a bottle of whiskey. Judge Cook held a coroner's hearing and bound the accused over for trial in the District Court.[51]

Bob Wright may have lost one of his Fort Dodge employees, but answering rumors afloat since the first of the year, he and Henry Beverley dissolved their six-year partnership on March 6, 1884. The new firm became R. M. Wright & Company. Beverley, though no longer a partner, remained associated with the firm as business manager: "We are pleased to announce to our many friends and customers that we have secured the services of Mr. H. M. Beverley, who will be glad to meet and entertain his many friends at his old place of business, The Brick Store."[52] Three weeks earlier Wright and former city marshal P. W. Beamer had ended their partnership in the blacksmith and wagon-repair business. "Andy the Swede" Johnson bought the stock and fixtures and added them to his own shop south of the tracks near Hamilton Bell's corner. Beamer soon left Dodge City for Arizona, eventually ending up in San Diego.

---

[50] *Dodge City Times*, February 14, 1884.

[51] State of Kansas vs. Henry Chambers, Records of the Ford County District Court, Criminal Appearance Docket A, 150. Also see *Ford County Globe*, February 19, 1884; *Dodge City Times*, February 21, 1884; and *Dodge City Democrat*, February 23, 1884.

[52] *Dodge City Times*, March 13, 1884. The breakup of Wright, Beverley & Company came as no surprise, the *Globe* having prematurely announced the change on January 8.

DEMOCRATIC VICTORY in the township elections reinforced Klaine's paranoia on the liquor question. He associated all Democrats with whiskey. Most dealers suspended advertising with the *Dodge City Times*. The last holdouts, wholesalers George M. Hoover and Henry Sturm, along with saloonman Walter Straeter, waited until the January 17 issue. Boycott made the editor more petulant than usual. Old Nick had become a martyr to his cause.

When the president of the Kansas State Temperance Union, the Reverend A. B. Campbell, arrived in late February to give three lectures—one in the morning at the Union Church, and two in the evening at the courthouse—Klaine devoted three columns to Campbell's ramblings. He then wrote, more in hope than as a claim, "A great temperance feeling has been produced and an interest awakened in temperance that cannot fail to arouse the entire community, and ultimately bring about a thorough and practical enforcement of the prohibitory law."[53]

All this nonsense caused Alonzo B. Webster to write from Hot Springs, Arkansas, where he had gone seeking relief from his chronic rheumatism: "I understand that Gospel Hill rung with their clamor for war, and that it is inevitable that the 'ides of March' will hardly have passed before the clash of the festive beer glass will no longer be heard in Dodge. I understand also that Generals Klaine and Sutton have shied their castors into the ring and sworn that prohibition shall no longer be a failure."[54] Webster, the saloonman, saw no reason for going to extremes.

Prohibition was all that mattered to voters in the city election. By March 11 the *Globe* claimed, "Politics will be ignored in the city issue, so the only question that is at all likely to come up is the saloon question, as against strict prohibition." The *Democrat*, too, dismissed the purpose of Klaine's crusade: "The *Times* has already defined 'the issue' upon which that paper intends to make its fight—that of prohibition of the liquor traffic in Ford county. The paper is frank enough to admit that 'to take away that trade would interfere with the commercial importance of the city,' but as the Republican party has decided that this shall be the issue, the *Times* proposes to fight it out on that line if there is not a business house left open in the city. The mandate of 'the party' has gone forth, and the *Times* has received a touch of the lash and wheeled into line."[55] Rev-

---

[53] Ibid., February 28, 1884.

[54] A. B. Webster to the editor, February 28, 1884. *Dodge City Democrat*, March 8, 1884.

[55] *Dodge City Democrat*, March 1, 1884.

erend Campbell returned for another temperance lecture, this time at the new Methodist church. His appearance changed few minds.

The Prohibition faction ran under the banner of the Peoples' Ticket. George S. Emerson headed the slate for mayor, with H. T. Drake, F. J. Durand, R. McElwain, P. G. Reynolds, and Oliver Marsh running for council seats. Incumbent R. E. Burns was renominated for police judge. The Democrats, running as the Citizens' Ticket, proposed George M. Hoover for mayor, with Henry Beverley, James H. Kelley, Hamilton Bell, George Cox, and John Kelsey for city council. This group supported R. G. Cook for police judge. Even Frost preferred his old foe Jim Kelley to anyone running as a Prohibitionist. On April Fool's Day he joked, characterizing Emerson's candidacy as the Holy Water Ticket, and Hoover's as Mixed Drinks. Carrying the jest one step further, the *Globe* listed a Straight Bourbon Ticket with James H. Kelley for mayor, and the Lemonade and Soda Pop Ticket headed by Joseph Modlin.

Reformers may have found Kelley's candidacy objectionable, but others felt the same about R. E. Burns as police judge. In early March, Frost questioned the propriety of that office, calling for an independent investigation of the judge's accounts. Resenting the implication, Burns confronted Frost at Gallagher's drug store, where the editor went "to buy his usual six-for-a-quarter lot of cigars." After harsh words the two exchanged blows: "No law Latin was indulged in by either the police judge or the ex-police judge, but the way in which the pure saxon was slung by the gladiators would have made Bobby Gill or [James H.] McGoodwin green with envy." Feeling bruised but vindicated, Burns supplied the *Democrat* with figures on fines collected from the first of the month—$350 from saloons, gamblers, and prostitutes. Burns congratulated the newspaper's plan to report the totals on a weekly basis instead of making "loud-mouthed assertions which they know were false." None of this convinced the battered Dan Frost, who continued to demand a complete investigation.[56]

Increasing the pressure, the *Times* championed the demise of the dance hall. Klaine found an unexpected ally in hotel proprietor Samuel Galland. The problem grew out of the doctor's plan to build a larger Great Western Hotel just east of his old place. The proposed two-story would offer forty-five guestrooms with modern conveniences. In the same block, how-

---

[56] Ibid., March 8, 1884; and *Ford County Globe*, March 11, 1884. The *Dodge City Times* stood silent on the Frost-Burns controversy.

ever, stood the notorious Bond and Nixon dance hall—occupying two lots on the southeast corner of Locust Street and Second Avenue, earlier site of the old Lady Gay and the Comique Theater. On New Year's Eve, only a week after Mayor Deger allowed dance halls to reopen, an employee of the New York Cattle Company named Al Thurmond stabbed railroad worker George Miller on those premises. With such activities, Dr. Galland considered the joint an obstacle to his plans to open a first-class establishment on the south side. He began devising steps to drive the two proprietors out of business, much to the delight of Nicholas Klaine.

Far from being a Prohibitionist, at least not at this stage of the debate, Galland had declared, "My interest in my own and my fellow citizens' welfare and prosperity, as well as my belief in the unalienable right of a man to govern his own stomach, would prevent such tomfoolery on my part."[57] Galland did, however, deplore prostitution and its chief ally—the dance hall.

Dr. Galland considered Bond and Nixon the worst offenders. On March 24, 1884, he ordered his attorney, the ubiquitous Michael Sutton, to file suit against both men for "contriving and maliciously intending to injure and damage the plaintiff in his said business of hotel keeper." On that same day Judge J. C. Strang issued a temporary injunction ordering Bond and Nixon to suspend operations.[58] That decision reflected frustration over prostitution, rather than saloons, and shows the lengths taken by Ford County authorities to protect legitimate business interests. The principals ended the controversy when the proprietors sold their property to Galland for twenty-five hundred dollars.[59]

Of course, Nicholas Klaine saw all this as affirmation. As Election Day neared, Mayor Deger, trying to appear fair minded, appointed H. T. Drake, George S. Emerson, and Hamilton Bell election judges. With both sides represented, although favoring the reformers, voters crowded the polls on April 7. Misjudging the mood, the *Times* claimed four days before, "The plans of the opposition have been disconcerted, and there is no united and scarcely a formidable opposition to the ticket headed by Geo. S. Emerson for Mayor."

[57] *Dodge City Democrat*, February 23, 1884.

[58] S. Galland vs. Bond and Nixon, Records of the Ford County District Court, Civil Appearance Docket A, 381. Also see, *Ford County Globe*, March 25, 1884; *Dodge City Times*, March 27, 1884 (Klaine published Galland's petition in full); and *Dodge City Democrat*, March 29, 1884.

[59] Ford County Register of Deeds, Book D, 238; and *Dodge City* Times, April 17, 1884. Bond and Nixon sold off both lots. The building on the corner, Lot 20, was the larger of the two in depth, but the structure on Lot 19 was two stories.

Imagine Klaine's embarrassment after Hoover crushed Emerson by the staggering total of 270 to 60. As for city council, the Democratic-supported Citizens' Ticket won all five seats with similar margins. In an understatement, Klaine tried explaining away the humiliation three days later: "The city election would indicate that the people of Dodge City were not ready for reform. The principle of reform must be cultivated it seems."

George Hoover assumed his duties on April 10, 1884, during a special meeting of the city council. On a motion from James Kelley, the new administration declared all city offices vacant. Hoover appointed Harry Gryden city attorney, Daniel Frost treasurer, and William M. Tilghman city marshal, with Tom Nixon his assistant. No surprise, the mayor and council picked the *Dodge City Democrat* to publish official proceedings. Frost declined to serve as treasurer, an appointment only made for political harmony. Hoover offered the post to bank vice president and former Long Branch co-proprietor William H. Harris.

Naming the notorious Tom Nixon the new assistant marshal did not set well with reformers. But Galland's purchase of the disputed property eased hard feelings. Marshal Tilghman, who owned a cattle ranch with Neil Brown, pulled out of the liquor trade by renting his south side Oasis Saloon to his younger brother. Frank Tilghman offered as a specialty "Methodist cocktails and hard-shell Baptist lemonades." Some appointments may have offended Klaine and his supporters, but Hoover and the council appeased reformers by passing an ordinance outlawing dance halls.[60]

Encouraged by changes in city government, cautious citizens planned major business improvements. Those interested in investing money in Dodge City's future included many of its original pioneers, such as Henry L. Sitler, George M. Hoover, Alonzo B. Webster, Richard Evans, Thomas L. McCarty, Jacob Collar, and Henry Sturm. Proposals included construction of major business blocks on the post office site and Webster's old corner. All the optimism demonstrated to townspeople and outsiders that Dodge City had not given up on itself. But the old town still had a few surprises left.

---

[60] Ordinance No. 83, May 22, 1884. Dodge City Ordinances, Book A, 153–54. Section 1 read: "That it shall be unlawful for any person or persons to keep or maintain in the City of Dodge City, Kansas, what is commonly known as a Dance Hall, or any other place where lewd women and men congregate for the purpose of dancing or other revelries." In writing Section 3, Hoover and the council must have kept in mind Dr. Galland's protests over Bond and Nixon's establishment: "it shall be unlawful for any saloon keeper to keep, maintain or allow in his or her place of business any violin, piano, or other musical instrument, and permit them to be used to the annoyance or inconvenience of any person." Violators of any of these provisions faced fines between ten and one hundred dollars.

Chapter 12

Moral Rumblings
and Other Diversions

As if tripping over the toes of Dodge City's saloonmen, Prohibition agitators negotiated a return engagement of the Reverend A. B. Campbell, along with former governor John P. St. John. Opponents cursed, believing "it detrimental to the business and social interest of Dodge City for [these two] to harangue our citizens on the subject of prohibition." Claiming everything could be handled locally—meaning nothing much needed to be done—they ended their appeal: "Our city is peaceable and prosperous and we do not desire any outside interference in regard to our local government, nor will it be tolerated by us." Thirty-eight signatures appeared on the petition dated May 5, a parade of citizens divided down the middle between Democrats and Republicans.[1]

Editors at the *Globe* and *Democrat* supported that sentiment. Nicholas Klaine covered his eyes and ears and, predictably, championed temperance in the *Dodge City Times*: "The social and financial conditions of a city must be in a sad plight if the advent of two distinguished speakers is likely to cause a panic in morals and finances. Dodge City is prosperous, healthy and in good condition, and if this condition is of the real and substantial kind, the coming and speaking of our distinguished visitors will not retard one iota."[2] Campbell and his co-conspirators saw Dodge City as just another challenge.

Determined to show support for the visiting lecturers, thirty-two likeminded souls, including the ever-agile Michael Sutton, organized a reception committee. Samuel Galland's name appeared on the list not so much

---

[1] *Dodge City Democrat*, May 10, 1884. The paper headlined its coverage of the meeting thus: "KEEP AWAY. That's What the People of Dodge Ask of the Fanatics." In this same issue, editor D. J. Van Meter made fun of the situation: "Luke Short is here from Fort Worth. He will remain until after the arrival of St. John and Campbell, as he is anxious to meet these learned gentlemen."

[2] *Dodge City Times*, May 15, 1884.

because he had changed his views on the issue, but rather from his opposition to dance halls and prostitution.[3] In Dodge City both were intertwined with the saloon and liquor trade.

At the last moment St. John, a long-time Prohibition supporter, declined the journey (citing that old excuse of illness in the family) and was replaced by R. B. Welch, "a one-horse lawyer" and president of the Shawnee County Temperance Union. Sheriff Sughrue escorted both to their rooms at the Great Western Hotel. The Methodist church was packed for the afternoon and evening lectures. Saloonmen sent observers, singling out attorney Thomas S. Jones to deliver their counter argument. To maintain order, City Marshal Tilghman and Sheriff Sughrue attended both harangues. Just how many converts, if any, Campbell and Welch succeeded in recruiting is unclear.[4]

Feelings against the saloons festered, especially among church regulars and women's groups, who saw the connection between liquor and violence. Not everyone attended the temperance free-for-all searching for salvation. Responding to a claim in a Topeka newspaper that "Bat Masterson was seen to draw his red silk wiper across the bridge of his nose two or three times," the *Democrat* explained. "We can vouch for the truth of the statement that the red wipe was out, but as Bat says he was trying to flirt with one of the young ladies in the choir, we will give both sides to the public. If Bat's story is true, however, we would advise his wife to watch him a little more. Dodge City young ladies are perfectly irresistible."[5] Masterson had returned to Dodge in February 1884 to avoid grand jury service at Trinidad, Colorado. Despite earlier disputes townspeople welcomed him home.

Prohibitionists applauded a ruling in early May assigning liquor cases to the district court, sidestepping the city-controlled police judge. With local authorities refusing to acknowledge Prohibition legislation, reform-

---

[3] Some weeks before, Galland had written, "To saloon men who are pressing dance houses to stay, I will say: I will have to take a life membership of enforcement of the prohibition law. I received notice from some lawless scoundrels that they will do some damage if I ever make any complaints. Come on, you lawless rascals, I fear no danger." *Dodge City Democrat*, March 22, 1884.

[4] One outside source commented on Campbell's first visit: "He induced at least one man, Mike Sutton, to take a life membership is his . . . association. But we notice that a prominent citizen of Dodge [Mayor George M. Hoover] yet publishes an advertisement announcing that he is a wholesale dealer in wines and liquors, and the sole agent for Anheuser beer. It must be concluded, then, that Dodge City has not been entirely converted." *Barber County Index*, as quoted in *Dodge City Democrat*, March 15, 1884. Little was changed by the reverend's second tirade. On May 24, 1884, the *Democrat* reported, "The number of converts made by Campbell and Welch in Dodge City last Sunday has been placed at—ooo,ooo,ooo!"

[5] *Dodge City Democrat*, May 24, 1884.

ers saw this as a victory. The city ignored the law, but the county's position seemed less rigid.

In June, based on complaints filed by H. T. Drake at the behest of Mike Sutton, Sheriff Sughrue arrested Dodge City's saloonkeepers for an appearance before the district court. Attempting to forestall the move, liquor supporters called for a boycott against those "narrow-minded, hide-bound, impecunious fanatics," since "The abolishing of saloons in Dodge is conceded by every responsible business man to be a direct blow to its welfare and prosperity."[6] This assault proved premature, as Ford County juries preferred ignoring a strict legal interpretation.

Klaine and the others found solace in Judge Strang's decision to bar liquor dealers from serving as jurors. This encouraged the filing of new complaints. Those indicted included Mayor George Hoover, Warren and Drake of the Long Branch, Hodkins and Johnson of Congress Hall— employing former assistant city marshal Nat Haywood as chief bartender, Z. T. Wingfield of the Junction, Nelson Cary of the Opera House, Charles Heinz of the Lone Star, City Marshal William Tilghman's brother, Frank, of the Oasis, and George Cox for his bar in the Dodge House, along with Henry Sturm and A. B. Webster. These indictments, too, fell on hard times. Annoyed by the reformers, Judge Strang dismissed the charges.[7] As the Fourth of July neared, Dodge City's saloons were as wide open and popular as ever. Visions of thirsty customers packing wads of cash obscured all thoughts of reform.

It was just as well. Businessmen were about to reap the benefits as organizers plotted a particularly memorable Independence Day. Only three months before, A. J. Anthony, Hamilton Bell, Adolphus Gluck, James H. Kelley, William Tilghman, and a few others began subscriptions to the Dodge City Driving Park and Fair Association. Its purpose was to build a racetrack and exhibition grounds for the July extravaganza. With success all but guaranteed, the group's directors toured possible sites. By late April they settled on a forty-acre parcel owned by Anthony about a mile west of town, nestled between the river and the railroad. Four weeks later A. J. and his wife sold the site to the association for twelve hundred dollars.[8]

---

[6] Ibid.

[7] Records of the Ford County District Court, Criminal Appearance Docket A, Case Nos. 643–50, 163–75; *Dodge City Times*, June 12, 1884; and *Globe Live Stock Journal*, October 28, 1884.

[8] Ford County Register of Deeds, Book D, 261. For more on the organization of the Driving Park and Fair Association, see *Dodge City Democrat*, April 19, 26, 1884; and *Dodge City Times*, April 24, 1884.

Locals had good reason to expect heavy attendance. Thanks to the imagination of Alonzo B. Webster, the festivities would include a Spanish bullfight: "This feature of the affair will alone draw thousands of people to Dodge. . . . The matter is in the hands of Ex-Mayor Webster, and he is already in correspondence with Spanish bull fighters in Old Mexico in regard to coming here. Delegations of sporting men will be here from Denver, Chicago, Kansas City, St. Louis, New York, New Orleans and other places. The bull fight will no doubt be a grand and thrilling affair."[9] As it turned out, this may very well have been the only *genuine* bull fight ever held in the United States, and the resulting controversy rippled across the nation.[10]

Dodge City ignored the notoriety. Business boomed along with the growing population. A hundred new houses sprang up, with two dozen more under construction. Citizens demanded a new courthouse: "The tumble-down brick structure needs remodeling or some fine morning our citizens may find Jailor Sughrue and his prisoners struggling for freedom from beneath the ruins."[11] Hamilton Bell seemed to be the most ambitious private developer. He launched a new enterprise on his property at Third and Locust, a one-and-a-half story monstrosity christened the Elephant Livery Stable, large enough to accommodate three hundred horses and seventy-five vehicles.

The anticipated bullfight did not provide Dodge City its only sporting interlude. Catering to the latest craze Henry Wright busied himself fitting up a building next to the government warehouse as a roller skating rink. Baseball also gripped people's imagination, with numerous unorganized but high-scoring contests. By late April devotees crowded Covert and Reudy's restaurant to start a local ball club. They elected a string of officers, including Bat Masterson as vice president, with A. B. Webster,

[9] *Dodge City Democrat*, May 17, 1884.

[10] Kirke Mechem, "The Bull Fight at Dodge," *Kansas Historical Quarterly* 2, no. 3 (August 1933): 294n1. As Mechem points out, "Cripple Creek, Colo., shares honors with Dodge City for the only fights where bulls were actually sworded." But elsewhere it has been said, "At Gillette [Colorado] was staged the only bullfight to be held in the United States." Frank Waters, *Midas of the Rockies: The Story of Stratton and Cripple Creek* (New York: Civici-Friede, 1937), 160. Despite these contrary claims, the affair at Dodge City seems the only instance of bull fighting on American soil carried out under strict Spanish rules. Of the affair at Gillett it has been said, "The preliminaries were colorful, to say the least. The bullfight was anything but. Several defenseless bulls were slaughtered without a fair trial." Perry Eberhart, *Guide to the Colorado Ghost Towns and Mining Camps* (Chicago: Sage Books, 1968), 446.

[11] *Ford County Globe*, May 20, 1884.

William H. Harris, and Adolphus Gluck directors. Committees were formed to recruit new members, as well as compose a written constitution and bylaws—all that just to play baseball. Dodge City had lost much of its spontaneity.

Even the town's attitude toward the cattle trade was changing by 1884. Local stock raisers feared outbreaks of Texas fever from the tens of thousands of invading longhorns. This represented an interesting shift of opinion, as these same men had downplayed the danger when dependent on Texas stock. Now, after spending years and thousands of dollars building their own herds, they voiced the arguments first raised at Abilene, Ellsworth, and Wichita. At meetings of the Western Kansas Stock Growers' Association, some members argued the quarantine should include the entire state. Lawmakers refused. This, together with the repeal of embargo legislation in New Mexico, encouraged continuation of old patterns. Matthew R. Draper, the one-time Fort Griffin agent for York, Parker & Draper, assured friends in Fort Worth that the Kansas trail would stay open for years. Time alone would decide Draper's skill as a prophet.

Despite opposition among stockmen in western Kansas, F. E. Conrad & Company reported from Albany, Texas, that 5,630 head had already passed that place for Dodge City by the first of May. Three weeks later reports estimated a drive so large that cattlemen spent much of their time searching for sufficient grass and water for staging purposes. Between the third and eighth of June, 28,830 through cattle arrived at Dodge, representing such old hands as Seth Mabry, James Ellison, and Shanghai Pierce. Texas sources predicted a season of a half-million animals. At Dodge City the figure reached 57,470 by June 17 and swelled to 117,480 a week later. The first shipment took place on the twenty-first. Still, drovers and local ranchers alike began to feel that perhaps 1884 might signal the last of the great drives.[12]

Ignoring the possibility, editor and publisher Samuel S. Prouty moved his newspaper, the *Kansas Cowboy*, south from Sidney and out of Ness County in time to get out his first issue on June 28. The new weekly devoted most of its space to livestock news and even featured a drawing of its colorful editor on its masthead—rakishly angled cowboy hat and all.

---

[12] Ibid., June 24, 1884. It was reported that "Many of the drovers as well as local ranchmen think this will be the last year cattle will be driven over the trail."

Surrendering to the spirit of the moment, Daniel Frost renamed his paper the *Globe Live Stock Journal* on July 15. Prouty got settled into business on the northeast corner of Front Street and Third Avenue just in time to report the Fourth of July festivities, finding space on the second floor of the building housing Oliver Marsh & Son's clothing store.

Opposition grew fierce as news spread of an actual bullfight on American soil. Many Kansas newspapers and large eastern dailies condemned the display. The Dodge City Driving Park and Fair Association dismissed the protests (while welcoming the publicity) and forged ahead. Members formed committees to organize such peripheral events as shooting and roping matches, foot races—with Bat Masterson on hand to oversee the details—as well as horse racing, for which Tom Nixon and Neil Brown assumed responsibility. Since it was his idea, Alonzo Webster headed the bullfight committee. The ex-mayor reported on his successful correspondence with El Paso lawyer W. K. Moore to engage genuine Mexican matadors.

Attorney Moore helped publicize the event, trying to dispel the notion of bullfighting as somehow uncivilized during a visit to the editorial office of Sam Prouty's *Kansas Cowboy*: "He says that fight is not the proper word; that athletic exhibition would be more suitable. There is nothing barbarous in the proceeding." The El Paso emissary went on to explain, "Only one animal in a fight is killed and he is dispatched so speedily by the sword of the matadors that the animal can scarcely realize that he has been hurt." Mindful of the pressure on Governor Glick to intercede, Moore ended his little chat on a flattering note, claiming great admiration for the governor, predicting that Glick "will yet be one of the representatives of Kansas in the United States Senate."[13]

George Glick never climbed that far up the political ladder, but then he did not interrupt the festivities either.[14] The town made light of the criticism; after all, its wide-open reputation remained important to the plan. No

---

[13] *Kansas Cowboy*, July 5, 1884.

[14] The president of the American Society for the Prevention of Cruelty to Animals sent a telegram from New York imploring the governor to prevent "such atrocities." The reply fell short of expectation: "The bull fight to which you refer was a tame and insignificant affair, and while advertisements gave it some importance it has little or no importance at Dodge City or any place else. Your telegram in relation to the matter dated July 4th was received but not until after the performance had taken place." G. W. Glick to Henry Bergh, Jr., July 14, 1884. Governors' Correspondence, Archives Division, Kansas State Historical Society.

matter that the image had lost much of its luster since the 1870s. Organizers saw only profits from the expected invasion of sporting men and other curious outsiders. Residents challenged: "Come on ye Eastern Piggamies [*sic*] and see what Kansas can do under the management of the citizens of Dodge City."[15] Backers prepared to make good on the pledge as each train brought in more wide-eyed easterners. Others—mostly drovers and nearby settlers—rode into Dodge from all compass points to enjoy the spectacle.

A reporter from the St. Louis *Globe-Democrat* named Charles Taylor jotted down an interesting portrait of a town in transition, concluding that Dodge City was at least safer than East St. Louis. Taylor wrote that three saloons per block was the average. Somewhat surprised, he claimed not to have seen any pistols, "except in the belts of the sheriff and marshal and their deputies," observing further: "Not a shot fired all day. Not a single, solitary fire-cracker—not a single cowboy coursing up and down the street as if he owned the town. All the profane language that your correspondent heard was in the hack while going to the bull fight, and that was enunciated by something that wore a Mother Hubbard dress."[16] Taylor did notice one legacy of the Dodge City War: the absence of music. Grumbling locals blamed it all on railroad coercion.

As Charlie Taylor walked the streets filling sheets of paper with scribbled notations, everything and everybody awaited the Big Day with unabashed enthusiasm. The Driving Park and Fair Association had done its work at the new forty-acre site. In little more than two months they had built a half-mile racetrack together with a 3,500-seat amphitheater fronting the arena. Business boomed as colorful crowds, mixing southwestern cowboys with eastern dudes, filled hotel lobbies, restaurants, and saloons. Jammed gaming tables delighted the sporting fraternity as large sums changed hands.

Shortly before two o'clock on the afternoon of July 4 the main event got started with A. B. Webster and W. K. Moore leading a procession to the fairgrounds. In close order came local dignitaries, the celebrated Cowboy Band, and five Mexican matadors. They stole the show: "Seen in the street parade the bull fighters presented a unique appearance, with their red jackets, blue tunics, white stockings and small dainty slippers. They all seemed the per-

---

[15] *Ford County Globe*, May 13, 1884.

[16] St. Louis *Globe-Democrat*, as quoted in *Kansas Cowboy*, July 19, 1884.

fection of litheness and quickness, and were heartily applauded as their dark handsome faces looked on the crowd gathered along the streets."[17]

At the amphitheater visiting journalists joined the band, filling seats overlooking the gate. To either side space was reserved for leading citizens and their families. Women and children made up nearly a third of the spectators, creating a minor problem, since a deputy sheriff had to be detailed to enforce the dividing line between respectable ladies and those possessing a less pedigreed lineage. Taylor observed: "Opposite the good citizens were seated the gentlemen of the cattle interest, with their girls, the cow-boy's ambition seemed to be to get a big fat girl and a high seat at the same time."[18] It was an example of segregated cosmopolitanism, Dodge City style.

Half of the dozen bulls selected by D. W. "Doc" Barton crowded adjacent pens. Men there removed the tips of the horns and rasped the ends. At 3:40 the matadors, adorned now in their fighting garb, entered the ring with the picadors amid wild applause from the expectant crowd.

The first bull, a ferocious-looking, red-colored animal, charged into the ring full of fight. Enraged by two decorative darts thrown into its neck, the bull charged matador Gregorio Gallardo, who took refuge behind one of the wooden escapes. Then, to the roar of the crowd, Gallardo, normally a merchant tailor from Chihuahua, deftly avoided the animal's stunted horns as the beast made pass after pass through the matador's mantle. After a time Gallardo retired and others came forward to test their skill against the bull, now standing in the middle of the arena, pawing the ground and covering himself with dirt. Maddened by more darts covering his shoulders and flanks, the animal lunged at his tormentors. After a half-hour, S. B. Chappell roped the exhausted animal and returned him to the pens, but not before he lunged and grazed Chappell's skittish horse. The crowd roared its approval.

The second animal proved cowardly compared with the first. After running from the advancing matador, he was driven out. The third bull, though not as tentative as the second, showed little fight and left the ring, its flanks studded with darts. The fourth, whose horns had been mistakenly sawed to the quick, ignored the matador and was also removed. The

[17] *Kansas Cowboy* and *Dodge City Democrat*, July 12, 1884. Both newspapers reprinted sections of Charles Taylor's articles from the St. Louis *Globe-Democrat*.

[18] Ibid.

fifth bull completely disappointed the crowd and had to be whipped from one of the escapes by a cowboy lounging on the lower bench.

Restive now, the spectators began demanding the first bull's return. Monotony gave way to excitement as the fierce red bull reappeared. At 5 P.M. Gregorio Gallardo stepped forward, sword in hand, as spectators shouted themselves hoarse. The skilled matador sidestepped repeated charges. The crowd then jumped to its feet and gasped—Gallardo was down. Fortunately the brave Mexican fell near one of the protective escapes and crawled to safety. The bull charged the wooden barrier and nearly demolished it before backing away. Bruised on the left thigh, Gallardo returned to the ring. Bowing to the cheering crowd he signaled the band to begin the finale. On the fourth charge Gallardo found his opening. Thrusting the tempered blade home, the matador watched the valiant animal stagger a step or two before stumbling to its knees. The crowd went wild as the first day's excitement ended.

Smaller crowds attended the fights on July 5. Perhaps they were having second thoughts, or, more likely, the novelty had worn thin. In any case, Daniel Frost wrote: "The second day's fight was with the exception of the killing of the last animal in the ring, more interesting than the first; a better selection of fighting bulls were introduced. Though not witnessed by near so large an assembly as the first, the second day was enthusiasm throughout. The first and last animals admittedly fought well and upon this occasion the matadors showed to the people of America what bull fighting really was." The editor went on to excuse the exhibition by claiming the punishment "was even less than that inflicted upon the animals in a branding pen," and that those killed suffered "no more than the steer would that is placed on the butcher's block."[19] Nicholas Klaine voiced a contrary opinion: "Many of our citizens who were present deeply regretted the affair and were heartily ashamed of their participation in the ancient custom. But there must be a good deal of penitence before the stain is fully wiped out."[20]

The last bullfight marked the close of the four-day series of events. Despite a smaller attendance than expected—owning, one source claimed, to washouts and other railroad delays—most seemed pleased with the

[19] *Ford County Globe*, July 8, 1884.
[20] *Dodge City Times*, July 10, 1884.

results. Editors at Larned entertained their readers with the observation: "Quite a number of our boys visited Dodge last week to see the bull fight. Some of them returned looking as though they had had a personal encounter with the animals."[21]

Press coverage generally pleased the organizers, who had purposefully plied reporters from New York, Chicago, St. Louis, Denver, San Francisco, and a dozen county papers with free beer and other delights. In one article, George William Gordon of the *New York Herald* remarked: "I would have less fear of molestation in this wild western town than I would have on the side streets of Kansas City or Chicago late in the evening." Describing Bat Masterson's reputation as a dangerous individual, Gordon explained: "but he is a peaceable sort of a man nevertheless. He might be considered a hard citizen by New Yorkers, but he is a sociable, good natured and kind hearted fellow, except when some one 'treads on his corns.' "[22]

Dodge had behaved itself for the most part, causing *Democrat* editor D. J. Van Meter to boast, "Not a disorderly row or a single arrest on the grounds during the week. How's that for Dodge City's reputed lawlessness?" The fairgrounds may have been orderly, but the town retained its robust characteristics. In that same issue it was reported that "Judge Cook and the city attorney have had their hands full during the past week in the police court."[23]

Van Meter soon regretted the phrase "reputed lawlessness." An hour or two past midnight on Sunday morning July 6, the sound of gunfire alerted Front Street pedestrians to another senseless tragedy. Standing with George Masterson at the doorway of the Stock Exchange, gambler Dave St. Clair had traded words with a number of Texans just beyond the threshold. Accepting the gambler's outburst as a challenge, the men followed Masterson and St. Clair into the saloon. One of them, a twenty-six-year-old cattleman from Goliad, K. B. "Bing" Choate, grabbed a friend's revolver. Banging the heavy weapon against the bar, he shouted for the special benefit of Dave St. Clair: "I am the fastest s—n of a b—h in the house; if anybody meant anything for me or any of this party."[24] Choate ordered drinks before handing the gun to bartender Mack Shelton.

---

[21] *Larned Optic,* July 11, 1884.

[22] *New York Herald,* as reprinted in *Kansas Cowboy,* July 12, 1884.

[23] *Dodge City Democrat,* July 5, 1884.

[24] *Globe Live Stock Journal,* July 15, 1884.

The Texans left but, convinced that St. Clair meant trouble, they armed themselves. Carrying a revolver in his right hand, Choate strolled back through the door of Webster's saloon inebriated and unappeased. He called St. Clair a coward and a son-of-a-bitch. The gambler later testified, corroborated by other witnesses, that Choate had warned him, after first striking his stomach and face with a cane he carried in his left hand, "If you make a move I'll kill you."[25] Dave clasped his hands in front of him and tried explaining he meant no harm. As they approached the bar Choate slipped the pistol into the left side waistband of his trousers. St. Clair then accused Choate of striking him with the cane, but the drunken man somehow seemed unable to recall the incident. Choate mumbled a half-hearted apology, but the disagreement continued.

Special Policeman William Bowles, who had just come through the door separating the saloon from Bob Wright's store, saw Choate reach for his gun. The officer shouted a warning. St. Clair pulled a pistol from his hip pocket and fired, striking Choate in the center of the chest. Benjamin F. Daniels, another special policeman standing just outside, watched the wounded man spin around and fall to his knees. "He lifted himself up by the door, and got hold of a rod at the window and acted as if he intended to shoot," Daniels later testified. "I knocked his pistol down, and this staggered him."[26] Daniels disarmed St. Clair while saloonman Nelson Cary, himself a deputy sheriff and township constable, stepped toward Choate and lifted the cocked revolver from the dying man's hand.

Under arrest, Dave St. Clair awaited the outcome of a coroner's inquest. Five of the six men hearing the evidence felt the gambler's response justified. St. Clair stood before Judge Rufus G. Cook. Reflecting on the testimony, County Attorney Whitelaw characterized the incident as "a sad case," but felt obliged to recommend the charges be dropped. The judge agreed. Released from custody on Wednesday, Dave St. Clair was seen on the streets that afternoon before leaving town that night on the westbound train.

This latest tragedy stirred up an old debate. Daniel Frost chided both ordinary citizens and town officials two days after the killing: "We are

[25] Testimony of Dave St. Clair before Judge R. G. Cook. *Dodge City Democrat*, July 12, 1884; and *Globe Live Stock Journal*, July 15, 1884.

[26] *Globe Live Stock Journal*, July 15, 1884.

more than ever inclined to hold to our former opinion as regards the carrying of deadly weapons and particularly the six-shooter. If this law was
more rigidly enforced there would be less killing done. Our officers should
see to it that this law was enforced and to the very letter. Our mayor
should exercise his power and authority in this direction, and see to it that
all those not officers of the law (and perhaps some of them), be made to
lay aside their shooting irons while in the city."[27] Two days later Nicholas
Klaine offered a personal observation: "Perhaps after the gambling table
has offered a few more victims some effort may be used to stamp out the
sources of so much blood, disorder and crime."[28]

None of this helped young Mr. Choate, as Drs. McCarty and C. A.
Milton embalmed his remains. Placed in a metallic shipping case, the slain
Texan traveled to Kansas City aboard the Sunday express, accompanied by
W. J. Mayfield and Mark Withers. There the casket waited at Stein's
funeral parlor for the arrival of the dead man's father, J. W. "Monroe"
Choate, and one of his older brothers. Married for only a year, Bing
Choate left behind a wife and infant child. After making arrangements to
ship his son's body back to Texas for burial at Goliad, the senior Choate—
a respected cattleman from Karnes County who had been among the first
to drive stock to the Kansas rail towns—traveled on alone to settle his
son's affairs in Ford County.[29]

No sooner had the dust settled over the Choate affair than more trouble erupted. Two months before, Nelson Cary, co-proprietor of the Opera
House saloon, began undercutting his competition by offering beer at a
nickel a glass. Nicholas Klaine welcomed Cary's reckless behavior, as he
saw it undermining saloon solidarity. Many in the business feared the
same. Within weeks one wholesaler refused to sell more brew to the Opera
House. Cary turned to a less fickle supplier. This revolution within the
ranks of the liquor fraternity amused the editor of the *Dodge City Times.*

In mid-July Mysterious Dave Mather and a partner—who had earlier
tried opening a dance hall in the Opera House—leased the saloon from
Cary and continued the nickel-beer policy. Mather had reason to believe
Assistant Marshal Tom Nixon had orchestrated the campaign against low-

---

[27] Ibid., July 8, 1884.

[28] *Dodge City Times,* July 10, 1884.

[29] Concerning the Choate family, see J. Marvin Hunter, *The Trail Drivers of Texas,* 2:736–38. For more on this
incident, besides the issues already cited, see *Dodge City Democrat,* July 12, 1884; and *Kansas Cowboy,* July 12, 19, 1884.

ering the retail beer price. In addition, "A feud of several months standing existed between the parties, growing out of the closing up of the dance hall in the Opera House. . . . Mather suspected Nixon of being the cause of the breaking up of the dance hall business."[30]

Nixon himself grew apprehensive over Mather's intentions, so much so that around nine o'clock on the evening of July 18 he tried to kill him. Mysterious Dave stood at the head of the stairs outside his place of business as Nixon walked by. Suddenly the assistant marshal pulled his revolver and fired. The shot went wild, striking the porch. A wooden splinter gouged Dave's little finger and powder residue burned his face. Mather claimed to have been unarmed. Sheriff Pat Sughrue arrested the assistant marshal on a charge of assault with intent to kill. Nixon posted an $800 bond before Judge Cook. "The shooting was the result of an old feud," reported the *Democrat*. "Mather claims to have been unarmed, while Nixon claims Dave reached for his gun before he attempted to draw his own. Mather says he will make no complaint, but from all appearances the end is not yet."[31]

Again on duty three days later, Tom Nixon walked east along Front Street from Bob Wright's store. As he reached the Opera House Saloon, Beatty & Kelley's old place at the corner of First Avenue (known as the Alhambra, before the partners replaced the site with a two-story saloon and meeting hall), Nixon heard someone call his name. Turning, the officer spotted Mysterious Dave, who raised his revolver and fired. Nixon had no time to draw as Mather advanced, firing three more shots at close range. The second round passed through the assistant marshal and lodged in the knee of bystander Archie Franklin, a teamster on the Mobeetie freighting run. Bat Masterson witnessed the affair. Sheriff Sughrue rushed forward to make the arrest. Nixon, leaving behind an invalid wife and several children, was buried amid all the trappings one might expect of a pioneer resident. The city then appointed Special Policeman Benjamin F. Daniels to the vacated post of assistant marshal, with its salary of one hundred dollars per month.

Mather's hearing was delayed as County Attorney Whitelaw tried to have the case moved to the district court. With the judge out of town,

---

[30] *Kansas Cowboy*, July 26, 1884.
[31] *Dodge City Democrat*, July 19, 1884.

Whitelaw hoped to at least have a justice of the state supreme court come out and hear the evidence. Failing again, the county attorney had no choice but to submit the case to Justice of the Peace W. H. LyBrand. All the delay caused considerable grumbling among those who saw the affair as a simple case of murder. Dan Frost, who hoped to challenge Whitelaw for state senator in the fall elections, tried to encourage feelings against the county attorney, without much success.

Listening to witnesses, Justice LyBrand ordered Mather back to jail to await trial in the district court. Judge Strang eventually released the prisoner on $6,000 bond. In October the court granted a change of venue to Edwards County. The trial at Kinsley ended on December 30 with a verdict of not guilty. How the jury reached their decision was never explained, but the *Dodge City Times* quoted the *Kinsley Graphic* as saying, "The jury is a good one, and the verdict is generally regarded as the right thing under the evidence." Bob Wright saw it as another "one of the cold-blooded deeds, frequently taking place in frontier days."[32]

Ignoring all the bloodshed, Dodge City saw itself as the cosmopolitan center of western Kansas. Convincing others was more difficult, a task not helped by the town's unsanitary setting. This situation became so pronounced during the hot summer months that dozens of citizens signed a petition demanding action. George Hoover issued a mayor's proclamation on August 16, threatening legal action against those who failed to comply within twelve hours. Even the irritable editor of the *Times* congratulated Hoover: "The proclamation is timely. The sink holes, privies and carcasses have made a stench almost unbearable in many parts of the city. The order for cleaning up might be extended to outside of the city limits. In many of the 'draws' dead animals are lying and the stench from these carcasses suggests cholera and pestilence."[33]

On August 29, just short of his forty-first birthday, City Attorney Harry Gryden died of what was described as "typhoid pneumonia." Nicholas Klaine, never one to pass up a chance to badmouth an enemy, even one on this deathbed, wrote: "As we go to press we learn that Harry

---

[32] Wright, *Dodge City, the Cowboy Capital*, 179. For more details on the case, see *Dodge City Democrat*, July 19, 26, August 2, 9, 16, 23, December 20, 1884, January 8, 1885; *Dodge City Times*, July 24, 31, August 7, 21, 1884, January 8, 1885; *Globe Live Stock Journal*, July 22, 29, August 5, 1884, January 6, 1885; and *Kansas Cowboy*, July 26, August 2, 9, 16, 23, 1884, January 3, 1885.

[33] *Dodge City Times*, August 21, 1884.

E. Gryden is dying. He has been in poor health for sometime, and a few days ago was removed to the county poor house. Gryden was one of the early settlers of Dodge and at one time had a considerable law practice. His dissolute habits soon wrecked his name and frame, and he is dying with the cold charity of the world around him. Being generous and genial he had many warm friends, 'but his worst enemy was himself.' "[34] The town's other editors offered a more traditional sendoff, without any reference to the dead man's personal failings.

Gryden's funeral was one of the city's largest, with the Glick Guards, members of the Grand Army of the Republic, the fire company, and the mayor and council, along with other members of the bar leading the procession to Prairie Grove Cemetery.[35] City officials, during their afternoon meeting of September 3, appointed Thomas S. Jones to fill the vacancy. Jones not only took the job but also moved into Gryden's old First Avenue law office. He then filed suit against Nicholas Klaine to recover a reputed shortage of nearly four hundred dollars from the editor's tenure as city treasurer.

Examining Klaine's ledgers, William H. Harris had reported this discrepancy to the council during their regular meeting the month before, adding he had notified Mr. Klaine of the problem but that the editor failed to reply. Councilman Beverley introduced a motion calling for the city attorney to file suit if Klaine did not make a satisfactory settlement by August 15. Only Harry Gryden's illness delayed things.

Klaine defended himself, claiming the case to be part of a long-standing feud with Harris over the question of gambling, dating from Klaine's days as a justice of the peace. As for the so-called missing funds, he explained, "Over $300 of this amount was paid out by me to A. B. Webster, Mayor, by order of the city council, for extra pay of policeman. . . . Some errors in additions of figures and copying are also reported against me, making claim of about $96.00, which the Mayor in name and the Mayor in fact are endeavoring to recover, for use of the city." As always, right or wrong, the combative editor stood firm: "Let the assassins continue their work."[36]

---

[34] Ibid., August 28, 1884.

[35] For more details on Gryden's demise, see *Dodge City Times*, September 4, 1884; *Globe Live Stock Journal*, August 26, September 4, 1884; *Dodge City Democrat*, August 30, September 6, 13, 1884; and *Kansas Cowboy*, September 6, 1884.

[36] *Dodge City Times*, September 18, 1884. Also see "Regular Meeting of the City Council," *Dodge City Democrat*, August 9, 1884.

Klaine's difficulties came as a welcomed respite—the city filing suit—
for in 1884 several people chose to sue the city. Larned attorney Nelson
Adams filed an action in Pawnee County for being denied access to Luke
Short during the Dodge City War. Not surprisingly the court awarded its
native son $4,500. In Dodge, despite threats of filing a motion for a new
trial, the mayor and the city council tried compromise. At a special session
on July 11 Adams agreed to accept $2,500, and city countered with $1,000.
Seven weeks later they settled. Adams would receive $1,750: $500 in cash,
with the balance paid in 6 percent bonds due in ten years. The agreement
upset citizens mindful of the previous administration's refusal to settle the
claim for $250. Klaine summed it up best: "The payment of $1750.00 to a
$10 lawyer is something that the tax-payers will take in hand."[37] For once
even Dan Frost sided with his rival: "The old city government is wholly
responsible to the tax-payers, not only for the trouble created, but the
present expense incurred."[38]

The spectacle of having both editors agree on anything of substance
soon evaporated over politics. With 1884 a presidential election year, party
loyalty assumed new meaning in Ford County. Dan Frost wanted the
Republican Party's nomination as senator for the Thirty-fifth District, an
area comprising twenty-five counties—nearly one quarter of the state. His
transparent quest prompted the remark, "For fear that some one wasn't
posted, Frost announces in his last issue that he is still running for office.
Now, the people want to know when he intends to stop running for
office."[39] Republicans snubbed the editor in favor of J. W. Rush. The
Democrats nominated James Whitelaw. Prohibitionists fielded their own
candidates but ignored the Senate race.

Personal attacks heightened interest among voters. Nicholas Klaine,
much to the amusement of those who remembered his support for James
H. Kelley, characterized the Democrats as vile examples of gang rule.
Frost, still blaming the *Times* for spoiling his own chances, ran stories
about the editor's troubles with alcohol while in Missouri. The Democrats
blasted everything tainted with Republicanism and Prohibition reform.
Klaine chided Bat Masterson for speaking out against Republicans,

---

[37] *Dodge City Times*, August 28, 1884.
[38] *Globe Live Stock Journal*, September 2, 1884.
[39] *Dodge City Democrat*, August 23, 1884.

including county attorney candidate R. E. Burns. Masterson responded through the *Globe*, reminding readers of Klaine's battles with the city over the missing four hundred dollars. Then, on November 1, 1884, he brought out the first and only issue of his own newspaper, a four-page handbill-sized effort called the *Vox Populi*.

Bat Masterson's brief entry into Dodge City journalism created a riotous atmosphere. He assured his readers that the *Vox Populi*'s "sentiments will be Republican of the Conklin stripe." Yet, of the eight offices listed on the ballot, he supported only three Republicans: J. W. Rush for state senator, J. Q. Sharp as representative, and L. E. McGarry for clerk of the district court.

Party loyalists questioned Masterson's motives even further after reading: "Old Nick Klaine has repeatedly been branded as a thief, liar and murderer, yet he never whimpers, or attempts to deny any of the accusations. We expect that proof of his being a rapist, barn burner and a poisoner of his neighbors horses could be obtained without much effort." "E. D. Swan would be a nice man to have charge of the poor widows and orphans of Ford county, after turning his aged and decrepit father out upon the streets to die of starvation." "Let Burns go back to Naperville [Illinois], and tell the people there, who were generous enough to purchase him a pauper ticket to Dodge City that the people here don't want him." "The Burns and Swan managers have advised them to keep away from portions of the county where they are not known, as this circumstance would certainly blight what little hopes they have of winning." "The Times says Burns has the 'requisite qualifications and experience for county attorney.' Heavens! how we must have been mistaken, we thought he only possessed the requisite qualifications and experience of a tramp." "HORACE GREELY [*sic*] once said that 'politics makes strange bed-fellows.' The old sage comes very near hitting the nail on the head, judging from where we saw Col. Prouty and Perry Wilden last night. Gentlemen we advise you to disenfect [*sic*] yourselves this morning." "A candidate is certainly out of luck that has old Nick Klaine supporting him. One puff from the columns of his foul sheet would defeat the best man in Ford county for any office that he would be an aspirant for."[40]

Four days later Masterson waited along with everyone else for the counting of ballots. Results favored the Democratic Party. Its candidates

---

[40] *Vox Populi*, November 1, 1884.

won seven of the eight local races, some by wide margins. August Crumbaugh crushed E. D. Swan for probate judge by 465 votes, much to the delight of Mr. Masterson. Benjamin F. Milton defeated Burns for county attorney. Democrat William F. Petillon lost his race to continue as clerk of the district court, but by only 39 votes. Cattleman R. J. Hardesty, another Democrat, won a seat as state representative. James Whitelaw lost the race for state senator to Republican J. W. Rush, but at least out polled his opponent at home, 659 to 586. Republican presidential hopeful James G. Blaine also defeated Grover Cleveland in Ford County, but lost nationwide. Former governor John P. St. John, running for president on the Prohibition ticket, polled a scant 15 votes countywide, and only 8 in Dodge Township. His miserable showing prompted Frost's sarcastic observation that, "Ex-Governor St. John could not be elected constable in this county."[41] In the governor's race, Republican John A. Martin unseated Democratic incumbent George W. Glick, although Glick did come out on top in Dodge Township.[42]

Controversy arose over returns from Clark City involving 70 votes and an additional 95 from Klaine Precinct. The most glaring irregularity involved the precinct judge, R. C. Lowery. He arrived in Dodge City on Wednesday evening, too late to turn over his returns to the county clerk. Instead of retiring to his hotel room until morning, Lowery went instead to George Hoover's saloon. There he either lost, or someone stole, his poll book. Lowery still held the ballots but, without the confirming poll book, county commissioners declined "to canvas the vote," in effect tossing out the results.[43]

Dodge City slipped back into routine after the Democratic Party's victory parade. After the dust settled, even the *Times* admitted, "The election in Kansas indicates that prohibition is endorsed. However, no one in this vicinity need go to Missouri for his drink of whisky. Whiskey is free in Dodge—free to whoever will buy."[44] In contrast to its early years, the town had mellowed. "Dodge City is not the town it used to be," explained a visiting editor from McPherson soon after the bullfight episode:

---

[41] *Globe Live Stock Journal*, November 11, 1884.

[42] Ford County Commissioners Journals, Book A, 478.

[43] Ibid., 479. See also *Globe Live Stock Journal*, November 11, 1884.

[44] *Dodge City Times*, November 6, 1884.

That is, it is not so bad a place in the eyes of people who do not sanction outlawry and lewdness. A few years ago at early candle-light nearly every saloon was turned into a public gambling or dance house. The "girls" came out from almost every nook and corner and solicited customers with as much effrontery as the waiter girls do for their counters at a church festival. It was trying on a man's virtue in those days. The cow boys with revolvers strapped upon each hip, swung these wicked beauties all night and made the sleeping hideous with their profanity and vulgarity. This has been stopped. No cow boy is allowed to carry weapons, few dance halls are allowed to run and gambling is only carried on in private quarters. The saloons are yet running in defiance of law, but prosecutions are pending against all of them.[45]

Other problems persisted: "Some of the small boys about town are carrying revolvers."[46] Nor had gunplay among older citizens gone completely out of style. One night in mid-October, City Marshal Tilghman and a party of drovers traded upwards of thirty shots with six-guns and Winchester rifles near the Arkansas River bridge. The only injury during this noisy melee seems to have been the wounding of a horse. Everyone else dove for cover. It was just as well, since "the balls came up the street like a young hailstorm striking in the road on the hill."[47]

CATTLE TRADING may have been on shaky ground, but numbers for 1884 seemed to promise Dodge City its best year ever. But numbers alone were deceiving. In July stock prices had fallen. Many owners held their herds hoping for a more favorable price, selling only enough stock to cover expenses. Not only did the trade suffer from price fluctuations, but that same July outbreaks of Texas fever were reported at the Chicago, St. Louis, and Kansas City stockyards. That information sent a chill through the entire industry, driving prices still lower. A threatened Illinois boycott of all cattle shipped from Kansas forced Governor Glick's hand. He called a conference at the State House at Topeka attended by the state veterinary and live stock sanitation commissioner, managers of the both the AT&SF and Union Pacific railroads, as well as the superintendent of the Kansas

[45] *McPherson Independent*, as quoted in *Globe Live Stock Journal*, July 22, 1884.
[46] *Globe Live Stock Journal*, December 16, 1884.
[47] Ibid., October 21, 1884.

City stockyards, together with representatives from cattle ranches in the Indian Territory and Texas.

A report from Dr. A. A. Holcombe, state veterinary surgeon, told of Texas fever outbreaks at eight separate points within Kansas. He included Dodge City, but locals denied the charge. Sam Prouty went so far as to say: "We have not heard of a single case of Texas fever within a hundred miles of Dodge City."[48] A committee advised the governor to place the entire state under quarantine, especially against cattle from south Texas. On August 13 Glick did just that, blocking until the first of November all cattle coming into Kansas, except those from the Indian Territory and the Panhandle of Texas with a certificate of health, and those from Colorado shipped through by rail. Within seven weeks he reinforced this edict with an even more detailed proclamation. Even so, months later it was noted with sarcasm, "Our law makers were very careful not to encroach upon the rights and interests of the railroad companies when they framed and passed the quarantine cattle bill."[49]

The governor's action all but ended the trailing of through cattle to Dodge City from central and southern Texas for the remainder of the season. Even so, 300,626 head had already made the journey by August 15. Glick asked the various sheriffs and county attorneys to enforce his proclamation. In Ford County Pat Sughrue proved equal to the task. Aside from other duties, including a trip to Galveston, Texas, to bring back an accused forger arrested by special detectives, Sheriff Sughrue rode south along the Western Trail to meet incoming herds. At least once he turned back an entire outfit. Shouldering this dangerous job with resolve, Sughrue won the praise of Governor Glick, who commended the officer's "discretion and firmness in this matter."[50]

Earlier the Santa Fe joined the fight by enlarging its stockyards at Lakin, some seventy miles west of Dodge City. The company then ordered some of its facilities at Coolidge dismantled and added to the Lakin site.

---

[48] *Kansas Cowboy*, August 30, 1884.

[49] *Globe Live Stock Journal*, March 17, 1885. Also see ibid., October 7, 1884; *Kansas Cowboy*, August 23, 1884; and James Humphrey, "The Administration of George W. Glick," *Transactions of the Kansas State Historical Society*, vol. 9, 1905–1906 (Topeka: State Printing Office, 1906), 405–406.

[50] Gov. G. W. Glick to Sheriff P. F. Sughrue, September 22, 1884. *Dodge City Democrat*, September 27, 1884. Another item, from the paper's edition of August 9, demonstrated Sughrue's resolve. While in Topeka attending a militia meeting, he "stopped a big row that occurred in one of the hotels, by simply producing his old '45's.' The scattering that took place was simply immense."

Many in Ford County acknowledged the need to keep infected stock seg-regated from local herds. The railroad talked of shipping stock from Cimarron and Howell Station, a point eight miles west.

Other facts suggested the demise of the great Texas drives. By that sum-mer nearly a quarter of all cattle leaving Texas did so by rail. Cattleman George Littlefield reiterated his own concerns: "I am tired of the trail. This year will be my last. In the future I will ship by rail. The annoyance of crossing the Indian reservation and getting through the settled up por-tion of the country with our cattle is enough to drive a man crazy."[51] The Department of the Interior allowed Texas herds to pass over Indian lands, but Comanches and Kiowas forced the Texans to pay for the privilege with large numbers of beeves.

The situation became so mixed up that drovers met at the Ford County courthouse early that summer to petition the federal government for relief. It is interesting, considering the earlier suggestion from the Western Kansas Stock Growers' Association to quarantine all Texas cattle, that such prominent locals as Robert M. Wright, Daniel Frost, and the saloon pro-prietor–turned–cattleman M. S. Culver now agreed to help the Texans. But it came too late; spreading settlement and barbed wire in Texas took a toll on the idea of continuing the fabled drives.

Texas fever dampened optimism well into September, but an outburst of activity over the next dozen weeks brightened hopes. By the time the ship-ping cycle ended in early December, 3,648 cars—each again holding twenty-two animals—had carried 80,256 head from the Dodge City stockyards. Those numbers, greater than the combined figures from all points along the Northern Pacific, stood as the town's crowning achievement. Although 1884 was Dodge City's most successful season, it also proved to be its last as a major terminus for the Texas cattle trade. After watching more than a mil-lion head shipped, the great decade-long era was about to end.

Dodge City owed its success to its isolation on the western Kansas grazing range. That position was now under threat from homesteaders. Ford County's population had nearly doubled within the last two years, with settlers spreading out over the once-pristine cattle lands to the south and west of the city. Local stock raisers, who only squatted on the range-

---

[51] *Colorado Live Stock Record,* as quoted in *Globe Life Stock Journal,* July 1, 1884.

land they used, felt pressure from these newcomers with their plows, sad-faced families, and single-room sod houses.

Everything seemed to conspire against Dodge City: "There are not so many men wanting to engage in the cattle business now, as there has been for the past three or four years," mused Dan Frost in mid-December. "There has been a regular craze among almost all classes of men to engage in some way in the cattle business. . . . It made no difference whether they knew anything about cattle or not, just so they got the stock. This craze is over."[52] The weak-hearted began selling out. Others scurried for pasture-land for their dwindling herds, searching for sanctuaries in the Neutral Strip, Texas Panhandle, and Indian Territory.

A. H. McCoy of the Western Kansas Stock Growers' Association joined Gross Longendyke, president of the Western Central Kansas Stock Association, and Ford County's newly elected state representative, Richard Hardesty, to arrange a year-end meeting with lame-duck governor George Glick. In what seemed a contradiction of purpose, they now opposed quarantining Texas stock, but not for the obvious reasons. Together they represented nearly 300,000 head. As they explained to the governor, local ranchers held 160,000 animals in the Neutral Strip between the Kansas border and the Texas Panhandle and did not expect to be denied access to their own market.

Glick was noncommittal, but it made little difference, as he would be stepping down after the inauguration of John A. Martin. The legislature began debating the quarantine bill in February, and for a time considered a summer embargo on the importation of all cattle south of the Kansas line. This terrified Dodge City ranchers who had been forced by settle-ment to pasture their herds below the border. Stunned by noisy and deter-mined protesters, the assembled legislators abandoned their idea of a summer embargo. Instead, they chose to bar all Texas stock from below the thirty-seventh parallel and all cattle from the Indian Territory south of the thirty-fourth parallel from entering Kansas between March 1 and the first of December. The days of the great Texas trail drives to Dodge City ended without so much as a whimper out of Ford County. As Nicholas Klaine noted somewhat prosaically on March 13, 1885, "The Texas cattle quaran-tine law passed the legislature. No more Texas cattle to Dodge City."

---

[52] *Globe Live Stock Journal*, December 16, 1884.

Chapter 13

THE ENDING OF AN ERA

As Texas stockmen pondered ways around the quarantine law, Dodge City showed off in November 1884 by sending its famous cowboy band to St. Louis to represent the town at the National Cattle Association meeting. Dreamed up years before by Chalkley Beeson to provide music at the Long Branch, the band had become a local institution. They enjoyed all the hoopla of the River City, costumed in their cowboy gear, complete with six-shooters and spurs.

Some were not amused. One Colorado delegate, sensitive to negative images of cattlemen, complained, "We feel that the cowboy band is out of place as long as they persisted in making a parade of their leggings and revolvers. . . . Times have changed and the necessity for revolvers no longer exists."[1] Others disagreed—within months the band was invited to the World's Exhibition at New Orleans. Several notables, including Bat Masterson, attended the festivities.

In his regular Saturday issue of January 17, 1885, Samuel Prouty of the *Kansas Cowboy* offered an observation: "Dodge City is a little paradise for fire insurance companies," adding, "there has never yet been any fires in the city, involving loss to insurance companies." The editor assigned credit for this peculiarity to the town's social customs: "Many of its business houses are never closed; its saloons are frequented by people at all hours, and at no time, day or night, are the streets destitute of pedestrians. Fires have broken out, but they are always discovered in their incipiency and squelched before harm is done."

---

[1] *Missouri Republican*, November 18, 1884, as quoted in Clifford P. Westermeier, "The Dodge City Cowboy Band," *Kansas Historical Quarterly* 19, no. 1 (February 1951): 5. One Texas delegate was especially upset: "We are not in favor of any such display as the so-called cowboy band is making. This leggin' revolver business is out of place in a great city like St. Louis. Besides we are not the desperadoes the band would seem to indicate we are. . . . They parade the streets with the handles of their revolvers protruding from their hip pockets and their leader keeping time with one." For more on this, see *Kansas Cowboy*, November 29, 1884, January 3, 1885; *Dodge City Times*, January 15, 1885; and *Dodge City Democrat*, February 7, 1885.

At four o'clock the following afternoon the paper's editor regretted those reassuring words. Flames engulfed the basement storage area of Front Street grocers Perry Wilden & Company. As it turned out the proprietor had been there earlier and while moving about overturned a candle by accident, igniting some rubbish. Stomping the flames, Wilden thought the fire out. Later a passerby discovered the street level filling with smoke, the entire basement aglow.

An alarm sounded as the flames spread. With nearby pumps frozen—it reached ten below the next morning—members of the Hook & Ladder Company stood by helpless as onlookers emptied stores, piling merchandise in the middle of the street. As they struggled to save what they could, fire burned out W. B. Smith's Union Restaurant to the west, followed in quick succession by Oliver Marsh & Son's "Cow-Boy" Clothing Depot and R. R. Robbins's tailor shop in the rear of that building. On the second floor the *Kansas Cowboy* lost its power press and much of its type. Volunteers salvaged five hundred dollars' worth of other materials from the burning newspaper office. Larry Deger and two or three others saved the Iowa House, west of the "Cow-Boy" across Third Avenue.

East of Wilden's grocery the fire burned out Gaede, Baker & Company's dry-goods emporium, Morris Collar's general store, Charles Shields's hardware and tin shop, as well as a storeroom used by jeweler F. J. Durand. At that point the flames reached the brick wall of Jacob Collar's new building, thus saving Keady Bros. grocery, J. Felkel's boot shop, Gorman and Reamer's grocery, H. P. Niess's boot and shoe repair, Ripple Bros. butcher shop, and the post office building, housing Dr. McCarty's City Drug store. The warehouses of Bob Wright and Morris Collar, facing the inferno near the railroad tracks, soon caught fire and were lost.

The only pump near enough to do any good was at the Wright House. From there a bucket brigade kept water flowing over roofs, holding back the flames at Collar's brick wall. City Marshal Tilghman ordered sheds along Chestnut Street torn down, creating a firebreak to the north. With the Wright and Collar warehouses burning, some feared flames spreading to freight cars parked alongside. Two railroad employees brought an engine through the smoking debris, coupled the cars, and pulled them to temporary safety. Jacob Collar's wife noticed one of the cars smoldering. Left unattended it threatened the gristmill. Struggling alone, Jennie Collar smothered the flames, much to the gratitude of the mill's new owner, Mayor George Hoover.

With nightfall Tilghman added extra policemen to guard all the property piled up on Front Street. They arrested a half-dozen looters, but most people behaved themselves during the crisis. Mother Nature also stood aloof, as Frost observed two days later: "There was but little wind or we would have had a fine piece of prairie where Dodge City now stands."[2] Officials estimated losses at seventy-five thousand dollars, only a portion of which was covered by insurance. Rebuilding began at once, with some proprietors reopening in temporary structures on their original sites within hours, albeit amid smoldering ruins and a disorganized sampling of merchandise. There was much talk of brick.

Even with its pump celebrated as a hero of the blaze, the Wright House closed for good in late February. Bob Wright sold the property to his one-time associate James Langton and Langton's new partner, W. G. Sherlock, for fifty-seven hundred dollars.[3] Those two converted the space into a hardware and agricultural supply store. Within weeks Frost drew distinctions to the future of Ford County: "Judging from the looks of the pile of plows and other farm utensils around Langton & Sherlock's place there is going to be some farming done in this county."[4]

Early February brought news of Herman Fringer's death from dropsy at Canton, Ohio. Ill for some months, he had traveled first to Topeka and then on to Hot Springs, Arkansas, seeking medical aid. Finding none, he journeyed home to Ohio and spent his last days with friends and family, dying at his mother's house on the sixth. He left instructions for his old friend Richard Evans to settle his Dodge City affairs. A forty-year-old bachelor, Fringer left an estate in excess of twenty-five thousand dollars. Next to Henry Sitler and Bob Wright, Fringer, a one-time deputy U.S. marshal at Hays City, had been one of the earliest settlers, arriving at Fort Dodge in 1867 as a quartermaster's clerk before becoming involved with the post sutlers.

Tragedy struck another pioneer resident when Charles Lane, an early associate of Wright's who had gone to Mobeetie to help manage Charlie

---

[2] *Globe Live Stock Journal,* January 20, 1885.

[3] Ford County Register of Deeds, Book D, 393.

[4] *Globe Live Stock Journal,* March 10, 1885.

Rath's business, was judged insane. In early April Sheriff Sughrue escorted him to the asylum at Topeka. Lane died there eight months later.

A tougher version of the state's Prohibition law took effect in early March 1885. The new statute still allowed sales of alcohol for medical, scientific, or mechanical purposes, but its enforcement provisions sent shock waves along Front Street. County attorneys remained the chief enforcement officers, but if they refused to act any private citizen could hire a lawyer and move against violators. Nor could county attorneys dismiss a case without the consent of these privately retained prosecutors. Dodge City's liquor dealers faced attacks from every side. Political alliances no longer guaranteed an easy way around the law. Since a successful prosecution meant confiscation and liquidation of assets—the proceeds going into the school fund—many turned away from this once-lucrative trade.

Some saw it coming and began diversifying even earlier. George M. Hoover, the town's first saloonman, had spent more than ten thousand dollars buying the gristmill from Oliver Marsh. Hoover signed contracts for flour in Colorado and New Mexico. Eyeing the wheat crop at Larned, he expected to run the mill day and night. Walter Straeter sold a large interest in his Old House saloon to Frost and Thompson (W. C. Frost, not Dan) and returned for a time to the boot-maker's trade in the basement of the Dodge House. Later, saloonman Alonzo B. Webster joined up with a new partner from Hunnewell and bought the Marble Hall Restaurant in Kansas City. Webster spent most of his time lounging around his Missouri eatery, while maintaining interests in Dodge.[5]

The town's largest liquor wholesalers, George Hoover and Henry Sturm, closed down two days before the new law went into effect. Many saloonmen followed suit. Walter Straeter, characterized by Dan Frost as one "who can always foretell the approach of a cyclone," disposed of his remaining interest in the Old House. Nye and Thompson sold out their south-side saloon business, renting the building to Sheriff Sughrue, who planned opening a feed store. Singer and Lahey followed, removing bar fixtures and offering the building for rent. One defiant saloon owner posted a sign in his window: "Palace of Women's Christian Temperance Ruin."

---

[5] Ford County Register of Deeds, Book D, 281. For more on changes in the liquor trade, see *Kansas Cowboy*, July 19, August 30, 1884; *Globe Live Stock Journal*, July 15, August 5, October 21, December 2, 1884; *Dodge City Democrat*, September 13, 20, November 22, December 6, 1884; and *Dodge City Times*, October 16, 1884.

Long Branch proprietors Drake and Warren talked of opening a restaurant, as did Atkinson and Romero at the St. James. Charles Heinz turned his popular Lone Star saloon into the Delmonico restaurant. Rumors told of the old Opera House saloon being turned into a granger hotel. Other locations began selling "Temperance Cocktails" as their owners pondered ways around the new law. George Hoover contented himself by selling off stock. A reporter from the *Cowboy* visited the mayor's business and noted, "The windows were placarded with announcements of great bargains in cigars. Messrs. Hoover and Phillips were sitting in easy chairs in front of the entrance. Moses Barber, the scientific and experienced manipulator of palatable liquids, was behind the bar, the only occupant of the house. He was engaged in scratching his chin. The appearance of the establishment was desolate and funereal. In answer to a question as to what they were doing, Mr. Phillips said, 'Selling cigars.' "[6] Dr. McCarty bought ten thousand Gold Tips for three hundred dollars. Sizable liquor sales followed.[7]

As reformers kept up their attacks, Dodge City paused long enough to choose a new mayor, five councilmen, and a police judge from four slates of candidates. The two most prominent groups characterized themselves as the true Peoples' Ticket. The so-called "law and order" coalition, popular among many Democrats, backed Hamilton Bell for mayor. The "liberals" ran Bob Wright, along with the likes of James Kelley and William H. Harris for city council.

For once the campaign produced no fireworks. Although it looked a lot like the old gang, the "liberals" swept into office—not surprising since that year's township elections saw Democratic candidates upset in some races by more than 200 votes. Out of 487 votes, Wright won the mayor's race by a margin of 101. The new city government retained William Tilghman and Ben Daniels as marshal and assistant marshal. Along with his council seat, William H. Harris also served as city treasurer. The council awarded its city-printing patronage to the *Globe*.

Sheriff Sughrue issued a warning on Election Day that "any person engaged in selling intoxicating liquors, in Dodge City, in violation of the law, on, and after May 1st, 1885, will be prosecuted to the full extent of the

---

[6] *Kansas Cowboy*, March 14, 1885.

[7] G. M. Hoover Account Book, April 11, 1885, 200. Archives Division, Kansas State Historical Society. For additional information on this phase of the saloon crisis, see *Dodge City Democrat*, March 7, 1885; *Kansas Cowboy*, March 21, 1885; and *Globe Live Stock Journal*, March 17, 1885.

law."[8] To avoid Sughrue's ultimatum, several saloonmen sought refuge under a provision of the new law exempting drug stores. A. B. Webster returned from Kansas City to help his partner make the conversion at the Stock Exchange. From George Hoover's dwindling reserves, Webster and Bond purchased 1,340½ gallons of whiskey for $2,526.90.[9] Webster arranged for additional stocks to be sent out from Missouri. The partners renamed their place the Palace Drug Store, advertising a complete line of drugs and patent medicines, including wine and fine Kentucky bourbon: "For Medicinal, Mechanical and Scientific Purposes."

So many saloonmen scrambled to follow Webster's lead that they prompted the *Globe's* humorous observation five days after Sughrue's deadline: "Dodge City is well supplied with drug stores, considering we are in the heart of the healthiest country on earth." By late May, Roy Drake and his new partner, William H. Harris (Frank Warren having joined up with Harry Atkinson at the St. James), reopened the Long Branch, jokingly referred to as the Long Branch Temperance Hall.

A. B. Webster sold the land under the Old House saloon to the Bank of Dodge City for $5,750.[10] George Hoover, who had rented his former liquor emporium across from the depot to Prohibitionist George S. Emerson for a grocery store, bought the actual Old House building at auction for $195. Putting the wooden structure on wheels, Hoover moved it east of the Dodge House, where it served as a blacksmith shop. Quitting the wholesale liquor trade, Hoover devoted most of his efforts to the flourmill.

Following Hoover's example, Henry Sturm priced his inventory for sale. These included eighty barrels of four-year-old whiskey, fifteen cases of champagne, six cases each of Rhine wine and Catawba, and three cases of London Swan Gin. To this Sturm added peach and apple brandy, rye, and Jamaica rum, as well as a No. 1 pool table, a 50-by-100-inch French mirror, a small iron safe, and a complete saloon outfit, together with "a lot of other goods too numerous to mention."[11] As Sughrue's deadline loomed, Sturm kept his warehouse open and invited citizens to help themselves to unsold merchandise. Despite the retreat, Dodge City's liquor wars were far from over.

---

[8] *Dodge City Times,* April 9, 1885. Also see *Dodge City Democrat,* April 11, 1885; and *Globe Live Stock Journal,* April 21, 1885.

[9] G. M. Hoover Account Book, April 30, 1885, 202.

[10] Ford County Register of Deeds, Book D, 517.

[11] *Globe Live Stock Journal,* April 28, 1885.

As the town turned away from dance halls and saloons, Dr. McCarty spent nine thousand dollars on an opera house capable of seating nearly two thousand devotees. It stood on the east side of Second Avenue between Walnut and Spruce, a block north and opposite the old Wright House. The place opened with a production of *Jane Eyre*, but its large auditorium mostly served as the center of the town's roller-skating craze. Of course Nick Klaine questioned the benefits of roller-skating. Frost replied in exasperation, "[Is it] not in fact a great improvement over dance halls, which he considered so harmless a few years ago?"[12] Not all the news was contentious. One Saturday baseball game against a visiting team from Cimarron resulted in a fifty-to-eleven victory for hometown fans.

Perry Wilden, the same unfortunate fellow whose carelessness caused the terrible fire in January, planned competition not only for Dodge City's other grocers, but for the town itself. In short, he proposed a rival townsite less than a mile south of the Arkansas River bridge on the old Camp Supply road. Filing an 800-acre plat, Wilden began offering commercial and residential property to prospective customers for five hundred dollars, on the site he named South Dodge City. To help lure merchants, Wilden advertised that lots would be given away to anyone erecting commercial buildings. Interest waned after a powerful storm destroyed Wilden's house, trapping the erstwhile impresario beneath a pile of rubble. By late August, Wilden and his family traveled to Circleville, Ohio, ostensibly to collect a promised loan of ten thousand dollars. He had, in fact, abandoned Ford County and his sizeable debts to the sheriff's care. The *Times* soon reported, "Perry Wilden is said to be rusticating in Canada."[13] South Dodge City faded from memory.

Local merchants were already looking southward from Dodge, but not because of Wilden's misadventure. Citizens finally saw the fulfillment of a promise announced by Alonzo W. Moore in the old *Dodge City Messenger* eleven years before: a free bridge over the Arkansas. County commissioners debated whether to call a special election to decide on $8,000 in bonds for a new bridge, or paying $6,000 for the existing structure. The strongest complaint came from someone who questioned the wisdom of more county debt, pointing out a nearly $70,000 burden to which he added $18,000 for a new courthouse and another $1,000 in floating county script.

[12] Ibid., June 9, 1885.

[13] *Dodge City Times*, November 12, 1885.

Later, this same fellow, who signed his letters TAX-PAYER, began blaming all sorts of financial shenanigans on county commission chairman Frederick Zimmerman, whom he characterized as a "blood-sucking leech," reminding voters of the scheme to build a poorhouse and courthouse wing, the lost bonds in the case of gambler Jack McCarty, the $1,000 paid to repair the Cimarron bridge—"for doing about six dollars worth of work"—and "for fifteen dollars allowed P. G. Reynolds for hauling a pauper to town, when it would have been better for them to have paid Mr. Reynolds fifteen dollars for hauling a pauper out of town."[14]

Those favoring the bridge pointed out what they saw as benefits if the growing numbers of south-side settlers could be induced against trading at Cimarron or Kinsley. But most county residents saw no need to raise taxes just to benefit Dodge City's merchant class. The final vote stood 734 against with only 460 in favor, 313 of these coming from Dodge Township.[15] Refusing defeat, township officers called their own election to authorize the six thousand dollars. As expected the measure passed 391 to 3.[16] After a delay to cover its expenses, the bridge company relinquished control on July 1. For the first time, all travelers could cross the Arkansas River into Dodge City for free.

Meanwhile, more ominous news brought back visions of the past: "Sunday evening, at half past eight, the quiet of the city was broken by the sharp quick reports of fire-arms in the saloon known as Junction's, and to those in the immediate vicinity it was evident that a desperate battle was going on within." So began the *Globe's* account, published two days later on May 12, of the town's latest brush with violence. About midway through that Sunday afternoon two brothers named David and John Barnes had ridden in from Clark County with three other men. Dave Barnes, who sold groceries from his home near Fowler City, planned to prove-up on a small land claim at the courthouse the next morning. Looking for a friend that evening after dinner, the brothers went to the Junction, originally Beatty & Kelley's restaurant, two doors west of Cary's Opera House.

---

[14] *Dodge City Democrat*, January 24, 31, 1885. Although the paper printed these remarks, it also suggested that the man "think a little, and weigh well what you are doing by voting against a free bridge." For more on the initial proposition, see Ford County Commissioners Journals, Book A, 483–84.

[15] *Globe Live Stock Journal*, February 10, 1885. For the complete results, see Ford County Commissioners Journals, Book A, 485.

[16] Ford County Commissioners Journals, Book A, 493.

Settling in, David Barnes began playing seven-up for fifty cents a game with Mysterious Dave Mather. They talked and even seemed to joke as Barnes won two of three hands. Suddenly Mather took all the money from the table, tossed the cards at Barnes, and began walking away. Barnes jumped up, demanding his winnings. Instead, Mather threw a punch. Sheriff Sughrue, who had earlier been standing behind Barnes watching the two men play cards in the crowded saloon, called out to Mysterious Dave, "Here, that won't do." At that instant someone at the back of the room yelled, "Look out, he is pulling a gun."[17]

Sughrue turned just in time to see John Barnes pull a revolver from his hip pocket. The sheriff grabbed the gun. At that moment David Barnes fired at Mather, the bullet cutting across the gambler's forehead and passing through his hat. From behind the bar Mather's brother, Josiah, started shooting. As the smoke cleared David Barnes lay dead near the door. Bystanders James Wall was hit in the right calf and C. P. Camp carried wounds in both legs. Sughrue arrested the two Mather brothers. He later admitted that Dave's gun had not been fired. Despite this testimony the coroner's jury assigned blame to both Josiah and Mysterious Dave, claiming "the said shooting was feloniously done."[18]

John Barnes hauled the body of his twenty-four-year-old brother back to his grieving widow and small children for burial, as Nicholas Klaine denounced the whole affair: "Our citizens strongly condemn the course of the officers who permit these gambling dens to exist in violation of law and decency, and another such occurrence will lead to the taking of desperate measures for the suppression of these hell holes."[19]

The Mather brothers spent time in jail awaiting trial in the district court, but eventually posted a $3,000 bond. In late July Mysterious Dave traveled to Topeka with liveryman and former city marshal Fred Singer. Three weeks later he joined the police force at New Kiowa in Barber County. Perhaps just happy to be rid of him, Klaine remarked, "Dave makes a good officer."[20] Neither of the brothers ever stood trial for the killing of David Barnes. Judge Strang moved the case to Edwards County,

---

[17] "Statement of Sheriff Sughrue," *Dodge City Democrat*, May 16, 1885.

[18] *Globe Live Stock Journal*, May 19, 1885.

[19] *Dodge City Times*, May 14, 1885.

[20] Ibid., August 20, 1885.

and by early December it was reported: "In the Mathers [*sic*] case they failed to appear, and their bonds were forfeited."[21]

Ignoring stories of Dodge City violence, as well as the Kansas quarantine law and similar legislation in Colorado, cattlemen from south Texas planned to drive their herds north. One of their ill-conceived schemes involved shipping herds over the Fort Worth & Denver Railroad to Harrold, that line's terminus south of Red River and east of Doan's Crossing in Wilbarger County, then drive them above the quarantine latitudes and await December before entering Kansas. That late in the year they hoped to ship from either Caldwell or Dodge City. They failed to consider reactions from stockmen in Kansas and the Panhandle who already occupied those lands—men who were not about to expose their animals to Spanish fever from south Texas.

The third annual meeting of the Western Kansas Stock Growers' Association took place at Dodge City in early April. Members spent most of the time discussing the possibility of Texas cattle invading lands south of the Kansas line, where they now held nearly two hundred thousand head. Resolutions condemned any introduction of south Texas cattle into the Indian Territory or Neutral Strip. In concert with allies in Kansas, people in Greer County, in what is now southwestern Oklahoma, protested rumors of Texans below San Antonio using their area as a quarantine ground. Panhandle stockmen, led by managers of the Francklyn Land & Cattle Company, showed the same determination displayed at Dodge City.

Willing to write off stock from south Texas, the old town hoped to benefit from cattle held within the quarantine zone. Responding to a report published in the *Colorado Live Stock Record*—"in the short cycle of the year the shifting sands of commerce has changed the scene. Dodge, like Abilene, so far as its cattle traffic goes, will only be known to history"— Dan Frost defended his home turf as "the greatest cattle exchange west of the Missouri river, Denver notwithstanding."[22]

Townspeople felt the same. With encouragement from the railroad, the city council called for a special election on June 10 to consider two thou-

---

[21] *Globe Live Stock Journal*, December 8, 1885. Also see State of Kansas vs. David Mather and Josiah H. Mather. Records of the Ford County District Court, Criminal Appearance Docket A, Case No. 732, 192, and Case No. 736, 197.

[22] *Globe Live Stock Journal*, April 7, 1885.

sand dollars in municipal bonds to purchase nearly 160 acres from Henry Beverley. This land, located south of the river and opposite the existing stockyards, was then to be used as a holding area for cattle awaiting shipment. Santa Fe stock agent W. P. Herring, visiting five days before the election, assured voters that if they passed the measure, "Dodge will stand a good show for the bulk of the range cattle south and west of here."[23] Those words fooled enough voters that even with a low turnout the result favored the scheme 279 to 3.[24]

Meanwhile, settlers continued to force cattle ranchers off public lands, a situation convincing locals, as well as others below the Kansas line, to organize small drives into Wyoming and Montana. Berry, Boin & Company bought three thousand head from J. M. Day for that very purpose. Towers and Gudgell did the same with five thousand of their cattle. The Francklyn Land & Cattle Company planned on moving twenty thousand head to northern grazing lands. Others, hoping to slow the assault, began shipping cattle out by rail. By early June an agent for the AT&SF requested five hundred cars. The company obliged.

It began looking like the old days, with Dodge City not only crowded with strangers but slipping back into some of its bad habits as well. The *Kansas Cowboy* could not help observing, "The town is beginning to fill up with cowboys and stockmen. The saloons, gambling halls and dance halls are in full blast again."[25]

As settlers swarmed into Ford County, grabbing up more land south and west of the city, merchants and others tried finding some way to get cattle into town from ranges farther south. In early June they gathered at Cary's Opera House to approve a possible solution. The trail committee, headed by jeweler Adolphus Gluck and backed by Bob Wright, Neil Brown, Dan Frost and others, presented a plan.

It represented a hodge-podge of compromise and negotiation. The new trail began in the Neutral Strip to a point about a mile east of the C.O.D. Ranch, still owned by Beeson and Harris, where it intersected the old Tuttle Trail. Beeson marked the route with a plowed furrow. From there cattle would move toward the Cornelius property on Sand Creek—the owner

---

[23] Ibid., June 1, 1885.

[24] *Dodge City Democrat*, June 13, 1885.

[25] *Kansas Cowboy*, May 30, 1885.

asking only that his plowed land be protected—then past the Lucas farm and over land occupied by two fellows named Fulton and Reese. At Reeseville, a small trading point, a storekeeper promised assistance to drovers. The trail then wound its way over some deeded but unoccupied land to a spot known as Twin Lakes. From that point to Mulberry Creek, it was believed, settlers were located far enough to either side of the trail to remain out of harm's way. Cattlemen at least hoped they could traverse this route without complaints.

It was asking a lot. Only a month before A. J. Anthony moved his cattle from Hodgeman County back into Ford, locating them south of the Arkansas some fifteen miles west of Dodge City. Others were pushed back. J. M. Day, who once occupied good range in southeast Ford County, was forced to sell off a large portion of his stock and drive the rest into Indian Territory. The Beverley brothers followed Day's example. Major Falls, managing the interests of the Harvey Cattle Company, moved ten thousand head back to their home range near Granada, Colorado. Robert Wright faced reality and sent five thousand steers into the northwestern corner of the state. The Weeks brothers moved their stock to Nebraska, while Pierce, Brown & Leuthstrom—who together held forth on the Bluff Creek range—decided to sell all their improved stock or retreat into the Neutral Strip.

Others, including George Anderson and Hi Kollar, did the same, but not without cost. Chalkley Beeson was forced to rent fenced land in the Strip at twenty-five cents per head per month while searching for empty range. Northeast of Dodge, Albert Boyd, the one-time partner in the Dodge House, joined with other Pawnee County stockmen planning to reduce their holdings. Vacant land could not be found, and wild fires did not help. Fearing lost revenue, Robert Wright opened a new supply store in the southeast corner of the Neutral Strip, 125 miles from Dodge. Housed in a large tent, Wright's latest enterprise managed sales of seventy-five to one hundred dollars from each passing herd.

Economic hardship crowded thousands of domestic cattle onto the Dodge City market. Outside buyers, who had contracted for south Texas stock before the new quarantine legislation became law, expected herd owners to disregard the statute and breakthrough. After all, Dodge City was known for ignoring laws not to its liking. Eastern buyers witnessed all this first hand, enjoying an afternoon whiskey in one of many illegal saloons. But now they waited in vain for the Texas herds.

By early June a Dodge City posse in the Indian Territory turned back thirty thousand head of through Texas cattle. This show of force upset stock raisers in and around Mobeetie, who feared those animals would be driven into the Panhandle, carrying with them the risk of Spanish fever. The men from south Texas had little choice, many facing ruin for failure to deliver animals already under contract. They prayed for compromise allowing passage across the quarantine line on a one-time basis, but the threat of Spanish fever hardened everyone's resolve.

The year before, Congress created the Bureau of Animal Industry. Included were provisions against the transportation of stock known to be carrying communicable diseases between states and territories. After learning that south Texas cattle had entered Indian land along the old Western Trail, United States Attorney J. R. Hallowell decided to act. Trail bosses J. R. Blocker and Oscar Woodley ignored Hallowell's warnings and found themselves arrested by Deputy U.S. Marshal Hamilton Bell. Taken to Dodge City, the men stood before United States Commissioner Rufus G. Cook.

Estimates of the number of cattle stopped by Hallowell's order reached one hundred thousand by mid-summer; before the secretary of the interior and former Confederate Lucius Quintus Cincinnatus Lamar confused the situation by issuing a directive prohibiting interference with noninfected south Texas stock moving along established routes through the Neutral Strip. Lamar implied that Gen. Philip Sheridan was willing to use force to keep open these avenues of legitimate commerce. But by now fewer Texans believed they could ignore the quarantine line. People acknowledged that the days of an uninterrupted cattle trail to Dodge City had ended.

Some felt the same about ignoring the state's Prohibition law. Albert Griffin, a former anti-slavery agitator, president of the Kansas State Temperance Union, and combative editor of the *Manhattan Nationalist*, came to Dodge City—more for personal political reasons than as a champion of moral reform—and delivered a well-attended temperance lecture at the Methodist church on the evening of June 21. Returning three days later, following a quick trip to Garden City, Griffin again attacked Dodge City's saloons while organizing a local chapter of the KSTU. He signed up sixty

converts and raised about three hundred dollars. That Friday he tried
swearing out complaints against the remaining saloonmen. Fearing open
rebellion, County Attorney Benjamin Milton refused to act. Griffin rushed
to Topeka hoping to persuade Attorney General Simeon Bradford to return
with him to Dodge and force compliance. Bradford declined the invitation,
but instead sent Abraham B. Jetmore as his deputized representative.

Forewarned, saloonmen closed their doors for the duration of the visit.
Unable to quench their thirst, a large group of irrigation-ditch diggers
idled by rain blamed Griffin and Jetmore for their inconvenience. These
ill-tempered men gathered at the Great Western Hotel shouting insults.
They manhandled Dr. Galland and several other Prohibition sympathiz-
ers who dared make an appearance. The doctor and one of the Junction
saloon's new owners came to blows.

The situation contained all the elements of serious trouble until Bat
Masterson intervened. Visiting with Griffin and Jetmore to quiet their
nerves, Masterson, a hastily appointed deputy sheriff, stepped from the
hotel and ordered the mob to the north side of Locust Street. He posted
himself outside Griffin and Jetmore's rooms before finally convincing the
thirsty laborers to retreat beyond the tracks. City officers jailed the most
belligerent combatants. The two reformers called off the public meeting
scheduled later that evening at the Methodist church. At noon the next
day the two interlopers, escorted by City Marshal Tilghman, assistant Ben
Daniels, another policeman, and two or three deputy sheriffs, boarded the
train and departed Dodge City, somewhat unnerved by their experiences.
With both agitators out of town the saloons reopened.

While Albert Griffin admitted at Topeka that "Mr. Masterson steadily
did all he could to prevent any attack being made upon us," the Kansas
press took up the incident with all the gusto shown the Dodge City War
some two years before.[26] Griffin may have credited Masterson with saving
his life, but from the safety of eastern Kansas he also characterized the ex-
sheriff "as the reputed leader of the lawless elements of Dodge City."
Later, while tucked away in his home town of Manhattan, Kansas, Griffin
added a parting shot at Masterson's expense: "He is smart and has many
elements of a leader, but is unquestionably a vicious man. He did not want
Assistant Attorney General Jetmore or myself killed, and the reason he is

---

[26] *Kansas Daily Commonwealth*, July 2, 1885.

said to have given his associates was that 'they could not afford to bring down upon themselves the vengeance of the State government and the State Temperance Union.'"[27] Griffin got carried away with his own rhetoric.

Some weeks later, Bat addressed a response to editor Sam Prouty, in which he called Griffin a "narrow-minded crank." Masterson dismissed the existence of a mob except to say, "The only individuals in this community that were ever engaged with a mob were those who were following Griffin and Jetmore." Then, with obvious reference to Luke Short's troubles in 1883, he added, "Sutton, Galland, Swan, Bullard, Emerson, Deger, et. al., have always been members of a mob, and the dirtiest and most villainous mob that ever went unhung."[28]

Dan Frost wasted no time chastising Griffin's cowardly performance: "he undoubtedly had a horrible nightmare when he conceived the idea that an arrangement had been made to form a line and fire off revolvers when he should leave town," the *Globe* crowed on July 7. "Heretofore Dodge City has not had the reputation of firing off revolvers just to scare an already scared man." A week later Frost continued his disparaging remarks: "Alfred Griffin is a good long range fighter, and is now pouring hot shot into Dodge City from the pulpit, on the streets, and his newspaper.... We do not claim that our city is a pink of perfection from a moral standpoint, but we do claim that we are the equal of Topeka, Atchison, Leavenworth, or any of the large places of Kansas, with the one exception, that our saloons are wide open in front, and not the back door."

Frost took exception to Griffin's complaint that three brothels stood "just across the street from the brick school house." A foul lie, challenged the editor with a sense of irony not lost on modern readers, "every body in this city knows better, for there is not a house of any kind within a block of the school house, and no house of prostitution within two or three blocks of the school house."[29]

On the subject of saloons, Griffin's hysterics misfired. Many questioned why Dodge City should be singled out when other towns defied the law, albeit in more subtle ways. At Wichita the *Beacon* went so far as to say, "When the light of practical experience shall have penetrated through the foggy ranting of the half crank, half shrewd reformers, Kansas will be

---

[27] *Manhattan Nationalist*, July 10, 1885.
[28] *Kansas Cowboy*, August 29, 1885.
[29] *Globe Live Stock Journal*, July 14, 1885.

ashamed of the funny law which Dodge City repudiates." Being laughed at helped doom Albert Griffin's gubernatorial ambitions.

Even before his tantrums subsided, Griffin tried convincing Governor Martin to send the militia into Dodge City to shut down all those saloons. Martin sought advice from cooler heads. In explaining the situation in Ford County from just that perspective, Judge Jeremiah Strang wrote the governor, blaming Griffin's personal motives for the trouble. Strang felt the preachy Prohibitionist wanted the saloons closed with fanfare so he could claim credit. The judge then pointed out the obvious: "Dodge City is in a transition state and will come all right soon of itself. . . . The festive cowboy is already becoming conspicuous by his absence in Dodge, and ere long he will be seen & heard there, in his glory, no more forever. The cowboy gone the gamblers and prostitutes will find their occupations gone, and, from necessity, must follow. The bulk of the saloons will then die out because there will be no sufficient support left, and the temperance people can close the rest as easily as they could in any other city in Kansas."[30]

Rather than call out the militia, the governor sent his attorney general to Dodge City. Mayor Wright and Sheriff Sughrue waited for their visitor at the Santa Fe depot. Simeon Bradford began his tour, asking the sheriff how many saloons existed before the new law. Seventeen, he was told, but now only ten were left. During his two-day visit Bradford spoke with all sides concerning the Albert Griffin incident, and of conditions generally. What he learned confirmed Judge Strang's assessment. Referring to the favorable impression Bradford made, Sam Prouty wrote, "He realizes the fact that Dodge City has an individuality of its own. . . . The town will work out its own salvation. It cannot be redeemed and purified by means of the lash in the hands of outside parties who are actuated by mercenary motives. . . . [H]ypocrisy does not exist here. Our wickedness is open to the glare of the sun."[31]

---

[30] Judge J. C. Strang to Gov. John A. Martin, July 5, 1885. Governors' Correspondence, Archives Division, Kansas State Historical Society. Some Kansas editors had reached the same conclusion, with the *Topeka Daily Capital* noting on August 6: "There are silent but irresistible forces at work to regenerate Dodge City. The passage of the Texas bill, the defeat of the trail bill and the rapid settlement of the country south and southwest of Dodge, have destroyed that place as a cattle town. The cowboys must go, and with him will go the gamblers, the courtesans, the desperadoes and the saloon."

[31] *Kansas Cowboy*, July 11, 1885. Even Albert Griffin eventually changed positions, it being claimed some years later: "He is now an uncompromising opponent of all laws for the prohibition or restriction of the liquor traffic, as he believes the results show that they supplant and prevent the work for total abstinence." Wilson, comp., *A Biographical History of Eminent Men*, 99.

This inability of the state to enforce its own laws encouraged the liquor men. By early October, perhaps bored swinging his cobbler's hammer, Walter Straeter sold his boot shop in the basement of the Dodge House and opened a small saloon on Front Street just west of the old Iowa House hotel. He soon added two billiard tables.

Residents may have argued over the state's liquor laws, but local cattle-men faced new threats. Not only did Governor Martin encourage the sheriff and others to enforce the quarantine law, reporting directly to the Live Stock Sanitary Commission, but President Grover Cleveland issued a proclamation on July 23 ordering all non-Indians to remove herds from the Cheyenne and Arapaho reservations within forty days. This would involve three hundred thousand cattle and horses, causing resentment among those cornered by an overstocked range.

General Philip H. Sheridan supported the plan as a way to calm dissat-isfaction among the tribes that had led to an Indian scare in early July. Some Indians resented the government's interference, concerned more with losing money from vacated stock leases. Other influential tribal members had always opposed the land-lease system, even refusing to accept their proportional share of the profits. Not wishing to defy both the president of United States and General Sheridan, cattlemen began moving their animals. Some drove herds to rangeland as far away as Ari-zona. By mid-August R. M. Wright & Company hired cowboys to drive out its stock. With his eyes on the future, Bob Wright bought out the Tas-cosa Mercantile Company in the Panhandle for twenty thousand dollars, in an effort to cement trading ties with Texas cattlemen.

Officials at Topeka were not only hearing from disgruntled cattlemen, but in late October an Edwards County deputy sheriff filed his own com-plaint. Warrant in hand, he had followed a gambler into Dodge City. Once there—reports to Governor Martin later suggested—the officer was sur-rounded by an angry mob. The governor might have considered interven-ing, until he discovered that the alleged mob consisted of only one man, Bat Masterson.

The Edwards County deputy had indeed come to Dodge to arrest the gambler. That man, identified only as Phelps, had obtained a license to run a game at Kinsley, but when told he could be arrested unless he paid an additional thirty dollars to a local "association," he skipped town. Masterson offered to pay the man's fine, but the deputy insisted that Phelps answer to the county attorney in person. Bat talked with the deputy in private, allowing Phelps to slip away. The disgusted Edwards County lawman handed his warrant to Deputy Sheriff Singer and took in a fight at the fairgrounds. Afterward he met with Phelps for an hour or so. Whatever was said, the officer retrieved his warrant and returned to Kinsley empty-handed.

Somewhat sensitive to rumors about mobs roaming the streets of Dodge City, Daniel Frost disavowed the incident, claiming tongue-in-cheek that had the deputy "made known to one of our officers, his business, as he ought to have done, Phelps would have gone to Kinsley on the first train, even if it had been necessary to make a corduroy road of dead men to walk on from Front street to the depot."[32]

Amid all this turmoil the 1885 county elections became the most controversial yet held, with the state supreme court finally deciding the issue. Democrats nominated Thomas J. Tate for sheriff, Henry M. Beverley as treasurer, and George M. Hoover (who later withdrew) for Third District commissioner. Anti-Prohibition Republicans and dissatisfied Democrats held a People's Convention and chose Patrick Sughrue to continue as sheriff, Robert Wright for treasurer, and Hamilton Bell as county commissioner. Then, crowding the ballot, a so-called Independent Ticket, made up primarily of out-county Prohibition Republicans, offered former-sheep-rancher-turned-cattleman R. W. Tarbox for sheriff and J. W. Gilbert, manger of the Eureka Irrigating Canal Company, as treasurer. The Independents also supported Hamilton Bell as county commissioner. The lines were drawn for an interesting contest, with the *Times* backing the Independents, the *Globe* supporting the People's County Ticket, and the *Democrat* praising its own party's candidates.

The campaign began with Bob Wright, Pat Sughrue, Dan Frost, and William H. Harris addressing the county's growing number of black citizens. Calling on them to support the People's Ticket, they stressed their group's allegiance to the Republican Party—invoking Lincoln while ignoring the three Democrats on the seven-man roster. Thirty-six members of the audience were so overcome by the performance they enrolled themselves in the so-called R. M. Wright Guards. Exactly what this group

---

[32] *Globe Live Stock Journal*, November 3, 1885.

was expected to do, aside from voting for candidate Wright, was never explained.

Tensions between Bob Wright and Henry Beverley seemed to rise as both men campaigned for the same office. Shortly before the convention, Beverley opened his own merchandising establishment on Chestnut Street. Someone signing himself "VOTER" wrote the *Dodge City Democrat* complaining of Wright's candidacy for treasurer as a ploy to gain control over county deposits for personal gain. Wright would not even mind J. W. Gilbert's victory, this man reasoned, since the Gilbert brothers did all their business and made their deposits with R. M. Wright & Company.[33] The People's Ticket accused Beverley of helping compose the offending letter. He, in turn, wrote Dan Frost expressing his distaste for the whole affair: "My relations with my worthy and honorable former partner and friend, R. M. Wright, have been of the most pleasant character. I entertain high regard for him, and defy any one to truthfully say I ever uttered a word derogatory to his character."[34]

Sparring continued right up to election day, with Bob Wright courting the Catholic vote to the very last. Opponents suspected a fraudulent People's victory, due to the large number of ballots cast in Dodge Township. An injunction was granted from the probate court restraining the commissioners from recording those votes. A procedural irregularity then convinced the court it had no jurisdiction. The judge ordered all the votes counted. As expected, candidates of the People's Ticket won handily. By contrast, the Independents carried all other precincts, except races for county clerk and surveyor, where the Democrats prevailed.[35]

With more than a thousand ballots cast in Dodge Precinct, opponents cried foul. Losing faith in Ford County justice, they took their grievances to the state supreme court on November 24. Many found it strange that Dodge City could suddenly find so many qualified voters. Frost explained: "Fact is, gentlemen, emigration had been pouring in here until we have got the votes."[36] It turned out to be true: estimates of Ford County's population had risen from 3,125 to 7,778 over the past five years. A subsequent

---

[33] "COMBINATION," *Dodge City Democrat*, October 17, 1885.

[34] H. M. Beverley to D. M. Frost, editor, October 23, 1885. *Globe Live Stock Journal*, October 27, 1885.

[35] Ford County Commissioners Journals, Book A, 515–17.

[36] *Globe Live Stock Journal*, November 17, 1885.

investigation showed the ratio increase of voters in Dodge City was no greater than in other county precincts.

On the very day Prohibition-minded Independents filed their lawsuit at Topeka, Attorney General Bradford returned, determined to close the saloons once and for all. Actually, the saloons and "drug stores" had closed on Election Day, and afterward Mayor Wright ordered all gambling stopped. The city hated to do it, since between July and October fines from gambling and prostitution poured $1,150 into city coffers, with another $275 rolling in from the police court.

Realizing Bradford planned to file suit in the district court, the saloon-men closed up before he stepped off the train. While touring the town, the mayor convinced the skeptical attorney general that the city would keep the saloons closed. A reporter from Newton claimed he was "at Dodge City the next day after Mr. Bradford was supposed to have put an end to the whole business there and saw the saloons running with open doors as they were previous to his visit. This thing of shutting saloons with 'shoot mouth' is becoming monotonous."[37] Others agreed, with many women responding to the farce by organizing a local chapter of the WCTU.

Ford County was then hit by a writ of mandamus from the Kansas State Supreme Court, ordering it to recount the November ballots without considering those from Dodge Township. Commissioners had little choice but to comply. They met in special session in the county clerk's office just before noon on December 11. An attorney for the People's Ticket objected to the recount on grounds that the time to do so, as indicated in the writ, had expired. Commissioners adjourned until 1:30, but decided to go ahead. Naturally, on this count the People's County Ticket lost.[38] The commissioners had now declared two sets of winners. Awaiting the supreme court's final say, the People's candidates took office in January, albeit under a cloud. Yet Dodge City had far more to worry about than lawsuits.

With year's end only five weeks away, many wondered what changes lay ahead. On November 21, Sam Prouty had predicted, "The old frontier appearance of Dodge City will be numbered among the things of the past, before another year departs." No one needed to wait that long. Six days

[37] *Newton Republican*, as quoted in *Dodge City Times*, December 17, 1885.
[38] Ford County Commissioners Journals, Book A, 518–19.

later an exploding kerosene lamp set fire to the second floor of the Junction saloon. Gaining strength in the wood-frame building, the flames spread quickly, to the east destroying councilman Henry Koch's barber shop, Cary and Wright's Opera House saloon, then north to the Opera House restaurant, Jones and Whitelaw's law office, and Crumbaugh and Fitzgerald's small real estate building.

Moving westward from the Junction, the fire claimed Dunn and Kirkpatrick's furniture store, York, Parker & Draper's mercantile, Charles Heinz's Delmonico restaurant, E. R. Garland's drug store (the real thing, not a camouflaged saloon), F. J. Durand's jewelry story, Zimmerman's hardware, Adolphus Gluck's jewelry store, and George Hinkle's four-month-old saloon to the rear and fronting Chestnut Street. The former sheriff had returned to Dodge from Garden City, after authorities there forced him out of the saloon business. West of Gluck's shop the fire continued, wiping out the St. James restaurant, saloon, and billiard hall; the Long Branch; Webster and Bond's "drug store"; and finally the brick building housing R. M. Wright & Company, together with its "fireproof" warehouse to the rear. Estimates of loss reached $150,000.

As in the January fire, no wind carried the flames beyond this single block. Citizens by the hundreds rushed forward, helping businessmen remove as much stock as possible. A few used the confusion to steal, but most came only to help. In doing so they put aside their moral differences, one account noting, "The question is not asked, 'do you keep a saloon or preach the gospel,' but let me help you save your property." This writer went on to explain, "By an over sight some awful good whiskey was allowed to burn up."[39] Bob Wright, after saving what he dared, told the crowd they were welcome to the rest, if they wished risking the flames. Several took the chance and survived with retrieved merchandise.

While onlookers piled goods onto Front Street, others fought to keep the flames from spreading to adjoining blocks, especially northward across Chestnut Street. There, on the east side corner, above the Odd Fellows Hall, were the *Globe* offices, and on the other corner, to the west, above Strange and Summersby's Bee Hive Dry Goods, Sam Prouty had relocated offices of his once-burned-out *Kansas Cowboy*. In adjacent blocks people kept soaked blankets spread out over roofs, or covered them with salt.

[39] *Globe Live Stock Journal*, December 1, 1885.

Many buildings blistered from the heat but did not burn. In their account of the blaze, *Globe* editors acknowledged aid from one class of citizen seldom praised: "To the two colored men who so ably assisted us in getting our material out of the office we say thanks."[40]

By evening's end Marshal Tilghman organized twenty special policemen to guard the area and protect exposed property. Even before the ruins cooled, businessmen began making arrangements for the construction of makeshift buildings or found temporary locations before contracting for permanent brick replacements on their destroyed sites.

Dodge City felt pride in the rather stoic acceptance of loss: "If anyone thinks that Dodge is a dead town let them come here now and get their illusion dispelled," boasted Sam Prouty on December 5, adding, "not a single murmur has been heard to escape from the lips of any of the sufferers of the late fire. One hundred and fifty thousand dollars went to glory at that time and yet nobody cares a cuspidor about it." Prouty saw some good coming from the blaze: "The old Dodge, with its world-wide celebrity has disappeared. The old rookeries and break-neck sidewalks that used to front the railroad have gone." Critics chastised the city for not spending the twelve hundred dollars requested by the fire company for a hand-pump and enough hose to reach the river.[41] Prouty joined the chorus, predicting with a tinge of humor: "After Dodge City is all burned up and a damage of a million dollars is experienced, it will then be about time to think about getting a fire engine."[42]

Ten days later all the heroic efforts to save the buildings facing south along Chestnut Street seemed unimportant. Another fire broke out near midnight in the middle of that same block, in a room "occupied by two 'fair young ladies' who were out visiting."[43] Actually the place housed members of the sporting crowd, and the two aforementioned lovelies were busy plying their trade in a south-side dive. The night being cold, one of the women, Flora Mansfield—known locally as Sawed-Off—asked the dance hall bootblack to go to her room and light the stove. A later passerby saw flames beside the chimney and sounded the alarm.

[40] Ibid.

[41] *Dodge City Democrat*, November 28, December 5, 1885.

[42] *Kansas Cowboy*, December 5, 1885.

[43] *Dodge City Democrat*, December 12, 1885.

Residents, by now accustomed to the procedure, pulled themselves out of bed and did their best to save goods and property. A strong north wind hampered efforts. Men tried pulling down a small wood-frame sporting house to the east with ropes, but the fire spread too fast. Next, firefighters stuffed 150 pounds of gunpowder into Mollie Whitecamp's house. It was hoped that taking out her abode would save the Odd Fellows Hall and the *Globe*'s office. Unfortunately, the blast failed to blow off the roof and the flames jumped across.

North of the *Globe* a vacant lot stopped the flames, which had engulfed M. S. Culver's stable but spared his house. West from its source, the fire destroyed H. P. Niess's relocated boot and shoe repair, J. A. Arment's paint shop, and the building on the corner occupied by the Bee Hive Dry Goods and *Kansas Cowboy*—this time Sam Prouty would not reopen. Northward, along Second Avenue, A. N. Ramseyer's grocery and two residences, one belonging to William H. Harris, were lost. On the northwest corner of the burning block the City of Paris millinery was saved, as were all the homes fronting Walnut Street eastward to Culver's house.

Of course the block south had burned ten days before, so the north wind could do no damage there. Sparks drifted toward the south side, where Hamilton Bell organized forty men to stop the fire from spreading below the tracks. Because of the wind and wooden construction, the fire did its damage in only an hour. Losses were set at twenty-five thousand dollars, only a portion of which was covered by insurance. Property owners began rebuilding, with appreciative eyes settling on Henry Sitler's brickyard.

Wild rumors circulated suggesting the town's Prohibitionists guilty of arson. Based on available evidence the claim seems groundless. Bob Wright, who suffered a $20,000 loss over that covered by insurance, did fire several shots into Mike Sutton's house. Earlier, concerned about the stories of arson, Sutton confronted Wright and demanded police protection. The merchant-turned-mayor later explained that he told the worried lawyer that he would personally handle the matter.

Claiming to have seen someone lurking in the shadows, Mayor Wright, six-gun in hand, ordered the figure to stand still. Instead, the man ran around Sutton's house with Bob Wright blasting away in hot pursuit. At least that was the mayor's story. Cyclone Mike convinced himself it was all prearranged to cover up an assassination. Wright's explanation prompted one Kansas editor to remark, "Even putting the most favorable construction upon this story it seems to us that it is not at all surprising that Mike should suppose that an attempt was being made upon his life and further more if that is the way the Dodge City mayor had of guarding people we don't want him for a guard of ours."[44] The skittish reformer swore out a criminal complaint against the mayor. City Marshal Tilghman arrested his boss. The case would carry over into 1886.

Dodge City welcomed the delay, and brought in the New Year in traditional fashion: orchestrated by three hundred gunshots fired at the moon. Yet there was much they could not celebrate, with nearly two blocks of businesses and housing destroyed, their elected slate of county officials in doubt, the mayor charged with the attempted murder of a prominent lawyer, the state attorney general threatening to suppress saloons, gambling, and other vices, along with their link to the Texas trade all but wiped out.

Settlement and quarantine legislation had taken their toll. The vast Texas through herds existed now only in memory. Numbers shipped from ranges north of the dead line put the lie to one mid-summer boast: "The fellows that said Dodge City was no longer a cattle shipping point, should drop in our city about now."[45] Despite all the encouraging language, shipping figures in no way matched those of 1884. Between May and early December 1885, the most active months, the AT&SF loaded only 42,174 animals, only slightly better than half those shipped during the previous record-breaking year. Much of Dodge City's uniqueness had faded away.

---

[44] *Medicine Lodge Cresset*, December 17, 1885. Also see *Globe Live Stock Journal*, December 15, 1885, *Dodge City Times*, December 17, 1885, and *Dodge City Democrat*, December 19, 1885.

[45] *Globe Live Stock Journal*, July 28, 1885.

EPILOGUE

As revelers awoke New Year's morning 1886, they faced an eerie white silence. A powerful blizzard had swept in during the night and plunged temperatures well below zero. Thirty-mile-per-hour winds drifted the snow. By the fourth day it seemed as if that winter might well be the worst since the town's founding fourteen years before. All travel stopped. Train schedules were delayed, then discarded altogether. Dodge City editors rationed newsprint by issuing half-sheet editions. Desperate travelers crowded hotels and restaurants. Outlying settlers, misled by the mild autumn weather, suffered more than most, with little fuel and few provisions.

After a few days some trains got through, only to have a second storm close the line. One got trapped six miles east of town. Drifting snow blocked the coaches, forcing access through a hole dug between cars. Some passengers walked into Dodge, where townspeople loaded wagons with fuel and food for those remaining on board. Women and children were evacuated on the return runs. Railroad agents provided stranded travelers free accommodations. The train was not freed for six days.

The storm brought advantages to some, compensating for the loss of freight and delayed mail service: "it has been a God-send to hundreds of unemployed men who have made very good wages at track clearing, and the hotel and restaurant men have reaped a harvest."[1] Two hundred men worked the line between Dodge City and Spearville, but shortages caused concern: "Provisions in the city were becoming scarce, some articles in the grocery line being nearly exhausted. The railroad company's coal pile replenished our coal dealers' supply. . . . Feed was scarce, but flour was plentiful."[2]

---

[1] *Dodge City Democrat,* January 23, 1886.

[2] *Dodge City Times,* January 28, 1886.

Over two hundred men, women, and children were trapped in Dodge City. Locals tried making their stay as pleasant as possible, even organizing a grand ball at McCarty's Opera House to help ease their sense of isolation. But Dodge City's menacing reputation clouded the festivities—only six couples showed up. The rest barricaded themselves in their lodgings, fearful of becoming victims of the deadly six-shooter or robbed by stick-up artists were they to venture out at night.

Losses from the storm, adding to the problems of dwindling rangeland, broke some local stockmen. Reports from Garden City, Spearville, Ness City, and Larned spoke of widespread damage. For some, losses remained light, perhaps a dozen head, but for others the numbers were frightening. Charley Ross lost 100 head. Sam Oxley counted forty dead steers from his herd of 130. Albert Hurst lost 150 cattle, while D. R. Menke lost the same number of sheep. Early estimates claimed 10,000 dead animals between Garden City and White Woman's Creek. "There is no exception to the rule," reported the *Globe* on January 19, "stock that died during the snow storms were the ones that were not sheltered or properly cared for. The day to allow cattle to shift for themselves in this country is over."

Smaller herdsmen were wiped out, while survivors faced losses of 25 to 50 percent. Railroad agents tried downplaying the disaster, one claiming to have seen only twenty-nine dead animals between Dodge City and Coolidge. Knowledgeable locals scoffed at those figures while also dismissing a report from the Associated Press telling of one hundred thousand dead cattle within a hundred-mile radius of Dodge City. The *Times* responded realistically on February 11: "The past two winters have been fatal to the cattle interests in Western Kansas . . . and other ways must be used in the rearing of stock on the plains. The settlement of the country will solve the problem." The blizzard of 1886 added to the difficulties facing Kansas stockmen, and the economic preeminence of the cattle business suffered as a consequence. Dodge City soon felt its effects.

Until then its citizens lived in a semi-dream world of never-ending prosperity. In fairness, it seemed likely to go on forever. Within the fire district and elsewhere construction began on impressive rows of brick buildings—eleven in all—much to the delight of Henry Sitler, who fired one hundred thousand bricks a week. By the end of February an electric light company and telephone and telegraph company had been organized, a board of trade established, and a new bank formed with fifty thousand dollars in capital stock.

C. W. Averill bought the last dance hall building and converted it into a warehouse packed floor to ceiling with household goods, thus ending that link to Dodge City's colorful past. James T. Whitelaw started another Democratic newspaper, a short-lived journal called the *Dodge City Sun*. New settlers kept coming: thirty cars of immigrants rolled in on a single day. Eyeing the future, Nicholas Klaine crowed on March 4, "A board of trade, a telephone line company, a telegraph line company, electric light, water works, more bridges across angry streams, better society, better business, more facilities for trade. These are demanded, and are receiving that attention due an enlighten and progressive people."

Amid all these symbols of progress, important political questions remained unanswered. On January 11 candidates representing the Independent Ticket tried claiming county offices to which they felt entitled from the recount ordered by the Kansas Supreme Court. Victors from the People's County Ticket refused to surrender as county commissioners approved their bonds.[3] To settle the matter once and for all, the Independents hauled their complaints back to Topeka.

Quo warranto proceedings began. Deputy Sheriff Singer served the writs on his boss, Patrick Sughrue, as well as on Sam Gallagher, Robert M. Wright, J. G. Jernigan, and Charles Van Tromp, ordering them to appear before the high court at Topeka on January 30. As is too often the case with legal controversies, delay followed delay so that the case was not decided until 1887, when, after more than a thousand pages of testimony, the court ruled in favor of the defendants.[4] Of course by then another county election had taken place, so it would not have mattered much had the Independent's won a favorable ruling.

Changes were in the wind. By early February a petition circulated calling on the city council to make Dodge what the state characterized as a City of the Second Class. More than three hundred voters and property owners signed the document. The mayor and council sanctioned the move

---

[3] Ford County Commissioners Journals, Book B, 5.

[4] A. M. F. Randolph, rep., *Reports of Cases Argued and Determined in the Supreme Court of the State of Kansas* (Topeka: Kansas Publishing House, 1887), R. W. Tarbox vs. P. F. Sughrue; L. W. Cherington vs. J. G. Jerningan [*sic*]; R. Gaede vs. S. Gallagher; and E. J. Beard vs. Chas. Van Tromp, January Term, 1887, 37, 225–36.

at their meeting on the seventeenth, forwarding the necessary papers to the
governor. Governor Martin issued a proclamation on March 5 elevating
the city's status. The town now had to register all voters and divide itself
into three wards. The first of these covered all of Dodge City south of the
railroad, the second ward took in everything north of that line and east of
First Avenue, including Wright's Addition and the developed area above
Military Avenue, with the third ward comprising all the remaining blocks.
The city council located polling places at the fire company building, the
Union Church, and the office at Dr. McCarty's skating rink.

As a city of the second class, Dodge would elect two councilmen from
each ward. Since they would hold office for two years, on an alternating
basis, this first election saw half the candidates running for a single year's
term and the others for a full term. This inconsistency was adjusted in 1887.
Other changes included two members of the board of education elected
from each ward. Dodge City voters also chose—besides the mayor and
council—the police judge, city treasurer, school board treasurer, two justices of the peace, and two constables. The mayor still appointed the city
marshal and his assistant, the city attorney, city clerk, and city assessor.

The question now was who should run for mayor. There seems to have
been a backlash of sorts against Bob Wright, as many voters were dissatisfied with his handling of the Griffin-Jetmore affair, pressures from Attorney General Bradford, and, of course, the embarrassing shooting episode
outside Mike Sutton's house. What Dodge City demanded was not so
much social respectability as stable government. The man they felt right
for the job was former mayor Alonzo B. Webster. By March 4, 1886, a petition had made the rounds calling on Webster to run.

A list of 223 names supported Webster's candidacy. What made it all so
remarkable was the wide range of political factions represented. Saloon
devotees Walter Straeter, Nelson Cary, Henry V. Cook, and George B. Cox
signed; but so did Prohibition supporters Nicholas Klaine, Samuel Galland, Larry Deger, and George S. Emerson. Republicans Daniel Frost and
Frederick Zimmerman signed, as did Democrats George M. Hoover,
Henry M. Beverley, and William F. Petillon. Businessmen and former officials all added their names, along with the likes of A. J. Anthony, M. S.
Culver, Richard Evans, Dr. Thomas McCarty, Walter Shinn, Hamilton
Bell, and Adobe Walls veteran "Andy the Swede" Johnson. An interesting

omission, considering the wide political voids being crossed, was that the name of the manipulative Michael W. Sutton was nowhere to be found. Bob Wright also avoided the festivities. Undeterred by Sutton's no-show but overwhelmed by the support, Webster agreed to run.[5]

More and more citizens wanted some sort of reform. A rash of robberies and an invasion of confidence men forced the city to hire six extra policemen. Gamblers and those saloonmen not represented on Webster's petition began worrying about desertions within their ranks. The future seemed uncertain, even with Webster's partnership in one of the quasi-drug stores.

The sporting crowd reacted from desperation, hoping to coerce their wayward brethren back into line. A week after publishing Webster's acceptance, the *Globe* added that saloonmen signing the petition had "brought about a revolt within their own ranks, and ex-Sheriff W. B. Masterson and present deputy sheriff of Ford county, entered complaint against every saloon-drug store in the city."[6] Masterson's action involved George B. Cox, Andy Johnson and Constant Brion, Walter Hart and Nathaniel Haynes, Harris and Drake, Henry Sturm—who had become a "druggist" seven months after disposing of his wholesale liquor business—Assistant Marshal Ben Daniels, Warren and Atkinson, Henry Wright and Harry Scott, Walter Straeter, Tom Marshall, as well as A. B. Webster himself, along with his partner Brick Bond.[7]

All this caused Spearville's editor to reflect: " 'Bat' Masterson seems to be a bigger man just now than Attorney General Bradford, as he has succeeded in closing the Dodge City saloons, which was more than Bradford could do—or did do."[8] But Masterson's ploy misfired. The court dis-

---

[5] *Globe Live Stock Journal*, March 9, 1886. Frost listed all 223 petitioners in full, as well as the ex-mayor's acceptance. Nick Klaine carried Webster's missive on March 11, followed by the *Democrat* two days later: "In my opinion we have reached that period in our existence as a city, when personal prejudice and factional feelings should be put aside and every man place his shoulder to the wheel and work for the prosperity of our city. . . . Although I know the duties are unpleasant, and the term of office oftimes [*sic*] ends in unthankfulness and ingratitude, if I am elected I wish it distinctly understood that I am a radical reformer only so far as the protection of life and property of our city is concerned. If this meets with your approval I consent to become a candidate."

[6] Ibid., March 16, 1886.

[7] Records of the Ford County District Court, Criminal Appearance Docket A, Case No.'s 857 through 867, 230–40, 243, 244, 246, 247, 248, 251, 253, 283, 286, 287.

[8] *Spearville Blade*, March 19, 1886. For an interesting look at this whole affair from a Prohibitionist's point of view, see M. W. Sutton to S. B. Bradford, March 10, 1886. Attorney Generals' Correspondence, Archives Division, Kansas State Historical Society.

missed the cases against George Cox and Andrew Johnson, while a jury found Constant Brion not guilty. Another jury failed to agree on the case of Walter Straeter after a week's deliberation and was discharged. Although Atkinson and Warren were found guilty, the court continued the other cases until the next term, owing to the absence of the complaining witness. Nick Klaine reported the departure of "Bat Masterson and his gang" on the westbound train, while Dan Frost explained, "W. B. Masterson left here Saturday night to go to Montana, where he expects to reside in the future."[9] Bat and his cronies traveled no farther than Denver, but he did not return to Dodge City for six months.

Masterson's maneuvering against the saloonmen failed to influence the voting, and Alonzo Webster won easily (he would be reelected over George Emerson by a 199-vote majority in 1887, only to die a week later at the home of his niece, Mrs. Michael Sutton). An editor in Finney County viewed the results: "The election at Dodge City on last Tuesday was the end of a gang rule in that city. The election was purely gang, anti-gang, with two candidates on the former ticket. As a city of the second class registration was necessary,—the consequence being no stuffing the ballot box, giving the anti-gang a good majority. Dodge is to be congratulated."[10]

Webster and the new six-man council took office on April 10. They wasted no time making appointments, including T. J. Tate as city marshal, replacing William Tilghman who had resigned a month earlier, and former railroad man I. J. Collier as Tate's assistant, taking over from Ben Daniels. Mayor Webster then ordered all saloons, front and back, closed on Sundays.

Few missed Ben Daniels as an officer. Three months earlier he had dropped his revolver in the Long Branch. Striking the floor, the weapon discharged, wounding a bystander in the leg. Now, five days after his dismissal, he got involved in a far more serious affair. Daniels kept a saloon on Locust Street between Second and Third avenues, next to a restaurant owned by Ed Julian, one of those signing Webster's petition. A feud of some sort existed between these two business neighbors. After Masterson's departure delayed the whiskey prosecutions, Julian filed his own complaint against Daniels.

Julian's difficulty with the former assistant marshal was not his first brush with the law. He was under indictment himself for firing a shot at

---

[9] *Dodge City Times*, April 1, 1886; *Globe Live Stock Journal*, March 30, 1886.

[10] *Garden City Sentinel*, as quoted in *Dodge City Times*, April 15, 1886.

Sheriff Sughrue. Following the escape of nine prisoners from the county jail on February 5, officers found one of the fugitives hiding in a backroom of Julian's restaurant. Chagrined by this exodus from his crowded cala-boose, Sughrue overreacted while making the arrest, pistol-whipping one of Julian's young employees. When Julian objected, Sughrue attacked him. Reporting the sheriff under the influence, the *Democrat* characterized his conduct as shameful. Julian maintained no knowledge of the prisoner hid-ing on his premises.

A week later Sughrue returned, claiming he only wanted to make peace. A deputy sheriff was having dinner as his boss approached the proprietor. Julian then saw one of the sheriff's friends come through the door. Fear-ing that "some advantage was going to be taken of him," Julian pulled a revolver from behind the counter. Sughrue slapped the gun aside just as it fired, the bullet scraping his head and powder residue burning his right eye. The sheriff disarmed Julian and handed the gun to his deputy, who arrested the offender. The hotheaded restaurateur secured his freedom on a $3,000 bond posted by two friends and was awaiting trial in the district court when the trouble with Ben Daniels erupted.[11]

Around six o'clock in the evening of April 15, the very day he had filed his complaint, Julian walked from his restaurant and headed two doors west to Utterback's hardware to get some money changed. Stepping from his saloon, Ben Daniels shot him from behind without warning. As Julian stumbled, he was hit a second time. Daniels approached the downed man and fired one shot through his head and another into his body. The for-mer assistant marshal turned away, walked calmly up Second Avenue and surrendered to City Marshal Thomas Tate.

Although friends claimed Julian had started to pull his own gun before Daniels fired, others described the affair as cold-blooded murder. True, Julian carried a weapon in his waistband, but he also held a number of sil-ver coins in his right hand and could not have easily pulled a gun. After a preliminary hearing, Justice of the Peace Harvey McGarry ordered Daniels held for trial. Released on $10,000 bond, he came before the dis-trict court near year's end. Thanks to the skill of defense attorney James Whitelaw, Daniels was acquitted, even though the jury required five bal-

[11] State of Kansas vs. Ed Julian, Records of the Ford County District Court, Criminal Appearance Docket A, Case No. 868, 241; *Dodge City Democrat*, February 13, 20, 1886; *Globe Live Stock Journal*, February 16, March 16, 1886; and *Dodge City Times*, February 18, 1886.

lots before reaching its verdict. Ben left Dodge City for other adventures. Because of services with the Rough Riders during the Spanish-American War, President Theodore Roosevelt appointed Benjamin F. Daniels United States marshal for the Arizona Territory, but not without some difficulty over his nominee's unsavory past.[12]

Dodge City recoiled from this latest outburst of violence, most people wanting nothing more to do with such things. Angry gunfire seemed so out of place alongside talk of electric lights and the sight of freight cars, stuffed with household goods and agricultural implements, arriving daily at the depot. The town would experience other incidents reminiscent of its early years—most notably the involvement of several citizens, including Billy Tilghman, Neil Brown, Jim Masterson, Fred Singer, and a visiting Ben Daniels, in the Gray County Seat War in 1889—but the future pointed away from these extremes. Even Dan Frost was forced to admit: "With this year Ford county begins anew, and this time as a farming country."[13]

The ending of the fabled trail drives, along with swarms of settlers spreading out over the open range, the fires of 1885, and the January storms of 1886, may have taken their toll on the town's image, but it all helped to establish a clear path to the future. It proved to be a painful transition. One could still buy a drink, but it took more imagination to do so. The days of wide-open saloons were over. In the years that followed, Dodge City's once-extensive freighting industry fell victim to railroad expansion. The Panic of 1893 undermined crop prices, driving wheat down to forty cents a bushel. Eventually, former mayor James Kelley was seen working on the streets as a day laborer; considered by some a more honorable calling than Michael Sutton's new position as U.S. revenue collector. Robert M. Wright characterized this entire period as the Great Decline, recalling:

> For ten long years, Dodge City suspended in reverses. But during this poverty stricken period, the process of liquidation was slowly being carried

---

[12] State of Kansas vs. Ben Daniels, Records of the Ford County District Court, Criminal Appearance Docket A, Case No. 887, 254, 272–76, 279–81; *Dodge City Democrat*, November 20, 1886; *Globe Live Stock Journal*, November 23, 1886; and *Dodge City Times*, November 25, 1886. Also see: James H. McClintock, *Arizona: Prehistoric—Aboriginal, Pioneer—Modern* (Chicago: The S. J. Clarke Publishing Company, 1916), 3:797–99; and Larry D. Ball, *The United States Marshals of New Mexico and Arizona Territories, 1846–1912* (Albuquerque: University of New Mexico Press, 1978), 215–17. Benjamin Franklin Daniels died of a heart attack at Tucson, Arizona, on April 20, 1923, at the age of seventy.

[13] *Globe Live Stock Journal*, April 6, 1886. The editor took his own prophesy to heart, and by the turn of the century Daniel M. Frost was listed as a "farmer," living with his wife and five children at Garden City. 1900 United States Census, Garden City, Finney County, Kansas, E.D. 41, Sheet 5A, lines 84–90.

out. Dodge City had had so much faith in her progress and former wealth, that a calamity was unexpected; she lost sight of the fact that the unnatural extravagance of that former wealth and progress was bound to bring a reaction, sooner or later. In this depression, property went down to five and ten cents on the dollar, in value, or you could buy it for a song and sing it yourself. People would not pay taxes, and the county became possessed of much valuable real estate, while hundreds of speculators were purchasers of tax titles. Many of the business houses closed, and large numbers of residences were without tenants. Parties were invited to live in them rent free, so the insurance could be kept up. And the same depression was felt in land and cattle. Good cows sold for eight to ten dollars. Land around Dodge sold as low as fifty cents per acre. The writer's land, a tract of seven thousand acres, was sold under the hammer, at less than fifty cents per acre; and some for less than that price.[14]

Wright's old partner and early Dodge City pioneer Charles Rath suffered for different reasons. Embroiled in an adulterous relationship at Mobeetie with a woman named Effie Miller during the spring and summer of 1885, Rath filed for divorce in Wheeler County, Texas, on July 3. Mrs. Rath traveled from Dodge City to the Panhandle with her attorney, W. E. Hendricks, and filed a cross complaint.[15] She prevailed, winning a settlement that proved costly to the once-proud plainsman. Financially strapped, Charlie Rath never fully recovered and died impoverished at his sister's Valencia Street home in Los Angeles in 1902, at the age of sixty-six.[16]

Others managed their later years more sensibly: Reluctant Prohibitionist Samuel Galland stayed on in the hotel business, as did Albert Boyd. Dr. Thomas McCarty still looked after the sick, joined by his son Claude, an 1897 graduate of the Rush Medical College in Chicago, and one of the first children born in early Dodge City. There was now little chance of either man treating gunshot wounds. Hamilton Bell became a farmer while his son served Ford County as a deputy sheriff. Patrick Sughrue gave up

---

[14] Wright, *Dodge City, the Cowboy Capital*, 328.

[15] *Globe Live Stock Journal*, July 21, November 17, 1885; and *Kansas Cowboy*, November 21, 1885.

[16] Rath, *The Rath Trail*, 186–96. Charles and Carrie R. Rath had had their share of difficulties, as their son, Robert W., later recalled: "I always liked papa, but mamma scolded him a lot because he didn't come home sooner. He would sit awhile and look around awhile like he didn't know what to do, then he would leave, going down town. When he came back, we knew he had been drinking. When manna began scolding, he would push her around; 'beat her up' she called it." Ibid., 183–84. In the end Charlie Rath rated less than a four-line death notice in the July 31, 1902, issue of the *Los Angeles Times*: "RATH—In this city, Charles Rath, aged 66 years. Funeral today at 2 o'clock from late residence, No. 1326 Valencia street. Funeral private."

on law enforcement and went back to working as a blacksmith. Even town-site pioneer Henry L. Sitler settled down as a farmer. Aging editor Nicholas Klaine continued scribbling out inflammatory articles. By 1900 Bob Wright listed his occupation as state forester, an amusing notation from an area with virtually no trees. His old partner at Fort Dodge, A. J. Anthony, raised cattle, while the venerable George M. Hoover, the town's pioneer saloonman, mill owner and political organizer, became a full-time banker.

After the turn of the century Dodge City began a fresh period of growth, based on agriculture, local stock raising, and regional commerce. Gone were the buffalo hunters, tracklayers, muleskinners, and gamblers and gunmen, along with concern over Indian raids or visions of cattle crowding the old trails from Texas. The celebrated romance of the frontier was replaced by reality. Dodge City became civilized—somehow sadly ordinary. No longer were its outrageous exploits debated in the nation's press. A good many citizens preferred it that way. In February 1926 a peti-tion circulated asking the city to acquire title to Boot Hill as "the last his-toric spot of our City." Others signed an opposing petition, claiming, "Boot Hill represents a history that should not be memoralized [sic]. It represents the history of the prostitute, the gambler and the thug. May its identity be forgotten."[17]

All the brick buildings erected along Front Street after the fires of 1885, from Bob Wright's store (later an outlet for F. W. Woolworth) past the Long Branch down toward Beatty & Kelley's old corner (gutted by fire again in 1912), fell victim to a wrecker's ball in 1970, with much of the space destined for off-street parking. Across First Avenue, the old Bank of Dodge City building, the original site of A. B. Webster's pioneer grocery and later the Old House saloon, followed this trend into oblivion.

Dodge City's most recent reincarnation has changed the place. With meat-packing operations leaving big cities for rural locations—reaching Dodge City in the 1980s—workers from Mexico poured in, transforming the community. The Associated Press reported in 2007: "Today, down-town has Mexican restaurants and stores more reminiscent of shops south of the border than Main Street Kansas. The city of 25,176 even has a new

---

[17] Original petitions in the possession of the author.

nickname: 'Little Mexico.'" Indeed, "about 70 percent of the 5,800 students who now attend Dodge City schools are Hispanic." But one must also consider, "at a time when other rural towns are slowly dying, Dodge City and meatpacking towns like it boast thriving economies."[18] Dan Frost would feel vindicated by all the feedlots and packing plants.

For others, thanks to published writings of varying length and quality, along with flickering images offered as history first on film and then on television, Dodge City became part of the mythical "Wild West," a process accelerated by the fictionalized exploits of its perennial heroes Bat Masterson and Wyatt Earp. Although resting on shaky historical and biographical ground, those two helped guarantee this Kansas town an honored place among America's pantheon of frontier shrines. Seduced by an entertainment culture, tourists are still lured to Dodge City by the residual notoriety, a turn of fate that might have surprised some of its speculative pioneers. Accepting the irony of it all, and appreciating the possibilities, James Kelley and the old gang would have loved it.

---

[18] Roxana Hegeman, The Associated Press, "Traditional farm towns struggle with immigrants. Influx of foreign workers changes U.S. midsection." *Arizona Daily Star,* Tucson, August 26, 2007.

BIBLIOGRAPHY

ARCHIVAL SOURCES, KANSAS

Boot Hill Petitions, Dodge City, February 1926. Author's collection.

Correspondence of the Adjutant Generals. Archives Division, Kansas State Historical Society.

Correspondence of the Attorney Generals. Archives Division, Kansas State Historical Society.

Dodge City Ordinances, 1875–86. Records of the City of Dodge City, Kansas. Microfilm copy, Kansas State Historical Society.

Dodge City War Collection, 1883. Manuscripts Department, Kansas State Historical Society.

Ford County Commissioners Journals, Books A and B. Board of County Commissioners, Ford County, Kansas. Microfilm copy, Kansas State Historical Society.

Ford County Marriages, Book A, 1874–86. Kansas Genealogical Society, Dodge City, Kansas, 1970. Copied from Original Records in Office of Probate Court, Dodge City, Kansas, by Donna Smyser Adams.

Ford County Register of Deeds, Books A through D. Microfilm copy, Kansas State Historical Society.

Governors' Correspondence. Archives Division, Kansas State Historical Society.

George M. Hoover Account Book, 1883–85. Archives Division, Kansas State Historical Society.

Kansas State Census 1875, Ellis, Ellsworth, Ford and Sedgwick counties; 1885, Ford County. Archives Division, Kansas State Historical Society.

Manuscripts Department, Kansas State Historical Society. Grenville M. Dodge to Joseph B. Thoburn, October 24, 1910; J. B. Edwards to H. B. Bell, October 25, 1936; and Henry H. Raymond to Merritt L. Beeson, September 25, 1936.

Police Judge Docket, City of Ellsworth, 1872–74. Microfilm copy, Kansas State Historical Society.

Proceedings of the Governing Body and Miscellaneous Papers, Records of the City of Wichita, 1874–75. Microfilm copy, Kansas State Historical Society.

Records of the City of Ellsworth, Minutes of the City Council, Journal Book, 1871–80. Microfilm copy, Kansas State Historical Society.

Records of the Ellsworth County District Court, August 1873. Microfilm copy, Kansas State Historical Society.

Records of the Ford County District Court: Civil Appearance Docket, Book A; Numbered and Unnumbered Civil Case Files; Criminal Appearance Docket, Book A; Numbered and Unnumbered Criminal Case Files; Judge's Journal, Book A; and Naturalization Records. Microfilm copy, Kansas State Historical Society.

Records of the Sedgwick County District Court, 1874. Microfilm copy, Kansas State Historical Society.

Wright, Beverley & Company Records: Sales Book, 1879–81; Ledger, 1883–85; R. M. Wright & Company, Petty Ledger, 1885–87. Archives Division, Kansas State Historical Society.

U.S. GOVERNMENT DOCUMENTS

House Misc. Doc. No. 45. "Town-site and County-seat Acts to June 30, 1880," 47th Congress, 2nd Sess., Pt. 4.

Military Service Records: Pettis L. Beatty, James Hobart Ford, Michael W. Sutton, Henry L. Sitler, Edward Palmer Turner. National Archives and Records Service.

Military Service Pension Files: Pettis L. Beatty, Richard W. Evans, James Hobart Ford's widow, Arabella, Henry L. Sitler, Alonzo B. Webster. National Archives and Records Service.

Letters Received by the Office of Indian Affairs, 1821–81: Central Superintendency, 1851–80; Kiowa Agency, 1864–80; Upper Arkansas Agency, 1855–74.

Nimmo, Joseph, Jr. "Range and Range Cattle Traffic in the Western States and Territories." House Ex. Doc. No. 267, 48th Congress, 2nd Sess.

Post Office Department, Records of Appointment of Postmasters, Vols. 21, 33, 40, 56. National Archives and Records Service.

Records of the Adjutant General's Office (RG 94): Medical History, Vol. 81, and Field Records of Hospitals, Records Relating to Fort Dodge, Kansas. National Archives and Records Service.

Records of United States Army Continental Commands, 1821–1920 (RG 393): Headquarters Records, Fort Dodge, Kansas, 1866–82; Camp/Fort Supply, Indian Territory, Letters Sent, 1872–74; Letters Received, 1872–74; and Department of the Missouri, Letters Sent, January–August 1874.

Returns from U.S. Military Posts: Fort Atkinson, Kansas, August 1850–September 1854 (Roll 48); and Fort Dodge, Kansas, January 1866–October 1882 (Roll 319). National Archives and Records Service.

United States Census 1870, Ellis, Ellsworth, and Ford counties; 1880 and 1900, Finney and Ford County, Kansas; 1900 and 1920, Archuleta County, Colorado.

U.S. Statutes, 14, March 2, 1867, "An Act for the Relief of the Inhabitants of Cities and Towns upon the Public Lands," 39th Congress, Sess. 2, Chap. 177.

U.S. Statutes, 16, March 3, 1871, "An Act making Appropriations for the current and contingent Expenses of the Indian Department," 41st Congress, Sess. 3, Chap. 120.

Other Archival Sources and Manuscripts

Campbell, Walter Stanley. Dodge City Collection, notes on primary sources. Manuscript Division. Western History Collection. University of Oklahoma Library.

Deposition of Wyatt S. Earp, with supporting documents, November 16, 1881, Territory of Arizona vs. Morgan Earp et al., Defendants, Document No. 94, in Justice Court, Township No. 1, Cochise County, A.T. Hayhurst typescript, WPA.

Fire Insurance Maps, Dodge City, Kansas, October 1884 and September 1887. Sanborn Map & Publishing Co., Limited, New York. Courtesy of the Sanborn Map Company, Inc., Pelham, New York, and the Library of Congress, Washington, D.C.

Forrest, Earle R. "Wicked Dodge." Manuscript and copies of miscellaneous correspondence. Copy from John Gilchriese Collection in author's possession.

Genealogical collections, various state and federal census records, county histories, and city directories. Walter Chiles Cox Memorial Library. Tucson, Arizona.

Gilchriese, John D. "Wyatt Earp." Various manuscript drafts, documents, and voluminous research notes. Originals in the author's collection.

Glenn, W. S. "Buffalo Hunt," manuscript. Copy from John Gilchriese Collection in author's possession.

Marriage Records. Book 15. Recorder of Deeds, St. Louis, Mo.

Mooar, J. Wright. Interviews and reminiscences, with J. Evetts Haley. Walter Stanley Campbell Files. Manuscript Division. Western History Collection. University of Oklahoma Library.

Moore, Lamar, comp. "The Cattle Drivers of Texas," manuscript. Copy from John Gilchriese Collection in author's possession.

———. "These Were the Texas Men," manuscript. Copy from John Gilchriese Collection in author's possession.

Recollections of Mary Katherine [Holliday] Cummings. From John D. Gilchriese Collection in author's possesstion.

Snell, Joseph W. Miscellaneous notes, Dodge City, Kansas. Copies graciously supplied for the author's collection.

Newspapers

Arizona Republican
Caldwell Journal
(Council Grove) Kansas Press
Dallas Morning News
Dodge City Daily Globe
Dodge City Democrat
Dodge City Globe-Republican
(Dodge City) Kansas Cowboy
Dodge City Messenger

Dodge City Times
(Dodge City) Vox Populi
Ellis County Star
Ellsworth Reporter
Ford County Globe
Globe Live Stock Journal
(Gunnison, Colorado) Daily News-Democrat
Hutchinson News
Junction City Weekly Union
Kansas City Commercial Indicator
Kansas City Evening Star
Kansas City Journal
Kansas City Times
Kinsley Graphic
Larned Optic
Las Vegas (New Mexico) Daily Optic
Leavenworth Daily Commercial
Leavenworth Daily Times
Los Angeles Times
Manhattan (Kansas) Nationalist
Medicine Lodge Cresset
New York Times
New York Tribune
Newton Kansan
Newton Republican
Oskaloosa (Iowa) Herald
Peoria (Illinois) Daily Transcript
Solomon Valley Pioneer
Spearville Blade
Spearville News
(St. Joseph, Missouri) Standard
Sumner County Press
Topeka Daily Blade
Topeka Daily Capital
(Topeka) Daily Kansas State Journal
(Topeka) Kansas Daily Commonwealth
(Tucson) Arizona Daily Star
Walnut Creek Blade
Walnut Valley Times
(Wichita) City Eagle
Wichita Weekly Beacon
Yates Center News

ARTICLES

Abel, Anna Heloise. "Indian Reservations in Kansas and the Extinguishment of Their Title," *Transactions of the Kansas State Historical Society*. Vol. 8, *1903–1904*. Topeka: State Printer, 1904

"A Noted Plainsman. Reminiscences in the Life of R. M. Wright, Esq., of Dodge City, Kan." *Kansas Daily Commonwealth*. August 19, 1874.

Barry, Louise. "Fort Aubrey." *Kansas Historical Quarterly* 39, no. 2 (Summer 1973).

———. "The Ranch at Cimarron Crossing." *Kansas Historical Quarterly* 39, no. 3 (Autumn 1973).

———. "The Ranch at Walnut Creek Crossing." *Kansas Historical Quarterly* 37, no. 2 (Summer 1971).

Campbell, C. E. "Down Among the Red Men." *Collections of the Kansas State Historical Society*. Vol. 17, *1926–1928*. Topeka: B. P. Walker, State Printer, 1928.

Coney, Capt. P. H., "Story of Mike Sutton of Kansas," *Topeka Daily Capital*, July 14, 1918.

Connelley, William, ed., "Life and Adventures of George W. Brown, Soldier, Pioneer, Scout, Plainsman and Buffalo Hunter," *Collections of the Kansas State Historical Society*. Vol. 17, *1926–1928*. Topeka: B. P. Walker, State Printer, 1928.

Cunningham, Gary L. "Gambling in the Kansas Cattle Towns; A Prominent and Somewhat Honorable Profession." *Kansas History: A Journal of the Central Plains* 5, no. 1 (Spring 1982).

Davis, Ronald L. "Soiled Doves and Ornamental Culture." *The American West* 4, no. 4 (November 1967).

"Desperate Fight at Adobe Walls." *Frontier Times* 1, no. 12 (September 1924).

Dick, Everett. "The Long Drive." *Collections of the Kansas State Historical Society*. Vol. 17, *1926–1928* (Topeka: B. P. Walker, State Printer, 1928).

Doster, Frank. "Eleventh Indian Cavalry in Kansas in 1865," *Collections of the Kansas State Historical Society*. Vol. 15, *1919–1922*. Topeka: State Printing Office, 1923.

Epp, Todd D. "The State of Kansas v. Wild Hog et al." *Kansas History: A Journal of the Central Plains* 5, no. 2 (Summer 1982).

"Field Notes by Joseph C. Brown, United States Surveying Expedition, 1825–1827." *Eighteenth Biennial Report of the Board of Directors of the Kansas State Historical Society*. Topeka: State Printing Office, 1913.

Foster, L. M. "An Eye-witness Account of The Last Indian Raid in Kansas, September 1878." *The Denver Westerners Monthly Roundup* 19, no. 8 (August 1963).

Galenson, David. "Origins of the Long Drive." *Journal of the West* 14, no. 3 (July 1975).

Gill, Helen G. "The Establishment of Counties in Kansas." *Transactions of the Kansas State Historical Society*. Vol. 8, *1903–1904*. Topeka: State Printer, 1904.

Hathaway, Seth. "The Adventures of a Buffalo Hunter." *Frontier Times* 9, no. 3 (December 1931).

Haywood, C. Robert. "Cowtown Courts: Dodge City Courts, 1876–1886." *Kansas History: A Journal of the Central Plains* 11, no. 1 (Spring 1988).

———. " 'No Less a Man' ": Blacks in Cow Town Dodge City, 1876–1886." *The Western Historical Quarterly* 19, no. 2 (May 1988).

———. "The Dodge City Census of 1880: Historians' Tool or Stumbling Block?" *Kansas History: A Journal of the Central Plains* 8, no. 2 (Summer 1985).

Hendricks, Carl Ludvig. "Recollections of a Swedish Buffalo Hunter, 1871–1873." *The Swedish Pioneer Historical Quarterly* 32, no. 3 (July 1981).

Hornaday, William T. "The Extermination of the American Bison, with a Sketch of its Discovery and Life History." *Smithsonian Report, 1887.* Part 2. Washington, D.C., 1889.

Humphrey, James. "The Administration of George W. Glick." *Transactions of the Kansas State Historical Society.* Vol. 9, *1905–1906.* Topeka: State Printing Office, 1906.

Hutchinson, W. H. "Billy Dixon and 'Big Fifty.' " *The Westerners, New York Posse Brand Book* 10, no. 4 (1963).

Karnes, Thomas L. "Gilpin's Volunteers on the Santa Fe Trail." *Kansas Historical Quarterly* 30, no. 1 (Spring 1964).

Leonard, Carol, and Isidor Wallimann. "Prostitution and Changing Morality in the Frontier Cattle Towns of Kansas." *Kansas History: A Journal of the Central Plains* 2, no. 1 (Spring 1979).

Lowe, Hon. Percival G. "Kansas, As Seen in the Indian Territory." *Transactions of the Kansas State Historical Society.* Vol. 4, *1886–1888.* Topeka: Kansas Publishing House, 1890.

Malin, James C. "Dodge City Varieties—A Summer Interlude of Entertainment, 1878." *Kansas Historical Quarterly* 22, no. 4 (Winter 1956).

"Marking an Epoch—The Last Indian Raid and Massacre." *Eighteenth Biennial Report of the Board of Directors of the Kansas State Historical Society.* Topeka: State Printing Office, 1913.

Mechem, Kirke. "The Bull Fight at Dodge." *Kansas Historical Quarterly* 2, no. 3 (August 1933).

Millbrook, Minnie Dubbs. "An Old Trail Plowed Under—Hays to Dodge." *Kansas Historical Quarterly* 43, no. 3 (Autumn 1977).

———. "The Jordan Massacre." *Kansas History: A Journal of the Central Plains* 2, no. 4 (Winter 1979).

Oliva, Leo E. "Fort Atkinson on the Santa Fe Trail, 1850–1854." *Kansas Historical Quarterly* 40, no. 2 (Summer 1974).

———. "Fortification on the Plains: Fort Dodge, Kansas, 1864–1882." *The 1960 Brand Book.* Vol. 16. Denver: Denver Posse of the Westerners, 1961.

Powers, Ramon, and Gene Younger. "Cholera on the Plains: The Epidemic of 1867 in Kansas." *Kansas Historical Quarterly* 37, no. 4 (Winter 1971).

Powers, Ramon S. "The Kansas Indian Claims Commission of 1879." *Kansas History: A Journal of the Central Plains* 7, no. 1 (Autumn 1984).

Reighard, George W. (as told to A. B. MacDonald). "What an Old Buffalo Hunter Saw Who Helped To Exterminate the Herds That Darkened the Plains." *Kansas City Star.* November 30, 1930.

Roberts, Gary L. "From Tin Star to Hanging Tree: The Short Career and Violent Times of Billy Brooks." *The Prairie Scout.* Abilene, Kans.: The Kansas Corral of the Westerners, Inc., 1975.

Schofield, Donald F. "W. M. D. Lee, Indian Trader." *Panhandle-Plains Historical Review* 54 (1981).

Shillingberg, Wm. B. "The John D. Gilchriese Collection: An Introduction." *Wyatt Earp, Tombstone, and the West from the Collections of John D. Gilchriese, Part I*. San Francisco: Johns' Western Gallery, 2004.

Snell, Joseph W., and Don W. Wilson. "The Birth of the Atchison, Topeka and Santa Fe Railroad." *Kansas Historical Quarterly* 34, no. 2 (Summer 1968) and 34, no. 3 (Autumn 1968).

Snell, Joseph W., ed. "By Wagon From Kansas to Arizona in 1875: The Travel Diary of Lydia E. English." *Kansas Historical Quarterly* 36, no. 4 (Winter 1970).

————. "Diary of a Dodge City Buffalo Hunter, 1872–1873." *Kansas Historical Quarterly* 31, no. 4 (Winter 1965).

"Some of the Lost Towns of Kansas." *Collections of the Kansas State Historical Society*. Vol. 12, *1911–1912*. Topeka: State Printing Office, 1912.

Thomas, James, and Carl N. Tyson. "Navigation on the Arkansas River, 1719–1886." *Kansas History: A Journal of the Central Plains* 2, no. 2 (Summer 1979).

Trautmann, Frederic, trans. and ed. "Across Kansas by Train in 1877: The Travels of Ernst von Hesse-Wartegg." *Kansas History: A Journal of the Central Plains* 6, no. 3 (Autumn 1983).

Unrau, William E. "Indian Agent vs. the Army: Some Background Notes on the Kiowa-Comanche Treaty of 1865." *Kansas Historical Quarterly* 30, no. 2 (Summer 1964).

Weichselbaum, Theodore. "Statement of Theodore Weichselbaum, of Ogden, Riley County, July 17, 1908." *Collections of the Kansas State Historical Society*. Vol. 11, *1909–1910*. Topeka: State Printing Office, 1910.

Westermeier, Clifford P. "The Dodge City Cowboy Band." *Kansas Historical Quarterly* 19, no. 1 (February 1951).

Wheeler, David L. "Winter On the Cattle Range: Western Kansas, 1884–1886." *Kansas History: A Journal of the Central Plains* 15, no. 1 (Spring 1992).

White, Lonnie J. "Indian Battles in the Texas Panhandle, 1874." *Journal of the West* 6, no. 2 (April, 1967).

Wright, Robert M. "Personal Reminiscences of Frontier Life in Southwest Kansas." *Transactions of the Kansas State Historical Society*. Vol. 7, *1901–1902* (Topeka: W. Y. Morgan, State Printer, 1902.

————. "Reminiscences of Dodge." *Transactions of the Kansas State Historical Society*. Vol. 9, *1905–1906*. Topeka: State Printing Office, 1906.

Books and Pamphlets

Anderson, Charles G. *In Search of the Buffalo: The Story of J. Wright Mooar*. Seagraves, Texas: Pioneer Book Publishers, 1974.

Anderson, George L. *Kansas West*. San Marino, Calif.: Golden West Books, 1963.

Annual Report of the Board of Directors of the Atchison, Topeka, and Santa Fe Railroad Co. . . . for the year ending December 31, 1875. Boston: Franklin Press: Rand, Avery, and Company, 1876.

Annual Report of the Board of Directors of the Atchison, Topeka, and Santa Fe Railroad Co. . . . for the year ending December 31, 1876. Boston: Franklin Press: Rand, Avery, and Company, 1877.

Annual Report of the Board of Directors of the Atchison, Topeka, and Santa Fe Railroad Co. . . . for the year ending December 31, 1877. Boston: Press of George H. Ellis, 1878.

Athearn, Robert G. *In Search of Canaan: Black Migration to Kansas, 1879–80.* Lawrence: The Regents Press of Kansas, 1978.

Atherton, Lewis. *The Cattle Kings.* Bloomington: Indiana University Press, 1961.

Bain, David Haward. *Empire Express: Building the First Transcontinental Railroad.* New York: Viking, 1999.

Baker, T. Lindsay, and Billy R. Harrison. *Adobe Walls: The History and Archeology of the 1874 Trading Post.* College Station: Texas A&M University Press, 1986.

Ball, Larry D. *The United States Marshals of the New Mexico and Arizona Territories, 1846–1912.* Albuquerque: University of New Mexico Press, 1978.

Barry, Louise. *The Beginning of the West: Annals of the Kansas Gateway to the American West, 1540–1854.* Topeka: Kansas State Historical Society, 1972.

Bartholomew, Ed. *Wyatt Earp, 1848 to 1880: The Untold Story.* Toyahvale, Tex.: The Frontier Book Company, 1963.

Battey, Thomas C. *The Life and Adventures of a Quaker Among the Indians.* Boston: Lee & Shepard, Publishers, 1875.

Baughman, Robert W. *Kansas Post Offices.* Topeka: Kansas Postal History Society & Kansas State Historical Society, 1961.

Bearss, Edwin C., and A. M. Gibson. *Fort Smith: Little Gibraltar on the Arkansas.* Norman: University of Oklahoma Press, 1969.

Bentley, Hon. O. H., ed. *History of Wichita and Sedgwick County, Kansas.* Vol. 2. Chicago: C. F. Cooper & Co., 1910.

Berthrong, Donald J. *The Cheyenne and Arapaho Ordeal: Reservation and Agency Life in the Indian Territory, 1875–1907.* Norman: University of Oklahoma Press, 1976.

Bieber, Ralph P., ed. *Exploring Southwestern Trails, 1846–1854.* Glendale, Calif.: The Arthur H. Clark Company, 1938.

————. *Marching with the Army of the West, 1846–1848.* Glendale, Calif.: The Arthur H. Clark Company, 1936.

Bigler, David L. and Will Bagley, ed. *Army of Israel: Mormon Battalion Narratives.* Spokane, Wash.: The Arthur H. Clark Company, 2000.

Biographical and Historical Record of Ringgold and Decatur Counties, Iowa. Chicago: The Lewis Publishing Company, 1887.

Blackmar, Frank W. *Kansas.* Vol. 2. Chicago: Standard Publishing Company, 1912.

Blanchard, Leola Howard. *Conquest of Southwest Kansas: A History and Thrilling Stories of Frontier Life in the State of Kansas.* Wichita, Kans.: The Wichita Eagle Press, 1931.

Bolton, Herbert Eugene. *Coronado: Knight of Pueblos and Plains.* New York: Whittlesey House and The University of New Mexico Press, 1949.

Braddock, Betty, and Jeanie Covalt. *Dodge City: Cowboy Capital—Beautiful Bibulous Babylon—Queen of the Cowtowns—Wicked Little City—the Delectable Burg.* Dodge City: Kansas Heritage Center, 1982.

Branch, E. Douglas. *The Hunting of the Buffalo.* New York: D. Appleton and Company, 1929.

Brewerton, George D. *In the Buffalo Country.* Ashland, Ore.: Lewis Osborne, 1970.

Brown, John Henry. *Indian Wars and Pioneers of Texas.* Austin: L. E. Daniell, Publishers, 1896.

Bryant, Keith L. *History of the Atchison, Topeka & Santa Fe Railway.* Lincoln: University of Nebraska Press, 1982.

Burns, Walter Noble. *Tombstone: An Iliad of the Southwest.* Garden City, N.Y.: Doubleday, Page & Company, 1927.

Busby, T. Addison, ed. *Biographical Directory of the Railway Officials of America.* Chicago: The Railway Age, 1901.

Butler, Lieut.-General The Rt. Hon. Sir W. F., G. C. B. *Sir William Butler: An Autobiography.* New York: Charles Scribner's Sons, 1913.

Campbell, John A., ed. *A Biographical History with Portraits of Prominent Men of the Great West.* Chicago: Western Biographical & Engraving Co., 1902.

Carriker, Robert G. *Fort Supply, Indian Territory: Frontier Outpost on the Plains.* Norman: University of Oklahoma Press, 1970.

Carter, Capt. Robert G. *The Old Sergeant's Story.* New York: Frederick H. Hitchcock, Publishers, 1926.

Chrisman, Harry E. *The Ladder of Rivers: The Story of I. P. (Print) Olive.* Denver: Sage Books, 1962.

———. *Lost Trials of the Cimarron.* Denver: Sage Books, 1961.

Clarke, Dwight L. *Stephen Watts Kearny, Soldier of the West.* Norman: University of Oklahoma Press, 1961.

Clarke, Dwight L., ed. *The Original Journals of Henry Smith Turner: With Stephen Watts Kearny to New Mexico and California, 1846.* Norman: University of Okalahoma Press, 1966.

Cockrell, Ewing. *History of Johnson County, Missouri.* Topeka: Historical Publishing Company, 1918.

Collins, Dennis. *The Indians' Last Fight; or, The Dull Knife Raid.* Girard, Kans.: The Appeal to Reason [1915].

The Commercial Agency Register for July, 1878. New York: McKillop & Sprague Co., 1878.

Connelley, William E. *A Standard History of Kansas and Kansans.* Vols. 2 and 3. Chicago: Lewis Publishing Company, 1918.

Cook, John R. *The Border and the Buffalo: An Untold Story of the Southwest Plains.* Chicago: The Lakeside Press, 1938.

Cox, James. *Historical and Biographical Record of the Cattle Industry and the Cattlemen of Texas and Adjacent Territory.* St. Louis: Woodward & Tiernan Printing Company, 1895.

Cox, William R. *Luke Short and His Era.* Garden City, N.Y.: Doubleday & Company, Inc., 1961.

Cozzens, Peter, ed. *Eyewitnesses to the Indian Wars, 1865–1890: Conquering the Southern Plains.* Mechanicsburg, Penn.: Stackpole Books, 2003.

———. *General John Pope: A Life for the Nation.* Urbana: University of Illinois Press, 2000.

Crumbine, Samuel J., M.D. *Frontier Doctor.* Philadelphia: Dorrance & Company, 1948.

Cullum, General George W. *Biographical Register of the Officers and Graduates of the U.S. Military Academy at West Point, N.Y.* Vols. 1 and 2. Boston: Houghton, Mifflin & Company, 1891.

Dale, Edward Everett. *Cow Country.* Norman: University of Oklahoma Press, 1965.

———. *The Range Cattle Industry: Ranching on the Great Plains from 1865 to 1925.* Norman: University of Oklahoma Press, 1969.

Dary, David. *The Buffalo Book: The Full Saga of the American Animal.* Chicago: The Swallow Press, Inc., 1974.

———. *The Santa Fe Trail: Its History, Legends, and Lore.* New York: Alfred A. Knopf, 2000.

Davis, Clyde Brion. *The Arkansas.* New York: Rinehart & Company, Inc., 1940.

DeArment, Robert K. *Bat Masterson: The Man and the Legend.* Norman: University of Oklahoma Press, 1979.

Decker, Leslie E. *Railroads, Lands, and Politics: The Taxation of the Railroad Land Grants, 1864–1897.* Providence, R.I.: Brown University Press, 1964.

Dixon, Olive K. *Life of "Billy" Dixon: Plainsman, Scout and Pioneer.* Dallas: P. L. Turner Company, 1927.

Dodge, Major-General Grenville M. *The Battle of Atlanta and Other Campaigns, Addresses, Etc.* Council Bluffs, Iowa: The Monarch Printing Company, 1910.

Dodge, Colonel Richard Irving. *Our Wild Indians: Thirty-three Years' Personal Experience Among the Red Men of the Great West.* Hartford: A. D. Worthington and Company, 1882.

———. *The Plains of the Great West.* New York: G. P. Putnam's Sons, 1877.

Drumm, Stella M., ed. *Down the Santa Fé Trail and Into Mexico: The Diary of Susan Shelby Magoffin, 1846–1847.* New Haven: Yale University Press, 1926.

Ducker, James H. *Men of the Steel Rails: Workers on the Atchison, Topeka & Santa Fe Railroad, 1869–1900.* Lincoln: University of Nebraska Press, 1983.

Dunlay, Tom. *Kit Carson and the Indians.* Lincoln: University of Nebraska Press, 2000.

Dyer, Frederick H. *A Compendium of the War of the Rebellion.* Des Moines, Iowa: The Dyer Publishing Company, 1908.

Dykstra, Robert R. *The Cattle Towns.* New York: Alfred A. Knopf, 1968.

Eberhart, Perry. *Guide to the Colorado Ghost Towns and Mining Camps.* Chicago: Sage Books, 1969.

Ellis, John N. *General Pope and U.S. Indian Policy.* Albuquerque: University of New Mexico Press, 1970.

Emmett, Chris. *Shanghai Pierce, A Fair Likeness.* Norman: University of Oklahoma Press, 1953.

Fehrenbach, T. R. *Comanches: The Destruction of a People.* New York: Alfred A. Knopf, 1974.

Fletcher, Baylis John. *Up the Trail in '79.* Norman: University of Oklahoma Press, 1968.

Foy, Eddie, and Alvin F. Harlow. *Clowning Through Life.* New York: E. P. Dutton & Company, 1928.

Frazer, Robert W. *Forts of the West: Military Forts and Presidios and Posts Commonly Called Forts West of the Mississippi River to 1898.* Norman: University of Oklahoma Press, 1965.

———, ed. *Over the Chihuahua and Santa Fe Trails, 1847–1848: George Rutledge Gibson's Journal.* Albuquerque: University of New Mexico Press, 1981.

Freeman, G. D. *Midnight and Noonday; or, The Incidental History of Southern Kansas and the Indian Territory.* Caldwell, Kans.: G. D. Freeman, 1892.

Gannett, Henry. *The Origin of Certain Place Names in the United States.* Washington, D.C.: Government Printing Office, 1902.

Gard, Wayne. *The Chisholm Trail.* Norman: University of Oklahoma Press, 1954.

———. *The Great Buffalo Hunt.* New York: Alfred A. Knopf, 1960.

Gardner, Mark L. *Wagons for the Santa Fe Trade: Wheeled Vehicles and Their Makers, 1822–1880.* Albuquerque: University of New Mexico Press, 2000.

Garrard, Lewis H. *Wah-To-Yah and the Taos Trail.* Glendale, Calif.: The Arthur H. Clark Company, 1938.

Garretson, Martin S. *The American Bison: The Story of its Extermination as a Wild Species and its Restoration Under Federal Protection.* New York: New York Zoological Society, 1938.

Goodnight, Charles, Emanuel Dubbs, John A. Hart and others. *Pioneer Days in the Southwest from 1850 to 1879.* Guthrie, Okla.: The State Capital Company, 1909.

Gould's St. Louis Directory for 1875. St. Louis, Mo.: David B. Gould, Publisher, 1875.

Gregg, Josiah. *Commerce of the Prairies: or the Journal of a Santa Fé Trader.* 2 vols. New York: Henry G. Langley, 1844.

Grinnell, George Bird. *The Fighting Cheyennes.* Norman: University of Oklahoma Press, 1956.

Guild, Thelma S., and Harvey L. Carter. *Kit Carson: A Pattern for Heroes.* Lincoln: University of Nebraska Press, 1984.

Hafen, LeRoy R., ed. *The Mountain Men and the Fur Trade of the Far West.* Vol. 5. Glendale, Calif.: The Arthur H. Clark Company, 1965–1972.

———, ed. *Ruxton of the Rockies.* Norman: University of Oklahoma Press, 1950.

Haines, Francis. *The Buffalo.* New York: Thomas Y. Crowell Company, 1970.

Hale, Edward E. *Kanzas and Nebraska . . . An Account of the Emigrant Aid Companies, and Directions to Emigrants.* Boston: Phillips, Sampson and Company, 1854.

Haley, J. Evetts. *Charles Goodnight: Cowman and Plainsman.* Norman: University of Oklahoma Press, 1949.

———. *George W. Littlefield, Texan.* Norman: University of Oklahoma Press, 1943.

Haley, James L. *The Buffalo War: The History of the Red River Uprising of 1874.* Garden City, N.Y.: Doubleday & Company, Inc., 1976.

———. *Sam Houston.* Norman: University of Oklahoma Press, 2002.

Hall, Jesse A., and Leroy T. Hand. *History of Leavenworth County, Kansas.* Topeka: Historical Publishing Company, 1921.

Hand-Book of Ford County, Kansas. Chicago: C. S. Burch Publishing Company, 1887.

Harman, S. W. *Hell on the Border; He Hanged Eighty-Eight Men.* Fort Smith, Ark.: The Phoenix Publishing Company, 1898.

Haywood, C. Robert. *Cowtown Lawyers: Dodge City and its Attorneys, 1876–1886.* Norman: University of Oklahoma Press, 1988.

———. *Merchant Prince of Dodge City: The Life and Times of Robert M. Wright.* Norman: University of Oklahoma Press, 1998.

———. *Trails South: The Wagon-Road Economy in the Dodge City-Panhandle Region.* Norman: University of Oklahoma Press, 1986.

———. *Victorian West: Class and Culture in Kansas Cattle Towns.* Lawrence: University Press of Kansas, 1991.

Heitman, Francis B. *Historical Register and Dictionary of the United States Army.* Vol. 1. Washington, D.C.: Government Printing Office, 1903.

Hening, H. B., ed. *George Curry, 1861–1947: An Autobiography.* Albuquerque: University of New Mexico Press, 1958.

Henry, Guy V. *Military Record of Civilian Appointments in the United States Army.* Vol. 1. New York: Carleton, Publisher, 1869.

Hirshson, Stanley P. *Grenville M. Dodge: Soldier, Politician, Railroad Pioneer.* Bloomington: Indiana University Press, 1967.

The History of Adams County, Illinois. Chicago: Murray, Williamson & Phelps, 1879.

History of Crawford County, Pennsylvania. Chicago: Warner, Beers & Co., 1885.

History of the Arkansas Valley, Colorado. Chicago: O. L. Baskin & Co., 1881.

History of Sangamon County, Illinois. Chicago: Inter-State Publishing Company, 1881.

History of the State of Kansas. Chicago: A. T. Andreas, 1883.

Hoig, Stan. *The Western Odyssey of John Simpson Smith: Frontiersman, Trapper, Trader, and Interpreter.* Glendale, Calif.: The Arthur H. Clark Company, 1974.

Holmes, Kenneth L., ed. *Covered Wagon Women: Diaries and Letters from the Western Trails, 1840–1890.* Vol. 2. Glendale, Calif.: The Arthur H. Clark Company, 1975.

Hunt, Elvid. *History of Fort Leavenworth, 1827–1927.* Fort Leavenworth, Kans.: The General Service Schools Press, 1926.

Hunter, J. Marvin. *The Trail Drivers of Texas.* 2 vols. New York: Argosy-Antiquarian, Ltd., 1963.

Hutchinson, C. C. *Resources and Development of Kansas.* Topeka: Published by the Author, 1871.

Hyde, George E. *Life of George Bent: Written From His Letters.* Norman: University of Oklahoma Press, 1968.

Hyslop, Stephen G. *Bound for Santa Fe: The Road to New Mexico and the American Conquest, 1806–1848.* Norman: University of Oklahoma Press, 2002.

Isenberg, Andrew C. *The Destruction of the Bison: An Environmental History, 1750–1920.* Cambridge, U.K.: Cambridge University Press, 2000.

Jackson, Donald, ed. *The Journals of Zebulon Montgomery Pike: With Letters and Related Documents.* 2 vols. Norman: University of Oklahoma Press, 1966.

Jones, Douglas C. *The Treaty of Medicine Lodge: The Story of the Great Treaty Council as Told by Eyewitnesses.* Norman: University of Oklahoma Press, 1966.

Kappler, Charles J., comp. *Indian Affairs, Laws and Treaties.* Vol. 2. Washington, D.C.: Government Printing Office, 1904.

Karnes, Thomas L. *William Gilpin, Western Nationalist.* Austin: University of Texas Press, 1970.

Kelsey, Harry E., Jr. *Frontier Capitalist: The Life of John Evans.* Denver: State Historical Society of Colorado, 1969.

Kenner, Charles L. *A History of New Mexican–Plains Indian Relations.* Norman: University of Oklahoma Press, 1969.

Kime. Wayne R. *Colonel Richard Irving Dodge: The Life and Times of a Career Army Officer.* Norman: University of Oklahoma Press, 2006.

————, ed. *The Indian Territory Journals of Colonel Richard Irving Dodge.* Norman: University of Oklahoma Press, 2000.

Klein, Maury. *Union Pacific: Birth of a Railroad, 1862–1893.* Garden City, N.Y.: Doubleday & Company, Inc., 1987.

Kraus, George. *High Road to Promontory: Building the Central Pacific Across the High Sierra.* Palo Alto, Calif.: American West Publishing Company, 1969.

Lake, Stuart N. *Wyatt Earp, Frontier Marshal.* Boston: Houghton Mifflin Company, 1931.

Laude, G. A. *Kansas Shorthorns: A History of the Breed in the State from 1857 to 1920.* Iola, Kans.: The Laude Printing Company, 1920.

Lavender, David. *Bent's Fort.* Garden City, N.Y.: Doubleday & Company, Inc., 1954.

Leckie, William H. *The Military Conquest of the Southern Plains.* Norman: University of Oklahoma Press, 1963.

Lockwood, Jeffrey A. *Locust: The Devastating Rise and Mysterious Disappearance of the Insect That Shaped the American Frontier.* New York: Basic Books, 2004.

Lowther, Charles C. *Dodge City, Kansas.* Philadelphia: Dorrance and Company, 1940.

Lynch, James D. *The Bench and Bar of Texas.* St. Louis: Nixon-Jones Printing Co., 1885.

Maddux, Vernon R., and Albert Glenn Maddux. *In Dull Knife's Wake: The True Story of the Northern Cheyenne Exodus of 1878.* Norman, Okla.: Horse Creek Publications, Inc., 2003.

Marshall, J. T. *The Miles Expedition of 1874–1875: An Eyewitness Account of the Red River War.* Austin: The Encino Press, 1971.

Marshall, James. *Santa Fe: The Railroad that Built an Empire.* New York: Random House, 1945.

Mayer, Frank H. and Charles B. Roth. *The Buffalo Harvest.* Denver: Sage Books, 1958.

McCarty, John L. *Adobe Walls Bride: The Story of Billy and Olive King Dixon.* San Antonio: The Naylor Company, 1955.

McClintock, James H. *Arizona: Prehistoric—Aboriginal, Pioneer—Modern.* Vol. 3. Chicago: The S. J. Clarke Publishing Co., 1916.

McCoy, Joseph G. *Historic Sketches of the Cattle Trade of the West and Southwest.* Kansas City, Mo.: Ramsey, Millett & Hudson, 1874.

McHugh, Tom. *The Time of the Buffalo.* New York: Alfred A. Knopf, 1972.

McIntire, Jim. *Early Days in Texas; A Trip to Hell and Heaven.* Kansas City, Mo.: McIntire Publishing Company, 1902.

Mead, James R. *Hunting and Trading on the Great Plains, 1859–1875.* Norman: University of Oklahoma Press, 1986.

Merrill, James M. *Spurs to Glory: The Story of the United States Cavalry.* Chicago: Rand McNally & Company, 1966.

Miles, General Nelson A. *Personal Recollections and Observations of General Nelson A. Miles.* Chicago: The Werner Company, 1896.

Miller, Nyle H., Edgar Langsdorf, and Robert W. Richmond. *Kansas in Newspapers.* Topeka: Kansas State Historical Society, 1963.

Miller, Nyle H., and Joseph W. Snell. *Why the West Was Wild: A Contemporary Look at the Antics of Some Highly Publicized Kansas Cowtown Personalities.* Topeka: Kansas State Historical Society, 1963.

Miller, Thomas Lloyd. *The Public Lands of Texas, 1519–1970*. Norman: University of Oklahoma Press, 1972.

Miner, H. Craig, and William E. Unrau. *The End of Indian Kansas: A Study of Cultural Revolution, 1854–1871*. Lawrence: The Regents Press of Kansas, 1978.

Morris, John W., and Edwin C. McReynolds. *Historical Atlas of Oklahoma*. Norman: University of Oklahoma Press, 1965.

Nimmo, Joseph, Jr. *Report on the Internal Commerce of the United States*. Washington, D.C.: Government Printing Office, 1879.

Official Military History of Kansas Regiments During the War for the Suppression of the Great Rebellion. Leavenworth, Kans.: W. S. Burke, 1870.

Oliva, Leo E. *Soldiers on the Santa Fe Trail*. Norman: University of Oklahoma Press, 1967.

Osgood, Ernest Staples. *The Day of the Cattleman*. Minneapolis: University of Minnesota Press, 1929.

Pace, Robert F., ed. *Buffalo Days: Stories from J. Wright Mooar As told to James Winford Hunt*. Abilene, Tex.: State House Press, McMurray University, 2005.

Paul, Rodman. *The Far West and the Great Plains in Transition, 1859–1900*. New York: Harper & Row, Publishers, 1988.

Pelzer, Louis. *The Cattlemen's Frontier: A record of the trans-Mississippi cattle industry from oxen trains to pooling companies, 1850–1890*. Glendale, Calif.: The Arthur H. Clark Company, 1936.

Perrigo, Lynn. *Gateway to Glorieta: A History of Las Vegas, New Mexico*. Boulder, Colo.: Pruett Publishing Company, 1982.

Portrait and Biographical Album of Jo Davies County, Illinois. Chicago: Chapman Brothers, 1889.

Portrait and Biographical Album of Sedgwick County, Kan. Chicago: Chapman Brothers, 1888.

Portrait and Biographical Record of Macon County, Illinois. Chicago: Lake City Publishing Co., 1893.

Powell, William H. *Records of Living Officers of the United States Army*. Philadelphia: L. R. Hamersly & Co., 1890.

Power, John Carroll. *History of the Early Settlers of Sangamon County, Illinois*. Springfield, Ill.: Edwin S. Wilson & Co., 1876.

Prose and Poetry of the Live Stock Industry of the United States. New York: Antiquarian Press, Ltd., 1959. Originally published in 1905 by the National Live Stock Historical Association.

Prucha, Francis Paul. *A Guide to the Military Posts of the United States, 1789–1895*. Madison: The State Historical Society of Wisconsin, 1964.

Quinn, John Philip. *Gambling and Gambling Devices*. Canton, Ohio: J. P. Quinn Co., 1912.

Randolph, A. M. F., rep. *Reports of Cases Argued and Determined in the Supreme Court of the State of Kansas*. Vol. 36. Topeka: Kansas Publishing House, 1887.

Rath, Ida Ellen. *Early Ford County*. North Newton, Kansas: Mennonite Press, 1964.

———. *The Rath Trail*. Wichita: McCormick-Armstrong Co., Inc., 1961.

Report of the Adjutant General of the State of Kansas, 1861–1865. Topeka: J. K. Hudson, State Printer, 1896.

Report on Barracks and Hospitals, with Descriptions of Military Posts, Circular No. 4. Washington: Government Printing Office, 1870.

Richardson, Rupert Norval. *The Comanche Barrier to South Plains Settlement: A century and a half of savage resistance to the advancing white frontier.* Glendale, Calif.: The Arthur H. Clark Company, 1933.

Ripley, John W., ed. *The Legacy of Sam Radges, Publisher and Historian.* Topeka: Shawnee County Historical Society, 1973.

Rister, Carl Coke. *Fort Griffin on the Texas Frontier.* Norman: University of Oklahoma Press, 1956.

Roberts, Gary L. *Doc Holliday: The Life and Legend.* New York: John Wiley & Sons, Inc., 2006.

The Rocky Mountain Directory and Colorado Gazetteer. Denver: S. S. Wallihan & Company, 1871.

Roe, Frank Gilbert. *The North American Buffalo: A Critical Study of the Species in Its Wild State.* Toronto: University of Toronto Press, 1951.

Root, O. C. *Root's Peoria City Directory For 1870–'71.* Peoria, Ill.: N. C. Nason, Printer, 1870.

Rosa, Joseph G. *The Called Him Wild Bill: The Life and Adventures of James Butler Hickok.* Norman: University of Oklahoma Press, 1974.

Rydjord, John. *Indian Place-Names: Their Origin, Evolution, and Meanings, Collected in Kansas from the Siouan, Algonquian, Shoshonean, Caddoan, Iroquoian, and Other Tongues.* Norman: University of Oklahoma Press, 1968.

————. *Kansas Place-Names.* Norman: University of Oklahoma Press, 1972.

Rye, Edgar. *The Quirt and The Spur: Vanishing Shadows of the Texas Frontier.* Chicago: W. B. Conkey Company, 1909.

Sabin, Edwin L. *Kit Carson Days, 1809–1868.* Vol. 2. New York: The Press of the Pioneers, Inc., 1935.

Self, Huber. *Environment and Man in Kansas: A Geographical Analysis.* Lawrence: The Regents Press of Kansas, 1978.

Sellers, Frank. *Sharps Firearms.* Los Angeles: Beinfeld Publishing Inc., 1978.

Sheffy, Lester Fields. *The Francklyn Land and Cattle Company: A Panhandle Enterprise, 1882–1957.* Austin: University of Texas Press, 1963.

Sheridan, General P. H. *Personal Memoirs of P. H. Sheridan, General United States Army.* Vol. 2. New York: Charles L. Webster & Company, 1888.

————. *Record of Engagements with Hostile Indians within the Military Division of the Missouri from 1868 to 1882.* Washington, D.C.: Government Printing Office, 1882.

Sherman, John. *John Sherman's Recollections of Forty Years in the House, Senate and Cabinet: An Autobiography.* Vol. 1. Chicago: The Werner Company, 1895.

Shillingberg, Wm. B. *Tombstone, A. T., A History of Early Mining, Milling, and Mayhem.* Spokane, Wash.: The Arthur H. Clark Company, 1999.

————. *Wyatt Earp and the "Buntline Special" Myth.* Tucson: Blaine Publishing Company, 1976.

Shirley, Glenn. *Guardian of the Law: The Life and Times of William Matthew Tilghman (1854–1924).* Austin: Eakin Press, 1988.

————. *Law West of Fort Smith: A History of Frontier Justice in the Indian Territory.* New York: Henry Holt and Company, 1957.

Simon, John Y., ed. *The Papers of Ulysses S. Grant, Volume 14: February 21, April 30, 1865.* Carbondale: Southern Illinois University Press, 1985.

Skaggs, Jimmy M. *The Cattle-Trailing Industry: Between Supply and Demand, 1866–1890.* Lawrence: The University Press of Kansas, 1973.

Snell, Joseph W. *Painted Ladies of the Cowtown Frontier.* Kansas City, Mo.: Kansas City Posse of the Westerners, 1965.

Socolofsky, Homer E., and Huber Self. *Historical Atlas of Kansas.* Norman: University of Oklahoma Press, 1972.

Souvenir of Settlement and Progress of Will County, Ill. Chicago: Historical Directory Publishing Co., 1884.

Stanley, F. *Clay Allison.* Denver: World Press, Inc., 1956.

———. *Dave Rudabaugh, Border Ruffian.* Denver: World Press, Inc., 1961.

———. *Satanta and the Kiowas.* Borger, Tex.: Jim Hess Printers, 1968.

Steinbach, Robert H. *A Long March: The Lives of Frank and Alice Baldwin.* Austin: University of Texas Press, 1989.

Strate, David Kay. *Sentinel to the Cimarron: The Frontier Experience of Fort Dodge, Kansas.* Dodge City: Cultural Heritage and Arts Center, 1970.

Streeter, Floyd Benjamin. *Ben Thompson: Man With a Gun.* New York: Frederick Fell, Inc., 1957.

———. *Prairie Trails and Cow Towns, the Opening of the Old West.* New York: The Devin-Adair Company, 1963.

Taylor, Morris F. *First Mail West: Stagecoach Lines on the Santa Fe Trail.* Albuquerque: University of New Mexico Press, 1971.

Thompson, George G. *Bat Masterson: The Dodge City Years.* Fort Hays Kansas State College Studies, General Series No. 6; Language and Literature Series, No. 1. Topeka: Kansas State Printing Plant, 1943.

Thorndike, Rachel Sherman, ed. *The Sherman Letters: Correspondence Between General and Senator Sherman from 1837 to 1891.* New York: Charles Scribner's Sons, 1894.

Tilghman, Zoe A. *Marshal of the Last Frontier: Life and Services of William Matthew (Bill) Tilghman.* Glendale, Calif.: The Arthur H. Clark Company, 1949.

Treadway, William E. *Cyrus K. Holliday: A Documentary Biography.* Topeka: Kansas State Historical Society, 1979.

The United States Biographical Dictionary, Kansas Volume. Chicago and Kansas City: S. Lewis & Co., Publishers, 1879.

Utley, Robert M. *Frontier Regulars: The United States Army and the Indian, 1866–1891.* New York: Macmillan Publishing Co., Inc., 1973.

———. *Frontiersmen in Blue: The United States Army and the Indian, 1848–1865.* New York: The Macmillan Company, 1967.

Vernon, Joseph S. *Dodge City and Ford County, Kansas: A History of the Old and a Story of the New.* Larned, Kans.: Tucker-Vernon Publishing Company, 1911.

Vestal, Stanley. *Queen of Cowtowns, Dodge City: "The Wickedest Little City in America," 1872–1886.* New York: Harper & Brothers, 1952.

Wallace, Ernest, ed. *Ranald S. Mackenzie's Official Correspondence Relating to Texas, 1873–1879.* Lubbock: West Texas Museum Association, 1968.

Wallace, Ernest, and E. Adamson Hoebel. *The Comanches: Lords of the South Plains.* Norman: University of Oklahoma Press, 1952.

Wallis, George A. *Cattle Kings of the Staked Plains.* Denver: Sage Books, 1964.

Walton, W. M. *Life and Adventures of Ben Thompson, the Famous Texan.* Austin: Published by the Author, 1884.

The War of the Rebellion: A Compilation of the Official Records of the Union and Confederate Armies. Ser. 1, Vol. 48, Pts. 1 and 2. Washington, D.C.: Government Printing Office 1896.

Waters, Frank. *Midas of the Rockies: The Story of Stratton and Cripple Creek.* New York: Civici-Friede, 1937.

Waters, L. L. *Steel Rails to Santa Fe.* Lawrence: University of Kansas Press, 1950.

Watkins, Ethel E. *Our First Century, An Historical Sketch: First Presbyterian Church, Dodge City, Kansas.* Dodge City: First Presbyterian Church, 1978.

Webb, James Josiah. *Adventures in the Santa Fé Trade, 1844–1847.* Glendale, Calif.: The Arthur H. Clark Company, 1931.

Webb, W. E. *Buffalo Land.* Cincinnati and Chicago: E. Hannaford & Company, 1872.

Webb, Walter Prescott. *The Great Plains.* Boston: Gin and Company, 1931.

Wenzl, Timothy F. *Discovering Dodge City's Landmarks.* Spearville, Kans.: Spearville News, Inc., 1980.

White, David A., comp. *News of the Plains and Rockies, 1803–1865.* Vols. 2, 3, 6, and 7. Spokane, Wash.: The Arthur H. Clark Company, 1996–2001.

White, Lonnie J., ed. *Chronicle of a Congressional Journey: The Doolittle Committee in the Southwest, 1865.* Boulder, Colo.: Pruett Publishing Company, 1975.

Wilson, Hill P., comp. *A Biographical History of Eminent Men of the State of Kansas.* Topeka: The Hall Lithographing Company, 1901.

Wilson, James Grant, and John Fiske, ed. *Appleton's Cyclopædia of American Biography.* New York: D. Appleton & Company, 1888.

Wilson, R. L. *The Colt Heritage: The Official History of Colt Firearms from 1836 to the Present.* New York: Simon and Schuster, 1979.

Wood, Richard G. *Stephen Harriman Long, 1784–1864: Army Engineer, Explorer, Inventor.* Glendale, Calif.: The Arthur H. Clark Company, 1966.

Woodruff, George H. *Fifteen Years Ago: Or the Patriotism of Will County.* Joliet, Ill.: Joliet Republican Book & Job Steam Printing House, 1876.

Worcester, Don. *The Chisholm Trail: High Road of the Cattle Kingdom.* Lincoln: University of Nebraska Press, 1980.

———. *The Texas Longhorn: Relic of the Past, Asset for the Future.* College Station: Texas A&M University Press, 1987.

Wormser, Richard. *The Yellowlegs: The Story of the United States Cavalry.* Garden City, N.Y.: Doubleday & Company, Inc., 1966.

Wright, Robert M. *Dodge City, the Cowboy Capital and the Great Southwest.* Wichita, Kans.: Wichita Eagle Press, 1913.

Young, Fredric R. *Dodge City: Up Through a Century in Story and Pictures.* Dodge City: Boot Hill Museum, Inc., 1972.

Young, Harry (Sam). *Hard Knocks: A Life Story of the Vanishing West.* Chicago: Laird & Lee, Inc., Publishers, 1915.

Young, Otis. *The West of Philip St. George Cooke, 1809–1895.* Glendale, Calif.: The Arthur H. Clark Company, 1955.

Youngblood, Charles L. *A Mighty Hunter: The Adventures of Charles L. Youngblood on the Plains and Mountains.* Chicago: Rand, McNally & Company, Publishers, 1890.

Zornow, William Frank. *Kansas: A History of the Jayhawk State.* Norman: University of Oklahoma Press, 1957.

Index

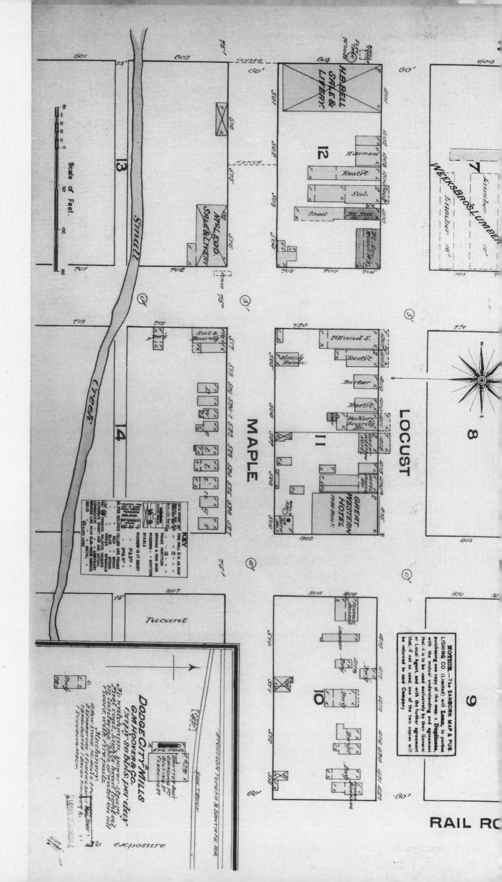